Pioneer Girl The Annotated Autobiography

THE PIONEER GIRL PROJECT

The Pioneer Girl Project is a research and publishing program of the South Dakota State Historical Society, working since 2010 to create a comprehensive edition of Laura Ingalls Wilder's *Pioneer Girl*.

For generations of

readers inspired by

Laura Ingalls Wilder's

life and work

PIONEER GIRL
The Annotated Autobiography

LAURA INGALLS WILDER

PAMELA SMITH HILL, *editor*

A publication of the Pioneer Girl Project

NANCY TYSTAD KOUPAL, *Director*

RODGER HARTLEY, *Associate Editor*

JEANNE KILEN ODE, *Associate Editor*

SOUTH DAKOTA HISTORICAL SOCIETY PRESS

Pierre

This publication is funded, in part, by the
Great Plains Education Foundation, Inc., Aberdeen, S.Dak.

Library of Congress Cataloging-in-Publication Data
Wilder, Laura Ingalls, 1867–1957.
Pioneer girl : the annotated autobiography / Laura Ingalls Wilder ;
Pamela Smith Hill, editor.
    pages cm
"A publication of the Pioneer Girl Project"
Includes bibliographical references and index.
ISBN 978-0-9845041-7-6 (alk. paper)
1. Wilder, Laura Ingalls, 1867–1957. 2. Women authors, American—20th century—
Biography. 3. Women pioneers—United States—Biography. 4. Frontier and
pioneer life—United States. I. Hill, Pamela Smith, editor. II. Title.
PS3545.I342Z46 2014
813'.52 dc23
[B]   2014027174

The paper in this book meets the guidelines for permanence and
durability of the committee on Production Guidelines for Book Longevity
of the Council on Library Resources.

Cover image: *Silver Lake Reflections* © 2014 Judy Thompson
Frontispiece: Laura Ingalls. *Laura Ingalls Wilder Historic Home and
Museum, Mansfield, Mo.*

Text and cover design by Rich Hendel
Typeset in Bulmer by Tseng Information Systems, Inc.

Please visit the Pioneer Girl Project website at www.pioneergirlproject.org.

Printed in Canada

18 17 16 15   3 4 5

The Pioneer Girl Project and the South Dakota Historical Society Press gratefully acknowledge generous support from the following:

The Great Plains Education Foundation, Inc., Aberdeen, S.Dak.

Dennis and Carol Anderson

De Smet Farm Mutual Insurance Company of South Dakota

National Park Service, South Dakota State Historical Society, Historic Preservation Office, Pierre, S.Dak.

BankWest, Pierre, S.Dak.

Canadian Pacific Railway Company

NorthWestern Energy

First PREMIER Bank/PREMIER BankCard

Growth Opportunities through Rail Access Coalition

John and Margaret Fowler

David and Mary Hartley

F. L. Clarkson Family Foundation

Laurie Hall Langland

And the hundreds of individual donors who have helped support the ongoing work of the South Dakota Historical Society Press through the South Dakota Historical Society Foundation.

Contents

Acknowledgments

Bringing *Pioneer Girl* to publication more than eighty years after it was written has involved a team of visionaries, scholars, and hardworking professionals committed to Wilder's work and literary legacy. Without them, this book would not be possible.

I am deeply grateful to Noel Silverman and the Little House Heritage Trust for giving this project life and entrusting Wilder's autobiography to the South Dakota Historical Society Press.

I am indebted to Nancy Tystad Koupal, director of the South Dakota Historical Society Press, who supported this project from the beginning and envisioned the beautiful book it has become. Rodger Hartley, production manager and associate editor at the Press, painstakingly transcribed Wilder's original handwritten manuscript and provided invaluable research assistance throughout the writing process, as did managing editor of *South Dakota History* and associate editor Jeanne Ode. Former marketing director Martyn Beeny and current marketing director Jennifer McIntyre supervised the Pioneer Girl Project website and gave interested readers access to the research process and Wilder's world. I am grateful for the entire staff's able and tireless contributions to this book.

The Laura Ingalls Wilder Historic Home and Museum in Mansfield, Missouri, granted the Press access to Wilder's homes and original archival materials. I am especially grateful to Director Jean Coday and tour guides Kathleen Forte and Vicki Johnston for their support and unique insights into Wilder's life at Rocky Ridge Farm. They helped make the photography shoot there absolutely magical.

Cheryl Palmlund, executive director at the Laura Ingalls Wilder Memorial Society in De Smet, South Dakota, expertly answered my questions and granted access to the society's archives and photograph collection. My thanks to her and the society's entire board for their cooperation and support.

Craig Wright at the Herbert Hoover Presidential Library provided essential scans from Rose Wilder Lane's original diaries and correspondence. His prompt and thorough responses to my requests helped me piece together the story behind the writing of *Pioneer Girl*.

Wilder expert William T. Anderson generously sent me a box of Wilder materials that added essential new perspectives to my interpretation of *Pioneer Girl* and then reviewed an early draft of this book. I appreciate his knowledge and guidance. Arian

Sheets, curator of stringed instruments at the National Music Museum answered questions about the origin of Charles Ingalls's fiddle swiftly and thoroughly. Research librarians at the West Slope Community Library and the Multnomah County Library tracked down all the obscure book and magazine articles I requested on interlibrary loan and then generously allowed me the time I needed with each title.

Phil Laumeyer, a retired United States Fish and Wildlife Service biologist, patiently answered my many questions about Great Plains wildlife, and poultry farmer Cheryl Tuttle gave me firsthand insights into the unique characteristics of leghorn chickens.

I am grateful to literary agent Ginger Clark and to Michael Gross of Authors Guild, Duane Bosworth of David Wright Tremaine, and my dear friend Jean Maneke for their legal counsel. My sister Angela Smith and her staff at ADsmith provided ongoing creative advice and support for the *Pioneer Girl* project. Special thanks go to Keli Tetzlaff at ADsmith; her photographs and short films bring Wilder's world at Rocky Ridge Farm to life.

Finally, I thank Chris Jacobson and my daughter Emily. Neither complained as *Pioneer Girl* took over my office and, ultimately, my life; both encouraged me to keep writing, even through the darkest and longest days.

Pamela Smith Hill

The editors of the Pioneer Girl Project and the South Dakota Historical Society Press wish to thank the Little House Heritage Trust for giving us the opportunity, privilege, and responsibility of publishing Laura Ingalls Wilder's *Pioneer Girl*. Special thanks go to Noel Silverman for his faith in the project, his sound advice, and his friendship.

We are indebted as well to William Anderson, who served as an expert reader on the project, troubleshooting the manuscript and sharing his knowledge. He also helped us locate photographs and documents in repositories across the country.

Without access to three important archival collections, this project could not have reached a successful conclusion. We thank Cheryl Palmlund at the Laura Ingalls Wilder Memorial Society in De Smet, South Dakota, who, in addition to allowing complete access to the society's archival collections, cheerfully performed additional research within the dusty vaults of the Kingsbury County Courthouse when we asked her to do so. She and her board have been enthusiastic supporters of the project from the beginning.

We are also grateful to the staff at the Herbert Hoover Presidential Library, most especially Craig Wright, Lynn Smith, and Spencer Howard, who have accommodated our endless requests for letters and documents from the Rose Wilder Lane Papers. They have also been tireless in arranging for the print-quality materials.

We also thank Director Jean Coday and her staff at the Laura Ingalls Wilder Historic Home and Museum in Mansfield, Missouri, where the original handwritten draft of *Pioneer Girl* is housed. The photographs and documents in the organization's archive give visual meaning to many passages in Wilder's *Pioneer Girl*.

Jill Hartke at the State Historical Society of Missouri provided timely and patient help in arranging loans of the Wilder Papers on microfilm. Marian Cramer of the Ingalls Homestead in De Smet graciously shared transcripts of her oral history interviews with early De Smet residents.

Special thanks go to the Reference Department of the Minnesota Historical Society. In particular, we wish to thank Deborah L. Miller, who helped us to track down the Congregational Conference of Minnesota Papers when all other efforts had failed, and Judy Calcote, who provided essential newspaper resources. We also thank David J. Ode, botanist/ecologist with the South Dakota Department of Game, Fish and Parks, for sharing his expertise on the flora and fauna of the region.

We gratefully acknowledge the willing assistance of the archival staff of the South Dakota State Historical Society, who have helped us track down maps, newspapers, photographs, and documents that illuminate the life and times of Laura Ingalls Wilder.

Nancy Tystad Koupal for the Pioneer Girl Project

Introduction

"Will It Come to Anything?": The Story of *Pioneer Girl*

PAMELA SMITH HILL

In 1925, a reporter from the *Kansas City Star* visited Rocky Ridge Farm in the Missouri Ozarks to interview the famous author who lived with her parents there in a "demure, rambling" farmhouse that boasted three unique writing "dens"—one for the famous author herself, Rose Wilder Lane; another for the working writers who sometimes visited—Dorothy Thompson, Catharine Brody, and Genevieve Parkhurst, for example; and the third for the famous author's mother, Laura Ingalls Wilder, who, the reporter explained, was "a writer, too."[1]

Five years later, Lane still lived and wrote in the rambling farmhouse with its three writing dens, but her mother had apparently stopped writing. Wilder and her husband Almanzo had moved into a new home, just over the hill within walking distance. It had been a gift from Lane, a handsome fieldstone English cottage that she had designed for her parents' comfort and ease, the perfect retirement home. Its modern conveniences were unique to rural Missouri at that time: hot and cold soft water, steel-casement windows, brass pipes, an electric range and refrigerator, a tiled bathroom, and even a detached garage for Isabelle, the Wilders' 1923 Buick sedan.[2] True, the cottage lacked a dedicated writing space for Wilder, but her career as a columnist and editor for the *Missouri Ruralist* (1911–1924) was clearly behind her. A life of ease and retirement beckoned. "I hope and sincerely wish your mother and father will find and enjoy much pleasure and comfort from their new home," the architect of the Rock House, as it came to be known, wrote in a letter to Lane.[3] And in a diary entry dated February 16, 1930, Lane noted with some satisfaction, "Parents comfortably established."[4] Her mother had just turned sixty-three.

Yet, a retiring life of comfort and ease was not exactly what Laura Ingalls Wilder

---

1. "The Heart and Home of Rose Wilder Lane," *Kansas City Star*, reprinted in *Springfield* (Mo.) *Leader*, July 5, 1925.

2. Rose Wilder Lane (RWL) to Fremont Older, Oct. 31, 1928, Box 10, file 137, Laura Ingalls Wilder (LIW) Series, Rose Wilder Lane Papers, Herbert Hoover Presidential Library, West Branch, Iowa.

3. Eugene F. Johnson to RWL, Dec. 21, 1928, Box 10, file 146, Lane Papers.

4. RWL, Diary #25 (1926–1930), Feb. 16, 1930, Box 21, item #25, Lane Papers.

envisioned for herself. At some point in 1929 or 1930, she purchased a supply of Fifty Fifty and Big Chief tablets and Number 2 lead pencils, found a space in the Rock House—perhaps at the new dining-room table—and began to write again. But this time, she was writing a book—not a newspaper column or a magazine article—and this book would focus on the story of her life and her family's pioneering experiences in the American West. She penciled the words "Pioneer Girl" across the cover of a Fifty Fifty tablet and began her original manuscript as so many stories begin, "Once upon a time. . . ."

The manuscript filled six tablets and spanned sixteen years of Wilder's life—her memories from age two until eighteen. *Pioneer Girl* was nonfiction, the truth as only Wilder remembered it. She wrote in first-person, creating an intimate bond between herself and her future readers. "I lay and looked through the opening in the wagon cover at the campfire and Pa and Ma sitting there," she wrote on the first page of the manuscript. "It was lonesome and so still with the stars shining down on the great, flat land where no one lived." This story was personal, a memoir about Wilder's past and her family's unique pioneering experience.

Pioneer Girl opens in what Wilder called Indian Territory, which is now southeastern Kansas, with her earliest childhood memories. She was just two years old when her family moved there in the late summer or early fall of 1869, but Wilder wrote convincingly about a pack of wolves "sitting in a ring around the house," the Indians who "camped by the creek not far away," and a pair of Indian "babies" with "bright, black eyes" that her younger self had wanted for her very own. As Wilder's memories grew more vivid, so too did her writing. She described the people and places from her past in greater detail. Pa's bugle-playing brother George frightened her all those years ago because he was "a wild man," forever changed by army life during the American Civil War. Grasshoppers along Plum Creek in Minnesota "rose and flew away into the west, clouding the sun again with their wings." Nellie Owens "had the most wonderful doll that she kept wrapped up in soft paper most of the time" so that young Wilder and her sister Mary could only yearn for it from afar. Wilder's baby brother Freddie made the whole family proud; she and Mary "always hurried home from school to see him." Wilder remembered neighbors, friends, and acquaintances, as well as the circumstances that had brought them into her family's life: George George, for example, a man who briefly traveled with the Ingalls family on their trek from Wisconsin to Minnesota; Teeny Peterson, who caught the eye of a young married man in Walnut Grove, Minnesota; and the Masters clan, who influenced Wilder's adolescence in Minnesota and Dakota Territory.

Rose Wilder Lane poses on the staircase of the farmhouse at Rocky Ridge, where she lived and wrote after building a home nearby for her parents. *Laura Ingalls Wilder Historic Home and Museum*

Laura and Almanzo stand at the front entrance to the Rock House shortly after their move from the Rocky Ridge farmhouse. *Laura Ingalls Wilder Historic Home and Museum*

Wilder also included vivid details from her family's everyday life—books, songs, toys, Christmas presents, boots, bonnets, jewelry, and dresses—objects that had woven themselves into the texture of her childhood. As Wilder moved on to her adolescent memories in *Pioneer Girl*, the manuscript became even richer, a compelling coming-of-age narrative that ended with her courtship by and marriage to Almanzo (Manly, as she called him) Wilder, ten years her senior. "I was a little awed by my new estate," she wrote on the last page of *Pioneer Girl*, "but I felt very much at home and very happy and among the other causes for happiness was the thought that I would not again have to go and live with strangers in their houses. I had a house and a home of my own." *Pioneer Girl* began with her family's quest to find a home; it ended with Wilder's discovery of her place in the world, her own little house.

Wilder wrote her life story straight through—the original manuscript has no section or chapter breaks. But because she was writing a rough draft, Wilder sometimes wrote out of sequence, rushing ahead with her story, then going back later to insert a scene or an episode. Usually, the scenes she added later appeared on the back of a manuscript page with directional notes about how Wilder intended the narrative to flow. But some of her marginal notes reveal that, from the beginning, she intended *Pioneer Girl* as both a private family narrative written from a mother to her daughter, and as a rough manuscript that would ultimately be edited for publication. In other words, Wilder imagined both an intimate, private audience and a much larger public one. Just four pages into the manuscript, for example, Wilder wrote the words "Not to be used" at the top of a page, and from the context of the scene that followed and the sentence that introduced it, Wilder worried that the general public might not find the episode credible. Yet she wrote it anyway—a scene in which wolves surrounded Pa as he rode his pony across the Kansas prairie. In Wilder's view, the scene did not fit into the main narrative; it was a digression, written entirely for her daughter's benefit.[5] Wilder finished her original draft of *Pioneer Girl* in the spring of 1930. On May 7, Lane noted, "My mother came in the afternoon bringing her manuscript. She & papa stayed to dinner."[6]

* * *

Wilder left no record of her thoughts, feelings, or attitudes about the process of writing *Pioneer Girl*. She kept diaries only a few times in her life, and they were all travel diaries.[7] Nor did Wilder leave a clear and illuminating trail of correspondence behind her. A collection of her letters, written to Manly during a trip Wilder made to visit Lane in San Francisco during 1915, was published as *West from Home* in 1974, but beyond that, little of Wilder's personal correspondence survives. The most revealing letters that still exist today were addressed to Lane and deal with the writing, editing, and publication of the Little House novels, which were written and published *after* Wilder wrote *Pioneer Girl*.

Lane, on the other hand, not only was an avid letter writer, but she kept multiple diaries throughout her lifetime, sometimes even simultaneously. During 1930, she wrote brief diary entries in a Walker's *"Year By Year" Book*, which also included daily postings for 1927, 1928, and 1929. Through Lane's diaries, it is possible to piece together a sequence of events for Wilder's writing of *Pioneer Girl*. This reconstruc-

---

5. *See ahead Pioneer Girl*, pp. 8–9n21. Later edited versions of the manuscript include the episode, as does *Little House on the Prairie*.

6. RWL, Diary #25, May 7, 1930.

7. Her first diary recorded her move from South Dakota to Mansfield, Missouri, in 1894. It was published in 1962, five years after her death, as *On the Way Home*. Another diary chronicled a three-week road trip she and Almanzo took in 1931, from Missouri back to South Dakota. It was published in 2006 as "The Road Back" in *A Little House Traveler: Writings from Laura Ingalls Wilder's Journeys across America* (New York: HarperCollins, 2006), pp. 285–344. The volume also included reprints of *On the Way Home* and *West from Home* (1974), Wilder's letters to her husband while in San Francisco in 1915. Wilder also kept brief trip diaries in 1915, 1925, and 1938. William Anderson to Nancy Tystad Koupal, Mar. 3, 2013.

tion is not, of course, a direct glimpse into Wilder's feelings or methods. It is filtered through Lane's perceptions, and like those of all diarists, those perceptions are sometimes fractured, indirect, incomplete, and even biased.

A diary's strengths—its intimacy and immediacy—are also its weaknesses. These qualities are magnified when a diary is used to reveal, not the diarist herself, but someone else who appears in its pages. No matter how intimate the diarist is with her subject, no matter how close her connection, her impressions are always projections of herself and her own feelings. Lane used her diaries not simply to record the events of the day, but to aspire, to validate, to dream, to praise, to criticize, to rant, and to remember. Lane's diaries deal with impressions and attitudes as well as everyday events. Yet, her entries for 1930 and a handful of her letters are all that is left to provide a tantalizing but clouded glimpse into the creation of *Pioneer Girl*.

From the context of her diary, for example, it is impossible to know if Lane had expected the manuscript on that afternoon of May 7, 1930, or if it caught her by surprise. On the next day, she recorded that she "worked all day copying" her mother's manuscript. She was still copying it on Friday, May 9, but stopped long enough to send a "sample" to Carl Brandt, her literary agent at the Brandt & Brandt agency in New York.[8] The text of that sample is unknown, although it probably was the manuscript's opening pages. Even today, writers often send the first five to ten pages of a manuscript to give agents and editors a feeling for its subject, voice, plot, and characters.

By 1930, Brandt had represented Lane's literary interests for over ten years. Although Wilder and Lane had launched their writing careers at roughly the same

Lane's writings and journals, including this five-year diary, give some insight into her mother's writing of *Pioneer Girl*. Herbert Hoover Presidential Library

8. RWL, Diary #25, May 7–9, 1930.

Wilder penned *Pioneer Girl* amidst the picturesque Ozark Mountain setting that surrounded the Rock House. *Laura Ingalls Wilder Historic Home and Museum*

time in the 1910s, Lane had swiftly become an international commercial and literary success. She wrote fiction and nonfiction for such magazines as *Sunset*, *Harper's*, and *Country Gentleman*. She traveled extensively and lived abroad for several years. As the reporter for the *Kansas City Star* had pointed out in 1925, "This astonishingly energetic person found time, in spite of other activities and the writing of many short stories and articles," to publish seven books: *Henry Ford's Own Story* (1917); *Diverging Roads* (1919); *White Shadows in the South Seas* (with Frederick O'Brien, 1919); *The Making of Herbert Hoover* (1920); *The Peaks of Shala* (1923); a translation of *The Dancer of Shamakha* (1922), and *He Was a Man* (1925).[9] By the late 1920s, Brandt was able to negotiate sizeable contracts for Lane, who commanded as much as ten thousand dollars for her serial fiction, the equivalent, by some estimates, of over one hundred twenty-five thousand dollars today.[10]

Lane's decision to send Brandt a sample from *Pioneer Girl* just two days after receiving it from her mother may have reflected her confidence in the manuscript. More likely, Lane submitted the sample as a favor to her mother or because Lane was desperate to bring in more income for the two Rocky Ridge Farm households, even if it came through her mother's writing rather than her own. The Great Depression had hit the American publishing industry hard. Magazines, the usual market for short and even long-form fiction and creative nonfiction throughout the first half of the twentieth century, had seen a dramatic drop in revenues. Advertisers slashed their budgets; readers canceled subscriptions. Moreover, magazine editors at such prestigious publications as the *Saturday Evening Post*, the *Ladies Home Journal*, and *Country Gentlemen* had snapped up substantial inventories of fiction and nonfiction manuscripts during the boom years leading up to the stock market crash of 1929. Given the lean realities of the early 1930s, editors published materials they had purchased earlier and

9. "Heart and Home of Rose Wilder Lane."

10. William Holtz, *The Ghost in the Little House: A Life of Rose Wilder Lane*, Missouri Biography Series (Columbia: University of Missouri Press, 1993), p. 177; "Historical Value of U.S. Dollar (Estimated)," mykindred.com/cloud/TX/Documents/dollar.

were reluctant to acquire new manuscripts, even from celebrated authors like Lane.[11] One of her colleagues sent Lane a letter pronouncing 1930 "a bad magazine year."[12]

This shift in the magazine market could not have happened at a worse time for her. In 1928, Lane had budgeted four thousand dollars to build her parents the Rock House; instead, she spent between eleven thousand and twelve thousand dollars on its design, materials, construction, and furnishings. At the same time, Lane had updated the farmhouse with extensive electrical, plumbing, and heating improvements. She had borrowed money from her parents as well as from long-time companion and house-mate Helen ("Troub") Boylston to meet expenses, but Lane had also relied on her own investments, most of which were with Palmer & Company, a financial firm in New York. The firm also handled Boylston's and the Wilders' investments, something Lane had advised. By mid-1930, the accounts with Palmer & Company had lost roughly fifty percent of their value.[13] Writing in 1932 about her personal recollections of the stock market crash and her own financial situation, Lane noted that she had not foreseen the impending crisis: "I believed everything was completely on the surface, up on the crest of the wave. Around $50,000. in Palmer account, every prospect of making it $100,000. Income was $100. a month, and I was spending about $400.00. Had built parents' new house, $12,000.00 with furnishings, in 1928. Owed bank about $2,100. My mother $2,700., Troub $5,000.00 and brokers loans on my marginal account around $25,000."[14]

When "market news" arrived a few days after the crash in 1929, Lane remembered telling Boylston, "'Our accounts are gone—this is the end," then noted the memory as "one of these feeling-white-faced-&-staring moments."[15] In the back of the five-year diary Lane kept from 1927 through 1930, she included brief notations about her goals, accomplishments, annual finances, and New Year's resolutions. For 1930, she wrote, "I will pay debts; save money."[16] But she admitted later that her initial financial fears "wore off," and "a kind of momentum carried us on."[17] Life at Rocky Ridge Farm con-

11. Pamela Smith Hill, *Laura Ingalls Wilder: A Writer's Life*, South Dakota Biography Series, no. 1 (Pierre: South Dakota State Historical Society Press, 2007), pp. 129, 133.

12. Quoted in RWL, Diary #25, Mar. 13, 1930.

13. Hill, *Laura Ingalls Wilder*, p.129; RWL, Diary #25, Aug. 15, 1930 and Memoranda 1928–1929; Holtz, *Ghost in the Little House*, p. 217.

14. RWL, Diary #21 (1924, 1926, 1932), May 14, 1932, Box 21, item #21, Lane Papers.

15. Ibid.

16. RWL, Diary #25, Memoranda 1930.

17. Ibid., #21, May 14, 1932.

tinued into the opening weeks of 1930 without any obvious changes in Lane's routine or that of her parents. A hired man and live-in cook did most of the mundane, everyday chores on the farm. Lane and Boylston bought a new mare for their fox hunts and rambling rides through the countryside; they played endless games of chess with local friends and house guests; and they attended meetings of the Justamere Club, a women's study group that Wilder had helped establish years earlier. Wilder and Lane baked French pastries together, shared tea and meals in each others' houses, and walked across the hilltop trail for afternoon visits.[18]

But, as Lane observed later, "Underneath, however, worry began."[19] Boylston paid the bills in January because Lane had just one hundred dollars left in the bank. Over the next four months, she struggled to write several new stories, but she confided to her diary her feeling that they did not measure up.[20] A letter from Brandt confirmed her suspicions. "Now about the new story ['Mrs. Smithers'']," he wrote. "Good gosh, what a swell piece of writing! But, Rose dear, I find myself absolutely at a loss to get just what you're shooting at."[21] Lane began to worry that her new material would not sell, and when another letter from Brandt arrived asking for more changes in one of the new stories, she wrote, "I feel blue as the devil." Her depression deepened as the winter wore on. "It seems to me," she wrote on February 28, "that in four years there's been nothing but dullness & growing old." The coming of spring did nothing to lighten her mood. In late March, Lane wrote, "So horribly blue that dying seems like a relief." On the next day, her entry hinted at the root of her depression, "Carl has sold nothing of mine."[22] Lane's career had stalled; when she received the *Pioneer Girl* manuscript on May 7, she may have turned to it with the hope that it would pay the bills until her own work found a market again.

Lane continued to "copy" what she called her mother's "pioneer manuscript" on May 10 and 11.[23] It is unclear exactly what the term "copy" meant in this context, but it is likely that Lane was *typing* her mother's manuscript and preparing it for submission. Even in the 1930s, the standard submission format for magazine and book publishers alike was a double-spaced, typewritten manuscript. Although Wilder herself

18. Ibid., #25, Jan. 27–Mar. 1, 1930.

19. Ibid., #21, May 14, 1932.

20. Ibid., #25, Jan. 3, 15, 20, 1930.

21. Carl Brandt to RWL, Jan. 31, 1930, Box 1, file 9, Lane Papers.

22. RWL, Diary #25, Feb. 14, 28, Mar. 30–31, 1930.

23. Ibid., May 10–11, 1930.

had learned to type at Lane's insistence shortly after she began to contribute regularly to the *Missouri Ruralist*, Lane was the better typist.[24]

On May 12, a telegram arrived with news that Brandt had sold Lane's revised story "State's Evidence" to the *Country Gentleman* for twelve hundred dollars. It was her first manuscript sale that year, but apparently it did little to reassure her doubts about the future because, two days later, she returned to *Pioneer Girl*. By May 17, she had finished "copying pioneer manuscript" and sent it to Brandt "for his opinion." She had received a note that same day from Brandt saying that the sample pages she had sent from *Pioneer Girl* the week before were "very fine."[25]

The manuscript submitted to Brandt on May 17, 1930, was in all likelihood what has since become known as the Brandt & Brandt version of *Pioneer Girl*. This 160-page, double-spaced, typewritten manuscript closely follows the structure, phrasing, and narrative of Wilder's handwritten original, but with one significant change: Lane revised the manuscript's opening line. She deleted "Once upon a time" because she may have felt the phrase was trite and implied that the manuscript was for children. Despite Wilder's original opening, *Pioneer Girl* was written for adult audiences; it was a remembrance of childhood, but its perspective and voice were mature, an older and wiser writer looking back on her past. Like Wilder's original, the Brandt & Brandt version had no chapter or section breaks. It was a continuous narrative.[26]

Once the manuscript was in the mail, the waiting game began. How would Carl Brandt respond to the entire manuscript? Did he feel there was a market for it? Would he be willing to represent it? Literary agents do not always agree to represent manuscripts, even from their established clients. Agents have to believe in the strength of the manuscript, its marketability, or ideally both. Even if *Pioneer Girl* had been written by Lane—and not by Wilder—Carl Brandt was under no obligation to represent the manuscript and then submit it to appropriate editors for their consideration.

On May 18, the day after Lane mailed *Pioneer Girl* to Brandt, her parents came for dinner, and "afterward," Lane noted in her diary, "my mother, Troub & [local friend] Corinne played bridge." Later that same evening, she taught them how to play "vingt-et-un"—blackjack.[27] Submitting a manuscript to an agent or editor is almost always a

---

24. Hill, *Laura Ingalls Wilder*, p. 100.

25. RWL, Diary #25, May 10–17, 1930.

26. The Brandt & Brandt version of *Pioneer Girl* is housed with the Lane Papers at the Herbert Hoover Presidential Library in West Branch, Iowa.

27. RWL, Diary #25, May 18, 1930.

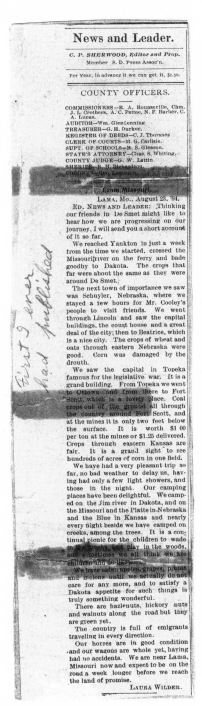

First I ever had published

In a letter to the editor that she clipped and saved as her first published piece, Wilder told readers of the *De Smet News and Leader* in 1894 about her move from South Dakota to Missouri. *Laura Ingalls Wilder Historic Home and Museum*

gamble; playing poker could not have been a more appropriate occupation at Rocky Ridge Farm that evening.

* * *

Lane's diary does not record how Wilder initially felt about submitting *Pioneer Girl* to the Brandt agency, but later in the summer of 1930, Lane wrote that Wilder hoped for "prestige rather than money" from publication.[28] Seven years later, when she was well on her way toward becoming a literary legend, Wilder said that she had decided to write about her own life partly to preserve her father's stories, that "they were [too] good to be altogether lost."[29] Yet, this explanation does not reveal *why* she chose to write her life story in 1929–1930 while in her early sixties. Why did she feel compelled to capture her family's history, stories, and traditions at that particular moment in time?

Wilder had launched her professional writing career almost twenty years earlier with a poultry column for the *St. Louis Star Farmer* and then moved on to the *Missouri Ruralist*, the major farm newspaper in the state. She wrote about farming techniques and innovations, the role of women on the farm and beyond, the changing seasons, war and peace. Wilder sometimes wrote personal sketches about her past. In 1917, for example, she published a column on "The Hard Winter" of 1880–1881; in 1924, her last year with the *Ruralist*, she wrote about the Christmas when she was sixteen. She ended that column this way, "Our hearts grow tender with childhood memories and love of kindred, and we are better throughout the year for having, in spirit, become a child again at Christmastime."[30]

Wilder's ambition to write professionally may have taken root when she was about sixteen. As a teenager in Dakota Territory, she wrote poetry and saved early writing projects that were important to her, including "Ambition," a theme written for her favorite schoolteacher Ven Owen. She also saved her first published piece, which appeared in the *De Smet News and Leader* in 1894. It was a letter to the folks back home, filled with Wilder's impressions as she and her young family moved from South Dakota to the Missouri Ozarks. "First I ever had published," she wrote in the clipping's margin.[31]

28. Ibid., July 31, 1930.

29. LIW, Detroit Book Fair (Book Week) Speech, 1937, p. 2, Box 13, file 197, Lane Papers.

30. LIW, reprinted as "Christmas When I Was Sixteen," in *Little House in the Ozarks: The Rediscovered Writings*, ed. Stephen W. Hines (Nashville: Thomas Nelson, 1991), p. 170. Wilder's original *Missouri Ruralist* columns were untitled.

31. Both the handwritten original of "Ambition" and the clipping from the *De Smet News and Leader*, 1894, can be found in the archives of the Laura Ingalls Wilder Historic Home and Museum, Mansfield, Mo.

Nine years later in 1903, Wilder drafted a short sketch based on memories of her family's experiences on Silver Lake in Dakota Territory and saved it in a file called "Ideas for Work."[32] Her father Charles Ingalls had died the previous year, and this unpublished fragment appears to be a response to his death, her first attempt at retelling family stories for a larger audience. The idea resurfaced a few years later, perhaps shortly after Wilder began her career with the *Missouri Ruralist*. In an undated letter written between 1911 and 1914, Lane referred to her mother's "life story" and gave Wilder this advice, "just think [that] you are writing a diary that no one anywhere will ever see, and put down all the things that you think, regardless."[33] If Wilder went on to write a cohesive memoir during this period, it does not survive.

She returned to the idea again in 1925, a year after her mother, Caroline Ingalls, died. Wilder wrote to her mother's sister, Martha Carpenter, asking for stories from her aunt's childhood. But by this time, Wilder herself was a professional writer, and the urgency of her request reflected a working writer's desire for authenticity. In urging her aunt to write, she echoed the advice she had received from Lane: "Just tell it in your own words as you would tell about those times if only you could talk to me. . . . As you begin to tell it so many things will come back to you about the little everyday happenings and what you and mother and Aunt Eliza and Uncle Tom and Uncle Henry did as children and young folks, going to parties and sleigh rides and spelling schools and dancing schools." Wilder was so eager for the

Wilder had been writing on farm-related topics for the *Missouri Ruralist* for seven years when this portrait ran with the column "Let's Visit Mrs. Wilder" on February 20, 1918. *Laura Ingalls Wilder Historic Home and Museum*

32. LIW, "Ideas for Work,"1903, Box 14, file 202, Lane Papers.

33. RWL to LIW, n.d. [1908-ca. 1914], Box 13, file 182, ibid. William Anderson has suggested that bits and pieces of this life story may survive, including "First Memories of Father," published in *A Little House Reader: A Collection of Writings by Laura Ingalls Wilder*, ed. Anderson (New York: HarperCollins, 1998), pp. 159–63. Anderson to Koupal, Mar. 3, 2013.

material that she even offered to pay a stenographer to transcribe Carpenter's memories. The stenographer proved unnecessary. Carpenter responded with a letter full of details—family recipes, stories about quiltings and corn-husking parties, memories of howling wolves and dangerous panthers.[34] Wilder filed her aunt's letter away and let those ideas simmer.

But when Wilder's sister Mary died at the age of sixty-three on October 17, 1928, Wilder apparently decided it was finally time to write her life story. Losing her sister may have increased her own sense of mortality. In any case, *Pioneer Girl's* time had come at last.

* * *

Anticipating news from an agent or editor can be agony for a writer, but Wilder's wait on *Pioneer Girl* was unusually harrowing. Less than a week after Lane submitted the manuscript to Carl Brandt, she decided to take Wilder to Saint Louis for a dental appointment; "a tooth" was troubling her mother. Two days later, on May 25, they drove to Springfield, Missouri, roughly fifty miles away, caught the train there, and arrived at their hotel in Saint Louis at around midnight. The next morning, a dentist named McGinnis decided Wilder's dental problem involved more than one tooth; he took out her lower teeth except for the front. Lane recorded in her diary that Wilder was "very ill" for the rest of the day and had retreated to bed at their hotel. The next day Wilder felt better and after an appointment at the clinic, she and Lane went shopping. They returned to the clinic in the afternoon for another appointment, this time with a Dr. Bartlett, who pronounced that all Wilder's upper teeth should be taken out as well. The procedure took place the next day. Lane reported that Wilder "stood it much better than the first operation." They left Saint Louis the following day and arrived in Springfield at 8 o'clock that night; Boylston was waiting for them there and drove them back to Rocky Ridge Farm.[35]

By the beginning of June, Lane was growing impatient. On the third, she asked Brandt to return her unsold manuscripts, the short stories she had sent him earlier in the year. On the next day, her anxiety had intensified, but now she worried about *Pioneer Girl*. "No word from Carl about my mother's story, which I think has been badly handled," she confided in her diary. Wilder and Lane were back in Saint Louis for another round of dental appointments in mid-June, again with Dr. Bartlett, who presumably also specialized in dentures. Wilder had several dental appointments during

34. LIW to Carpenter, June 22, 1925, and Carpenter to LIW, Sept. 2, 1925, Box 14, file 204, ibid.

35. RWL, Diary #25, May 23–29, 1930.

the week of June 16, and on Friday, "got her teeth." In between, she and Lane attended a performance of *Desert Song* at the Saint Louis Municipal Opera, took in shows at the Ambassador and Fox theaters, and shopped at the Union Market. They bought "Brönsweiger sausage for papa" before returning home on Saturday, June 21. Lane wrote, "No good news in mail, nothing sold, & Carl returns my mother's story."[36]

If Wilder was disappointed with Brandt's decision not to represent *Pioneer Girl*, Lane did not record it in her diary. On June 22, her entry focused on the summer heat, writing letters, and eating "ice cream and cake" with "papa & Mama Bess," Lane's nickname for Wilder. Nor did Lane express any disappointment herself. She dreamed of being in New York and began work on two new stories, both with Ozark themes. And for the next month, Wilder and Lane seemed preoccupied with the heat, routine errands to nearby Mountain Grove and Springfield, a farm sale outside of Hartville, and a round of visitors and house guests. But by the end of July, Lane had reached a decision: *Pioneer Girl* needed to be edited heavily to succeed in the marketplace. She began "rewriting" *Pioneer Girl* on July 31, 1930, at the same time Wilder declared her hope that the manuscript would bring her "prestige rather than money."[37]

* * *

Lane had been "rewriting" or editing manuscripts for other writers, including Wilder, for about fifteen years when she took on *Pioneer Girl*. Furthermore, based on Wilder's notes to Lane in the original *Pioneer Girl* manuscript, it is clear that Wilder expected her daughter to review and edit it for publication. The process was familiar to them both. Fifteen years earlier, Wilder had visited her daughter in San Francisco, where Lane worked for the *San Francisco Bulletin*; the purpose of the trip, aside from a lengthy mother-daughter visit, was business: Lane would teach Wilder how to write for bigger, more prestigious publications. Wilder lacked this experience; the *Missouri Ruralist* was the biggest farm publication in the state, but its audience and their interests were narrow. Even in 1915, Lane was beginning to move into the national literary spotlight and understood the demands of writing for what she later called the "big market."[38] She eagerly embraced the role of professional mentor from the beginning. In a letter from San Francisco that fall, Wilder told her husband: "Rose and I are blocking out a story of the Ozarks for me to finish when I get home. If I can only make it sell, it ought to help a lot and besides, I am learning so that I can write for the

36. Ibid., June 3–4, 16–21, 1930.
37. Ibid., June 22–July 31, 1930.
38. Lane used the term in RWL to LIW, Apr. 11, 1919, file 185, and [Nov. 1924?], file 186, Box 13, Lane Papers.

magazines."[39] Ultimately, Wilder landed an assignment with the *Missouri Ruralist* to cover San Francisco's Panama-Pacific International Exposition. Her story made the publication's front page in December 1915.

Working under Lane's editorial supervision, Wilder also published a handful of articles in two national magazines. Before submitting her articles to editors, Wilder shared her rough drafts with her daughter. In 1919, while working on a piece entitled "Whom Will You Marry?" for *McCall's*, Wilder was disheartened by the extent of Lane's revisions to the manuscript. "Don't be absurd about my doing the work on your article," Lane assured her mother. "I didn't re-write it a bit more than I rewrite Mary Heaton Vorse's articles, or Inez Haynes Irwin's stories."[40] A few years later, she pointed out that her mother's work for the *Missouri Ruralist* was "extraordinarily good," but that audiences for national publications like *McCall's* or the *Country Gentlemen*, which accepted two of Wilder's articles in the 1920s, demanded a different kind of writing.[41] Wilder had to learn to adapt to different audiences, genres, and publications. She began to accept her daughter's editorial advice, and she rarely questioned it until much later in her writing career when she found her own voice as a writer of fiction for young readers.

But in 1930, Wilder clearly had confidence in Lane's editorial instincts. In one of Wilder's last columns for the *Missouri Ruralist*, she listed her daughter among the distinguished personalities Wright County, Missouri, had produced. She described Lane as a "writer and world traveler whose books and short stories" had been published "in the United States and England" and translated into "foreign languages."[42] Her daughter's career had outstripped Wilder's modest success. Why would she question Lane's editorial recommendations?

Lane herself had boundless confidence in her editing and rewriting skills. During the 1920s, she began to run manuscripts "through the typewriter" for established writers as well as for those just breaking into the business: Frederick O'Brien, Louis Stellman, Helen ("Troub") Boylston, and even Lowell Thomas in 1930.[43] Lane came from an aggressive editing tradition — the daily newspaper business. Editors rewrote

39. LIW to Almanzo Wilder, Sept. 21, 1915, in *Little House Traveler*, p. 212.

40. RWL to LIW, Apr. 11, 1919.

41. Ibid., [Nov. 1924?].

42. LIW, "Our Little Place in the Ozarks," in *Little House in the Ozarks*, p. 27.

43. Holtz, *Ghost in the Little House*, p. 200. Lane met Boylston in 1920 when they worked together for the Red Cross. With Lane's encouragement, Boylston took up writing and became famous for her Sue Barton books, a series about nurses for teenage readers. *See* Michael Cart, *From Romance to Realism: 50 Years of Growth and Change in Young Adult Literature* (New York: HarperCollins, 1996), pp. 14–15.

Wilder recorded her childhood memories, which became *Pioneer Girl*, on these lined tablets. *Laura Ingalls Wilder Historic Home and Museum*

leads, moved paragraphs around, added details and information, or cut entire sections out of stories, usually without a reporter's knowledge or approval. Wilder had initially bristled at this approach and had questioned Lane about it in 1919, when they worked together on an article for *McCall's* magazine. Lane responded by comparing her mother's work favorably to other manuscripts, telling her, "at least your copy was all the meat of the article."[44]

When Lane set out to edit *Pioneer Girl* on July 31, 1930, she retained the "meat" of the story, but she cut away sections that seemed too childish: the story about Grandpa's childhood struggles to endure long Sunday afternoons in prayer and contemplation; Pa's boyhood memory of failing to get the cows home before dark; an episode about Wilder's naughty cousin Charley who cried wolf one too many times. She used the existing Brandt & Brandt manuscript, which had been returned from New York on June 21, to make her initial edits. Pencil lines slash through whole pages; line edits with new words or phrases in Lane's handwriting appear above and below the original typewritten text. But she must have abandoned this approach in favor of typing a new version. No handwritten edits appear in the Brandt & Brandt manuscript after page 59, where a notation in Lane's handwriting reads, "Pick up other ms."

44. RWL to LIW, Apr. 11, 1919.

The "other" manuscript has been identified as the Brandt Revised version of *Pioneer Girl*.[45] It, too, is typewritten and double-spaced, but it runs to just one hundred and twenty-seven pages. It is a leaner, meaner manuscript, a work in progress, filled with line edits in Lane's handwriting, some of them completely filling the margins and the spaces between lines. This version of *Pioneer Girl* attempts to impose a clearer narrative path through Wilder's story and includes section breaks between key scenes or important periods in the family's personal history. The manuscript also introduces new material, most notably a chilling episode about the Ingalls family's brush with the notorious Bender family in southeastern Kansas.

The Benders were accused of mass murder on the Kansas frontier in the 1870s, and their case was never formally resolved. In fact, the Benders were not arrested and brought to trial for their crimes. Newspaper accounts from the period, however, were grisly and sensational. The story captured the nation's attention and continued to do so well into the 1930s. Although Lane's diary is silent about this addition to *Pioneer Girl*, it is possible she reasoned that the new Bender material would make *Pioneer Girl* more marketable. She placed it early in the manuscript, on page six, where it would get an editor's attention right away. Is the episode authentic? Probably not, although Wilder herself mentioned the Benders in a speech she delivered during the Detroit Book Fair in 1937, and she may have thought it was authentic.

The story might have been an Ingalls family tradition, something Wilder's father Charles Ingalls could have invented to entertain his children, although even this seems unlikely. It is out of character with Wilder's depiction of him in the original *Pioneer Girl* manuscript. More importantly, however, the most sensational aspects of the Benders' story occurred after the Ingalls family had left Kansas and were living in Wisconsin; the full sequence of events presented in the Brandt Revised and the subsequent version of *Pioneer Girl* could not have happened because the Ingallses were not there to experience it (*see* Appendix B).

It is important to point out that Lane had built her professional career by fictionalizing what she published as nonfiction. Beginning as early as 1915 with "Ed Monroe, Manhunter" and "Behind the Headlight," both appearing serially in the *San Francisco Bulletin*, Lane wrote what was presented to her audience as "true" stories, but they were loosely based on interviews and factual material that Lane embellished or re-imagined to heighten their market appeal. In the case of detective Ed Monroe, the

45. What I have named the "Brandt Revised" version is also housed among the Lane Papers at the Herbert Hoover Presidential Library.

incidents were essentially factual, but Lane changed not only his name and occupation but even his character. The real Ed Monroe was a crook, not a detective.[46] Lane biographer William Holtz maintained that these stories demonstrated Lane's "easy ethical slide" from truth to fiction. In the series "Behind the Headlight," purportedly "edited by Rose Wilder Lane," the "recreated dialogue and setting, its careful pacing of dramatic incident, and its strong romantic plot make it a fictionalized narrative however true its main outline and incidents may have been," Holtz argued.[47]

Such fictionalized "true stories" led Lane to more prestigious, nonfiction assignments about the lives of famous men—Charlie Chaplin, Henry Ford, and Jack London. Her writing career blossomed. The Bobbs-Merrill Company reissued her *San Francisco Bulletin* series on Charlie Chaplin in book form. *Sunset*, a "big market" national magazine, entrusted Lane with a series on Jack London, which the Century Company then offered to publish in book form. Lane had added invented dialogue, created fictional sequences, and even transformed historical characters in these biographical stories. Henry Ford repudiated the biography Lane wrote about him for its inaccuracies, and Chaplin was apparently so outraged at the literary liberties she had taken with his life story that he threatened to bring legal action against Bobbs-Merrill. Although copies of the book had already been printed, the company canceled its distribution.[48] Even before Lane's series on Jack London had run its course in *Sunset*, London's widow and sister contacted Lane directly to register their dismay. "What Jack London himself wrote about his own life is mixed with fiction," his sister told Lane. "But *you* are supposed to be writing his biography."[49]

Before the London series saw print, Lane had tried to explain to his widow, Charmian, that *Sunset* had commissioned "a semi-biography, . . . a sort of free-hand sketch of his entire life."[50] Lane later conceded, "Of course the whole thing is fictionalized—but I hope, merely in the matter of color and handling." She added that her aim was to get "at the truth rather than at the facts,"[51] a hairline distinction

46. LIW to Almanzo Wilder, Sept. 11, 1915, in *Little House Traveler*, pp. 188–89.

47. Holtz, *Ghost in the Little House*, p. 66. Although Lane apparently interviewed several retired railroad engineers for her serial "Behind the Headlight," it was published as an autobiography of a single engineer. Lane had created a composite, embellishing the account with her mother's memories of the Hard Winter in Dakota Territory. *See Little House Traveler*, p. 270.

48. Ibid., pp. 67, 394n14.

49. Eliza Shepard to RWL, Oct. 13, 1917, Papers of Jack London, 1866–1977, Huntington Library, San Moreno, Calif.

50. RWL to Charmian London, May 22, 1917, Box 13, folder 14, Jack and Charmian London Correspondence and Papers, Utah State University Special Collections and Archives, Logan.

51. Ibid., Sept, 22, 1917.

Confident in her own skills as a writer, Rose Wilder Lane guided her mother's career. *Laura Ingalls Wilder Historic Home and Museum*

that the London family ultimately rejected. After the *Sunset* series had run its course in the magazine, Charmian London expressed how "hurt" and "enraged" she was that a writer as talented as Lane had set so many "misleading" and "false impressions" in print without first "taking the trouble to find out their truth."[52]

Yet, for Lane, mixing fiction with fact was simply good business—it strengthened the popular appeal of an important public figure like London and attracted book publishers. "Century publishing company offers me fifteen percent royalty," she wrote Charmian, inquiring if there were any way to revise the book that would make it acceptable to the family. "The royalty is not as high as I have been offered," Lane continued, "but I like the connection with Century. I like the connection, indeed, more than the money. It might be possible to arrive at some financial arrangement with you."[53] Charmian London refused, saying that she considered the book "largely an erroneous interpretation of Jack London" that could not be fixed.[54] Century did not publish Lane's series on London in book form.

But the following year, in 1919, Century Company did publish Lane's first novel, *Diverging Roads*, an *autobiographical* story loosely based on her own experiences in California and her marriage to Gillette Lane, which officially ended in divorce in 1918. From Lane's perspective, fictionalizing nonfiction had paid off again,[55] but this time, she had transformed the facts of her own life into a novel, an inherently fictional art form. During the 1920s, her career continued to prosper, although a dispute over Frederick O'Brien's memoir *White Shadows on the South Sea*, which became a best-

52. Charmian London to RWL, Apr. 28, 1918, Box 10, folder 5, ibid.

53. RWL to Charmian London, May 2, 1918, Box 13, folder 14, ibid.

54. Charmian London to RWL, May 6, 1918, Box 10, folder 5, ibid.

55. Holtz, *Ghost in the Little House*, pp. 76–77. It is interesting to note that Charmian London believed that Lane could market an alternative book idea to Century. She wrote Lane, "If CENTURY PUB. CO. wants you 15%-worth, you can certainly demand it by delivering them something upon a subject otherwise than my late husband" (London to RWL, May 6, 1918).

seller, again brought up questions of fact versus fiction. O'Brien had asked Lane to help him revise his manuscript in 1918 and paid her five hundred dollars for her services. He also agreed to give her a share of his royalties if the book was successfully published. Lane's edits were so extensive that she essentially functioned as a ghost writer on the project, creating a "wholesale revision" of the original manuscript.[56] What was fact and what was fiction in this memoir? How much material came from O'Brien's memories and Lane's imagination? The issue boiled to the surface when Lane sued O'Brien for her share of the royalties. Lane won her case in 1926, but in the process her creative approach—fictionalizing what was marketed as nonfiction— became an issue, at least for some readers. As late as 1929, she felt compelled to address the subject directly. "The important fact," she wrote, "is that WHITE SHADOWS was not an attempt to cheat the public by selling it lies as facts. So far as I know, there was no misrepresentation in the book."[57]

Much of Rose Wilder Lane's work from the late 1910s and 1920s certainly qualifies as "literary journalism," or creative nonfiction, a genre that emerged at the turn of the twentieth century. It gained momentum in the 1960s and early 1970s through the work of such writers as Tom Wolfe, Joan Didion, and Edward Abbey. Creative nonfiction draws on established literary techniques: depicting three-dimensional characters, forming a structured narrative, conveying a vivid sense of place or scene, and, perhaps most importantly, creating a unique and personal authorial voice. A writer of creative nonfiction concentrates on "the drama and intensity of ordinary people living unusual, stressful, and compelling lives."[58] Like fiction, literary nonfiction seeks to explore or reveal the greater truth existing beneath or behind the particular details of a story. In nonfiction, however, those details are *factual*. As scholar Amy Mattson Lauters explained, a work of literary journalism "must be factually verifiable."[59] Not all the work Lane published as nonfiction prior to 1930 met that standard.

Yet, Lane's rapid rise in the publishing world seemed to vindicate her approach. Would it work for her mother as well? Why not include the Bender episode in *Pioneer Girl* if it resulted in a sale, especially if there was some tentative connection? Her diary reveals that as she was editing the new version of *Pioneer Girl*, Lane was eager to sell

56. Ibid., p. 88.

57. RWL to Mr. Colcord, July 8, 1929, Box 10, file 147, Lane Papers.

58. Lee Gutkind, Introduction to *The Art of Creative Nonfiction: Writing and Selling the Literature of Reality* (New York: John Wiley & Sons, 1997), p. 2.

59. Lauters, Introduction to *The Rediscovered Writings of Rose Wilder Lane, Literary Journalist* (Columbia: University of Missouri Press, 2007), p. 3. For discussions of creative nonfiction, *see* Brenda Miller and Suzanne Paola, *Tell It Slant: Creating, Refining and Publishing Creative Nonfiction*, 2d ed. (New York: McGraw Hill, 2012).

it. On August 1, she wrote Brandt "asking his opinion" about entering the manuscript in contests." Lane was also severely depressed and worried about money. "Bad night," she wrote on August 4, after working all day on *Pioneer Girl*, "smothering & very much depressed about money, failure, old age, death, etc."[60] Perhaps Lane's desperation further influenced her decision to add a fictional episode to her mother's memoir.

Wilder herself was at least partially aware of Lane's approach to writing "true stories." Fifteen years before, she had provided her daughter with details and background information that Lane then presented as coming from the fictionalized engineer in "Behind the Headlight," published in 1915. Wilder had explained this technique to her husband and justified it because "every incident in it is true."[61] Perhaps she applied a similar standard when evaluating whether to add the Bender account to *Pioneer Girl*.

* * *

Lane abruptly set *Pioneer Girl* aside on August 5, 1930, and the next day began working on a new short story entitled "A Methodist Lady." She also learned that Brandt had sold another one of her manuscripts—"Grandmother's Silver"—to *Good Housekeeping* magazine for twelve hundred dollars. Lane gave it a new title, "A Man in the House," and rewrote it for markets in Great Britain. In the meantime, the extreme heat persisted. Wilder and Lane visited each other regularly, but they apparently argued about an anniversary gift Lane had proposed to give her parents: a trip to South Dakota. After spending the whole afternoon of August 14 with Wilder, Lane learned that her parents did not want the trip after all; they preferred to spend the money on "ponds & meadows here—and may go south in the winter." Lane ended her diary entry with the lines, "God! I need money. Dreamed a worry all night."[62]

But something else had apparently shifted after that visit, for on the next day and the next, Lane wrote that she "worked on my mother's copy." Then on August 17, Lane noted that she had "worked on & finished my mother's 'juvenile.'"[63] Never before had Lane referred to *Pioneer Girl* as a "juvenile" project, nor does her diary—until August 17. In fact, the juvenile Lane had finished was an excerpt from Wilder's original *Pioneer Girl* manuscript, a compact narrative based on episodes of the family's life in Wisconsin. Lane, however, had embellished this juvenile version with dialogue and more description. She also switched point of view, from Wilder's original first-person voice to a fictionalized, third-person perspective. The opening lines began: "When

60. RWL, Diary #25, Aug. 1–4, 1930.

61. LIW to Almanzo Wilder, Oct. 22, 1915, in *Little House Traveler*, p. 270.

62. RWL, Diary #25, Aug. 5–14, 1930.

63. Ibid., Aug. 15–17.

Grandma was a little girl, she lived in a little gray house made of logs. The house was in the Big Woods, in Michigan." A line runs through "Michigan," which is replaced with the word "Wisconsin" in a handwritten correction (*see* Appendix A). Wilder herself would rework and expand this juvenile in 1931, but in August 1930, Lane had apparently prepared the excerpt without her mother's knowledge.

Lane's diary provides no clues that explain why she decided to take this new approach with her mother's pioneer material. Many Wilder scholars maintain that Lane's old friends, Elmer and Berta Hader, who wrote and illustrated children's books, influenced this decision.[64] But nothing exists to document a conversation or correspondence between Lane and the Haders at this time. In February, 1930, Lane had written Berta Hader a chatty letter about books, mutual friends, and life on Rocky Ridge Farm that winter. It also included a paragraph about a writing competition, a subject Lane raised later with Carl Brandt as a possible publication opportunity for *Pioneer Girl*. Otherwise, the letter has nothing to do with children's literature in general, or *Pioneer Girl* in particular. It is clear that Lane and Berta Hader discussed the juvenile version of *Pioneer Girl* later in 1931, but the context of that discussion was not about adapting Wilder's autobiography for young readers but about finding a publisher for the children's manuscript.[65]

It is possible that the seed for a juvenile adaptation originated with Wilder herself, not in 1930, but much earlier—in 1919, when Lane was still living in San Francisco. While working on a second and ultimately unfinished project for *McCall's* magazine, Wilder wrote Lane for advice but also sent her a selection of children's stories. These stories no longer survive, but Lane wrote back to Wilder and pronounced the stories "good." Yet, at the time, Lane advised her mother against writing for children, "for there is no opportunity to make a name with children's stories."[66] In 1930, Lane changed her mind.

Although it may be impossible to know with certainty why Lane decided to adapt a slice of *Pioneer Girl* for children, it is clear from her edits that much of the material she apparently deemed inappropriate for adult readers and cut from the Brandt Revised version of *Pioneer Girl* went into the juvenile excerpt. For example, Pa's story about failing to bring the cows home one night and Grandpa's boyhood memory of

64. *See*, for example, Janet Spaeth, *Laura Ingalls Wilder*, Twayne's United States Authors Series (Boston: Twayne Publishers, 1987), p. 8.

65. RWL to Berta Hader, Feb. 18, 1930, Box 5, file 64, and Marion Fiery to LIW, Feb. 12, 1931, Box 13, file 189, Lane Papers.

66. RWL to LIW, Apr. 11, 1919.

the Sunday afternoon he and his brothers got into trouble reappear in the juvenile manuscript. In fact, Wilder's desire to preserve her father's stories may have been the guiding principle that Lane used to shape the juvenile manuscript, for the narrative essentially provides a frame to showcase the stories that Charles Ingalls told his children.[67] Yet, Lane not only switched audiences, she switched genres—from nonfiction to fiction. When she replaced Wilder's intimate first-person voice, her "I" narrator, with a third-person narrator, the juvenile manuscript instantly became fiction. Now known as "When Grandma Was a Little Girl," the original juvenile *Pioneer Girl* manuscript survives today as a rough draft, complete with typewritten strike-outs and Lane's handwritten edits and notes. It is a twenty-one-page, double-spaced typescript (Appendix A).

On August 18, 1930, Lane wrote, "Had to recopy part of juvenile, which was then mailed." The diary does not reveal to whom Lane submitted the manuscript, but on the next day, August 19, she was back at work on the adult revisions of *Pioneer Girl*. "Working on my mothers story—stupidly," she wrote, "for will it come to anything?"[68]

* * *

Lane edited her mother's adult manuscript through the end of August and into early September. "I finished the pioneer copy," she wrote on September 2, without noting if she decided to submit this final draft to Brandt, although she probably did.[69] Lane continued to worry about finances at Rocky Ridge Farm, and after so much effort, it seems unlikely that she would hide the manuscript away in a file. This final edited version is probably the manuscript now known as the George T. Bye version.[70] It is a typewritten, double-spaced manuscript covering 203 pages and contains no handwritten notes or revisions, a defining characteristic of a final draft. The Bye version, which takes its name from Lane's and Wilder's literary agent from 1931 until his death in 1957, is by far the most developed, polished, and literary version of *Pioneer Girl*. Like its predecessors, the Bye manuscript is not divided into chapters, although section breaks give the narrative structure and shape.

The final editing of the Bye manuscript, coming as it did on the heels of her work on

67. The opening line of Wilder's 1937 Detroit Book Fair speech referred to her desire to preserve her father's stories: "Many years ago, in the Little House in the Big Woods, Sister Mary and I listened to fathers stories," she began. She reiterated the point to reporter Fred Kiewit in 1955: "It seemed a shame to let die those stories that father told us of his boyhood on a New York farm. . . . I hated to see them lost" ("Stories That Had to Be Told," *Kansas City Star*, May 22, 1955). Wilder may have told Lane much the same thing as Lane worked to shape *Pioneer Girl*.

68. RWL, Diary #25, Aug. 18–19.

69. Ibid., Sept. 2, 1930.

70. The George T. Bye version of *Pioneer Girl* is also housed as part of the Lane Papers.

the juvenile manuscript, exhausted Lane. She reported feeling "horribly depressed" in early September and found it difficult to work on her own new material. "Started new story," she observed on September 9, "not much good."[71] Friction had deepened that month between Lane and Wilder, who perhaps was beginning to worry about money, too. Despite all the talk about celebrating Wilder and Manly's forty-fifth wedding anniversary in August with a trip to Dakota or improvements to Rocky Ridge Farm, the day itself had turned out to be a miserable occasion, at least for Wilder. Lane took a trip to Hollister, Missouri, with Boylston, their neighbors the Craigs, and house-guest Catharine Brody; Manly worked with the hired man all day; and Wilder was left, "sitting alone."[72] On September 14, Lane wrote that she hoped that the anniversary was not "an omen." But she and her mother quarreled frequently that month. On September 10, Lane "walked over & spent afternoon with my mother, who walked home with me, I heartsick at all this wrangling & eternal pulling & tugging at me from all sides. Why can't I be left alone?" Wilder wanted a new will and worried about "property." She and Lane walked the hilltop trail between their houses frequently that month and even had tea together. But the bickering continued. "Said I wished I'd never made a cent," Lane told her mother on the twentieth, "then she & papa could be supporting me."[73]

The emotional tension between Wilder and Lane certainly had its roots in money and the anxiety they both felt as the Great Depression deepened. Furthermore, their personal finances had become hopelessly entangled—their accounts at Palmer & Company; their two houses—Lane, living in a house her parents had built, while they lived in one she had built and paid for; and the property they lived on—Rocky Ridge Farm, which had been mortgaged until Wilder made the last payment in 1929. Even as Lane supported her parents financially, she borrowed money from them. To complicate matters further, Wilder and Lane had totally different visions of how to live economically. Wilder preferred to face financial hardships by cutting back on what she perceived as luxuries, even such modern conveniences as electricity.[74] Writing in her journal three years later, Lane complained of her "mother's scorn, fear, fury, from her agonizing finger-tip hold on economic safety."[75] Yet, Lane also recognized in a

71. RWL, Diary #25, Sept. 8–9, 1930.

72. Ibid., Aug. 25, 1930.

73. Ibid., Sept. 10–20, 1930.

74. RWL, Diary #21, May 14, 1932; RWL, Diary #47 (1933–34, 1940, 1949–50, 1960), Apr. 10, 1933, Box 23, item #47, Lane Papers.

75. RWL, Diary #45 (1932–1933), Jan. 5, 1933, Box 22, item #45, ibid.

moment of candor that she had long been part of what she called the "irresponsible 'artist' class" and that she had to struggle to become a member of the "responsible householder class."[76] But household economy, even during hard times, was a difficult concept for Lane to embrace. During September 1930, even as she and Wilder quarreled about money, Lane and Boylston made frequent shopping trips to Springfield, including stops at the exclusive Levy Wolf department store, where they charged their purchases. On one of their visits, Lane came home with a "brown wool tailored dress." She returned a week later to try on more.[77]

Although Lane does not directly refer to *Pioneer Girl* in her diary after mailing it off to Carl Brandt, the manuscript must have cast a shadow over the tensions at Rocky Ridge Farm and likely intensified the friction between mother and daughter that September. Weeks went by without any word from the agent. When he did write on September 27, it was merely to say that he had sent one of Lane's stories on to *Ladies Home Journal* and that he would "wire any good news" as it developed. While silent on the subject of *Pioneer Girl*, Brandt urged Lane to come to New York, but she noted, "he is really indifferent." By October 8, there was still "no word from Carl."[78]

Ultimately she decided to go to New York, and on October 13, Wilder and Boylston saw Lane off. Armed with a trunk and her typewriter, she caught the noon train from Lebanon, Missouri, to Saint Louis. It was running twenty minutes late, so she missed her connecting train and arrived in New York a day later than she had planned, on October 15. She met with Carl Brandt in his office two days later. "Carl advises not to try to sell my mother's story," she wrote in her diary on the seventeenth. Reading between the lines, Brandt remained unimpressed with the entire project; Lane's most recent revision had not changed his initial opinion of *Pioneer Girl*. If Lane wrote Wilder of his decision, the letter does not survive, but she seemed determined to sell *Pioneer Girl* and took on the role of literary agent for the manuscript herself. Four days later, she met Graeme Lorimer of the Curtis Publishing Company in Brandt's office and made a lunch date for the following week.[79] Curtis Publishing owned such distinguished magazine titles as the *Ladies Home Journal* and the *Saturday Evening Post*. The *Ladies Home Journal* had published a handful of Lane's short stories over the past two years, but she had not sold anything to the *Post*. Lorimer was an important contact for Lane.

76. RWL, Diary #21, May 14, 1932.
77. Ibid., #25, Sept. 23, 30, 1930.
78. Ibid., Sept. 27, Oct. 8, 1930.
79. Ibid., Oct. 13–21, 1930.

She "lunched" with Lorimer on October 28, and instead of concentrating on selling her own material, she "gave him a sales talk on Pioneer Girl." Lane was so persuasive that he followed her to the apartment where she was staying and picked up the manuscript.[80] Again it is impossible to know whether Lane's focus on *Pioneer Girl* was based on her conviction that her mother's autobiography was inherently strong or whether Lane was merely trying to appease her mother's desire for the prestige of publication. But personally handing over a manuscript to someone as important as Lorimer could not have been a casual decision on Lane's part. It was not in her professional interest to promote a manuscript to him if she believed it was inferior; to do so would damage her credibility and her own future submissions, even if they came through Carl Brandt.

Just over two weeks later, Lorimer telephoned Lane to give her his verdict. *Pioneer Girl* was a manuscript that exhibited "most intelligent writing," but he could not accept it for *Ladies Home Journal*. Lane told Wilder, "they would undoubtedly have taken it, only they have in their safe some material which, broadly speaking, covers the same field." In the same letter, addressed to "Dearest Mama Bess" in November, Lane added, "There's nothing to do but try it somewhere else. . . . I haven't any doubt at all that it will go in book, but what I want to do is to exhaust serial possibilities before offering it for book publication."[81] In other words, Lane hoped to sell *Pioneer Girl* as a magazine serial before selling the rights again to a book publisher. She hoped to earn more money for her mother as well as prestige.

Later in the same letter, Lane wrote, "I have taken your manuscript to [William F.] Bigelow at *Good Housekeeping*, he promised to read it. . . . I gave him the best sales-talk I could on it." But she prepared Wilder for another rejection, "I doubt myself that it will be quite suitable for G.H., but don't want to leave any stone unturned." Obviously Lane had decided to persevere in her efforts to market *Pioneer Girl* and would continue to act as a kind of literary agent for the manuscript. She ended the letter with a quick overview of the New York literary market in 1930. Her tone was pragmatic, efficient but encouraging, a summary from one professional writer to another. Lane complained that although such publications as *Ladies Home Journal* and *Woman's Home Companion* had "cleared" millions of dollars, they were "cutting down on writers and artists," paying them less, buying fewer manuscripts and illustrations. Editors were being forced to use the "manuscripts in their safes." But Lane's last lines were opti-

80. Ibid., Oct. 28, 1930.
81. RWL to LIW, [Nov. 12, 1930], Box 13, file 188, Lane Papers.

mistic: "Fortunately this just can't continue for long. Eventually the safes are bound to be empty."[82]

Pioneer Girl's editorial trail goes cold for the rest of the year. Lane stopped writing in her diary after an entry for November 8, 1930, briefly resumed writing again on November 30, then stopped completely on December 6, noting that she was "frightfully sick."[83] No written accounts exist to document Wilder's feelings at year's end. Was she discouraged or encouraged by the news from New York? At least, she had a persistent and well-connected literary advocate in her daughter.

Lane started a new five-year diary on January 1, 1931, noting, "This year begins with a very strong bright expectation that it will be a good year." But on the next day, she wrote that "Mr. Bigelow" of *Good Housekeeping* had "refused *Pioneer Girl*." For the rest of the month and well into February, Lane's diary is silent on the subject of *Pioneer Girl*. Then on February 15, 1931, Lane recorded that she took the train to the home of Berta Hader in Nyack, New York. There she met Marion Fiery of the Children's Book Department at Alfred A. Knopf. "She takes Pioneer Girl juvenile," Lane wrote.[84]

The manuscript that impressed Fiery was the children's version of *Pioneer Girl*, which begins with the line "When Grandma was a little girl." Hader had submitted the manuscript to Fiery on Wilder's behalf, probably late in 1930. Nothing survives from this period to indicate precisely when Hader first received the manuscript from Lane, or if the two of them even discussed it. But Lane and Hader had met at least three times during the fall of 1930, once at Hader's home in Nyack, twice in the city for dinner and shopping. Given Fiery's interest in the manuscript early in February, Lane and Hader must have discussed marketing ideas for the manuscript during at least one of those visits.[85]

Lane's observation, however, that Fiery had decided to take the juvenile on February 15, 1931, was premature. Three days earlier, Fiery herself had written Wilder about the manuscript, saying she had read it with "the greatest interest." She did not make an outright offer on the book but asked: "Would you be willing to make some editorial changes on your manuscript? It is not long enough in its present state to make the kind of book which I have in mind." Fiery wanted "more details" about "the everyday life of the pioneers"; she envisioned a longer and richer story, a novel for children aged

82. Ibid.
83. RWL, Diary #25, Dec. 6, 1930.
84. RWL, Diary #37 (1931–1935), Jan. 1–2, Feb. 15, 1931, Box 22, item #37, Lane Papers.
85. Fiery to LIW, Feb. 12, 1931, Box 13, file 189, Lane Papers; RWL, Diary #25, Oct. 25, 29, Dec. 4, 1930.

eight to ten. Still, Fiery's interest was promising and represented the first glimmer of hope for Wilder's autobiographical material.[86]

It is not unusual, even today, for children's book editors to ask for revisions before offering a first-time, or even an experienced, writer a contract. Under such circumstances, there is no guarantee that the writer will receive a contract after completing a revised manuscript. Three weeks later, Fiery clarified Alfred A. Knopf's position to Wilder: "Our interest in having this book is very definite, and if the complete book is as well done as the part you have submitted, there is no reason in the world why we will not accept it. Of course, you understand a definite contract cannot be made until we receive the complete manuscript."[87]

Lane wasted no time in coaching Wilder about Fiery's expectations for the manuscript. "Knopf's will take the juvenile in book, if you can make it twice as long," Lane wrote Wilder on February 16, the day after the meeting with Fiery. "I do not think you will have any trouble doing that." But before Lane could explain exactly what changes Knopf expected, she had to describe the manuscript itself. "It is your father's stories," Lane wrote, "taken out of the long PIONEER GIRL manuscript, and strung together, as you will see." Clearly, Wilder had no idea this version of her autobiographical story even existed. "Of course I have said nothing about having run the manuscript through my own typewriter, because the changes I made, as you will see, are so slight that they could not even probably be called editing," Lane assured her mother. "It is really your own work, practically word for word." Lane also made sure she conveyed Fiery's enthusiasm for the manuscript, saying, "Marian [sic] Fiery is crazy about your writing; indeed, everyone is who has seen it."[88]

Lane then launched into a detailed discussion of the changes Fiery wanted, directing Wilder back to the original handwritten *Pioneer Girl* for episodes, scenes, and details to bring this new juvenile version to life. "There is a very lovely bit in your tablets," Lane wrote, "about your big cousin [aunt] who comes to visit, and your quarrel with Mary about whose hair is the prettier. That should be put back in." Lane even told her mother where to find the handwritten original tablets; they were at the Rocky Ridge farmhouse, "somewhere on the sleeping porch."[89]

One strategic shift Lane had made in the *Pioneer Girl* juvenile needed special clarification: the shift from first-person to third-person point of view. She did not tell her

---

86. Fiery to LIW, Feb 12, 1931. *See also* RWL to LIW, Feb. 16, 1931, Box 13, file 189, Lane Papers.
87. Fiery to LIW, Mar. 3, 1931, ibid.
88. RWL to LIW, Feb. 16, 1931.
89. Ibid.

mother that this change moved *Pioneer Girl* from nonfiction to fiction; instead she explained, "For juveniles you can not use the first person, because the 'I' books do not sell well." And she emphasized the need for her mother to write "from the point of view of the child" when adding new material to this version of *Pioneer Girl*. If Wilder found the shift too daunting, Lane encouraged her to continue to write in first person and promised that she herself could change the narrative "into the third person later." For the moment, Lane wrote, "I wish you would just get another tablet, and put down in it somehow the other 15,000 words that Marian [*sic*] wants."[90]

That is exactly what Wilder did. She found the original *Pioneer Girl* on the sleeping porch, bought a fresh supply of tablets, and began work on the revisions Fiery had requested. Undaunted by Lane's concern that the shift in point of view would be too much for her, Wilder began her children's version of the story in third-person with the line, "Once upon a time, long ago, a little girl lived in the Big Woods of Wisconsin in a little gray house made of logs."[91] Wilder filled two tablets; she labeled them "Pioneer Girl, Number 1" and "Number 2" on their covers, then renumbered the first three original tablets.[92] On May 8, 1931, a year and a day after she had given the original *Pioneer Girl* manuscript to Lane, Wilder presented her daughter with the new manuscript, a children's version of *Pioneer Girl* that depicted a year in the life of the Ingalls family, pioneers living in the Big Woods of Wisconsin.[93]

* * *

Lane had remained in New York through the end of February and into March 1931. She worked on her own creative projects, dined with literary friends and acquaintances, shopped for pajamas and an eggshell blouse, attended parties, saw movies,

90. Ibid.

91. LIW, "Pioneer Girl, Number 1" [*Little House in the Big Woods*], p. 1, Folder 7, Laura Ingalls Wilder Papers, Laura Ingalls Wilder Home Association, Mansfield, Mo., Microfilm ed., LIW Papers, 1894–1943, Western Historical Manuscript Collection, Ellis Library, University of Missouri, Columbia, Mo.

92. When she revised what Lane called the "juvenile Pioneer Girl" manuscript, Wilder continued to use the "Pioneer Girl" title. She renumbered the first three original tablets as 3, 4, and 5, striking out 1, 2, 3, but she maintained the original numbering on tablets 4 through 6. As a result, there are eight tablets of "Pioneer Girl" labeled in her handwriting, with duplicate numbers 4 and 5. These eight tablets are housed together as a unit at the Laura Ingalls Wilder Historic Home and Museum in Mansfield, Missouri. When the University of Missouri microfilmed Wilder's papers, the organizer of the microfilm edition relabeled the newer tablets as *Little House in the Big Woods*, attaching a handwritten slip of paper to the cover of the Fifty-Fifty tablet that Wilder had designated "Pioneer Girl, Number 1." As a result, the microfilm edition organizes the original six tablets of *Pioneer Girl* as Folders 1 through 6, while the two additional tablets constitute Folders 7 and 8. Folder 9 is another handwritten tablet that appears to be an earlier version of parts of Folder 7. Most of the organizing labels used in the microfilm edition of the Wilder Papers have since been removed from the original manuscripts.

93. RWL, Diary # 37, May 8, 1931.

and read. All the while her dissatisfaction with her literary agent deepened. On March 12, she wrote, "Saw Carl at 11:30 and—this is a mistake." She may have fired Brandt during this meeting. Four days later, on March 16, she met with a different literary agent, George Bye from the George T. Bye literary agency on Fifth Avenue.[94] The meeting apparently went well; on March 19, one of Bye's associates wrote her, confirming, "This office would be pleased to handle your current and future stories for magazine and book publication."[95] Although she met with Fiery for lunch later that same day, Lane did not discuss her mother's potential children's book deal with Bye.[96]

Lane left New York on March 19 and arrived in Mansfield on the morning of March 20. "Father, mother, . . . & Troub met the train." Lane felt "bum" and "heartsunk" at the prospect of resuming life in the Ozarks, and she struggled with depression during her first few days back at Rocky Ridge Farm.[97] But soon she was at work on her own projects again and corresponding regularly with George Bye. At some point in late March or early April, Lane sent Bye a copy of the final draft of *Pioneer Girl*, the adult version she had completed in September 1930. On April 6, he wrote back, "'Pioneer Girl' didn't warm me enough the first reading. It didn't seem to have enough high points or crescendo. A fine old lady was sitting in a rocking chair and telling a story chronologically but with no benefit of perspective or theatre." He added, "However, we are trying—."[98]

Perhaps because the working relationship with Lane was still so new, Bye decided to market *Pioneer Girl* even though he lacked professional confidence in it. He prepared a new cover sheet for the manuscript, bound it in his agency's "rhododendron blue jackets with buff labels," and began the submission process.[99] On April 22, he wrote Lane that the *Saturday Evening Post* described *Pioneer Girl* as "a good autobiography and well written" but had returned the manuscript, saying, "in light of the large amount of historical material we have printed in the past year or so, we dare not make a place for it on a long article list."[100] *Country Home* magazine also rejected the manuscript; its editorial staff noted that while it "contains some very interesting pioneer reminiscences," the magazine had "no place for non-fiction serials."[101]

94. Ibid., Mar. 12, 16, 1931.

95. Robert S. Bassler to RWL, Mar.19, 1931, Box 1, file 11, Lane Papers.

96. Lane waited until September to do so. *See* RWL to Bye, Sept. 25, 1931, Box 13, file 189, ibid.

97. RWL, Diary #37, Mar. 19–21, 1931.

98. Bye to RWL, Apr. 6, 1931, Box 13, file 189, Lane Papers.

99. Ibid., May 28, 1931, Box 1, file 11.

100. Ibid., Apr. 22, 1931, Box 13, file 189.

101. Andrew S. Wing to Bye, May 1, 1931, ibid.

The news was disappointing, of course, but Wilder was focused primarily on revisions for Knopf. On May 8, she had tea with Lane at the farmhouse and dropped off her new juvenile *Pioneer Girl* manuscript. Two weeks later, she returned to the farmhouse "at breakfast time" and "roughed out 15,000 words of her juvenile" with Lane. From the context of Lane's diary entry, it appears that the two spent the entire day together working through these revisions. On May 23, Wilder returned to read and review the revisions with Lane. On the next day, Lane completed her final edits and began "copying"—probably typing—the manuscript for Fiery. It was finished at 4:30 in the afternoon on May 26, when Wilder came over for a final reading. On May 27, Lane recorded that she "got juvenile ready for mailing, wrote Marian [*sic*] Fiery."[102]

She began the letter to Fiery, which served as a cover letter to her mother's revised manuscript, with an explanation about the book's emphasis. It was based on "those tales" of Wilder's "childhood in the Big Woods." Lane does not refer to the manuscript's title, although a list of potential ideas included "Trundle-bed Tales," "Long Ago in the Big Woods," "Little Girl in the Big Woods," and "Long Ago Yesterday." The second title on the list was "Little Pioneer Girl." The rest of Lane's letter focused on editorial and business issues. She advised Fiery to correspond directly with herself, rather than Wilder, "because my mother naturally consults me about everything concerning her writing." Furthermore, Lane said, her parents were leaving the following week "for a long motor trip," and it would be virtually impossible to reach them if Fiery had urgent editorial questions. George Bye, Lane went on, should be consulted about all business details but not editorial ones, for even "the best of agents always seems to me to be a little bit in the way between writer and editor." Lane added that Bye was handling her mother's "other manuscripts," presumably a hint that the adult version of *Pioneer Girl* was still in circulation.[103]

For all practical purposes, Wilder's full-length autobiography had lost its momentum as a marketable manuscript. Lane's diary does not refer to it for the rest of 1931; two of her letters, however, include a final sales pitch. On September 25, Lane wrote Bye, saying, "It occurs to me that Marian [*sic*] Fiery at Knopf might be interested in PIONEER GIRL, if it were rewritten in the third person."[104] She then mentioned the adult manuscript to Fiery a few days later. "George Bye is handling another book of my mothers [*sic*], PIONEER GIRL," Lane wrote. "It is slightly older autobiography,

. . . full of fascinating material, about pioneer life in the Dakotas, the building of the railroads, home-steading, the coming of the grasshoppers, sod shanties, and the memorable HARD Winter of 1870 [*sic*], when the little town of 100 people was snowed under for months, without adequate food or fuel. It is told in the first person, but it occurs to me that you might like it enormously for slightly older juvenile readers, if it were rewritten in the third person."[105] As Lane and Wilder were soon to find out, however, Fiery was not in the position to buy another manuscript, from Wilder or anyone else.

In the summer of 1931, as Wilder awaited a verdict on her revised juvenile *Pioneer Girl*—and perhaps a contract—she seemed to have pushed concerns about selling the adult version of *Pioneer Girl* aside. She and Manly left Mansfield with their dog Nero on June 6 in their 1923 Buick for the trip to South Dakota they had been discussing for nearly a year. They planned to retrace the route they had taken in 1894, when they had moved from South Dakota to Missouri when Lane was seven years old. Wilder once again kept a travel diary and sent her entries back to her daughter, who recorded that the first of them arrived on June 15.[106] Wilder had not been back to South Dakota since her father's death in 1902, so the trip was bittersweet. She and Manly stopped in Manchester, South Dakota, where Wilder's sister Grace

The Wilders traveled back to South Dakota in 1931. Among the places they visited was what is now Badlands National Park, not far from the Black Hills home of Wilder's sister Carrie. *Laura Ingalls Wilder Historic Home and Museum*

105. RWL to Fiery, Oct. 3, 1931, Box 13, file 189, Lane Papers.
106. RWL, Diary #37, June 15, 1931.

and her husband were living. "Grace seems like a stranger now," Wilder wrote, "only now and then something familiar about her face. I suppose it is the same with me."[107]

Wilder and Manly then drove out toward her father's farm "on the road from town across the slough, nearly in the place were Carrie and I walked to school and Manly used to drive Barnum and Skip as he came dashing out to take me on those long Sunday afternoon drives when I was seventeen." The landscape had changed, but Wilder's memories from *Pioneer Girl* seemed vivid and fresh. Wilder and Manly next headed west out of De Smet toward the Black Hills, where Wilder's sister Carrie Ingalls Swanzey lived with her husband David in Keystone. After several days in the Black Hills, Wilder and Manly turned their Buick east and headed for home. "I said," Wilder wrote in her diary, "'The hot wind is blowing us out of Dakota àgain,' and Manly said, 'It's the last time it will ever have a chance.'"[108] They arrived back home at Rocky Ridge Farm on June 29. "Parents arrived, . . . saying, 'East, west, home's best.' Utter complacency of that point of view—& so 'dated,' too," Lane complained to her diary.[109]

The rest of the summer dragged by with no news from either Bye or Fiery. "Feeling dull & sunk," Lane wrote on September 11. A few days later, she decided to write Fiery, and on September 19, Fiery herself wrote that Knopf had decided to purchase Wilder's manuscript. There is no record of how Wilder felt about this, but Lane wrote, "My mother's juvenile is accepted. . . . Am feeling grand."[110] Fiery offered Wilder a three-book contract, which included plans to release the first book in 1932. Lane wrote to Bye, asking him to "handle the business arrangements" with Knopf as they prepared the contract and, for the first time, identified her mother's manuscript by its new title: "Little House in the Woods."[111] A month later, on October 23, Bye wrote Lane that he planned to meet with Marion Fiery at Knopf on the following day. The meeting was postponed until October 27, when Bye wrote Lane to brief her on other things. "Miss Fiery," Bye added in a handwritten postscript, "says children's books are the most snobbish things in the world, therefore they crave permission to change Pa and Ma to Father and Mother excepting in dialogue."[112]

Just ten days later, this request from Knopf was irrelevant. "This is just a little note

107. LIW, "The Road Back," p. 307.
108. Ibid., pp. 311, 337.
109. RWL, Diary #37, June 29, 1931.
110. Ibid., Sept. 11–19, 1931.
111. RWL to Bye, Sept. 25, 1931.
112. Bye to RWL, Oct. 23, 27, 1931, Box 1, file 11, Lane Papers.

to tell you," Fiery wrote Lane, "that Mr. Knopf has decided to give up the children's department the first of the year, so I shall not be here after that time. Under the circumstances," Fiery continued, "I do not believe it would be wise for you to sign a three book contract here for your mother as heaven knows what will happen in the next three years."[113] George Bye wired from New York with the same news on November 6. "My mother came over to discuss this," Lane wrote in her diary.[114] Although no account survives of Wilder's response to this development, the news was certainly devastating. If Wilder decided to sign the three-book deal with Knopf, "Little House in the Woods" would be orphaned, without an editor or children's department to support it through publication or market it to schools and libraries. If Wilder decided not to sign, she would have to launch a new search for another publisher.

In a letter to Fiery, Lane confessed, "My mother does not know what to do and I dare not advise her, because I know nothing whatever of the juvenile field." But, she added, "My mother is telegraphing you to hold up the contract, . . . until I have time to make a few inquiries about the possibility of selling it elsewhere. . . . So much depends, not upon the quality of the book per se, but upon the personal tastes of the heads of juvenile departments. . . . Could you hold the contract a little while, and then put it through with Knopf if my mother's too scared to take the chance of refusing them and trying the book's fate elsewhere?"[115] Wilder, however, was not too scared to try submitting the manuscript elsewhere. On November 7, she and Lane "air mailed" her manuscript to Lane's old friend Ernestine Evans, who oversaw children's publications at Lippincott. Meanwhile, Fiery herself had quietly contacted a children's book editor at Harper's and given her the manuscript.[116] During this crisis, neither Lane nor Wilder appeared to consider a more aggressive marketing approach for the adult version of *Pioneer Girl*. The focus was entirely on the children's manuscript.

Lane continued to write letters during early November, perhaps on her mother's behalf. The month dragged on. Lane was "bothered & worried" by her teeth on the ninth; struggled to work on her own creative projects on the thirteenth; and then learned of another set-back on the nineteenth, when she wrote in bold pencil with a double underline: "Palmer Income Stopped." Although her parents had invested

113. Fiery to RWL, Nov. 3, 1931, Box 13, file 189, ibid.

114. RWL, Diary #37, Nov. 6, 1931.

115. RWL to Fiery, n.d. [1931], Box 13, file 189, Lane Papers.

116. RWL, Diary #37, Nov. 7, 1931; William T. Anderson, "The Literary Apprenticeship of Laura Ingalls Wilder," *South Dakota History* 13 (Winter 1983): 328; Virginia Kirkus, "The Discovery of Laura Ingalls Wilder," *The Horn Book Magazine* 29 (Dec. 1953): 428–29.

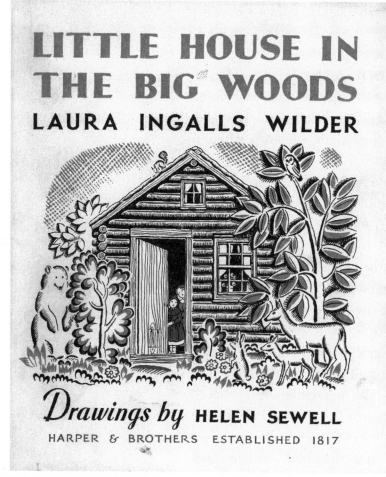

LITTLE HOUSE IN THE BIG WOODS
LAURA INGALLS WILDER

Drawings by HELEN SEWELL

HARPER & BROTHERS ESTABLISHED 1817

Little House in the Big Woods was the first of Wilder's novels based on *Pioneer Girl*. Harper & Brothers published it in the spring of 1932.

in Palmer & Company, too, Lane decided to delay telling them that the firm had failed; perhaps she wanted to spare her mother any more anxiety that autumn.[117] Yet, Palmer's failure made finding a new home for "Little House in the Woods" even more important.

Then on Thanksgiving Day, November 26, Marion Fiery wired with news that Harper & Brothers had decided to buy Wilder's manuscript.[118] Wilder then "telegraphed Knopf direct" and withdrew "Little House in the Woods." Lane wrote Bye with instructions that any contract from Harper's that appeared "satisfactory to you will suit us." She even directed him to sign the contract on Wilder's behalf.[119] Both Lane and her mother wanted to get the book into publication as quickly as possible.

Virginia Kirkus, who directed the children's division at Harper & Brothers, wrote Wilder on December 8, confirming the sale. "I am notifying Mr. Bye today that we are accepting your manuscript, LITTLE HOUSE IN THE WOODS," she wrote.[120] Bye mailed Wilder three copies of the contract for her signature the next day; clearly he thought it wise for her to see the contract herself before she committed to work with Harper & Brothers. Unlike Knopf, Harper offered Wilder a contract for only one book, but the publication process moved quickly once Wilder had signed. By December 15, Kirkus was requesting photographs for the illustrator and, shortly thereafter, made one last change to the title, which became *Little House in the Big Woods*. On April 6, 1932, the book was published and debuted as a Junior Literary Guild Selection.[121]

117. RWL, Diary #37, Nov. 7–19, Dec. 10, 1931.
118. Ibid., Nov. 26, 1931.
119. RWL to Bye, Nov. 27, 1931, Box 13, file 189, Lane Papers.
120. Kirkus to LIW, Dec. 8, 1931, ibid.
121. Bye to LIW, Dec. 9, 1931, and Kirkus to LIW, Dec. 15, 31, 1931, all ibid.; Anderson, "Literary Apprenticeship," pp. 329–30. The Junior Literary Guild was established in 1929 as a children's book club, marketing its own imprints of newly published children's books to libraries, young readers, and their families. Eleanor Roosevelt served on its edi-

At some point in late 1931 or early 1932, Wilder had started work on another manuscript for children, perhaps initially encouraged by the three-book offer from Knopf. In March, she showed it to Lane, who began editing it on March 6, 1932. Its working title was "Farmer Boy."[122] Wilder had found a voice as a writer of historical/biographical fiction for children and seemed to lose interest in marketing the adult version of *Pioneer Girl*. As Lane explained to Bye, "My mother will continue to write juveniles and I'll go on placing them, and I hope the dribbling commissions will be worth while to you."[123]

In mid-April that same spring, Graeme Lorimer, writing on behalf of the *Saturday Evening Post*, asked Bye if Lane would consider submitting "an article in the form of a first person experience" about "pioneer conditions in the middle West," which would "remind people of what that [frontier] spirit" was all about. He had remembered Lane's sales pitch for *Pioneer Girl* a year and a half earlier and decided the time was right for such a piece.[124] Bye forwarded Lorimer's letter to Lane with the note, "I think that Graeme Lorimer confused your mother's manuscript with your authorship."[125]

Yet, *Pioneer Girl* as an active, marketable project dropped from sight. The Bye agency referred to it one last time in 1933, as an entry to the *Atlantic Monthly*-Little, Brown writing contest.[126] It did not win, and the manuscript was never published. Instead, Wilder used the original draft of *Pioneer Girl* as the foundation for one novel after another, beginning in 1935 with the publication of *Little House on the Prairie* and continuing until 1943, when she published the last novel in the series, *These Happy Golden Years*.[127] Her autobiography influenced, informed, and inspired her fiction and shaped her career and literary legacy.

---

torial board from 1929 until her death in 1962. The organization changed its name to Junior Library Guild in 1988 and currently markets its imprints exclusively to libraries. The Junior Literary Guild edition of *Little House in the Big Woods* no longer remains in the organization's collection, but according to its editorial director Susan Marston, the book club edition would have differed only slightly from the Harper & Brothers version with simple "black plate changes" to the text on the copyright page and jacket. The original card catalogue entry for *Little House in the Big Woods* remains in the organization's files and reveals that its edition included Helen Sewell's illustrations, which, "have the homespun flavor and humor of the story itself" (Marston email to Hill, Aug. 15, 2013, with entry card attachments).

122. RWL, Diary #37, Mar. 6, 1932.

123. RWL to Bye, Nov. 27, 1931.

124. Lorimer to Bye, Apr. 15, 1932, Box 1, file 12, Lane Papers.

125. Bye to RWL, Apr. 28, 1932, ibid.

126. Jasper Spock to RWL, Feb. 24, 1933, Box 13, file 192, Lane Papers.

127. Wilder's final novel, *The First Four Years*, was published posthumously in 1971, and only the opening scenes were inspired by *Pioneer Girl*. The book was Wilder's second attempt to write for an adult audience. A complete discussion of this novel appears in Hill, *Laura Ingalls Wilder*, pp. 66–79.

LET THE
HURRICANE ROAR

By

Rose Wilder Lane

Let the hurricane roar !
'Twill the sooner be o'er !
We'll weather the blast and land at last,
On Canaan's happy shore !

Lane drew on the stories that her mother had recorded in *Pioneer Girl* for her own novel *Let the Hurricane Roar*, shown here in the first English edition.

* * *

Pioneer Girl also had a profound influence on her daughter's career. In 1931, shortly after Marion Fiery at Knopf accepted *Little House in the Big Woods*, Lane wrote that she "walked over to my mother's in the afternoon and contemplated what I'm coming to in twice ten years." The next day, she referred for the first time to a new writing project that she called "Courage."[128] What this diary entry does not reveal is that "Courage" was based on *Pioneer Girl*; it would be a short novel, written for adults, drawing on characters, scenes, and episodes from her mother's material. Lane had been depressed and worried throughout 1931 that her own career was over. Her short fiction had not sold well that year, and although the adult version of *Pioneer Girl* had fared even worse, the positive comments about its subject matter and speculation that it would be more marketable as fiction may have influenced Lane's decision to mine the manuscript.

It is also interesting to speculate on her earlier decision to develop the "juvenile" version of *Pioneer Girl* in 1930 and allocate that project to her mother. As the new year dawned in 1931, Lane wrote: "I think I must stay in America and write American stuff. Sometimes I can almost feel this."[129] Perhaps Lane had directed her mother toward writing for children so that she herself could shape *Pioneer Girl's* rich store of characters and situations for adult readers. Lane considered writing for children to be an inferior artistic occupation. She routinely dismissed her mother's "stuff" as "small fry" and apologized to Bye for the "dribbling commissions" that would come his way from Wilder's juvenile fiction.[130] She could have believed that her mother was simply un-

128. RWL, Diary #37, Oct. 7–8, 1931.
129. Ibid., Memoranda [following Jan.], 1931.
130. RWL to Bye, Oct. 5, Nov. 27, 1931, file 189, and May 15, 1933, file 192, Box 13, Lane Papers.

able to take on what Lane considered to be the greater artistic challenge—to deliver *Pioneer Girl's* unique and fundamentally American stories to discriminating adult readers. But she could also have wanted to take on this task herself.

For her work on "Courage," Lane drew on episodes primarily from the middle of *Pioneer Girl*, melding and condensing sections dealing with the railroad in Dakota Territory, the grasshoppers at Plum Creek, and a blizzard as terrifying as those Wilder's family had endured during the Hard Winter. Lane named her main characters Charles and Caroline. She worked on the novel throughout early 1932, changed its title to *Let the Hurricane Roar*, and sold it to the *Saturday Evening Post*. It was published as a serial novel in October and November 1932, then released as a hardcover book by Longmans, Green and Company. Lane apparently disclosed nothing about the project to her mother—until it appeared in print. When Wilder realized that her own material had been fictionalized without her knowledge, she expressed her deep unhappiness at Lane's actions. It was a major betrayal of her trust in her daughter as editor and confidant. Wilder may also have worried that Lane's novel would undercut *Little House in the Big Woods*, which had been pub-

Wilder had come into her own as a writer and was working on her fifth novel, *By the Shores of Silver Lake*, when she posed for this portrait at the age of seventy in 1937. *Laura Ingalls Wilder Historic Home and Museum*

lished in the spring, or diminish the appeal of *Pioneer Girl*, which was still circulating. Furthermore, *Let the Hurricane Roar* was published almost simultaneously with news of Harper & Brothers' initial dissatisfaction with Wilder's second novel, *Farmer Boy*. Wilder may have feared that her career was over, even as her daughter's was blossoming again, due in large part to Wilder's own *Pioneer Girl*.[131]

But it eventually became clear that both mother and daughter could draw inspiration from *Pioneer Girl* simultaneously and successfully. In spite of the unpleasantness surrounding *Let the Hurricane Roar*, Wilder and Lane continued to work together

131. Hill, *Laura Ingalls Wilder*, pp. 149–53.

in revising *Farmer Boy*, which was published in 1933, and *Little House on the Prairie* in 1935. By then *Pioneer Girl* had been retired as an active book project with George Bye's literary agency, and financial insecurities at Rocky Ridge Farm had been resolved.

In July 1935, a writing and research project prompted Lane to move to Columbia, Missouri, and take up residence in the Tiger Hotel. The next year, Wilder and Manly moved back into the Rocky Ridge farmhouse and rented out the Rock House.[132] When Wilder finished a draft of her fourth novel, *On the Banks of Plum Creek*, during the summer of 1936, she sent it to Lane for her editorial review. The subsequent correspondence between Wilder and Lane on this novel, as well as her next one, *By the Shores of Silver Lake*, reveals the working relationship that had developed between the pair—Wilder as writer, Lane as editor—and illustrates Wilder's deepening insights into her characters, their stories, and the overarching themes of her series. The correspondence also reveals that *Pioneer Girl* continued to play a role in Wilder's creative process. Lane had taken the *Pioneer Girl* files with her, and Wilder requested the return of sections of the manuscript. "Thanks for the pages from Pioneer Girl," she wrote Lane in 1937 while writing *By the Shores of Silver Lake*. "They will help. All that time is rather dull to me now for some reason. Not nearly so vivid as when I wrote P.G."[133] By this time, Wilder was seventy.

She, of course, had already used material from the *Pioneer Girl* manuscripts in her previous novels, expanding and embellishing scenes, transforming them into fiction. The autobiography gave Wilder a personal historical foundation for her novels and their narrative thread, but her evolving series of children's books was "not a history but a true story founded on historical fact."[134] *Pioneer Girl* also gave her a plot, complete with action and forward motion. After all, the memoir was an inherent coming-of-age story, which could readily be repackaged as fiction across multiple book titles. The *Pioneer Girl* autobiography also provided a theme: a tightly-knit, pioneer family, moving west, always facing adversity with courage, love, and hope. Wilder had long

132. Ibid., p. 164; John E. Miller, *Becoming Laura Ingalls Wilder: The Woman behind the Legend*, Missouri Biography Series (Columbia: University of Missouri Press, 1998), pp. 208–13. Wilder and Lane began to reconcile their differences when Lane left Rocky Ridge Farm in late 1932 for a trip to New York and visited the Wilder family farm in Malone. She sent back descriptions of the farm and surrounding countryside that helped Wilder get a clearer picture of the setting for her second book. When Lane returned to Rocky Ridge in 1933, the two women seemed to fall back into their familiar patterns. Wilder started work on "Indian Country," which became *Little House on the Prairie*, and that summer, the two women took a road trip into Kansas and Oklahoma, looking for the site of the Ingalls family cabin.

133. LIW to RWL, [3/22/37?], Box 13, file 197, Lane Papers.

134. LIW to Aubrey Sherwood, Nov. 18, 1939, Archives, Laura Ingalls Wilder Memorial Society, De Smet, S.Dak.

Wilder wrote her later novels at this writing desk in the Rocky Ridge farmhouse (below) near Mansfield, Missouri. Photographs by Keli Tetzlaff, *South Dakota Historical Society Press*

believed her family's story had the power to inspire readers, which is one reason why she had decided to experiment with a long-form narrative in the first place. As she told the Detroit Book Fair audience in 1937, "I realized that I had seen and lived it all—all the successive phases of the frontier, first the frontiersman then the pioneer, then the farmers and the towns. Then I understood that in my own life I represented a whole period of American history."[135] That spark existed from the beginning in *Pioneer Girl*; it blazed to life in Wilder's fiction.

Even so, Wilder made deliberate creative changes in her family's narrative when she moved from nonfiction to fiction. *Pioneer Girl* had taught her that nonfiction, no matter how compelling, does not always make a good story. During the Hard Winter, for example, the real Ingalls family had shared their storefront home with a young married couple and their newborn. Wilder wrote them out of *The Long Winter* and argued with Lane about this decision. Wilder persevered, saying that it "would spoil the story" and diminish the hardships the fictional family faced if anyone else lived under the same roof with them during that memorable winter.[136] In fact, when Wilder turned to fiction she decided to eliminate whole chunks of Ingalls family history, most notably the birth and death of her infant brother Freddie and her family's experiences in Burr Oak, Iowa. As she explained to Lane, "It [the time in Burr Oak] is a story in itself, but does not belong in the picture I am making of the family." Wilder also imagined new situations for her fictional characters, adding action and scenes that were clearly not autobiographical. In *By the Shores of Silver Lake*, Pa takes Laura to see the building of the railroad, but as Wilder explained to Lane, "I stretched a point when I had Laura go with Pa to see the work. I never did. He would not have taken me."[137] According to Wilder, she created the scene "to have Laura see it first hand and get her reaction."[138] As a writer, Wilder had clearly moved from memoirist to novelist and understood how to manipulate the raw material in *Pioneer Girl* to create stronger, more memorable fiction.

She also made decisions about eliminating material that she considered inappropriate, omitting several stories from *Pioneer Girl* with adult themes: the couple who run away together after singing a beautiful whippoorwill duet; the married shopkeeper's infatuation with hired girl Teeny Peterson; Dr. Hoyt's courtship of Matie Masters. But Wilder did not shy away from adult material that she felt was essential to her un-

135. LIW, Detroit Book Fair Speech, p. 2.
136. LIW to RWL, Mar. 7, 1938, Box 13, file 194, Lane Papers.
137. Ibid., n.d. [1937], file 193.
138. Ibid., Jan. 25, 1938, file 194.

folding story and its themes, or that she intuitively believed would appeal to young readers. As the fictional Laura matured and moved into adolescence, Wilder maintained that the situations, feelings, and ideas her main character experienced had to be more adult. "I don't see how we can spare what you call adult stuff," Wilder told Lane while working on *By the Shores of Silver Lake*, "for that makes the story. It was there and Laura knew and understood it."[139]

* * *

Wilder found her voice as an author in writing fiction for young readers. *Pioneer Girl* was an essential step in that process. Perhaps the original concept for *Pioneer Girl* was ill-conceived—a coming-of-age memoir dealing with childhood and adolescent experiences written for adults from an adult's perspective. But as Wilder transformed her original material into fiction for young readers, she grew both as a writer and ultimately as an artist, creating dynamic characters, building more suspenseful stories, and manipulating her themes more masterfully. Lane's great literary gift to her mother may not have been in the days, weeks, months, and years she spent editing first *Pioneer Girl* and then eight of Wilder's novels; instead, her great gift may have been in steering Wilder toward young readers in the first place, in seeing that within *Pioneer Girl* there were stories and characters with intrinsic and universal appeal to children.

Wilder offered her daughter advice and assistance as she wrote *Free Land*, Lane's second novel based on material from *Pioneer Girl*.

But Wilder, in turn, gave her daughter a great gift: Lane's most enduring novels and much of her short fiction, published in the 1930s, came directly from the pages of *Pioneer Girl*. When Lane took the handwritten tablets and files with her to Columbia, she was about to embark on a second novel based on her mother's autobiography. This time, however, she and Wilder communicated openly about the project, which

139. Ibid., Jan. 26, 1938.

became *Free Land*, and both Wilder and Almanzo provided additional research support for it. In one letter to Lane, Wilder recounted a story about how her Uncle Hi had cheated the railroad when he worked on its construction through Dakota Territory. "I can't use [this episode] in a child's story, but you could use it if you have a place for it," Wilder suggested.[140] Lane used the episode, lifting even a snippet of dialogue that her mother had suggested. Lane also included dozens of characters and episodes from *Pioneer Girl*, often making only minor variations in names, circumstances, and plot points. She created two characters—David Beaton and Nettie Peters—who were thinly disguised versions of her parents. Wilder's Big Jerry became Lane's Halfbreed Jack; Old Stebbins of *Pioneer Girl* became Lane's Mr. Gebbert. In some instances, Lane did not even bother to change names. David Beaton's older sister was named Eliza, for example; and the hellfire and brimstone preacher in Lane's bustling new town on the prairie was named "Rev. Brown." At this point in their careers, both women possessed enough professional self-confidence to share and swap materials as well as advice. Lane's *Free Land* was again published in serial form by the *Saturday Evening Post*, then released in book form by Longmans, Green and Company in 1938. Like *Let the Hurricane Roar*, it became a bestseller. Throughout the 1930s, Lane continued to draw on characters, setting, and episodes from *Pioneer Girl*, including such short stories as "Long Skirts" and "Object, Matrimony."[141] Wilder's autobiography thus supplied both Wilder and Lane with character after character, story after story. Although the original is only now being published, its influence and literary importance are undeniable. Without *Pioneer Girl*, neither Wilder nor Lane would be read or remembered today.

So, all these years later, does *Pioneer Girl* merit publication, and if so, why publish Wilder's rough draft? Few writers would agree to share their rough drafts with the reading public. A first draft is an experiment, an attempt to capture the essence of a story on paper. It is raw material, designed to be pruned or expanded, revised or even abandoned during a writer's attempt to find a story and give it shape, voice, and meaning.

Yet, Wilder's handwritten draft of *Pioneer Girl* is unique for many reasons. As noted, Wilder relied heavily on this version of the manuscript when she created her series. Moreover, some critics have charged that Wilder could not write and that Lane

---

140. Ibid., Feb. 5, 1937, Box 13, file 193.

141. Hill, *Laura Ingalls Wilder*, pp. 153, 172–73; RWL, *Free Land* (Longmans, Green & Co., 1938), pp. 4, 81, 107, 130, 193. "Long Skirts" appeared in *Ladies' Home Journal* in April 1933, and "Object, Matrimony" in *Saturday Evening Post* in September 1934.

was the creative genius behind the Little House books. The transcription of the hand-written *Pioneer Girl* illustrates instead that Wilder possessed raw talent and descriptive genius. Consider, for example, this passage from the family's trip into Dakota Territory: "The sun sank lower and lower until, looking like a ball of pulsing, liquid light it sank gloriously in clouds of crimson and silver. Cold purple shadows rose in the east; crept slowly around the horizon, then gathered above in depth on depth of darkness from which the stars swung low and bright" (p. 158).[142]

The original draft of the manuscript also demonstrates that Wilder's years as a columnist for the *Missouri Ruralist* served her well and shows her evolution as writer—from columnist to memoirist to novelist. Some of the opening scenes in the hand-written original draft of *Pioneer Girl* are episodic, perhaps a reflection of the nature of the author's earliest recollections, those vivid but often fragmented images that universally seem to characterize memories from early childhood. In a single paragraph, she describes Pa building a house of logs and, in another, a ring of wolves surrounding the cabin. Wilder's more developed scenes, however, are structured much like the short, concentrated newspaper columns she wrote for the *Missouri Ruralist* from 1911 through 1924. Each *Ruralist* column averaged between six to eight short paragraphs—or ten to twelve even shorter paragraphs if the column included extensive dialogue or quotations. They used spare but vivid vocabulary to draw readers in, linger a moment, then take them back out.

The same pattern emerges in the opening scene of *Pioneer Girl*. It includes one line of dialogue—" 'Well Caroline,' [Pa] said, 'here's the place we've been looking for. Might as well camp' "—and then covers just seven paragraphs. Yet, this episode has a distinct beginning, middle, and end. A scene a few pages later—when American Indians enter the house, eat a meal, and smoke Pa's pipe—has the same structure. The action covers seven paragraphs, an ideal length for a *Missouri Ruralist* column. The opening pages of Wilder's handwritten draft of *Pioneer Girl* repeat this pattern again and again.

As Wilder gained more confidence with a long-form, nonfiction narrative and as her memories grew more distinct and sequential, episodes in *Pioneer Girl* became fuller and more developed. One scene built on the next, creating tension and suspense. This development is especially visible in Wilder's original depiction of the grasshopper plague that struck Walnut Grove, Minnesota, when her family lived there from 1874 to

142. Compare this original to Lane's version: "Sunset spread in rainbow colors around the level rim of the earth and purple shadows rose. The low stars were huge and quivering" (*Free Land*, p. 37).

Once upon a time years and years ago, Pa stopped the horses and the wagon they were hauling away out on the prairie in Indian Territory.

"Well Caroline," he said "here's the place we've been looking for. Might as well camp."

So Pa and Ma got down from the wagon. Pa unhitched the horses and picketed them, tied them to long ropes fastened to wooden pegs driven in the ground, so they could eat the grass. Then he made the campfire out of bits of willow twigs from the creek nearby.

Ma cooked supper over the fire and after we had eaten, sister Mary and I were put to bed in the wagon and Pa and Ma sat awhile by the fire. Pa would bring the horses and tie them to the wagon before he and Ma came to sleep in the wagon too.

I lay and looked through the opening in the wagon cover at the campfire and Pa and Ma sitting there. It was lonesome and so still with the stars shining down on the great, flat land where no one lived.

There was a long, scared sound off in the night

1876. Wilder used dialogue, description, and suspense to carry readers through the four-page episode. Another example is Wilder's original narrative of the Hard Winter of 1880–1881. It begins with a rare reference to a specific date — September 25, 1880 — and then covers roughly twenty-nine handwritten pages, ending in April 1881, with the arrival of the family's Christmas barrel.

By the end of *Pioneer Girl*, Wilder had strengthened her narrative voice and technical skill as a memoirist. She would go on to create an entire novel — *The Long Winter*, published in 1940 — out of those twenty-nine pages. And, indeed, the last four novels in the series parallel the original version of *Pioneer Girl* closely. These books, *By the Shores of Silver Lake, The Long Winter, Little Town on the Prairie*, and *These Happy Golden Years*, were all Newbery Honor books. Publishing the initial material from which these books emerged provides fresh insights into Wilder's creative process.

More importantly, however, this draft of *Pioneer Girl* takes modern readers closer to Wilder's unique and personal voice. She wrote this version of her autobiography for Lane, as well as for a larger audience. Her voice is intimate, conversational, and unguarded. Reading this transcript of Wilder's handwritten draft is perhaps as close as modern readers can get to the experience of hearing the author's life story in her own words. *Pioneer Girl* does what Wilder had asked her Aunt Martha Carpenter to do back in 1925; it tells the story in her "own words as you would tell about those times if only you could talk to me."[143]

143. LIW to Carpenter, June 22, 1925.

The *Pioneer Girl* Manuscripts

PAMELA SMITH HILL

HANDWRITTEN ROUGH DRAFT (PG)

Laura Ingalls Wilder completed the original, handwritten draft of her autobiography, now known as *Pioneer Girl*, in the spring of 1930 and presented it to her daughter Rose Wilder Lane on May 7. The narrative filled four Fifty Fifty and two Big Chief lined tablets and covered sixteen years of Wilder's life, from age two through eighteen. This version of *Pioneer Girl* has no page numbers, section breaks, or chapters. The only breaks in the narrative occur when Wilder completely filled one tablet and moved to the next, sometimes midsentence. Wilder wrote the words "Pioneer Girl" across the first two tablet covers and numbered all six in sequence. She used Number 2 lead pencils and sometimes wrote both on the front and back of a page and in the margins. Occasionally, she included notes to indicate how she intended her narrative to flow; a few of these notes were addressed directly to her daughter and often appeared adjacent to scenes or episodes that Wilder intended only for Lane—and not for publication. It is clear from these handwritten notes, however, that Wilder envisioned a broader audience for this manuscript. She assumed that Lane, a successful author herself by 1930, would edit and type the manuscript before sending it to her literary agent, Carl Brandt of the Brandt & Brandt agency in New York.

The original handwritten manuscript is part of the archival collection housed at the Laura Ingalls Wilder Historic Home and Museum in Mansfield, Missouri. The manuscript is also available on microfilm through the Ellis Library's Western Historical Manuscript Collection at the University of Missouri in Columbia. Rodger Hartley, associate editor at the South Dakota Historical Society Press, transcribed the text that serves as the basis for this edition of *Pioneer Girl* from a digital copy of the original.

BRANDT & BRANDT VERSION (BRANDT)

From Wilder's handwritten draft, Lane prepared a typewritten manuscript of *Pioneer Girl* that she submitted to her literary agent in New York, Carl Brandt. Lane made minor line edits as she typed, but the narrative in this version closely resembles Wilder's original text. Lane mailed this version of the manuscript to Brandt on May 17, 1930. Like Wilder's original, the Brandt manuscript has no section breaks or chapters; it is 162 pages long and double-spaced, the standard format for nonfiction and fiction manuscripts. The agency supplied a cover page for this version of *Pioneer Girl*. It reads, "Serial Department/Pioneer Girl/by/Laura Ingalls Wilder/from/Brandt & Brandt/101 Park Avenue/New York," indicating that the copy was submitted to magazines for serialization.

Five weeks later, on June 21, 1930, Brandt returned the manuscript to Lane and Wilder. He did not consider the manuscript marketable. Lane then decided to edit *Pioneer Girl* more aggressively, and by the end of July 1930, she was at work on another version.[1] She used the typewritten manuscript that Brandt had returned to make her initial edits for the new, revised manuscript, and as a result, the copy of the initial Brandt manuscript that survives in the Rose Wilder Lane Papers at the Herbert Hoover Presidential Library in West Branch, Iowa, includes Lane's preliminary handwritten line edits, deletions, and notes. Pages 56 through 59 are heavily edited. Page 2 is missing, and there are two different pages numbered 86 and 152. No handwritten notations appear in the Brandt manuscript after page 59, where a line in Lane's handwriting reads, "Pick up other ms."

BRANDT & BRANDT REVISED VERSION (BRANDT REVISED)

This version of *Pioneer Girl* is probably the "other manuscript" Lane referred to on page 59 of the Brandt manuscript. Also housed at the Herbert Hoover Presidential Library, the Brandt Revised manuscript appears to be a transitional draft between the Brandt and the final, more polished George T. Bye version of *Pioneer Girl*. The Brandt Revised is a leaner manuscript, coming in at just 129 pages, and it is heavily edited, a work in progress. Edits in Lane's handwriting sometimes fill the margins and spaces between lines. The Brandt Revised manuscript attempts to impose a clearer narrative on Wilder's personal story and includes section breaks between key episodes. This manuscript also includes new material, most notably an episode focused on the murderous Bender family of southeastern Kansas (Appendix B).

Lane set the Brandt Revised version of *Pioneer Girl* aside in August 1930 and began work on what she called "juvenile Pioneer Girl." When this short project was completed, Lane returned to the adult version of *Pioneer Girl*, but, in the process, apparently abandoned this Brandt Revised version in favor of a more developed, longer approach to her mother's memoir.

1. Rose Wilder Lane (RWL) Diary #25 (1926–1930), July 31, 1930, Box 21, item #25, Rose Wilder Lane Papers, Herbert Hoover Presidential Library, West Branch, Iowa.

"JUVENILE PIONEER GIRL" (JPG)

Also known as "When Grandma Was a Little Girl," which is the manuscript's opening line, this version of Wilder's *Pioneer Girl* story was developed for young readers and has traditionally been interpreted as an independent project, unrelated to Wilder's original memoir. But Lane prepared this manuscript as she was editing the longer, adult version of *Pioneer Girl* and used the term "juvenile Pioneer Girl" to describe it in her diary. The manuscript focuses on Wilder's early stories and impressions of life in and near the Big Woods of Wisconsin and contains material Lane had cut from the Brandt Revised version.

Lane approached the juvenile version of *Pioneer Girl* as fiction, writing in third person and introducing an elderly grandmother as narrator. She finished typing this manuscript on August 17, 1930, and mailed it the following day to an unspecified recipient. The earliest surviving copy of JPG is a twenty-one-page (there is no page 13), double-spaced manuscript, complete with typewritten strike-outs, Lane's hand-written notes, and one false start on the reverse of page 10. It, too, is part of the Lane Papers in the Herbert Hoover Presidential Library and is reproduced here in facsimile as Appendix A.

Wilder herself revised and expanded this manuscript in early 1931, using it as the basis for her first novel, *Little House in the Big Woods*, published in 1932. Wilder apparently considered her revisions to be part of the larger *Pioneer Girl* story. She labeled her finished handwritten copy, which filled two Fifty Fifty tablets, as "Pioneer Girl, Number 1" and "Number 2," then renumbered the first three original *Pioneer Girl* tablets to correspond to the story's new sequence.[2]

GEORGE T. BYE VERSION (BYE)

Lane returned to revising the adult version of *Pioneer Girl* in mid-August and finished an updated version of her mother's memoir on September 2, 1930. This final edited version is the manuscript now known as the George T. Bye manuscript, and it includes the last editorial changes made to *Pioneer Girl* during Wilder's and Lane's lifetimes.[3] Most of the handwritten notes from the Brandt Revised manuscript found

---

2. Laura Ingalls Wilder (LIW), "Pioneer Girl, Number 1" and "Number 2" [*Little House in the Big Woods*], Folder 7, Laura Ingalls Wilder Papers, Laura Ingalls Wilder Home Association, Mansfield, Mo., Microfilm ed., LIW Papers, 1894–1943, Western Historical Manuscript Collection, Ellis Library, University of Missouri, Columbia, Mo.

3. In 1985, Rodger MacBride, the literary executor of Lane's estate, worked with William T. Anderson to develop a version of *Pioneer Girl* for young readers. The manuscript that emerged from this collaboration drew on multiple sources, including the various versions of *Pioneer Girl* itself, Wilder's rough drafts for the Little House series, her let-

their way into the Bye version, which takes its name from literary agent George T. Bye. After firing Brandt, Lane hired Bye in March 1931 and sent him a copy of *Pioneer Girl* shortly thereafter. Bye, however, failed to find a home for *Pioneer Girl*, and within a year or two, it was retired as an active, marketable project. Bye eventually returned the manuscript to Lane in 1938, with Wilder's blessings.[4]

The name "Laura Ingalls Wilder" appears on the top of Page 1 on this version of the manuscript. A rubber-stamped image reads "GEORGE T. BYE INC./535 FIFTH AVE., NEW YORK." The Bye manuscript covers 195 double-spaced, typewritten pages with section breaks but no chapters. Because it was a final, circulating draft, it contains no handwritten revisions. This manuscript is part of the Lane Papers at the Herbert Hoover Presidential Library. The Laura Ingalls Wilder Historic Home and Museum in Mansfield holds a copy of this version as well. It is identical to the one at the Hoover library with two exceptions: (1) it does not have the rubber-stamped image from the Bye agency on its opening page; and (2) it is missing pages 151, 193, and 194.

---

ters, correspondence, and interviews. MacBride's idea was "to include only new material in this book," which would be "reflective of the past," and to then blend and edit the various sources so that they became "'present' in their attitude toward events" (MacBride to Anderson, July 24, 1985, Private Collection). The manuscript was titled "Pioneer Girl: More Stories from the 'Little Houses' by Laura Ingalls Wilder." Typewritten and divided into nine chapters with an introduction, this version is the longest *Pioneer Girl* manuscript at 323 pages. Although *Laura Ingalls Wilder Lore*, the newsletter of the Laura Ingalls Wilder Memorial Society, Inc., of De Smet, S.Dak., announced the forthcoming publication of this version in the spring of 1983, the manuscript was never published. A copy is part of the society's archives in De Smet. Because this version of *Pioneer Girl* was created after Wilder's and Lane's deaths and because it draws on multiple sources that relate primarily to Wilder's Little House novels rather than the memoir itself, an examination of this manuscript is not included in the annotations that follow.

4. LIW to RWL, Sept. 26, 1938, Box 13, file 194, Laura Ingalls Wilder (LIW) Series, Rose Wilder Lane Papers, Herbert Hoover Presidential Library, West Branch, Iowa. In this letter, Wilder wrote Lane that George Bye had mailed *Pioneer Girl* to Lane so that she could "have it for reference."

Editorial Procedures

NANCY TYSTAD KOUPAL AND RODGER HARTLEY

TEXT

Written in pencil on inexpensive school tablets, Wilder's original *Pioneer Girl* manuscript is a product of the decades before modern technology, and, as such, it presents unique editorial challenges. In preparing the text for publication, our goal has been to provide readers with a text as close as possible to Wilder's original. As a result, spelling and punctuation errors appear as they occur in the original, and while words are sometimes corrected in brackets, the word *sic* is not used; readers can assume that all errors were in the original. Wilder sometimes forgot to provide closing quotation marks for sections of dialogue, and in those instances, we provided the missing marks in brackets. In some instances, we included a missing word within brackets, but for the most part, the text of the manuscript is as Wilder left it—with a few exceptions.

The main narrative of Wilder's manuscript is written on the front side of each tablet page. The text is relatively clean, with few deletions and almost no false starts, suggesting that it is not her first draft of the manuscript but, instead, a "fair" copy prepared for Rose Wilder Lane to read and type from. Even so, Wilder appended forgotten material or additional episodes, and in the age before computers, her insertions were of three types. One was the simple addition of text, sometimes written in between the lines of the tablets, along the margins, or on whole pages laid into the manuscript. On one or two occasions, the author appears to have employed the cut-and-paste method, attaching slips of paper containing additional text to the original pages and/or cutting off parts of pages. On many occasions, she gave directions to additions written on the back of a page. In these ways, Wilder amended her text without having to recopy the whole manuscript. Where Wilder's intentions are clear, we have presented the narrative as she intended it, rearranging the text seamlessly as a typist would have done. We have walked the reader through the first instance of each of these types of correction in the annotations.

In other instances, Wilder's directions led to what could be considered editorial notes to her daughter. Wilder headed one example with the words "Not to be used." In these cases, we have put the text in a different typeface, retained Wilder's notes, and inserted the material where Lane herself inserted it in the Brandt version. In a few other cases, Wilder failed to indicate where she wanted additional material inserted, and Lane either chose not to include it or edited the surrounding material to incorporate it in the middle of an original sentence or paragraph. In those instances, we have inserted the copy in the next most logical place and again signaled the addition with a different typeface.

Another peculiarity of the original text of *Pioneer Girl* is that it contains no pauses except the arbitrary breaks caused by the end of a tablet of paper; such breaks may come in the middle of an episode or scene. In the interests of readability, we have broken the text into sections or chapters based on dates and geography. This division also allows the annotation numbers to begin anew in each section.

MAPS

The maps provided in this book are based on primary research of the various locations in early map collections and in relevant secondary sources, but we do not guarantee the precise accuracy of any location, place, or route indicated on the maps, especially those of Kansas and Missouri where Wilder herself was unclear as to her precise location. In many cases, early sources also did not agree, and the early maps themselves varied. The maps drawn for this book, therefore, are not intended to be definitive, but they are designed to allow readers a good general understanding of each locale.

ANNOTATIONS AND SOURCES

In the interest of keeping the annotative material from overwhelming Wilder's text, the documentation style used within the notes has been simplified. An abbreviated citation for each direct quotation appears in parentheses immediately following the quotation. For full references, the reader is advised to consult the bibliography. The major collections of primary documents used in preparing the annotations are the Rose Wilder Lane Papers at the Herbert Hoover Presidential Library in West Branch, Iowa, which are cited as the Lane Papers, and the Laura Ingalls Wilder Papers at the Laura Ingalls Wilder Historic Home and Museum in Mansfield, Missouri, which are available on microfilm from the University of Missouri at Columbia. This collection is cited as the Wilder Papers. Additional primary material can be found in the various Wilder homes and museums, which are located as follows:

> Laura Ingalls Wilder Historic Home and Museum
> Mansfield, Mo.
> Laura Ingalls Wilder Memorial Society
> De Smet, S.Dak.

Laura Ingalls Wilder Museum
  Walnut Grove, Minn.
Laura Ingalls Wilder Park and Museum
  Burr Oak, Iowa

Again, Wilder's letters are quoted as they appear, and *sic* is used sparingly. In citations of specific letters, diaries, or manuscripts, the following abbreviations are used:

Laura Ingalls Wilder   LIW
Rose Wilder Lane   RWL
Almanzo James Wilder   AJW

The main sources of biographical information about Wilder and her family are William T. Anderson, *Laura Ingalls Wilder: A Biography* (New York: HarperCollins, 1992); Pamela Smith Hill, *Laura Ingalls Wilder: A Writer's Life* (Pierre: South Dakota State Historical Society Press, 2007); William Holtz, *The Ghost in the Little House: A Life of Rose Wilder Lane* (Columbia: University of Missouri Press, 1993); John E. Miller, *Becoming Laura Ingalls Wilder: The Woman behind the Legend* (Columbia: University of Missouri Press, 1998); and Donald Zochert, *Laura: The Life of Laura Ingalls Wilder* (Chicago: Contemporary Books, 1976). The bibliography contains a full listing of all sources consulted in the compiling of the annotations.

In determining the identity of the many people Wilder mentioned throughout *Pioneer Girl*, census records, compiled by federal or state agencies and made available online through sites such as ancestrylibrary.com, have been most useful in establishing the basic fact of a person's existence at a given time and place. The federal decennial census is taken in every state and territory on years ending in zero, while state censuses were usually taken in years ending in five. Thus a listing in 1880, for example, appears on the federal census, while a listing in 1885 refers to the relevant state census. While the censuses are not formally cited in each annotation, they were heavily used in determining the identity and location of individuals.

Because census forms changed from year to year, censuses vary in their utility. The 1880 census, for example, can clarify family structures because, unlike prior censuses, it asked for each person's relationship to the head of household. The 1900 census asked for both month and year of birth, making it a more specific resource than those that asked only for a person's age at enumeration. State censuses generally recorded less information than federal ones. Regardless of how clear a record might seem, we have attempted to consider each one carefully, recognizing that inaccuracy, imprecision, and variability across time are normal phenomena in census data. For example, a person's age may appear to fluctuate unpredictably, and even a name may change from one enumeration to the next. People self-reported, and changing situations and memories (or even reports by third parties), along with the abilities of census takers, affected the quality of the data. Moreover, especially in the fluid conditions of the frontier, a person might easily be missed entirely or counted twice. Finally, some records simply do not exist. Virtually the entire 1890 federal census was destroyed in a fire, and other censuses (the 1885 Dakota territorial census and 1895 South Dakota census, for example) exist only in partial form. These drawbacks aside, census data is still the most useful first resource for establishing a given person's historical existence.

State-compiled birth, marriage, and death indices, often also available through ancestrylibrary.com, have also been used to provide or corroborate some of the same information and can be subject to similar drawbacks. Also noteworthy and important as a source but not specifically mentioned in each annotation is a national user-maintained database of information recorded on grave markers, *Find a Grave*, online at findagrave.com. This website, accessed by name of the deceased, often includes photographs of the grave markers, which are themselves primary sources subject to errors of fact. Many records on the site include additional biographical details contributed by users, and we have also employed caution in utilizing this information, especially when a user's sources cannot be determined. Again, however, when state-maintained death records do not exist or are not readily accessible, we have had to assume that information recorded on grave markers is accurate.

Another set of records that proved immensely useful in tracking down individuals were the Land Entry Files of the United States General Land Office. These were accessed in two ways. Copies of the most critical land entry files, such as the homestead records of the Ingalls family, were obtained from the National Archives and Records Administration, Record Group 49, Washington, D.C. To access the essential facts of other land entry files, including the location, type of entry, and final patent number, we searched for the name of the patentee through the website of the United States Department of the Interior, Bureau of Land Management, which is abbreviated: BLM-GLO Records.

Finally, a resource that proved especially useful in locating people and events and giving life to dry facts was the local newspapers of the various towns that Wilder lived in or near as she grew older. In most cases, these small new towns did not have their own newspapers at the time, and we have tried to find nearby newspapers that published news from correspondents in Wilder's home communities. In other cases, copies of early newspapers have not survived. For example, De Smet did not have its own newspaper during 1879, and issues from 1880 through 1882 are no longer extant. In those instances, we used papers from nearby towns to fill in what we could. The single most useful newspaper proved to be the *De Smet Leader*, the first issue of which appeared on January 27, 1883. The titles of some often-used newspapers are abbreviated as follows:

Brookings County Press	BCP
De Smet Leader	DSL
Redwood Gazette	RG

References to the *Pioneer Girl* manuscripts are abbreviated as follows:

Brandt & Brandt Version	Brandt
Brandt & Brandt Revised Version	Brandt Revised
"Juvenile Pioneer Girl"	JPG
George T. Bye Version	Bye

Unless the first edition is specified, page references to and quotations from Wilder's novels, published by Harper & Brothers and Harper & Row, refer to the 1953 revised editions with illustrations by Garth Williams (there appear to be slight variations in page numbers in later printings of these editions). Helen Sewell and Mildred Boyle illustrated the first editions. The books are abbreviated as follows:

Little House in the Big Woods (1932)	BW
Farmer Boy (1933)	FB
Little House on the Prairie (1935)	LHOP
On the Banks of Plum Creek (1937)	PC
By the Shores of Silver Lake (1939)	SL
The Long Winter (1940)	LW
Little Town on the Prairie (1941)	LTOP
These Happy Golden Years (1943)	HGY

After Wilder's death in 1957, Harper & Row or HarperCollins published books based on her manuscripts, diaries, and letters. Those abbreviated here are:

The First Four Years (1971)	FFY
A Little House Traveler (2006)	LHT

PIONEER GIRL

MAP OF KANSAS, MISSOURI, AND INDIAN TERRITORY, 1869~1871

This map shows the region in which Charles Ingalls built the family's cabin in 1869. While established settlements and political boundaries can be pinpointed with accuracy, the region's trails, which varied over time, are more difficult to place with precision. The routes of the two trails shown here, the Osage Trace and the First Buffalo Trail, are approximations based on numerous historical maps and secondary sources.

The Osage Trace was a combination of several trails with various formal and informal names, including the Great Osage Trail, Shawnee Trail, Sedalia Trail, and Kansas Trail. The segment depicted on this map was also known as the Military Road or the Fort Leavenworth to Fort Gibson Road. An offshoot from the Osage Trace near the point where it turned northeast to Sibley connected it with Fort Leavenworth.

The First Buffalo Trail was also called the Osage Trail. It represented a spur off from the main Osage Trace between the approximate locations of Independence and Osage Mission, where it merged with or paralleled the Osage Trace. It is possible that the Ingalls family followed the First Buffalo Trail on their way out of Kansas.

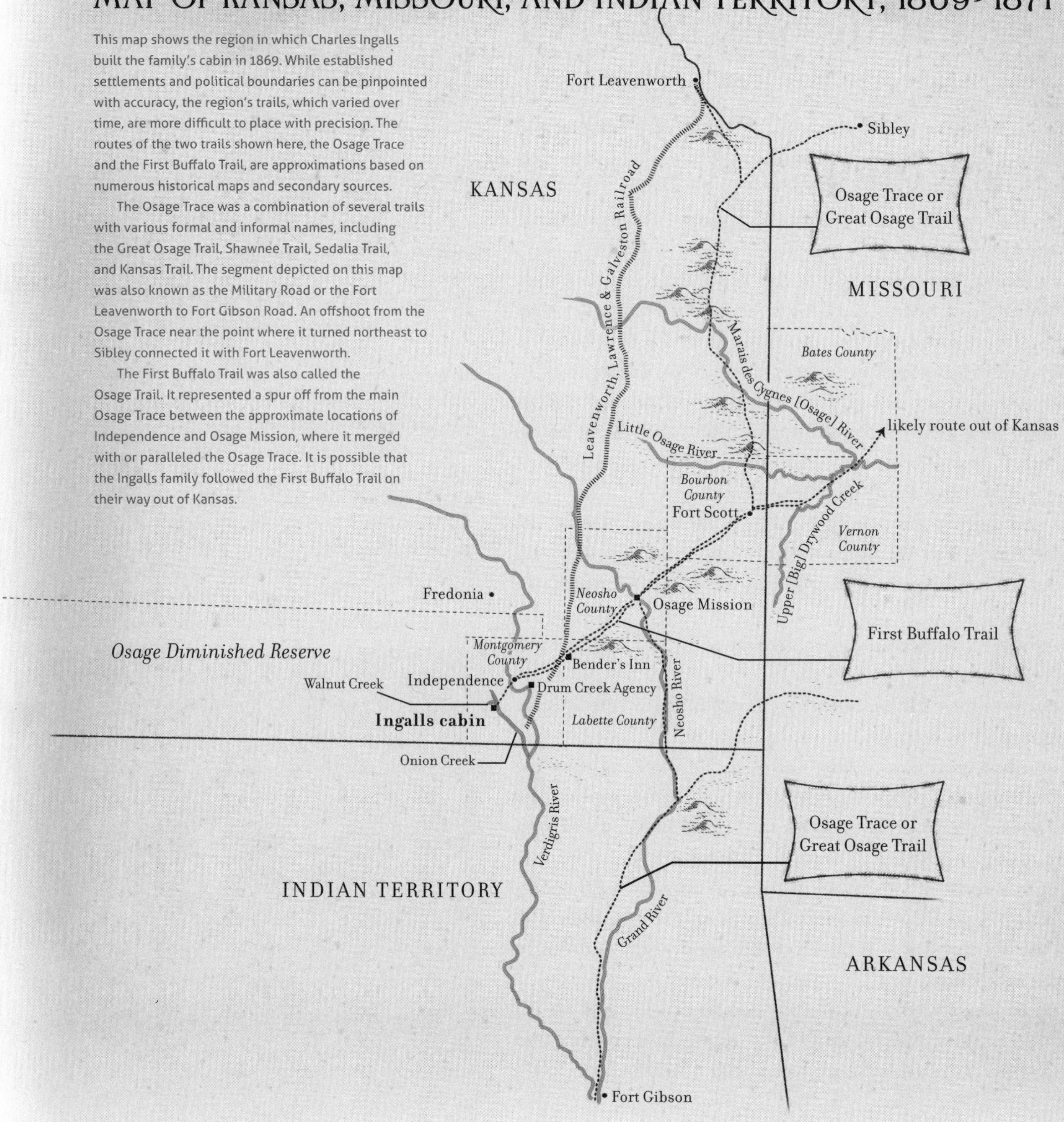

Fort Leavenworth

Sibley

KANSAS

Osage Trace or Great Osage Trail

MISSOURI

Leavenworth, Lawrence & Galveston Railroad

Bates County

Marais des Cygnes [Osage] River

Little Osage River

likely route out of Kansas

Bourbon County

Fort Scott

Upper [Big] Drywood Creek

Vernon County

Fredonia

Neosho County

Osage Mission

First Buffalo Trail

Osage Diminished Reserve

Montgomery County

Bender's Inn

Neosho River

Walnut Creek

Independence

Drum Creek Agency

Ingalls cabin

Labette County

Onion Creek

Osage Trace or Great Osage Trail

Verdigris River

INDIAN TERRITORY

Grand River

ARKANSAS

Fort Gibson

Kansas and Missouri, 1869–1871

Once upon a time years and years ago,[1] Pa[2] stopped the horses and the wagon they were hauling away out on the prairie in Indian Territory.[3]

"Well Caroline," he said "here's the place we've been looking for.[4] Might as well camp."

So Pa and Ma[5] got down from the wagon. Pa unhitched the horses and picketed them, tied them to long ropes fastened to wooden pegs driven in the ground, so they could eat the grass. Then he made the campfire out of bits of willow twigs from the creek nearby.

Ma cooked supper over the fire and after we had eaten, sister Mary and I were put to bed in the wagon and Pa and Ma sat awhile by the fire. Pa would bring the horses and tie them to the wagon before he and Ma came to sleep in the wagon too.

I lay and looked[6] through the opening in the wagon cover at the campfire and Pa and Ma sitting there. It was lonesome and so still with the stars shining down on the great, flat land where no one lived.[7]

There was a long, scared sound off in the night and Pa said it was a wolf howling.

It frightened me a little, but we were safe in the wagon with its nice tight cover to keep out the wind and the rain.[8] The wagon was home, we had lived in it so long and Pa's rifle was hanging at the side where he could get it quickly to shoot the wolf. He wouldn't let wolves nor anything hurt us and Jack the brindle bull dog was lying under the wagon guarding us too and so we fell asleep.

Pa built a house of logs[9] from the trees in the nearby creek bottom and when we moved into it, there was only a hole in the wall where the window was to be and a quilt hung over the doorway to keep the weather out.

At night Jack always lay across the doorway inside and when I was waked by the wolves howling, I would hear Jack growling and Pa would say, "Go back to sleep! Jack wont let them in."

1. *Once upon a time years and years ago.* Brandt, Brandt Revised, and Bye omit this original opening phrase and begin with the sentence, "Pa stopped the horses." This editing decision may reflect assumptions about readership. *Pioneer Girl* was intended for adult readers. The first edition of Wilder's first novel, *Little House in the Big Woods*, which relied heavily on the original draft of *Pioneer Girl*, was intended for young readers and opens with "Once upon a time, sixty years ago" (*BW*, p. 1).

2. *Pa.* Wilder's father, Charles Philip Ingalls, was born near Cuba, New York, on January 10, 1836. When he was nine years old, his parents—Lansford and Laura Ingalls—moved the family to Illinois and then, in 1853, to Jefferson County, Wisconsin. There Charles met and married Caroline Lake Quiner on February 1, 1860. Two years later, the Ingalls clan moved to Pepin County, Wisconsin (the Big Woods). Laura Ingalls Wilder was born there on February 7, 1867. The next year, Charles Ingalls sold his farm in Wisconsin, bought another one in north-central

Caroline Quiner Ingalls and Charles Ingalls, 1860.
Laura Ingalls Wilder Historic Home and Museum

Missouri, and possibly moved his young family there. If so, they would have been traveling from central Missouri rather than Wisconsin as *Pioneer Girl* opens. No matter where their journey began, the family's movements illustrate the fundamental restlessness at the heart of Charles Ingalls's character—in fiction as well as in real life. In 1868 or 1869, he set his small family in motion and inspired an essential theme for Wilder's novels: a pioneering family moving west. In *Pioneer Girl*, however, Wilder recounted the family's moves as closely as she could recall them, and in reality, her family backtracked and meandered throughout the Midwest, searching for a better life. But the optimistic pioneering spirit that defines Charles Ingalls's character in the novels clearly emerges in her autobiography as well. Even after the family settled in Dakota Territory in 1879, he still longed to move as far west as he could possibly go. "Pa was no business man," Wilder told Lane. "He was a hunter and trapper, a musician and poet" (LIW to RWL, Mar. 23, 1937, Box 13, file 193, Lane Papers). At various times, he was also a carpenter, farmer, and an innkeeper. Charles Ingalls died in De Smet, South Dakota, on June 8, 1902, at the age of sixty-six. Miller, *Becoming*, pp. 16, 18, 22; Hill, *Laura Ingalls Wilder*, p. 397n8.

3. *Indian Territory*. Unlike Wilder's novels, her autobiography begins in Kansas, not Wisconsin. This discrepancy is one of many between the lives of the real Ingalls family and its fictional counterpart. In 1869, the real Ingalls family was part of an illegal movement to settle the Osage Diminished Indian Reserve, what Wilder calls "Indian Territory," in southeastern Kansas. In a series of treaties from 1808 through 1825, the Osage people ceded sizable tracts of land in what is now Missouri, Arkansas, Oklahoma, and Kansas to the United States. The Treaty of 1825 established a reserve for them that was roughly fifty miles wide and about one hundred and twenty-five miles long; under the terms of the treaty, this land was to remain in Osage possession "so long as they may choose to occupy the same" (quoted in Burns, *History of the Osage People*, p. 163).

At the close of the American Civil War in 1865, however, people displaced by the conflict swarmed over the Missouri border onto Osage lands. To appease this land grab, the Osages sold the eastern part of their reserve to the United States in 1865 and moved into what was thereafter known as the Osage Diminished Indian Reserve, but the sale did nothing to stem the tide of intruders. In 1867, the superintendent of Indian Affairs at Atchison, Kansas, wrote, "nothing less than a military force would suffice to

keep them [American settlers] off the Osage Reserve" (quoted in Mathews, *Osages*, p. 660).

In 1868, facing dire economic hardships, the Osage people signed what became known as the Sturges Treaty. They agreed to sell their lands in southern Kansas to the Leavenworth, Lawrence & Galveston Railroad and use the proceeds to purchase land on the Cherokee reserve and move there, but Congress refused to ratify the treaty, and it was formally withdrawn in February 1870. The mere prospect of a sale, however, had sent more trespassers surging across the Missouri border into Osage lands. Charles and Caroline Ingalls were among them.

The Ingallses settled their young family on Osage lands illegally in 1869 and remained on the reserve until the spring of 1871. According to the 1870 census, taken in August of that year, the "Ingles" family, including daughters Mary, Laura, and Caroline ("Carrie"), lived about thirteen miles from Independence, Kansas, in Montgomery County. The text of *Pioneer Girl* does not specify whether the family moved to the reserve from Wisconsin or Missouri, but given the general pattern of settlement onto Osage lands, it is possible that the family moved there from Chariton County, Missouri. Charles Ingalls and his brother-in-law Henry Quiner had purchased property there in 1868, although no documentation exists that indicates the Ingallses actually lived there. Burns, *History of the Osage People*, pp. 152–71, 281–91; Chapman, "Removal of the Osages," pp. 287–88; Mathews, *Osages*, pp. 658–60; Linsenmayer, "Kansas Settlers," p. 173; Miller, *Becoming*, pp. 24–25.

4. *"Well, Caroline," he said "here's the place we've been looking for."* A similar line appears in the fifth chapter of *Little House on the Prairie*. "'Here we are, Caroline!' he said. 'Right here we'll build our house'" (p. 52). In the first four chapters of the novel, Wilder recounted the family's trek west from Wisconsin to Kansas. To create those fictional scenes, she drew on her memories of the family's trek from Kansas back to Wisconsin in 1871, recorded later in this section of *Pioneer Girl*.

5. *Ma*. Caroline Quiner Ingalls "was a school teacher and well educated for her time and place, rather above Pa socially," Wilder told her daughter Rose Wilder Lane (LIW to RWL [fragment], ca. Feb.–Mar. 1931, Folder 19, Wilder Papers). Caroline Quiner's parents, Henry and Charlotte Quiner, were New Englanders who ultimately settled in Wisconsin, where Caroline was born on December 12, 1839. Not quite five years later, her father drowned in an accident on Lake Michigan, and her mother struggled to main-

tain the family farm, remarrying when Caroline was nine. Despite the family's hardships, Charlotte Quiner, a schoolteacher herself, instilled the importance of education in her daughter. Caroline followed in her mother's footsteps and was certified to teach in Concord Township at age sixteen. Her teaching certificate, preserved in De Smet, indicates that she received ten dollars a month plus board. After her marriage to Charles Ingalls, Caroline insisted that their children receive a solid education, even on the frontier, and her fictional counterpart is largely responsible for the family's decision to remain permanently in Dakota Territory. In *These Happy Golden Years*, Pa "must stay in a settled country for the sake of them all" (p. 142). Caroline Ingalls outlived her husband by twenty-two years. She died in De Smet, South Dakota, on Easter Sunday, April 20, 1924, at the age of eighty-four. Hill, *Laura Ingalls Wilder*, pp. 5–6; Miller, *Becoming*, p. 17; Zochert, *Laura*, p. 11; Anderson to Koupal, Mar. 3, 2013.

6. *I lay and looked.* This phrase signals that *Pioneer Girl* is a memoir, Wilder's personal narrative of her childhood and adolescence. Memoirs, by their nature, are written in first-person, from the author's unique and personal perspective. In *Pioneer Girl*, Wilder conveyed her memories, impressions, and feelings directly, in her own voice, using the "I" pronoun. Wilder's novels, however, employed a different point of view — third-person limited. Why did she make this shift and why is it important? Unlike writers of memoir, writers of fiction have more choices when it comes to point of view: first-person, third-person omniscient, third-person objective, third-person limited, even (though rarely) second-person. In a novel written in first-person, for example, a fictional character within the story relates the action as he or she experiences, sees, hears, and understands it. In a novel written in third-person omniscient, the author moves freely from the thoughts of one character into another. Most of the great Victorian novelists, including Charles Dickens and George Eliot, relied on this technique to give their novels greater range, insight, and perspective.

Wilder's first novel, *Little House in the Big Woods*, had its beginnings as an excerpt from *Pioneer Girl*. Probably without Wilder's knowledge, her daughter selected episodes from the original manuscript and shifted point of view from first-person to third-person, creating an elderly narrator to relay the story's action. Lane referred to the resulting twenty-one-page version as "juvenile Pioneer Girl" (Appendix A). It opened with the line, "When Grandma was a little girl," which became its title as a circulating manuscript. Marion Fiery at Alfred A. Knopf Company

admired the excerpt and met personally with Lane to discuss revisions. In a subsequent letter to her mother, Lane discussed point of view. Evidently Lane's third-person grandma narrator had not appealed to Fiery, but neither had the original first-person point of view of *Pioneer Girl*. "You can not use the first person," Lane told her mother, "because the 'I' books do not sell well" (RWL to LIW, Feb. 16, 1931, Box 13, file 189, Lane Papers).

Initially the shift in point of view hinged on a business decision — what was selling in the juvenile book market of 1931. Over time, however, Wilder and Lane settled on third-person limited. The action unfolded almost entirely from the fictional Laura's point of view, giving the series its unique, childlike voice and establishing Laura as the main character. It avoided what were then considered the distractions of an "I" narrator, yet it added a sense of reality. Young readers saw the author's world from a single perspective, much like their own. Most literary critics continue to praise the voice and point of view Wilder adopted in her fiction; it is, perhaps, one reason the books have remained so popular. Although the market has since shifted and first-person novels for young readers are now common, J. K. Rowling's Harry Potter series is also written in third-person limited.

7. *flat land where no one lived.* This line, which occurs in all versions of *Pioneer Girl*, is perhaps the shadowy original of a line that prompted a rare change in the text of one of Wilder's published novels. On the first page of the first edition of *Little House on the Prairie*, Wilder wrote: "There the wild animals wandered and fed as though they were in a pasture that stretched much farther than a man could see, and there were no people. Only the Indians lived there." In 1952, seventeen years after the book's publication, a reader who was offended by these lines wrote to Wilder in care of her publisher, Harper & Brothers. Wilder's editor responded directly to the reader. "I must admit to you," wrote Ursula Nordstrom, "that no one here realized that those words read as they did. Reading them now it seems unbelievable to me that you are the only person who has picked them up and written to us about them in the twenty years since the book was published." Nordstrom contacted Wilder and proposed a change. "You are perfectly right about the fault in *Little House on the Prairie*," Wilder responded, "and have my permission to make the correction you suggest. It was a stupid blunder of mine" (both women quoted in Marcus, *Dear Genius*, p. 54). In 1953, the newly re-illustrated edition of *Little House on the Prairie* contained these revised lines: "There the wild animals wandered and fed as though they were in

a pasture that stretched much farther than a man could see, and there were no settlers. Only Indians lived there" (p. 2). Although the original draft of *Little House on the Prairie* (Folder 16, Wilder Papers) does not include the offensive line or the variation found in *Pioneer Girl*, it is possible that the idea found its way back into the text when Rose Wilder Lane worked with Wilder on editorial changes for the final draft of the novel.

8. *its nice tight cover to keep out the wind and the rain.* All the edited versions of Wilder's memoir describe the wagon as having a "good tight cover to keep out the rain," with "good" replacing "nice." Bye made an additional shift: the wagon has a "good tight cover that keeps out the rain"; "that keeps" replaced "to keep." These kinds of minor revisions in words and phrases appear throughout the edited manuscripts, and unless such revisions are stylistically or editorially significant, they will not be addressed further.

9. *Pa built a house of logs.* In *Little House on the Prairie*, Wilder devoted two chapters to the construction of the house and the family's move inside. "The House on the Prairie" (pp. 52–70) and "Moving In" (pp. 71–79) include extended descriptions of the cabin's construction, multiple action scenes, and the introduction of the fictional character Mr. Edwards. Ma also helps Pa build the cabin and is injured when a log slips. In both *Pioneer Girl* and the novel, the house is termed "finished" with just an opening for one window and a quilt as a door, but Wilder wrote three more chapters to complete the fictional house—"Two Stout Doors," "A Fire on the Hearth," and "A Roof and a Floor" (pp. 99–131).

One night Pa picked me up[10] out of bed and carried me to the window so I could see the wolves. There were so many of them all sitting in a ring around the house, with their noses pointed up at the big, bright moon, howling as loud and long as they could,[11] while Jack paced before the door and growled.

Pa went to the town forty miles away[12] and brought back a cook stove a window to put in the window hole and some lumber to make a door.

Some other people had come to live along the creek so we had neighbors. ~~Some of them had broken the land and planted some crops for next winter.~~[13]

When summer came everyone was sick with chills and fever[14] so when the beautiful large watermelons[15] were ripe we were not allowed to eat them. No one could eat them for to do so made their chills much worse.

We were all sick in bed at the same time except Pa. I think he was as sick as any of us but he staggered around and waited on the rest. When I waked and cried for a drink of water Pa would bring it to me but his hand shook so he would spill some of the water out of the cup when I drank.

One time I waked and there was a great, big, black man[16] looking at me. He raised my head and poured some awfully bitter medicine down my throat from a spoon. He was the doctor but I was afraid of him[17] for I had never seen a colored person before.[18] Some time later we were all well again.

Our house was on the cattle trail[19] where so many cattle were driven north and when one great herd was driven by, Pa got a black cow with great long white horns; and her little black calf.

We had such an exciting time with that cow, for she did not want to let us have any milk and would kick Pa over whenever he tried to milk her. Finally he built a pen, against the fence, that was so small she could not turn around in it. He would drive her in and put up the bars behind her so close she couldn't kick. Then he would milk her through the fence and she couldn't kick him.

10. *One night Pa picked me up.* The short, intense scene in this paragraph illustrates the episodic structure of *Pioneer Girl* and reflects Wilder's experience as a newspaper columnist with the *Missouri Ruralist*. Throughout the manuscript, Wilder developed compact episodes that are virtually self-contained. Structurally they resemble newspaper columns—they are tightly written, evocative, dramatic, and revealing. They usually convey a single experience through a few well-chosen words and brushstroke details, creating, as here, a visual picture that is charged with emotional intensity and drama. Words were a luxury for a newspaper columnist; Wilder had learned to use them sparingly—and effectively.

It is also interesting to speculate on the personal significance of this scene. Was this event one of Wilder's earliest memories? She placed it near the beginning of *Pioneer Girl* and would develop it further in her third novel, *Little House on the Prairie.* But by then, Wilder had begun to shed the inherent constraints of writing for newspapers. She expanded the scene from this one paragraph into five pages, devoting an entire chapter to it ("The Wolf-Pack," pp. 80–98). She had also mastered an essential principle of writing fiction: show don't tell. Rather than tell readers, as she did here, that the wolves "howled as loud and long as they could," she pulled readers into the fictional scene when a wolf howls "right in Laura's ear" (p. 95). Then, through Laura's eyes,

"Laura looked and looked at that wolf."
Helen Sewell, 1935

readers actually see the wolves: "They sat on their haunches and looked at Laura in the window, and she looked at them" (p. 96). Fiction, as opposed to nonfiction, also offered another kind of freedom. Wilder could pluck a memory from one part of her childhood and place it anywhere within her fiction. This episode, for example, appears much later in the novel than in the autobiography. She could also create scenes or parts of scenes that did not exist in her memories, adding depth to the experiences of her fictional alter-ego. An examination of scenes like this one suggests that Wilder had quickly embraced the creative freedom fiction provided.

11. *howling as loud and long as they could.* Wilder's original phrasing in her memoir was direct and conversational. It survived Lane's initial editorial scrutiny, but a line runs through it on the Brandt manuscript (p. 1), and Brandt Revised (p. 1) and Bye (p. 2) contain a different sentence: "Long and loud they howled, from side to side." The new wording lacks the immediacy and spontaneity of Wilder's original and strikes a slightly different tone. This small change illustrates how an editor can subtly alter an author's voice.

12. *the town forty miles away.* Independence, Kansas, was founded in August 1869, just weeks before the Ingalls family crossed into Kansas. The town was located on the banks of the Verdigris River, about four miles from the Drum Creek Agency, the federal Indian Affairs field office that functioned as a liaison to the Osage people. The Osages called Independence Hay-House Town because townspeople roofed buildings with prairie grasses. In reality, however, the town was about thirteen miles—not forty—from the spot where Charles Ingalls decided to settle. By the 1930s when Wilder wrote first *Pioneer Girl* and then *Little House on the Prairie*, which fictionalized her family's experiences in Indian Territory,

Independence, Kansas, ca. 1870. *Kansas State Historical Society*

she could not remember the location of the cabin site. This lapse of memory is not surprising since she had been just four years old when the family left Kansas in 1871. The term "Indian Territory" may have confused her. In the early twentieth century, that phrase was largely associated with Indian lands in Oklahoma. If that was Wilder's assumption, then Independence—as the nearest town she remembered from childhood—would indeed have been about forty miles north of the Oklahoma state line. In 1933, while writing *Little House on the Prairie*, Wilder tried to locate the place where her family had lived. She and Lane took a road trip into Kansas and Oklahoma but failed to find any trace of the little house—because they were looking in the wrong place. In the 1970s, a local Kansas historian located the probable Ingalls cabin site in section thirty-six of Rutland Township, Montgomery County, Kansas, just about thirteen miles southwest of Independence. Burns, *History of the Osage People*, pp. 61, 309; Mathews, *Osages*, p. 693; Miller, *Laura Ingalls Wilder and Rose Wilder Lane*, pp. 171–72; Linsenmayer, "Kansas Settlers," p. 175n27.

13. *Some of them had broken the land and planted some crops for next winter.* This line is crossed out on the original manuscript, but it remains legible. Brandt Revised includes the following sentence instead: "Here and there the prairie sod was broken and the land planted to crops for next winter. From what Pa said to Ma, I knew that the Indians did not want us to live here." The phrase "us to live here" has been crossed out, and Lane's handwritten edit reads: "I knew that the Indians did not want so many white people living on their land" (p. 2), which Bye incorporates.

14. *When summer came everyone was sick with chills and fever.* Wilder devoted an entire chapter ("Fever 'n' Ague," pp. 182–98), in *Little House on the Prairie* to this episode. During the nineteenth century, the phrase "fever and ague" was commonly used to describe malaria; contemporary definitions of the word "ague" continue to link it to the disease and its symptoms: persistent chills, fever, and waves of hot and cold sweats. While it is impossible to know with certainty if malaria is what struck the Ingalls family, the symptoms Wilder described in the novel match those typically associated with the disease, including the haze and hallucinations of fever: "Something dwindled slowly, smaller and smaller, till it was tinier than the tiniest thing. Then slowly it swelled till it was larger than anything could be. . . . Laura cried because she was so cold. Then she was burning up" (pp. 186–87). During the American Civil War (1861–1865), Union forces alone reported almost a million cases of malaria, which "became so common that one soldier wrote home saying that if the Union forces could synchronize

their chills, they could shake the rebels into submission" (Bollet, *Civil War Medicine*, p. 289). At the time, malaria was treated with quinine, often administered in a bitter powdered form dissolved in liquid. *In Little House on the Prairie*, when Laura receives a cup of liquid with the promise that it will make her well, she drinks "the whole bitter dose" (p. 190). In 1880, a French army surgeon discovered that malaria was caused by a parasite, and seventeen years later, a British medical officer demonstrated that the parasite, in turn, was transmitted by mosquitoes. Wilder was aware of these discoveries and ended the chapter with these lines: "No one knew, in those days, that fever 'n' ague was malaria, and that some mosquitoes give it to people when they bite them" (p. 198). Bollet, *Civil War Medicine*, pp. 236–38; "Civil War and Medicine."

15. *watermelons*. The reference to watermelons in connection with the family's chills and fever is somewhat baffling, but Wilder developed this idea more fully in *Little House on the Prairie*, where the character of Mrs. Scott is convinced that eating watermelons caused the fever and ague. The fictional Pa disagrees with her, and when the family recovers, he brings home a giant watermelon to prove his point. Over a century later, modern medicine confirms Pa's faith in watermelons, which "may play an important part in decreasing the incidence of certain cancers, cardiovascular problems, and other aging diseases" ("Research: Watermelons and human health").

16. *a great, big, black man.* George A. Tann (spelled "Tan" in LHOP, pp. 191–92) was an African American homeopathic doctor who settled on the Osage Diminished Indian Reserve in 1869. Listed as a physician on the 1870 Rutland Township census, he lived roughly one mile from the Ingalls cabin with his parents. The census listing appeared just above the one for "Ingles, C. P." Dr. Tann was born on November 27, 1835, in Pennsylvania, making him the same age as Charles Ingalls. Tann served in the Union Army dur-

ing the Civil War and went on to become a doctor to the Osage Indians. He died on March 30, 1909, and is buried in Independence, Kansas. Homeopathic medicine dates to the early nineteenth century when a German doctor began to espouse what is known as the "law of similars," maintaining that medical conditions can best be treated by remedies that produce similar symptoms in healthy people. Zochert, *Laura*, p. 34; "Dr. George Tann"; "What is Homeopathy."

17. *I was afraid of him.* This passage is the first of many instances in *Pioneer Girl* when Wilder's personal recollection of feelings contrasted with those she gave to the fictional Laura Ingalls. In *Little House on the Prairie*, she wrote, "Laura had never seen a black man before. . . . He was so very black. She would have been afraid of him if she had not liked him so much" (p. 191).

18. *I had never seen a colored person before.* In Brandt Revised (p. 4) and Bye (p. 5), this line reads, "I had never seen a negro before." The change from "colored" to "negro" reflects the broader societal changes taking place in the 1930s concerning what was considered appropriate when referring to people of African American descent. *See* Bennett, "What's in a Name," pp. 48, 50.

19. *Our house was on the cattle trail.* The Shawnee Trail, also known as the Sedalia Trail or the Kansas Trail, was the first north-south cattle trail, extending from Texas to Missouri. It sliced through eastern Kansas, including the Osage Diminished Indian Reserve. The trail fell out of use during the Civil War, but longhorn cattle drives resumed shortly thereafter. Cattlemen continued to use this trail through the early 1870s. In *Little House on the Prairie*, Wilder also placed the Ingalls cabin near an Indian trail (p. 55), and, in fact, large portions of the Shawnee Trail had originated as the Osage Trace, or the Great Osage Trail, which linked north and south bands of the Osages. "Shawnee Trail"; Burns, *History of the Osage People*, pp. 50, 76.

Not to be used.[20]

XX This story would be called "nature faking"[21] if anyone read it, but it is true.

One day when Pa was riding Patty, the pony, across the prairie he went down into a little wash and found himself surrounded by a pack of wolves. The wolves must have just eaten well for they paid no attention to him. Patty was terrified and wanted to run but Pa held her down. He knew she could not run so fast as the wolves; that if she started the wolves would chase her and after chasing would surely kill them, for Pa couldn't kill a whole pack of wolves with just one muzzel loading gun.

Patty trembled with fear, but Pa made her walk and the wolves carelessly ran on by.

When they had passed Patty was shaking and actually sweating with fear and Pa wasn't much better. It took some nerve I'd say!

He came on home as fast as he could and told us about it.

Indians often came to the house and asked for anything they liked.[22] Pa or Ma always gave them what they wanted to keep them good natured. Jack hated them and was kept chained[23] so he could not hurt anyone.

The neighbors were afraid of him too and used to climb up on the wood pile quite a ways from the house and call, "Is the dog chained?" before they would come on to the house.

When the Indians took the notion[24] of hanging around the barn and looking at Pet and Patty the black horses, Pa left Jack chained at the barn door to keep the Indians from stealing them.

As Mary[25] and I were playing with Jack at the barn we saw two Indians go into the house.[26] They looked awful. Their faces were painted, their heads were shaved, except for a bunch of hair on top that was tied so it stood straight up, and they were all naked except for a skin around the middle.

We were frightened and cuddled close to Jack with our arms around his neck for we felt safe with him. We said we would stay

20. *Not to be used.* In Wilder's original manuscript, the main narrative reaches the end of a tablet page with the incomplete line, "Indians often came to the house and asked for anything," and concludes the sentence on the first line of the next page. On the back of the first page, however, is additional text that begins with this heading concerning its use. This message is the first that Wilder wrote exclusively for Lane, implying that the material would be edited. Wilder seemed at once to be writing a private memoir for her daughter and a public one for publication.

21. *"nature faking."* The handwritten words here are almost illegible and unfamiliar, but the mystery phrase appears to be "nature faking," which is probably derived from Theodore Roosevelt's term "nature fakers." In 1907, President Roosevelt, an outdoors-

man and writer, first used the term when he took sides in a literary debate then raging over so-called realist authors who exaggerated or romanticized the traits and habits of wild animals. In an article in *Everybody's Magazine*, the president suggested that contemporary writer Jack London, among others, was guilty of filling "credulous strangers with impossible stories of wild beasts" ("Nature Fakers," p. 428). Once the president weighed in on the topic, it became a public phenomenon, and the term "entered the American language as an instant colloquialism" (Carson, "T. R. and the "Nature Fakers," p. 2). *See also* Clark, "Roosevelt," pp. 771–72.

Clearly, Wilder had doubts about including this episode in her memoir, but the scene appears on the second page of both Brandt Revised and Bye, ahead of the sequence about Indians visiting the Ingalls cabin. It may also have been part of the Brandt manuscript, but page 2 is missing. In these edited versions of *Pioneer Girl*, the story about Pa, Patty, and the wolves unfolds immediately after he travels to Independence, Kansas. In *Little House on the Prairie*, Wilder expanded the story into "The Wolf-Pack" (pp. 80–98), in which Pa leaves his gun behind, making the situation more dangerous. Wilder also inserted colorful details directly into the dialogue: "'It was a big pack,' Pa said. 'All of fifty wolves. . . . Their leader's a big gray brute that stands three feet at the shoulder'" (p. 89).

22. *Indians . . . asked for anything they liked.* The American Indian people who appear in the opening scenes of *Pioneer Girl* and in *Little House on the Prairie* are Osage Indians. Part of the larger Dhegiha Sioux group, they originated east of the Mississippi, but by the late eighteenth and early nineteenth centuries, they occupied most of present-day Missouri, Kansas, Arkansas, and Oklahoma. "The Osages are the finest-looking Indians I have seen in the West," noted Washington Irving in *A Tour on the Prairies*, published in 1835. By then, the Osage people had already begun ceding their lands to the United States, and when the Ingalls family crossed into Kansas in 1869, all the Osage villages were clustered near the Verdigris River in the Osage Diminished Indian Reserve. Agent Isaac Gibson estimated the Osage population to be between thirty-five and thirty-nine hundred in 1873, two years after the Ingalls family left Kansas.

The Ingalls family's cabin was just two to three miles west of an Osage village on Onion Creek, which may explain the Indians' frequent visits to them, but such encounters were not unusual. Contemporary historian William G. Cutler wrote that settlers were "obliged to secure consent from the Indians" before occupying a "squatter's claim" such as the Ingalls claim and that individual Osages made frequent visits to their tenants' property to ensure ongoing payment in one form or another ("Montgomery County," pt. 1). For the Osages, however, it was not simply a question of land rights; they were impoverished and hungry. Shortly before the American Civil War, the federal government had stopped making their annuity payments, and that, coupled with the extremities of the war itself, had left the Osage nation "on the edge of extinction" (Burns, *History of the Osage People*, p. 283). The Osages' "crops were destroyed by herds of cattle and other stock belonging to white settlers; and lawless white men stole their horses and robbed their corn cribs" (Chapman, "Removal of the Osages," p. 289n8). As a result, the Indians began to take what they needed from those they viewed as trespassers, and "tensions mounted between the two groups" (Linsenmayer, "Kansas Settlers," pp. 175–76).

23. *Jack hated them and was kept chained.* Throughout her handwritten memoir and in her novel *Little House on the Prairie*, Wilder made it clear that Jack disliked all strangers. He chases the fictional Mr. Edwards up a woodpile in the chapter "When Pa Goes to Town" (*LHOP*, p. 212) and makes only one exception when the family is sick: "Jack, who hated strangers and never let one come near the house until Pa or Ma told him to, had gone to meet Dr. Tan and begged him to come in" (*LHOP*, p. 192). In contrast, Brandt Revised and Bye focus entirely on the dog's dislike of Indians: "We were all afraid that some day he might hurt an Indian" (Brandt Revised, p. 2), and "Pa was afraid that some day he might hurt an Indian and start bad trouble" (Bye, p. 2).

"Laura tried to comfort Jack." *Helen Sewell, 1935*

24. *When the Indians took the notion.* In *Little House on the Prairie*, Wilder painted a more vivid picture of such visits: "Indians often came to the house. Some were friendly, some were surly and cross. All of them wanted food and tobacco, and Ma gave them what they wanted. She was afraid not to" (pp. 275-76). Wilder also built entire chapters around the fictional family's interactions with the Osages: "Indians in the House" (pp. 132-46), "The Tall Indian" (pp. 226-37), and the three chapters that provide the climax of the book, "Indian Jamboree" (pp. 263-73), "Indian War-Cry" (pp. 263-73), and "Indians Ride Away" (pp. 302-11). Once again, fiction gave Wilder more freedom to shape and transform her memories, allowing her to create a more suspenseful plot with sustained action.

25. *Mary.* Wilder's older sister, Mary Amelia Ingalls, was born on January 10, 1865, on the Ingalls farm near Pepin, Wisconsin. "Mary was a very good little girl," Wilder wrote in *Little House in the Big Woods*, "who always did exactly as she was told" (pp. 181-82). In *Pioneer Girl*, the author painted a similar portrait of Mary Ingalls as poised, obedient, and ladylike, suggesting that her temperament was radically different from the young Wilder's, which led to childhood squabbles. In adolescence, however, the girls outgrew their rivalries and forged a supportive relationship. The fictional Laura even lived out her sister's dreams, as outlined in *These Happy Golden Years*: "'I am planning to write a book some day,' she [Mary] confided. Then she laughed. 'But I planned to teach school, and you are doing that for me, so maybe you will write the book'" (p. 136). *Pioneer Girl* does not include a similar scene; yet, the autobiography may owe its existence to Mary Ingalls. She died on October 17, 1928, and shortly thereafter, Wilder was at work on her memoir. The death of her mother in 1924 had inspired Wilder to think more creatively about her pioneer childhood, but Mary's death may have convinced her that time was running out. Hill, *Laura Ingalls Wilder*, p. 130.

26. *we saw two Indians go into the house.* The passage that follows this observation is Wilder's first developed scene in *Pioneer Girl*. It contains specific descriptions of the Indians, important insights into Ingalls family dynamics, and remembered feelings and emotions. But it still reads like a newspaper column. The Bye version creates a slightly more colorful scene. The Indians, for example, have painted their faces "in streaks of red and yellow and white" (p. 3), and they make Ma light Pa's pipe for them (p. 4). Wilder developed this episode further in *Little House on the Prairie* ("Indians in the House," pp. 132-46), where Pa leaves to go hunting, chains Jack to the stable, and orders Laura and Mary not to let him loose. Later in the morning, two Indians arrive, dressed as Wilder described them here, but Laura and Mary argue about whether to cut Jack free, and Laura alone decides to rush into the cabin. From that point on, Laura is the focus of the chapter, and readers experience the scene through her eyes. Only toward the end do we discover that Mary is standing beside Ma, holding on to her sleeve (p. 141). Baby Carrie is also in the house with Ma, an added incentive for Laura to feel protective. And Carrie, not Mary, clings to Ma's skirts (pp. 136-37). In all versions of *Pioneer Girl*, however, Baby Carrie has not yet been born when this incident occurs. In the novel, this episode delivers an important lesson when Laura admits that she considered letting Jack loose. Pa's response is dramatic: "'After this,' he said, in a terrible voice, 'you girls remember always to do as you're told. Don't you even think of disobeying me'" (pp. 145-46). Perhaps because it was written for an adult audience, *Pioneer Girl* contains no such moralizing.

with him and then we thought that Ma was all alone in the house with the Indians.

We did not dare turn Jack loose for we had been told we must never, never do that. If we went to help Ma we must leave Jack and he couldn't take care of us then.

We hesitated and swallowed hard and then we left Jack and ran as fast as we could to the house to help Ma if she needed us.

My! But we were two scared little mites[27] when we got there. I was two years the littlest and I hid behind the stove. Mary clung to Ma's skirt. Ma was cooking food for the Indians and I knew she was afraid too. The Indians were looking at everything and taking all Pa's tobacco. The room smelled awful for the skins the Indians were wearing were skunk skins and they were fresh.

After a long time when the Indians had eaten all the food and taken Pa's pipe and all the meat we had they went away.

A great many Indians came and camped by the creek not far away and in the night we would hear the most frightful shouting and screaming.[28] It sounded much worse than the wolves. Pa said the Indians were having their war dances and to go back to sleep for they were afraid of Jack and wouldn't come but whenever I opened my eyes, I would see Pa all dressed and walking around. Once I thought he was carrying his gun.

At last we didn't hear them any more at night and Pa said they had all gone away.

It was very dark outside. I could not see even one star through the window, the night I was waked by hearing Pa say "But Caroline I must go. I'm sure it was some one calling for help. Sounded like a woman and came from down the creek toward Robertson's.[29] I must go and see what's the trouble." Then Pa went out into the dark and shut the door.

I didn't know when he came back, but in the morning he was there and he told Mary and I we must stay in the house because there was a panther[30] in the creek bottom.

"Last night," said he "I thought I heard Mrs Robertson calling and I went down there to see if anything was wrong. But the house was dark, everyone asleep and everything quiet. I started back won-

27. *My! But we were two scared little mites.* Later versions of *Pioneer Girl* convey Wilder's fear differently. Brandt reads, "My! but we were scared when we got there" (p. 3). Bye changes that to, "When we got there, I was so scared that I felt sick" (p. 3). All versions express Wilder's feelings, but they fail to pull readers into the scene so that they too can experience a child's fear and wonder. By the time Wilder fictionalized the scene, she had mastered some basic principles of creative writing, and the scene is gripping: "When Laura peeked out from behind the slab again, both Indians were looking straight at her. Her heart jumped into her throat and choked her with its pounding. Two black eyes glittered down into her eyes. The Indian did not move. . . . Laura didn't move, either. She didn't even breathe" (*LHOP*, p. 140).

28. *A great many Indians came and camped by the creek . . . we would hear the most frightful shouting and screaming.* Brandt Revised (p. 3) and Bye (pp. 2–3) place this episode before the two Indians visited the Ingalls cabin and emphasize Wilder's personal encounter with the two Indians in the house, not those terrifying nights when Pa stood with his gun at the ready. In *Little House on the Prairie*, however, Wilder used the inherent drama of the material to build toward the climax of the novel ("Indian War Cry," pp. 286–301). "Night crept toward the little house, and the darkness was frightening," Wilder wrote. "It yelped with Indian yells, and one night it began to throb with Indian drums" (p. 287). The situation escalates, but suddenly the Indian camp breaks up and all is quiet. Pa credits an Osage chief named Soldat du Chêne with bringing a peaceful resolution to the crisis (pp. 300–301).

In recent years, Wilder has come under attack for her fictional depiction of events. Critic Frances W. Kaye maintained that, at best, Wilder misunderstood the nature of the Osage encampment. The sounds Wilder and her family overheard were part of "traditional [Osage] ceremonies asking for success on their buffalo hunt" or Osage women mourning their leaders' decision to leave the reserve in Kansas ("Little Squatter," p. 134). Cultural misunderstand-

The historical Le Soldat du Chêne. McKinney, *History of the Indian Tribes of North America*, vol. 2.

ing and panic, Kaye reasoned, caused the family and their neighbors to overreact, or perhaps Charles Ingalls had embellished the truth to entertain his children in the years after they left Kansas. In *Little House on the Prairie*, the episode comes in late winter or early spring; the Osages move away; and the Ingalls family leaves Indian Territory later that summer before Pa can harvest his corn. If viewed within the actual chronology of the family's time in Kansas, this sequence of events would have unfolded in the early spring of 1871, just before the family actually left, giving Kaye's interpretation of events some validity. By then, not only had the Osages agreed to sell their lands in Kansas, but most of them were already moving away and the settlers' fears had been laid to rest.

Wilder, however, was writing fiction, and to tell a more com-

pelling story, she had rearranged the sequence of her family's experiences in *Little House on the Prairie*. The original draft of *Pioneer Girl* presents a different sequence of events, and that sequence corresponds to the historic escalation of hostilities between the Osages and the settlers. The "war dances" as Wilder remembered them in *Pioneer Girl* appear to have taken place in the late winter or early spring of 1870, when tensions were running high. In January 1870, Agent Isaac Gibson wrote the superintendent of Indian Affairs that the Osages "could massacre the inhabitants of this valley in a few hours; and if they should be driven to do so this spring, I would not be surprised." The superintendent agreed. If the Osages and settlers continued to live side by side, he wrote, "war may result therefrom" (both men quoted in Linsenmayer, "Kansas Settlers," p. 178). The Ingallses themselves "may have been close enough to the Claremore village [two to three miles away] to hear Osage nightly debates. In addition, Walnut Creek flowed through the quarter section on which the Ingalls family was living, and Agent Gibson wrote that he had received reports of the Osages assuming a hostile stance near the mouth of Walnut Creek in mid-January 1870" (ibid., p. 179). A few pages after her mention of Indian war dances in *Pioneer Girl*, Wilder wrote that the Indian activities ceased and her sister Carrie was born, which occurred on August 3, 1870. The remaining paragraphs about Osage activities are consistent with events that unfolded between late 1870 and the spring of 1871, when the Ingalls family as well as the Osages left Kansas. *See also* Chapman, "Removal of the Osages," p. 290.

The name Soldat du Chêne does not appear in *Pioneer Girl*, nor did Wilder allude to an influential Indian chief anywhere in its pages. She launched a search for his name only after she began writing fiction. "I thought perhaps you could tell me the name of an Indian Chief that I have forgotten," she wrote in a letter to R. B. Selvidge in Oklahoma, whom she perceived as an authority on the subject (LIW to Dear Sir, June 26, 1933, Folder 14, Wilder Papers). He wrote back, suggesting that the Osage chief in question was Le-Soldat-du-Chêne, who "was very friendly to the white people" (Selvidge to LIW, July 5, 1933, Box 14, file 219, Lane Papers). Wilder also sought information from the Kansas State Historical Society (KSHS). "I have been unable to find a reference to your story of the Indian chief who was friendly to the white settlers," the representative wrote back (Helen M. McFarland to LIW, June 19, 1933, Box 14, folder 219, Lane Papers). Yet, Wilder was apparently convinced that an Osage chief had played a critical role in ending the crisis. In the end, she accepted Selvidge's suggestion and settled on her own interpretation of the past.

Contemporary critics and scholars have condemned and sometimes ridiculed Wilder's decision to portray Le Soldat du Chêne as she did in *Little House on the Prairie*. Kaye, for example, objected to the character's French name and Pa's assumption that the Osages had spoken French. "The French had had no official role in the Missouri valley since 1803, and since 1808 the Osages had been making treaties with the Americans in English," Kaye wrote. She then theorized that the French name of the chief had come from Charles Ingalls's misreading of American history, and that Wilder had decided to use it because it "sounded more noble . . . than . . . Not-Afraid-of-Longhairs or Black Dog or Arrow-Going-Home" ("Little Squatter," p. 135). This argument does not take into account Wilder's correspondence with Oklahoma and Kansas historians. Wilder initially wrote to *ask* for the name of the man she remembered. And, in fact, Le Soldat du Chêne was the name of an Osage chief who sat for his portrait in Philadelphia in the early 1800s. Granted, he was not Wilder's Osage chief, but the name itself had historical legitimacy. Wilder's Oklahoma correspondent apparently failed to note that the author was searching for someone who had been influential in 1870 and 1871, something she clearly specified in her original letter. Furthermore, the fragment of correspondence that remains from KSHS suggests that Wilder had later asked not simply for confirmation of the name Le Soldat du Chêne but for his "Indian name" as well ([Kirke Mechem] to LIW, Jan. 10, 1934, Folder 14, Wilder Papers). Finally, contrary to Kaye's assertion about use of the French language among the Osages, historian Louis Burns reported that language was a major barrier between the Osages and the federal government in treaty negotiations as late as 1865. Few "full-bloods," he wrote, were "fluent in English, and "most of the mixed-bloods were more accustomed to French" (*History of the Osage People*, p. 284).

In the context of writing fiction, Wilder's decision to introduce Le Soldat du Chêne into *Little House on the Prairie* is consistent with the creative license inherent in this genre. She checked with two legitimate historical sources, then made her own interpretation of the past. Wilder claimed that her novel was true to the spirit of its age and to her own childhood memories of her family's experiences. Today's readers may agree with Kaye that the novel sends up "red flags for contemporary critics who believe in diversity, multiculturalism, and human rights," but Kaye also observed that Wilder "was shaping her narrative to meet her idea of poetic truth" ("Little Squatter," pp. 123, 132), which is what all writers of fiction do, whether they write for young readers or adults. Artistically, Wilder's choice was a valid one, although readers and scholars alike may question its cultural, political, and social validity as society's attitudes and perceptions about the American frontier continue to evolve.

29. *Robertson's*. No one named Robertson appears on the 1870 census of Rutland Township. None of the Ingalls family's neighbors in Indian Territory can be identified with any certainty except Dr. George Tann. The families who probably lived in the closest proximity were named Johnson, Lunker (possibly a misspelling of Longcor), and Gilmore. A. K. Johnson and his wife had four children, ranging in age from five to eleven. He was thirty-six in 1870; his wife was twenty-eight. The Lunkers or Longcors were perhaps newlyweds (she was just eighteen) and had no children. Robert Gilmore and his wife, Mary, had five children; he was fifty-two, and she was forty-four in August 1870. Johnson, Lunker or Longcor, and Gilmore were all farmers; their wives were "keeping house." Wilder devoted an entire chapter to this episode in *Little House on the Prairie* ("Scream in the Night," pp. 253–62), where she changed the neighbors' name to Scott. No one named Scott appears on the 1870 census either.

30. *panther*. Throughout the nineteenth century, settlers identified the big cats they encountered in the wild as panthers, mountain lions, pumas, and cougars; yet, these terms all refer to one species—*Puma concolor*. It ranged throughout most of North America and preyed on deer, elk, moose, and livestock. It weighed between one hundred and one hundred forty-five pounds, was about six to seven feet long, and had a tawny coat. Commonly known as cougars today, the big cats growl, hiss, purr, and scream. They are capable of great speeds for short distances. While Charles Ingalls sought to reassure his children by suggesting that he could outrun the panther, he would have needed a lengthy head start. Laumeyer to Hill, Aug. 10, 2010; Danz, *Cougar*, p. 47.

31. *But we heard no more of the panther.* In the revised manuscripts, Pa kills the panther. Brandt Revised and Bye insert the end of the story into the family's bout with chills and fever: "every night we asked Pa if he had killed the panther. But before he had done it, everyone came down sick with chills and fever" (Bye, p. 5). Did Charles Ingalls actually shoot the panther, or were Wilder and Lane already revising the family's personal history to tell a better story? It is impossible to know for sure, but Wilder imagined yet another ending in *Little House on the Prairie*, where Pa continues to hunt the panther until he meets an Indian in the woods who communicates that he has killed the animal. Laura decides that the Indian "had killed that panther" to protect his own "little papoose" (p. 262). Pa and the Indian are thus united by a father's love and concern for his family.

32. *one of these old camps. . . . finding a great many pretty beads.* Charles Ingalls could have taken his daughters to the Claremore village two to three miles east of the Ingalls cabin. In June 1870, the Osages left for their summer hunt and did not return to the area until early September. In "Indian Camp," a chapter in *Little House on the Prairie* (pp. 172–81), the fictional Pa demonstrates his skills in interpreting how the Indians lived and in reading moccasin tracks, while Laura and Mary collect beads. But the

"Mary and Laura sat side by side and strung the beads."
Helen Sewell, 1935

dering what it could have been I had heard and just as I got near the place where the trees are thickest by the creek, I heard a panther scream down there. My hair stood straight up! It fairly lifted my hat and I made time getting home. Run! I should say I did run! I'm sure no panther could have caught me, but you girls can't run that fast, so you stay in the house until I say you may go out." But we heard no more of the panther.[31]

Indians often stopped for a while by the creek, living there in their tents while they fished & hunted. One morning early Pa put me on Jack's back to ride and with Mary walking beside him took us to one of these old camps to see what we could see. We stayed there all morning hunting around finding a great many pretty beads[32] that the Indian women had lost from their bead work. There were white beads and blue beads and yellow beads and a great many red ones.

When finally we went back to the house, the black Dr. was there and Mrs Robertson and Baby Carrie had come.[33] Ma haden't got up yet and Carrie was lying beside her. Such a tiny, tiny baby but Ma said she would soon be big enough to play with us. We were very busy then for awhile putting all the pretty beads we had found on thread to make a string of beads for Carrie to wear.

So we had a baby sister to watch and laugh at.[34]

It did not rain for a long time. The creek got low and the tall prairie grass turned dry and brown.

For days it looked smokey all around the edge of the sky and Pa said it was Indian summer.

One day the smoke seemed thicker[35] at one side of the sky and Ma often looked that way.

Pa came to the door and said something to her, then went hurrying to where Pet and Patty were on their picket ropes. He hitched them to the plow and began to break a furrow in the sod, a little way from the house, on the side where the smoke cloud was. He made the horses go as fast as they could, back and forth turning up the black ground. When there was a strip of plowed ground on that side, he made some furrows clear around the house and stable. Then he drove the horses inside the furrows and tied them tightly to

fictional trip is not simply a diversion as it is in *Pioneer Girl*. Instead, Wilder used the chapter to underscore fundamental differences between the girls. Mary offers her beads to the baby, but Laura wants to keep hers: "Her chest felt all hot inside, and she wished with all her might that Mary wouldn't always be such a good little girl" (p. 179).

33. *Baby Carrie had come*. Named for her mother, Carrie's full name was Caroline Celestia Ingalls; she shared a middle name with her Aunt Ruby Celestia Ingalls. She was born on August 3, 1870, and was listed on the census when it was taken just ten days later. Dr. George Tann attended her birth, as did one of the family's neighbors; yet, in Wilder's fiction, Carrie is a baby in Wisconsin and goes west with the rest of the family. This change is one of many significant alterations that Wilder made when she shifted from autobiography to fiction. The decision to include Baby Carrie in the story right from the beginning may have been a consequence of the juvenile manuscript that Lane had pieced together from later sections of *Pioneer Girl* and submitted on her mother's behalf to editor Marion Fiery. The second paragraph of that manuscript concludes with the line, "Grandma lived with her father and her mother, her sister Mary and baby Carrie" (Appendix A). Since an editor was already interested in the story, it might have been awkward to write Carrie out of it. Furthermore, Wilder had not yet envisioned a series of children's books in 1931 when she began the revisions that would turn the shorter manuscript into *Little House in the Big Woods*, and she may have wanted her sister to be a part of that book. She still hoped to sell *Pioneer Girl*, which would relay her family's entire pioneering experience. Wilder's portrayal of Carrie as the timid and frail younger sister is consistent in both her fiction and her autobiography. The real Carrie Ingalls, however, would prove to be an enterprising and independent adult. She worked as a typesetter for her hometown newspaper, the *De Smet Leader*; homesteaded alone in a tar-paper shack near Philip, South Dakota; and managed several newspapers in the Black Hills. In her early forties, she married widower David N. Swanzey on August 1, 1912. He was sixteen years her senior and had two young children. After her husband's death, she managed the Keystone, South Dakota, railway station. She died at the age of seventy-five on June 2, 1946. Hill, *Laura Ingalls Wilder*, p. 10; Miller, *Becoming*, p. 89; *Ingalls Family of De Smet*, pp. 21–24.

34. At this point in Wilder's handwritten draft she puts an "X" in the text and the note "(On back of page)," directing Lane to

the reverse of the sheet, where a full page of text on the prairie fire can be found. The lengthy insert ends with the note "(Back to begin at X)." Although the rest of the original page contains Wilder's Christmas memories, she clearly intended that the narrative should continue with the prairie fire scene. Wilder's notes made her intention clear, and this narrative puts the material in the sequence that she intended. Subsequent directions and insertions of this sort will not be pointed out if they have no effect on the narrative.

35. *One day the smoke seemed thicker*. In *Little House on the Prairie*, Wilder explored the episode that follows more fully. The girls are inside with Ma when they notice, "suddenly the sunshine was gone" (p. 276). Pa takes essentially the same actions as he did in *Pioneer Girl*, but the fictional Laura understands what is happening as the young Wilder herself did not. In the novel, "Laura wanted to do something, but inside her head was a roaring and whirling like the fire" (p. 280). Changing from nonfiction to fiction gave Wilder the freedom to develop a bolder main character. The prairie fire also happens *after* Christmas in a subtle shift in chronology that adds tension to the novel as it builds toward its dramatic conclusion. Mr. Edwards and Mr. Scott tell Pa, "perhaps the Indians had started that fire on purpose to burn out the white settlers" (p. 283). Pa disagrees and tries to reason with his neighbors. The next chapter is "Indian War-Cry" (pp. 274–85). In Brandt Revised (p. 5) and Bye (p. 6), the prairie fire scene ends with the line, "Mr. Robertson said to Pa that he believed the Indians had set the fire, to burn us out." Nowhere in the original draft nor in Brandt did Wilder hint that the fire was set by American Indians.

In the fall of 1870, when the fire probably took place, the Osages had approved the Removal Act of 1870, in which they agreed to sell their lands in Kansas and move to a new reservation in Indian Territory, which is now part of Oklahoma. They had no incentive to set a fire to flush out Kansas intruders. Furthermore, as historian Louis Burns pointed out, almost three thousand Osages then left the Kansas reserve for the fall hunt of 1870–1871. Another three hundred went with Agent Isaac Gibson to take up temporary winter quarters on Cherokee lands. Quite simply, there were not any Osages left in that part of Montgomery County to set a fire in the autumn of 1870. Burns, *History of the Osage People*, pp. 321, 345; Chapman, "Removal of the Osages," p. 297; Linsenmayer, "Kansas Settlers," p. 184.

36. *Mr Brown*. Wilder transformed Mr. Brown of *Pioneer Girl* into Mr. Edwards, the "wildcat from Tennessee," who makes his first appearance in *Little House on the Prairie* when he helps Pa build the family's cabin in Indian Territory (p. 63). Later in the novel, he crosses the swollen creek to bring the girls their Christmas presents from Independence (pp. 243-52). The fictional Mr. Edwards returns in *By the Shores of Silver Lake* to help Pa successfully file his claim at the land office in Dakota Territory (pp. 236-37). The 1870 census of Rutland Township does not include a listing for anyone named Brown or Edwards. Nor does it include a listing for a bachelor farmer from Tennessee. It does, however, reveal that a twenty-five-year-old bachelor farmer lived relatively close to the Ingalls cabin; he was an Englishman named Edward Mason.

37. The Brandt manuscript concludes the Christmas episode with the line, "So we had the most beautiful Christmas, after all." The sentence is circled, and a phrase in Lane's handwriting reads, "Later I know—" (p. 5). If this comment is an editorial message to Wilder, it would indicate that Wilder read and reviewed Lane's typewritten drafts. It is unclear, however, what the notation means in the context of the scene or the manuscript as a whole. Both Brandt Revised and Bye have section breaks after this scene, and both include variations of a conclusion in which Wilder looks back with the maturity of an adult: "No one told us, then, that Mr. Brown had walked forty miles to Independence, Kansas, and forty miles back, in the rain, to bring those presents to us so that we should not be disappointed on Christmas morning" (Bye, p. 7).

38. *We all had the whooping cough*. Pertussis—whooping cough—is a contagious bacterial infection that causes intense fits of coughing along with a high-pitched, whooping sound between breaths. Until the 1920s, when a vaccine was developed, pertussis frequently caused death. Wilder did not fictionalize the family's struggle with whooping cough in *Little House on the Prairie*, perhaps because she had already dealt with fever and ague and one major disease in the novel was enough. The three revised

a corner of the house. Patty's little mule colt had been following her, but now it seemed afraid and kept running around and whinnying, so Pa caught it by the little halter, it always wore, and tied it to the end of another log of the house. The cow was already on her picket rope inside the furrows.

Mary and I were much excited, though I didn't understand what it was all about. But just as the colt was tied a cloud of smoke blew around us and then I saw the prairie fire coming. The wind was blowing hard and the dead grass burned quickly. The flames came running across the prairie, leaping high and the smoke rolled above them. After that it was over in a few moments. The fire went roaring past, leaving us and our house and barn safe inside the ring of plowed ground, while all around as far as we could see the prairie was burned black.

Indians didn't come any more after the fire and we were all very happy and quiet until before Christmas it began to rain. It rained so much that Pa couldn't go to town to tell Santa Clause what we wanted for Christmas.

He said the creek was up so high he was afraid Santa Clause couldn't get across it to bring us anything.

But when we waked on Christmas morning our stockings were hanging on the back of a chair by our bed and out of the top of each showed a bright shining new tin cup. Farther down was a long, flat stick of red and white striped peppermint candy all beautifully notched along each edge.

Mr Brown[36] the neighbor from across the creek stood looking at us. He said Santa Clause couldn't cross the creek the night before so left the presents with him and he swam over that morning.[37]

We all had the whooping cough[38] that winter, even Baby Carrie, but spring came at last and we played out doors with Jack again.[39]

Then the Indians came back. I sat on the doorstep one day and watched them pass on their path that went right by the door.[40] As far as I could see, looking one way, they were coming, riding their ponies. First came the big Indians. On black ponies, and gray ponies, and spotted ponies and yellow ponies and red ponies they rode past. Then came the women and children riding too, and then

manuscripts also skip this episode. "Whooping Cough"; "Pertussis, Whooping Cough."

39. At this point, both Brandt Revised and Bye begin a new section with the sentence, "In the spring when the creek had gone down, Pa went to Independence again." What then follows is an extended sequence—a set piece that reads more like a short story—covering two full typewritten pages in Brandt Revised (pp. 6, 6a–6b) and about three pages in Bye (pp. 7–10). The narrative explores Pa's encounter with the infamous serial killers, the Benders of Kansas, and implies that Charles Ingalls rode with vigilantes who attempted to track down the murderers. *See* Appendix B.

40. *Then the Indians came back. . . . right by the door.* In March 1871, the Osages returned from their buffalo hunt. Although most of them went directly from their hunting grounds to their new reserve in what is now Oklahoma, "others returned to Kansas to salvage what they could of their possessions" (Burns, *History of the Osage People*, p. 345). Since the Ingalls family lived on a well-traveled Indian trail, it is possible that Wilder's memories stem from this slice of history. On the other hand, in August 1870 or later that fall, Indian Agent Isaac Gibson had led small parties of Osages from Kansas on a route that "would have passed in close proximity to the Ingalls's claim" (Linsenmayer, "Kansas Settlers," p. 184). If Wilder's memories in *Pioneer Girl* are sequential, however, the Indian removal she remembered likely occurred in March 1871, a short time before the Ingallses themselves left. Regardless, the Indians' departure is the climactic episode in *Little House on the Prairie*, where Wilder devoted an entire chapter to it ("Indians Ride Away," pp. 302–11).

Issac T. Gibson (standing), ca. 1868. *Oklahoma Historical Society*

Picture copyright 1953 by Garth Williams, copyright © renewed 1981 by Garth Williams. Used by permission of HarperCollins Publishers

41. *bright, black eyes. . . . I wanted those babies*. Here, *Pioneer Girl* and *Little House on the Prairie* are consistent. The bright, black eyes of an Indian child clearly triggered an indescribable longing and powerful memory in the young Wilder. "'Its eyes are so black,'" her fictional counterpart sobs. "She could not say what she meant" (*LHOP*, p. 309). Wilder built toward this fictional moment throughout her novel, starting in Chapter 5 when Laura tells Ma, "I want to see a papoose." Ma scolds, "Don't get such an idea into your head" (p. 46), but in the next chapter, Laura asks again. She raises the question one more time in Chapter 10, and when Pa meets the Indian who killed the panther in Chapter 20, "Laura asked if a panther would carry off a little papoose and kill and eat her, too" (p. 262). On some level, Wilder, who was barely four years old in March 1871, seemed to have forged a deep connection with the images she remembered of Osage children and, as an adult, used that fascination to forge another connection with her young readers, generations of whom seem to have understood Laura's longing for the Osage baby with bright, black eyes.

This theme in *Little House on the Prairie* has offended contemporary critics such as Frances Kaye, who described Laura's desire as a propensity for "kidnapping" ("Little Squatter," p. 136). Yet, the most potent childhood fantasies are rarely politically correct. Writing for children brings with it great moral responsibility, but it also requires an

as far as I could see in both directions were Indians riding one behind the other.

Some of the women had babies in baskets fastened on their ponies and some had little babies tied on their backs.

When a woman rode by with a baby in a basket on each side of her pony and they looked at me with their bright, black eyes, I could keep still no longer. I wanted those babies[41] and when Pa said "no": I cried and was very naughty so that Pa picked me up and set me down in the house. "We have a baby," said he. ["]I don't see what you [want] those papooses for."

But I did want them their eyes were so bright.

Soon after this Pa put the cover on the wagon again and hitched Pet and Patty to it. Then he and Ma took everything out of the house and put it in the wagon. Then we all got in the wagon and with Jack running under it we drove away leaving our little house standing empty and lonely on the prairie. The soldiers were taking all the white people off the Indian's land.[42]

On this journey out of Indian territory,[43] before we got to Independence Kansas, we passed a covered wagon standing beside the trail.

A man and woman and some children were sitting on the wagon tongue but there were no horses.

Pa stopped to find out what was the trouble and see if he could help.

They told him their horses had been stolen in the night.

Pa offered to take them to Independence, but they would not leave their wagon and things, so there was nothing he could do.

We drove away and left them sitting stolidly on the wagon tongue, looking off across the empty prairie.

Pa told some men in Independence about them, but we never knew if help was sent them or not.

All the neighbors went with us for awhile,[44] then they scattered but we went on into Missouri. It was bad going for it rained making the roads muddy and the creeks and rivers high.[45]

emotional honesty that sometimes offends and frightens adults. As author Madeleine L'Engle observed: "Children will read and accept stories which would be frightening to their parents. Children are still in touch with dragons and seraphim" (Chase, ed., *Madeleine L'Engle Herself*, p. 166). As a result, writers of children's books often tread into what adults consider dangerous, irresponsible, or offensive territory. "Children . . . often like books that anxious adults would consider scary or immoral or both" (Lurie, *Boys and Girls Forever*, p. xii). Even so, Wilder grounded this memorable scene in adult wisdom. In *Pioneer Girl*, her father delivered a stern reprimand that Laura should be contented with her own baby sister. In the novel, her mother admonished her with the same message. In both accounts, however, the Indian baby's bright eyes linger in the imagination as a longing that defies reason.

42. *The soldiers were taking all the white people off the Indian's land.* Wilder's explanation for her family's decision to leave the Osage Diminished Indian Reserve during the spring of 1871 is sketchy. Later versions of *Pioneer Girl* are equally vague, although Lane made one subtle but significant editorial change: the "soldiers were *driving* [emphasis added] all the white people off the Indians' land" (Brandt, p. 6; Brandt Revised, p. 6b; Bye, p. 11). Wilder elaborated on this idea in *Little House on the Prairie*. When Pa learns that the federal government is sending the military to escort whites out of Indian Territory, he says, "If some blasted politicians in Washington hadn't sent out word it would be all right to settle here, I'd never have been three miles over the line into Indian Territory" (*LHOP*, p. 316). In reality, the family had settled fourteen miles west of the reserve's eastern boundary and six miles north of its southern one, but with this strategic piece of dialogue, Wilder cleared the fictional Charles Ingalls of wrongdoing in squatting on Indian land: the government had misled him. Although politicians in Washington had not officially encouraged settlement on the Osage Diminished Indian Reserve, politicians in Kansas had. Governor Samuel J. Crawford, for example, advertised the state extensively, claiming that Kansas "cannot afford to remain idle while other states are using every honorable means in their power to encourage immigrants to settle within their borders" (quoted in Burns, *History of the Osage People*, pp. 309–10).

Was the threat of eviction real in the spring of 1871? Scholar Frances Kaye has argued that it was not but that it might have been implied. "The soldiers who had come to southern Kansas in 1870 and stayed through the fall had not been allowed to evict squatters," Kaye said, "but they might have suggested the idea"

("Little Squatter," p. 138). In the fall of 1870, federal troops were in fact ordered to remove white intruders who had settled on Cherokee lands — soon to be Osage lands — in Indian Territory (Oklahoma). At least one Kansas newspaper misunderstood these orders and reported that the troops intended to remove white families from Osage lands in Kansas. Agent Isaac Gibson also distributed an announcement that the government had decided "to remove all settlers and intruders in the Indian Territory." Even though the order was intended to include trespassers only in what is now Oklahoma, at the time, the term "Indian Territory" was also used to describe the Osage Diminished Indian Reserve. A later order also seemed to give the army authority to force intruders from "the alleged boundaries of the Osage Indian Reservation or other Reservations in South Eastern Kansas" (both orders quoted in Linsenmayer, "Kansas Settlers," pp. 182–83). Such official statements could have created misunderstanding and confusion among the settlers.

Even so, by the late fall of 1870, Charles Ingalls should have known that land in Montgomery County would soon be available for legitimate settlement. What he did not know was how much it was going to cost. The Osages were then advocating sale of their reserve to the federal government; in that case, settlers would be charged $1.25 an acre, the same price the Osage people would be paid for it. But in 1868, the Osages had agreed to sell the reserve to the Leavenworth, Lawrence & Galveston Railroad Company, and the railroad continued to press for rights to the land. If the company prevailed, settlers would pay more for their claims. It is possible that Charles Ingalls believed the land he prized would cost more than he could afford.

So why did the Ingalls family leave? Wilder herself revealed another probable motivation when she mentioned the status of their land in Wisconsin later in *Pioneer Girl* (*see* p. 22). Perhaps a combination of circumstances sent the family northeast in 1871. Clearly, however, neither *Pioneer Girl* nor *Little House on the Prairie* portrays the social, political, and cultural complexities at work on the Osage Diminished Indian Reserve in the late 1860s and early 1870s. Wilder completely omitted, for example, the influence railroads and land speculators played during this period. *Pioneer Girl* is her personal narrative, based on her own memories and family stories; *Little House on the Prairie* is a middle-grade children's novel in which she chose to focus on the larger themes of Manifest Destiny and one family's attempt to fulfill that promise. Still, Wilder hinted at what is now perceived as the greed and self-interest that motivated families to settle on land that was not theirs.

"When white settlers come into a country, the Indians have to move on," Pa tells Laura. "The government is going to move these Indians farther west, any time now. That's why we're here, Laura. White people are going to settle all this country, and we get the best land because we get here first and take our pick" (p. 237). Kaye, "Little Squatter," pp. 137–38; Linsenmayer, "Kansas Settlers," pp. 172–74, 182–85; Burns, *History of the Osage People*, pp. 300–13.

43. *On this journey out of Indian territory*. This section is a self-contained digression in the original manuscript. It appears on the back of the tablet page that begins the Ingallses' journey out of Kansas, but Wilder made no indication of where it was to be inserted. In Brandt (p. 6), Brandt Revised (p. 7), and Bye (p. 11), Lane smoothly incorporated the episode into the unfolding narrative, placing this vignette in the middle of a paragraph between the neighbors traveling with the family and the rain making the roads bad. These later versions also offer slightly more detail, including this line from Pa: "Hanging is too good for horse thieves." The Bye manuscript notes that the Ingalls family reached Independence the following day.

44. *All the neighbors went with us for awhile*. This line adds credibility to Wilder's explanation that white settlers in Rutland Township believed they were threatened with eviction. Apparently several families left together. Other settlers, however, remained in the region. They purchased land on the Osage reserve for $200 per quarter section, or $1.25 per acre. In *Little House on the Prairie*,

the fictional family leaves by itself. Pa invites Mr. Edwards to go with them, but he prefers to head south. This novel was Wilder's third, and she was beginning to see her personal story set against larger American themes. By striking out on their own, the fictional family becomes almost mythic, archetypal characters who embody the frontier experience in the American West.

45. *we went on into Missouri. It was bad going . . . the creeks and rivers high*. It is unclear where the Ingalls family entered Missouri, or which swollen river they crossed, but it is interesting to speculate. A. J. Johnson's map of Kansas and Nebraska, published in 1870, shows no roads leading out of Independence, Kansas, toward Missouri. In fact, the map indicates only one road out of Independence—heading north toward Fredonia. This lack of roads is not especially surprising; Montgomery County was, after all, part of the Osage Diminished Indian Reserve. But if the Ingalls family had traveled northeast into Neosho County, Kansas, they could have found a road that cut northeast through Bourbon County, Kansas, to Fort Scott, and from there into Vernon County, Missouri. Along this route, Wilder and her family would have crossed Big Dry Woods Creek and eventually the Little Osage River in Vernon County. Farther on, they would have crossed the Marais des Cygnes River in Bates County. Perhaps one of these rivers is the source of Wilder's vivid childhood memory of fording a flooded river in Missouri. For more discussion of their route, *see* Appendix B.

As we drove into one river to cross it[46] Ma dropped baby Carrie down on the bed in the bottom of the wagon where Mary and I were and covered us over head and all with a blanket. "Lie still," she said.

I heard the horses making a great splashing in the water and the wagon went sort of funny. Then I heard Pa say, "Take the reins Caroline!"

Things seemed strange and Pa's voice sounded queer so I stuck my head out from under the blanket. I saw the horses splashing in the water and Pa was most all covered with water. He was at the side of Pet's head pulling at her. Ma was driving but she saw me and said in a very firm voice, "Get back under the blanket and be still!"

'What makes the horses walk so funny?' I whimpered as I covered my head and Ma said they were swimming.

It was hard to stay covered and hear the horses splashing and once in awhile Pa's voice talking to them.

Presently I felt the wagon move differently and dared to peep. Ma looked funny and white and there was Pa all dripping wet leading the horses up the steep bank of the river.

The water was behind us.

"Whew!" said Pa as he and the horses stopped to rest, "They'd never have made it without help!"[47]

We waited then for the weather to settle and the waters to go down. We stayed for awhile in a log house with a big fireplace.[48] Pa worked for the man who owned the house so we were alone with Ma all day.

Once when we were sitting by the fireplace we heard a great crackling up the chimney. Ma put baby Carrie in Mary's arms and ran outdoors to see. She found the chimney on fire at the top. It was made of sticks and mud and the top sticks had caught on fire from a spark.

Ma took a long pole and knocked the blazing sticks off the top of the chimney. Some of the pieces of fire fell down the chimney inside and dropped right at Mary's feet. She was so frightened she could not move, but I grabbed the back of the chair and jerked chair, Mary, baby and all clear across the room. Ma said I did well for a four year old.[49]

46. *As we drove into one river to cross it.* Wilder used this episode as the basis for the chapter "Crossing the Creek" (pp. 16–27) at the beginning of *Little House on the Prairie* when the fictional Ingalls family moves *toward* Indian Territory, where it strengthens the plot and heightens the drama. In *Pioneer Girl*, this vivid scene hints at Wilder's later mastery of dialogue, description, and characterization.

47. *"Whew!" said Pa . . . without help!"* In Brandt (p. 7), Brandt Revised (p. 8), and Bye (p. 12), this line and the ending of the scene are different:

> "Whew!" Pa said, as he and the horses stopped to rest. "Awhile there, I thought we couldn't make it."
> Ma did not say anything (Bye, p. 12).

In the corresponding scene in *Little House on the Prairie*, Pa delivers a line that is more consistent with the original: "Pet and Patty are good swimmers, but I guess they wouldn't have made it if I hadn't helped them'" (pp. 23–24).

48. *We stayed for awhile in a log house with a big fireplace.* This log cabin is another example of how Wilder mined later sections of *Pioneer Girl* for details to embellish the opening of *Little House on the Prairie*. In the first chapter ("Going West," pp. 1–15), the fictional family temporarily stays in "a little log house" along the way (pp. 7–8). Brandt (p. 7) included an abbreviated version of the scene, but Brandt Revised eliminated it. Wilder and Lane may have cut the Missouri scenes from later drafts to make room for the Bender episode (*see* Appendix B).

49. *She found the chimney on fire at the top. . . . Ma said I did well for a four year old.* Wilder transferred her memories of the chimney fire in the log house in Missouri to the fictional family's home in Kansas. The similarities are striking. In *Little House on the Prairie*, Ma also "seized a long pole and struck and struck at the roaring fire." Flaming debris falls near Mary and frightens her. The fictional Laura grabs "the back of the heavy rocking-chair and pulled with all her might." Ma praises Laura for her bravery (pp. 201–4). There are also significant differences.

The novel contains concrete details and dialogue that make the passage more vivid and suspenseful, demonstrating Wilder's deepening understanding of her craft, and there is no reference to Laura's age. This scene does not appear in the revised versions of *Pioneer Girl*.

50. *Jack wanted to stay with Pet and Patty . . . Pa gave him to the man who had them.* In Wilder's novels, Jack remains a beloved member of the fictional family until his death of old age in *By the Shores of Silver Lake*, just before the family's move to Dakota Territory. The fictional Laura remembers Jack as Wilder herself may have remembered him, running "on the beautiful wild prairies of Indian Territory" (pp. 13–14). Jack's death marks an important transition for Laura, who moves from childhood into adolescence and can no longer depend on Jack or even Pa to look out for her.

51. *The land was Pa's again.* Gustaf Gustafson had bought the Ingalls Wisconsin farm in 1868, but he could not continue to make payments on it by 1871. This circumstance may be the real reason why Charles Ingalls left the Osage Diminished Indian Reserve. With little to show for their ventures in Missouri and Kansas, it made financial sense for the family to reclaim their farm near Pepin, Wisconsin. They arrived back in Wisconsin sometime in May 1871.

Soon the water in the creeks went down and the weather was warmer. Pa traded the horses Pet and Patty for some larger horses and because Jack wanted to stay with Pet and Patty as he always did Pa gave him to the man who had them.[50]

Then we went on our way in the covered wagon. After driving for days and days, sleeping in the wagon at night, until we were all very tired we came at last to the place we had left when we went west. The land was Pa's again[51] because the man who bought it from him had not paid for it.

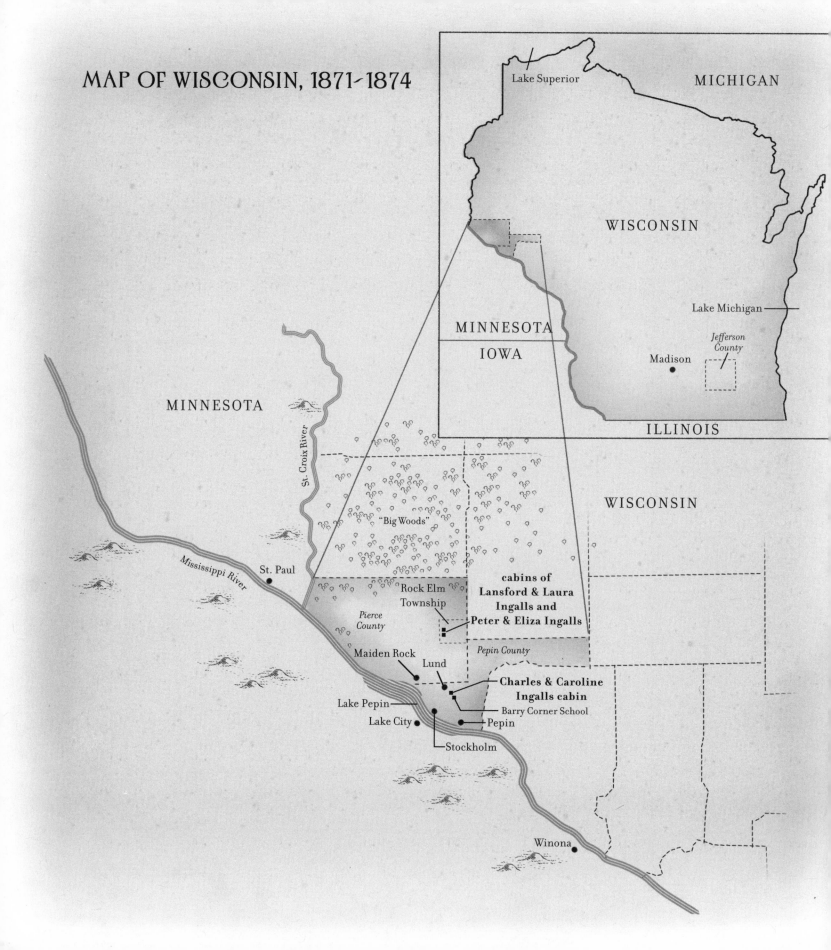

MAP OF WISCONSIN, 1871–1874

MICHIGAN

Lake Superior

WISCONSIN

Lake Michigan

MINNESOTA

IOWA

Madison

Jefferson County

ILLINOIS

MINNESOTA

St. Croix River

"Big Woods"

Mississippi River

St. Paul

WISCONSIN

Rock Elm Township

cabins of Lansford & Laura Ingalls and Peter & Eliza Ingalls

Pierce County

Pepin County

Maiden Rock

Lund

Charles & Caroline Ingalls cabin

Lake Pepin

Barry Corner School

Lake City

Pepin

Stockholm

Winona

Wisconsin, 1871–1874

Uncle Henry and Aunt Polly lived close by and we were so glad to drive into their yard and go into a house again. We lived with them[1] until the people who were in our house moved away.

Uncle Henry was Ma's brother; Aunt Polly was Pa's sister and we learned that the cousins were double cousins almost like sisters and brothers. There were Louisa and Charley, then Albert and Lottie[2] the baby a little older than Baby Carrie.

We had great times playing together, but after all we were glad when we could go home.

The house was larger than the one we left on the prairie. It was made of logs, but there were three rooms besides the attic. There were lots of windows and the house was very comfortable and cozy set down among the hills in the Wisconsin woods.[3]

There were trees all around the house outside the yard and in the front yard were two great, beautiful oak trees.

One morning as soon as I was up I ran to look out of the window and there was a deer hang[ing] from a branch of each tree.

Father[4] had shot the deer and didn't get them home until after I went to bed the night before. He had hung them up in the tree so that nothing could reach them in the night. They were so pretty I felt badly because they could not run around any more.

We ate some of the venison but most of the meat was salted and put away to eat in the winter,[5] for winter was coming.

The days were shorter and frost came in the night.

~~Father~~ Pa went away one morning with the horses and wagon and came back at night with a load of fish. The wagon box was full and some of them were so long the[y] more than reached across the wagon box. Father had been to Lake Pepin,[6] seven miles away and caught them with a net. There were so many fish and so few people, in those days, that it was not wrong to do so.[7]

We feasted on fish. Mother could cut large slices from the backs,

1. *Uncle Henry and Aunt Polly. . . . We lived with them.* Henry Quiner was Caroline Quiner Ingalls's older brother. Aunt Polly was one of Charles Ingalls's four younger sisters. In 1859, Henry and Polly were the first of three Quiner/Ingalls couples to marry in as many years. Charles and Caroline were wed the following year, and in 1861, Peter Ingalls married Eliza Quiner. In Brandt, Brandt Revised, and Bye, Charles Ingalls and his family moved directly into their own log house in Wisconsin, and the paragraphs about the Quiners were omitted. Miller, *Becoming*, p. 17.

2. *Louisa and Charley, then Albert and Lottie.* Louisa Quiner was born in 1860; Charles in 1862; and Albert in 1865. Baby Lottie—Charlotte—was born in 1867, the same year as Wilder herself. It is unclear why Wilder portrayed Lottie as Carrie's contemporary.

3. *Wisconsin woods.* All the adult *Pioneer Girl* manuscripts identify the Ingalls farm as being in the "Wisconsin woods." The fictional family, however, lives "in the Big Woods of Wisconsin, in a little gray house made of logs" (*BW*, p. 1). This change dates back to the opening lines of the transitional "juvenile Pioneer Girl," which read: "When Grandma was a little girl she lived in a little gray house made of logs. The house was in the Big Woods, in Michigan" (*JPG*, p. 1, *see* Appendix A). The word "Michigan" is crossed out and replaced with "Wisconsin." Apparently, the term "Big Woods" sounded more archetypally American than "Wisconsin woods." Even so, the title for the book when Alfred A. Knopf accepted it for publication was "Little House in the Woods." After the Knopf deal fell through, Harper & Brothers bought the manuscript and later re-titled it *Little House in the Big Woods*.

4. *Father.* In this section of the manuscript, Wilder identified Charles Ingalls as "Father." Three para-

graphs later, she crossed out the word "Father" and replaced it with "Pa." She did the same thing in the scene in which Pa buys a pig from Uncle Henry. She also failed to catch the word "Mother" for "Ma" in this same section. Such inconsistencies are not unusual in early drafts of a manuscript; in the edited, typewritten versions of *Pioneer Girl*, these inconsistencies are gone. When Lane pieced together the juvenile draft of her mother's autobiography, she included a brief explanation within the narrative for the names "Ma" and "Pa" (JPG, p. 1), but Marion Fiery at Alfred Knopf questioned the usage, calling it "a little colloquial" despite its authenticity (Fiery to LIW, Feb. 12, 1931, Box 13, file 189, Lane Papers). After Harper & Brothers accepted the manuscript, overt editorial concerns regarding the use of Ma and Pa disappeared, but *Little House in the Big Woods* contains a variation of Lane's original explanation: "The little girl was named Laura, and she called her father, Pa, and her mother, Ma. In those days and in that place, children did not say Father and Mother, nor Mamma and Papa, as they do now" (pp. 2–3).

5. *the meat was salted and put away to eat in the winter.* Dry-salting meat, also called corning, is one of the oldest methods of preserving food. Rubbed onto the surface of the meat, the salt inhibits microbial growth by drawing out water. The salt can also be dis-solved in liquid and the meat soaked in the brine. The resulting cured meat can be used in small pieces to flavor food or can be boiled or soaked to remove excess salt prior to cooking as the main protein. "Curing and Smoking Meats."

6. *Lake Pepin.* Lake Pepin is a natural lake on the Mississippi River about sixty miles downstream from Saint Paul, Minnesota. A large natural lake, it has a surface area of about forty square miles. Along with the county and town, the lake was probably named for two brothers, Pierre Pepin and Jean Pepin du Cardonnets, who were among the first Europeans to explore and trade with the American Indian population in the region. The British took possession of what is now Wisconsin in 1763, then lost it to the United States in 1783. American settlement along Lake Pepin came much later—in the late 1840s, at about the same time that Wisconsin formally became a state. Pepin County itself was not formed until 1858. "History of Pepin County."

7. *not wrong to do so.* Wilder's recognition that fishing laws had changed or been imposed since pioneer times did not make it into subsequent versions of the manuscript. The large size of the fish—long enough to reach across the wagon box—is a common feature of early pioneer tales of freshwater fishing in a time when there were fewer people and less pressure on the resource.

Lake Pepin at Lake City, Minn., 1870.
Lake City Historical Society

of some of them, that would not have a bone, so Mary and I could eat it safely.

The fish we did not eat were salted down in barrels to be eaten later.

~~Father~~ Pa had bought a pig[8] from Uncle Henry. They caught it out in the woods; where everyones hogs ran, nearly wild; and put it in a pen to fatten. Pa would butcher it when the weather was cold enough to keep the meat frozen.

One night we heard the pig squealing[9] terribly and Pa snatched his gun and ran out to see what was hurting it. A big bear stood by the pig pen as just as Pa got there it reached in to grab the pig. Pa saw him in the starlight and shot at him so quickly he missed.

The bear ran away in the woods so we lost the bear meat, but Pa said he had saved our bacon anyway.

We had the garden that had been raised by the people who moved away[10] and now the potatoes and carrots, the beets and turnips and cabbage were gathered and stored in the cellar for the winter for freezing nights had come. Onions were strung in long ropes and hung in the attic. Pumpkin and squash were stored where they would not freeze. Mary and I played in the house now for it was cold out doors and the leaves were all brown and falling off the trees.

One day the sun was nearly hidden by smoke all day and when dark came the sky was reddened by fire. We stood in the door watching it and soon we could see fire run up to the tops of some trees on a hill and then the trees stood there burning like great candles.[11]

We heard gunshots off in the woods and Pa said, "Somebody's lost." He took down his rifle and fired it up at the sky several times and after awhile a man came to the door. He was a stranger and lost in the woods. Pa told him, if he had gone on the way he was headed, there was nothing but woods between him and the North Pole, whatever that was, but he turned and came in the direction of the shots Pa had fired. It seemed the "Big Woods" as Pa called them were just north of us a ways[12] and they went on and on into the north. I thought our woods were big enough and was going to ask questions about the bigger one when Pa and the strange man went

8. *Pa had bought a pig.* In JPG, the ownership of the pig is simplified to "Pa owned a pig" (p. 2), which is retained in *Little House in the Big Woods* (p. 10).

9. *we heard the pig squealing.* In a seemingly small shift in the juvenile *Pioneer Girl* manuscript, Lane edited this line so that Laura alone wakes up and hears the pig (p. 2). This change of focus became more prominent within *Little House in the Big Woods*, due in part to constructive criticism from Knopf editor Marion Fiery. In children's literature, the main character should almost always be a child, but JPG presented the action from a grandmother's perspective. Fiery met with Lane in New York to discuss revisions of "When Grandma was a Little Girl" and must have addressed this issue. A few days later, Lane wrote Wilder, "We will start right off with Laura, and not say anything about Grandma" (RWL to LIW, Feb. 16, 1931, Box 13, file 189, Lane Papers).

10. *the garden . . . raised by the people who moved away.* In preparing the JPG manuscript, Lane edited this line to read, "The garden behind the house had been growing all summer" (p. 3), neatly avoiding the need to explain that the previous residents had planted it. Thus, in *Little House in the Big Woods*, the fictional Ingalls family seems always to have lived in the "little house" (BW, pp. 11–12).

11. *burning like great candles.* This scene illustrates Wilder's natural talent for description, especially this vivid image of the trees. All the existing adult versions include a similar description, but Wilder chose not to include the episode in *Little House in the Big Woods*, perhaps because this seemingly random incident was not consistent with the snug, cozy world the novel portrays.

12. *the "Big Woods" as Pa called them were just north of us a ways.* For the real Ingalls family, the Big Woods was a specific geographical area that did not extend as far south as Charles Ingalls's property, which was seven miles north of the town of Pepin, Wisconsin. But Brandt Revised moved them closer: "The Big Woods, Pa said, began just north of us and ran on and on to the north, with not another house in them" (p. 9). In Bye, the Big Woods "began where

we were, and ran on and on to the north" (p. 14). Despite these descriptions of an uninhabited forest, all versions of *Pioneer Girl* place Grandpa Ingalls's house squarely within the Big Woods. Apparently neither Wilder nor Lane caught this contradiction. The novel puts the fictional family within the Big Woods right from its first line: "Once upon a time, sixty years ago, a little girl lived in the Big Woods of Wisconsin" (p. 1).

13. *Father. . . . Mother.* Wilder did not correct the use of "Father" and "Mother" here, although she quickly returned to "Ma." Fictionalized in the chapter "Two Big Bears" (*BW*, pp. 101–16), this scene unfolds in early spring, when Pa goes to town "to trade the furs of the wild animals he had been trapping all winter" (p. 101).

14. *by the bars that opened into the house yard.* In this context, the bars refer to horizontal slats or split logs in a wooden fence than can be adjusted to "bar" or allow entrance into an enclosed space.

15. *Ma hurried down to let her in.* In the novel, Laura helps Ma with the chores and is standing beside her when she discovers the black bear. This change, which was first introduced in the juvenile *Pioneer Girl* manuscript (p. 18), makes the scene much more relevant to young readers. The heroine is at risk as well as her mother. Wilder intensified the tension even more as Ma and the girls wait for Pa to return: "All around the house the wind went crying as though it were lost in the dark and the cold. The wind sounded frightened" (*BW*, p. 107).

16. *Pa shot the bear . . . he had them both.* In the fictionalized account of this episode, which appears early in *Little House in the Big Woods* (pp. 24–26), the only significant change comes toward the end of the scene. Wilder gave the character of Pa one of his many obvious yet somehow charming observations: "Pa shot the bear, and there was no way of knowing where the pig came from nor whose pig it was. 'So I just brought home the bacon,' Pa said" (*BW*, p. 26).

out to fight the fire and Ma put Mary and me to bed in the trundle bed, the little bed that in the daytime was pushed out of the way under the big bed.

Father took his gun and went hunting one day and was not home when it began to get dark. Mother[13] fed the horses and the pigs and wanted to do the milking, but black Sukey the cow did not come home. Sukey still ran loose in the woods finding a little grass here and there and Ma was afraid something had hurt her.

Ma was watching out of the window for Sukey, ready to go, when she did come, and let down the bars so she could go into the barn yard. At last Ma thought she saw her standing by the bars that opened into the house yard.[14] It looked like Sukey standing by the bars in the dusk, but she stood so still that her bell did not ring and she did not call as she usually did when she came home at night. Ma hurried down to let her in[15] before it got any darker, but when she came near the bars, she turned around and ran as fast as she could back into the house and shut the door tight. She was scared and shaking for it had not been Sukey at all but a big black bear standing there looking through the bars into the yard at Ma.

After awhile Pa came home bringing Sukey from where he had found her hiding in the woods. The bear was gone!

The first snow came and the cold. Pa took his gun and traps and was gone all day setting the traps for muskrats and mink along the creek and for wolves and foxes and the big bear trap hoping to get a fat bear before they all went into their dens to sleep all winter.

One morning he came back took the horses and sled and hurried away again. Ma said he had shot a bear and came for the team to haul it home. Mary liked best to eat the drumstick of a chicken and, never thinking how much larger a bears leg would be, she jumped up and down saying, "I want the drumstick! I want the drumstick!"

When Pa came he had both a bear and a pig in the wagon. He had come on the bear just as he killed the pig and began to eat it, standing up on his hind legs and holding the pig in his forepaws just as though they were hands.

Pa shot the bear and as there was no way to learn whose pig it was, he had them both.[16]

There was plenty of fresh meat now to last a long time but when Mary saw the great bear she did not want the drumstick.

The snow kept coming until it was drifted and banked against the house.

When the work was done, Ma would cut out paper dolls[17] for us and let us cook on the stove[18] for our play house dinners.

She taught Mary to knit, I was too little, she said, but sitting by watching I caught the trick first. Then with some bits of yarn she helped me start knitting a mitten for Baby Carrie. Taking great pains, with much hard work for days I finished one mitten. I wanted to stop then, but Ma said, one must always finish what she began[19] and besides Carrie could not go with only one mitten, the other little hand would be so cold. So I began the second mitten and kept on knitting though it was much harder to do than the first, for I wanted so much to be doing something else.

At last after days and days I finished the mitten and put it on Carrie's hand. And then I couldn't find the first one!

We all hunted and at last we found it. Wolf, the black and white spotted puppy[20] had it under the bed and was chewing it. It was all in bits, completely ruined, so after all my work, Baby Carrie had only one mitten at the last. I cried some but Ma said, never mind I had learned to knit and had done wonderfully well for a little girl not quite four years old.[21]

I stopped crying then[22] because I didn't have to knit any more so it wasn't so very bad after all.

Pa went to his traps every day and came back with the skins of the animals he caught in the traps or shot. The trapping was good he said and he would have a lot of furs to sell later.

He would come in from his tramp to his traps, with icles [icicles] on the ends of his whiskers, hang his gun over the door, throw off his coat and cap and mittens and call "Where's my little half pint of cider half drank up?"[23] That was me because I was so small. Mary and I would climb on his knees while he warmed a bit, then he would put on his coat and cap again and do the chores and bring in wood to keep a good fire.

We were very warm and snug and happy in our little log house[24]

17. *Ma would cut out paper dolls*. In *Little House in the Big Woods*, Wilder added concrete details. Ma cut them "out of stiff white paper, and drew the faces with a pencil. Then from bits of colored paper she cut dresses and hats, ribbons and laces, so that Laura and Mary could dress their dolls beautifully" (p. 33). By providing a few key details, Wilder pulled her readers into the unfolding action and brought the scene to life, a process she had quickly learned to master.

18. *let us cook on the stove*. The Bye version added that Ma also "taught us to peel potatoes so thinly that not a bit was wasted, and how to cook simple things and to wash dishes properly" (p. 14). These tasks are impressive for a preschooler. A few paragraphs later, the Bye manuscript reveals that Wilder was just four years old at the time.

19. *but Ma said, one must always finish what she began*. In Bye, "Ma said that one mitten was not a pair and that one must always finish whatever she began" (p. 14). Even though this episode does not appear in *Little House in the Big Woods*, Ma's voice is consistent with the one Wilder created for Caroline Ingalls in the novels. She is a conscientious, hardworking homemaker who teaches wholesome, conventional principles to her children.

20. *Wolf, the black and white spotted puppy*. In *Little House in the Big Woods*, the family dog is Jack the bulldog, but the real Ingalls family had actually left Jack behind in Kansas. Wolf appears in all adult versions of *Pioneer Girl*.

21. *a little girl not quite four years old*. Wilder had actually turned four in February 1871, shortly before the family left Kansas. In both Brandt (p. 9) and Brandt Revised (p. 10), Wilder is "three years old" when she knits the mitten. In Bye, Wilder and Lane corrected this mistake: "I had learned to knit, and was doing wonderfully well for a little girl only four years old" (p. 14).

22. *I stopped crying then*. Wilder drew on her own remembered frustration to create the feelings and attitudes of her fictional counterpart. The Laura Ingalls of the Little House books is high-spirited and capable, but she is also impatient and quick-tempered.

23. *little half pint of cider half drank up?"* A form of this endearment appears in all versions of *Pioneer Girl*, as well as in the Little House novels. Wilder introduced it in the second chapter of *Little House in the Big Woods* (p. 33), where it is rendered "little half-pint of sweet cider half drunk up." Throughout the rest of the novels, Pa often calls Laura "Half-Pint."

24. *warm and snug and happy in our little log house.* With just a few words, Wilder evoked the loving and secure home that her father had provided in the wilderness. This coziness became a hallmark of the fictional series.

in the woods, especially at night with the fire shining on the hearth and the dark and the snow and wild beasts shut out but Wolf and Black Susan,[25] the cat, with us by the fire.

Sometimes Pa would make bullets for the rifle to take with him in his hunting next day. He would melt bits of lead in a large spoon over the coals of fire. While it was hot as hot he would pour it through a little hole into the bullet molds and after a minute he would open the molds and drop out a bright, shiny new bullet onto the hearth. When he had made enough he would let them cool, then trim off with his jacknife, the little lump where he had poured the lead into the mold. When they were all finished he would put them in his bullet pouch. The pouch was a bag made of buckskin.

It was fun for us to watch Pa load his gun. He would pour some powder down into the barrel[26] from his powder horn. Then he would pull the ramrod from its place at the side of the gun, drop it into the barrel and pound the powder down hard. Next he would take a little patch of greased cloth from the small tin box he carried them in, lay it over the mouth of the gun barrel put the bullet on it and with the ramrod push it down the gun barrel pounding it hard against the patch and the powder. He would put the ramrod back in its place on the gun, then take his box of gun caps from his pocket, take one out, raise the hammer of the gun slip the little bright cap over the pin that was under the hammer and let the hammer down over it carefully. When the hammer went down hard as it did when Pa raised it, cocking the gun, and then pulled the trigger with his finger, the gun would go off and kill anything that was in front of it. When the gun was at home, it hung over the door. When Pa went hunting, he carried his bullet pouch full of bullets, his patches and box of caps in his pockets. The horn filled with powder and a small hatchet were hung at his waist and he carried his gun all loaded on his shoulder. Every time he shot at anything he had to stop and load his gun before he could shoot again.

Sometimes Pa would come home early from his day with the traps and guns. Then we would have great fun playing. One game we liked to play we called 'mad-dog.'[27]

25. *Black Susan.* Black Susan makes her first appearance in *Little House in the Big Woods*, where she has her own swinging "cat-hole in the bottom of the front door" (p. 22).

26. *pour some powder down into the barrel.* A gun loaded in this way is called a muzzleloader, and the first rifles, developed in the eighteenth century, were single-shot guns of this type. Charles Ingalls's muzzleloading long rifle is not among the family artifacts preserved in Mansfield or De Smet, probably because it was obsolete by the time of his death. By the 1880s, muzzleloading guns were giving way to breechloading rifles capable of rapid reloading and firing. All versions of *Pioneer Girl* included an extended narrative about making bullets and loading the gun, and this episode ultimately formed the basis for the chapter "The Long Rifle" (*BW*, pp. 45–58). Throughout, Wilder added details to such scenes to describe how the fictional family lived. This approach originated from an editorial suggestion from Marion Fiery, who asked for more details "about the everyday life of the pioneers, such as the making of the bullets, what they eat and wear, etc." (Fiery to LIW, Feb. 12, 1931).

27. *'mad-dog.'* Wilder's description of this game is one of her most fully realized scenes in *Pioneer Girl* and provides a glimpse into the everyday life of the real Ingalls family. It appears with only minor variations in the chapter "Winter Days and Winter Nights" (*BW*, pp. 24–44). Brandt and Brandt Revised include this lively scene as well, but the Bye version replaces

"One game was called mad dog." *Helen Sewell, 1932*

the game with a more composed and expanded version of Pa's fiddle playing.

28. *by jinks. . . . You shouldn't frighten the children so Charl[e]s," Ma said.* From Charles Ingalls's use of slang—"by jinks"—to Caroline Ingalls's gentle admonition to her husband not to "frighten the children," Wilder used dialogue in her autobiography to reveal essential differences between her parents and their unique personalities. She used virtually the same lines in her novel:

> "Well!" [Pa] said to her. "You're only a little half-pint of cider half drunk up, but by Jinks! you're as strong as a little French horse."
>
> "You shouldn't frighten the children so, Charles," Ma said. "Look how big their eyes are" (*BW*, p. 36).

For her part, Lane took the cue from her mother and added more such dialogue to the juvenile version of *Pioneer Girl*. When Wilder began revising the juvenile, however, she reminded her daughter of the importance of *accurate* dialogue and voice in revealing insights about character. "A lady like Ma would never use such expressions [as "I'll be darned" or "great Gehosaphat" or "I vow"]," she wrote Lane, because Ma "was a school teacher and well educated for her time and place, rather above Pa socially" (fragment, ca. Feb.–Mar. 1931, Folder 19, Wilder Papers). She was objecting to Lane's line, "Ma said she vowed she didn't believe those young ones ever *were* going to sleep" (*JPG*, p. 11). For Wilder, getting the dialogue right was an essential part of writing both fiction and nonfiction. Her preoccupation with dialogue and voice may have been linked to her father's storytelling tradition or to her own experience as columnist and farm journalist.

29. *Pa took his fiddle.* Charles Ingalls's fiddle is now on display at the Laura Ingalls Wilder Historic Home and Museum in Mansfield, Missouri. The words Amati, Nicolana, and Cremonensia are inscribed inside the fiddle. The original case is dated 1850. Nicolò Amati of Cremona, Italy, was a master violinmaker in the early seventeenth century, but Ingalls's fiddle was probably made in Germany as a mass-

Pa would run his fingers through his hair standing it all on end; then he'd get down on all fours and growling would chase us around the room, trying to corner us so we couldn't get away. We were quick at dodging him but once he caught us by the woodbox behind the stove. Then Pa growled so terribly, his hair looked so wild and his eyes so fierce, that it all seemed real to us instead of just play.

Mary was so frightened she could not move, but I gave a scream as he started to come nearer and with a wild leap I went over the woodbox dragging Mary after me.

Then there was no dog at all, only Pa standing there with his blue eyes so bright and shining looking at me.

"Well," he said, "you may be only a half pint of cider half drank up, but by jinks you're strong as a little French horse!"

"You shouldn't frighten the children so Charl[e]s," Ma said.[28] But Pa took his fiddle[29] and began to play "Yankee Doodle." When he began to sing, "Yankee Doodle went to town he wore his striped trousers," we were so interested we forgot all about the mad dog and leaned against his knee to listen as he sang on. "And there he saw some great big guns big as a log of maple and every time they turned [em] round it took 2 yoke of cattle & every time they fired [em off] it took a horn of powder. It made a noise like fathers gun only a nation louder."[30]

The day before Christmas,[31] Aunt Eliza and Uncle Peter with the cousins Peter and Alice and Ella[32] came over the snow to spend Christmas. Uncle Peter was Pa's brother and Aunt Eliza was Ma's sister, so these were double cousins too. The little log house was full and running over. Black Susan ran out of the cat hole in the door and hid in the stable and Wolf was very much excited and ran and barked in the door yard.

We played so hard that when night came we were to excited to sleep and a little afraid to go to bed after Pa told about Grandpa and the panther.[33]

Grandpa lived in the Big Woods[34] in a log house like ours. He went to town[35] one day and was late starting home. It was dark as he rode his horse through the woods and when he heard a panther scream behind him he was frightened for he didn't have his gun.

Charles Ingalls's fiddle. Photograph by Keli Tetzlaff,
South Dakota Historical Society Press

produced instrument "in the style of Amati." According to Arian Sheets, curator of stringed instruments at the National Music Museum, Vermillion, South Dakota, the words inside the fiddle functioned as a label denoting its model. "The violin is absolutely right for a mid-nineteenth-century German commercially produced violin," Sheets noted. "The workmanship and varnish appear correct for the region of Upper Saxony known as the Vogtland, with commercial center Markneukirchen, from which the majority of imported German instruments originated." Sheets observed that other details on the fiddle—its fingerboard and its finish—are "also typical of this time and place" (Sheets to Hill, Feb. 21, 2010).

30. *"Yankee Doodle."*. . . *only a nation louder."* This song originated with British soldiers who made up the tune's satirical lyrics to insult American rebels during the Revolutionary War. The colonists, however, embraced the song, and by the end of the American Revolution, "Yankee Doodle" had become a patriotic favorite in the new United States. Because it is a folk tune, there are many variations. Wilder's handwriting makes it hard to read the original manuscript. She added the lyrics later, cramming them in between lines of the previously written text. Careful reading suggests "em" and "em off," shown in brackets here, for the least legible parts of the manuscript, and corresponding lyrics in *Little House in the Big Woods* (p. 37) confirm that reading. The Bye manu-

script (p. 16) includes four verses with minor variations, including Yankee Doodle wearing "trousies" (which also appears in the novel) instead of trousers. "Lyrical Legacy."

31. *The day before Christmas.* The Christmas scenes in Brandt and Brandt Revised closely follow the sequence presented here, but both JPG and Bye add more details, some involving preparation:

> All one week Ma was busy cooking good things for Christmas. She baked loaves of salt-rising bread, she baked vinegar pies and dried apple pies and a cream-of-tartar cake. She boiled down a kettle of molasses, and Pa brought in from outdoors two pans of clean snow, one for Mary and one for me. We poured the thick molasses in tiny streams onto the snow, and it hardened and was candy. We were each allowed to eat one curleycue then, but the rest we must save for company (Bye, pp. 16–16½).

32. *Aunt Eliza and Uncle Peter with the cousins Peter and Alice and Ella.* Eliza Ann Quiner and Peter Ingalls were married in 1861.

Cousin Peter Ingalls. *Laura Ingalls Wilder Memorial Society*

Eliza was three years younger than her sister Caroline; Peter was three years older than his brother Charles. Eliza and Peter Ingalls and their children lived roughly thirteen miles from Charles and Caroline in Rock Elm Township, Pierce County, Wisconsin. Alice Josephine Ingalls was born in 1862; Ella Estella Ingalls in 1865; and Peter Franklin Ingalls in 1866. Three more children were born to the family later: Lansford, Edith, and Edmond. William Anderson noted in *Laura's Album* that these children looked so much like Charles and Caroline's girls that people frequently thought they were siblings (p. 11). Eliza and Peter's children were the Ingalls sisters' second set of double cousins. Zochert, *Laura*, p. 68; Miller, *Becoming*, p. 17.

33. *Grandpa and the panther.* All the adult *Pioneer Girl* manuscripts place this story in the Christmas scene. In the juvenile manuscript, Pa tells the story to Laura and Mary, not the entire clan of cousins. In *Little House in the Big Woods*, "The Story of Grandpa and the Panther" (pp. 40–41) appears in the chapter entitled "Winter Days and Winter Nights" and again is told only to Mary and Laura.

34. *Grandpa lived in the Big Woods.* Lansford Whiting Ingalls, Charles Ingalls's father, was born in Canada in 1812, although his family returned to the United States shortly after his birth and settled in New York. He married Laura Louise Colby, and together they moved their family west to Illinois in the mid-1840s. They moved again in 1853 to Jefferson County, Wisconsin. He mortgaged his farm there in the late 1850s and, at the dawn of the American Civil War, was unable to repay his loan. The entire family, including his adult sons, moved again to the woods of northwestern Wisconsin in 1862. In 1870, he, his wife, and two of their teen-aged children were living in Pierce County, Wisconsin, roughly thirteen miles north of Wilder's childhood home. In *Pioneer Girl*, Wilder made a distinction between the location of her own family's cabin, "set down among the hills in the Wisconsin woods," and her grandfather's and Uncle Peter's houses, which were in the "Big Woods" to the north. Lane, with less attention to such geographical subtleties, moved the Charles Ingalls home into the Big Woods in the first line of the juvenile manuscript. Miller, *Becoming*, pp. 16–18; Zochert, *Laura*, pp. 12–14; Anderson, *Laura's Album*, p. 13.

Lansford and Laura Ingalls (seated, center) with children Lydia and Ruby (front) and Lansford James, George, and Hiram (standing, from left). *William Anderson Collection*

35. *He went to town.* Lansford and Laura Ingalls's home in Pierce County would have been near the community of Lund, on the Pepin/Pierce County line, and the villages of Stockholm and Maiden Rock (originally known as Harrisburg).

"How did a pa[n]ther scream?" we asked. "Oh like a woman," Pa said, "just like this." Then he screamed and we all shivered.

Well the horse, with Grandpa on him, ran and ran for it was scared too and the panther kept following and once in awhile would scream. It sounded first from one side of the road and then from the other. At last Grandpa had a glimpse of it as it crossed the road behind him, but he was almost home then. As the horse ran up to the house, Grandpa jumped off against the door fell through into the house and slammed the door shut behind him.

Grandpa grabbed his rifle from over the door and jumped to the window just as the panther sprang on the horse.[36] The horse screamed awfully and started to run with the panther on his back and Grandpa shot the panther dead. He said he'd never go in the woods again without his gun.

We huddled closer together and Ma said, "you shouldn't frighten the children so just before bed time Charles. Look how big their eyes are."

But Pa said, "Oh well, I'll play the fiddle to them and it will be all right.["] So we hung our stockings by the fire and were put to bed, Mary and Alice and Ella and I all in one big bed on the floor and Pa played Old Zip Coon and Money Musk, The Red Hiefer, the Arkansas Traveler and we went to sleep with the fiddle and Pa both singing My Darling Nellie Gray.[37]

In the morning we found candy and red mittens[38] in all our stockings. We ate good things and played all morning. Mary played out doors in the snow with the cousins, sliding down the drifts and making snowballs, but because I was so small, I could be out only a little while.

After the Christmas dinner Aunt Eliza and Uncle Peter bundled the cousins into the big sled among the blankets and they all went home.

After Christmas we began to be tired of staying in the house an[d] especially on Sundays the day seemed long. We were dressed all in clean clothes with fresh ribbons in our hair and were not allowed to knit or sew or be noisy in our play.

Ma read us stories out of the Bible or about lions and tigers and

36. *Grandpa grabbed his rifle . . . and jumped to the window just as the panther sprang on the horse.* While this scene is dramatic, it became even more so once the transition to fiction began. In the juvenile manuscript, the panther was "a huge, black panther" that leaped onto the horse's back just as Grandpa jumped off (JPG, p. 5). The panther in the novel is also black (BW, p. 41). References to black panthers appear frequently in pioneer narratives and dime novels of the nineteenth and early twentieth centuries. Yet, according to wildlife biologists, North American black panthers, or melanistic color variants of the *Puma concolor*, have never existed in the wild. Despite these scientific disclaimers, black panther sightings persist, and the *New Orleans Times-Picayune* published a photograph of what appeared to be a black panther in Saint Tammany Parish on November 30, 2011.

37. *Old Zip Coon . . . My Darling Nellie Gray.* A similar list of tunes is part of the Christmas segment in *Little House in the Big Woods* (p. 73). Not listed there is "Old Zip Coon," which used the same music as "Turkey in the Straw." "Money Musk" was an old fiddle and dance song from the 1700s. "The Red Heifer" may have been a corrupted reference to either "The Red Steer" or the "Yellow Heifer." "The Arkansas Traveler" and "Darling Nellie Gray" were composed in the nineteenth century. All the songs were popular in minstrel shows. For more on the music in Wilder's writings, *see* Garson, *Laura Ingalls Wilder Songbook*, and Cockrell, *Ingalls Wilder Family Songbook*.

38. *candy and red mittens.* These simple gifts form part of all the *Pioneer Girl* manuscripts, but in *Little House in the Big Woods*, Wilder embellished the occasion with a gift that she actually received later in *Pioneer Girl*. On Christmas morning, the character of Laura receives Charlotte, her first rag doll, and is forced to share the gift with Mary and her cousins (BW, p. 77), a painful situation that especially resonates with young readers.

39. *Pa's big, green book "The Polar and Tropical Worlds."* Charles Ingalls's copy of this book, with the inscription "Mr. C. P. Ingalls" on the inside, is part of the Laura Ingalls Wilder Memorial Society's collection in De Smet, South Dakota. *The Polar and Tropical Worlds: A Description of Man and Nature in the Polar and Equatorial Regions of the Globe* was published simultaneously in 1871 by several American publishing houses, including Bill, Nicols & Company of Springfield, Massachusetts, the publisher of Charles Ingalls's copy. Written by Dr. George Hartwig and edited by Dr. Alfred H. Guernsey, the book contained two hundred black-and-white engravings.

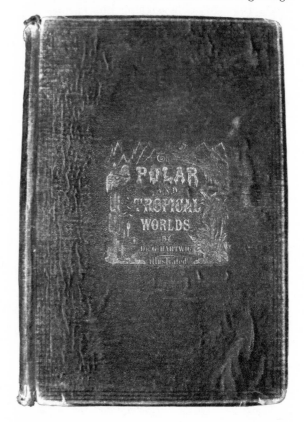

Charles Ingalls's copy of *The Polar and Tropical Worlds,* with his signature. *Laura Ingalls Wilder Memorial Society*

white bears out of Pa's big, green book "The Polar and Tropical Worlds."[39]

We liked best to look at the pictures in the big paper covered Bible[40] and there were two we always lingered over. One was Adam naming the animals. Adam was sitting on a big rock and all the animals big and little were standing or sitting around him. Adam looked so comfortable. He didn't have to be careful of his clothes for he had none on except a skin around his waist and the animals wouldn't get that dirty even if they did put their paws on him as Wolf was always doing to me. It must have been fun naming the animals for we had so much trying to tell Ma the names of them all.

The other picture we liked was of the Flood with people and animals all mixed together climbing out of the water onto a big rock.

But Sunday at best was a long, tiresome day.

One Sunday afternoon I was naughty[41] and made such a disturbance playing with Wolf that I was told to sit in a chair and keep quiet for awhile. Then I was naughtier still and cried and kicked until Pa had to speak to me.

After supper he said "Come here Laura and I'll tell you about one Sunday when Grandpa was a boy.["] So he lifted me up on his knee and with Mary sitting close began—

"When your Grandpa was a boy,[42] Sunday began at sundown on Saturday night, then everyone stopped working and playing. Your Grandpa and his brothers James and George[43] didn't mind stopping work but sometimes they did not want to stop playing. When bed time came, your Grandpa's father read aloud a chapter from the Bible while everyone sat very still and straight, then they all knelt down by their chairs and their father said a long prayer. When he said 'Amen': everyone got up from their knees and went to bed.

Sunday morning after breakfast, they all dressed in their best clothes and went to church.

In the church while the preacher preached for an hour or maybe two hours, your Grandpa and his brothers must sit very still on their bench. They dare not whisper nor swing their feet; but sat still with their eyes on the preacher. It was much longer than you had to be still Laura.

Given the book's publication date, it would have been a new and lavish acquisition in the Ingalls household, illustrating the importance that Caroline and Charles Ingalls placed on books, reading, and education. In *Little House in the Big Woods*, Wilder changed the book's title to *The Wonders of the Animal World* (p. 85). It makes another appearance in *The Long Winter*, when the family attempts to identify a bird found after a blizzard (*LW*, p. 51). Palmlund to Hill, Feb. 23, 2012.

40. *pictures in the big paper covered Bible*. While the scene that follows this line does not appear in the juvenile *Pioneer Girl* manuscript, Wilder folded it back into *Little House on the Prairie*, adding a conversation between Laura and Ma to reinforce her main character's dislike of wearing "good clothes" on Sundays (*BW*, p. 85).

41. *I was naughty*. This entire scene and the story about Grandpa that follows were cut from Brandt (pp. 13–15) with a diagonal slash through the copy. It does not appear in either Brandt Revised or Bye, although it does appear in JPG.

42. *"When your Grandpa was a boy."* Perhaps because Wilder had heard it so often from her father as she was growing up, this story is well developed from the beginning. "The Story of Grandpa's Sled and the Pig" (pp. 87–97) appears in *Little House in the Big Woods* in only slightly more detail. As her novels became more successful, Wilder frequently told readers that her father's stories had inspired her to write fiction. "I loved Pa's stories best," she wrote in a speech crafted for a 1937 Detroit book fair. "We never forgot them and I have always felt they were too good to be altogether lost" ("Detroit Book Week Speech," p. 2, Box 13, file 197, Lane Papers). The well-developed nature of the stories and the wish to preserve them also seem to have been the driving forces behind the creation of the juvenile *Pioneer Girl* manuscript, which Lane described to Wilder as "your father's stories, taken out of the long PIONEER GIRL manuscript, and strung together, as you will see" (RWL to LIW, Feb. 16, 1931, Lane Papers).

43. *Grandpa and his brothers James and George*. Biographer Donald Zochert stated that Lansford Ingalls and his brothers James and George were boys together in western New York, and, as adults, the three moved their families to Illinois. According to the 1850 census, a Lansford "Ingols" or "Ingals" (the handwriting is difficult to read) settled his large family in Campton Township in Kane County, Illinois. Using the same census records, however, it is difficult to ascertain which of Lansford's brothers may have joined him in Illinois and impossible to determine the difference in their ages. Zochert, *Laura*, p. 5.

When preaching was over, they went home and ate dinner that had been cooked the day before. Then all afternoon your Grandpa and his brothers could not play but sat quiet and studied their catechism until the sun went down and Sunday was over.

Your Grandpa's fathers house was about half way down the side of a steep hill. The road went from the top of the hill right down past the front door and on to the bottom of the hill. It was a wonderful place to slide down hill in the winter.

One week you[r] Grandpa and his brothers James and George worked hard all their play time making a wonderful new hand sled, long enough so all three could ride it at once down the hill. They tried their best to have it ready to play with Saturday but their father kept them working longer in the woods, so that they finished their sled just as the sun went down and Sunday began.

Of course they couldn't slide down the hill even once for that would be breaking the Sabbath and their father wouldn't allow that. So they put the sled in the shed behind the house to stay until Sunday was over.

But all the time they were sitting in church next day, keeping their feet still and their eyes on the preacher, they were thinking about the new sled.

At home after dinner their father sat and read the Bible while your Grandpa and James and George sat as quiet as mice on their bench and studied their catechism. The sun shone brightly outside and the snow was smooth and glistening on the road, they could see out of the window. They kept thinking of the new sled instead of learning their lesson and it seemed as though sundown would never come.

After awhile they heard their father snore and looking at him they saw that his head had fallen against the back of his chair and he was fast asleep.

Then James looked at George and tiptoed out of the room through the back door. George looked at your Grandpa and tiptoed after James and your Grandpa looked fearfully at their father but on tiptoe followed George and left him snoring.

The boys got their new sled and went quietly up to the top of the

"This pig sat down on James." *Helen Sewell, 1932*

hill. They thought they could coast down just once, walk back up, put the sled away and slip back into the house before their father waked.

James sat first on the sled, then George and then your Grandpa because he was the littlest, like you Laura.

The sled went beautifully, but they dare not shout. Instead they kept quiet as mice to slip by the house without waking their father.

Then just before they got to the house an old sow, you know, a mother hog, walked out of the woods at one side and into the road. They couldn't stop and the sled slipped under her. She sat down on the front of it with an awful squeal and rode on past the house screaming "Squ-e-e Squ-e-e["] as loud as she could.

Just as they flashed by the door, the hog sitting in front, then James, then George, then your Grandpa, they saw their father standing in the door looking at them. Then on down to the bottom of the hill they went, the hog squealing all the way.

Back up the hill they walked while the hog ran off into the woods still squealing.

They put the sled away, slipped quietly in at the back door and sat down on their bench. Their father was reading his Bible. He looked up at them never saying a word, but when the sun set and the Sabbath day was over, he took them out into the woodshed and tanned their jackets good, first James, then George, then your Grandpa.

Now run along and let Ma put you to bed and be glad you don't have to be still as long as children did on Sunday when your Grandpa was a boy."

Then Pa took up his fiddle and we went to bed and to sleep while he played and sang, "There is a Fountain," and Rock of Ages.[44]

Uncle Tom Quiner, Ma's brother,[45] came to make us a visit. I liked Uncle Tom, he was always so pleasant and he dressed so nicely. He brought Ma a book called "Millbank."[46] Ma said it was a novel and not for little girls but she read it aloud to Pa at night by the light of the glass lamp and Ma read it aloud to us all in the evenings.

Pa's brother George[47] came too, but I did not like him so well. I heard Pa say to Ma that George had been wild ever since he came from the army and any little girl would be afraid of a wild man.

44. *"There is a Fountain," and Rock of Ages*. William Cowper, an eighteenth-century English poet, wrote the lyrics to the hymn "There is a Fountain." In the United States, Cowper's lyrics were often paired with a melody attributed to American composer Lowell Mason. "Rock of Ages" has been a favorite Christian hymn since it was introduced in the late eighteenth century. Thomas Hastings composed the music; the words were by Augustus M. Toplady. The Brandt version of *Pioneer Girl* (p. 15) includes another hymn, "There is a Happy Land," which dates from 1838. Also known as "The Happy Land," its lyrics were written by Andrew Young, a Scottish schoolmaster, with music composed by Robert Archibald Smith. Ma sings this hymn to Laura in *Little House on the Prairie* (p. 220). Sanderson, *Christian Hymns*, pp. 49, 79; Cockrell, *Ingalls Wilder Family Songbook*, p. 384.

45. *Uncle Tom Quiner, Ma's brother*. Born a few weeks after the death of his father in 1844, Thomas Lewis Quiner was five years younger than his sister Caroline Quiner Ingalls. Wilder admired not just his nice clothes but his sense of adventure. He was part of the Gordon Party that illegally crossed into the Black Hills of Dakota Territory searching for gold in 1874 (*see* Appendix C). He married in 1879, fathered six children, and was a long-time employee of the Laird, Norton Lumber Company headquartered in Winona, Minnesota. When he was in his late fifties, he ventured west one more time to Eugene, Oregon, where he worked as a foreman on a logging crew until his death in an accident in a flume on the Columbia River in 1903. "Thomas Lewis Quiner"; LIW to RWL, [1938], Box 13, file 194, Lane Papers; Anderson to Koupal, Feb. 2014.

46. *"Millbank."* Copyrighted in 1871, *Millbank; or, Roger Irving's Ward* was written by Mary Jane Holmes, a best-selling novelist of the period. When she died in 1907, the *Nation* reflected: "It is an eternal paradox of our world of letters that the books which enjoy the largest sale are barely recognized as existing by the guardians of literary tradition. Mrs. Mary Jane Holmes . . . wrote thirty-nine novels with aggregate sales, it is said, of more than two mil-

lion copies, and yet she had not even a paragraph devoted to her life and works in the histories of American Literature" (quoted in "Mary Jane Holmes"). Her work is largely forgotten today, but she was known for her self-sufficient and socially conscious heroines.

47. *Pa's brother George.* George Whiting Ingalls was born on July 15, 1851, making him not quite ten years old when Southern forces bombarded Fort Sumter in April 1861, launching the American Civil War. The Bye manuscript adds that the bugle he played at Grandpa Ingalls's house "was the bugle he had blown in the army" and that he "had joined the army when he was fourteen" (p. 20). *Little House in the Big Woods* also says that George ran away when he was fourteen "to be a drummer boy" (p. 137), but George would have been only thirteen when the war ended at Virginia's Appomattox Court House on April 9, 1865. Could he have enlisted at a younger age than the family remembered? Possibly. Like his older brother Charles, he had musical ability, and a Union Army regulation of 1863 encouraged recruiters to enlist anyone possessing "a natural talent for music, to be instructed on the fife, bugle, and drum, and other military instruments" ("Union Drum").

It is impossible, however, to trace George's military service with any certainty. The official roster of Wisconsin volunteers reveals that a George A. Ingalls of Georgetown, Wisconsin, served as a private with the Twentieth Wisconsin Infantry. He enlisted on July 10, 1862, five days before George W. Ingalls's eleventh birthday, and then deserted on October 13, 1862. Could young George have fibbed about his real name and hometown when he ran away to enlist? It is an intriguing possibility. In the fall of 1862, the Twentieth Wisconsin was engaged in a series of forced marches and skirmishes in parts of southwest Missouri and northwest Arkansas. If young George W. Ingalls had deserted there at that time, he could have fallen in with other Union deserters and raiders who preyed indiscriminately on families throughout the area during the remaining years of the war, stealing livestock, grain, and other goods at will.

The Brandt Revised and Bye versions of *Pioneer Girl* note that his experiences during the Civil War transformed George into a wild and even lawless young man:

"Afterward Uncle George stole a cow and was arrested. . . . Pa said, What could you expect of a boy who had joined the army when he was fourteen, and lived off the country all those years? In the South, when the Union soldiers wanted anything they just took it, and George had got used to that way of doing. All that was wrong with George was that he couldn't seem to realize the war was over and that he was in the North, where he couldn't live off the country any more (Bye, p. 20).

If George had indeed come of age in Missouri, Arkansas, and Kansas during the Civil War, the experience could explain his behavior. In any case, he went on to marry Julia Bard and died in Burnett County, Wisconsin, on February 15, 1901, five months short of his fiftieth birthday. Wisconsin, *Roster of Wisconsin Volunteers*; Love, *Wisconsin in the War*.

We went to a dance at Grandpa Ingall's house[48] in the Big Woods and Uncle George blew his bugal for us.

Uncle James[49] was there too. He had been in the army the same as Uncle George but he was not wild for I asked him and he said he wasn't. He had a little girl named Laura too.

Aunt Libby[50] and Aunt Docia[51] looked so pretty but they couldn't dance a bit better than Grandma and her dress was as pretty as theirs.[52]

There was a dance at Mr Huleatt's too and we all went, riding all bundled up in the big sled. Mr Huleatt was an Irish gentleman[53] Ma said. His place was called Summer Hill and everyone was proud to be invited there. When the dance began, Carrie was put to sleep on the bed among our wraps while Ma danced with the rest. Mary and I sat at the side of the room and watched and listened to the music. Pa played his fiddle[54] part of the time. Right in the midst of the liveliest dance, I heard Carrie cry. Out I went into the middle of the floor, seized Ma's skirts and pulled. "Carrie is crying," I said. Everyone stopped and it was awful until Ma smiled at me and said "Go stay with her! I'll come in a minute.["] Then I ran to the bedroom while the dance went on.

After awhile I had a birthday. I didn't know anything about it until when I got up in the morning, Pa played spank me, four spanks,[55] one for each year. Then he gave me a little wooden man he had whittled out of a stick. Ma and Mary gave me a rag doll[56] that Ma had made and Mary helped dress. And I was a great girl 4 years old![57]

Early one morning Pa tucked us all into the big sled and drove us away to spend a day and a night at Aunt Martha's. Aunt Martha was Ma's sister[58] and Will and Joe, Letty and Nannie and Millie and the twin babies[59] were just cousins, not double.

It was a long drive and only Millie and the babies were at home with Aunt Martha when we got there. The others were in school. All the other boys and girls in the school were Swedes[60] and the cousins could talk in their language as well as English. Mary and I went back to school with them after dinner, the school house was so close.

48. *a dance at Grandpa Ingall's house.* Wilder built one of the most vivid chapters ("Dance at Grandpa's," pp. 131–55) in *Little House in the Big Woods* around this dance. She had started the process in Brandt Revised and Bye:

> Grandpa Ingalls lived in a log house like ours. It was the house to which the panther had chased him, and his horse in the barn had the scars of the claws on his back. There seemed to be nothing but trees for miles all around Grandpa's house, but so many people came to the dance that the three rooms could hardly hold them.
>
> All the beds except one for the babies were taken down, to make room for the dancing. Beds weren't needed, for nobody went to bed that night. They danced till morning.
>
> Pa played the fiddle. Sometimes he stood by the wall and played it, and sometimes he danced, keeping right on playing. There were other fiddlers there, too, and a banjo.
>
> The babies slept on the bed and little girls like me stood around and watched the dancers' skirts and boots going by, and listened to the music and the stamping and the caller's shouts, till everything blurred. I went to sleep on the floor in a corner and woke up on the bed with the babies. Then we came home, riding bundled up in the bob-sled through the cold woods (Bye, pp. 20–21).

49. *Uncle James.* Lansford James Ingalls was born on March 14, 1842, and was nineteen in 1861 when the American Civil War began. He and his younger brother, Hiram Lemuel Ingalls, enlisted with the First Regiment, Minnesota Heavy Artillery. Biographer Donald Zochert recorded that the two brothers ran off to enlist in January 1865 and that their father ran after them, "because he said James was too young to go to war" (*Laura*, pp. 19–20). Yet, James was twenty-three; Hiram, however, was only sixteen (born April 27, 1848). Lansford Ingalls was unable to convince either son to return home, and their regiment was sent to Chattanooga, Tennessee, where it saw no combat. James married twice and had nine

Hiram L. Ingalls. *Laura Ingalls Wilder Memorial Society*

"Aunt Ruby and Aunt Docia." *Helen Sewell, 1932*

children. He died in 1928. "1ˢᵗ Minnesota Artillery"; "List of real-life individuals."

50. *Aunt Libby*. Wilder has confused the name of Charles Ingalls's youngest sister, who was named Ruby Celestia Ingalls, not Libby. Born in 1855, Ruby would have been a teenager in the early 1870s. She married Joseph Card but died in 1881 at the age of "25 years 6 m 7 da in the town of Inman, Holt Co, NEB" (Lansford Ingalls family Bible, quoted in "Colby Family & Others"). Perhaps her early death, when Wilder herself was a teenager, contributed to the confusion over her name in *Pioneer Girl* and could explain why Brandt, Brandt Revised, and Bye do not mention the aunts by name in the dance sequence. In *Little House in the Big Woods*, Wilder corrected the mistake and devoted several paragraphs to Aunt Ruby's and Aunt Docia's preparations for the dance, including a detailed description of their coiled and braided hair (pp. 139–41).

51. *Aunt Docia*. Aunt Docia's full name was Laura Ladocia. Born in 1845 or 1846, she married August Waldvogel in the mid-1860s and had two children—Lena and August Eugene. August Waldvogel was imprisoned for shooting someone who attempted to enter their home, and shortly after the birth of their son in 1870, Docia divorced him and moved back into her parents' home. Neither Wilder's fiction nor the existing versions of *Pioneer Girl* mention the divorce. Although George Ingalls's theft of a cow could be explained away by his Civil War experiences, Aunt Docia's failed marriage apparently deserved only silence. There is, however, a hint of disapproval in *By the Shores of Silver Lake* when Caroline Ingalls says that Docia's daughter Lena is "a good, capable girl," but she is "boisterous, and Docia has not curbed her as much as she might" (p. 96), the implication being that Docia's style of living was not good for her children. "Colby Family & Others"; "Docia Waldvogel Forbes."

52. The Bye manuscript added this paragraph here:

After the dance at Grandpa's, Pa and Ma talked sometimes about going to Kansas. Pa's cousin, John J. Ingalls, had gone to Kansas, or was going to Kansas. Pa thought he would like Kansas, but Ma said all he had was an itching foot. She liked the hills and the trees better than the flat, bare plains in Kansas (p. 21).

The paragraph does not say that Wilder's parents talked about going *back* to Kansas. It reads as if they had never lived there. Yet, within the context of all the adult *Pioneer Girl* manuscripts, the Ingallses' experiment in Kansas had already failed. Wilder and Lane may have intended the paragraph to set up what happens on the next page in the Bye manuscript, where Charles Ingalls decides to move the family west to Minnesota. In any case, it probably reflects the assumption by both Wilder and Lane that the Ingalls family had earlier settled in present-day Oklahoma, not Kansas.

53. *Mr Huleatt was an Irish gentleman.* Thomas P. Huleatt of Summer Hill was born in Ireland in 1809 and died in Pepin County in 1896. He and his wife, Jane, farmed in Pepin County as early as 1860. Wilder did not write about this dance or these neighbors in *Little House in the Big Woods* (although she did write about Huleatt's grandchildren, *see below* Annotation 79). Presumably one dance was enough for the novel, but this decision may have related to Wilder's larger themes, as well. The novel emphasizes the isolation and independence of the tightly knit extended Ingalls family, who rely almost exclusively on themselves to build a life on the frontier. Zochert, *Laura*, p. 63.

54. *Pa played his fiddle.* In Brandt Revised and Bye, Wilder added that her father played "The Irish Washerwoman" during a lively "Irish reel." The "Irish Washerwoman" is a traditional Celtic tune that was popular in North America during the nineteenth century. The song is also part of the dance in *Little House in the Big Woods* (p. 146).

55. *I had a birthday. . . . four spanks.* This birthday appears to be connected to the earlier memory lapse concerning age. Wilder had turned four in 1871, when the family was still living in Kansas; she would have celebrated her fifth (1872) and sixth (1873) birthdays in Wisconsin. The Bye version corrected Wilder's mistake. Pa gives her "five spanks, one for each year." The scene ends with the line, "And I was a great girl five years old" (Bye, p. 21). In *Little House in the Big Woods*, this scene, with the correct age, takes place at the end of the chapter entitled "Sundays" (p. 98). During the promotion of the book, Wilder's editor at Harper & Brothers asked for clarification about the autobiographical aspects of her work. "Won't you send us an autobiographical sketch," her editor wrote in 1931, "so that we can see just how this material fits into your own background?" (Virginia Kirkus to LIW, Dec. 15, 1931, Box 13, file 189, Lane Papers). Wilder realized that she would have to age her fictional self for her third book, *Little House on*

the Prairie, to make Laura more believable and appealing to both young readers and her editors. Thus, as *Little House on the Prairie* opens, the fictional Laura is six years old, not two as Wilder really was, when she first arrives in Indian Territory.

56. *Ma and Mary gave me a rag doll.* In *Little House in the Big Woods*, Laura receives her rag doll at Christmas and names her Charlotte (pp. 74–75). On Laura's fifth birthday, she receives a new dress for Charlotte (p. 98). Later in *Pioneer Girl*, Wilder revealed that she actually named her rag doll Roxy or Roxey, not Charlotte.

57. At this point, Wilder instructed her daughter to go to the back of the page, where she described the long visit to her Aunt Martha's that follows. Brandt, Brandt Revised, and Bye do not include this episode, nor does the novel.

58. *Aunt Martha was Ma's sister.* Martha Jane Quiner was two years older than Caroline. She married Charles Carpenter in 1860, and they had fourteen children. She died in 1927 at the age of eighty-nine in Plainview, Minnesota. In 1925, Wilder had written her Aunt Martha asking for help with an article she was writing for *The Ladies Home Journal* on "our grandmother's cooking." What she really wanted, however, was information about the past. Her mother had died in 1924, and Wilder now asked her aunt for details "about the little everyday happenings and what you and mother and Aunt Eliza and Uncle Tom and Uncle Henry did as children" (LIW to Carpenter, June 22, 1925, Box 14, file 204, Lane Papers). Her aunt responded a few months later with a lengthy letter full of recipes and memories of maple-sugar parties, quiltings, and sleddings. Wilder did not complete the magazine article, but she held on to Aunt Martha's letter, which may have inspired her when she began to write *Pioneer Girl*. "Obit of Mrs. Charles . . . Carpenter"; Carpenter to LIW, Sept. 2, 1925, Lane Papers.

59. *Will and Joe, Letty and Nannie and Millie and the twin babies.* Wilder identified five of her Carpenter cousins by name in the order of their births. William Augustus, born in 1861, was the oldest of Charles and Martha Carpenter's fourteen children. Joseph Quiner Carpenter came two years later, followed by Lettice Jane ("Letty") in 1864 and Nancy Cora ("Nannie") in 1865. Wilder skipped over Martha Eliza, who died in 1871 at the age of three, to get to Millicent Ann ("Millie"), born in 1869. But Wilder also skipped over Charles Carr (1871). She may have skipped over Emma Bertha (1873) and Etta Minerva (1874), as well, or she may have thought they were "the twin babies." The Carpenters actually had two sets of twins born after Wilder left Wisconsin. Marion Caroline and Myrtle Emmeline were born in 1879,

the same year Wilder moved to Dakota Territory. Their twin boys, Thomas Quiner and George Lockwood, were born in 1882. Thomas Quiner Carpenter eventually bought the family farm in Pepin County, and his mother's funeral took place there in the old family farmhouse in 1927. "Obit of Mrs. Charles . . . Carpenter"; "List of real-life characters."

60. *the other boys and girls in the school were Swedes.* Martha Carpenter and her family lived near the village of Stockholm, about six miles from Pepin, and this episode probably took place in the school there. Swedish immigrants had established the town in the 1850s, which would explain Wilder's memory that many of the students spoke their parents' native language. The Carpenters had settled in Stockholm in 1860. Thurman, *Ingalls-Wilder Homesites*, p. 3.

A crowd of boys and girls were playing in the yard as we came up, snowballing and washing each others faces in the snow. "They are so rough they hurt you" Letty said and then "Run, Laura, Gus[61] will get you!"

I ran, but Gus caught me, held me under one arm and began washing my face with the cold hard snow. He was barehanded and his hands were big and red. I fought but couldn't get away, then as his hand came up to my face with a fresh handful of snow, his thumb was right before my mouth. I set my teeth in it as hard as ever I could. Gus yelled and let go of me shaking his hand while blood dripped from his thumb, just as cousin Will came running up to help me. He stopped looked at me, then at the thumb and said "Well Gus, I guess you'll learn to leave Laura alone!"

I didn't like school and was glad when it was time to go home. We played up stairs in the big loft while Aunt Martha and Ma got supper. We fought a little and made lots of noise so that Ma opened the stair door to tell us to be still. Nannie was crying because Will had pulled her hair; Joe was chasing me around the room threatening me because I had scratched his face and Mary and Letty were trying to catch Joe. I heard Aunt Martha say to Ma "You go up Caroline and spank them all. I'll go next time." Ma came up and spanked Will and Joe for being rough, Nannie for crying and me for scratching and Mary and Letty for helping make such a noise. Then she went down and we were quiet.[62] Aunt Martha didn't have to come up.

It wasn't long then until one day Pa said it would soon be spring. The snow had begun to thaw and he must go to town with the furs and hides he had got with his hunting and trapping all winter. So early in the morning he made a big bundle of them, fastened the pack on his back and started out to walk the seven miles to town. There were so many furs to carry he did not take his gun.

He was gone all day and was not back when Mary and I were put to bed so we went to sleep without the music of the violin.[63]

In the morning he was there. Ma gave us some candy he had bought for us and there was some pretty calico[64] he had brought for us each a dress. Ma had calico for a new dress too we were all glad

61. *Gus.* The identity of Gus is a mystery. He was not one of Wilder's Carpenter cousins, and although Aunt Docia's son was named August Eugene, he would have been a baby at the time. Furthermore, he was known as Gene or Jean, not Gus. This episode appears only in the original manuscript of *Pioneer Girl*, but clearly this Wisconsin schoolboy left a lasting impression on Wilder.

62. *Ma came up and spanked Will and Joe. . . . and we were quiet.* In this scene, readers see a different side of Caroline Ingalls, a far tougher disciplinarian than her fictional counterpart.

63. *violin.* This instance is one of the few times in *Pioneer Girl* that Wilder identified Pa's fiddle as a violin.

64. *some pretty calico.* Calico was plain woven-cotton cloth printed with a figured pattern. In *Little House in the Big Woods*, Mary's calico is "a china-blue pattern on a white ground, and Laura's was dark red with little golden-brown dots on it." Ma's is "brown, with a big, feathery white pattern all over it" (p. 108). The concrete details make the scene more vivid.

65. *Pa told us about how he came home from town.* Wilder titled this episode "The Story of Pa and the Bear in the Way" in *Little House in the Big Woods* (pp. 109–14), where it contains minor changes in phrasing and more dialogue. It does not appear in the other adult versions of *Pioneer Girl*, but it is included as one of Pa's stories in JPG (pp. 19–21).

66. *my hair stood straight up like this."* The original line in *Pioneer Girl* is more immediate and dramatic than the version that appears in *Little House in the Big Woods*. In JPG (p. 20) and the novel (p. 111), Charles Ingalls does not demonstrate how his hair stood up on end.

67. *I had been thinking about bears you see, afraid I would meet one.* This original line in *Pioneer Girl* is also more satisfying than the one Wilder and Lane settled on for *Little House in the Big Woods*, which reads, "I only thought it was a bear, because I had been thinking all the time about bears and being afraid I'd meet one" (pp. 113–14). Not all editorial decisions are good ones.

68. *"Pop Goes The Weasel."* This song originated in England and jumped to the United States in the mid-1850s. Americans changed some of the lyrics but kept the original refrain and tune. According to Cockrell in the *Ingalls Wilder Family Songbook*, "'pop' meant 'to pawn' and a 'weasel' referred to the tools of a trade, . . . hence, the pawning of one's tools because 'Pop!—the money's gone!'" (p. 346). The fictional Charles Ingalls plays this tune for Laura on her fifth birthday in *Little House in the Big Woods* (p. 99).

he had got so much money for the furs that he could buy us such nice presents.

That night Pa told us about how he came home from town.[65]

The walking had been hard on the slipery snow and it had taken him a long time to sell his furs and do his trading.

"It was sundown when I got started home," said Pa, "and then it got dark. I tried to hurry, but the walking was bad and I was tired, so I hadn't gone far when it got dark.

"It got darker and darker and I wished I had my gun for some of the bears had waked up from their winters sleep and come out of their dens. They were hungry and cross as they always are then and I didn't know but I might meet one. I had seen some of their tracks beside the road as I went to town in the morning.

["]It was so dark, it was black as pitch where the woods were thick, but by and by I came to an open place in the woods. I could see the road ahead a little way and there right in the middle of the road stood a big black bear.

["]He was standing up on his hind legs looking at me. I could even see his eyes shine like Susan's eyes shine in the night you know.

["]I thought if I could scare him he would get out of the road and let me go by, so I hollerd and hollerd but he never moved. I was scared! My scalp prickled and my hair stood straight up like this,"[66] and Pa ran his fingers through his thick hair standing it all on end.

"I just had to get past that bear to get home, so I gathered me a good, big club from the woods beside the road. I went straight at that bear yelling and swinging my club as hard as I could I brought it down, Bang! on his head. And there he still stood but he was just a big, black, burned stump that I passed every time I went to town. It wasn't a bear at all. I had been thinking about bears you see, afraid I would meet one[67] and things look different when you're scared.

["]And now, if you'll climb down off my knee Laura, I'll let the weasel pop out of the fiddle."

Then he took the fiddle out of its box and began to play the tune we knew was "Pop Goes The Weasel."[68] "Watch close"! Pa said, "there where my fingers are and he'll pop out pretty soon.["]

Mary and I drew closer and breathlessly watched Pa's fingers on the strings. We knew we were going to be startled and loved it. Then the fiddle said plain as plain: 'Pop' goes the weasel and we both jumped and screamed and the fun was over.

When spring came Mary and I moved out under the big trees in the front yard. One tree was my house and one was Mary's. Each of us had her dolls and housekeeping things under her tree and I had besides a swing made of tough bark fastened to one limb of my tree.

One day I wanted so much to be out under my tree for I had the most beautiful china cup with only one crack in it to add to my store of dishes, but Ma would not let me go. She was unrolling my hair[69] from the strings of cloth on which it had been tightly wound and tied to curl. Aunt Lottie[70] was coming to visit and I must be made pretty for her to see. Mary was all ready, with her golden hair hanging in long curls and her pretty blue dress so fresh and clean. I liked my dress better because it was red, but Ma pulled my hair dreadfully and it was brown instead of golden and no one noticed it as they did Mary's.[71]

"There," said Ma ["]at last your hair is curled beautifully and Aunt Lottie is coming. Run meet her both of you and ask her which she likes best brown curls or golden curls!"[72]

We ran out the door and down the path for there came Aunt Lottie through the yard from the road. She was a great big girl twelve years old. Her dress was a lovely pink and she was swinging a pink sunbonnet by one string. She took each of us by the hand, and one on either side we danced along to the door where Ma stood.

We went on into the room with the cookstove so bright and shining, the table with the red cover and the sunshine streaming through the windows. I could see into father's and mother's room, with the trundle bed showing underneath. The pantry door stood wide open giving us the sight and smell of goodies within and Black Susan came purring down the stairs from the loft where she had been sleeping on the company bed. It was all so pleasant and I felt so gay, you never would have thought I would be so naughty as I was in just a little while.

Aunt Lottie had gone and Mary and I were tired and cross. We were out behind the house getting a pan of chips for Ma to kindle

69. *She was unrolling my hair.* This highly developed sequence concerning the sisters' hair, which is emotionally gripping, reveals Wilder's natural understanding of storytelling and foreshadows her success as a writer of fiction. The Brandt version (p. 17) of *Pioneer Girl* also includes the episode; JPG, Brandt Revised, and Bye do not. Wilder and Lane may have decided that the material did not belong in an adult story, and Lane excluded it from JPG for reasons of length. However, as Wilder began expanding the juvenile manuscript for publication, Lane reminded her of this material: "There is a very lovely bit in your tablets, about your big cousin [*sic*] who comes to visit, and your quarrel with Mary about whose hair is the prettier. That should be put back in" (RWL to LIW, Feb. 16, 1931). Not surprisingly, much of this scene appears with only slight variations in *Little House in the Big Woods* (pp. 180–85).

70. *Aunt Lottie.* Charlotte E. Holbrook, born in 1854, was Caroline Ingalls's half-sister. Their mother had married Frederick Holbrook in 1849, five years after her first husband's death. Lottie, as she was known to the family, was their only child and her mother's namesake. She married Henry Moore, raised a family, and died in 1939.

71. *no one noticed it as they did Mary's.* This line reveals the twinge of jealousy Wilder felt concerning her older sister, an emotion she transferred to Laura in *Little House in the Big Woods.* In the novel, Wilder prepared readers for Laura's jealous feelings in an earlier chapter, when a shopkeeper "admired Mary's golden curls" but said nothing about Laura's "ugly and brown" ones (p. 167). Wilder had earlier shared this episode in a 1917 newspaper column, where she portrayed Mary as having "a sharp tongue" and herself as "slow to speak but quick to act" (reprinted in Hines, *Little House in the Ozarks*, pp. 297–98).

72. *"There," said Ma. . . . ask her which she likes best brown curls or golden curls!"* With minor changes in punctuation, Wilder lifted this piece of dialogue from *Pioneer Girl* and placed it directly into *Little House in the Big Woods.* In the novel, Aunt Lottie answers, "I like both kinds best" (pp. 181–82). Her diplomatic response, which triggers so much trouble

between Laura and Mary, does not appear in either the original *Pioneer Girl* manuscript or the Brandt version, although the aftermath does.

73. *Pa said*—. Fiction gave Wilder the freedom to create a more satisfying ending to this episode. In the novel, as Pa gathers Laura in his arms, she asks if he likes golden hair better than brown, and he replies, "Well, Laura, my hair is brown" (p. 184).

74. *"When I was a little boy.* This story appears as "The Story of Pa and the Voice in the Woods" in the chapter "The Long Rifle" in *Little House in the Big Woods* (pp. 53–58).

the fire in the morning. I grabbed the biggest chip and Mary said "Aunt Lottie likes my hair the best anyway. Golden hair is lots prettier than brown." My throat swelled up and I couldn't answer for I knew golden hair was prettier than brown. I couldn't think of anything to say, so I just reached out quickly and slapped her face. Then I heard Pa's voice, "Come here Laura!" he said and I went dragging my feet to where he sat just inside the door.

"You remember," said he, "I told you girls never to strike each other?"

"But Mary said"—I began.

"That makes no difference" said Pa and he took down a little strap from the wall, laid me across his knee and spanked me with the strap. Then I sat in a corner and sobbed and sulked for awhile.

At last just when I had noticed that it was getting dark outside, Pa said, "Come here Laura!" and when I went he took me on his knee again but right side up this time. Mary sat on her little chair beside us. (She had to get the whole pan of chips by herself.)

I sat within the crook of Pa's arm with his long, brown whiskers partly covering my eyes and Pa said—[73]

"When I was a little boy,[74] I used to have to go find the cows in the woods and drive them up at night. My father told me never to play by the way but to hurry along and get the cows home before dark for there were bears and wolves and wildcats in the woods.

One evening I started early but there were so many things to look at along the way that I forgot about dark coming. There were red squirrels playing in the trees, chipmunks scurrying through the leaves and rabbits running and playing before they went to bed.

I played I was a mighty hunter stalking the game and fighting Indians until the woods seemed full of wild men and beasts and then all at once I heard the birds twittering good night and saw that it was dusky in the path where I was and and quite dark back in the woods.

And then I couldn't find the cows!

I listened but I couldn't hear the bell. I called and called, but they didn't come nor answer. I was afraid of the dark and the Indians and the wild beasts, but I dare not go back without the cows so I ran here and there calling and getting more and more scared.

Then something right over my head cried 'Who-o-o-o.' My hair stood straight on end and then I did run for home. I ran and ran! Once something seemed to reach out and grab me by the foot. Down I went, but I jumped up and ran faster than ever. Not even a wolf could have caught me I'm sure.

Two or three times I heard 'Who-o-o-o' behind me but at last I came out of the woods by the barn and there stood all the cows waiting to be let through the bars. I let them through into the yard and sneaked into the house. My big toe hurt and I looked down and saw that the nail had been torn clear off, when I snagged it and fell I suppose but I had been so scared I never felt it hurt until that minute.

My father looked up and said [']Young man what made you so late? Been playing by the way?['] And then he tanned my jacket because I hadn't minded. 'If,' said he [']you'd do as you are told you wouldn't be scared by an owl.'

"Now run along," said Pa "and let Ma put you to bed. I'll make the old fiddle sing for you a little.["]

When we had said our prayers, for Ma, and she had tucked us into the trundle bed I lay awake awhile thinking how much better it was to mind fathers who knew all about owls and things.[75] Then I fell asleep while the fiddle sang 'Home Sweet Home.'[76] I knew that tune for Pa had taught me which one it was.

When the warm weather really came Mary went to school for the school house was only a little way down the road.[77] She had a beautiful new book and a bright new dinner pail. I wanted to go too but Ma said I was too little and must wait until I grew more. It was lonesome at home all day without Mary for Carrie was so little. I would run down the road to meet Mary when it was time for her to come and carry her dinner bucket. Nearly always she had left bits of her dinner for me and always she brought her primmer. While Ma was getting supper Mary would show me the letters and the words she had learned that day, until, to Ma's surprise, I could read[78] as well as Mary.

75. *owls and things.* The Brandt version eliminated this paragraph and the preceding one, possibly in the interest of creating a leaner, more marketable manuscript. Yet, the original paragraphs provided a frame and context for Wilder's memory of this dramatic episode from her childhood. They also softened the portrayal of Charles Ingalls as a tough disciplinarian.

76. *'Home Sweet Home.'* This popular song dates from the early 1820s, with music by Englishman Henry Rowley Bishop and lyrics by American John Howard Payne. Cockrell, *Ingalls Wilder Family Songbook*, p. 366.

77. *Mary went to school . . . only a little way down the road.* The Barry Corner School was within a mile of the Ingalls cabin. Wilder biographer William Anderson discovered that old school records indicate that both Mary and Laura Ingalls attended from 1871 to 1873 and that Charles Ingalls had acted as treasurer for the school district in 1868 before the family moved to Kansas. In Wilder's fiction, Laura and Mary attend school for the first time in *On the Banks of Plum Creek* (pp. 140–52), Wilder's fourth novel and the third that deals with the Ingalls family. Wilder's decision not to fictionalize her experiences at the Barry Corner School may relate to the way she chose to portray her family in *Little House in the Big Woods*. The fictional characters are self-reliant, facing the dangers and delights of the frontier with only their extended family to support them. This isolation gives them a more archetypal quality. Once Wilder realized she was writing a series, she retained the focus on family but allowed her fictional characters to deepen their ties with the outside world, culminating with their roles as active, upstanding citizens in De Smet, South Dakota, where the series ends. Over the course of seven novels, the Ingalls family tames and transforms the frontier.

78. *to Ma's surprise, I could read.* The character of Laura does not know how to read when she first goes to school in *On the Banks of Plum Creek* (p. 150).

Clarence and Eva Huleatt. *Laura Ingalls Wilder Historic Home and Museum*

79. *Eva and Clarence Huleatt.* Eva and Clarence were the children of Thomas P. Huleatt, Jr., and his wife Maria, who lived not quite a mile from the Ingalls cabin. Like his father, Thomas was born in Ireland; his wife hailed from Pennsylvania. Their son Clarence was a year older than Wilder, born in 1866. Eva was about Carrie's age, making it surprising that Wilder placed her at school on that Friday. Clarence remained a favorite of Wilder's. Later in *Pioneer Girl*, she revealed that even as a teenager in De Smet she continued to write to him. Perhaps her lingering fondness for Clarence influenced her decision to write the family into *Little House in the Big Woods*, where he and Laura climb trees while Mary and Eva play "carefully" (pp. 179–80). The scene in the novel is one of the few involving neighbors who are not somehow related to the family. As an adult, Clarence moved west and went into the hardware business. He died in Chandler, Arizona, in 1947. His sister Eva married a man named Leitch and moved to Illinois. Zochert, *Laura*, p. 63; Miller, *Becoming*, p. 27.

80. *Ann Berry.* According to the 1870 census, Ann or Anna Barry (not Berry) was a twenty-three-year-old schoolteacher living at home with her parents and fourteen-year-old brother James in Pepin County. She taught school all her life and was buried in Pepin in 1941.

81. *Captain Berry had brought a Negro boy home.* Born

The book was so pretty with pictures of cats and dogs and birds and trees. I was proud when I could read for Ma, about the tree.

"The sun is up and it is day,
The dew is on the new mown hay,
But it did not wet the old oak."

But I was horrified when one day I read a little story beginning "Laura was a glutton," and Ma explained to me what a glutton was. I could hardly be comforted even when she said it did not mean me, and I need not be like that though my name was Laura.

One Friday, when Mary was to speak a piece at school, Ma said I might go with her. She put my dinner in the pail with Mary's and dressed me in a pretty white dress. Mary and I went down the road to the school house, swinging the dinner pail between us. I had a wonderful day. Cousin Louisa and Charley were there and Eva and Clarence Huleatt[79] whose Grandpa lived at Summer Hill besides lots of boys and girls I didn't know at all.

Ann Berry[80] was the teacher. Her father Captain Berry had brought a Negro boy home[81] with him from the war. Everyone called him Captain Berry's nigger.[82]

This black boy came over to watch us play at the last recess and stood laughing at us with the whites of his eyes and his white teeth shining and then a dreadful thing happened. I ran so fast in my play that I stubbed my toe and fell hard in the soft, green grass and there on my pretty white dress was a great grass stain. Cousin Louisa said it would never come out and I cried, but Mary told me she was sure Ma could fix it and I felt better.

Mary and I saw Eva and Clarance Huealett quite often, because their father and mother and ours were great friends. They called their farm Okland.

Eva was a pretty girl with black hair and dark eyes. Her dresses were always pretty. Clarence' hair was red and his face was freckled, but he was always laughing and great fun to play with. His clothes were pretty too with braid and bright gilt buttons and copper toes on his shoes. When we played house Mary and Eva always kept

in Ireland, James Barry emigrated to the United States and met his wife, Elizabeth, usually identified as Eliza, in Pennsylvania. By 1860, however, they were living in Pepin County, Wisconsin. The 1870 census identified James Barry as a farmer with a wife and two children still living at home. A fourteen-year-old farm laborer named George Wieb was part of the household. Wieb was born in Tennessee, but he is listed as white. A Captain James "Berry" served with the Twenty-fifth Wisconsin Infantry during the American Civil War. This regiment traveled throughout most of the slaveholding states, including Tennessee, over the course of the war. It is not clear, however, if the two men are the same. The James Barry of Pepin County died in 1883; his wife Eliza died ten years later. Both are buried in Oakwood Cemetery in Pepin.

82. *Everyone called him Captain Berry's nigger.* Although Wilder carefully did not ascribe use of this epithet to herself, she reported its prevalence in the culture. This term, considered offensive today, was in common usage in the 1870s.

83. *Mrs Peterson*. Without a first name or a husband's name, it is impossible to identify Mrs. Peterson with any certainty. The 1870 census of Pepin County lists several women of that surname who were born in Sweden. Most lived near Stockholm, home to Wilder's Aunt Martha, about six miles from the Ingalls cabin. The Sven Peterson family, however, is listed just two households away from Henry and Polly Quiner, Wilder's aunt and uncle. No first name is given for this Mrs. Sven Peterson, but she was thirty years old in 1870, the mother of a six-year-old girl and a one-year-old boy, which contradicts the portrait of Mrs. Peterson in *Little House in the Big Woods*, where she keeps a tidy house because she has "no little girls to muss it up" (p. 178). If Wilder had confused the name Peterson with Anderson, as she apparently did a few pages later, the identity becomes even more uncertain.

84. *When the grain got ripe in the fields*. Wilder transformed this episode of reaping grain into the chapter "Harvest" (pp. 199–211) in *Little House in the Big Woods*), where it helps to round out the single year's activities chronicled in that volume.

85. *He was a big boy*. If this memory dates from Charles Ingalls's last harvest in Wisconsin in 1873—before the family moved to Minnesota—Charley Quiner would have been about eleven years old.

86. *Charley was a bad boy*. In *Little House in the Big Woods*, Wilder was less direct about Charley's character, skillfully introducing his shortcomings through Pa's eyes. "At home," Wilder wrote, "Pa had said to Ma that Uncle Henry and Aunt Polly spoiled Charley. When Pa was eleven years old, he had done a good day's work every day in the fields, driving a team. But Charley did hardly any work at all" (p. 203).

house together and Clarance and I. I heard Ma say to Mrs Huealett that maybe we would some day. Who knew?

It was a happy summer. We went with Ma to gather berries and brought home buckets full; we found birds nest; we gathered flowers and played out doors all the long bright days.

Sometimes we would go down the hill to see Mrs Peterson,[83] the Swedish woman who showed us pretty things she had brought from Sweden and who always gave us each a cookie when started home.

We nibbled them as we went up the hill but we each always saved half a cookie for Baby Carrie.

We saw that it would not be fair for Mary to save half of hers for Carrie while I ate all mine. Neither would it be fair for me to save half mine while Mary ate all hers, but if we each ate only half and saved the other half for Carrie, it must be right.

When the grain got ripe in the fields[84] Uncle Henry helped Pa cut his and then we all went to spe[n]d the day at Uncle Henry's while he and Pa cut his grain. Ma and Aunt Polly worked in the house but we cousins played in the yard all except Charley. He was a big boy[85] and went to the field with the men in the afternoon to carry the water jug to them when they wanted a drink.

Pa and Uncle Henry were cutting the grain with cradels, a steel blade fastened to a wooden frame with slats that caught the grain as it was cut and a curved handle to swing it by. It was hard work to cut the grain that way, walking around and around the field, swinging the heavy cradels and dropping the grain in little piles and they were glad it was only a little field.

Charley was a bad boy[86] and made all the trouble he could, getting in the way and hiding the whetstone so they could not sharpen their blades.

Finally he began to follow them around the field talking to them. They were too busy to pay much attention to him, but stopped quickly and ran to him when he screamed. They thought a snake had bitten him, but nothing was wrong and Charley just laughed, at them so They took a drink of water and went back to work.

Three times Charley fooled them and laughed. Then again he

screamed louder than ever, but Pa and Uncle Henry were tired and hurrying to get the cutting finished before night, so when they looked back and saw Charley just jumping up and down screaming as he had before, they went on with their work.

But he kept screaming and at last they went back to him. He was jumping up and down on a yellow jackets nest. The bees were stinging him all over and the more he jumped and screamed and threw his hands around the more they stung him.

He was pretty badly hurt[87] because Pa and Uncle Henry had been fooled so many times, they didn't run quickly to help him.

Pa was too tired that night to tell us any stories. His hands were tired and he couldn't even make the fiddle sing us to sleep, but we had played so hard we were sleepy anyway.

Only I did wonder how Charley lied.[88] Pa had said "It served the little liar right" but I couldn't understand how Charley could have told a lie when he hadn't said a word.

Mary's tree, out in the yard, with her play things under it, was struck by lightening one day in a storm. The tree wasn't killed but one side of it was made dead and the branches broken off.

Summer was over and Jack Frost came again. The leaves on the trees were all brightly colored. Carrie was old enough now to sleep in our trundle bed and Mary and I slept in the attic with Susan the cat sleeping at the foot of the bed to keep our feet warm.

Pa sold Sukey, the cow, and when I cried, he said we were going to Uncle Peter's[89] to stay and could not take her. He said we could not take Wolf or Susan, but Mrs Peterson was coming to live in our house[90] and she would keep them.

Then one day Ma put our things in boxes,[91] Pa loaded them into the wagon we all got in and Pa drove a long time through the woods.

The farther we went the bigger the trees were and nearer together, until at last we came to Uncle Peter's. Uncle Peter lived in the Big Woods. His house was made of logs and stood in a little cleared place with the great, tall, dark trees all around it.

Uncle Peter, Aunt Eliza and the cousins Alice and Peter and Ella were glad to see us. Baby Edith[92] was to small to know us but

"He was jumping up and down." *Helen Sewell, 1932*

87. *He was pretty badly hurt.* When Wilder fictionalized this scene, she made a significant change: Laura herself sees her cousin after the event, thereby giving readers a chance to see him, too, with his face "so swollen that the tears could hardly squeeze out of his eyes" (p. 208). Not only is this description more dramatic, it also provides a vivid lesson in the virtues of hard work and obedience.

88. *Only I did wonder how Charley lied.* Both here and in *Little House in the Big Woods*, the story of Charley's misbehavior is essentially a retelling of the classic Aesopian fable "The Boy Who Cried Wolf." An 1867 translation rendered the moral of that Greek tale of false alarms in this manner: "There is

no believing a liar, even when he speaks the truth" (Townsend, *Aesop's Fables*). Clearly, both Wilder as author and her father as storyteller knew their Aesop. Wilder's youthful bewilderment, however, is preserved as the last two sentences of the "Harvest" chapter: "But she didn't understand why Pa had called him a liar. She didn't understand how Charley could be a liar, when he had not said a word" (*BW*, p. 211).

89. *we were going to Uncle Peter's.* In the opening chapter of *Little House on the Prairie*, the fictional Ingalls family loads up the wagon and leaves Wisconsin for Indian Territory (pp. 2–7). They do not stay with Uncle Peter, nor do they stay or travel with extended family when they move from Indian Territory to Minnesota, which is where *On the Banks of Plum Creek* begins. Even though the timeline and movements these novels depict are fictional, Wilder drew some details from this scene for *Little House on the Prairie*. By eliminating the short stays with extended family that occurred on both sides of the trip to Kansas, however, Wilder focused on the self-sufficiency of her fictional family rather than on the reality of her own personal history.

90. *Mrs Peterson was coming to live in our house.* Charles and Caroline Ingalls sold their farm in October 1873 to Andrew Anderson for one thousand dollars. Wilder may have confused the names Peterson and Anderson. The census does include a listing for an Andrew Anderson, his wife Annie, and three teenage sons near Pepin in 1880. Miller, *Becoming*, p. 30.

91. *Then one day Ma put our things in boxes.* Corrections in Brandt Revised amend this sentence to read, "In the warm spring weather, when I was five years old, we went west into Minnesota" (p. 15). Obviously, the confusion about Wilder's age persisted, which is not surprising. In this section of the memoir, there are no dates and no clear progression of time. One year seems to blend into the next. In reality, Wilder was six, almost seven, in the fall of 1873 as the family prepared to move to Minnesota.

92. *Baby Edith.* Edith Florence Ingalls was born in June 1872, the fifth of Peter and Eliza Ingalls's six children. She married Heil Nelson Bingham in the early 1890s, and they had eight children together. She died in 1951 and is buried in Sunset Memorial Park in Minneapolis, Minnesota.

she laughed at me and held out her little hands. They all called her Dolly Varden because she had a pretty dress of calico that was called that.[93]

Mary and the cousins began going to school the next week. The log schoolhouse was only a little way down the road and sometimes they would take me, drawing me over the snow on their sled. They took lunch in a bright tin pail and ate it with all the other children in the school house.

At home we played out doors in the snow for it was soft and deep. Where the trees had been cut down around the house their stumps were so close together that Mary and Alice and Peter could jump from one to the other.

Ella and I couldn't jump so far, but we would climb up on a stump, spread our arms wide and fall off into the snow face down, then get up carefully not to spoil the marks. We called it making our pictures.[94]

Then we took the Scarlet Fever.[95] We couldn't go to school nor play out doors but had to lie in bed and take nasty medicine. We were all going west in the spring and this sickness worried the fathers and mothers for we must drive across the lake before the ice got soft and thin. Sometimes people were drowned in the lake by trying to cross to late.

Presently everyone was well but me. There were signs of a thaw so it was decided not to wait any longer.

Pa and Uncle Peter hitched the horses to the big bobsleds and we all got in. I was carried out all rolled up in blankets, even my head covered so I would not take cold. I couldn't see the horses as they took us over the long road to the lake and then across the ice on the lake for a long time. But when we were on the lake I heard the horses feet go 'splash! splash'! in water and I was terrified. I thought we were breaking throug and would all be drowned in the lake under the ice, but Ma put her arm over me,[96] drew me close and said it was all right. It was only a little water on top of the ice, so I went to sleep and waked up when they were putting me to bed in the hotel at Lake City,[97] safely across the lake.

93. *Dolly Varden because she had a pretty dress of calico that was called that.* Dolly Varden is a character from Charles Dickens's novel *Barnaby Rudge*, published in 1841. Dickens described her as "the very pink and pattern of good looks, in a smart little cherry-coloured mantle, with a hood of the same drawn over her head, and upon the top of that hood, a little straw hat trimmed with cherry-coloured ribbons, and worn the merest trifle on one side—just enough in short to make it the wickedest and most provoking head-dress that ever malicious milliner devised" (pp. 41–42). The character of Dolly Varden became the darling of popular culture on both sides of the Atlantic, inspiring songs, dances, paintings, and fashion. Women donned Dolly Varden straw hats and floral-patterned dresses of cotton, silk, and linen. Her influence extended even to the Big Woods of Wisconsin. Ferguson, "Brief History."

94. *We called it making our pictures.* In the juvenile *Pioneer Girl* manuscript, Lane placed this game on Christmas Eve afternoon (JPG, p. 11), where it also appears in *Little House in the Big Woods*. Wilder ended the scene in the novel with a variation of this line, "They called these their pictures" (p. 66).

95. *Scarlet Fever.* In the nineteenth century, scarlet fever was a dreaded and often deadly childhood illness. Charles and Emma Darwin lost two children to it, and some accounts contend that it caused Helen Keller's blindness. It also played a central role in American fiction of the period. In *Little Women*, for example, Beth March contracts the disease and never completely recovers from it. Wilder attributed Mary's blindness to scarlet fever in *By the Shores of Silver Lake*, writing that it "had settled in Mary's eyes, and Mary was blind" (p. 2). Scarlet fever usually begins with a sore throat and fever, followed by chills, body aches, loss of appetite, nausea, and vomiting. Its telltale sign is a rash that spreads from the neck and face, down the chest and back, and eventually to the arms and legs. Sometimes even the tongue becomes inflamed. Scarlet fever is highly contagious but is no longer considered life-threatening, in large part because of the

Washington Street, Lake City, about 1864. *Lake City Historical Society*

development of antibiotics in the twentieth century. In 1873, however, the Ingalls children were fortunate to survive it with so few repercussions. Alcott, *Little Women*, pp. 202–3; Smith, "Scarlet fever"; Nettleman, "Aetiology"; Allexan et al., "Blindness in Walnut Grove," pp. 1–3.

96. *we were breaking throug . . . but Ma put her arm over me.* The fictional Ingalls family's crossing of Lake Pepin is less dramatic, but it contains a significant change. When Pa drives the wagon onto the ice: "Laura didn't like it. But . . . she knew that nothing could hurt her while Pa and Jack were there" (p. 7). The fictional version

reinforces Pa's role as the defender of the family. He and Jack, not Ma, provide reassurance to Laura. Throughout the Little House series, Pa is the dominant influence in Laura's life. Ma, more passive, less direct, always plays second fiddle to Pa.

97. *Lake City.* Platted in 1856, Lake City, Minnesota, had a deep-water grain port when the Ingalls family paused there after crossing Lake Pepin. Brown's Hotel, established in the early 1850s, would have been a possible lodging place for the Ingallses in 1874. *Minnesota Place Names*; "Local History Items."

MAP OF MINNESOTA, 1874~1876

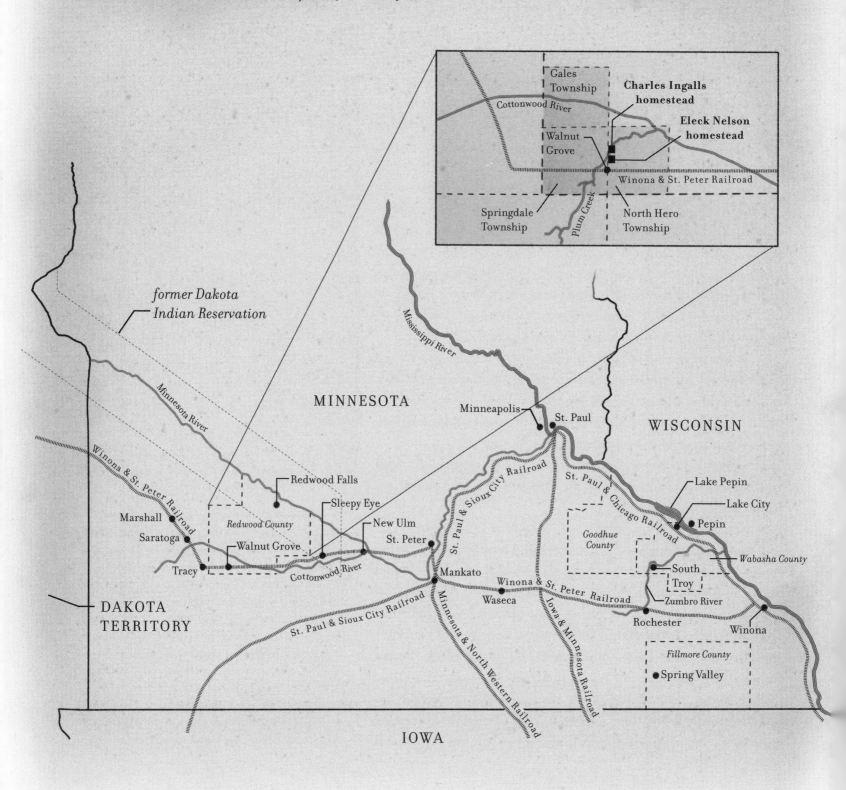

Gales
Township

**Charles Ingalls
homestead**

Cottonwood River

**Eleck Nelson
homestead**

Walnut
Grove

Winona & St. Peter Railroad

Springdale
Township

Plum Creek

North Hero
Township

*former Dakota
Indian Reservation*

Mississippi River

Minnesota River

MINNESOTA

Minneapolis

St. Paul

WISCONSIN

Winona & St. Peter Railroad

Redwood Falls

Sleepy Eye

St. Paul & Sioux City Railroad

St. Paul & Chicago Railroad

Lake Pepin

Lake City

Marshall

New Ulm

St. Peter

*Goodhue
County*

Pepin

Saratoga

Redwood County

Walnut Grove

Cottonwood River

Wabasha County

Tracy

Mankato

South
Troy

DAKOTA
TERRITORY

Winona & St. Peter Railroad

Zumbro River

Waseca

Iowa & Minnesota Railroad

Rochester

Winona

St. Paul & Sioux City Railroad

Minnesota & North Western Railroad

Fillmore County

Spring Valley

IOWA

Minnesota, 1874–1876

The next I knew I waked and Pa was standing by the bed. It was late; the lamps were all lighted and I knew Pa was tired, but he had been out in town and bought me the pretty little book of verses called "The Floweret"[1] for it was another birthday and I was five years old.[2]

After a few days we went on into the country and lived in a house on the bank of a creek,[3] so close to the creek that if we had fallen out of the back window we would have dropped in the water. For the thaw did come[4] and the creek raised as the ice went out. The water went foaming and racing past the house! The cellar filled with water and it ran out through a hole on the other side, when the trap door in the floor was raised we could see and hear it running. The house was on rock so it was safe enough, Pa and Uncle Peter said.

It was fun to watch the water and play with the cousins by the creek. One time we found a big fish in a little pool where the water had washed him, then left him there when it went down a little.

We all plunged into the pool and chased around and around until we caught it, then Alice carried it home in her apron.

Sometimes my ears hurt me so much I couldn't play. Ma and Aunt Eliza said it was because of the scarlet fever, that I must have caught a little cold in the moving.

One morning when my eart [ear hurt] so badly I couldn't keep from crying and Mary and the cousins stood around almost crying from sympathy, Aunt Eliza said if only she had some warm wool fresh from a black sheep to put in my ear and keep the air out, it would cure the ache,[5] but she didn't know how she could get any.

Cousin Ella turned and ran out of the door saying nothing. After some time she came back with both hands full of black sheep's wool. "How!" said Ma and "Where in the world!" said Aunt Eliza.

Ella had seen a black sheep with others in a pasture, so she ran and ran until she found them. She was afraid of the black sheep for he put down his head and stamped his foot at her, but she wanted

The Floweret. Laura Ingalls Wilder Museum

1. "*The Floweret.*" Written by Anna Maria Wells, *The Floweret: A Gift of Love*, first published in 1842, contained a selection of poems for children illustrated with miniature engravings. This poem appears on the title page: "A simple flower to you I bring,—/ In solitude it grew;/Accept the humble offering,—/ I gathered it for you."

2. *I was five years old.* Wilder turned seven on February 7, 1874. Throughout *Pioneer Girl*, Wilder recorded her memories without using dates, marking the passage of time principally in seasons and birthdays rather than years. The fictionalized version of the Ingallses' sojourn in Wisconsin from May of 1871 to February of 1874 compounded the problem:

the action of *Little House in the Big Woods* takes place roughly within one year, combining and compressing Wilder's Wisconsin memories into a single twelve-month cycle of activities. As a result, Wilder and Lane never completely sorted out the early time frame in the various versions of *Pioneer Girl*, but their failure to nail down dates and ages worked to Wilder's advantage when she began the third novel (*Little House on the Prairie*) and had to fit the Kansas years into a fictional time frame. Only when *On the Banks of Plum Creek* opens do Wilder's true age and fiction correspond: "Laura was a big girl, seven years old" (*PC*, p. 6). Wilder, however, remained confused about her exact age. For example, in a letter to Lane with details about the Plum Creek footbridge, Wilder reminded her daughter, "After all I was only six and very busy about my affairs" (LIW to RWL, July 3, [1936], File 19, Wilder Papers).

3. *lived in a house on the bank of a creek*. This house is the second abandoned shelter the Ingalls family occupied during their cross-country treks. They stayed in an empty log house on their way out of Kansas to Wisconsin, as well. One of these houses was the inspiration for the description of the "little log house" among the trees that makes a brief appearance in *Little House on the Prairie* (pp. 7–8).

4. *For the thaw did come*. With these words, Wilder emphasized that the threat of melting ice was real, a point she made to much more dramatic effect in *Little House on the Prairie*. The fictional Laura wakes to the sound of ice breaking on Lake Pepin, "sharper and longer than a shot," and realizes that the family could have "all gone down into the cold water in the middle of that vast lake" (p. 8).

5. *warm wool fresh from a black sheep . . . would cure the ache*. It is a folk tradition, especially among the Irish, that wool "from a black sheep will cure earache" (Bergen, *Animal and Plant Lore*, p. 72).

so much to cure my earache that she ran right at him, grabbed with both hands into his wool, screamed and stood still. The black sheep ran away as fast as he could leaving his black wool in her hands.

Ma put some of it in my ear while I laughed at Ella's story and sure enough my ear stopped aching.

When night came, Mary and I went quickly to sleep in our little bed on the floor. Sometimes we made believe we were in a ship for we could hear the water in the creek running by and the water gurgling in the cellar.

One night Mary lay sleeping beside me,[6] but I lay awake looking through the bedroom door at the firelight flickering and the shadows moving in the room outside. Pa was sitting in the shadows where I couldn't see him, but I could hear his fiddle singing.

It was all so beautiful it made my throat ache. And then I thought again of something I had been trying to forget since we lived in the Big Woods in Uncle Peter's house.

On sunny days, the snow on the roof of that house would melt and dripping off the edge make long icicles. I used to break them down and eat the pieces until Ma said I must not do so any more.

But after that I saw a particularly nice piece—I think I really forgot when I picked it up, but I remembered as I came in the door and put the whole big piece in my mouth to hide it.

Ma suspected for she asked "Laura are you eating ice?" Then I swallowed the whole piece at one gulp to clear my mouth so I could speak and told my first lie. "No-m," I said.

The ice felt awfully cold in my tummy! I was frightened to have been so wicked and ashamed when I saw that Ma believed me, so that I was very quiet until I went to sleep. I thought of it next morning and then forgot.

But this night as I lay watching the firelight and the shadows and everything was still but the murmur of the waters and the fiddle singing, it all came back to me. My heart hurt, because everything was so sweet and lovely but me and I was a liar.

Then my throat filled up so that a big sob popped out of my mouth, and then they kept coming.

The fiddle stopped singing and Ma hurried in to see what was the

6. *One night Mary lay sleeping beside me.* Wilder transformed the experience contained in this paragraph and the eight that follow into the chapter "Strange Animal" (pp. 28–36) in *On the Banks of Plum Creek.* The fictional Laura's transgression is more serious (she had slipped away without permission to go to the swimming hole), but the two scenes are strikingly similar. In both, Laura awakens in the night, and Pa's fiddle playing stirs feelings of guilt and remorse. "Everything was beautiful and good, except Laura," Wilder wrote. "She had broken her promise to Pa. Breaking a promise was as bad as telling a lie" (p. 32). Laura slides out of bed and goes straight to Pa, not Ma. He then provides the stern but wise reprimand that is consistent with the primary role he plays in the fictional Laura's life. This episode from *Pioneer Girl* and its counterpart in *On the Banks of Plum Creek* illustrate the way in which Wilder drew experiences and emotions from her real life and reshaped them to give depth to her fictional character. In the Brandt version of *Pioneer Girl* (p. 25), a big handwritten "x" indicates the decision to cut the scene from subsequent versions.

Peter Ingalls and Eliza Quiner, wedding photograph.
Laura Ingalls Wilder Museum

7. *Uncle Peter's folks moved to a farm he had rented.*
   Peter and Eliza Ingalls settled their family in Wabasha County, Minnesota, along the Zumbro River. Wilder and her family would visit them there in 1876 en route to Burr Oak, Iowa.

8. *David and Sampson (Sam for short).* When the real family left Kansas, Charles Ingalls traded Pet and Patty, along with Jack, for a larger pair of horses—presumably David and Sampson. In *On the Banks of Plum Creek*, however, Pa trades Pet and Patty for the Plum Creek property, which includes a team of oxen—Bright and Pete (pp. 14–15). David and Sam will make their appearance in the novel as the Christmas horses that Laura and Mary find standing in the stable "in Pete's and Bright's places" (p. 94).

9. *I . . . saw the train and the engine.* If Wilder's recollections here are sequential, she probably saw her first train in either Wabasha or Goodhue County. According to an 1874 Minnesota township and railroad map, the St. Paul & Chicago Railroad followed the Missis-

trouble. It was such a comfort to tell her all about it. She smoothed my hair and said of course she would forgive me, because I had told her I was sorry and that now I must say a little prayer and ask God to forgive me too. She told me to say "Dear God please forgive me for telling a lie?" And when I did, Ma said she was sure I would never be so naughty again, then she tucked me in kissed me and went away. The fiddle was singing again as I went to sleep.

When warm weather came Uncle Peter's folks moved to a farm he had rented,[7] but we went west.

The grass along the road was fresh and green in the springtime and it was a delight to camp at night in a little nook somewhere beside the way. Nearly always we stopped by a creek or a small river, where was were plenty of water and sticks to make the campfire.

We'd see the sun go down, hear the birds twitter their sleepy good nights and sleep with David and Sampson (Sam for short)[8] crunching their oats in their feed box at the back of the wagon, with just the thin wagon cover between their heads and ours.

Sometimes Pa would sit awhile by the campfire and play his violin.

We were camped one night in a lovely creek bottom a little way from the road and I had just gone to sleep, when I heard a clear, wonderful call.

"Oh what was that," I said and Ma answered that it was the whistle of a R. R. engine and if I would look quickly I could see the train. I looked and in the twilight saw the train and the engine,[9] the first I'd ever seen. 'I thought it was calling me', I said and Ma laughed.

One day, on the road, we overtook a strange man all alone in a covered wagon. For several days he drove along with us and camped with us at night.

His name was George George.[10] He was pleasant company and we liked his little dog, who rode all day on the wagon seat with him.

As we neared New Ulm[11] we came, one day, to a large, square house, with green grounds around it and a large red, white and blue flag flying above it. Pa said it was a beer garden.[12] Mr George went up to the house and brought back a shining pail filled with beer all

Schell's Brewery in New Ulm, Minn., ca. 1885, including August Schell's pet crane at left. *August Schell Brewing Company, New Ulm, Minn.*

sippi River down the southeastern edge of the state. Other railroad companies that operated in southern Minnesota during this period were the Winona & St. Peter, the Minnesota & North Western, the St. Paul & Sioux City, and the Iowa & Minnesota. This passage received unusual editorial attention from Wilder and Lane. Brandt followed the original closely, but Brandt Revised added: "We were all silent, watching until they were out of sight. Then Pa spoke of the building of railroads across the Great American Desert, and said that we were living in an age of wonderful invention and enterprise" (p. 15). In Bye, the episode became a mini-scene:

> I looked, and in the twilight saw an engine and a train, the first I had ever seen. I held my breath while it went by, the engine puffing and the wheels rattling on the iron rails. One of the cars had lighted windows, and through them I could see people sitting, riding on, through the dark. We were all silent, watching till the train was out of sight.
>
> Then Pa said we were living in a great age. He said that in a day a train covered more distance than an ox-team could travel in a week, and he spoke of railroads conquering the Great American Desert (p. [22]).

The first extended description of a train in Wilder's fiction appears in the chapter "Riding the Cars" (pp. 15–27) in *By the Shores of Silver Lake*.

10. *George George.* It is impossible to identify this traveler with any certainty because Wilder's description provides no traceable details. The 1870 census, however, lists a forty-six-year-old Englishman named George George living in Merton, Minnesota, a town in the southeastern part of the state and in the general vicinity of the Ingallses' route west. Ten years later, this same George George lived in Island Lake, Minnesota, in the southwestern part of the state.

11. *New Ulm.* German immigrants settled New Ulm in south-central Minnesota in the mid-1850s, naming the new settlement for the old city of Ulm on the Danube River in what is now Germany.

12. *it was a beer garden.* In 1860, August Schell and Jacob Bernhardt started the August Schell Brewing Company two miles from New Ulm on the Cottonwood River to serve the nearby community of German immigrants. During its first year, the company produced only two hundred barrels, but the owners had chosen the location well, with a natural spring for fresh water and a river for transport, and the enterprise prospered. Today it is the oldest brewery in Minnesota and is famous for its gardens and grounds. Whether the Ingallses stopped at the brewery itself or at a local outdoor tavern, or German *biergarten*, the beer likely came from Schell's.

13. *we saw some grassy mounds . . . an Indian masacree.* For years, this part of Minnesota had been the hunting grounds of the Santee Dakota, who signed the Treaty of Traverse des Sioux in 1851, ceding the bulk of their lands "in return for annuities and a ten-mile-wide strip of land along each side of the Minnesota River" (Miller, *Becoming*, p. 31). On August 17, 1862, four young Santee Dakota men decided to steal eggs from white farmers in south-central Minnesota; in the process, they killed five settlers. The incident ignited a deadly six-week conflict known by several names, including the Dakota Conflict, the Sioux Outbreak of 1862, and the United States–Dakota War of 1862. Although the Santee people did not unanimously embrace this war, the provocations were many: treaty violations, government agency corruption, drought, and famine. Furthermore, the United States government, preoccupied with funding its war against the Confederacy, had failed to make annuity payments to the Santee. "Had I been an Indian," said Charles E. Flandrau, one of the defenders of New Ulm during the conflict, "I would have rebelled, too" (quoted in Karolevitz, *Challenge*, p. 64). Between four and six hundred white settlers and soldiers were killed during the six-week period; the number of Santee deaths is unknown. Most of the warring Santee surrendered in late September 1862, and thirty-eight American Indian men were publicly hanged on December 26, 1862, an event that remains the largest public execution in American history. The reservation along the Minnesota River was disbanded in 1863, and many of the Santee who surrendered were relocated to the Crow Creek Indian Reservation in Dakota Territory. Some of the fiercest fighting of the conflict had taken place on August 19 and 23, 1862, in New Ulm, when close to two hundred structures were burned or otherwise destroyed. When the Ingalls family passed through the town just twelve years later, these events were still fresh in the collective memory. Minnesota Historical Society, *U.S.–Dakota War*; Fridley, "Charles E. Flandrau," pp. 116–17.

14. *a pretty place . . . Pa said it was ours.* According to the Land Entry Files of the General Land Office,

foamy over the top. It looked cool and good, but Mary and I did not like it because it was bitter.

It was near here we camped for the night and I went with Pa to a near by house to get some milk. The door yard was full of big white geese and they all stretched their long necks at us and said "hiss-s-s-s[."]

They kept hissing at us and crowding close around while the woman was getting the milk. One stretched out his long neck, opened his big yellow bill said hiss and bit me on the leg. I yelled and another one bit me. Then Pa picked me up from among them, took the milk from the woman and went away leaving the geese hissing. West of New Ulm we saw some grassy mounds that Pa said were ruins of houses where Indians had killed the settlers in an Indian masacree[13] years before.

We drove on and on until we came to such a pretty place by the very nicest creek we had seen and were so glad when Pa said it was ours.[14] The creek was named Plum creek[15] because wild plums grew along its banks.

It was a funny little house that we moved into, not much more room than in the wagon, for it had only one room. It was dug in the side of the creek bank near the top.[16] Willows were laid over the top of the hole and grass sods laid on them. Then the grass grew over the roof tall and thick and it looked just like the rest of the creek bank. Once when a herd of cattle came by, a big, old ox couldent tell the difference. He walked right over the top of the house and one foot came down through.[17]

There was a shelf dug in the bank before the door of the house, just wide enough to walk on. From that steps were cut in the bank[18] down to the creek and at the foot of the steps a plank was laid across the creek for a foot bridge.

Mary and I had wonderful times playing in the creek and along its banks, but we couldn't play all the time now.[19] We had to help take care of Carrie and watch her so she wouldn't fall out of the door down into the creek and when the herd boy drove up the herd of neighborhood cattle at night we must go help him drive our cow out from among the others and into her yard.

housed in the National Archives, Charles Ingalls paid two dollars on June 26, 1874, at the federal land office in New Ulm to file a preemption claim on the northwest quarter of Section 18, Township 109, Range 38, Redwood County, Minnesota, roughly two miles north of the town of Walnut Grove in North Hero Township. Ingalls had settled on the land on May 28, 1874. Under the terms of the Preemption Act of 1841, he had to establish residency for six months, make improvements, and pay a per-acre fee for the land (in this case $2.50 per acre because the property was close to a railroad) within thirty-three months of the filing date. Two years later, on June 29, 1876, he would sign an affidavit affirming his eligibility for the land, and on July 7, 1876, Elias Bedal would specify the improvements Ingalls had made: "built a dwelling house on said land 20 × 24 feet square, and 10 feet high, [which] has a good roof and floor, and contains 5 doors and 3 windows, and is a comfortable house for a family to live in." In addition, Ingalls had "plowed and cultivated forty acres of said land, built two stables — one 12 × 20 feet square and the other 12 × 16 feet square, and dug a well" (Cash Entry File, Final Certificate #7410). Ingalls paid $430.18 for the property, which measured slightly over 172 acres, on the same day. Because of a procedural or other error, he would have to file a second affidavit of eligibility later, and the final patent for the land would not be issued until December 30, 1879. By then, however, the Ingalls family had left Minnesota and was living in Dakota Territory. Cash Entry File, Final Certificate #7410; Redwood County, Deed Record Book, no. 5; Cleaveland and Linsenmayer, *Charles Ingalls*, p. 2.

15. *Plum creek*. An early history of Redwood County, Minnesota, described Plum Creek as being one of "numerous creeks of considerable size" that "join the Cottonwood river from the south." It cut through a "rolling, well-watered prairie" with "little timber" (Curtiss-Wedge, *History of Redwood County*, pp. 2, 358). An early settler recalled "only one tree on the prairie, with the exception of the growth along Plum creek, and the natural grove a mile southwest of the present village of Walnut Grove" (ibid., p. 359). Wilder herself described Plum Creek in detail to Lane as the two prepared *On the Banks of Plum Creek* for publication: "The creek was a prairie creek running between grass grown banks, deeper where the banks narrowed and spreading out shallower where the banks set back. The creek water was low in the hot weather" (LIW to RWL, July 3 [1936]). In the novel, Wilder described Plum creek as "rippling and glistening in the sunshine. The willow trees grew up beyond the creek" (p. 3).

16. *It was dug in the side of the creek bank near the top*. Settlers ex-

cavated and built into the sides of hills, slopes, ravines, or creek banks throughout the Great Plains, usually as temporary dwellings until a family could afford a frame house. These dugouts were especially prevalent in locations such as Redwood County, Minnesota, where trees were few and far between and settlers had limited access to milled lumber. Although dugouts were warm in winter and cool in summer, they posed unique problems with lighting, ventilation, flooding, basic housekeeping, and unwelcome intruders such as insects, rodents, and snakes. Wilder devoted an entire chapter to the house in in *On the Banks of Plum Creek* (pp. 8–21). In an editorial letter to Lane in the summer of 1936, Wilder described the setting: "The high bank was a gentle swell and not so terribly high, if you figure the dugout at 8 ft high. . . . it was just high enough for a low ceilinged room probably not more than seven feet from the path before the door to the top of the roof which was smooth with the bank. . . . From the dugout door we looked across the creek and the low bank on the other side to the sweep of prairie beyond" (LIW to RWL, [summer 1936], File 19, Wilder Papers). In another undated letter in the same collection, she added, "Wild morning glory vines would grow on the sod wall of the dugout . . . and bloom in the morning." Despite

Plum Creek, circa 1970. *Laura Ingalls Wilder Memorial Society*

Picture copyright 1953 by Garth Williams, copyright © renewed 1981
by Garth Williams. Used by permission of HarperCollins Publishers

the extensive notes Wilder made, including two diagrams of the Plum Creek property, Lane struggled to understand the prairie landscape surrounding the dugout and continued to pepper her mother with questions. At one point, Wilder wrote, "Get these [Missouri] hills and our gorge out of your mind. The character of the place was altogether different" (ibid.). Finally Lane was able to visualize it and wrote back, "I have the creek all right now" (RWL to LIW, [summer 1936], ibid.). Greiner, "Dugout"; Giezentanner, "In Dugouts and Sod Houses," pp. 140, 143.

17. *one foot came down through.* For *On the Banks of Plum Creek,* Wilder created an entire chapter out of this incident—"Ox on the Roof" (pp. 45–51). It "was funny," Laura reflects, "to live in a house where a steer could step through the roof. It was like being rabbits" (p. 50).

18. *steps were cut in the bank.* In a letter to Lane, Wilder wrote, "I think there were five steps down from the door to the creek" (LIW to RWL, [summer 1936]).

19. *playing in the creek . . . we couldn't play all the time now.* In both Brandt Revised (p. 15) and Bye (p. 23), Wilder explained that Mary and she could not play because they "were old enough to help with the work." She then went on to list their ages incorrectly as eight and "nearly six." In the novel, Wilder devoted a chapter to work and play—"Rushes and Flags" (PC, pp. 18–21).

David and Sam were gone and Pa drove a yoke of cattle, Bright and Broad. Broad was a good ox, but Bright was ugly and would run away whenever he could.

Coming home from town one time, he ran away with while Ma sat in the bottom of the wagon bed and held Carrie tight so they wouldn't be thrown out. Mary and I had been left at home and were sitting on the creek bank near the house watching for them, when they came. Pa was running beside Bright, between him and the creek, beating him over the head with the whip, trying to make him turn so he wouldn't run off the bank and maybe kill Ma and Carrie. Pa couldn't turn him, but good old Broad saw the barnyard and turned toward it pulling bright with him. He stopped by the yard gate so Bright had to stop too[20] and no one was hurt but we were all badly frightened.

Mary and I each had a big flat rock for a play house up on the top of the bank, then down in the creek bottom was a wonderful place to play. There was a perfectly round table land[21] there of about a half acre, Pa said, that rose straight up on the sides about six feet from the lower ground. It was so steep we could not climb straight up but had to go sideways up it. We used to play it was our fort and that Indians were hiding in the willows along the creek.

There had been only a little crop planted in the spring[22] and there was not much work with that but Pa worked hard all summer,[23] making hay, digging a well where he was going to build a new house in the spring and doing the fall breaking for the crop next summer.

We were very snug in the dug out house through the winter which was mild. The winds blew over above our heads and the snow banked deep along the creek but the shelf before our door was easily kept bare.[24] It was a sight to see when the snow melted and the ice went out of the creek in the spring. Yellow water swirled and foamed before our door; the footbridge was covered[25] and our tableland was a little island with deep water all around it.

The water soon went down and Pa could work on the land. When his crops were planted he built the new house[26] and we moved in.

It was a busy summer, with the building and moving the care of the crops, haying and harvesting and all the rest. Mary and I helped

20. *he ran away. . . . so Bright had to stop too.* The Bye manuscript placed Laura at the center of this scene: "I ran as fast as I could along the creek bank, waving my arms and trying to head the oxen. Shouting with all my might, it seemed to me that I did not make a sound" (Bye, p. 23). The chapter "Runaway" (pp. 73–79) in *On the Banks of Plum Creek* fictionalizes this incident. The oxen are named Bright and Pete, and Pa saves the day through sheer force of will.

21. *a perfectly round table land.* Wilder included the tableland in both diagrams of the Plum Creek property that she drew for Lane. In *On the Banks of Plum Creek*, Laura and Mary discover the tableland with Pa. "It really was like a table," Wilder wrote. "That ground rose up high above the tall grasses, and it was round, and flat on top" (p. 27).

22. *only a little crop planted in the spring.* In the years before Charles Ingalls filed his preemption claim, two other men had filed on the land. Neither stayed to prove up, but one of them had probably broken the sod for a small field, and perhaps a squatter or a neighbor had seeded the field on the empty claim in the spring before the Ingalls family took residence. At this point in *Pioneer Girl*, Wilder did not hint at the grasshopper plague to come, but early historical accounts of Redwood County included the summer of 1874 in the agricultural tragedy that hit southwestern Minnesota between 1873 and 1877. The small size of the crop planted on the Plum Creek property that spring may have been a direct response to the previous year's grasshopper infestation. In the novel, Pa puzzled over the size and quality of the field planted by a fictional former owner: "I can't make out why Hanson sowed such a small field. It must have been a dry season, or Hanson's no farmer, his wheat is so thin and light" (p. 6).

23. *Pa worked hard all summer.* Brandt Revised and Bye added a sentence to this paragraph: "He would come in at night white and worn out from struggling with that prairie sod which had never known a plow" (Brandt Revised, p. 16). In *On the Banks of Plum Creek*, Wilder stretched this material over several chapters in which Pa takes a job with a neighbor and begins to make hay from the prairie grasses. An

One of Wilder's Plum Creek property diagrams, ca. 1936. *Laura Ingalls Wilder Historic Home and Museum*

entire chapter is devoted to building a straw stack (pp. 52–60). In the following chapter, Pa plows "all the land across the creek." It "was going to be a very big wheat-field," and once "Pa made a wheat crop," the family "would have a house, and horses, and candy" (pp. 61–62). Wilder not only built tension in this way, she also used the family's aspirations as a central theme. "The wheat is what they are working and waiting for," Wilder explained to Lane. "The Banks of Plum Creek are the stage setting where all these things happen while waiting for the wheat" (LIW to RWL, Aug. 6, 1936, File 19, Wilder Papers).

24. *We were very snug. . . . easily kept bare.* The Bye manuscript divided this paragraph between the seasons. The winter portion ended with a new sentence: "The winds could not penetrate through the warm, deep snow, and the howling of the storms was drowned by the music of Pa's fiddle" (p. 24). In the novel, Wilder used the mild weather to foreshadow the grasshopper plague. As Thanksgiving nears, Pa comments: "I never saw weather like this. Nelson says the old-timers call it grasshopper weather" (p. 66). When there is still no snow at Thanksgiving, Laura thinks "of grasshoppers' long, folded wings and their high-jointed hind legs" (p. 80). Such thoughts reinforce the idea that the weather is unusual and disturbing. Modern scientists suggest that mild fall weather is conducive to a higher survival rate for grasshopper eggs.

Although *On the Banks of Plum Creek* moves smoothly ahead to Christmas and the surprise of new horses, Wilder had struggled to find a path through the novel, primarily because she had decided that the fictional Ingalls family would spend more time along Plum Creek than the real one had. In the novel, the family will spend three Christmases near Walnut Grove rather than two. They will also stay there until they move on to Dakota Territory in *By the Shores of Silver Lake* when Laura is almost thirteen. In reality, the family moved from Walnut Grove to Burr Oak, Iowa, in the fall of 1876 and then back to Walnut Grove in 1877.

Wilder not only had to fictionalize her memories from this period, she had to change and transform their sequence. "I don't know what to do with that first Christmas if we don't have the horses," Wilder wrote to Lane. "There could only be a sameness to those before. And if Laura and Mary do not learn about Santa Clause, what are we going to do with the next Christmas and the Christmas tree and Mr Alden's gifts" (LIW to RWL, [summer 1936]). As this letter indicates, Wilder constructed a totally fictitious first Christmas for the novel and moved the Christmas tree party at the Congregational church in Walnut Grove, which was probably based on an actual event in December 1874, to the fictional family's second winter, toward the end of *On the Banks of Plum Creek*. Wilder then condensed one more year of life along Plum Creek and ended the book with a third Christmas in Minnesota.

25. *yellow water swirled . . . the footbridge was covered.* Wilder combined the imagery of this spring thaw with a later incident to create the chapter called "Spring Freshet" (*PC*, pp. 97–100). On April 15, 1875, the *Redwood Gazette* of Redwood Falls, Minnesota, reported that the "freshet in the various streams in this vicinity" was at last subsiding, but that the water had been higher and more destructive than in previous years.

26. *he built the new house.* In *Pioneer Girl*, the timing suggests that Charles Ingalls built a frame house in 1875, after they had spent roughly a year in the dugout. However, the affidavit that described the actual dimensions of the frame dwelling, twenty by twenty-four feet and ten feet high, claimed that the Ingalls family lived in this house starting on June 26, 1874, the same day that Charles Ingalls filed on the preemption claim. Did the family spend only four weeks in the dugout, or did the affidavit describe the house that the Ingalls family was occupying on July 7, 1876, the date the affidavit was signed, and omit the time spent in the dugout? As described, the house had five doors and three windows. In *On the Banks of Plum Creek*, Wilder devoted two chapters to this change

all we could, running errands, washing dishes, driving the cows to and from the herd and watching over Carrie.

Soon it was winter again and, it was a terrible winter.[27] There was blizzard after blizzard when the wind blew the snow in such whirling fury tha[t] one could not see into it at all nor tell where he was going. We learned that a dark cloud lying close to the horizon in the north west meant that a blizzard was coming and that it moved so swiftly it would be on us soon, sometimes in only a few minutes.

In one of these storms two balls of fire rolled down the stovepipe, onto the floor. We were frightened thinking the house would burn, but the balls though they looked like fire didn't burn anything. They would follow Ma's knitting needle around the floor and soon seemed to melt away and disappeared. Pa said they were electricity.[28]

Pa fastened one end of a long rope[29] to the corner of the house nearest the barn; the other end he fastened at the barn door. In a blizzard he would go from house to barn with one hand on the rope to keep from getting lost. As soon as he saw the cloud in the west, he would hurry to the barn to feed the stock and make everything snug against the storm. Usually he came back to the house with his hand on the rope. People froze to death, in blizzards, within a few feet of their own houses, not able to find them.

One man got lost and wandered[30] until he was tired out. Then he took shelter under the creek bank and the snow drifted over him while he went to sleep. They found him in the spring when the snow went off.

On a nice pleasant day Pa and Ma left us girls at home, comfortably in the house, while they walked to town to do some trading. We enjoyed being by ourselves for awhile, but after we had played for some time and eaten our lunch, the time seemed long and we wished Pa and Ma would come. Watching for them we saw the long, low cloud in the west and watched it climb up toward the sun, while there still was no sign of Pa and Ma.

Then we remembered a tale of some children freezing to death in the house, while their parents were away, because they had no fire.

There was a big pile of wood a little way outside our door and we

in the family's fortunes: "The Wonderful House" (pp. 107–17) and "Moving In" (pp. 118–24). Pa buys the materials for the house on credit (p. 109) and selects "boughten doors" (p. 113) and a "shiny-black cookstove" (p. 114) for Ma. These luxuries contribute to the tension later in the novel when the fictional family faces financial disaster after grasshoppers descend right before harvest.

27. *a terrible winter.* Because this paragraph appears after the reference to the house that Charles Ingalls built in the summer of 1875, the "terrible winter" should have been the winter of 1875–1876, but many of the incidents Wilder described in subsequent pages of *Pioneer Girl* appear to be out of sequence, so this winter or parts of it could be, too. Wilder wrote to Lane when they were working on revisions for *On the Banks of Plum Creek,* "What I remember is of course only a series of pictures" (LIW to RWL, July 3, [1936]). Neither the winter of 1874–1875 or 1875–1876 lingered in the collective memory of other Redwood County citizens as particularly hard, but a close reading of the *Redwood Gazette* from 1874 to the fall of 1876 reveals that the worst winter weather in this period occurred from January through March of 1875. After a mild November and December 1874, the temperature plunged to 26 degrees below zero on the fifth of January. Deaths during blizzards began to occur late in the month, and on February 18, the editor reported, "Storms occur about often enough to make suspension of trains west of New Ulm a settled thing." In contrast, the same newspaper noted a year later, on April 6, 1876, that the Winona & St. Peter Railroad "has not been blockaded this winter and that has added greatly to [people's] comfort and convenience." In any case, Wilder constructed most of the episodes for the third and fictional Minnesota winter in *On the Banks of Plum Creek* (pp. 282–339) from the few sketchy details in this section of *Pioneer Girl.*

28. *two balls of fire rolled down the stovepipe. . . . Pa said they were electricity.* The Brandt manuscript added details: the balls of fire followed Ma's knitting needle and "seemed to be playing like kittens." After Pa's explanation, a new paragraph continued: "Mary

and I had never heard of electricity before. But Pa told us that it was everywhere—like God, I thought; that it was the lightning and that it was the crackling in a cat's fur when you stroked it" (p. 28). In *On the Banks of Plum Creek*, Wilder placed the incident within the chapter "The Long Blizzard" (pp. 299–312). Pa has gone to town when a blizzard strikes. The stovepipe rattles, and a ball "bigger than Ma's big ball of yarn" rolls across the stove and drops to the floor. It follows Ma's knitting needles as another and another ball of fire descend. They soon disappear, and Ma says, "That is the strangest thing I ever saw" (pp. 309–10). For centuries, people have described ball lightning, from the small size Wilder described to much larger examples, but the scientific community offers little explanation for or verification of the phenomenon. Handwerk, "Ball Lightning."

29. *Pa fastened one end of a long rope.* Wilder modified a few details and built a scene around this rope and Pa's chores for the chapter "Prairie Winter" (*PC*, pp. 293–98). Later when Pa is away, the rope guides Ma to the stable during a blizzard as she struggles to do the chores alone (*PC*, pp. 304–8).

30. *One man got lost and wandered.* In Wilder's original depiction of this episode, the man, found in an unspecified location, was unknown to the family. The paragraph simply illustrated the dangers of prairie blizzards. In Brandt, Brandt Revised, and Bye, the man became a neighbor, and in Bye, his body was found near the Ingallses' barn (p. 25). In *On the Banks of Plum Creek*, Pa himself gets lost on his way home from town during the final, long blizzard and shelters in a snow den. After the storm, he digs himself out, only to realize that he was "on the bank of Plum Creek" (p. 333) within sight of home all along. The family celebrates his return—on Christmas Eve—and the novel ends.

decided we wouldn't freeze even if Pa and Ma couldn't get home. So we carried in the wood armload after armload and piled it on the floor around the stove.

Just as the first gust of wind from the blizzard hit us and the snow whirled in our faces we were carrying in the last armfulls of wood. And Oh Joy! Pa and Ma burst out of the storm and in at the door with us. They were all out of breath for they had run most of the way home, trying to beat the storm.

"You are good girls," Pa said, "I wont have to carry in the wood,"[31] then he hurried to the stable to care for the stock. After a while he came back with his hand on the rope and we sat by the fire all snug and warm, while the wind howled and howled and the snow blew outside.

When Christmas came, there was a Christmas tree in the church in town. Walnut Grove[32] was only a tiny town, with two small stores, a blacksmith shop a little school house and a few houses[33] where people lived, but the summer before they had built a church.[34] There was Sunday school every sunday and a sermon preached by the Home Missionary Rev. Alden.[35]

We loved to go to Sunday school. Our teacher, Mrs Tower,[36] would gather us close around her and tell us Bible stories and every Sunday she taught us a verse from the Bible that we must remember and tell her the next.

Ma would get books from the Sunday school library to read to us through the week. There was one book that we asked her to get again and again, until we nearly knew it by heart. We did learn to repeat from it one whole poem which began, —

"Twenty froggies went to school[37]
Down beside a rushy pool.
Twenty little coats of green
Twenty vests all white and clean."

— — — — — — —

"Master Bullfrog grave and stern,
Taught the classes in their turn
Showed them how to leap and dive

31. *Pa said, "I wont have to carry in the wood."* The Bye version added: "He and Ma burst out laughing so heartily that in a minute we, too, began to laugh and laughed till we almost cried. We had carried the whole woodpile into the house!" (pp. 25–26).

32. *Walnut Grove.* Walnut Grove, Minnesota, was platted in April 1874, shortly before the Ingalls family arrived, and was incorporated in 1879. Because the town straddles two townships in Redwood County, its settlement history has more than one narrative. It took its name from a naturally occurring grove of black walnuts in Springdale Township, in which a settler named Frink or Burns (accounts disagree) built a cabin in about 1860 but abandoned it during the United States–Dakota War in 1862. Primarily because of this conflict and the fact that the Indian reservation sliced across part of Redwood County, settlement came slowly to the area. In 1866, Joseph Steves built a new house in the grove over Frink's or Burns's old cellar, but other families did not arrive until 1871. The eastern part of the town of Walnut Grove is in North Hero Township, where Charles Ingalls purchased his property (two miles north). Eleck C. Nelson, the family's closest neighbor, had been the region's first settler, arriving in 1870 or 1871. The Winona & Saint Peter Railroad, an offshoot of the Chicago & North Western,

Walnut Grove, 1880. *Laura Ingalls Wilder Museum*

arrived in 1873, and, in the beginning, the settlement was called Walnut Station. Elias Bedal erected the first building on the site of present-day Walnut Grove in 1873, and Gustave Sunwall and J. H. Anderson established the first store that same year. The grasshopper scourge, however, slowed the settlement's growth, and blizzards gave the region a bad name. Moreover, the rapid settlement of eastern Dakota Territory, known as the Great Dakota Boom, which began in 1878, caused settlers to bypass the area. Howe, *Half Century*, pp. 3–4; Neill, *History of Minnesota Valley*, pp. 781–82.

33. *a tiny town, with two small stores, . . . and a few houses*. When working on revisions with Lane for *On the Banks of Plum Creek*, Wilder sketched a diagram of Walnut Grove. It included the railroad, post office, blacksmith shop, Oleson and Fitch stores, church, schoolhouse, and two houses—the Ensign and Anderson homes. A dotted line labeled "path" runs diagonally from a line marked "our road" to the schoolhouse. "Just a little wide place beside the tracks," Wilder said of the town in the paragraph below the diagram. "We came in on our road [from the north], passed in front of Fitches store on main street, then took the path to the schoolhouse" (LIW to RWL, [summer 1936], File 19, Wilder Papers). In another undated note to Lane in the summer of 1936, Wilder wrote, "There were no sidewalks in town, [j]ust the dusty road between the two stores and the ground trampled in front of them" (ibid.).

Wilder's diagram of Walnut Grove, ca. 1936.
Laura Ingalls Wilder Historic Home and Museum

34. *they had built a church*. In the summer of 1874, fourteen citizens of Walnut Grove, including Charles and Caroline Ingalls, formed the "Union Congregation society," which met in the home of James Kennedy until a frame church could be completed.

The congregation dedicated the Union Congregational Church of Christ, the first in town, on December 20, 1874. It had cost roughly two thousand dollars to build and was "the only church of any pretentions between Sleepy Eye lake and the Pacific ocean" (F. Ensign to the Editor, RG, Dec. 31, 1874). Charles P. Ingalls was an elected trustee in 1874 and 1875. Congregational Conference of Minnesota Papers, Box 5, vol. 10, pp. 16, 125, 141, 143 (hereafter cited as Congregational Papers).

35. *Rev. Alden*. In 1864, Edwin H. Alden was ordained by the American Missionary Association, an interdenominational Protestant organization that founded hundreds of schools for freedmen, and was assigned to manage a freedman school in New Orleans. According to the 1860 census, he had already been in the South, working as a teacher and living in Irwinton, Georgia. Alden, who had been born in Vermont in 1836, attended Dartmouth College and the Bangor Theological Seminary in Maine. After the Civil War, he returned to Vermont, where he served as a minister in Turnbridge before accepting an assignment with the American Home Missionary Society to help establish churches in Minnesota. By 1870, he lived about a hundred miles east of Wal-

Reverend Edwin H. Alden. *Laura Ingalls Wilder Museum*

nut Grove in Waseca, Minnesota, with his wife, Anna, and their three-year-old son, George. The Reverend Alden followed the railroad line west from Waseca, regularly preaching in New Ulm, Sleepy Eye, Barnston, Walnut Grove, Saratoga, and Marshall. In her novel, Wilder explained: "Three or four Sundays they went to Sunday school, and then again the Reverend Alden was there, and that was a church Sunday. . . . This was his home missionary church, in the West" (p. 188). Alden was thirty-eight years old when the Ingalls family first met him in Walnut Grove. Zochert, *Laura*, pp. 74, 83; Calloway, *Indian History*, p. 110; "Historical Note"; Miller, *Becoming*, p. 34.

36. *Mrs Tower.* Julia Tower, Wilder's Sunday school teacher, was born in Vermont in about 1842 and married New York native Amasa Tower. By 1875, the couple had moved to Springdale Township, just west of Walnut Grove. Amasa Tower was elected Redwood County treasurer on the "People's County Ticket" that fall. Charles P. Ingalls had served as North Hero Township delegate at the party's nominating convention in October. The Towers eventually moved to Dakota Territory, where Amasa was struck and killed by lightning in 1885. Church records indicated that Mrs. Tower then "drowned in a well during an attack of insanity" (Congregational Papers, p. 17), but a Julia Tower, widow of Amasa, was living in Grand Rapids, Michigan, as late as 1914, so perhaps her story was not as tragic after all. "Lamberton" and "The Election," *RG*, Oct. 21, Nov. 4, 1875.

37. *"Twenty froggies went to school.* The book that Wilder's mother checked out could have been a bound copy of *The Nursery: A Monthly Magazine for Youngest Readers*, vol. 16 (Boston: John L. Shorey, 1874). "Frogs at School," by poet George Cooper (1840–1927), appears on page 101. A hit with schoolchildren like the Ingalls girls, the poem was reprinted in anthologies through the 1920s and was set to music in 1993. The verses Wilder remembered are shortened versions of the first two (of three) verses printed in *The Nursery*.

"The little fur cape and muff still hung on the tree."
Helen Sewell, 1937

38. *the Christmas tree, the first we had ever seen.* This three-paragraph memory of the Christmas tree, which Wilder added on the back of a page almost as an afterthought, is possibly out of sequence. The dedication of the Union Congregational Church took place on December 20, 1874, which is when the Christmas celebration that Wilder remembered as her first probably took place. That occasion featured many representatives from the eastern congregations who had helped to fund the church, and the tree would have been well festooned with presents. However, the Christmas tree became an annual event during Wilder's time in Walnut Grove, and she could have remembered a later occasion. For an account of later trees, *see* "Walnut Station Items," *RG*, Jan. 2, 1879. In *On the Banks of Plum Creek*, the novelist added another layer to the Christmas tree

Taught them how to nobly strive
Likewise how to dodge the blow
From the stick which bad boys throw."

We went to Sunday School and church every pleasant sunday and so we went to the Christmas tree, the first we had ever seen.[38]

It was a beautiful tree, all decorated with colored paper and little bags of candy and candles.

People had given each other presents of things that were needed. There was a washboard on that tree; and new shoes and boots and mittens an[d] calico for dresses and shirts, besides dolls and hand-sleds. Some church in the east had sent a barrel of toys and clothing to our sunday-school and my present from this barrel was a little fur collar or tippet, to keep my throat warm. I was so pleased I could hardly speak and just managed to say 'Thank You' to Rev. Alden when Ma told me to.

Pa had trapped some along the creek in the fall and soon after Christmas he took the furs to town to sell. He was going to get him some new boots because his old ones had holes in them, but when he came back there were no new boots. Ma asked him about them and he said they were trying to get money enough to buy a bell for the church and he had given Rev. Alden his boot money[39] to help. Ma looked so sorry and said "Oh Charles!" But Pa said, he could mend his old boots and they would do.

We were glad when the long cold winter was over and the grass grew green and wild flowers bloomed.

Pa was so busy breaking ground and sowing grain that he did not have time to go fishing, so he made a fish trap of lath and put it in the creek. The lath were fastened together like a box but were far enough apart to let all the smaller fish go through, but the big fish would go in at the top and couldn't go on through. Pa never took more than a few to eat and would let the others go.[40] He said there were so many fish in the creek, it was all right to take some, but it was wicked to kill anything one didn't need.

Ma and I, walking by the creek one day, saw a gray animal[41] as large as a small dog lying in the grass. Its legs were short and it lay

story. During the fall, Laura's fictional rival Nellie Oleson flaunts a beautiful fur cape that Laura covets, and when Laura sees a "little fur cape, and a muff to match" hanging on the Christmas tree, she thinks it is "the most wonderful thing of all" (p. 252). As in *Pioneer Girl*, she is all but speechless when the coveted gift becomes hers. Ensign to the Editor, *RG*, Dec. 31, 1874.

39. *he had given Rev. Alden his boot money.* Congregational church documents record that on November 28, 1874 or 1875, Charles Ingalls gave the treasurer $26.15, a sizable sum for the period. However, it is probable that the amount represented the combined contributions of church members rather than his personal donation. As a church trustee, Ingalls was responsible for holding church property and superintending "the raising of the minister's salary" (Congregational Papers, pp. 135, 144). In *On the Banks of Plum Creek*, Pa contributes just three dollars to the church bell fund, but even that amount is a sacrifice. Within the context of the novel, his contribution reinforces the family's financial hardships and illustrates their longing to be out of debt after Pa harvests the wheat.

40. *so he made a fish trap. . . . would let the others go.* Wilder placed the fish trap along the creek between the tableland and the dugout in one of the two diagrams of the Plum Creek property that she created for Lane while working on revisions to *On the Banks of Plum Creek* (LIW to RWL, [summer 1936]). This memory has been cut from Brandt Revised and Bye, but in the novel, Wilder created an entire chapter called "The Fish-Trap" (pp. 133–39), weaving the device into the unfolding story. Dreading her first day of school, Laura finds Pa building the fish trap, "a long, narrow box without a top, and Pa left wide cracks between the strips of wood" (p. 134). After they place it in the creek, Pa stresses the importance of education. "That's why we stopped here," he explains, "so close to a town that has a school" (p. 138). The conversation advances the plot, and the chapter reveals that Pa never takes more fish than the family needs (p. 139), a character trait lifted directly from *Pioneer Girl*. The chapter also reinforces the unifying theme of the novel, for when Ma praises Pa for being a good provider, he replies: "Wait till I harvest that wheat! . . . Then we'll have salt pork every day. Yes, by gravy, and fresh beef!" (p. 139).

41. *saw a gray animal.* This episode only appears in the Brandt manu-

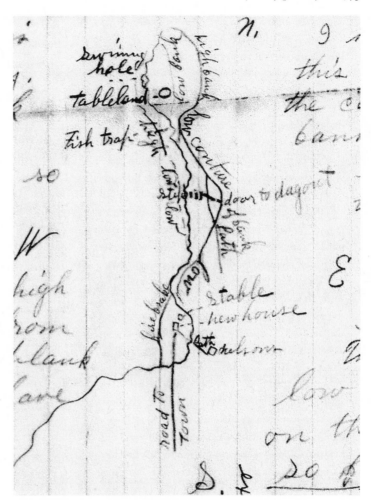

Wilder's second diagram of the Plum Creek property, ca. 1936.
Laura Ingalls Wilder Historic Home and Museum

script (p. 30), where a line slices through it, indicating the cut from subsequent drafts. Wilder used this material in "Strange Animal" (pp. 28–36), a chapter toward the beginning of *On the Banks of Plum Creek*. The American badger, *Taxidea taxus*, is a member of the weasel family. It is about two to three feet long, short-legged, and usually nocturnal, although it can be active in the daytime in quiet settings and is fiercely territorial. Its short stature and broad width give it a flattened look. "American Badger."

42. *the pocket gopher. . . . a great pest, carrying off grain and potatoes.* In Bye, Wilder observed: "We planted the potatoes again and again, and killed as many gophers as we could. But we did not hope for much of a potato crop" (p. 28). Wilder did not include this episode in *On the Banks of Plum Creek*, where the emphasis is entirely on the wheat, but rodents of this type were a bane to early farmers. When settlers began to plant new crops in areas not previously cultivated, pests such as gophers thrived on the increased food supply. Minnesota is home to two types of pocket gopher, the rare northern pocket gopher, *Thomomys talpoides*, and the common plains pocket gopher, *Geomys bursarius*. They are named for their fur-lined, food-carrying cheek pouches. The creatures dig, burrow, mound, and tunnel through fields and gardens, wreaking havoc along the way. The animal continues to be a garden pest in the twenty-first century. "Northern Pocket Gopher"; "Pocket Gophers"; "Gopher Removal."

43. *Mr & Mrs Nelson.* In 1870 or 1871 (historical accounts disagree), Eleck C. Nelson was the first settler to arrive in North Hero Township. When the Minnesota state census was taken in Redwood County in 1875, Eleck was twenty-eight years old; his wife Olena was twenty-four; and they had two daughters, Anna and Mary. Both adults had emigrated from Norway. By 1885, they had six children. Eventually the Nelsons moved into Walnut

Eleck C. Nelson and family. *Laura Ingalls Wilder Museum*

very flat to the ground on its stomache. We were all surprised. We looked at it and it looked at us, lying very still until Ma poked at it with a stick to drive it away. Then it snarled fiercely at us, its gray, stiff hairs bristled and it came toward us a little.

We went away and left it there. Pa said it must have been a badger. Later he found his hole, near where we had seen him. But I never went again, where the old, gray badger lived.

There were mounds of fine dirt, as large as a half bushel scattered here and there in the grass where Pa had planted potatoes. He didn't know what made them. I was with him finishing the planting when we saw a small gray animal running along the plowing as though it were carrying something heavy. Pa hit it with a clod of dirt just as it was going into a hole in the ground. He killed it and we saw that it had a pouch of skin on each cheek and in each pouch was a piece of potatoe Pa had planted.

Pa dug along the hole and found that it was a runway leading to one of the mounds of dirt. Several such runways came in under the mound and there he found a pile of his seed potatoes that the pocket gopher had dug and carried there in the pockets in its cheeks. Mr Nelson told us what it was and that it was a great pest, carrying off grain and potatoes[42] from the fields and ruining meadows with its mounds. When it dug its holes it carried the dirt in its pockets and pushed it up to make the mounds.

Mr & Mrs Nelson,[43] our nearest neighbors, had a little girl named Anna. Once when they were at our house Anna wanted Roxy my rag doll.[44] Roxy was old but I had kept her so carefully that she was still nice and I thought her beautiful, with her curled black yarn hair, her red mouth and her black bead eyes. When Anna cried for her, Ma said I was getting to be too big a girl to play with dolls and she thought I would better give Roxey to Anna.

I didn't want to let my doll go, but when Anna left she took Roxey with her and the very next time I went to Mrs Nelsons I saw her lying face down in a mud puddle in the door yard.

I often went to Mrs Nelson's, not to play with Anna, she was too little, but to be with Mrs Nelson. She taught me to milk[45] her big, old, gentle cow, the only one who would stand still and let me try,

Grove, where Eleck served on the town council. Olena died in 1921; Eleck died ten years later. In *On the Banks of Plum Creek*, the Nelsons live just half a mile down the creek from the Ingallses' dugout. The fictional Nelsons prove to be good neighbors, providing work for Pa and helping him build the frame house (p. 109). When Mr. Nelson helps put out a prairie fire while Pa is away, Ma says, "There is nothing in the world so good as good neighbors" (p. 275). The real Eleck and Olena Nelson, as *Pioneer Girl* indicates, played an even more crucial role in the daily lives of Wilder and her family during their years along Plum Creek. Without the Nelsons, the Ingalls family's struggle against grasshoppers, prairie fire, debt, and illness would have been even more daunting. Curtiss-Wedge, *History of Redwood County*, p. 360; Neill, *History of Minnesota Valley*, p. 781.

44. *Anna wanted Roxy my rag doll*. Anna Nelson was just two years old in May 1875, when she was listed on the Minnesota state census. Her fictional counterpart "talked Norwegian. It was no fun to play with her" (*PC*, p. 229). In this original *Pioneer Girl* manu-script, Wilder spelled her doll's name as both Roxy and Roxey. She used Roxy in Brandt (p. 31) and Bye (p. 28); Brandt Revised excluded the episode. In the novels, the fictional Laura names her doll Charlotte. In the chapter "The Darkest Hour Is Just Before Dawn" (*PC*, pp. 228-39), this story has a happy ending. After Laura finds the discarded doll, Ma repairs her "as good as new" (p. 236). The added details and emotional depth make the chapter one of the most memorable in *On the Banks of Plum Creek*. It illustrates Wilder's mastery of using concrete details to pull readers into a scene to share her characters' experiences.

45. *Mrs Nelson. . . . taught me to milk*. Wilder made significant changes to a similar episode in *On the Banks of Plum Creek*. Pa gets a cow from the Nelsons and pays for it by "haying and harvesting" (p. 41). The Ingalls name her Wreath of Roses, which is also the name for the chapter (pp. 37-44). Laura instantly begins to milk the cow because "she had watched Pa do it" (p. 42). Pa—and not Mrs. Nelson—is Laura's fictional mentor.

46. *Mrs Nelson was Swede*. Olena Nelson was Norwegian, not Swedish, a fact that Wilder noted a few paragraphs later in *Pioneer Girl* when she wrote that Mrs. Nelson forgot "her Norwegion speech in her excitement." In *On the Banks of Plum Creek*, Wilder described the fictional Mrs. Nelson as "plump and pretty," with golden hair (p. 229).

47. *whipoorwill's song!*" "The Whip-Poor-Will's Song" dates from 1865, with words and music by Harrison Millard. This Fourth of July outing does not appear in *On the Banks of Plum Creek*, but Wilder quoted from the song's lyrics in *Little Town on the Prairie* (p. 136). The editor of the *Redwood Gazette* announced on June 22, 1876, "The Walnut Station people are making arrangements for a grand Celeb[ra]tion at that place on the 4th. . . . Toasts, Speeches and Music are all liberally provided for." Cockrell, *Ingalls Wilder Family Songbook*, p. 393.

48. *I heard Pa tell Ma. . . . I wondered why they had run away.* The climax of this story—an elopement and possibly an illicit love affair—targeted an adult audience. But the last line, which appears in all adult versions of *Pioneer Girl*, is written from a child's point of view. It underscores the innocence Wilder—and by extension, her audience—had once possessed. It provides a touch of humor but also a sense of longing for something lost. In the Brandt manuscript, a handwritten line appears under the words "together" and "I wondered why."

until she got tired of my fooling, when she would push me over carefully with her foot not hurting me a bit. Ma was so surprised when I ran out ahead of her to our barn yard and milked my tin cup full from our own, old, spotted cow before she got there.

Mrs Nelson was Swede[46] and she taught me Swede words. I was with her so much that Pa said I talked English like a Swede and I could easily understand when Mrs Nelson talked her language with the other Swede neighbors.

Mrs Nelson was very clean about her house. She kept everything scrubbed and shining and pink misqueto bar over the pictures on the wall to keep the flys from specking them.

But when she milked the cows she would set a full bucket of milk down on the ground and let the cats drink out of it. When I drove them away, she said let them be, the poor cats wanted their milk.

When the 4th of July came we went to the picnic at Walnut Grove. Mary and I had never been to a 4th of July celebration and we were excited about it all. Ma packed fried chicken, bread and butter, cake and a lemon pie in our basket and all dressed up in our best we rode in the wagon to the picnic grounds. A platform had been made of rough lumber and board seats fixed around it. I got tired sitting still while a man read out of a book and other men talked, but I liked the singing. Several men and women on the platform led while everyone sang "The Star Spangled Banner" and other songs. Then a man and woman sang by themselves. She was very pretty, dressed all in white, and he was nice looking. They looked at each other while they sang "Then meet me, Oh meet me, when you hear the first whipoorwill's song!"[47] His voice was deep and tender and hers was clear and sweet. When he sang "Whipoorwill" and she answered "Whipoorwill," it was just like birds calling to each other.

After the speaking and singing a big cloth was spread on the grass, the dinner baskets were emptied onto it and we all sat around on the grass and ate. Then everyone visited until time to go home. Several days afterward I heard Pa tell Ma that the man and woman who sang the Whipoorwill song had run away together. I wondered why they had run away[48] and what from.

The weather was just right and the crops grew and grew. At dinner one day, Pa was telling us that the wheat in our field was so tall[49] it would just stand under his arms, with long, beautiful heads and filling nicely. He said the grain was all soft and milky yet but was so well grown he felt sure we would have a wonderful crop.

Just then we heard some one call and Mrs Nelson was in the doorway.[50] She was all out of breath with running, wringing her hands and almost crying. "The grasshoppers are coming! The grasshoppers are coming!" she shrieked. "Come and look!"

We all ran to the door and looked around. Now and then a grasshopper dropped on the ground, but we couldn't see anything to be so excited about. [erasures]

"Look at the sun! Yoost look at the sun!" cried Mrs Nelson, pointing to the sky.

We raised our faces and looked straight into the sun. It had been shining brightly but now there was a light colored, fleecy cloud over its face so it did not hurt our eyes.

And then we saw that the cloud was grasshoppers,[51] their wings a shiny white making a screen between us and the sun. They were dropping to the ground like hail in a hailstorm faster and faster. "Ta will ruin ta crops, alretty ta eat ta wheat!" wailed Mrs Nelson forgetting her Norwegion speech in her excitment.

Our dinner was forgotten, Mrs Nelson ran home sobbing. Pa put on his hat and went out toward his beautiful wheat field while Ma stood in the door and watched the cloud of grasshoppers settling on the land.

Pa tried to save his wheat.[52] He hauled straw and manure and put it in piles around and through the field, then set it on fire, hoping that the smoke might keep the grasshoppers away. He worked all the rest of the day and all night, but the grasshoppers paid no attention to the smoke. They ate throught the stems of the tall wheat as well as the heads of grain so that it all fell down and was eaten and destroyed. They ate every green thing, the garden, the grass, the leaves on the trees. Our chickens ate grasshoppers[53] until they would eat no more. The fish in the creek ate all they could hold. Everywhere we stepped we mashed grasshoppers and they crawled up under our skirts and down the backs of our necks.

49. *the crops grew and grew. . . . Pa was telling us that the wheat . . . was so tall.* In Brandt (p. 32), Brandt Revised (p. 21), and Bye (p. 30), "the crops grew wonderfully." The new phrase lacks the original's simple, childlike rhythm. The adverb "wonderfully" is a weak substitute for the active verb "grew," which Wilder repeated for emphasis. In a parallel passage in *On the Banks of Plum Creek*, Wilder returned to her more direct and childlike style: "Now the wheat was almost ready to cut. Every day Pa looked at it. Every night he talked about it" (p. 192). All adult *Pioneer Girl* manuscripts also include Pa's enthusiasm at the table. The whole family knew what a good wheat crop meant: "Everything would be easier now. We did not think of clothes and food, exactly. It was more a feeling we had, that everything was larger, and easier, and that it was a good world" (Bye, p. 30). In *On the Banks of Plum Creek*, the fictional family also gathers around the dinner table to talk about the "greeny-gold" wheat field (p. 193).

50. *Mrs Nelson was in the doorway.* In the *Pioneer Girl* manuscripts, it was always Mrs. Nelson who warned the Ingalls family about the grasshoppers, perhaps because she had seen them arrive in this way before. In the Brandt manuscript, Lane's handwritten edits change the dialect slightly, attempting to convey more of Mrs. Nelson's Norwegian accent: "'Ta grashoopers coom! Ta grashoopers coom!'" (p. 33). In contrast, the scene in *On the Banks of Plum Creek* focuses exclusively on the Ingalls family and Laura's premonition as the light turned "queer. . . . Laura was frightened, she did not know why" (pp. 193–94). By centering this episode entirely on the family and presenting the action from Laura's point of view, Wilder gave the scene a mythic quality.

51. *fleecy cloud. . . . the cloud was grasshoppers.* An early historian of Redwood County wrote, "The deepest cause of discouragement and delay in the settlement of the county was the visit of the Rocky mountain locusts, lasting from 1873 to 1877, during which time very little was harvested" (Curtiss-Wedge, *History of Redwood County*, p. 568). Like *Pioneer Girl*, this early account used the phrase "fleecy cloud . . . between the observer and the sun" to describe how the

hordes of grasshoppers looked against the horizon (p. 569). Rocky Mountain locusts, *Melanoplus spretus*, descended on some counties of southwestern Minnesota in June 1873, devouring crops and laying their eggs for the following season. The eggs hatched in 1874, "just in time for the young hoppers to move into the wheat fields, when the tender blades were two or three inches high" (ibid., pp. 568–69). There is, however, disagreement about exactly when the grasshoppers arrived in Redwood County, with some accounts saying 1873 and some 1874. The Ingallses arrived in May 1874, so it is hard to imagine that the family escaped at least a brush with grasshoppers that first year, although the seven-year-old Wilder may not have noticed. Charles Ingalls must have known that the area had been stricken; farmers throughout the region were suffering. In a letter written to the governor of Minnesota in July 1874, a landholder in a county to the southeast wrote, "our crops has now ben [*sic*] destroyed two year in succession and we can see nothing but starvation in the future" (quoted in Fite, "Some Farmers' Accounts," p. 207). Perhaps Wilder's father thought the odds were in his family's favor: who could have foreseen a four-year run of locusts? For example, the *Redwood Gazette* opined that the locusts "have never been known to breed in their new found home beyond the second generation" (July 16, 1874). Everyone hoped the scourge had passed by 1875, and with high hopes, farmers planted crops in North Hero and surrounding townships that spring. On August 12, however, the editor of the *Gazette* reported that things looked bad for the southern part of the county. During the flight of grasshoppers from four "counties to the south west, several squads of them lit and remained long enough to do serious damage. In the lower tier of Towns, through which the Winona & St. Peter rail road passes, the oats crop is just about destroyed, and wheat is not more than half a crop." The Rocky Mountain locust, North America's only swarming grasshopper, is now considered extinct. Its last official sighting was in 1902. Entomologists are not certain why the species disappeared, but some scientists hypothesize that farming itself obliterated the pest by transforming its original habitat. *See* Yoon, "Looking Back."

52. *Pa tried to save his wheat*. The Bye text reads, "We worked all day until after dark, and Pa kept on working all night," implying that the entire family tried to save the wheat. In *On the Banks of Plum Creek*, Laura, Mary, and Carrie remain in the house while Ma works alongside Pa, lighting "little piles of stuff" afire to smoke away the descending grasshoppers (p. 197).

53. *Our chickens ate grasshoppers*. In *On the Banks of Plum Creek*, Wilder created a vivid scene from this brief memory:

> The hens were funny. The two hens and their gawky pullets were eating grasshoppers with all their might. They were used to stretching their necks out low and running fast after grasshoppers and not catching them.
>
> Every time they stretched out now, they got a grasshopper right then. They were surprised. They kept stretching out their necks and trying to turn in all directions at once" (pp. 198–99).

By the summer of 1936 when she was revising this section of the novel, Wilder's years of raising chickens had made her a keen observer of their behavior. The fact that "wild hoppers" were plentiful in Missouri that summer may also have revived her memory and contributed to the liveliness of the scene (LIW to RWL, [summer 1936]).

Picture copyright 1953 by Garth Williams, copyright © renewed 1981 by Garth Williams. Used by permission of HarperCollins Publishers

The second day at noon Pa gave up fighting them. He came in the house all tired out, with his eyes all swollen and red from the smoke and lack of sleep. He told us the wheat was gone and that the grasshoppers were laying their eggs.[54]

The day after this which was the third day since they came, the grasshoppers began to walk[55] toward the west. Every one was walking in the same direction like an army. They did not stop nor go around anything but went straight on over or through whatever they came to. They came to the east side of the house walked up it, over the roof and down the other side. There was an open window up stairs on the east side and those that came to the window walked on in. There were hundreds of them in the room when Ma thought of it and ran to shut the window. Pa tried with a stick to turn some of them, but they wouldn't go a step in any direction except west.

When they came to the creek, they walked out on the water and drowned. Others came up and walked out on the drowned ones, until they drowned too, when others walked out over them until finally the creek was choked with drowned grasshoppers and others walked safely across on the bodies.

All day they walked west and in the night they kept walking by. Next morning grasshoppers were still walking until the sun was warm and bright, towards noon, then they all rose and flew away into the west,[56] clouding the sun again with their wings.

We looked around as though we were just waked from a bad dream. There was not a grasshopper in sight except a few with broken wings that could not fly. Neither was there any green thing in sight and the ground looked like a honey comb it was so full of the little round holes where the grasshoppers had laid their eggs.

There were no crops to be harvested nor anything to live on until crops could grow again and there was no money to buy food.

And so one day, Pa told us all goodby, put on his hat and carrying his coat over his shoulder started walking east to where there was harvesting to be done.[57] He walked because there was no money to pay for a ride on the train[58] and he must go where he could get work in the harvest fields to earn money for us to live on through the winter.

54. *Pa gave up fighting them. . . . grasshoppers were laying their eggs.* Early historians reported on the futility of fighting the locusts. "While millions of the insects were killed," one recalled, "their numbers did not seem to be diminished" (Curtiss-Wedge, *History of Redwood County*, p. 569). Another put it more colorfully, "many millions of them were destroyed, . . . but it was about as effectual as fighting a Northwestern blizzard with a lady's fan" (Flandrau, *History of Minnesota*, p. 120). In *On the Banks of Plum Creek*, Laura looks down "at Pa's patched boots under the table and her throat swelled and ached. Pa could not have new boots now" (p. 202). Pa's generosity in contributing to the church bell fund has cost him money the family needs for basic necessities. After the noon meal, Pa lies "down on the floor" to sleep (p. 203), symbolizing his resignation. As people begin to leave, "going back east" (p. 204), Pa nevertheless declares: "No pesky mess of grasshoppers can beat us! . . . We'll get along somehow" (p. 209). Even as other families are pulling up stakes, the Ingalls family are real pioneers, enduring this epic hardship.

55. *the grasshoppers began to walk.* In the novel, Wilder shifted this scene to the following summer and devoted an entire chapter to it—"Grasshoppers Walking" (pp. 250–67). Although the scene in *Pioneer Girl* is well developed, Wilder added more gripping touches in the novel. Grasshoppers, for example, walk right over Carrie in her high chair (p. 263). According to natural science professor Jeffrey A. Lockwood, the nymphs, or immature Rocky Mountain locusts, walk across the land in "bands" and the mature grasshoppers fly in swarms. An outbreak cycle typically lasted four to five years, rather than the two depicted in the novel, with the adults swarming in from the West, settling where there was plenty of forage, mating, and laying eggs in pods of thirty or more in the ground. The adults died off shortly after, and the embryos hibernated through the winter, emerging the next spring and "forming into immense aggregations" of immature bands that marched across the land. The nymphs would molt five times until their adult wings emerged, and

they would be ready to swarm back toward the Rocky Mountains (Lockwood, *Locust*, p. 21).

56. *they all rose and flew away into the west.* At this point in the novel, Pa delivers this haunting line, "I would like some one to tell me how they all knew at once that it was time to go, and how they knew which way was west and their ancestral home" (*PC*, pp. 266–67). As Professor Lockwood commented, "Locusts were then—and still are—mysterious creatures, whose sudden irruptions are their defining attribute" (*Locust*, p. 27).

57. *started walking east to where there was harvesting to be done.* Writing in 1898, one Redwood County historian observed: "The farmers lost courage and in many cases were driven away altogether from the places where they had hoped to make their homes. Many others were compelled to leave their claims temporarily to procure means of subsistence for themselves and their families" (Turrell, "Early Settlement," p. 289). In 1874, the grasshopper invasion affected twenty-eight counties in southwestern Minnesota. "The grasshoppers went only about a hundred miles east of here," Pa explains in the novel. "Beyond that there's crops"

and jobs in the fields (*PC*, p. 210). The state of Minnesota also set up direct relief programs that dispersed flour, bacon, and seed wheat.

58. *He walked because . . . no money to pay for . . . the train.* Living close to railroad service but being unable to afford it proved frustrating for many during this period. In 1874, for example, a woman from a nearby county wrote the governor of Minnesota, "I heard through a friend . . . that persons who had there crops distroyed by grasshoppers were allowed to travel on the cars free of charge, to th[eir] friends where they could be helped, or a place where they were going to work[;] now if this is the case I would be very thankfull" (quoted in Fite, "Some Farmers' Accounts," p. 208). The Bye version of *Pioneer Girl* added that Pa walked, not only because there was not enough money for a train ticket, but also because he could not afford to keep the horses. "Our horses were sold," Wilder recalled, "and the little money they brought was left with Ma" (Bye, pp. 32–33). In *On the Banks of Plum Creek*, Pa leaves Sam and David behind in the stable. The novel does not address why Pa did not consider riding east.

It was lonesome with Pa gone, but Mr and Mrs Nelson were good neighbors. The grass grew again so that he cut some for hay for us. Then when the frost came and made the grass all dry and brown he came and plowed a firebreak[59] around the house and barn to keep them safe from prairie fires.

We were glad of that strip of bare fresh earth where nothing could burn, when the prairie fire did come. The wind was behind the fire and blowing strong, sending the flames before it.

We felt safe until we saw the great tumble weeds, some as large around as a tub. They had been dead and dry so that the wind blew them loose from the ground and now all ablaze they were rolling ahead of the fire like wheels[60] setting fire to everything they touched. They began rolling across the firebreak and Ma had started to go put out the fire on some of them when Mr Nelson came up on his gray horse as fast as it could run. He sent Ma in the house and he watched for the tumble weeds stopping them as they came across the plowed [firebreak]. It was soon all over.[61] The fire ran around us and went on.

We had several letters from Pa with some money[62] and before the cold came, he was at home with us again.

We went to town, that winter,[63] to live in a little house behind the church, and not far from the schoolhouse, so that Mary and I could go to school.

Coming home from school one day, we found a strange woman getting supper and a little brother[64] beside Ma in the bed. We were very proud of him and always hurried home from school to see him.

Private[65]

And then we caught the itch at school and couldn't touch the baby. Gosh how it did itch and Ma rubbed us with sulpher and grease and turned us before the fire to heat it in. We had an awful time.

We didn't think much of school anyway and were glad when we left town and went back home while the snow and ice were still on the ground and the creek.

59. *he came and plowed a firebreak.* In *On the Banks of Plum Creek*, Pa—not Mr. Nelson—plows the "firebreak" (p. 269) west of the house before leaving for the wheat harvests in the east. This simple shift makes Pa look all the more responsible as he prepares to leave his family alone on the unpredictable prairie.

60. *the great tumble weeds. . . . were rolling ahead of the fire like wheels.* The common name "tumbleweed" refers to "any of several plants that have globelike growth forms with stems that [when dry] break off at ground level and allow the plants to bounce off with the prairie wind, scattering their seeds hither and yon" (Ode, *Dakota Flora*, p. 172). Russian thistle is a common plant of this type. The Bye manuscript used the phrase "fire like balls," but Wilder returned to the wheel image for the chapter "Wheels of Fire" (*PC*, pp. 268–75). Fire was a perennial problem on the prairie, especially in late summer and fall, a situation that appears to have intensified during the grasshopper years. "The entire southern part of this County seems to have been run over by prairie fires," the *Redwood Gazette* reported on October 22, 1874. At "a Grasshopper convention" held in September 1875, many resolutions concerned prairie fires, offering rewards for information about people who set them and recommending the best prevention methods, which included plowing firebreaks around whole towns ("Local News," *RG*, Sept. 9, 1875). Although unstated, farmers probably started fires to fight the locusts and lost control of the blazes. Sparks from locomotives also contributed to fall fires, and railroad men often burned down overgrowth around bridges and fences as a preventive measure, a risky strategy. Wilder could have been remembering a fire that got "away from the section men west of Walnut Station and burned over about three sections of prairie, greatly endangering the premises of several settlers" in the fall of 1875 ("Local News," *RG*, Oct. 28, 1875).

61. *Mr Nelson came up. . . . He sent Ma in the house. . . . all over.* Here, Mr. Nelson saved the Ingalls family, but in later versions, Ma continued to help fight the fire. In Brandt, Mr. Nelson helped Ma "stop the

tumble weeds, and stamped out the little fires" (p. 35). In Brandt Revised, however, Wilder herself dragged a tumbleweed away from the house, although "it was too big for me to stamp out" (p. 23). At the end of the episode, Lane added in longhand: "I was very tired, and wanted to cry. But Mary or I had never cried if we could possibly help it. We would have been ashamed to give way like that" (p. 24). This particular editorial addition did not make it into Bye, but it is clear that Lane, probably in consultation with her mother, was attempting to add detail and refine the point of view of the manuscript, centering it firmly on the young Wilder's thoughts and emotions. Their motivation may have been to make the Ingalls family appear more heroic and render *Pioneer Girl* more marketable, but in any case, they were moving the manuscript toward fiction. In *On the Banks of Plum Creek*, the transformation is complete. Mr. Nelson helps Ma, but he also engages Laura and Mary in the task. Although frightened, Laura beats "that burning wheel to death with a wet gunny sack" (p. 274).

62. *letters from Pa with some money.* In *On the Banks of Plum Creek*, as the family waits for a letter from Pa, Laura begins to worry: "Perhaps his boots had fallen to pieces and he was limping barefooted. Perhaps cattle had hurt him. . . . perhaps wolves had got him. Maybe in dark woods at night a panther had leaped on him from a tree" (pp. 225–26). Weaving together elements from the present novel with frightening episodes from earlier ones, Wilder made Laura's fears for Pa's safety seem believable. Finally Pa sends Ma five dollars (pp. 226–27.) The Ingalls family's circumstances that fall were much starker than the picture Wilder painted in either her autobiography or her fiction. Given her young age, she was probably unaware that at the end of November 1875, Charles Ingalls found himself without means to buy food for his family. He was forced to go to the county commissioners to ask for relief supplies that the state of Minnesota had made available to people in the grasshopper-ravaged areas. By law, he had to sign a document stating that he was a petitioner "wholly without means," and in return, he received two half-barrels of flour worth $5.25 (Ingalls petition [copy], Dec. 3, 1875, Laura Ingalls Wilder Museum, Walnut Grove). *See also* Minnesota, *General Laws of 1875.*

63. *We went to town, that winter.* The fact that Caroline Ingalls was pregnant with her fourth child may have prompted this temporary move into the relative security of Walnut Grove, where the family had better access to doctors via the railroad. The fictional Ingalls family, however, remains in the house that Pa built for them on Plum Creek until they leave for Dakota Territory in the opening pages of *By the Shores of Silver Lake.*

64. *a little brother.* Wilder's brother, Charles Frederick Ingalls, was born November 1, 1875. While the eight-year-old Wilder may not have noticed or understood her mother's pregnancy, it is curious that the adult Wilder did not prepare her readers for this impending birth. Instead, she allows the reader to experience the birth as abruptly as she would have done as a child, which is in keeping with the innocent tone of much of the manuscript. It also reflects the way in which pregnancy and childbirth were rarely mentioned in the era in which Wilder came of age.

65. *Private.* This notation is another indication that Wilder intended both a public and private audience for her original draft of *Pioneer Girl*. On the handwritten manuscript, she literally boxed this paragraph off from the main text. None of the remaining *Pioneer Girl* manuscripts included this incident, probably because of the perceived social stigma associated with the condition Wilder described. The itch, sometimes called the seven-year itch, was most likely scabies, a common problem for all social classes throughout human history, especially in eras when "bath-tubs were unknown and family bathing rare" (McKnight, *Pioneer Outline History*, p. 400). Caused by microscopic mites that burrow under the skin, the symptoms include intense itching and rash. The mite is spread by direct skin-to-skin contact. A concentrated sulfur soap is still one method of treatment. Grease and sulfur were also historical treatments for head lice, which remain a perennial problem among school children. "Parasites–Scabies."

It soon thawed and the creek raised until the water spread over all the low ground.

And right in the midst of the spring freshet Ma was taken desperately sick.[66]

One early morning she was in such pain that Pa dare not leave her. He must have forgotten about the high water for he told me to run to Mr Nelson's and tell him to hurry to town and telegraph for a Dr. The only Dr. was (40) forty miles away[67] and would have to come on the train.

I ran as fast as I could down the path to the creek, for the creek was between us and Mr Nelson's.

When I saw the creek, it terrified me for the footbridge was standing away out in the middle of the stream, with yellow, foamy water running on both sides and just over the top of it. I didn't want to go on, but[68] Pa had told me to go and Ma was awfully sick, so in I waded.

The water was at my knees[69] when I heard someone shout "Go back!"

I looked up and there was Mr Nelson on the far bank, swinging his arms wildly and shouting, "You'll drown! You'll drown! You're crazy!" he said.

I called to him and gave him Pa's message. He hurried away while I went back to the house. Ma was quieter and when Pa saw me all wet he asked about it. When I told him he said "By Jinks!"

The Dr. came the next day. Pa had to bring him, and the women who came from town to help, across the creek and take them back in his boat. The Dr. came twice and after awhile Ma got well and the creek was down again.

Pa got some seed off the train[70] and sowed a small field of grain. He said he would not sow much because if the grasshoppers hatched they would eat it anyway.

Mary and I walked to school that summer.[71]

I was a big girl now seven years old[72] and did not mind walking 2½ miles each way.

It was jolly when we got there too.[73] We could hear the boys shouting at their play a long time before we could see the schoolhouse.

66. *in the midst of the spring freshet Ma was taken desperately sick.* Wilder gave the title "Spring Freshet" to a chapter early in *On the Banks of Plum Creek*, where the focus is on the "rushing and roaring" creek (p. 98). The decision not to include Ma's illness in the novel was an editorial one. "I am doubtful about Ma's sickness," Lane wrote her mother on June 13, 1936. "It is such a wretched miserable time, and in that kind of nasty grasshopper atmosphere. I think the grasshoppers are enough. I believe it would be better to cut out Ma's sickness altogether." But, she added, "the part about the creek is a pity to leave out" (RWL to LIW, June 13, 1936, File 19, Wilder Papers). Wilder, however, considered the entire episode important. She wrote Lane, "I do think the picture of two little girls doing what they did while Ma was sick and the fact that it was nothing for a Dr to be 40 miles away and no auto, would make a great impression on children who are so carefully doctored in schools and all" (LIW to RWL, [summer 1936], ibid.). This kind of exchange is routine in publishing fiction. Editors and writers often discuss issues related to the structure, style, tone, and even content of a manuscript before settling on the final draft for publication. What is unusual, however, is that this editorial process was a private one, between mother and daughter. Wilder's editors at Harper & Brothers were unaware that Lane was acting as her mother's editor (*see* Marcus, *Dear Genius*, pp. 234, 289). Ultimately Lane's editorial position prevailed, and Ma's illness was cut from the final version of the *On the Banks of Plum Creek*, but the flooding creek remained.

67. *Dr. was (40) forty miles away.* Redwood Falls, Minnesota, is roughly forty miles northeast of Walnut Grove and is the county seat of Redwood County. As many as three doctors had set up practice there by the mid-1870s, and perhaps Charles Ingalls asked one of them to care for Caroline, but it is more likely that he sent for the doctor in Sleepy Eye, also about forty miles away. Dr. J. W. B. Wellcome established his practice there in the mid-1870s, and Wilder mentioned him later in *Pioneer Girl* as the family's

Dr. J. W. B. Wellcome. *Sleepy Eye Area Historical Society*

old doctor. He had originally established his practice in New Ulm. By 1879, Dr. Wellcome would be the official surgeon of the Winona & St. Peter Railroad. Curtiss-Wedge, *History of Redwood County*, p. 288; "Walnut Station Items," *Redwood Gazette*, June 26, 1879.

68. At this point, in mid-sentence but at the end of a tablet page, Wilder inserted eight pages into the manuscript. They appear to have been bound differently from those before and after them. There is also evidence that they were once stapled together. The scenes depicted on the pages do not appear to be sequential.

69. *The water was at my knees.* In Brandt, the wording is more dramatic: "The current was very strong and I could hardly keep my footing. I went on until the water was rushing at my knees" (p. 36). In *On the Banks of Plum Creek*, Laura nearly drowns but manages to pull herself out of the water. In the novel, the episode reveals Laura's grit and determination; in *Pioneer Girl*, it illus-

trates Wilder's loyalty and bravery—she would have crossed the creek, despite her fear, if Mr. Nelson had not intervened.

70. *Pa got some seed off the train.* Brandt Revised and Bye added, "There was hardly any seed left in the country, because the grasshoppers had eaten it all" (Bye, p. 35). The wheat "off the train" was likely part of the seed wheat that the state of Minnesota purchased for farmers in the devastated areas. By 1876, the grasshopper plague had spread to forty counties in southwestern Minnesota, and the legislature had increased its appropriations for relief food supplies and seed wheat for farmers. Fite, "Some Farmers' Accounts," pp. 210–11.

71. *Mary and I walked to school that summer.* In an editorial letter, Lane asked her mother, "Was school in the summer-time, in July?" (RWL to LIW, June 13, 1936). Wilder wrote back, "School began in the spring when the first flowers came and was still going on when it was very warm. . . . Each school was a law to itself in those days" (LIW to RWL, [summer 1936]). In the novel, Mary and Laura go to school during the first summer after the fictional family moves into their new house (*PC*, p. 140), which may match the time frame for the first term of school held in Walnut Grove. In the late summer of 1874, the citizens of North Hero Township voted six hundred dollars in bonds to build a two-story schoolhouse, and the township school district was organized shortly thereafter. "Local News," *RG*, Sept. 10, 1874.

72. *I was a big girl now seven years old.* This section of *Pioneer Girl* is episodic, and while the description that follows is out of sequence, it could relate to Wilder's first memories of attending school in Walnut Grove when she was seven. Wilder used elements from this passage to describe Laura's first day of school in *On the Banks of Plum Creek* (pp. 143–45). Even so, this reference could also reflect Wilder's ongoing confusion about her age. She had been seven years old in 1874, the Ingallses' first summer in Walnut Grove, eight when her brother Freddie was born in November 1875, and nine during the summer of 1876. In the Brandt manuscript (p. 36), her age is crossed out, and Brandt Revised (p. 25) and Bye (p. 35) do not give her age.

73. *It was jolly when we got there too.* The fictional Laura's first experience at the school in town is tense, not jolly. Although the scene opens with Laura and Mary hearing voices from the schoolyard, the mood shifts. The noisy children grow suddenly silent when they see the two sisters. Laura calls out, "You all sounded just like a flock of prairie chickens!" One boy instantly retaliates, pointing at the dresses Laura and Mary have outgrown and yelling, "Snipes, yourselves! Snipes! Snipes! Long-legged snipes!" (p. 145).

After we were in town we went between the two stores[74] passed Mr Kennedy's house where Daniel and Christy and Sandy and Nettie[75] would be starting for school, then by the church to the school house. We usually had time to play anti-over or ring-around-the-rosie awhile before school.[76]

I liked Nettie Kennedy very much.[77] The Kennedys were Scotch. Mr Kennedy was an enormous big red-headed man; Mrs Kennedy was little and dark. Daniel and Christy were dark and their black hair curled tightly. Sandy was red headed and freckled and Nettie's hair was a brownish red that I thought wonderfully pretty.

Not many children were in the school but we made several friends.

The ones we came to know best were the Kennedys and Nellie and Willie Owens.[78]

Mr Owens kept one of the stores[79] and we were sometimes allowed to go home with them and stay a little while after school.

They had such wonderful toys, tops and jumping jacks and beautiful picture books.[80] [It was a treat to see such toys, though they would][81] not let us play with them.

Nellie had the most wonderful doll that she kept wrapped up in soft paper most of the time. She would take it out and hold it up before our eyes, then wrap it up again and put it back in its box.[82]

She and Willie would help themselves to candy out of the store and eat it before us never offering us any.

We would not have been allowed to be so rude and selfish but Mrs Owen never seemed to care.[83]

Mr and Mrs Fitch, whos store was across the street had no children we could play with,[84] but they often called us in, as we were passing and gave us candy to eat on the way home.

One day we saw a beautiful, high, back comb[85] in their store. Ma hadn't any pretty combs for her hair and we wanted her to have this one. The price was 50¢ and Mr Fitch said he would keep it for us until we could save enough to buy it.

We each already had 10¢ so we saved the pennies Pa gave us and earned a little by doing errands. We wanted to surprise Pa too, so he did not know [how badly we needed money].[86]

74. *the two stores.* The map Wilder drew of Walnut Grove when she was revising *On the Banks of Plum Creek* showed that she and Mary passed by the "Oleson" (Owens) store and the Fitch store on their way to the schoolhouse.

75. *Mr Kennedy's house . . . Daniel and Christy and Sandy and Nettie.* The 1875 Minnesota census places James Kennedy and his wife, Margaret, in North Hero Township, or east Walnut Grove, where the Union Congregation society initially met in their home. Both James and Margaret Kennedy were born in Canada, but their parents had emigrated there from Scotland. James Kennedy was fourteen years older than his wife. Wilder mentioned four of James and Margaret Kennedy's eight children. In 1875, Daniel was twelve; Christina ("Christy") was fifteen; Alexander ("Sandy") was ten; and Nettie was eight. Perhaps Wilder could not remember the names of the entire Kennedy clan, for she did not mention Catherine ("Cassie"), who was thirteen, or Elizabeth, who would have been six in 1876. John and Edwin were toddlers. Twenty-five years later, some of the Kennedys were still living in Tracy, Minnesota.

76. *before school.* In Brandt Revised, this phrase is replaced with "before teacher rang the bell" in Lane's handwriting (p. 25; Bye, p. 35). While working on editorial changes to *On the Banks of Plum Creek,* Wilder wrote Lane: "I thought I said the teacher rang a large hand bell to call school. She came to the door and rang the bell. The bell stood on top of her desk at other times" (LIW to RWL, [summer 1936]).

77. *I liked Nettie Kennedy very much.* In *On the Banks of Plum Creek,* Wilder changed Nettie's name to Christy, who has red hair, just as Wilder recalled here that Nettie did. In the novel, Wilder gave Nettie's name to an older sister, who strikes up an acquaintance with Mary. Daniel Kennedy becomes Donald in the novel; Cassie and Sandy also make appearances (pp. 146–48). It is unclear why Wilder jumbled Kennedy family names in the published version of the novel, for she had originally identified "Nettie" as Laura's special friend (draft, "On the

Banks of Plum Creek," p. 20, File 21, Wilder Papers). Wilder and Lane may have decided that "Nettie" was too similar to "Nellie," the name they settled on for Laura's fictional antagonist, who appears for the first time in *On the Banks of Plum Creek*. The real Nettie Kennedy was still living with her parents in Tracy, Minnesota, as late as 1900.

78. *Nellie and Willie Owens.* Nellie Owens, along with two other girls Wilder met later (Genevieve Masters and Stella Gilbert), was the model for Nellie Oleson, Laura's fictional rival. At their first meeting, Nellie wrinkles her nose at Laura and Mary and dismisses them with two words, "Country girls" (*PC*, p. 148). From the beginning, Nellie Oleson is conceited, selfish, and mean, the kind of character readers love to hate. One subtle clue exists in the editorial correspondence between Wilder and Lane to indicate that the two women discussed fictionalizing this character's name while working on revisions for *On the Banks of Plum Creek*. In a letter to Lane, Wilder used Nellie's name and then corrected herself with "or what is her name," implying that it had not yet been finalized (LIW to RWL, Aug. 6, 1936, File 19, Wilder Papers). Ultimately, the name "Nellie" remained; Owens, however, became Oleson.

The real Nellie W. Owens was born in Minnesota in 1868 or 1869 (Waskin, "Nellie Olson," p. 3, says 1868, and the 1870 census concurs, but her grave marker says 1869). The Owens family even-

The William and Margaret Owens family: (standing from left) adopted son Frank Bedal, Nellie, and Willie. *Laura Ingalls Wilder Museum*

tually moved to Oregon, where Nellie married Henry Frank Kirry in 1893. They had three children. She is buried in the Forest View Cemetery in Forest Grove, Oregon, beside her father and brother. Nellie's younger brother, William R. Owens, became the model for Willie Oleson in the Little House series. He was born in 1869 or 1870, married in Oregon, and had three children. William was partially blinded during a fireworks accident in Walnut Grove. He died in Portland in 1934 at the age of sixty-four. Nothing exists to indicate whether Nellie Owens Kirry read Wilder's books or knew that she and her brother were the models for such memorable characters.

79. *Mr Owens kept one of the stores.* The 1880 census lists William H. Owens's occupation as "General Merchandise." A New York native, he and his wife, Margaret, a Canadian, had moved to Minnesota by 1870 to farm in Fillmore County. Wilder changed the family's surname to Oleson in *On the Banks of Plum Creek* and described the fictional family's store in the chapter "Nellie Oleson" (pp. 153–59). Like any general store of the time, it stocked tin pots and pans, lamps, bolts of cloth, plows, nails, wires, saws, hammers, hatchets, and knives. "A large, round, yellow cheese was on the counter," Wilder wrote, "and on the floor in front of it was a barrel of molasses, and a whole keg of pickles, and a big wooden box full of crackers, and two tall wooden pails of candy" (p. 154). The Brandt Revised (p. 25) and Bye (p. 35) versions of *Pioneer Girl* reveal that the Owens family "lived upstairs over the store," but the fictional Olesons live in rooms at the back of their establishment (*PC*, p. 161). By 1900, William H. Owens was farming in Tillamook County, Oregon, with his wife and son. The television series *Little House on the Prairie* based its fictional characters Nels and Harriet Oleson on William and Margaret Owens.

80. *They had such wonderful toys . . . and beautiful picture books.* In the chapter "Town Party" (*PC*, pp. 160–68), Wilder described the fictional Oleson children's toys in lavish detail, including a beautiful copy of *Mother Goose* (p. 167). In a letter to Lane, Wilder described her memory of the episode that served as the foundation for the fictional scene. "I think I said all the children at the party, except me, played in the yard after we had looked at the toys. I was fascinated by so many books and sat on the floor by the book-cupboard, instead of going out to play" (LIW to RWL, [summer 1936]).

81. *[It was a treat to see such toys, though they would].* The bottom edges of a few pages of the original manuscript are damaged, possibly because the inserted pages were more brittle and not uni-

form with the tablet in which they had been inserted. Part of the original text is no longer readable on this page and a later one. The text in brackets here comes from the Brandt manuscript (p. 36).

82. *Nellie had the most wonderful doll. . . . back in its box*. In Lane's handwriting, the Brandt Revised version of this scene adds: "We did want so much just to touch her, once. I would have given anything to hold her in my arms" (p. 25; Bye, p. 36). In *On the Banks of Plum Creek*, when Laura reaches for the doll without thinking, Nellie snatches it away: "'Don't you touch her!' Nellie screeched" (p. 166). Wilder's deliberate vocabulary choices enhanced Nellie Oleson's image as a naughty little girl and later as a self-centered young woman. Throughout the series, the fictional Nellie screeches, flounces, punches, kicks, screams, pouts, schemes, and brags. Her actions are clearly at odds with her physical beauty.

"They walked out of the store." *Helen Sewell, 1937*

83. *but Mrs Owen never seemed to care*. The Brandt manuscript added, "Or perhaps she did not know, but at that time we did not know that children would ever disobey their mothers so we thought that Mrs. Owen did not care" (p. 37). In *On the Banks of Plum Creek*, it is Mr. Oleson, and not his wife, who ignores the children's behavior.

84. *Mr and Mrs Fitch, . . . had no children we could play with*. Wilder's diagram of Walnut Grove includes the Fitch general store across the street from the Owens establishment. John R. Fitch and his wife, Josephine, are listed on the 1875 Minnesota census along with their baby daughter, Ada. By 1880, the family had grown to

include another child, Lester, and John Fitch's sister, Ellen. The city directory listed his business as "general store and farm implements" (quoted in Curtiss-Wedge, *History of Redwood County*, p. 551). By 1910, John Fitch was the president of a bank in Tracy, Minnesota, where he died in 1913. His wife died there ten years later.

85. *high, back comb*. In a tintype dating from the late 1870s or early 1880s, Caroline Ingalls wears a back comb, perhaps the one from Mr. and Mrs. Fitch's general store. Her hair is parted down the middle, and the comb rises like a crown from the back of her head. Also known as Spanish mantilla combs, these ornate hair accessories, originally made of tortoiseshell, became popular

Charles and Caroline Ingalls, with Caroline wearing a high back comb. *Laura Ingalls Wilder Historic Home and Museum*

in the mid-1870s. Georges Bizet's opera *Carmen*, performed in Paris in 1875, may have inspired the fashion. During this period, "elaborate hairstyles . . . festooned with ornaments and false hairpieces" also became fashionable and increased demand for the combs (Blum, *Victorian Fashions and Costumes*, p. 77). Tortoiseshell combs were highly prized and usually handcrafted, but beginning in the mid-nineteenth century, mass production of such ornaments made them affordable, even for limited budgets like the one the Ingalls girls had scraped together. Judging from the tintype, Caroline Ingalls eschewed the elaborate hairstyles of the period, but she embraced the mantilla comb, probably because it was a gift from her children. Her hair is pulled back severely, not piled high on her head. "Victorian Combs."

86. *[how badly we needed money]*. Again, the bottom of the page of the original handwritten manuscript is tattered, making the last words in this sentence illegible. The text in brackets comes from the Brandt manuscript (p. 37), which is probably the closest to the original.

At last we had 40¢ and then days went by and it seemed as though we could never get the other 10¢. We were terribly discouraged and one night we went in the store just to look at the comb. It was more beautiful than ever but we couldn't get it.

Mr Fitch asked how much we had and when we told him, he wrapped the comb in soft paper and handed it to us, telling us to bring him the 40¢ when we came to school next day and never mind about the other 10¢.

We nearly ran all the way home and Ma was so surprised and pleased when we gave it to her that we couldn't understand why her eyes were so shiny and wet. The comb looked awfully pretty in her hair.

Mr Fitche's clerk John Anderson and his wife lived in the little house where we had lived in town. They were only just married and Anna[87] kept the little place wonderfully bright and clean. I could see my face in her shining black cookstove.

But one day, when Mary and I stopped on an errand after school, Anna had been crying. The place was clean as ever, but it didn't seem bright someway and we hurried away.

In a few days we overheard Mrs Nelson talking to Ma about Anna and John. She said Anna would better do less work and be with John at the store some of the time for "that Teeney Peterson[88] was hanging around him most of her time."

She said Teeny had tried her best to get John before he married Anna and now she was trying to make trouble.

I wondered how that could be and wished Anna wouldn't cry, I liked her so much.

I felt better about it soon, for going home from school we would see Anna in her pretty pink dress all smiling and beautiful, standing by John in the store. She was so pretty with her blue eyes and hair more golden than Mary's.

Teeny Peterson was very dark and her hair was black. I didn't think her pretty and didn't like her, but it didn't matter for she went away from town.

Mary and I were glad when Saturday came, for we didn't have to go to school.

87. *clerk John Anderson and his wife. . . . Anna*. A twenty-year-old bachelor named John H. Anderson appears on the 1875 Minnesota census, just below the listing for John and Josephine Fitch. Early histories record that a J. H. Anderson established the first store in town in 1873, along with his partner Gustave Sunwall. In August 1874, Anderson and John Fitch became partners and operated the store together until January 1879, when they dissolved the arrangement, and Anderson began to study law with attorney D. M. Thorp. Shortly thereafter, Anderson began working with Dr. Robert Hoyt in a drugstore and also became the town's postmaster. By 1880, the twenty-six-year-old Anderson was married to a woman named Carril, not Anna. At that time, they had a one-year-old son. Several Anna Andersons are listed on census records in Minnesota from 1880 on, but none are married to a John Anderson. During her second stay in Walnut Grove, Wilder again mentioned an Anna Anderson, whom she identified in Bye as "a Swedish girl" working in town (p. 59). It is possible that Wilder confused the two Anderson women. *Redwood Gazette*, Jan. 30, Feb. 20, 27, Oct. 30, 1879.

88. *Teeney Peterson*. No census records exist for a Teeney or Teeny Peterson living in Walnut Grove between the years 1875 and 1880. Nor are there records for a young Tina Peterson. But a Mary Peterson was part of John and Josephine Fitch's household in 1880, working as a servant. She was nineteen. "Teeny" or "Teeney" might have been her nickname. The soap-opera implications Wilder made in this brief episode about the Andersons and Teeney Peterson reinforce the fact that she had written *Pioneer Girl* for adult audiences. This story is the first of several, usually set in town, that deal with mature themes—forbidden love, seduction, deceit, even adultery. Apparently in real life, the Ingalls girls were not as sheltered as their fictional counterparts. Still, although this episode appeared in the Brandt manuscript (pp. 37–38), it was cut from Brandt Revised and Bye.

"On the Banks of Plum Creek." *Helen Sewell, 1937*

89. *Or we waded and played in the water.* In Brandt Revised, this sentence simply reads, "Then we played," followed by a line that alerts the reader to what is coming, "We had not been playing by the creek very long before I thought of a way to get even with Nellie & Willie, who wouldn't let us touch their toys" (p. 26). In *On the Banks of Plum Creek*, Laura decides to get even with Nellie Oleson during the chapter "Country Party" (pp. 169–76) after Nellie tells Ma, "Of course I didn't wear my best dress to just a country party" (p. 171). As here, what Laura has in mind for Nellie is not revealed until the action begins to unfold along Plum Creek, allowing readers to be almost as surprised as Nellie is.

90. *below the footbridge, in a sunny spot.* In a letter to Lane, Wilder included another description: "When the creek came from there out into the sunshine it ran over the sandy pebbly bottom where we waded and played so much after we lived in the new house" (LIW to RWL, July 3 [1936], File 19, Wilder Papers).

91. *a big old crab.* When working on revisions to *On the Banks of Plum Creek*, Lane wrote her mother: "Surely it could not be a crab. Are there any fresh-

After we had washed the dishes and helped Ma clean up the house we went to the creek and fished with hook and line, often catching a good mess of fish for dinner. Or we waded and played in the water.[89] Mary didn't care much about going and I had to coax her a lot, for Ma wouldn't let me go down to the creek alone.

Around the footbridge was the nicest place to play.

A big willow grew at our end of the bridge and shaded the pool just above the bridge, where there were always fish that would take the bait.

Mary wouldn't bait her hook nor take a fish off it, so when we fished, I did all that for us both.

Just below the footbridge, in a sunny spot,[90] the bottom of the creek was nice clean sand, a nice place to wade with the water so cool and clear, running over our feet.

Next was the stone where a big old crab[91] lived. If we went near the stone he would run out at us and we teased him until he got very cross. Down the creek from the crab's stone was a shady little pool with a muddy bottom, where blood-suckers (leaches)[92] lived. If we waded in the pool they would fasten themselves on our feet and legs. They didn't hurt a bit, but they were shiny and flat and mud colored, very unpleasant looking. To get them off, we must take hold of them with our fingers and pull. They would hardly come loose for they were fastened on tight all over like a plaster. They were sucking the blood all over and when we pulled them loose a tiny trickle of blood would run down from where they had been.

When we were playing by ourselves we didn't wade in that pool, for we didn't like the bloodsuckers they seemed such nasty things.

But when the girls from town came out, as they often did to play with us, we would lead them by the old crab's stone and when he would chase them, they would run screaming on into the bloodsuckers pool.

When they came out on the bank and saw the little, long, flat bloodsuckers stuck on their feet and legs, they would try to brush them off. When they found they couldn't they would dance around and kick and scream while I would roll on the grass and laugh, until Mary would make me come and help her pull them off.

Orconectes virilis. Casey D. Swecker

water crabs in prairie creeks? How big was it? What color? What shape? Could it have been a crawdad? (crayfish). A crab is about as big as a turtle (yep, all sizes) and with a shell, smoother than a turtles [*sic*], and all its legs have shells, too. Its eyes are on feelers like a snail's. It has six legs and general impression is like a spider, I mean as to legs. It is a sort of greenery-yaller in color" (RWL to LIW, [summer 1936]). Wilder wrote back that the crab was indeed a "crawdad." She went on, "It was not the crab you de-

scribe though we always called them crabs." Later, she added that it "lived under the rock. I assure you he was enormous" (LIW to RWL, [summer 1936]). As Lane surmised, there are no indigenous freshwater crabs in Minnesota, but three species of crayfish occur in the southwestern portion. Wilder's crab could have been *Cambarus diogenes*, known as the devil crayfish; *Orconectes immunis*, called the calico crayfish; or *Orconectes virilis*, commonly named the virile crayfish. Of the three, the present-day *Orconectes virilis* is the largest at up to five inches in length. Crayfish, called crawdads or crawfish in some locales, look like miniature lobsters with two pincer claws and a long tail. "State of Minnesota Crayfish."

92. *blood-suckers (leaches)*. Wilder slightly expanded her description of a bloodsucker, or leech, in *On the Banks of Plum Creek* when Laura and Mary first discover them: "The thing stretched out long, and longer, and longer, and still it hung on" (p. 131). The vivid writing allows readers to share Laura's emotional response, and when the bloodsuckers return later in the novel and Laura exacts her revenge on Nellie Oleson (pp. 174–76), readers delight in Nellie's reaction. Minnesota has a number of leech varieties, including *Erpobdella punctata*, which is now a popular bait with walleye fishermen in the Midwest. Laumeyer to Hill, May 10, 2012; Nachtrieb, *Leeches of Minnesota*, p. 121.

93. *they wouldn't let us handle their toys, . . . so I just would play my way.* This line finally clarifies who the targets of these pranks were—Willie and Nellie Owens. In *On the Banks of Plum Creek*, the scene unfolds in much the same way, although only Nellie ventures into the bloodsuckers' pool. Laura's friend Christy later says, "I never had such a good time! And it just served Nellie right!" (p. 176). If Wilder had cast the rivalry between Laura and Nellie as simply good girl versus bad girl, the conflict would have been predictable and unsatisfying, far too didactic to resonate with young readers. But Laura fights back and sometimes fights dirty. She is delighted with the outcome of her prank, and, just as here, she laughed "till she fell on the grass and rolled" (p. 174).

94. *Ma said . . . but Pa's blue eyes twinkled when he heard about it.* From Laura's feistiness and Mary's tenderheartedness to Ma's reprimand and Pa's delight at the mischief, the traits that define the fictional Ingallses are present in this episode from *Pioneer Girl*. Wilder had depicted her revenge on Nellie Owens much earlier in her writing career, featuring it in a column for the *Missouri Ruralist* in 1920 (LIW, "How Laura Got Even," *Little House Sampler*, pp. 19–23). Except that Mary's "cry of warning" kept the old crab from having "Nellie by the toe" (p. 22), this column about little girls at play does not show the same character development present in *Pioneer Girl*, where the story is more intimate and personal.

95. *Pa said he'd had enough.* The fictional Charles Ingalls does not give up on the Plum Creek farm. Instead, he clings to the land until he is offered a job on the railroad in Dakota Territory, where he can also file a claim (SL, p. 4). Once again, Wilder made it clear that a desire to move west motivates the fictional Charles Ingalls, who maintains a restless optimism that refuses to accept defeat.

96. The inserted pages end here.

97. *Burr Oak, Iowa.* Burr Oak is a small community three miles south of the Minnesota state line in Winneshiek County in eastern Iowa.

98. *a man who would buy the farm and we would all go . . . to Uncle Peter's.* Charles Ingalls sold the Plum

They would come again but they never caught us at our little trick of leading them into the pool on purpose and the[y] never learned that the old crab lived under the stone and that the pool was the home of the bloodsuckers.

Mary was tender hearted and sometimes said we ought not to frighten our company so, but I said, when we went to town to see them they wouldn't let us handle their toys, the wonderful doll that would open and shut it eyes we were not allowed to hold and we could only look at their other things while they showed them to us; so I just would play my way[93] when they came to see us. Finally Ma said we must not do so any more, but Pa's blue eyes twinkled when he heard about it.[94]

The warm summer sun hatched the grasshoppers eggs. The little grasshoppers came up out of the holes in the ground, tiny at first but they aid [ate?] the grain and grass and leaves and grew larger and larger. We smashed them when we walked; they got up under our skirts when we walked to school and Sunday-school; they dropped down our necks and spit "tobacco juce" on us making brown, ugly spots on our clothes.

The crops were ruined again and Pa said he'd had enough.[95] He wouldn't stay in such a [erasure] "blasted country!"[96]

One of the friends in town had traded for a hotel in Burr Oak, Iowa[97] and was going there late in the fall. He wanted Pa and Ma to go and be partners with them and it was so decided. But Pa said there was no use to wait, he had found a man who would buy the farm and we would all go now, back east to Uncle Peter's.[98] He had written for us to come and Pa could work in the harvest fields and at the fall work until time to go to Iowa.

The wagon was covered; our things were loaded and early on a bright morning the horses were hitched on, we all climbed in and started east.[99]

I felt sorry to leave Plum Creek and our play ground by the footbridge, but it was nice to be in the wagon again and going on and on.[100] We stopped that first day in such a nice, clean, grassy place to eat our cold lunch at noon, but Ma would not eat until she had combed and braided our long hair, Mary's still golden, but Carrie's

Creek property to Abraham and Margaret Keller on July 7, 1876, the same day he filed his first preemption affidavit and paid $430.18 for the property. He received four hundred dollars from the Kellers, losing thirty dollars in the transaction. Taking a loss on property blighted by grasshoppers probably seemed prudent. Ingalls may have hoped to recoup his losses by working the harvest with his brother Peter in eastern Minnesota before traveling south to Burr Oak. Redwood County, Deed Record Book, no. 5, p. 412.

99. *we all climbed in and started east.* From this point on in all adult versions of *Pioneer Girl*, Wilder described what happened to her family as they journeyed east, settled in Iowa, and remained there from the fall of 1876 until their return to Walnut Grove, Minnesota, in the fall of 1877. She deliberately chose not to depict this part of her family's experiences in her fiction. "It is a story in itself," Wilder explained to Lane in 1937, "but does not belong in the picture I am making of the [fictional Ingalls] family" (LIW to RWL, [Dec. 1937 or Jan. 1938], Box 13, file 193, Lane Papers). Moving the fictional family east and not west would have undermined Wilder's optimistic portrait of their resilient pioneer spirit. Furthermore, her experiences in Burr Oak were more urban, gritty, even edgy. Although Wilder introduced some adult ideas and themes into her later novels, she waited until the fictional family had moved west once more into Dakota Territory, where her main character was a more mature adolescent. Wilder herself was just nine years old when the family moved to Burr Oak.

100. *nice to be in the wagon again and going on and on.* The Bye manuscript offers additional perspective on Wilder's feelings: "I wished we were going west. Pa did not like to turn his back on the west, either; I knew this, though he didn't say so. There was no reason why we should want to go west, but we had that feeling" (p. 38). Brandt Revised adds: "We wanted to face the west and keep on going, like the grasshoppers" (p. 28).

101. *he was going west to Oregon. He kept bees.* Later in *Pioneer Girl*, Wilder revealed that Charles Ingalls and this unidentified beekeeper continued to correspond over the years.

102. *Lansford, just a little older than Baby Freddy.* Named for the Ingalls family patriarch, Lansford Newcomb Ingalls was born on April 5, 1870, which made him six years old in 1876, much older than Baby Freddy. Lansford Newcomb married Melissa Funk in 1894 and appears to have lived out his life in Wabasha County, Minnesota. He was buried there in 1946.

103. *Zumbro River.* A tributary of the Mississippi, the Zumbro River flows through southeastern Minnesota. Peter and Eliza Ingalls rented a farm along the Zumbro in Wabasha County near South Troy. Their farm was outside the area of the grasshopper ravages. Zochert, *Laura,* p. 105.

104. *several kinds of red plums and the Frost Plum.* Wild plums, *Prunus americana*, are native to Minnesota and often grow in thickets at the edges of prairies and woodlands. Their reddish-purple fruit ripens in August and September. Several modern plum cultivars are descendants of American wild plums, but none are called frost plums. "Plant Guide."

brown like mine. Little Brother Freddy didn't have much hair to comb. There had been so much to do that morning getting started that our hair couldn't get done, but Ma said nice girls would have their hair combed sometime in the morning anyway. It was nice to be in the big, fresh outdoors all the days and nights and we found so many nice camping places.

One night we stopped near a house and three little girls came out to the wagon and played "Hide and Go Seek" and "Ring Around the Rosie" with us until it was dark and we had to go to bed. Their father was leaving the grasshopper country too, but he was going west to Oregon.

He kept bees[101] and had rows and rows of hives.

The grasshoppers had eaten all the flowers and everything so the bees could not find any honey to store for eating in the winter. Then because they had nothing to feed them, the bees stung all their baby bees to death and threw them out of the hives.

The man nearly cried when he told about the poor bees and he said he would not stay any longer in a country where even a bee couldn't make a living.

Uncle Peters folks were so glad to see us when, after driving for days, we came to their house. The cousins had grown and there was a new cousin, Lansford, just a little older than Baby Freddy.[102]

Mary and I were glad to be with the cousins, but we did not play so much as we used to.

There was work to be done, washing dishes, bringing wood, running errands and helping take care of the babies.

Late in the afternoon Ella, Peter and I must go hunt the cows in the pasture and drive them home to be milked. I loved to go after the cows for their pasture was on the Zumbro River[103] and the river was so pretty running along in the sunshine and shade with trees and flowers on the banks. The grass was soft on our bare feet and the cow bells would "tinkle, tinkle" telling us just where to look for the cows.

The wild plums along the river were ripe and sweet. There were several kinds of red plums and the Frost Plum[104] a big, beautiful, purple kind with a dusting of white that made it look as if it were frosted. They were best after the frost came. When we would get to the plum thickets we would eat and eat. Sometimes we would forget about the cows while we were stuffing ourselves with plums; until dark would come and listening we would hear the cow bells ahead of us going home. Then we would run like anything to catch up and go home with the cows and we would get scolded for being late.

After some time the cows were taken out of the river pasture and Ella, Peter and I herded them on the meadows where the hay had been cut. We had to keep them away from the haystacks and see that they did not stray away.

The fall rains came on and it was cold, but we wore warm coats and built little camp fires in sheltered places over which we roasted wild crab apples and bits of meat and toasted pieces of bread so we played even when we worked.

Little Brother was not well and the Dr. came.[105] I thought that would cure him as it had Ma when the Dr. came to see her. But little Brother got worse instead of better and one awful day he straightened out his little body and was dead.[106]

105. *the Dr. came.* It is impossible to identify the doctor who attended Wilder's baby brother, but several physicians were practicing in Wabasha County at the time, and many were members of the Wabasha County Medical Society, organized in 1869. *See* Curtiss-Wedge, *History of Wabasha County*, p. 55.

106. *one awful day he straightened out his little body and was dead.* Charles Frederick Ingalls died on August 27, 1876, and was buried near the home of Peter and Eliza Ingalls. He was nine months old. His grave location is unknown. Other versions of *Pioneer Girl* shed no additional light on the nature of his illness or the cause of his death. Anderson, *Laura Ingalls Wilder*, p. 64.

MAP OF NORTHEASTERN IOWA, 1876~1877

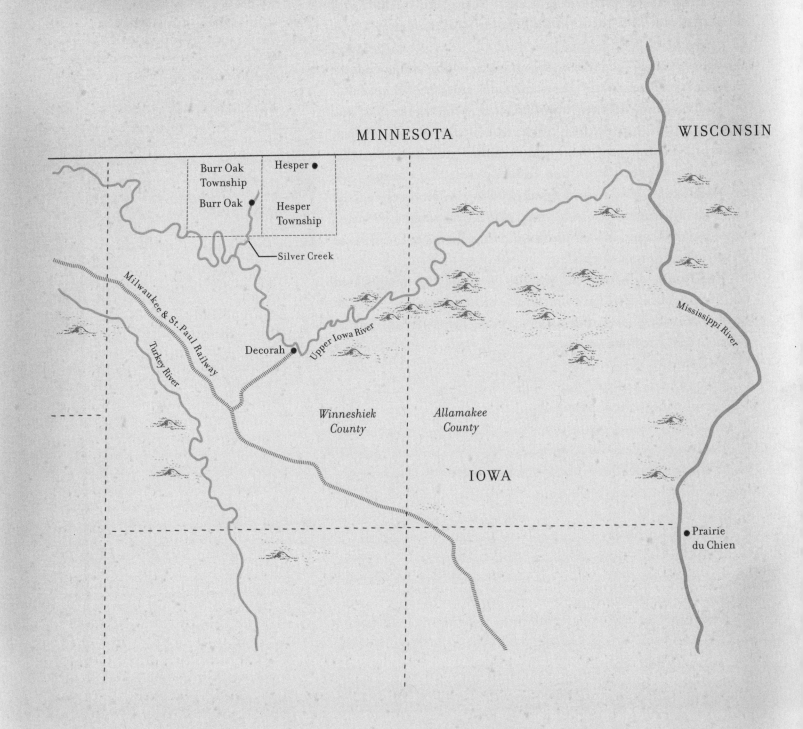

MINNESOTA

WISCONSIN

Burr Oak
Township

Hesper •

Burr Oak •

Hesper
Township

Silver Creek

Milwaukee & St. Paul Railway

Turkey River

Decorah •

Upper Iowa River

Mississippi River

Winneshiek
County

Allamakee
County

IOWA

• Prairie
du Chien

Iowa, 1876–1877

We felt so badly to go on and leave Freddy, but in a little while we had to go on to Iowa to help keep the hotel. It was a cold miserable little journey and we were glad when we drove into Burr Oak[1] and got out of the wagon into the warmth and comfort of the house.

Mr & Mrs Steadman[2] the friends from Walnut Grove were there and their two boys Johnny and Ruben were our playmates now. There was a baby boy named Tommy[3] who was always crying and no wonder for his mother was always shaking, or slapping him.

Johnny was lame, one leg was shorter than the other and he wore a wooden support under his foot and strapped to his leg. We always had to be good to Johnny because he was a cripple but it was hard not to fight back when he would pull our hair, pinch us, tear our books or break our playthings as he was always doing. Neither Johnny or Ruben were like the cousins who had always been good playfellows.

The hotel was built on a side hill.[4] A door off the front street opened into the barroom; across the hall was the parlor also with a front door onto the street. At the back of the hall was a stair going up to the bedrooms above and another stair going down to the dining room, kitchen and kitchen bedroom. A side door opened from the hillside into the dining room and the outside kitchen door opened onto the hillside farther down. From there the yard sloped down to a little, level yard with a fishpond in the center. At the side of the path to the pond was a spring with a springhouse over it. The spring was boxed in and a place made to keep milk and butter, in the cold water, in the summer time.

It was all a very pretty place, but in the door between the dining room and kitchen were several bullet holes made by the son of the man who had sold us the hotel,[5] when he shot at his wife as she ran from him through the door. He had been drunk! It was because of his drinking that his father had taken him west away from the saloon next door. Pa and Ma didn't like the saloon next door either and we

Burr Oak, Iowa. *Laura Ingalls Wilder Memorial Society*

1. *we drove into Burr Oak.* The Ingalls family arrived in Burr Oak, Iowa, during the autumn of 1876. The town had been settled in 1850 and, by the fall of 1851, boasted a store, blacksmith shop, and the hotel that had drawn the Ingalls family to town. Early in its history, wagonloads of settlers passed through the town on a major north-south route connecting Iowa to Minnesota and Wisconsin, and as many as two to three hundred wagons camped in Burr Oak daily. An early visitor described the "beautiful groves" that surrounded the village "on every side" and praised "the undulating country in every direction, the limpid stream of pure and sparkling water, cold and clear, that wound its way through the place." He concluded: "I could not fail to admire the judgment and discernment of the men who decided upon the place for a site of a town" (quoted in Alexander, *History of Winneshiek*, p. 301). By the time the Ingalls family arrived in the fall of 1876, however, Burr Oak's heyday had passed. Later in *Pioneer Girl*, Wilder described it as "an old settled place," a "dead town . . . without even a railroad."

2. *Mr & Mrs Steadman.* William and Mary Steadman, both born in England in the 1830s, had moved to Pennsylvania by the mid-1860s when their first son was born. In 1875, they were living in North Hero

Township in Minnesota, where, like the Ingallses, they were charter members of the Congregational church in Walnut Grove. The Steadmans purchased the Burr Oak House from William Masters in 1876 and less than a year later, in April 1877, sold it to William McLaughlin, who intended "to re-model it into a [dry goods and grocery] store" ("Burr Oak Items," *Decorah Iowa Republican*, Apr. 13, June 8, 1877). By 1880, the Steadmans had moved with their three sons and a four-year-old daughter to Oskaloosa, Iowa, almost two hundred miles south of Burr Oak. At that time, Steadman worked as a butcher.

3. *Johnny and Ruben. . . .Tommy.* Johnny, the oldest Steadman boy, had been born in Pennsylvania and was fifteen years old in 1880; the census that year notes that he was "born a cripple in the left lower limb." Born in Iowa, Reuben was twelve years old in 1880; Tommy was nine. Brandt Revised and Bye do not include descriptions of the Steadman family. Instead, those manuscripts moved directly to a description of Burr Oak and the hotel.

4. *The hotel was built on a side hill.* The Burr Oak House, also known as the Masters Hotel for its previous owner, had been established in 1851, shortly after the community of Burr Oak had been settled. It was one of two hotels in town. Over twenty years before, when hundreds of people had followed the main road on their way west, the town had easily supported two hotels, but in 1876, Burr Oak could no longer sustain both establishments. "It was undoubtedly a measure of the family's financial desperation in Walnut Grove," observed biographer John Miller, "that Charles and Caroline had decided to take their chances in a partnership with the Steadmans" (*Becoming*, p. 37). By 1876, the Burr Oak House depended on long-term guests, local people who resided in the hotel. While the Steadmans stayed in the business longer than the Ingallses

The Masters Hotel. *Laura Ingalls Wilder Memorial Society*

did, they, too, had given up on the enterprise by April 1877. The building, which still stands in its original location, is now the headquarters of the Laura Ingalls Wilder Park and Museum. Photographs clearly show the way in which the builder took advantage of the hillside in constructing the hotel. "Take a Tour."

5. *several bullet holes made by the son of the man who had sold us the hotel.* William J. Masters sold the hotel to William Steadman and moved to Walnut Grove in 1876. Later in *Pioneer Girl*, Wilder identified Masters's son "Will" as the man "who had made the bullet holes in the door shooting at his wife Nannie." The Masters family, who had moved west from New York, lived in Burr Oak as early as 1860. William J. and his wife Emeline had three children: Eugene, William or Willie, and Mary. William A. Masters would have been about twenty years old in 1876; his wife's name was Nancy, which Wilder rendered as "Nannie" or "Nan." In 1880, the couple was still living with his parents in Walnut Grove.

were a little afraid of the men who were always hanging around its door.

The hired girl, Amy's[6] beau was there a good deal. His name was Jim, but the crowd at the saloon called him Hairpin, because he was so tall and thin.

Burr Oak was a small town, but it was not a new, clean little town like Walnut Grove. It was an old, old town[7] and always seemed to me dark and dirty. But there was a nice big school house up on a hill in the sunshine.

The Principal, Mr Reed lived at our hotel and Johnny and Ruben, Mary and I went to school.

While Mr Reed was a slim young man, just 21 years old,[8] some of the boys in his room were big men 24 and 25 years old. They went to school only in the winter time and always before the winter was over they started a fight with the teacher and drove him away.[9]

Awhile before Christmas these boys began to act ugly. They were late at school, noisy in school hours and didn't learn their lessons. Downtown they said that Reed wouldn't be there after Christmas.

One morning the week before Christmas, they were very late and made a great disturbance as they came in.

The oldest and biggest one, named Mose, was the worst of the lot.

Mr Reed sat in his chair by his desk with his ruler in one hand, idly spatting it against the other. It was a large, flat, very strong ruler he had just had made. Mose was the last one in and before he sat down Mr Reed told him to come to him.

Mose was all ready to fight and came swaggering up expecting Mr Reed to stand up so he could knock him down. But Mr Reed sat still and, just as Mose stood in front of him, reached up with his left hand, grabbed Mose by the collar and jerked, tripping him with his foot at the same time and layed him neatly across his knees, with one leg across Mose's legs. It all happened so quickly and Mose was so surprised that, before he knew what had happened, he lay there like a bad little boy and was being soundly spanked with the flat, strong ruler.[10] He looked so funny that every one in the room laughed, even the other big boys "Haw! Hawed!" at him.

6. *hired girl, Amy's*. In the Bye manuscript, "Amy, the hired girl," was the person who imparted the information that the son's wife "Nannie had been running from him" when the dining room door came to be riddled with bullet holes (p. 41).

7. *an old, old town*. Burr Oak was only a little over twenty years older than Walnut Grove.

8. *Mr Reed was a slim young man, just 21 years old*. In fact, William Herbert Reed was only sixteen in 1876—not twenty-one—when he began teaching at the Burr Oak school. The son of William and Phoebe Reed, he had grown up on the family farm near Waukon, Iowa, and, like Wilder herself, was

William H. Reed. *Laura Ingalls Wilder Park and Museum*

educated in the local schools. He probably received his first teaching certificate in 1875 or 1876. He acted as principal and taught school for at least two years in Burr Oak before accepting an assignment at the Webster school, six miles west of town. In the early 1880s, Reed worked for a time on the family farm before accepting a teaching post near Fort Ransom in Dakota Territory in 1883. He eventually returned to Iowa to marry one of his former students. He died at the age of ninety-two in Canton, Minnesota. *See* Reed and Willford, "Genealogy and History." In 1947, in an article about Burr Oak written for the *Decorah Public Opinion*, Wilder recalled Reed fondly. "He was an elocutionist," she wrote, "and I have always been grateful to him for the training I was given in reading" (LIW, *Little House Sampler*, p. 27).

9. *They went to school only in the winter time . . . and drove him away.* This episode is reminiscent of the situation that forms the tension in the first few chapters of Wilder's second novel, *Farmer Boy*. There, the big boys "were sixteen or seventeen years old and they came to school only in the middle of the winter term. They came to thrash the teacher and break up the school" (p. 5). In *Farmer Boy*, Wilder told the story of Almanzo Wilder's youth near Malone, New York, and nine-year-old Almanzo is the main character. While older boys disrupting classrooms could have been a universal problem in small rural schools, Wilder may have taken the elements of this story from her own life and adapted it for her fictional portrayal of Almanzo's school days.

10. *soundly spanked with the flat, strong ruler.* In *Farmer Boy*, the teacher uses a bullwhip to keep the big boys at a distance and off balance (pp. 44–45). Both here and in the novel, the teacher is poised, confident, and completely in control of the situation.

When Mr Reed let Mose up, he went toward his seat, but as he passed the door he went out and he never came back to school again. Everyone in town was laughing at him and he went away somewhere. The other big boys left too and school went on peacefully. When we were at home, Mary and I helped wash dishes and wait on table. We took care of Tommy all day saturdays and Sundays. Mrs Steadman had said if we would, she would give us something nice for Christmas and so though we couldn't like Tommy we did our best to keep him clean and happy.

The snow was fine for coasting and there was a wonderful place for it from the front gate of the yard down past the barroom, the dining room, the kitchen; past the spring-house and out on the little flat yard at the bottom of the hill. But we had no sled of our own and Johnny wouldn't let us use his, but at times when I knew he was away I would take it anyhow and slide down a few times then hurry to put it up before he got back.

Christmas was disappointing. Ma was always tired; Pa was always busy and Mrs Steadman did not give us anything at all for taking care of her disagreable baby, Tommy!

Then we all had the measels![11] Mary and Ruben and I had them all at the same time and Johnny would slip in where we were and snatch the pillows from under our heads and pinch us. I was glad when he had the measeles himself and was awfully sick. We were all well again when spring came and when our school and work were done we played out by the pond.

My play time was cut short because Mr Bisbee,[12] one of the boarders, took a notion to teach me to sing and I had to waste some time every day practicing the scales up and down and mixed. I would rather play but Mr Bisbee was one of the richest men in Burr Oak and our best paying, steady boarder. He must be pleased if possible and so I patiently learned to sing "do ra me fa sol la see do."

And so the summer passed but, before winter came again, we moved out of the hotel[13] to rooms over a grocery store[14] on the other side of the saloon. We didn't help with the hotel any more.[15] (Funny but I don't remember of ever seeing Johnny and Ruben again) Pa

11. *Then we all had the measels!* Throughout the late fall of 1876, the *Decorah Iowa Republican* reported that measles were "raging to quite a lively extent" and "seriously" interfering with schools in the state ("State News," Nov. 17, Dec. 15, 1876). Measles, or rubeola, is a contagious respiratory illness that causes fever, cough, runny nose, and a full-body rash. Complications can include ear infections, pneumonia, diarrhea, hearing loss, encephalitis, and death. Until well into the twentieth century, measles was such a common childhood illness that most people worldwide contracted it before they were fifteen years of age. The first measles vaccine was tested in 1958 and licensed in 1963. In a letter written as she worked on *By the Shores of Silver Lake*, Wilder wrote, "Mary had the measles in Burr Oak and the illness, they called it brain fever, that caused her blindness was the effects of the measels" (LIW to RWL, [1937], Box 13, file 193, Lane Papers). Mary Ingalls would not go blind until the spring of 1879, and this diagnosis of her condition was not made until she saw a specialist in Chicago sometime after that. A recent study in the journal *Pediatrics* concluded, "[T]he physicians' attribution of Mary's blindness to measles that had not fully resolved is improbable." The authors noted that, in rare cases, measles can go dormant and "later develop into subacute sclerosing panencephalitis," but this condition "leads to progressive neurologic deterioration and death" (Allexan et al., "Blindness in Walnut Grove," p. 2). Mary Ingalls did not die from the illness that caused her blindness; she lived to be sixty-three years old.

12. *Mr Bisbee.* Benjamin L. Bisby was a prosperous farmer whose property was valued at close to ten thousand dollars in 1870. Both he and his wife, Roxy, were originally from New York. By 1880, the couple lived in Decorah, Iowa, where Bisby listed his occupation as retired farmer. He died in Decorah in 1895; his wife died in Burr Oak in 1918.

13. *before winter came again, we moved out of the hotel.* Wilder's timing here is out of sequence. The Ingalls family probably moved out of their accommoda-

tions at the hotel early in 1877, not in the fall as the text implies. This error may explain why subsequent versions of *Pioneer Girl* presented Wilder's earliest memories of Burr Oak in a different order. The Bye version, which includes multiple section breaks, used this sequence: (1) a description of Burr Oak and the hotel; (2) introduction of Amy, the hired girl; (3) Mr. Reed and Mose; (4) Christmas; (5) measles; (6) singing lessons with Mr. Bisbee; (7) the move to rooms above the grocery store; (8) memories of Mr. Pifer; (9) the town fire; (10) reading from the *Fifth Reader*; (11) Amy's beau and the fatal cigar; (12) Pa saving the grocer's wife; (13) the little brick house (pp. 40–45).

14. *rooms over a grocery store*. In 1947, in a short piece for the *Decorah Public Opinion*, Wilder identified the store as Kimball's grocery. It belonged to George Kimball, who was a justice of the peace in 1876 and is listed as a "retail grocer" on the 1880 census, and his wife, Sarah. Later in *Pioneer Girl*, Wilder identified the store-owners as a Mr. and Mrs. Cameron. The Kimballs may have bought the store after the Ingalls family left Burr Oak. LIW, *Little House Sampler*, p. 27; "Burr Oak," *Decorah Iowa Republican*, Sept. 29, 1876.

15. *We didn't help with the hotel any more*. In 1937, Wilder wrote Lane: "Pa & Ma worked as partners with Steadmans in the hotel. Steadman handled the money and someway beat Pa out of his share. I don't suppose there was much" (LIW to RWL, Mar. 23, 1937, Box 13, file 193, Lane Papers).

had a good job running a feed mill,[16] grinding the corn and wheat with our horses, and Ma just kept her house again, while Mary and I went to school and helped her out of school hours. There was an outside stairway to get up to our rooms but we always hurried up and down it, for it was almost against the saloon. The town pump was in the middle of the street right in front of the store below us.

One night Ma waked Mary and me and told us to dress quickly. The saloon was on fire and our place might catch fire any minute.[17] All the men in town came running with buckets to carry water from the town pump to put out the fire.

Pa was out there and Ma, Mary and I stood at the windows and watched. The men were standing in a long line waiting their turn at the pump to fill their buckets. They didn't seem to be moving up and Ma kept saying "why don't they hurry."

Mr Bisbee was standing at the pump. He was pumping water fast enough and every time he worked the pump handle up and down he would shout "Fire! Fire!" And Ma kept saying "Why don't they hurry?"

Then there was a great shout and some one jerked Mr Bisbee away from the pump, filled his bucket and went on the run, and every one filled his bucket quickly and ran. They put the fire out and when Pa came, he told us Mr Bisbee was pumping water into a bucket without any bottom and yelling fire while they all stood and waited and the fire burned merrily.

Pa said if the darned saloon could have burned up without burning the town, he wouldn't have carried a drop of water. And Ma said she guessed Mrs Cameron would have been glad.

Mr and Mrs Cameron owned the store[18] below us and lived in rooms at the back. Mr Cameron spent a good deal of his time in the saloon and left his wife to tend the store.

One night we heard Mrs Cameron scream and Pa dressed quickly and went down. He found Mr Cameron dragging her around the room, by her long hair, with one hand and in the other hand he carried a lamp bottom side up. The kerosine was running out of the lamp, catching fire and flaming up around his hand.

16. *Pa had a good job running a feed mill*. Zochert identified the grist mill owner as J. H. Porter, although a newspaper item in March 1877 suggested that Porter and Ingalls ran the place as partners. According to the census, James H. Porter had been farming in the Burr Oak area as early as 1860. A month or so after selling the grist mill, in April 1877, Porter bought the American House, which was the only hotel in town after Steadman sold the Burr Oak House earlier that same month. "Burr Oak Items," *Decorah Iowa Republican*, Mar. 9, Apr. 20, 1877.

The American House. *Laura Ingalls Wilder Park and Museum*

17. *The saloon was on fire and our place might catch fire any minute*. This fire probably took place on February 5, 1877. Like most weekly newspapers of the period, the *Decorah Iowa Republican* relied on correspondents for its news of small outlying towns like Burr Oak. On February 9, a writer who signed the letter "A. M. P." submitted this report: "On Monday night M. J. Ervin, the proprietor of the billiard hall in Burr Oak, in putting out the lights, one of the lamps exploded, the oil running down and igniting, set the building on fire in the ceiling. The alarm was given, although late, and the people gathered, and in a few minutes had the flames under control. If the building had burned down the Burr Oak hotel would have gone with it, as the two join." The Ingalls family may still have been living at the hotel when the fire took place.

18. *Mr and Mrs Cameron owned the store*. A number of Camerons lived within a mile of Burr Oak in 1870. It is possible that someone from these families ran

a store in Burr Oak while the Ingalls family lived there. In 1947, Wilder identified the owners of the store as the Kimballs. Brandt Revised (p. 33) and Bye (p. 45) do not identify the grocer and his wife by name.

19. *sing the multiplication table.* In 1947, Wilder recalled that the students sang the table "to the tune of 'Yankee Doodle'" (*Little House Sampler*, p. 27).

20. *the fifth reader.* The title page of *Independent Fifth Reader*, compiled by J. Madison Watson, promised that this standard textbook of the period was "a simple, practical, and complete treatise on elocution, illustrated with diagrams; select and classified readings and recitations; with copious notes, and a complete supplementary index." In 1947, Wilder wrote, "I still have the old *Independent Fifth Reader* from which [Mr. Reed] taught us to give life to 'Old Tubal Cain,' 'The Polish Boy,' and 'Paul Revere'" (*Little House Sampler*, p. 27).

21. *"The Polish Boy, . . . The Village Blacksmith.["]* With the exception of "The Burial of Sir John Moore at Corunna" (written by Charles Wolfe in 1816), all these poems appeared in the *Independent Fifth Reader.* Ann S. Stephens wrote "The Polish Boy" (pp. 249–53); Jean Ingelow was the author of "The High Tide" (pp. 141–46); Bayard Taylor wrote "The Bison Track" (pp. 211–12); Henry Wadsworth Longfellow penned both "Paul Revere's Ride" (pp. 257–61) and "The Village Blacksmith" (pp. 308–9); Robert Browning wrote "The Pied Piper" (pp. 270–80); and Charles Mackay was the author of "Tubal Cain" (pp. 312–14).

22. *we went upstairs to Mr Reed's room but we stayed in the downstairs school room the rest of the time.* In 1947, Wilder wrote: "It seemed to us a big school, but as I remember there were only two rooms. One began in the downstairs room and when advanced enough was promoted upstairs" (*Little House Sampler*, p. 27). Mr. Reed, as principal, taught the older students in the upstairs room, and, the *Decorah Iowa Republican* correspondent reported, the school "is a grand success. Mr Reed . . . is one of the few who may be styled a first-class teacher. He

Pa made him stop; put him to bed and came back to bed himself saying it was a mercy we were not all burned to death in our sleep.

Mary and I liked to go to school this winter. I learned to sing the multiplication table[19] and was put in the fifth reader.[20] We liked our reading lessons very much and used to practice reading them aloud at home nights.

Pa knew, but did not tell us until later, that a crowd used to gather in the store beneath to hear us read, "The Polish Boy, The Burial of Sir John Moore, The High Tide, The Bison Track, Paul Revere's Ride, The Pied Piper, Tubal Cain, The Village Blacksmith["][21] and many others.

For our reading lessons we went upstairs to Mr Reed's room but we stayed in the downstairs school room the rest of the time.[22] We could bring our school books home and study without any boys to bother. It was so nice not to be in the hotel any more and the rooms where we lived were very pleasant and sunny and clean. From our front windows we could look into the beautiful, terraced, lawn of a big, white house across the street. The house and grounds filled all of two blocks.

Mr Pifer, the man who owned it, was very rich and the house was beautiful inside as well as out. There were wide open stairways and beautiful marble fireplaces but the place seemed chill and unhomelike. Mr Pifers widowed daughter and her two daughters lived there[23] and kept the house. The girls were much to large to be our playmates but they often came to sit with Ma in our pleasant front room, because, they said, it was so bright and cheerful.

Then a dreadful thing happened at the saloon! Amy's beau, Hairpin, who had been lying there drunk for several days came to and took another drink to sober up. Before he had well got it swallowed he put a cigar in his mouth and lit it. He brought the flame of the match close to his mouth and the fumes from the whiskey caught fire. He breathed the flame into his lungs burning them and died almost at once.

Pa said we should not live near the saloon any longer. It was coming spring and there was no more grinding to do.[24] The work he

The Burr Oak schoolhouse, built 1867–1868.
Laura Ingalls Wilder Park and Museum

and his assistant in the lower room are giving general satisfaction" ("Burr Oak Items," June 18, 1877).

23. *Mr Pifer . . . was very rich. . . . Mr Pifers widowed daughter and her two daughters lived there.* Census records for 1870 and 1880 present a different picture of Peter Pfeiffer's household. During those years, he lived with his wife, Mary, and their daughters, May and Isidore (or Isa), in the home of Mary's parents, John and Elizabeth May. The household was large and, in 1870, included the Mays' son George, his wife (also named Mary), and their two-year-old son, Raymond. The Mays were English; Pfeiffer was German. In 1870, Pfeiffer listed his occupation as store clerk, but John May was a wealthy retired architect and builder who estimated his real estate and personal property holdings at close to twelve thousand dollars. George May was a stonecutter. In 1877, the Pfeiffer girls would have been fifteen and twelve, the latter certainly not too old to play with Mary Ingalls, who was the same age. Wilder may have confused Peter and Mary Pfeiffer with John and Elizabeth May, whose daughter, Mary May Pfeiffer, would have been thirty-five, and whose daughter-in-law, Mary May, would have been thirty-three.

24. *no more grinding to do.* On March 9, 1877, the *Decorah Iowa Republican* contained this brief notice, "Porter & Ingals [*sic*] have sold their grist-mill to Paris Baker" ("Burr Oak Items"). The sale may have taken place in early February, suggesting that Charles Ingalls was involved in the enterprise for, at most, five months.

25. *a little red brick house out on the very edge of town.* The house was located a few blocks northwest of the hotel, near the Congregational church. Torn down in the 1970s, it was "a two story house with front bay windows" (Thurman, *Ingalls-Wilder Homesites*, p. 21).

26. *Wild Iris, or flags.* A variety of iris, *Iris virginica* L., commonly known as blue flags, grows near woodlands and damp meadows in Iowa and flowers in the spring. U.S. Forest Service, *Celebrating Wildflowers*.

27. *an old stone quarry.* An early visitor to Winneshiek County observed that two "excellent quarries of blue limestone unsurpassed for building purposes" were located in the area of Burr Oak (Alexander, *History of Winneshiek*, p. 301). Wilder remembered in 1947 that she "could see the old stone quarry, but was forbidden to go to it as it was filled with water" (*Little House Sampler*, p. 28).

28. *Grace.* Grace Pearl Ingalls was born in Burr Oak on May 23, 1877. Her fictional counterpart made her first appearance in the Little House series on the opening page of *By the Shores of Silver Lake* as

Grace Pearl Ingalls, ca. 1878. *Laura Ingalls Wilder Historic Home and Museum*

would have in the spring would keep him away from home a great part of the time and we must not live where we were.

So he rented, from Mr Bisbee, a little red brick house out on the very edge of town[25] and we moved into it in the spring.

It was a wonderful place, to live, right beside an oak wood that was filled with sunshine and shadows, where birds sang and wildwood flowers grew.

We had a cow again and it was my happy task to take her to pasture in the morning and bring her back at night.

The pasture was a little open meadow through which a small brook wandered. Wild Iris, or flags[26] as we called them, sweet Williams, buttercups and dandilions grew among the grass near the water. There was an old stone quarry[27] in the side of a little hill; water from the brook ran into it, just before it left the pasture and made a little pool. I loved to wander along the creek and look at the flowers and wriggle my toes among the cool, lush grasses. I was such a great girl now that I wore my shoes all day, but I always went barefoot after the cow.

My greatest trouble this spring was that I couldn't get past the multiplication table at school. I just couldn't memorize it and we couldn't go on in the arithmetic until we could say the multiplication table. Those who passed were going up stairs next term and I would have to stay behind. So I was glad when Ma said she needed me to help her and I would have to stay out of school for awhile.

I helped Ma with the work, ran errands and every day worked sums in multiplication looking back at the multiplication table to help me when I couldn't remember.

One day when I came back from an errand that had taken me a long time, I found a new little sister. We named her Grace.[28] Her hair was golden like Mary's and her eyes were blue and bright like Pa's.

I stayed at home to help for awhile longer, then I went back to school and I knew my multiplication so well that I went up stairs where my class was.

That was a delightful summer! Work and play were so mixed that I could not tell them apart. Of course it was work, helping Ma take

"baby Grace." Wilder waited until the third chapter to describe her briefly: "Grace sat still in her little starched white lawn dress and bonnet, her feet in small new shoes sticking straight out" (p. 16). In both *Pioneer Girl* and Wilder's fiction, Grace Ingalls plays a minor role, perhaps because she was so much younger than Wilder. Grace was only eight years old when her big sister married Almanzo Wilder in 1885. However, Grace's diary, which she began keeping as a nine-year-old, gives us glimpses into the Wilders' early married life. "Laura and Manly were sick with diphtheria," Grace wrote on March 5, 1888, "and are just getting over it so we have Rose here. She is the best girl I ever saw." A year later, on August 27, Grace noted: "A great many things have happened since I last wrote in this book. Laura's little baby boy only a month old died a little while ago, he looked just like Manly" (quoted in Anderson, *Little House Reader*, pp. 25, 27).

Grace Ingalls attended Redfield College, a Congregational school about sixty miles northwest of De Smet, and then taught country schools near Manchester, South Dakota, a small town west of De Smet. She met local farmer Nathan William Dow, about eighteen years her senior, and the two were married in 1901, the year before Charles Ingalls died. Grace and Nate, who had no children, lived on the Dow farm near Manchester for many years, but they eventually moved into the Ingalls family home in De Smet to care for Caroline and Mary Ingalls. After Mary's death in 1928, the Dows returned to Manchester. Grace died November 10, 1941, at the age of sixty-four; Nate died in 1943. His nephew Harvey Dunn grew up near Manchester and went on to become a celebrated illustrator and artist. *Ingalls Family of De Smet*, pp. 26-27.

29. *I would go with my chum to the old graveyard.* Wilder later identified her chum as Alice Ward and wrote that their graveyard rambles usually took place on Sunday afternoons. Alice Ward was older than Wilder; she would have been twelve in 1877. Her father, Benjamin, was a carpenter. The oldest cemetery in Burr Oak dates from 1853 and was located on land donated by William H. Willsie, a prosperous early merchant. LIW, *Little House Sampler*, p. 28; "Burr Oak Township."

30. *A boy lived there who, people said, was an idiot.* In the nineteenth and early twentieth centuries, idiocy and idiot were the terms used to describe severe cases of intellectual disability.

31. *an old woman, his grandmother.* In 1947, Wilder identified the residents of the little stone house as the "Sims" (*Little House Sampler*, p. 28). Donald Zochert spelled the name "Symms" (*Laura*, p. 122), but a search of census and grave records proved inconclusive. A George D. Symms, his wife Mary, and their year-old-son Richard lived in Burr Oak in 1870, but they drop from sight in later census records. A farmer named John O. Sims appears on the federal agriculture record in 1880, but it is impossible to ascertain details about the composition of his household. Adaliza A. Symms, who died in 1878, is buried in the Burr Oak cemetery and would have been the right age for the grandmotherly figure Wilder remembered.

32. *our Dr's wife Mrs Starr.* In 1880, Dr. Alfred H. Starr and his wife, Eunice, lived alone in their home in Burr Oak. In 1877, Dr. Starr would have been about forty-seven; his wife, forty-four. Dr. Starr, who advertised weekly in the Decorah newspaper, billed himself as a "physician and surgeon" who kept "on hand a supply of fresh drugs, for prescription purposes" (*Decorah Iowa Republican*, Aug. 31, 1877).

33. *Ida and Fanny, were grown and gone away teaching.* In 1880, Fannie Starr was a schoolteacher living in nearby Hesper with her married sister Ida, whose husband, D. Burr Willis, was also a schoolteacher. The Brandt version of *Pioneer Girl* does not in-

care of Grace but it was the best kind of play too. Going after the cow was work but it was the best part of the day. Even if it rained the wet was nice on my feet and the rain felt good on my face and on my body through my thin, summer clothes. The oak woods were always a delight and sometimes, on saturdays, I would go with my chum to the old graveyard[29] on the other side of town. On the way we passed a little stone house all covered with ivy with a front yard full of roses.

A boy lived there who, people said, was an idiot[30] whatever that could be. Sometimes he would be leaning on the picket fence and he acted so strange we didn't like to see him, but an old woman, his grandmother,[31] always called to us and gave us cookies and roses from the yard.

The graveyard was a beautiful place. The grass was so soft and green and short like velvet; there were mossy places in little hollows and growing on some of the tombstones; and there were tall, dark, evergreen trees and lovely flowers everywhere. We might look at the flowers and smell them but never, never pick them.

The white stones standing among all this beauty didn't look lonesome. We could wander for a whole afternoon looking at them and reading the names and verses on them. It seemed a very pleasant place to lie and sleep forever.

But we always went away before sundown.

Coming home from one such afternoon I found our Dr's wife Mrs Starr[32] visiting with Ma. As I came in the door she put her arm around me and went on with her talk. She said she wanted me to go and live with her; that her own girls, Ida and Fanny, were grown and gone away teaching[33] and she wanted a little girl to help her around the house and keep her from being lonesome. She said if I would come she would adopt me and treat me just like her own. But Ma smiled at me and said she couldn't possibly spare me. So Mrs Star went away looking very disappointed.[34]

Toward the last of the summer I knew that Pa and Ma were troubled. Pa's work kept him away from home most of the time and the pay was not much. I knew we needed money and besides Pa did

Dr. Alfred H. Starr. *Laura Ingalls Wilder Park and Museum*

Eunice Starr. *Laura Ingalls Wilder Park and Museum*

clude this episode; Brandt Revised and Bye placed it later in the sequence of the Ingalls family's last days in Burr Oak.

34. *So Mrs Star went away looking very disappointed*. The Bye manuscript added that Laura then felt much better: "But afterward, whenever I thought of her, the queer feeling came back.

It seemed to be possible that I could go on being me—Laura Ingalls—even without Pa and Ma and Mary and Carrie and Grace. Mrs. Starr might have taken me away from them. It seemed strange and I always tried to forget about it as quickly as I could" (p. 49).

35. *"My Old Kentucky Home, . . . "John Brown's Body"* or *"Johnny Comes Marching Home."* These songs date from the nineteenth century. Stephen Foster composed both "My Old Kentucky Home, Good Night" and "Old Folks at Home" (or "Swanee River") in the early 1850s. The lyrics of "The Happy Land" were written by Andrew Young in 1838 and set to a popular tune by Robert Archibald Smith; Ma sings this song to Laura in *Little House on the Prairie* (p. 220). "John Brown's Body" was a popular abolitionist march and shares a melody with the "Battle Hymn of the Republic." Also from the Civil War era, "When Johnny Comes Marching Home" was first published in 1863 with lyrics by Louis Lambert, a pseudonym for Patrick Sarsfield Gilmore. Cockrell, *Ingalls Wilder Family Songbook*, pp. 370, 372, 380, 393; "John Brown's Body."

36. *Pa was very angry. . . . he always had paid all he owed.* At this point in the text, the Bye manuscript included a paragraph that underscored the family's desperation: "But there seemed to be no way we could leave Burr Oak. The law was on Mr. Bisbee's side, and he could have Pa arrested if we tried to go without paying him" (p. 48). Mrs. Starr's offer to adopt Laura was then placed here to emphasize further the Ingallses' financial crisis and their resolve to keep the family together. In this context, Charles Ingalls's decision to skip town seemed justified: he needed a fresh start to support his family and keep them under one roof.

37. *drove away in the darkness.* The Bye manuscript provided a slightly different ending: " 'I never thought,' Pa said, 'that I'd be leaving any place between two days.' And he said he had half a notion to get even with that rich old skinflint by never sending him one red cent. But Ma said, 'Now Charles' " (p. 50).

38. *once more driving into the west.* Wilder supplied one last line to this paragraph in Bye: "Burr Oak seemed like a dream from which we had awakened" (p. 50).

not like an old settled place like Burr Oak; a dead town, he said it was, without even a railroad.

Pa was restless and nights when he was home he played on the fiddle sort of lonsome, longing music, "My Old Kentucky Home, Suanne River, There Is a Happy Land Far, Far Away," but always afterward he would play some marching tune, "John Brown's Body" or "Johnny Comes Marching Home."[35]

So I was not at all surprised, hearing Pa and Ma talking to learn that we were going back west. I learned too that if all the debts were paid, Dr. bills, grocery bills and rent, we couldn't go, for we wouldn't have any money to pay our expenses.

Pa had asked Mr Bisbee to wait for the rent, promising to send it to him in a little while, but he would not wait. He said if we tried to go he would take our team and sell it to get the rent.

Pa was very angry. He said he always had paid all he owed[36] and he would pay everyone else but he'd "be darned if he'd ever pay that rich old skinflint Bisbee a cent.["]

The man Pa had been working for, came one night and bought the cow, paying Pa the money. He told Pa goodby and wished him good luck.

Sometime in the night we children were waked to find the wagon with a cover on standing by the door and everything but our bed and the stove loaded in. While we were dressing with Ma's help, for we were awfully sleepy, Pa put our bed in the wagon and hitched the horses on; then we climbed in and drove away in the darkness.[37]

Before daylight we were in another county. Then Pa stopped, unhitched and fed the horses. We had breakfast while they ate and then went on again, once more driving into the west.[38]

Oh those sunrises by the light of which we ate our breakfasts; those sunsets into which we drove looking for a good camping place!

The first camp we made was a little late and as Pa hurried building the campfire he pointed over his shoulder and said "Old Sol has beaten us this time. There's his campfire."

And there, looking like a fire, through a grove of trees, was the great round moon just rising; "Old Sol's campfire."

I am sure Pa was happy to be going back west. He said the air was fresher where there were not so many people and he played his fiddle by the campfires. "Marching Through Georga, The Star Spangled Banner, Yankee Doodle, Buffalo Gals, Arkansas Traveler"[39] were scattered on the air all the way from Burr Oak Iowa to Walnut Grove Minn.[40]

39. *"Marching Through Georga, . . . Arkansas Traveler."* Wilder mentioned "Yankee Doodle," "Buffalo Gals," and "The Arkansas Traveler" earlier in *Pioneer Girl*. "Marching through Georgia" was composed by Henry Clay Work in 1865 and celebrated William Tecumseh Sherman's March to the Sea late in the American Civil War. "The Star Spangled Banner," with lyrics by Francis Scott Key and music by John Stafford Smith, dates from 1814; it became the United States national anthem in 1931. Cockrell, *Ingalls Wilder Family Songbook*, pp. 390–91, 400.

40. *all the way from Burr Oak Iowa to Walnut Grove Minn.* Given the apparent good weather, this journey probably took place during August and/or September of 1877, possibly after the summer term of the Burr Oak school ended on July 28. "Burr Oak Notes," *Decorah Iowa Republican*, Aug. 3, 1877.

MAP OF REDWOOD COUNTY, MINNESOTA, 1877~1879

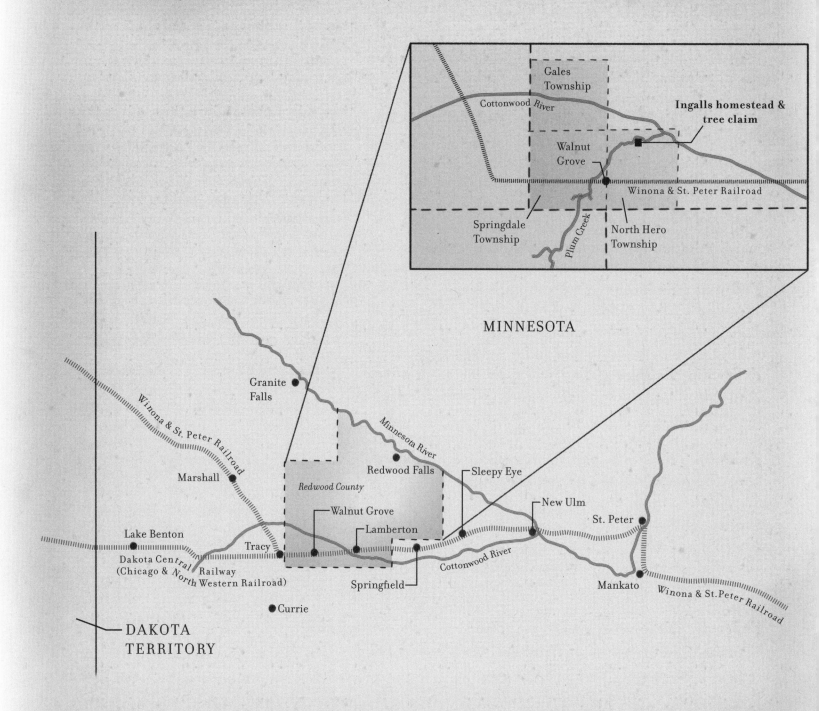

Gales
Township

Cottonwood River

**Ingalls homestead &
tree claim**

Walnut
Grove

Winona & St. Peter Railroad

Springdale
Township

Plum Creek

North Hero
Township

MINNESOTA

Granite
Falls

Minnesota River

Redwood Falls

Sleepy Eye

New Ulm

St. Peter

Marshall

Redwood County

Walnut Grove

Lamberton

Cottonwood River

Mankato

Winona & St. Peter Railroad

Lake Benton

Tracy

Springfield

Dakota Central Railway
(Chicago & North Western Railroad)

Currie

DAKOTA
TERRITORY

Winona & St. Peter Railroad

Minnesota, 1877–1879

When we drove up to Mr Ensign's[1] house in Walnut Grove we were welcomed as though we had come home. When Pa was going, the next day, to find a place for us to live, they said "No!" we were to stay with them until Pa could build a house for us.

So we lived at Mr Ensign's, Pa paying half the family living expenses and working in a store down town.[2] Willard, Anna and Howard Ensign,[3] Mary, and I went to school.

We all studied the same books, only I was at the begining of the grammar, Arithmetic, history and geography, Mary was quite a ways farther over and Anna and Willard were quite in the back of the book. We were all in the fifth reader.

There were two spelling classes and I was in the highest. We all stood up in a row, each in his own place. When anyone missed a word it was given to the next to spell and so on down the line until some one spelled it right when they went up the line above the one who first misspelled the word. When class was dismissed we knew our number in the line so that we could take the right place next time. It was a great honor to stay at the head of the class for a week. There was a foolish boy in the class and if I could not go up I would go down to keep from standing beside him.

Every Friday afternoon at school we did not have our regular lessons but instead spoke pieces and spelled down to find who was the best speller in school.

Friday night there was the spelling school. All the grown folks came to this, bringing lamps and lanterns to light the schoolhouse. Everyone talked and laughed and visited until the teacher rang the bell, then they all took their seats and were quiet.

The teacher chose two leaders, the best spellers in school who stood one on each side of the teachers platform. They each in turn chose one person to stand on their side until everyone was chosen and all were standing in two long lines facing each other across the room.

1. *Mr Ensign's.* John Ensign and his wife, Louperlia or Lupeda, and their children moved to the Walnut Grove area to farm between 1870 and 1875 from Elgin, Minnesota; both he and his wife were born in New York. The Ensigns and Ingalls families became acquainted through their membership at Walnut Grove's Union Congregational Church, where John Ensign served as a deacon. Congregational Papers, Box 5, vol. 10, p. 4.

2. *we lived at Mr Ensign's, Pa . . . working in a store down town.* Brandt Revised and Bye do not mention that the Ingalls family lived with the Ensigns. Instead, the Bye manuscript simply recorded: "We lived in town that winter. Walnut Grove was growing, and Pa had all the carpenter work he could do" (p. 51). In neither manuscript did Charles Ingalls work in a store. But Walnut Grove was in fact growing. In April 1878, the editor of the *Redwood Gazette* pronounced it "one of the liveliest places on the railroad this spring. There are two new general stores, with new two story buildings and Masonic Hall in one." The town also boasted new hardware and grocery stores and a meat market. Eight or nine houses were under construction. "The farmers who went away during the hard times have returned and many new ones have come in," the editor concluded ("Local News," Apr. 11, 1878).

3. *Willard, Anna and Howard Ensign.* In 1877, William or Willie was about seventeen; Anna was about thirteen; and Howard was about nine.

4. *we were all happy to go to the old church*. Charles and Caroline renewed their membership with the Union Congregational Church in Walnut Grove. This time, Mary Ingalls also joined the church. Charles Ingalls was again elected a church trustee in 1878 and was re-elected in 1879. Congregational Papers, pp. 18, 161, 169.

Union Congregational Church. *Laura Ingalls Wilder Museum*

5. *a new preacher*. The Reverend Leonard H. Moses was born in Maine, moved with his parents to Minnesota, and married Alameda Cook in 1862. He attended Wheaton College in Illinois and served with Union forces during the American Civil War. After the death of his first wife, he married Urena Jane Denison in 1866. By 1875, the family was in Walnut Grove; by 1880, they had moved to Rose Creek, Minnesota. While he served as minister to several Congregational churches in Minnesota, Moses spent the final years of his life in Manhattan, Kansas, where he died in 1938. "Rev Leonard H. Moses"; "Leonard Hathaway Rev. Moses."

6. *Lura and Albert Moses*. Lura or Laura Moses was the Reverend Moses's oldest daughter, born to his first wife Alameda in 1863. Albert Curtiss Moses was Wilder's age, born in 1867, the first of six children the Reverend Moses had with his second wife Urena. Two other children—Lurton, born in 1870, and Nina, born in 1875, were part of the Moses household during the period the family was in Walnut Grove.

The teacher then gave out the words from the spelling book first to one leader then to the other leader across the room to the next in line back and forth from one line to the other. Whenever a person misspelled a word he took his seat and the next in the other line tried to spell it and so on back and forth across the line until some one spelled it right.

Words were given out and spelled in this way, while the lamp flames flared in the drafts and the fire roared in the red hot stove, until all but one were spelled down and seated. The teacher gave out words to the person left standing until one was misspelled, then school was out.

Mary and I liked to go to school in the same little old school house where we used to go and we were all happy to go to the old church[4] and sunday-school again.

A parsonage had been buil[t] while we were away and a new preacher[5] lived in it. His childre[n] Lura and Albert Moses[6] walked with us to and from school while we snowballed and played all the way. Howard Ensign wanted me to promise to marry him[7] when I grew up and I thought quite seriously about it but when he cried because I played with Albert Moses I was disgusted and told him "No!"

Mr Masters, who had owned the hotel in Burr Oak before we went there, had built a hotel in Walnut Grove and his son Will who had made the bullet holes[8] in the door shooting at his wife Nannie, still lived with him. Besides the hotel, Mr Masters owned a large pasture, joining and back of his town lots.

During the winter Pa worked for him and paid for a lot in the pasture near the hotel. When spring came he built a little house on the lot[9] and we moved in as soon as we could while Pa finished the house afterward.

We had all enjoyed living with the Ensigns but it was nice to be in our own home again, where it didn't bother anyone if Grace cried a little in the night and there was only just ourselves.

After the house was finished and a garden made, Pa rented a room down town and kept a butcher shop.[10] Everyone had used up their supply of home butchered meat by that time in the spring so that he had a very good business.

Reverend Leonard H. Moses. *Laura Ingalls Wilder Museum*

7. *Howard Ensign wanted me to promise to marry him.* Brandt Revised and Bye did not include this episode.

8. *his son Will who had made the bullet holes.* In Bye, Wilder relayed this idea more tentatively: "His son Will, who was said to have made the bullet holes in the door shooting at his wife Nannie. . . . There was no saloon in Walnut Grove and Will did not drink much now" (Bye, p. 52).

9. *he built a little house on the lot.* While Masters did own land just west of town, there appears to be no record that Charles Ingalls ever owned a lot in the area. And aside from this description in *Pioneer Girl*, there are no other records that document the house.

Instead, in 1875, Charles Ingalls had filed on a tree claim about three miles from his original preemption claim. After his return to the area in the fall of 1877, he relinquished his tree claim and, in May 1878, filed on a portion of it as a homestead claim. The Homestead Act of 1862 required that a claimant establish residency within six months of filing, but during the grasshopper years, such requirements were eased if no other claimant appeared. Because Wilder did not mention this claim in *Pioneer Girl* or elsewhere, there is no way of knowing if the family ever lived on this acreage about five miles northeast along Plum Creek from Walnut Grove. Ingalls relinquished the claim in 1880 after he had filed on a homestead in Dakota Territory. Cleaveland and Linsenmayer, *Charles Ingalls*, p. 9; "The bill, providing for the relief of," *RG*, May 30, 1878.

10. *Pa rented a room down town and kept a butcher shop.* This business may be the new meat market the *Redwood Gazette* mentioned in April 1878. A "butcher shop" is also mentioned in November 1878 as one of the things that made Walnut Station "a promising little town on the C. & N. W. R. R. fifty-four miles west of New Ulm and twenty-six east of Marshall, with a population of about one hundred and sixty inhabitants" ("Walnut Station Letter and Items," *RG*, Nov. 28, 1878). "Before he started the butcher shop," Wilder explained in Bye, "people had not been able to have fresh meat, except chicken, in the summer, for no one would kill a beef or hog when the hot weather would spoil the meat before it could all be eaten. Now when Pa butchered, so many people wanted a piece of the meat that he could sell it all while it was still good, and make a nice little profit" (p. 52). As they did later with the books, Wilder and Lane probably conferred over the revised *Pioneer Girl* manuscripts, and such details may have come straight from Wilder's memories. In a speech about her work, Wilder said, "I have learned that if the mind is allowed to dwell on a circumstance more and more details will present themselves and the memory becomes much more distinct" (*Little House Sampler*, p. 179).

11. *A milliner. . . . divorced.* In 1880, four women in Redwood County, Minnesota, listed their occupation as "milliner" or "keeps milliner store," but none of them lived in Walnut Grove. Two were married, and two were single. Only two women in all of Redwood County in 1880 revealed to federal census takers that they were divorced, and neither woman lived in Walnut Grove. The unknown Walnut Grove hat maker may have sold her wares through the town's general stores, where the "latest style of Ladies trimed and untrimed [*sic*] hats" could be secured ("Walnut Station Items," RG, Apr. 17, 1879).

12. *Mr Master's brother. We all called him "Uncle Sam."* In 1870, Samuel O. Masters and his wife, Margaret, lived in Hornby, New York, with their four children. He was a farmer with property valued at about nine thousand dollars. Sometime after 1875, he, his wife, and their two youngest children moved to Walnut Grove, where Masters listed his occupation as "surveyor." Masters had received his degree in civil engineering from Cornell University and had been a school administrator, surveyor, and merchant in New York. His wife had worked as a schoolteacher. The Masters family would move to De Smet, Dakota Territory, in 1880. In the Bye manuscript, Wilder clarified the reason for his nickname: "We all called him Uncle Sam, he was so tall and thin, needing only a star-spangled coat and striped trousers" (p. 52).

13. *with bad teeth and a bad breath. . . . would . . . fondle any of the girls hands.* Brandt and Brandt Revised did not include this unsavory description of Samuel Masters and his habits, but the Bye manuscript restored Wilder's original story.

14. *George and . . . Gussie . . . Jessie and Jenieve.* In 1870, the four Masters children—George, Augusta, Jesse (a boy, although Wilder identified this child as a girl in Brandt), and Genevieve ("Jenny")—lived at home with their parents in Hornby, New York. George, who was seventeen, listed his occupation as "farm laborer." Augusta ("Gussie"), who later went by her middle name of Elgetha, was eleven and attending school. Jesse was six; Jenny was two. By 1880, Genevieve (there are multiple spellings of her

Mr Ensign moved out on his farm and Anna stayed with us to finish the school term.

A milliner had rented the Ensign house and she made such beautiful hats with lace and ribbon and artifical flowers, that I decided I would be a milliner when I grew up. Mary and I used to stop with her little girl on the way home from school to watch her work. I could not understand how any one who handled such lovely things, making of them something still more beautiful, could be so gloomy as the milliner was. I never saw her smile and often she would give deep, sad sighs. I asked her little girl why her mother was like that and she said her Mamma was divorced[11] from her Pappa. There must be something terrible about being divorced, I thought, to make anyone so miserable.

Our teacher this spring and summer was Mr Master's brother. We all called him "Uncle Sam."[12] He was tall and thin, with bad teeth and a bad breath and small brown eyes and a bald head. He had an unpleasant habit of putting his face to close to ours when he talked to us and would absent-mindedly pick up and fondle any of the girls hands[13] that happened to be handy. He captured mine one day when I had a pin in my fingers and I turned the pin quickly, so it jabbed deep when he squeezed. After that he let my hands alone.

Sam Masters oldest boy George and girl Gussie had not come west with the family but Jessie and Jenieve[14] his other children were about my age. Genieve sneered at the other girls[15] in school because they were westerners. She thought herself much above us because she came from New York. She was much nicer dressed than we were and lisped a little when she talked; if she could not have her way in any thing she cried or rather sniveled. Everyone gave up to her and tried to please her because they liked to appear friends with the new girl. Every one that is except Nellie Owens. Nellie was still a leader among the girls when Genieve came and did not intend to give up her leadership. She tried to hold it by being free with candy and bits of ribbon from her father's store. So my crowd divided.

Mary and her crowd were older. Carrie just starting school was with the little girls. That left me alone for I would not be led by either Nellie or Genieve but took sides first with one and then the

name in census records, but her gravestone uses this spelling) was the only Masters child still living at home in Walnut Grove. Wilder called her Jenieve and Genieve in the original draft; Jeneve in Brandt; and Genevee in Brandt Revised and Bye. During the winter of 1880–1881, George Masters and his wife lived with the Ingalls family in Dakota Territory. Anderson to Koupal, Feb. 2014.

15. *Genieve sneered at the other girls.* Along with Nellie Owens and Stella Gilbert, Genevieve Masters served as a model for the fictional character Nellie Oleson in *On the Banks of Plum Creek, Little Town on the Prairie*, and *These Happy Golden Years*. Genevieve was born in New York on November 12, 1867. She attended college in Pierre, Dakota Territory, and taught schools in Hamlin County before taking over the Wilkin school near De Smet in September 1885. She married William Renwick in 1888 and moved to Chicago, where he worked as an accountant. They had one daughter, born in 1900. Genevieve Masters Renwick died at the age of forty-one in 1909 and is buried in the De Smet Cemetery. "Genevieve Masters Renwick"; "Town and Country," *De Smet Leader*, Apr. 11, July 11, Sept. 19, 1885.

Genevieve Masters. *Laura Ingalls Wilder Museum*

16. *Anti-over, Pullaway, Prisoners Base and hand ball.*
All these children's games except handball involved
variations on the game of tag. In anti-over or anti-
i-over, two teams gathered on opposite sides of a
small building, and a designated player from one
team threw the ball over the rooftop, shouting "anti-
over" as a warning. Players on the opposite side of
the building tried to catch the ball before it hit the
ground. When someone caught it, the entire team
dashed around the building, and the person with
the ball tried to tag his or her opponents. The team
that captured the most players won. Pullaway, also
known as pom-pom pullaway, pump-pump pullaway, or similar variations, was also a chasing game.
A player usually stood in the center of a field, with
a group of children lined up on the other side of the
schoolyard. When the player in the center called out
"pom, pom pullaway," the remaining players raced
toward her. Those she tagged became her team-
mates, who tried to catch the remaining players
when she next called out. The game was over when
everyone had been tagged. Prisoner's base was a
similar running and chasing game. Opposing teams
tried to catch each other's players and bring them
to a designated base or prison. Handball, as Wilder
might have played it, probably involved hitting a
ball against a schoolhouse wall, although she could
be referring to baseball or a catching game. Brandt,
"Children's Games"; Rice, "Traditional Games."

17. *Only one boy . . . could run faster than me. . . . we
played that the rest of the summer.* In her novels,
Wilder also presented her fictional counterpart as
a capable tomboy, but she did not describe schoolyard games or Laura's athleticism as directly as she
did in *Pioneer Girl*. In *The Long Winter*, set in 1880–
1881, Cap Garland unexpectedly throws Laura the
ball, and "before she could think, she had made a
running leap and caught it" (p. 78). The boys urge
Laura to play, but she decides that she is too old to
play boys' games.

18. *to the scandle of . . . Anna, Lura and Christy and
Ida and May Cockrhan.* These big girls were Mary's
friends: Anna Ensign, Lura Moses, and Christy

other as I had a notion, until to my surprise I found myself the
leader of them all, because Genieve and Nellie each being eager to
win me to her side would play what I wanted to play and do as I said
in order to please me.

Genieve lived in the little, old house where brother Freddy had
been born. She asked me to stop as I passed going home from
school to eat cookies when her mother had baked and Nellie gave
me her pretty carnelian ring.

Being, as sister Mary said, a tomboy, I led the girls into the boys
games. We played Anti-over, Pullaway, Prisoners Base and hand
ball.[16] Only one boy in the school could run faster than me and not
always could he do it. When the boys saw how well we could play,
in an hour of triumph they took us into their baseball game and we
played that the rest of the summer,[17] much to the scandle of Mary
and Anna, Lura and Christy and Ida and May Cockrhan[18] all big
girls, being ladies.

Early in the summer [erasure] the Sunday school suprentendent,
invited all the Sunday-school to go on a picnic to the walnut grove,
two miles from town. We were to pack our lunch baskets and go to
Mr Moses' house. A big wagon would be there to take us all to the
grove. Swings had been put up and there would be plenty of lemonade and ice-cream. Ma made us a delicious lunch and packed it in
our basket. There was a whole lemon pie, which was the only kind
of pie I liked. Ma said there would be a piece each for Mary and I
and the rest for some one else.

Pa bought me a new pair of shoes because my old ones were
shabby and early in the morning, Mary and I went gaily to the meeting place.

The ride to the grove was crowded but fun. When we got there
we found two swings and played with them awhile, taking our turn
at swinging with all the others.

The lemonade and ice cream were there too, but the lemonade
was 5¢ a glass and the ice-cream 10¢ a dish.[19] As we had understood
the lemonade and icecream were provided for the sunday school
scholars we had taken no money, so we went without any. As Mary

Christie Kennedy. *Laura Ingalls Wilder Museum*

Kennedy. Ida A. Cochran was the daughter of Andrew and Martha Cochran; at the age of eighteen in 1880, she was "teaching school" in the Walnut Grove area. May Cochran was probably a sister. Brandt Revised (p. 38) and Bye contain an additional paragraph to conclude Wilder's memories of being a tomboy: "Mary was always telling Ma that a great girl like me, eleven years old, should walk and talk and sit properly, like a lady, instead of racing across the schoolyard and throwing balls. Ma agreed with her and would gently remonstrate with me, but as long as she did not actually forbid me I went on playing. And sometimes stuck out my tongue at Mary and called her tattle-tale" (Bye, p. 54).

19. *the ice-cream 10¢ a dish.* The first hand-cranked ice-cream freezer had been patented in the United States in 1843, and ice cream, as well as lemonade, was a summertime treat on the American frontier in the 1870s. Many church and service groups held ice-cream socials as fund-raisers. The "ice cream festival" held in Walnut Grove on June 6, 1879, for example, netted the church women who organized it "over twenty-one dollars" ("Walnut Station Items," *RG*, June 12, 1879). At the 1879 Sunday school picnic, held a week later, "Ice-cream was free to all." Apparently, the organizers had not made the mistake of the previous year, for, unlike the Ingalls girls in 1878, the scholars of 1879 "came home feeling happy and tired" (ibid., June 19). In the era before electricity, ice to make the ice cream and cool the lemonade was cut from frozen rivers and ponds in blocks during the winter, covered with sawdust to insulate it, and kept in a separate structure through the hot months. Wilder gave an account of this process in "Filling the Ice-House," a chapter in *Farmer Boy* (pp. 65–74). Likewise, in Walnut Grove during the last week in January 1879, "quite a number [of people] were engaged . . . in hauling ice for next summers [*sic*] use" ("Walnut Station Items," *RG*, Jan. 30, 1879).

20. *Mrs Masters*. Emeline Hurley Masters was the wife of William J. Masters, who had built the new hotel in Walnut Grove. They married on October 9, 1850, in Hornby, New York.

21. *Nannie's baby, Little Nan*. Nancy ("Nannie") Masters was married to William and Emeline's son William A. Masters. Little Nan, who appears as Eugenia on the 1880 census, was their infant daughter.

22. *Matie Masters . . . was very much the fine lady.* Mary L. ("Mattie") Masters, born in New York, was twelve years old and attending school in Burr Oak, Iowa, in 1870. By the time Wilder met her in Walnut Grove, Mattie would have been about twenty. A writer for the *Redwood Gazette* suggested that Mattie, as an only daughter and "very delicate," had "been cherished as a tender plant" ("Walnut Station Items," Jan. 23, 1879).

23. *a cousin Lotie*. Lotie, or Lottie as it is spelled in revised manuscripts, is identified later in *Pioneer Girl* as the sister of Sadie Hurley, and a "Miss Lottie Hurley" is mentioned in the *Currie Pioneer* of May 8, 1879, as being a newly installed officer of the Good Templar's lodge ("Walnut Grove Items").

and I agreed we would not have asked Pa to give us money for them anyway so it didn't really matter.

At noon the teachers took the lunches out of all the baskets and spread them on a large, white cloth on the ground.

Someway I didn't care much for any of the dinner and I couldn't see the lemon pie that had been in our basket. I went away from the food and wandered by a large box at one side just as a couple of the teachers came to it.

"Here," said one, "I saved this lemon pie out for us teachers. There was'n't enough of it to go all around anyhow." I looked and there was my lemon pie, under a paper, on the box.

Then I went and sat down in the shade of a tree. When they called me to come play, I said I didn't want to play any more, my foot hurt.

After awhile, Mary and I went picking flowers in the wood away from the sight of the ice-cream and lemonade and soon it was time to go home.

We all crowded into the wagon and rode quietly back to town; Mary and I said goodby and walked on home where I took off my new shoes and found a big blister on the heel of my right foot.

When vacation time came, Mrs Masters[20] wanted me to help a[t] the hotel, washing dishes, waiting on table and helping take [care] of Nannie's baby, Little Nan.[21] She said she would give me 50¢ a week and not let me work too hard, so Ma said I might go. The work was easy and there were interesting things happening all the time.

Matie Masters was Will's sister and she was very much the fine lady.[22] She never helped with the work, not even making her own bed. Her room was the parlor bedroom, furnished expensively. And in her bed, with its snowy linen and silk draperies, Matie would sleep until ten oclock in the morning, while her mother and Nannie and a cousin Lotie[23] were busy as they could be. They worked hard all day but I never saw Matie even do a bit of sewing. When Matie came out into the dining room at 10 oclock, in her pretty wrapper and soft slippers with her fair hair hanging loose, Lotie or Nannie or her mother would bring her a warm breakfast with usually some special, dainty dish.

Lotie was a pretty girl, with wonderful, long, thick hair that she wore in two braids wound around her head. She was a poor relation with no other home and lived like an ordinary daughter, not like Matie, getting nothing for her work but her board and clothes. Nannie was a tiny, little, brown woman, a nice English girl.[24] Of course living as she did in her father-in-laws house with her husband and baby she was expected to work as long as there was work to do, which she did cheerfully.

On Monday morning Lotie and Nannie did the hotel and family washing out in the yard, such stacks and stacks of clothes. On that day at 10 oclock Mrs Masters and I always gave them a warm lunch with coffee at the same time Matie had her breakfast but Nannie and Lotie ate in the kitchen. Then they went back and finished the washing while Mrs Masters, with my help, cooked the dinner.

I washed dishes and swept and dusted and played with Little Nan. I never liked to wait on the table but I did like to set it, with the silver castor, its bottles filled with salt and pepper, vinegar and mustard in the center. Near the castor were the sugar bowl, cream pitcher and spoon holder, the silver spoons standing bowls up looking like a boquet.

I liked to put the wire screens, looking like round bee hives over the food, the little one over the butter, larger ones over the cake and bread the vegetables, cooked fruit and other food.

The flys could come in the open doors and windows, as they pleased, but could only crawl disappointedly over the round, wire-screen caps that covered the food.

When my work was done and Little Nan sleeping, I could curl up in a corner out of the way and read the stories in the New York Ledger.[25] Great stories they were of beautiful ladies and brave, handsome men; of dwarfs and villians of jewels and secret caverns. I would lose myself in them and come to, with a start if Little Nan cried or Mrs Masters said it was time to set the table for supper.

Dr. Robert Hoyt[26] was a regular boarder and Matie always smiled her sweetest and dressed her prettiest when she would see him. At the noon dinner and at supper Dr Hoyt always ate with the family sitting beside Matie and after supper, before my dishes were done so I could go home, Matie and the Dr. would be in the parlor, playing the piano and singing or sitting on the sofa talking.

24. *a nice English girl.* Census records confirm that Nancy Masters was English; she was twenty-two in 1878.

25. *stories in the New York Ledger.* The *New York Ledger* was a popular family journal published by Robert Bonner from the early 1850s through 1887. It contained verse, moral essays, and fiction by such writers as Harriet Beecher Stowe, Louisa May Alcott, William Cullen Bryant, Alfred, Lord Tennyson, and Charles Dickens. Mott, *History of American Magazines*, pp. 356–63; "The *New York Ledger*."

26. *Dr. Robert Hoyt.* According to a biographical profile in an 1882 history of Redwood County, Dr. Robert W. Hoyt was born in New Haven, Vermont, on February 14, 1852. His family moved to Iowa when he was eight and then on to Fillmore County in Minnesota. He graduated from Rush Medical College in Chicago in 1875 and settled in Walnut Grove in 1876. In addition to his medical practice, Hoyt established a drugstore and became Red-

Dr. Robert W. Hoyt. *Laura Ingalls Wilder Museum*

wood County superintendent of schools in 1878. Neill, *History of the Minnesota Valley*, p. 782; "Local News," *RG*, Jan. 24, Feb. 14, 1878; "Walnut Station Items," *RG*, Oct. 30, 1879.

27. *Fanny Star.* The unmarried daughter of Dr. Alfred and Eunice Starr of Burr Oak, Fannie was about twenty-three years old in 1878. She was a schoolteacher who lived with her married sister in Hesper, Iowa.

28. *Dr Hoyt had learned to be a Dr. studing with Dr Star.* While the profile of Robert Hoyt published in 1882 did not mention any training with Dr. Alfred Starr in Burr Oak, the opportunity for such training certainly existed. In 1870, the eighteen-year-old Hoyt lived in Hesper Township, adjacent to Burr Oak Township, where he could easily have worked with Dr. Starr before or in the year after he went to medical school in Chicago. Perhaps the failed relationship with Fannie Starr led him to omit the connection in his biographical profile.

29. *"Under The Dasies."* American composer Harrison Millard is usually credited with writing both the music and the lyrics to this mournful love song. The first two lines differ slightly from those Wilder quoted:

> And far better than life with two hearts estranged,
> Is a low grave starred with daisies— ("Under the Daisies!").

The lyrics of this song actually originated as a poem written by Hattie Tyng Griswold in 1842. "Hattie T. Griswold," p. 425.

Then Fanny Star[27] came to visit Matie. Fanny was one of Mrs Star's big girls who had gone away from Burr Oak to teach leaving Mrs Star lonesome. Dr Hoyt had learned to be a Dr. studing with Dr Star.[28]

The first I knew of Fanny's coming was when Matie was having her breakfast. She read a letter that was beside her plate, then told her mother that Fanny Star was coming to make her a visit. "And I just know," Matie said almost crying "that she is coming to try to get Robby back. It doesn't make any difference if he did engage himself to her when he was studying with her father, she shan't have him!" Matie threw the letter on the floor and stamped on it, then went to her room and slammed the door so that we heard it out in the dining room.

The next morning, Matie was all smiles at her breakfast. "What a storm in the night," she said. "My window was open and it rained right in on me and waked me up. It was lightening something terrible and you know I'm so afraid of lightening," she went on in her lisping voice. "I was terribly frightened but I heard Robbie going up stairs to his room and I called to him and he came in and shut the window." And she laughed softly.

Fanny came and Matie met her all smiles, but I had a feeling that underneath the smiles was a sneer, and I could see that she tried to hurt Fanny by showing off her friendship with Dr Hoyt and calling him "Yobbie," instead of his proper name. I thought Matie was mean and silly and I liked Fanny who was a tall, dark, handsome girl always kind and considerate and sensible.

The three of them went on picnics and played croquet. They played cards evenings and played the piano and sang.

Fanny was a good singer with a deep, rich voice that I thought was wonderful compared with Matie's little soprano squeak.

Fanny sometimes sang "Under The Dasies,"[29] and her voice trembled a little, I thought as she sang,

> "Better far better than a love unblest,
> Is a low grave under the dasies
> The beautiful, beautiful dasies
> The snowy, snow dasies."

Fanny came intending to stay two weeks, but only one week had past, when on my way home one night as I passed the parlor, I heard angry voices and some one crying. I knew Fanny and Matie and Dr. Hoyt where there and I wondered.

When I came back in the morning, Fanny was having breakfast alone so she could catch the early morning train. Mrs Masters and Lotie were there but very quiet. Fanny did not go into Matie's room at all, but after cool good bys to Mrs Masters and Lotie went to the train with Mr Masters.

Matie did not come out of her room until noon. Her eyes were red and swollen and she was very angry at Fannie, muttering something like "I'll never forgive her for insulting me."

Right away Mrs Masters began to get Matie ready for her wedding.[30] Ma sewed on her pretty clothes and went to her wedding in a few weeks.

Will Masters was as good for nothing as ever but he could not get as much as he wanted to drink[31] so he and Dr Hoyt persuaded our old neighbor on the farm, Mr Nelson, to come to town and keep a saloon.[32]

It got to be a pretty rough place and because of so much drinking and fighting there, the constable[33] was going to arrest Mr Nelson. He went to the saloon to get him, but Anna Anderson[34] had sent Mrs Nelson word of it. Mrs Nelson beat the constable to the saloon and had Mr Nelson in the wagon ready to start home to the farm when the constable got there. Pa said Mrs Nelson used some dreadful language and dared the constable to touch them and they let her drive away home with Mr Nelson drunk in the bottom of the wagon. We were all very glad for Pa was Justice of the Peace that year[35] and did not want Mr Nelson brought before him.[36]

So there was no saloon in town,[37] but Dr. Hoyt would get whiskey somewhere and give it to Will so that he was drunk most of the time. Pa said he was trying to help Will drink himself to death so that his wife Matie would get all their father's property.

Pa's Justice office was in our front room; when he had a trial we all went into the kitchen,[38] but we could hear very well through the door between the rooms and whenever I could I would sit by the

30. *her wedding.* Mattie Masters married Robert W. Hoyt on October 24, 1878, and they went on a wedding tour in the East, from which they returned a month later. "Gleanings," *RG,* Nov. 28, 1878; news items, *Currie Pioneer,* Oct. 24, 1878.

31. *Will Masters was as good for nothing as ever . . . as he wanted to drink.* In revised versions, Wilder diplomatically omitted these comments about Will Masters.

32. *Mr Nelson, to come to town and keep a saloon.* Eleck C. Nelson and his wife, Olena, had been neighbors and friends during the Ingalls family's first stay in the Walnut Grove area. In the winter of 1878, a newspaper correspondent called Walnut Grove "a temperance town, and we intend it shall remain so . . . so many here who were once addicted to liquor drinking have quit and joined the temperance ranks" ("Walnut Station Items," *RG,* Dec. 5, 1878). By April, however, business had "commenced pretty lively" at the new establishment (ibid., Apr. 17, 1879).

33. *the constable.* The first constable in Walnut Grove was a J. Russell, who was elected to the position on March 10, 1879. Curtiss-Wedge, *History of Redwood County,* p. 553.

34. *Anna Anderson.* In Bye, Wilder explained that Anna Anderson was "a Swedish girl who was working in town" (p. 59). Wilder may have earlier confused this Anna Anderson with John Anderson's wife, whose name was Carril.

35. *Pa was Justice of the Peace that year.* Charles Ingalls was elected "justice" of Walnut Grove on March 10, 1879. He was one of six town officers, including the constable, who won administrative positions in the newly formed civic government that took shape after Walnut Grove was incorporated by the legislature on March 3, 1879. William H. Owens, father of Nellie and Willie, was elected treasurer. Charles Ingalls had also been politically active during the family's first stay in Walnut Grove, serving as North Hero delegate to the county convention that drew up the successful "Peoples County Ticket." Curtiss-Wedge, *History of Redwood County,* p. 553; "Lamberton,"

RG, Oct. 21, 1875; "Walnut Grove Items," *Currie Pioneer*, Mar. 20, 1879.

36. *did not want Mr Nelson brought before him.* The duties of justices of the peace vary over time and place, but it is clear that Charles Ingalls's duties included presiding over local trials. In revising, Wilder added more perspective to the story: "Pa told us this at home and we were all very much troubled about it. . . . The charges against his saloon were true, and Pa was one of many who thought the town would be better off without a saloon. But Mr. Nelson had been such a good neighbor to us in the hard times after the grasshoppers came. . . . It would go hard for Pa to be obliged to fine him or close his place of business" (Bye, p. 59).

37. *So there was no saloon in town.* This situation did not last long. The Walnut Grove business directory for 1880 recorded that Paul Sandquist & Co. was then operating a saloon there. E. C. Nelson, on the other hand, was running a meat market.

38. *Pa's Justice office was in our front room; when he had a trial we all went into the kitchen.* Rose Wilder Lane used this setting in a short story. When a client approached a county officer's house, his wife "shooed the children out of the front room and moved the lamp from the center table, while Harvey pulled the box of county papers from beneath one of the beds" ("Object, Matrimony," p. 5).

door and listen. There was a lawyer in town now, a stranger named Thorpe.[39] It was said that he was part Mexican, he was so very dark with such straight black hair and black eyes. He had an awful temper and I enjoyed hearing him argue a case for he nearly always got mad at someone or something.

One day some people came in from their farm to sign papers before Pa. They were Mr Welch and his wife[40] a large, coarse looking red-headed woman, her sister, a tiny little white haird woman, who had been crying and her husband, Mr & Mrs Ray, and their grown son Will Ray.[41]

There were queer stories about Mrs Welch, her awful temper, the quarrels she had with her husband and the outlandish things she did. Mr Welch had advertised, in a paper, for a wife and this woman had answered the advertisement.

After exchanging a few letters she had come to Walnut Grove on the train; hired a rig, took the preacher and driven out to Mr Welch's farm. There they were married beside a hay stack. "And what," people said, "could you expect of a woman like that!"

She had later sent for her nephew Will Ray who made his home with her, worked for Mr Welch and held a homestead he took near by.

This spring Mrs Welch had persuaded Will to have his father and mother make him a visit. She had sent them money to buy their railroad tickets and when they came was very nice to them, insisting that they make their visit longer and longer, until it had lasted the whole summer.

When at last they were determined to go home, they learned from the east that they had no home to go to. They had given a mortgage ont it when Will went west, under a contract that they could not be turned out so long as they lived, but the contract was so worded that if they gave up residence on it then the mortgage could be foreclosed. They had been away so long, they had lost residence, the mortgage had been foreclosed and a quit claim deed sent them to sign as a further security to the title for which they were to be paid a small sum.[42]

They had come to sign the deed before Pa. From the deed as Pa

39. *a lawyer . . . named Thorpe.* Lawyer David M. Thorp was born in Ohio and moved to Walnut Grove after 1875. In 1880, he and his wife, Emma, had two young children. Thorp's parents were from New York. His ethnic heritage is not discernible from the available records.

40. *Mr Welch and his wife.* A search of census records proved inconclusive for this couple. A Richard Walsh and his wife Ann, both Irish, lived in North Hero Township in 1880, but they had been married for over twenty years and had two children.

41. *Mr & Mrs Ray, and their grown son Will Ray.* According to the 1880 census, Samuel and Mary Ray lived northwest of Walnut Grove in Gales Township with their son William J., who was twenty-four and a farmer. Samuel Ray was a seventy-year-old marble cutter; his wife was sixty-one. William had been born in New York, which fits Wilder's profile of the family; his parents were Irish. The *Currie Pioneer* recorded that the "parents of W. J. Ray" arrived in Walnut Grove on July 3, 1879 ("Walnut Grove Items," July 10, 1879). Brandt (p. 54), Brandt Revised (p. 42), and Bye (p. 60) changed the family's surname to Roy.

42. *They had given a mortgage. . . . a small sum.* The Homestead Act of 1862 included a residency requirement in which claimants could not leave their claims for more than six months at a time. This act may have inspired the money lender to write a similar requirement into the fine print of the Rays' mortgage. According to the terms as sketched here, the Rays could not be absent from their property for more than a certain length of time; otherwise the mortgage holder could foreclose on the loan regardless of their payments. When they stayed away too long, the mortgage holder exercised this right and then paid the Rays "a small sum" to sign a quit-claim deed, an instrument renouncing whatever claim they might have on the property, presumably to ensure that they could not litigate the matter later.

43. *But they had wanted so much to go home!* Rose Wilder Lane used this story of the vindictive wife and her hapless sister as the basis for a short story entitled "Object, Matrimony," which appeared in *The Saturday Evening Post* on September 1, 1934. In Lane's much longer retelling, the women are cousins rather than sisters, and the revenge took twenty years to mature. In the end, the husband talks his mail-order bride into letting her cousin and husband return east to live on the farm until their deaths. Not only the plot, but much of the atmosphere and setting of Lane's story derive from *Pioneer Girl*.

44. *It did so well that Mr Masters had him try it out in the pasture.* Although the Brandt manuscript followed Wilder's original story closely (p. 56), handwritten notes reveal that Lane thought this episode would benefit from heavy editing. The story does not

Samuel O. Masters. *Lucille (Masters) Mone Collection*

read it I knew it must have been a beautiful old place. It was in New York and the description read from a certain tree on a hillside to a certain stone in a valley, then following the course of a brook to another stone, twisting and turning here and there, not square with straight lines like the farms I knew.

Everyone was very quiet, with Mrs Ray touching her handkerchief to her eyes now and then, until the deed was read and signed.

Then Mrs Welch snatched the deed, while the red flew into her face and her eyes blazed. "It's mine!" she screamed at her sister. "That's where I put the money I earned teaching school. I was the one held that mortgage and no one but the lawyer knew. That's why I hired Will to come out; that's why I had you come and kept you from going back. I planned it all from the begining! All these years I've waited, but I told you I would get even with you when you married the man I wanted!"

Then she began to call her sister names and curse her, until Mr Welch took her roughly by the shoulders, pushed her out into the yard and shut the door, while she screamed and kicked and clawed, scratching his face, till her nails drew blood.

Mrs Ray looked tinyier than ever crumpled in her chair, with her sweet, dark eyes looking frightened in her white face.

I looked at Mr Ray, a feeble, small, old man and wondered why anyone should make such a fuss over him, but when I saw him put his arm around his wife, heard his voice as he spoke to her and saw her eyes light up, I almost understood.

Will took them over to the hotel, while Mr Welch to[ok] his wife home. Mr Masters loaned Will some money and he paid Mrs Welch the money she had sent his mother to bring them west; built an addition to the claim shanty on his homestead and took his father and mother home to live with him. But they had wanted so much to go home![43]

Uncle Sam Masters had invented a machine he said would find gold, silver or iron wherever it was. He used to try it and show how it worked by finding gold or silver watch which had been hidden in the house. It did so well that Mr Masters had him try it out in the pasture.[44] Mr Masters thought there was some kind of ore there.

appear in Brandt Revised, but a more developed episode is included in Bye:

> Uncle Sam Masters, the school teacher, had been inventing a machine which he said would find gold, silver or iron wherever they were. Now it was finished, and it worked. He used to show it and prove that it worked by finding a gold or silver watch which had been hidden in a house. It did so well that Mr. Masters had him try it out in the pasture behind the hotel. Mr. Masters thought there was some kind of ore there.
>
> Everyone was very much excited. And sure enough, Uncle Sam's instrument said there was ore on the bank of a dry wash a little way from our house.
>
> The instrument couldn't tell what kind of ore was there, whether gold, silver, or iron, but Mr. Masters got a well drill and began drilling to find out.
>
> Then what excitement! People hardly talked of anything else. Suppose the drill found gold? We might all be rich. Even a silver strike would make fortunes. All day long men stood around the hole, and looked at the earth that came up when the drillers cleaned the hole.
>
> When the drill had gone down a hundred feet, it was blown clear out of the hole, and a stream of water followed it. It was no use trying to drill any farther. Mr. Masters had a pipe put into the hole and there was a flowing well. The water ran out of the pipe into a barrel, overflowed from that and ran off, making a little brook in what had been the dry wash. This was all that came of our hopes.
>
> But the water tasted strongly of iron and turned the ground a rusty red where it ran, so Uncle Sam's machine had made no mistake, it had found iron ore down in the ground (p. 63).

45. *a cattle buyer came.* This eight-paragraph episode does not appear in Brandt Revised or Bye.

And sure enough Uncle Sam's instrument said there was on the far bank of a dry wash a little ways back of our house. The instrument didn't tell what kind of ore was there but Mr Masters got a drill and began drilling to find out. When the drill had gone down a hundred feet, it was blown out of the hole and a stream of water followed it. It was no use trying to drill any farther, so they put a pipe around the hole that stood up from the ground and there was a flowing well. The water ran out the top of the pipe into a barrel, overflowed from that and ran off making a little brook out of what had been the dry wash. The water tasted strong of iron and turned everything it ran over a rusty red, so Pa and Mr Masters thought likely there was iron ore down in the ground.

Our house sat in the big pasture without any yard fence around it, but I wished we were not there when a cattle buyer came [45] from the west driving 200 cattle he had bought and was taking to his farm in Iowa to fatten.

He rented the pasture to put them in over night and hired Pa to watch them, while he and his men slept.

Such a bawling and a pawing as there was around our little house as they drove the cattle in the gate, but they drove them on past to the running water and left them drinking and eating grass.

After awhile they all lay down, while Pa walked around the outside of the fence and the dark settled quietly over everything.

Ma said I was to stay dressed because I might have to go call the men if Pa needed them and along in the night sometime she shook me awake and told me to run to the hotel as fast as I could and call the men. I heard the cattle bawling and Pa shout and when Ma opened the door I jumped to the fence, rolled under it and ran. I couldn't tell which way the cattle were going, but I could hear them bawling and trampling and I lost no time to the hotel door where I pounded and shouted. The men came running, jumped on their horses and went after the cattle. They didn't get them back until daylight.

Pa said they were all sleeping quietly when one big steer jumped to his feet and bawled. Instantly all were up bellowing and away they went. The fence might as well not have been there for all the good it did.

I never saw a stampede, but hearing one is enough.

Late in the summer, Pa sold his butcher business,[46] because, he said, folks would soon be butchering their own meat.

Mr Masters was putting up a store building, with a hall above, beside the hotel and Pa did carpenter work on that until it was finished before winter came.[47]

We had a new teacher when school began that winter. Mr Thorpe did not have law business to keep him busy or pay him much so he took the school to help out. He was a good school teacher and we were getting along nicely in our books. Also we were playing particularly hard at recess and noon. The snow was deeper and softer than usual and we chose sides and had snow-ball fights that were gorgeous.

Mary objected to my playing such rough games out doors with the boys, but she could not keep me in and once when she took both hands full of my loose, long hair and tried to hold me[48] I stiffened my neck and dragged her to the door where she caught some of the snowballs herself befor she let me go. Then she told Ma about it and Ma said I was to large a girl to play that way any more. I would soon be thirteen[49] and must be more of a lady. After that I stayed with the big girls and the very little ones in the house. The other girls of my crowd would not go because I didn't and soon the boys had all the outdoor fun to themselves except on the way to and from school. When Genieve got her face washed in the snow she would cry helplessly but I was busy giving as good as I got.

There were three new boys in school. Clarance and Maylon Spurr[50] were brothers. Clarance was man grown but Maylon and Silas Rude[51] the other new boy were about my age.

There was quite a rivelery among the big girls over Clarance, especially between Anna Ensign and Lura Moses. They were both pretty girls, tall, with black hair and brown eyes, but Anna's hair was straight and long in braids around her head; her eyes were cold and her face pale and fine.

Lura's hair was short and thick and curley. She wore it in crisp ringlets. She was not so slender as Anna; her eyes were large and soft her cheeks red and her lips very red and full. I thought they

46. *Pa sold his butcher business.* In the 1880 city directory, Eleck Nelson owned a meat market. Perhaps he bought it from his friend Charles Ingalls.

47. *Mr Masters was putting up a store building, . . . before winter came.* Wilder's time frame is faulty. Some of the anecdotes she has just related occurred in the spring of 1879, most notably Charles Ingalls's election as justice of the peace. The Masters store building, on the other hand, was one of the new two-story general stores under construction in April 1878. It contained a "Masonic Hall," which was often called Masters Hall ("Local News," *RG*, Apr. 11, 1878). *See also Currie Pioneer*, Apr. 18, 1878.

48. *she took both hands full of my loose, long hair and tried to hold me.* This depiction of the final childhood struggle between Wilder and her sister Mary is far more physical and aggressive than the conflicts between Laura and Mary in Wilder's fiction. This episode, which appears in all versions of *Pioneer Girl*, underscored Wilder's physicality and her reluctance to grow up.

49. *I would soon be thirteen.* Wilder would turn thirteen in February 1880, when the family was in Dakota Territory.

50. *Clarance and Maylon Spurr.* The Spurr family had moved from Fillmore County, Minnesota, to Walnut Grove. The boys' father, Cyrus B. Spurr, was a blacksmith. In 1880, nineteen-year-old Clarance was a laborer; his eleven-year-old-brother Mahlon was still in school.

51. *Silas Rude.* In 1880, sixteen-year-old Silas Rood lived with his sister Ida C. Kenyon, her husband Herbert J. Kenyon, and their six-year-old daughter in Springdale on the west side of Walnut Grove. Silas had left school by then and worked on the farm.

52. *a new boy from the east*. In Brandt, a handwritten edit added that the three new boys in school—Clarence and Maylon Spurr and Silas Rude—were "all from the east" (p. 58). Census records show that Clarence Spurr and his parents were born in Maine, but Mahlon was born in Minnesota. Silas Rood was born in New York.

53. *he shook him . . . then he slapped his face . . . and slammed him down in his seat*. As Wilder related this episode, Mr. Thorp's temper was on display rather than any standardized form of corporal punishment, which usually involved paddling or hitting hands with a ruler as a public reprimand. In any case, corporal punishment was not banned in Minnesota schools until 1989. In Bye, Thorp's temper is described as "ungovernable" (p. 60).

54. *Daniel and Sandy Kennedy . . . Christy and Nettie stayed*. The Kennedys were the Ingalls sisters' friends from their first stay in Minnesota. The Bye manuscript also identified "the four Kennedys" as the only friends in Wilder's circle to stay behind at school (p. 65).

were silly to care at all about Clarance. He was rather a prissy, thinking himself smart, he was sometimes impudent to Mr Thorpe. The other boys did not like him, but I suppose being a new boy from the east[52] made him interesting to the girls.

The boys had been careless in their play about throwing snow in the door and Mr Thorpe told them to stay out when they were snowballing, not be dodging in the door bringing the snow with them.

Clarance Spurr never condesended to snowball with the other boys, but one noon as he came back to school he made some balls and threw them at the boys as he dodged for the door. He opened it and ran in just as the snow balls all the boys threw at him got there and ~~the~~ a perfect shower of snowballs came in with him causing him to slip on the snow and fall on the floor.

Mr Thorpe was there before he could get up and his eyes were blazing. "What do you mean by this?" he said and Clarance answered "None of your business!" Mr Thorpe took him by the collar, jerked him to his feet and great boy that he was, as large as Mr Thorpe, he shook him as though he were a small child until his teeth must have rattled, then he slapped his face on both cheeks with his open hand and slammed him down in his seat.[53]

Clarance sat there sullenly, with his hair on end and his tie undone, while we girls huddled together fearfully, until Mr Thorpe rang the bell. Then Clarance got up took his cap and walked out of the door, Mr Thorpe watching him and saying nothing.

Anna and Lura were very angry they said they would not come to school any more and at recess they took all their books and went home. Because they were the oldest and the rest of us looked up to them Mary and I and several of the others took our books too. Daniel and Sandy Kennedy said it served Clarance right and Christy and Nettie stayed.[54]

When Mary and I got home, Pa and Ma wanted an explanation and when we told them about it he said we were to go right back to school in the morning. We hated to do it thinking the others would not be there, but in the morning there they all were, with their books, looking rather sheepish.

Clarance did not com[e] but Maylon came and took Clarance's

books and his own and went away again. They didn't come back any more and I thought school was much pleasanter without Clarance strutting around.

The girls of my crowd missed Maylon. We had liked him. He and Silas Rude were so different from Howard and Alber[t] and Sandy[55] with their rough hair and freckled faces. Like Clarance, Maylon and Silas wore collars and ties. Silas said he was "Rude by name and rude by nature," but if so he hid it well, for his manners were very nice and instead of treating us girls like playmates only a little less good than boys, he was very polite and treated us like grown ladies, which was strange and somehow thrilling, though really not so much fun.

Any of us were proud to have a note from him slipped to us in school hours or to walk with him on the way to school.

Genieve used to watch from her window until she saw him coming, then start to school in time to meet and walk on with him.

I could do nothing like that for I lived in another part of town, but one night, when I knew he was going down town, I went around that way home so I could walk with him.

Of course Ma wanted to know why I went down town and I didn't have a good excuse, so she said I should stop being silly over Silas Rude or she would take me out of school and Pa said any boy who would fool around with the girls, instead of playing with the other boys like a man, was no good, only a sissy.

I knew all this but someway I couldn't tell them that I didn't really even like Silas, but I just didn't want Genieve to have his attentions.

But soon we were rid of Silas Rude! It happened this way.

A Good Templars Lodge was organized in town and all the nice, older people in town joined it. Pa and Ma joined although they were angry at the lecturer who organized it, because he had been drinking and when he was lecturing for temperance and telling the evils of drinking, he had a bottle of whiskey in his pocket. But he went away as soon as the Lodge was started and the people used to have good times at the lodge meetings.[56]

On the nights of those meetings I stayed at Mrs Goffs[57] to take care of the baby while they were away. I always locked the door care-

55. *Howard and Alber[t] and Sandy.* In Bye, Howard Ensign, Albert Moses, and Sandy Kennedy are simply identified as "the other boys we knew" (p. 66).

56. *Good Templars Lodge. . . . people used to have good times at the lodge meetings.* The Independent Order of Good Templars, founded during the nineteenth century with local chapters, or lodges, across the country, had as its main objective "to secure personal abstinence from the use of all intoxicating drinks as a beverage, and the prohibition of the manufacture, importation, and sale of intoxicating drinks." The "great aim" of the Good Templars was "to secure a sober world" (Turnbull, *Good Templars*, p. 5). The Walnut Grove lodge organized in April 1878 with fourteen members. By December, their ranks had swelled to fifty, and they were holding dramatic performances and other events in Masters Hall. In February 1879, the membership elected Charles Ingalls as an officer. "Walnut Station Items" and "Gleanings," *RG*, Dec. 5, 1878; "Walnut Grove Items," *Currie Pioneer*, Feb. 6, 1879.

57. *Mrs Goffs.* A Fred and Delia Goff lived in Springdale Township, adjoining Walnut Grove on the west, as did Silas Rood. Goff was a carpenter; he and his wife were both originally from New York. The 1880 census reported that they were childless.

58. *had just come from Lodge.* According to the *Redwood Gazette*, this incident took place in December 1878 during the Ladies' Sewing Circle's "weekly sociable" held at the house of W. J. Masters ("Walnut Station Items," Dec. 26, 1878).

59. *his face bleeding, his wrists cut, a piece of rope hanging to one.* This description (and Wilder's story overall) corresponds with the one published in the newspaper: "The deep marks on his wrists showed plainly that his hands had been bound, and he carried the gag in his hand which consisted of a short stick with a notch in it and rope tied in the notch" (ibid.).

60. *It was plain that Silas had bruised his own face . . . and made up the whole story.* "Some seem to think that it is only a ruse of the boy," the newspaper correspondent wrote at the time, adding, "but the boy has told the story several times in my hearing and his story agrees with what he told on his arrival at Mr. Masters" (ibid.).

fully after they went away and would read while the baby slept or rock it if it waked.

One night as I sat reading there came a knock at the door and when I asked who was there a voice said "Silas Rude." I opened the door and he asked for Mr Goff. When I told him where Mr Goff was he ran towards town as fast as he could.

I locked the door again wondering what could be the matter that Silas should look so wild and be without a cap outdoors in the cold.

Silas lived with his sister and her husband out a little ways in the country. He passed Mr Goffs on the way to town, but I wondered why he had not stayed home as he always did alone until his folks came from lodge.

In a few minutes there was another pounding on the door and Mrs Goff calling "Open the door! Open the door!" I did so quickly and she rushed in, snatched the baby from the cradle where it was, sound asleep, and asked in one breath, "Are you all right? Has anyone been here?"

She sent Mr Goff home with me though I usually ran home alone.

It was only when I was home where Pa and Ma had just come from Lodge,[58] that I learned what it was all about:

Silas Rude had burst into the Lodge room with his face bleeding, his wrists cut, a piece of rope hanging to one[59] and told how two strange men had come into the house, beaten and gagged him, tied his feet and hands together, then gone and left him lying on the floor. After a long, hard struggle he had got his hands loose untied the gag and his feet and ran for help.

There was wild excitement in the Lodge room and everyone ran home to see if their children were safe. Then they hurried out to see if they could find any trace of the men.

They found no sign of them, nor could they the next day when they went back to search by daylight. No strangers were seen or heard of in the neighborhood, no one that at all answerd the description of the men that Silas had given.

It was plain that Silas had bruised his own face and wrists, tied the rope around his wrist and made up the whole story,[60] to make of himself a sort of hero and create excitement.

He had made an excitement but he was no hero. Everyone despised him and his sister took him out of school and sent him home because he could not face the redicule of the town.

There was a revival in our church that winter.[61] I enjoyed going, hearing the singing and watching the crowd. One man named Will Knight[62] was very amusing. He was tall and dark with a deep bass voice and sang as loud as he could. When the meetings were at the greatest pitch of excitement, he one night left off singing and with a great shout went forward among the mourners. This was the first revival I had ever attended and I didn't understand the process. It rather sickened me to hear Will Knight groan and sob and take on calling on the Lord to forgive him for his many sins. After a couple of meetings he stopped groaning and imploring and shouted and sang joyfully. Pa said he was all right now until he backslid again. When I asked what he meant, he said Will Knight always got religion every revival meeting, but backslid and was a sinner all the time between.

Will Ray was there too. He sang tenor and I loved to sit or stand beside him and follow his tenor with my piping soprano.

Will Ray loved to sing and when he was reaching a high note with his voice would raise himself on his tiptoes. The higher the note the higher he stood seeming to raise himself that he might pick it out of the air above him, lifting his voice with his feet.

Will Ray was a church member who never backslid, but he was very quiet in the meetings, the opposite of Will Knight in every way even in his looks for though he was tall too, it was a slim tallness and he was very light, with pale hair. His little mother sometimes came to church with him and one could see how proud of him she was.

When the revival meeting at the Congregational church stopped, the Methodists began one in the hall over Masters' new store where they had their preaching and Sunday-school.

This was much more exciting. Will Knight was there shouting and singing and helping with the sinners. Pa said this was where he belonged instead of at the other church.

The preacher and his wife were English people[63] who had come from England after they were married. They always put their Hs in

61. *a revival in our church that winter.* Rev. Leonard H. Moses began a series of prayer meetings the week after Christmas 1878 that extended, with some interruptions due to cold weather, through the first week of February 1879. Rev. H. C. Simmons of Marshall, Minnesota, assisted for a few days, and "the house has been crowded most of the time," the Walnut Grove correspondent reported ("Walnut Station Items," *Redwood Gazette*, Feb. 13, 1879).

62. *Will Knight.* In 1875, a W. T. Knight lived with his parents, B. M. and M. D. Knight, and a brother, M. H. Knight, in North Hero Township, the eastern half of Walnut Grove. W. T. Knight would have been about twenty years old in 1879.

63. *The preacher and his wife were English people.* "Mr. Gimpson the Methodist Minister from Tracy has commenced meetings again in the congregational church and will continue the evening meetings as long as a good interest is shown," the *Redwood Gazette* announced on February 13, 1879. Gimpson, who was actually the Reverend John Gimson, served rural congregations on a Methodist Episcopal circuit that included Walnut Grove. He regularly held services at the Masonic Hall in the Masters store building, as Wilder noted. By 1880, John Gimson had moved from Tracy to Lamberton, Minnesota, about ten miles east of Walnut Grove. He was English, and his wife was Irish; their children had been born in New York, Connecticut, and Minnesota. "M. E. Appointments," *Currie Pioneer*, Feb. 7, 1878.

64. *Mary . . . was not very well all winter.* Brandt (p. 62) and Brandt Revised (p. 47) included this detail, but a handwritten line cuts through this sentence in Brandt Revised, and the line does not appear in Bye. Perhaps this editorial decision was an attempt to bring more consistency to the narrative. Later in *Pioneer Girl*, Wilder characterized Mary's illness as sudden.

65. *Golden Texts and Central Truths for the entire year.* Nineteenth-century Sunday school lessons were often structured around a Bible verse and the central truth it exhibited. A text from 1889, for example, combined Bible verses with contemporary stories to illustrate how to apply Biblical concepts to everyday lives. Every Sunday of every month had its own verse and story. Some golden texts were simple: "Prepare ye the way of the Lord" (Mark 1:3); others were more complex: "Whosoever will come after me, let him deny himself" (Mark 8:34). *See* Hale, *Sunday-School Stories*, pp. 1, 99. According to Brandt Revised (p. 47) and Bye (p. 77), this Sunday school contest at Walnut Grove's Methodist church included "one hundred and four Bible verses."

the wrong place and were queer in some of their ways, but they certainly knew how to handle a crowd and sway them as they pleased. At times the whole congregation would be on their knees with groanings and shoutings breaking out in all parts of the room. Again everyone would be singing and shouting at the same time.

All that winter we all went to our church and Sunday-school on Sunday morning and in the afternoon I went to the Methodist church and Sunday-school.

Mary did not go in the afternoon, because she was not very well all winter.[64] Sometimes Pa went with me but I never failed because there was a contest in the Sunday-school. A prize was offered to the pupil who at the end of the year could repeat from memory, in their proper order, all the Golden Texts and Central Truths for the entire year,[65] which would be two Bible verses for each Sunday of the year. When the time came for the test, we stood up one at a time before the whole Sunday-school and beginning with the first lesson of the year repeated first the Golden Text then the Central truth of each lesson, one after the other as they came, without any prompting or help of any kind. The prize was a reference Bible.

One after the other they tried and failed until my turn came and I was perfect. But alas so was Howard Ensign when his turn came and there were both of us winners with only one prize between us.

My teacher, the preacher's wife, said if I would wait until she could send and get another Bible she would get me one with a clasp, so I was glad to wait.

Howard Ensign had joined the Congregational church after their revival and would testify at prayer meeting every Wednesday night. It someway offended my sense of privacy. It seemed to me that the things between one and God should be between him and God like loving ones mother. One didn't go around saying 'I love my mother, she has been so good to me.' One just loved her and did things that she liked one to do.

On stormy winter evenings, Pa loved to play his violin and he took great pains to teach Carrie and me to dance together nicely all the round dances. With him playing, and watching our steps to see that we did them right, we learned to waltz and shottice (that is not spelled right but it is not in my dictionary) and polka.[66]

Pa had taught me some of the steps before but I had to dance alone. Now Carrie was big enough to dance with me, we became quite expert and were often called on to dance when some one came in for the evening.

I had been away from home a good many days that winter helping Mrs Goff on Saturdays and holidays and soon after the Methodist meeting was over, Mrs Masters asked Ma to let me go and stay with Lotie's sister Sadie Hurley. Sadie's husband, John,[67] had to be away at his work a good deal and Sadie not being very well ought not to be left alone.

Ma hated to take me out of school but finally consented, so taking my school books with me I went with John driving through the cold and the snow to a little two roomed house in the country. My bed was curtained off with a calico curtain from the front room.

I stayed with Sadie two weeks while John made up his crop of broom straw into brooms to sell in town. One day to my pleased surprise I found Pa helping him, when I went to call him to dinner.

The rest of the days were lonely and I was homesick. I knew things were not going well at home, because Pa could not get much work and we needed more money to live on.

One night while saying my prayers, as I always did before going to bed, this feeling of homesickness and worry was worse than usual, but gradually I had a feeling of a hovering, encompassing Presence of a Power, comforting and sustaining and thought in surprise 'That is what men call God!'

I was no more than back home again when Matie now Mrs Hoyt was taken sick. Ma went every day to help take care of her and they had Dr Fred Welcome, our old Dr.'s son come,[68] but after all she died. No one ever said what the sickness was but I heard Ma tell Pa that Dr. Hoyt had been trying some experiment and she said, "Matie would better have let Fanny Star have him than to have gotten him that way."[69]

The winter which had not been so bad, this far, turned stormy

66. *waltz and shottice . . . and polka.* The waltz, schottische, and polka are partnered dances that were popular in the nineteenth century and continue to be performed today. The waltz originated in Austria and southern Germany in the sixteenth century, but the elegant, flowing style associated with the dance as it is performed now dates from the eighteenth century. The waltz is performed to music with a 3/4 meter. The polka originated in Bohemia in the 1830s and is a lively, energetic dance performed to music with a 2/4 meter; its basic dance pattern is hop-step-close-step. The schottische is a variation of the polka. The spelling of "shottice" was corrected to "schottiche" in the revised versions of *Pioneer Girl*. In Bye, Wilder added this brief sentence to the dance episode: "Though this [dancing] was very shocking to the Methodists, Pa and Ma saw nothing wrong in it, and the evenings passed gaily with Pa's music and our dancing" (p. 78). In *By the Shores of Silver Lake*, Pa plays a waltz and polka for Laura and Carrie to dance to (pp. 156–57).

67. *Sadie Hurley. Sadie's husband, John.* Sarah and John Holly, a married couple from New York, lived in Walnut Grove when the 1880 census was taken. Probably the same John Holly, born around 1842 in New York, had been part of the William J. Masters household in Burr Oak, Iowa, in 1860. It is possible that census takers heard "Holly" instead of Hurley," and that John Holly was Emeline Hurley Masters's younger brother. If so, then Lottie would have been Sarah Holly/Sadie Hurley's sister-in-law. According to the 1880 census, John and Sarah Holly/Hurley had a two-year-old daughter. Sarah Hurley could have been pregnant during the winter of 1877–1878, making Wilder's company especially welcome. It is possible that "not being very well" was nineteenth-century code for "pregnant." Wilder's timeline in this section is jumbled, making it hard to tell when she stayed with the Hurleys.

68. *Dr Fred Welcome, our old Dr.'s son come.* Dr. Florado Houser Wellcome was the son of Dr. J. W. B. Wellcome, who had perhaps cared for Caroline Ingalls during an earlier illness. Dr. Florado Wellcome

graduated from Rush Medical College in Chicago at the age of twenty and briefly practiced medicine in Sleepy Eye, Minnesota. He married in 1878 or 1879 and moved with his wife to Granite Falls, Minnesota. Newspaper reports of Mattie Hoyt's illness, however, suggest that a Dr. Berry of New Ulm attended the sick woman. Shutter, *History of Minneapolis*, p. 302; "Walnut Station Items," *RG*, Jan. 23, Mar. 13, 1879.

69. *she died. . . . "Matie would better . . . than to have gotten him that way."* Mattie Masters Hoyt died on March 5, 1879. The implication in *Pioneer Girl* is that Mattie cemented her relationship with Dr. Hoyt by having sexual relations prior to the marriage and that this circumstance contributed to her death. The newspaper reported that she became ill in January 1879 with what the local correspondent called "billious [*sic*] colic which turned to inflammation of the bowels" ("Walnut Station Items," *RG*, Jan. 23, Mar. 13, 1879). For a time, she seemed to improve, but she died within five months of her marriage. Her father and mother took her body to Burr Oak for burial. For his part, Dr. Hoyt failed to mention this brief marriage in his profile published in 1882. He was still living with the Masters family as a boarder when the census was taken in June 1880, but within the month, he had married Myra E. Tester of Wisconsin. Neill, *History of the Minnesota Valley*, p. 782.

and the awful blizzards came again out of the north-west as they had when we lived on the farm. We stopped going to school for we were not very warmly dressed[70] and on our path was quite a ways where there were no houses and the wind swept harder there.

One morning, after a blizzard, Pa went down town early, then came hurrying back to dress himself warmer. He was going, he said to help find Robbins' children, who were all lost in the storm.[71]

Pa didn't know how it had happened and he hurried back to go with the other men out to Mr Robbins farm about three miles from town. The morning was clear and still with the sun shining brightly, but it was very cold and they must hurry to try to save the children from freezing to death, though they didn't have much hope.

Mr and Mrs Robbins had been in town the day before when the storm struck and they stayed until the wind began to go down in the night, then they hurried home. They found the house cold and empty, no sign of the children anywhere, but the stovepipe had fallen down and was lying on the floor.

They and a neighbor who lived a half mile away had been looking for the children ever since and the neighbors boy had ridden to town for help.

When Pa came home, about noon, he told us that the men had started in a circle from the house, spreading as they went, looking into every drift and pile of snow and at last they found the children in a snow drift. There were five. They hurriedly carried them to the house and began to work over them.

The oldest a girl twelve years old was alive but badly frozen. The baby wrapped close against her under her coat was alive and only chilled. The others, two boys and a girl were frozen to death.

They packed snow around the frozen arms and legs of the girl who was alive to thaw them out. Pa said it was terrible with the dead children lying there and this girl swearing horribly as her legs and arms hurt thawing out. They thought she would be all right, but she had been so badly frozen that later the Dr. had to cut off one leg.

When the stovepipe fell down in the night, the room filled with smoke and sparks from the fire and the children thought the house was on fire. They wrapped themselves up the best they could,

70. *for we were not very warmly dressed*. In Brandt Revised and Bye, Wilder stated this more directly: "for we could not afford to dress warmly" (p. 49/78).

71. *Robbins' children, who were all lost in the storm*. Census records from the period do not include a match for a Robbins, Robinson, or Roberts family, and neither the *Redwood Gazette* nor the *Currie Pioneer* shed light on this incident.

72. *Chinook wind.* A chinook wind is usually a wind from the Pacific Northwest that brings warmer temperatures in late winter or early spring. In *The Long Winter*, Wilder defined the term for her readers: "The Chinook, the wind of spring, was blowing. Winter was ended" (p. 312).

73. *spring had come.* The revised versions of *Pioneer Girl* presented Wilder's memories of her last fall and winter in Walnut Grove in different sequences. In Brandt, for example, Mattie Masters Hoyt died shortly after the cattle stampede and before Mr. Thorp began to teach school. Brandt Revised not only changed the sequencing of these episodes, but it eliminated several. In that version, Mattie died shortly after the conflict between the Welches and Rays. The cattle stampede, Sam Masters's attempt to find gold, Mr. Thorp's showdown with Clarence, and the descriptions of Anna Ensign and Lura Moses were not included (pp. 44–45). The Bye manuscript restored much of what was cut from Brandt Revised but eliminated the cattle stampede. In many ways, *Pioneer Girl* is an impressionistic memoir, less concerned with pinpointing historical moments in time and more focused on recreating a general historical atmosphere. Such variations probably reflected Wilder and Lane's attempts to find a narrative thread that would sustain readers' interest through the middle sections of the manuscript. The Bye manuscript, however, essentially restored Wilder's original chronology.

74. *Mr & Mrs Masters would have nothing to do with him.* In 1880, Dr. Hoyt was still a boarder with the Masters family, which seems to contradict Wilder's memory—or perhaps Dr. Hoyt's continued residence with the family intensified the differences between them. Hoyt remarried later in 1880 and, presumably, moved out of the Masters household.

quickly, and ran out into the night and the storm trying to go to the nearest neighbors.

In a few minutes they were lost, but kept on trying to find their way until they could go no farther. Being wrapped under Nora's coat, so close to her body had saved the baby.

That was the last, bad storm of the winter. Soon a warm wind came out of the north west instead of a blizzard and Pa called it the Chinook wind[72] and said spring had come.[73]

Pa got work to do when the days were warmer, repairing the pasture fence for Mr Masters and doing carpentering. He got Mr Masters team and plowed our little garden and I helped him plant the seeds. Mary and I made some flower beds and planted seeds and set out plants that Missouri Pool gave us. Mary liked to [dig?] in the flower beds, but I did hate to get my fingers in the dirt.

Will and Nannie Masters had moved into rooms over the Masters' store and Mrs Masters persuaded Ma to let me stay with Nannie, because she had falling spells and it was not safe for her to stay alone with Little Nan.

There was'n't much work to do. The washing was done down at the hotel and Nannie and I together cooked and washed dishes made the beds swept the floors and took care of Little Nan.

But it was not pleasant, for I never knew at what moment Nannie would fall without a word or a sign and lie as if dead. Then I must loosen her clothes and sprinkle water on her face until she opened her eyes, then in a few minutes I would help her up and to a chair.

I did not like either to be where Will was. He was drinking more than ever. His eyes were red rimmed and he had such a silly look on his face. Dr. Hoyt was always giving him whiskey, sometimes bringing it into the rooms and giving it to him there. He seemed to be doing it more for spite than anything for since Matie was dead Mr & Mrs Masters would have nothing to do with him[74] and Fanny Star wouldn't take him back.

I hadn't stayed with Nannie very long when one night I waked from a sound sleep to find Will leaning over me. I could smell the whiskey on his breath. I sat up quickly.

'Is Nannie sick,' I asked.

"No," he answered, ["]lie down and be still!"

'Go away quick,' I said, 'or I will scream for Nannie.'

He went and the next day Ma said I could come home.[75]

Old Mr & Mrs Pool, with their grown daughter, Missouri,[76] lived in a queer little house near us. There was a fireplace and Missouri never let the fire go out on the hearth, carefully covering the coals with ashes to keep them when the fire was not needed. Missouri did all the work, caring for her father and mother for they were old. She kept the house and herself always spotless. I never saw a speck of dirt on her dress or apron or sunbonnet, not even when she was working in her garden. She had a wonderful garden and the house yard was filled with all kinds of beautiful flowers, mingonnett and moss roses on the borders, tall hollyhocks against the back fence and poppies all over the place. I loved the poppies best, with their wonderful colors and the texture of their petals, the blossoms were like silken banners blowing in the wind.

Mr & Mrs Pool and Missouri all smoked pipes, Missouri's was a very small, white clay pipe. She used to bring it with her when she came to visit and tell us stories of Missouri, the state for which she was named. She had five sisters and six brothers all married and still living there, but she said whenever she had a beau, something happened to drive him away.

She couldn't understand it until she overheard her mother telling a neighbor woman that she "aimed to keep Missoury at home to take care of me in my old age and so far I've managed to drive her beaus away."[77]

Missouri was homesick for the old place in Missouri where she used to ride horseback and pick wild fruit in the woods. She was a great help and comfort when Mary was taken sick and we were all so sorry when we learned later, that having at last married an old sweetheart and gone back to Missouri, she died in childbirth, it having been much harder for her because of her age.

Mary was taken suddenly sick[78] with a pain in her head and grew worse quickly. She was dilierous with an awful fever and Ma cut off her long, beautiful hair[79] to keep her head cooler.

We feared for several days that she would not get well and one

75. *He went and the next day Ma said I could come home.* This disturbing scene between Wilder and Will Masters is not included in any of the revised *Pioneer Girl* manuscripts.

76. *Old Mr & Mrs Pool, with their grown daughter, Missouri.* The 1870 census lists a Thomas Pool, wife Annie or Anna, and a twenty-nine-year-old daughter named Missouri who was still living at home in Adair County, Missouri. The couple and their daughter, along with eight other children no longer at home, had all been born in Virginia. Sometime before 1876, the Pools moved to Walnut Grove, where the *Redwood Gazette* recorded that Thomas Pool owed back taxes on two lots in the original plat of the town ("Delinquent Tax List," July 13, 1876). In October 1879, Thomas Pool sold his house and lots and "with his wife and daughter [went] to spend the winter with their friends near Burns Station" ("Walnut Station Items," Oct. 30, 1879). By the 1880 census, Thomas and Anna were living with their married daughter Amy Dotson (forty-eight years old) in North Star Township, Brown County, Minnesota, three townships away from Walnut Grove, near Burns Station (Springfield) on the Winona & St. Peter Railroad. Missouri Pool was no longer part of the household, and there is no further trace of her. She would have been about forty years old.

77. *she "aimed to keep Missoury at home . . . and so far I've managed to drive her beaus away."* Lane adapted the Missouri Pool material for her short story "Long Skirts," published in *Ladies' Home Journal* in 1933, then republished as part of *Old Home Town* in 1935. Lane changed Missouri Pool's name to Minty Bates, a hardworking spinster prevented from marriage when her mother intervened and turned away her suitors.

78. *Mary was taken suddenly sick.* Earlier in the manuscript, Wilder suggested that Mary "was not very well all winter."

79. *Ma cut off her long, beautiful hair.* In *By the Shores of Silver Lake*, Pa shaves Mary's head, perhaps because the fictional Ma would have been too ill to do so (p. 2).

80. *Mary had, had a stroke. . . . she could not see well.* On April 24, 1879, the *Redwood Gazette* reported: "Miss Mary Ingalls has been confined to her bed about ten days with severe headache. It was feared that hemorrhage of the brain had set in [and] one side of her face became partially paralyzed. She is now slowly convalescing." Three weeks later, Mary was still confined to bed and suffering, but on June 12, there was some good news: "Miss Mary Ingalls is recovering, but very slowly. Her eye sight which she had almost lost is improving as she gains strength." By June 26, however, her health had continued to improve, but her sight was "so much impaired that she cannot distinguish one object from another. She can discern day from night but even this slight vision is also failing." Wilder provided few details about the fictional Mary's illness in *By the Shores of Silver Lake*, perhaps because she and Lane had argued over how to deal with Mary's blindness. Wilder wanted to include her sister's loss of sight but did not want the fifth book in her series to "begin . . . with a recital of discouragement and calamities" (LIW to RWL, Jan. 25, 1938, Box 13, file 194, Lane Papers). Ultimately, the novel begins with a revelation about Mary's eyesight, but Wilder provided only brush-stroke details to convey what happened to her characters between the end of *On the Banks of Plum Creek* and the beginning of *By the Shores of Silver Lake*.

81. *Pa had Dr Welcome come . . . but . . . nothing could be done.* It is not clear whether Dr. J. W. B. Wellcome or his son Florado Wellcome tended Mary at Charles Ingalls's request. The elder Dr. Wellcome was the official surgeon for the railroad and would "stop off occasionally to see his friends in this burg" ("Walnut Station Items," *RG*, June 26, 1879), so it is possible that he dropped in to see Mary, as well. Charles and Caroline Ingalls did more than request local aid, however. The newspaper reported that they were planning to take their daughter to Saint Paul "in a short time in hopes that they can have something done for her eyesight. Although entirely blind she is very patient and submissive" (ibid., July 31, 1879). "We learned later," Wilder told Lane in

morning when I looked at her I saw one side of her face drawn out of shape. Ma said Mary had, had a stroke and as I looked at her I remembered her oak tree away back in Wisconsin that had been struck by lightening all down one side.

After the stroke Mary began to get better, but she could not see well.[80] Pa had Dr Welcome come to help Dr Hoyt with them, but he said the nerves of her eyes had the worst of the stroke and were dying, that nothing could be done.[81]

They had a long name for her sickness and said it was the results of the measels[82] from which she had never wholly recovered.

As Mary grew stronger her eyes grew weaker until when she could sit up in the big chair among the pillows she could hardly see at all. The last thing Mary ever saw[83] was the bright blue of Grace's eyes as Grace stood holding by her chair, looking up at her.

Mary was getting strong again sitting up most of the day and her face was almost straight once more, when, one day, Pa's sister Aunt Docia Holms[84] drove up to the door, taking us by surprise.

She was on her way west, where Uncle High had a contract grading for the Chicago and Northwestern which was being extended westward[85] from Tracy[86] that spring.

Aunt Docia was alone with her horse and buggy and had come to get Pa to go with her to the camp where Uncle High[87] was. They wanted Pa for book-keeper, company store keeper and time-keeper and would pay him a good salary.[88]

Pa was glad of the chance and Ma told him to go along,[89] we would be all right until we could come later.

So the next day, Pa sold our house and lot to Mr Masters[90] and drove away with Aunt Docia the morning after.

There had not been much idle time for me that summer, what with working away from home and then helping at home with the house and garden and taking care of Grace while Mary had been so sick. I had hardly seen any of the girls. Anna Ensign would come from the farm some days to see us; Maud Blair[91] my chum at Sunday-school came once in a while to see me and I walked out to where Nettie Kennedy lived two miles from town and spent a long, lazy day with her.[92]

1937, "when Pa took her from De Smet to Chicago to a specialist that the nerves of her eyes were paralyzed and there was no hope. You can see that all this cost money. I would have no idea how much. I know Pa sent home money for Dr. bills after he was working on the R.R." (LIW to RWL, Mar. 23, 1937, Box 13, file 193, Lane Papers).

82. *They had a long name for her sickness and said it was the results of the measels.* In 1937, Wilder wrote: "Mary had ~~spinal mengitis~~ some sort of spinal sickness. I am not sure if the Dr. named it" (LIW to RWL, Mar. 23, 1937). The doctor may not have named the disease, but in 2013, a team of medical researchers explored the possibilities and concluded that her blindness was not the result of the measles but most likely of "viral meningoencephalitis" (Allexan et al., "Blindness in Walnut Grove," p. 2). In *By the Shores of Silver Lake*, Wilder attributed Mary's illness to scarlet fever, a disease that she and her sister had actually contracted in 1874. The only correspondence that survives to explain this decision suggests that it might have come about almost by accident. Lane, who argued for omitting Mary's blindness from the story, had capitulated to her mother's logic for keeping it but had insisted that the condition be introduced "as the end of an illness." She then quickly sketched how it should go: "Times have been hard, Grace has been born, Jack has died, Mary has had—scarlet fever, was it?—between plum Creek and this volume" (RWL to LIW, Dec. 19, 1937, Box 13, file 193, Lane Papers). In the end, the two women may have decided that scarlet fever, given its prevalence in novels such as Louisa May Alcott's *Little Women*, worked better than measles.

83. *the last thing Mary ever saw.* When Lane advised Wilder to drop Mary's blindness from the Little House series, Wilder argued fiercely that it was a necessary source of conflict and change for the entire family. "A touch of tragedy makes the story truer to life," she insisted, "and showing the way we all took it illustrates the spirit of the times and the frontier" (LIW to RWL, [Dec.1937], Box 13, file 193, Lane Papers). In the novel, Wilder made Mary's blindness a challenge for both sisters, and Laura takes on the responsibility of describing the visual world for Mary, becoming her eyes (*SL*, p. 2).

84. *Aunt Docia Holms.* Sometime in the 1870s, after her divorce from her first husband (August Waldvogel), Wilder's Aunt Docia married Hiram Forbes. It is unclear why Wilder used the surname Holms or Holmes in all versions of *Pioneer Girl*. Docia, whose full name was Laura Ladocia, sometimes went by Lorrey; she was thirty-three in 1879.

85. *the Chicago and Northwestern which was being extended westward.* The Chicago & North Western Railway was formed through the merger of smaller railroads in Illinois and Wisconsin in the late 1850s. In 1877, the company's manager, Marvin Hughitt, visited eastern Dakota Territory and recommended that the company expand its rail service from Tracy, Minnesota, all the way to Pierre, Dakota Territory. The first news of the extension came in February 1879, when large numbers of rail ties were being collected at Tracy in preparation for spring work. Railroad surveyors, headed by C. W. Irish, arrived in March or April, and by May 8, surveys of the Dakota Central Division of the Chicago & North Western were almost complete, and contracts for grading and other work were being let. *Encyclopedia of Chicago*, s.v. "Chicago & North Western Railway Co."; Schell, *History of South Dakota*, p. 161; news items, *RG*, Feb. 13, May 8, 1879, *Currie Pioneer*, Apr. 10, 1879; *Brookings County Press*, Mar. 3, Dec. 11, 1879.

86. *Tracy.* The town of Tracy, Minnesota, just seven miles west of Walnut Grove, was established in 1875 and named for a director of the Chicago & North Western Railway. "During the first four years of its history," an early historian noted, "the aspirations of Tracy were not great, and few had the temerity to predict that it would ever become aught but a little trading point." But in 1879, "the town was lively all summer because of the activity in railroad construction, and there was a large increase in population" (Rose, *Illustrated History of Lyon County*, p. 163).

Aunt Docia. *Helen Sewell, 1939*

87. *Uncle High.* According to census records, Hiram Forbes had been born in Prussia and was forty-one years old in 1879.

88. *They wanted Pa for book-keeper, . . . and would pay him a good salary.* On July 24, 1879, the *Redwood Gazette* reported that Charles Ingalls had taken "charge of a gang of men near Lake Benton," where work was "progressing rapidly." Ingalls later wrote that he worked for "A. L. Wells and Co selling goods to the graders on the Dakota Central Railroad" ("Settlement of De Smet," p. [1]). This company may have been the one identified as H. D. Wells and Company of Milwaukee in the *Currie Pioneer* of June 5, 1879; its owners had just contracted to build a portion of the new railroad. In any case, it was a substantial operation—by the end of June 1879, Hiram Forbes had one hundred eighty teams and four hundred eighty men working for him, according to the *Brookings County Press* (June 19, 1879). As bookkeeper and company store keeper, Charles Ingalls was taking on a significant position in the enterprise. Given the costs of Mary's illness, the job must have seemed providential. *By the Shores of Silver Lake* captured his reaction to the offer of fifty dollars a month: "A kind of tightness smoothed out of Pa's thin cheeks and his blue eyes lighted up" (p. 4). Later in the novel, Pa explains that he would run the store, keep track of the men's charges against their wages, and "when the paymaster brought the money each payday, Pa would pay every man" (p. 61).

89. *Ma told him to go along.* All versions of *Pioneer Girl* agree that Caroline Ingalls supported her husband's decision to move west (Brandt, pp. 66–67; Brandt Revised, p. 52; Bye, p. 82). Her fictional counterpart, however, needs to be persuaded. "But we're settled here. We've got the farm," she argues. She also worries about traveling so soon after Mary's illness, but ultimately she agrees (*SL*, p. 4).

90. *Pa sold our house and lot to Mr Masters.* When *By the Shores of Silver Lake* opens, the fictional Ingalls family still lives in the house Pa built on the original Plum Creek farm. In the novel, Wilder explained that two years have passed in Laura's life and that Pa "had made only two poor wheat crops since the grasshoppers came" (p. 3). Wilder's decision to keep the fictional family in the Plum Creek house was a sensible solution to the challenging creative problem of skipping over the Burr Oak period. It also allowed her to maintain the image of the fictional family as pioneering homesteaders *until* they settled down at last in Dakota Territory. Lane encouraged Wilder to make this creative decision. "It is not a fact," Lane wrote her mother, "but it is perfectly true to take them west from the house on Plum Creek, where everything that has happened during this time might as truthfully have occurred as where it did occur" (RWL to LIW, Jan. 21, 1938, Box 13, file 194, Lane papers). In the novel, Pa sells the Plum Creek farm to Mr. Nelson, who pays two hundred dollars cash for it (*SL*, p. 6).

91. *Maud Blair.* Maud Blair would have been thirteen in 1879. She lived with her parents, Luther and Emma Blair, in Springdale Township on the west side of Walnut Grove. Brandt Revised and Bye do not mention Maud.

92. *I walked out to where Nettie Kennedy lived . . . and spent a long, lazy day with her.* Bye added: "That last day I had all to myself, because Ma said I had worked so hard that I deserved it" (p. 82). In 1875, the Kennedy family lived in North Hero Township, east of Walnut Grove.

How I did enjoy that day with Nettie and Sandy. Christy and her mother made an extra good dinner and wouldn't let Nettie do any of her work, so we had the day to ourselves with her books and pictures and the sunshine and flowers. Sandy, with his red head and freckled face, his pant legs rolled up from his bear feet was on his good behavior and he and Nettie walked part way home with me when it was time to go. I never saw them again.

After Pa went away, Ma and I were busy getting all our clothes in order, sorting out and packing the things we were to take with us and selling or giving away the rest. When a month had gone by[93] Pa sent Ma his first pay check; she bought our tickets to Tracy which was as far as the train ran and once more we started west, but on the train this time instead of with horses and wagon.

This was my first ride on a train[94] and was all too short for leaving Walnut Grove in the morning we were at Tracy by noon, but short as it was I enjoyed it, while I helped Ma with Grace and the sat*chel*s (?)[95] and told Mary about every thing I saw,[96] for we were on our way again and going in the direction which always brought the happiest changes.[97]

Pa was driving in from the camp to meet us at Tracy that night and take us out the next morning, so when we got off the train we went to the hotel to wait. The man carrying our satchels took us into the parlor and left us. We stayed there looking at pictures and books seeing no one for some time, then two little boys came in looked at us and went out again. A few minutes after a man came in leaning on a cane. He said he was sorry there was no one to make us welcome. His wife and her sister used to make the place pleasant, but they were dead and gone. There was no one left but him and the little boys and the hired help didn't do very well by themselves.

The man sat down in a big chair with pillows in it and told Ma his story.[98]

He and his wife and the twin boys, with his wife's sister and her sweetheart had gone for a drive one Sunday afternoon. A storm had come up and they were trying to get home before it struck. That was

93. *When a month had gone by.* In *By the Shores of Silver Lake*, Wilder implied that "weeks and months" had gone by before the rest of the family set out to join Pa in Dakota Territory (*SL*, p. 15–16). The exact timeline of Charles Ingalls's employment is not clear, but he would have taken the job sometime after May 8 and before June 3, 1879. He later wrote that his family arrived at Silver Lake on September 9, 1879. "Settlement of De Smet," p. [1]; LIW to RWL, [1937 or 1938], Box 13, file 193, Lane Papers.

94. *This was my first ride on a train.* On September 6, 1879, "Mrs. C. P. Ingalls and family started for Dakota. She goes to rejoin her husband who is at work on the Chicago & Dakota R. R. west of Lake Benton," the *Currie Pioneer* correspondent wrote. "We are sorry to lose them but what is our lose [*sic*] is their gain" ("Walnut Grove Items," Sept. 11, 1879). Wilder devoted a chapter, "Riding in the Cars" (*SL*, pp. 15–27), to the family's seven-mile train trip to Tracy, emphasizing the danger and adventure Laura feels during the experience.

Depot, Tracy, Minn., early 1880s. *Wheels Across the Prairie Museum, Tracy, Minn.*

95. *sat*chel*s (?).* Wilder underlined the *t*, *h*, *l*, and *s* in the original manuscript, and the question mark in parentheses signaled her uncertainty about the word's spelling. In a speech she delivered to the

Mountain Grove Sorosis Club in Missouri, she told the audience, "The only stupid thing about words is the spelling of them" (*Little House Sampler*, p. 179).

96. *and told Mary about every thing I saw*. This instance marks the first time in *Pioneer Girl* that Wilder acted as her sister's eyes.

97. *going in the direction which always brought the happiest changes*. This memorable line was omitted from the Bye manuscript (p. 83), a change indicated in Lane's handwriting in Brandt Revised (p. 52). This westward yearning would become a hallmark of Wilder's novels.

98. *The man . . . told Ma his story*. The first hotel in Tracy, the Commercial, was built in 1875; Henry H. Welch was its proprietor until the autumn of 1879. M. ("Dad") Finch presided over the rival Tracy Exchange. Both establishments added on to their buildings during the railroad boom. Brandt Revised and Bye do not include the hotel proprietor's story, nor does *By the Shores of Silver Lake*. Rose, *Illustrated History of Lyon County*, p. 162; "Tracy Tracings," Mar. 27, May 22, 1879, and "Tracy Notes," Aug. 28, 1879, *Currie Pioneer*.

the last he knew until he waked up in bed not able to move seemingly paralized.

People caring for him told him the storm had come with a great deal of thunder and lightening and a deluge of rain.

The open prairie came up to the hotel on the back and some time after the storm was over, the hired girl saw the little boys come walking down the road. They acted strangely, walking a little ways, then stopping and whispering to each other, then coming a little farther and stopping again appearing very frightened. She ran out to them and brought them in, but when she asked where their father and mother were they would not talk at first, but finally said they were all asleep out there in the road.

People went hurrying along the road until two miles from town they came on the four people and the horses lying in the road. They were indeed all fast asleep and none of them ever waked, except the boys' father. Lightening had struck them and when the man talking to us, had waked in bed, he had been unconcious so long that his wife, her sister and the sister's sweetheart were buried.

No one knew whether the boys had not been touched or if they had been stunned and revived by the rain. The boys would not talk about it and for a long time would just sit and stare at nothing. Even yet they would not play, but wandered around the house and still seemed strange and frightened.

After a short time, as the man still lay helpless, boils began to break out on his body and limbs and as far as the swelling and inflamation of a boil reached the body came back to life. By now he had so far recovered that he could hobble around with a cane. He showed us the gold watch he had been wearing when the lightening struck him. It was full of round holes and the inside all melted together.

It was no wonder the hotel was quiet and gloomy. We were so glad and felt much better when Pa came. In the morning after an early breakfast Pa loaded all our things from the depot and the hotel into the lumber wagon he had driven in and we started on to Uncle High's camp.

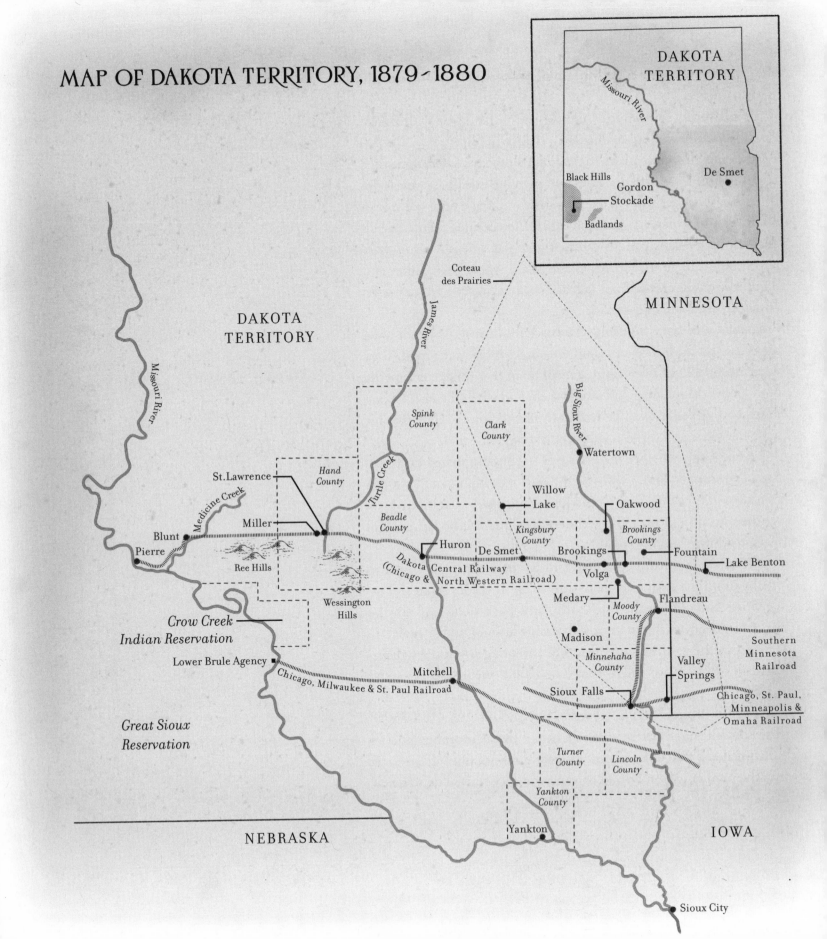

MAP OF DAKOTA TERRITORY, 1879~1880

DAKOTA
TERRITORY

Missouri River

Black Hills

Gordon
Stockade

Badlands

De Smet

Coteau
des Prairies

MINNESOTA

DAKOTA
TERRITORY

Missouri River

James River

*Spink
County*

*Clark
County*

Big Sioux River

Watertown

Willow
Lake

Oakwood

St.Lawrence

*Hand
County*

Turtle Creek

Miller

Medicine Creek

Blunt

Pierre

*Beadle
County*

Ree Hills

Huron

*Kingsbury
County*

De Smet

Brookings

*Brookings
County*

Fountain

Lake Benton

Dakota (Chicago &
Central Railway
North Western Railroad)

Volga

Medary

*Moody
County*

Flandreau

*Wessington
Hills*

Madison

Southern
Minnesota
Railroad

*Crow Creek
Indian Reservation*

Lower Brule Agency

*Minnehaha
County*

Valley
Springs

Mitchell

Sioux Falls

Chicago, Milwaukee & St. Paul Railroad

Chicago, St. Paul,
Minneapolis &
Omaha Railroad

*Great Sioux
Reservation*

*Turner
County*

*Lincoln
County*

*Yankton
County*

NEBRASKA

Yankton

IOWA

Sioux City

MAP OF KINGSBURY COUNTY

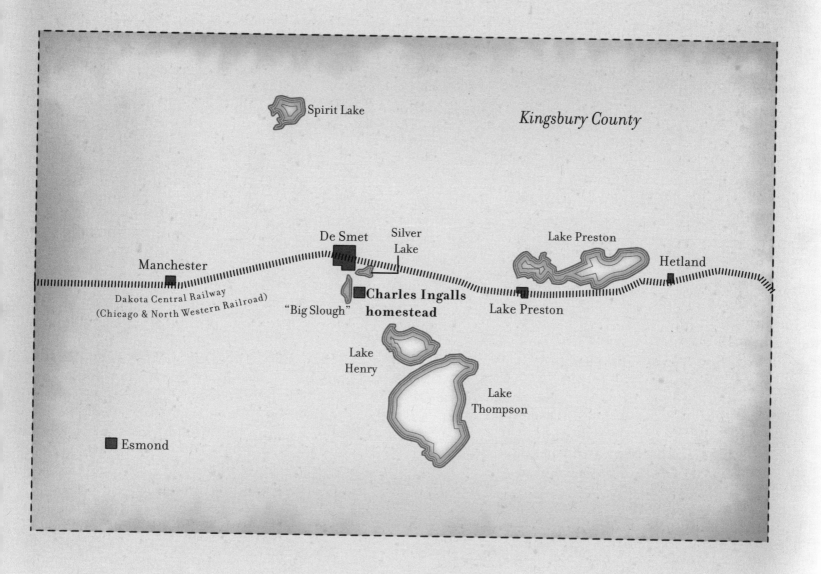

Spirit Lake

Kingsbury County

De Smet

Silver
Lake

Lake Preston

Hetland

Manchester

Dakota Central Railway
(Chicago & North Western Railroad)

"Big Slough"

**Charles Ingalls
homestead**

Lake Preston

Lake
Henry

Lake
Thompson

Esmond

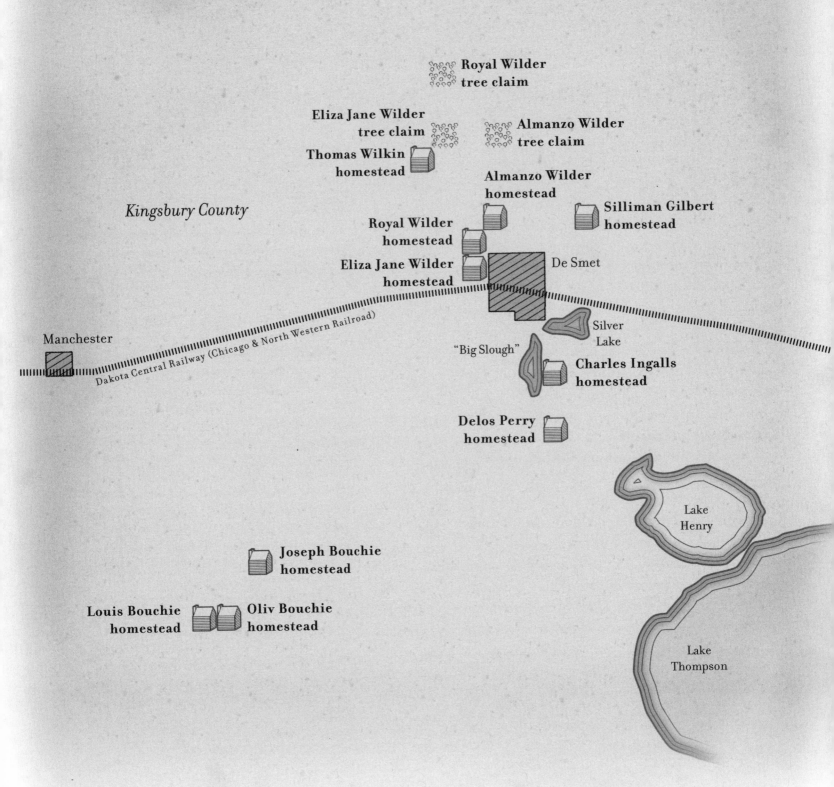

MAP OF DE SMET VICINITY

Royal Wilder
tree claim

Eliza Jane Wilder
tree claim

Almanzo Wilder
tree claim

Thomas Wilkin
homestead

Kingsbury County

Almanzo Wilder
homestead

Silliman Gilbert
homestead

Royal Wilder
homestead

Eliza Jane Wilder
homestead

De Smet

Silver
Lake

"Big Slough"

Manchester

Dakota Central Railway (Chicago & North Western Railroad)

Charles Ingalls
homestead

Delos Perry
homestead

Lake
Henry

Joseph Bouchie
homestead

Louis Bouchie
homestead

Oliv Bouchie
homestead

Lake
Thompson

Dakota Territory, 1879–1880

Nothing happened on the way and the road looked all the same. At noon we stopped, fed the horses and ate the cold lunch we had brought from the hotel, then went on again.

It was after dark when we got to the camp, but Aunt Docia had a good warm supper waiting for us.

Gene and Lena were two cousins I had never seen before.[1] Lena was a very pretty girl about my age with black eyes and black curley hair. Gene was very dark too a little younger than Lena.

There was room in Aunt Docia's shanty for all except Gene and Lena and me. Gene went to stay in the bunk house with the men and Lena and I slept on a quilt on the ground in a tent. It was all very strange and rather unpleasant. If I had been up in the wagon I wouldn't have minded, but I didn't like to sleep on the ground where there might be snakes and bugs and I was away from Pa and Ma and the girls in a strange country. It didn't seem as though I ought to mind any of these things but taken all together I felt lonesome. Just as I was dropping off to sleep there was a scratching on the tent by our heads and a screech almost in our ears. It gave me a frightful start, but Lena shouted "Hey! I wasn't brought up in the woods to be scared by an owl. It's Gene trying to scare us," she said and was asleep at once, so I went to sleep too.[2]

We didn't stay long at this place. The camp was already breaking up and going farther west to the next camp, for the grade was finished here and a town called Brookins started.[3]

Aunt Docia's family and Pa were staying on for a final acceptance of the work and settlement with the railroad company. I understood that Aunt Docia and Uncle High[4] were bitterly disappointed for after their hard summer's work with themselves and four big teams they were coming out behind, in debt to the railroad company for the price they were paid for making the grade would not cover the expense of building it allowing nothing for the work of themselves

1. *Gene and Lena were two cousins I had never seen before.* Lena and Gene were Docia Ingalls Forbes's children by her first husband, August Waldvogel or Wanfogle, whom she divorced in the early 1870s. Lena, born in 1866, was slightly older than Wilder, and August Eugene ("Gene"), who is called Jean in *By the Shores of Silver Lake*, was two years younger. Lena and Gene had lived in Wisconsin in the early 1870s when Wilder and her family were there and must have been among the babies and children at the dance Wilder recalled at Grandpa Ingalls's house, although she apparently did not remember them. In *By the Shores of Silver Lake*, Wilder wrote that Aunt Docia "had married a widower with two children" (p. 3), making Lena and Gene her cousins by marriage. She made this fictional change because she had included Aunt Docia as a young single woman in *Little House in the Big Woods*. "Lena and Jean could not be Aunt Docias children," Wilder explained to Lane, "for [Docia] was a girl in the [fictional] Big Woods when Laura was 5[.] Lena was older than Laura" (LIW to RWL, [1938], Box 13, file 194, Lane Papers). By 1880, the Forbes household also included five-year-old Ida, three-year-old Abby, and eight-month-old Emmie. Docia Forbes had apparently been pregnant during the summer of 1879.

2. *Lena shouted. . . . so I went to sleep too.* The corresponding passage in *By the Shores of Silver Lake* (pp. 42–43) uses similar vocabulary to evoke the same action, mood, and characterization of Laura, Lena, and Jean.

3. *The camp . . . a town called Brookins started.* Charles Ingalls had been bookkeeper for the grading operations at this camp on the Big Sioux River since early June 1879. In platting Brookings, Dakota Territory, on or near the spot of the camp, the Chicago & North Western Railway Company bypassed three already established communities in Brook-

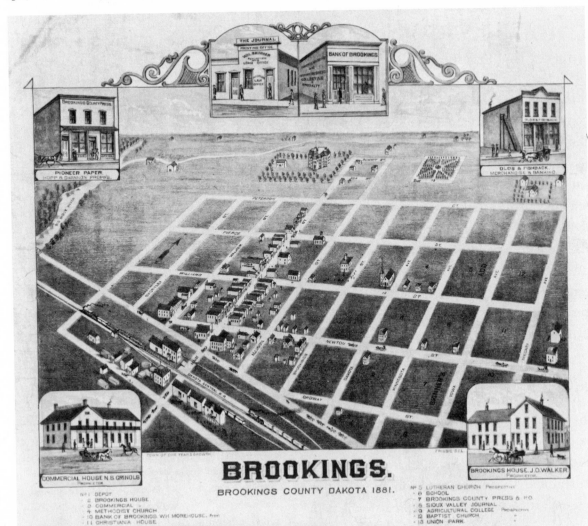

Bird's-eye view, Brookings, 1881. *South Dakota State Historical Society*

ings County: Medary, Oakwood, and Fountain, the original home of the *Brookings County Press*. Both the town and county were named for territorial judge Wilmot W. Brookings, who settled in eastern Dakota Territory in the late 1850s and played an active role in territorial politics into the 1870s. A Dakota Central Railroad engine chugged into Brookings for the first time in mid-October 1879; the *Brookings County Press* was not far behind. In all versions of *Pioneer Girl*, the town's name is spelled "Brookins" (Brandt, p. 69; Brandt Revised, p. 53; Bye, p. 84). Wilder similarly misspelled it in *By the Shores of Silver Lake* and wrote a

family friend in De Smet, who had pointed out the mistake, that the book contained "several typographical errors in the spelling, besides leaving the 'g' out of Brookings" (LIW to Aubrey Sherwood, 18 Nov. 1939, Laura Ingalls Wilder Memorial Society). LIW to RWL, [1937 or 1938], Box 13, file 193, Lane Papers; *History of Southeastern Dakota*, p. 138; "History of Brookings"; Schell, *History of South Dakota*, p. 161–62.

4. *Uncle High*. In Brandt (p. 69), Brandt Revised (p. 53), and Bye (p. 84), Wilder abbreviated Hiram Forbes's name as "Uncle Hi," as she did in *By the Shores of Silver Lake* (p. 4).

and teams.[5] On the contract at the camp ahead[6] they hoped to pay what they owed the company and make a little for themselves.

Besides the big work horses, Uncle High had two black ponies one for Lena and one for Gene. These were on picket ropes near the camp. Gene loaned me his pony and I rode around with Lena a little, but I was timid for I had never ridden a horse.[7] Lena could leap on her pony from the ground and ride it bareback on the run. She and Gene raced each other from the ground trying which could sooner mount and reach a certain place.

Lena and I drove both ponies hitched to a light wagon several miles into the country to bring home the washing a farmer's wife had done for us all.

It would be hard to tell which enjoyed it most the ponies or Lena and I. They ran most of the way with their long, black manes and tails blowing in the wind while we shouted and sang. When we slowed the ponies down to rest, they were quiet only a few minutes, then would touch noses and break into a run of their own accord.

We found the reason the washerwoman had not brought the washing back was because her daughter had just been married and she had been busy with the wedding. "She is only thirteen," she said proudly, "but it is just as well to be married young." The bride was just my age and a year younger than Lena. As we talked about it going back, we were glad we were not in her place but could run around and play as we were doing. We decided we didn't mind helping with the work and the babies but as for us let some one else be responsible.[8]

The next day aunt Docia's folks moved on to the new camp, but we had to wait another day for Pa to be checked out of the Company store.[9]

Then very early in the morning we put all our things in the big wagon; Pa hitched on the big team and we went on west. Almost at once we drove through the breaks along the river; crossed the Sioux river[10] and were out on the broad prairie that looked like a big meadow as far as we could see in every direction.

There was no cover on the wagon for we were going only forty miles and the sky was clear and cloudless.

5. *bitterly disappointed . . . nothing for the work of themselves and teams.* Later in *Pioneer Girl*, Wilder explained that a contractor did not get money for running his own teams because "on the face of it that would be simply paying himself." The railroad company docked the contractor for all supplies related to his teams, however, and the situation profited the railroad, which controlled the capital and the contracts, as Wilder also explained later (*see* p. 172). A 1906 review of railroad grading contracts concluded that the "usual railway contract is . . . a very one-sided agreement, altogether in the interests of the railway company." Given that the railroad company engineers held authority over the work, the railroad contractor was not running a "business proposition," but "a hazardous risk" ("Notes on Classification," p. 159).

6. *On the contract at the camp ahead.* Hiram Forbes and his company had the contract for "twenty miles more, west of the Sioux River, which is heavy work," the *Brookings County Press* reported on June 19, 1879. The headquarters camp for this new contract would be at Silver Lake.

7. *two black ponies. . . . I was timid for I had never ridden a horse.* Wilder devoted an entire chapter, "The Black Ponies" (*SL*, pp. 45-55), to her adventures with Lena and the horses, but in the novel, Laura is far from timid. She falls off the pony, but she gets back on. "Her hair came unbraided and her throat grew hoarse from laughing and screeching" (p. 54). Illustrator Garth Williams chose this image as the cover illustration of the new edition of *By the Shores of Silver Lake* published in 1953. Yet, the color rendering featured a sorrel-colored pony, not a black one.

8. *The bride was just my age. . . . let some one else be responsible.* Wilder was actually twelve during the fall of 1879, and Lena turned thirteen in November of that year. For Wilder, their actual ages were less important than their proximity in age. As she wrote in *By the Shores of Silver Lake*, the bride "was only a little older" (p. 50) than Laura and about to assume the responsibilities of a married woman. In *Pioneer Girl* as well as the novel, the fate of the young bride is sobering, an unexpected reminder that childhood

is slipping away and new responsibilities are ahead if the girls follow a conventional path. Wilder embellished this episode in the novel, even giving the bride a name (Lizzie). The scene also introduced a coming-of-age theme, which Wilder developed throughout the remaining novels and which now places them squarely in the Young Adult category. In *By the Shores of Silver Lake*, Wilder placed the wild ride on the ponies immediately after Laura and Lena decide they are not ready for the responsibilities of marriage, reinforcing the desire for freedom (p. 51). Wilder, however, married at the age of eighteen. Lena married a farmer named Samuel A. Heikes at the age of twenty-one in 1888 and had seven children; the family settled in Dakota City, Nebraska. Baldwin and Baldwin, *Nebraskana*, p. 534.

9. *Company store*. The company store was the source of all goods for the workers and teamsters who were grading the railroad. In a letter to Lane, Wilder included notations from Charles Ingalls's railroad account book for the Big Sioux River camp. This example is from June 3, 1879:

1 thousand feet lumber	$13.
20 lbs nails	.80
50 " flour	$1.50
3 shovels	3.75
2 scrapers	$20.00
1 Big Plug Tobaco	.40

(LIW to RWL, [1937 or 1938]).

10. *Sioux river*. The Big Sioux River flows southward for over four hundred miles through eastern South Dakota and joins the Missouri River at Sioux City, Iowa. All versions of *Pioneer Girl* identify the Big Sioux as simply the Sioux River. Wilder corrected this mistake in *By the Shores of Silver Lake*, where Laura describes it to Mary as "a big river sometimes, but now it's dried up till it's no bigger than Plum Creek. It trickles along from pool to pool, by dry gravel stretches and cracked dry mud flats" (p. 58).

The weather was warm, but not too warm and the wind was blowing, waving the tall prairie grass that had turned brown in the summer sun.

At noon we stopped, fed the horses and ate our lunch quite in the old way, then hitched up again and went on mile after mile, never seeing a house or any sign of people, the trail we were following showing only broken and bent down grasses to mark it.

There were old buffalo paths worn deep in the ground but grassed over and round depressions of perhaps a quarter or a half an acre that had once been buffalo wallows but where now also the grass was growing.[11]

Late in the afternoon a man on horseback showed on the prairie behind us and followed gaining a little and so drawing nearer as we went on. Pa seemed uneasy and kept glancing back.

Then a man on a white horse overtook the other and they came on. Ma didn't like their coming but Pa said the last man was Big Jerry and everything was all right.[12]

When they overtook us the first man went on, but Jerry rode beside the wagon and talked to Pa. He was a very tall, broad man, but not a bit fat, very dark, with high cheek bones a large nose and straight, black hair. He wore no hat. His shirt was a flaming red and he rode his snow-white pony without saddle or bridle, guiding it with his knees. In a few minutes he touched his pony with his heel and away it went in the smoothest, prettiest run, down into a little draw, up on the other side and away.[13]

Ma was afraid[14] they might wait for us in some draw to rob us, but Pa said Jerry was perfectly safe. He didn't like the looks of the other fellow but Jerry had promised to keep with him. Jerry, Pa said was a half breed, Indian and French,[15] a gambler, some said a horse thief, but a darned good fellow.

For some time the sky had been full of flocks of wild ducks and V shaped flocks of wild geese, the leader flying at the point of the V and calling on his flock to follow. They always answered him all along the lines and the air was full of their "Honk! Honk!" They were flying low to light and rest for the night on the chain of little lakes not far to the west of us.[16]

11. *buffalo paths . . . buffalo wallows . . . where . . . the grass was growing.* Buffalo trails and wallows were once common throughout North America, where an estimated sixty million bison roamed before the arrival of Europeans. The buffalo, or American bison (*Bison bison*), can reach six feet tall at the shoulder and weigh more than one ton. Traveling in herds, the animals carved distinct trails, "the only natural roads in the wilderness" (McHugh, *Time of the Buffalo*, p. 49), which served as routes for both American Indian and white travelers. Wallows were large depressions carved into the prairie when bison repeatedly rolled in the dust to shed fur and insects. Plains Indians relied for food and shelter on the bison, which were nearly exterminated by the late 1800s. In a similar passage in *By the Shores of Silver Lake*, Wilder added: "Laura had never seen a buffalo, and Pa said it was not likely that she would ever see one. . . . They had been the Indians' cattle, and white men had slaughtered them all" (pp. 61–62). Recent research has shown that buffalo populations started to decline once American Indians began to build large horse herds and employ "more effective hunting techniques." Thus, bison populations "were falling even before American soldiers, hunters, and ranchers began to destroy the herds in the second half of the nineteenth century" (Calloway, *One Vast Winter Count*, pp. 311–12). By 1879, bison were so rare that it made the papers when "a buffalo was seen eighteen miles northwest of Fargo" ("Dakota Items," *Dakota Pantagraph*, June 18, 1879). Higgins, *Wild Mammals*, pp. 241–43; Lott, *American Bison*, pp. 9, 66–67, 88; Dary, *Buffalo Book*, pp. 40–41, 180–81.

12. *Big Jerry and everything was all right.* This man's full name is probably not recoverable given the clues in the text, but like Soldat du Chêne, Big Jerry fulfilled an almost mythic role within the framework of the Ingalls family's pioneer experience. He intervened at key moments to protect the family and, for Wilder, became an archetypal frontier hero, combining the untamed spirit of the West with an inherent integrity. Rose Wilder Lane found this role equally compelling; in her novel *Free Land*, which drew

Picture copyright 1953 by Garth Williams, copyright © renewed 1981 by Garth Williams. Used by permission of HarperCollins Publishers

thus deepened her fictional counterpart's character at the same time that she created a transcendent image of an American Indian forever riding west across the prairie, unencumbered by encroaching settlement and its inevitable conflicts.

14. *Ma was afraid.* In *By the Shores of Silver Lake*, Wilder used Ma's fear to reinforce the unspoken conflict between her parents and their views of the American West: "[Ma] did not say anything because nothing she could say would make any difference. But Laura knew that Ma had never wanted to leave Plum Creek and did not like to be here now" (p. 66).

Helen Sewell, 1939

heavily from *Pioneer Girl*, she named a similar character "Half-breed Jack" (p. 130). For a discussion of the role of such characters in Wilder's fiction, *see* Campbell, "'Wild Men' and Dissenting Voices," pp. 111–22. .

13. *he touched his pony with his heel . . . up on the other side and away.* In *By the Shores of Silver Lake*, Wilder used this moment to reinforce Big Jerry's mythic quality and underscore the fundamental difference between Laura and Mary: .

> Laura let out her breath. "Oh, Mary! The snow-white horse and the tall, brown man, with such a black head and a bright red shirt! The brown prairie all around—and they rode right into the sun as it was going down. They'll go on in the sun around the world."
>
> Mary thought a moment. Then she said, "Laura, you know he couldn't ride into the sun. He's just riding along on the ground like anybody."
>
> But Laura did not feel that she had told a lie. What she had said was true too. Somehow that moment when the beautiful, free pony and the wild man rode into the sun would last forever (p. 65).

In this scene, Laura recognizes that truth is not simply fact and that a single experience can transcend time. Mary, however, is restricted by the inherent limitations of her imagination. Wilder

15. *Jerry, Pa said was a half breed, Indian and French.* While not considered appropriate today, the term half-breed was in common usage in the nineteenth and early twentieth centuries to refer to people of mixed racial heritage. Because of the strong influence of the French in the American fur trade of the late eighteenth and early nineteenth centuries, people of French and American Indian extraction were (and are) numerous in Minnesota and Dakota Territory. If he was born in the area, Big Jerry's American Indian heritage would most likely have been Sioux (Dakota, Lakota, Nakota), Three Affiliated Tribes (Mandan, Hidatsa, Arikara), or Ojibway. However, Wilder later identified him as the brother-in-law of Fred Fields, who was probably from Canada, which opens up other possibilities.

16. *sky had been full of flocks. . . . on the chain of little lakes not far to the west of us.* The region that Wilder and her family passed through on their way to Silver Lake lies within the Coteau des Prairies, or Prairie Coteau, a high plateau dotted with lakes and wetlands that extends through what is now eastern South Dakota from the North Dakota border south. It rises up to nine hundred feet above the surrounding prairie and averages fifty miles wide. Small lakes and depressions created by melting glaciers punctuate the rolling landscape and give the area its alternate name, the "prairie pothole" region. Because of its abundance of wetlands and grasslands, this region became a stopping point on the Central Flyway, one of several natural passageways for waterfowl (ducks, geese, and swans) and other water dependent birds (loons, grebes, cranes, shorebirds) as they migrated in the spring and fall from their wintering grounds on the Gulf Coast of the United States and Mexico to their nesting grounds in the Dakotas and farther north. Schell, *History of South Dakota*, pp. 4–5; Gries, *Roadside Geology*, pp. 12–13, 20, 42–43; Johnsgard, *Wings over the Great Plains*, pp. 9–18.

17. *The sun sank lower and lower. . . . tucking them gently in.* This passage illustrates Wilder's gift for writing descriptive prose. It appears in all adult versions of *Pioneer Girl*, where minor edits undercut its original lyricism. In Bye, for example, the opening line has been chopped into two sentences: "The sun sank lower and lower still. A ball of pulsing, liquid light, it sank in clouds of crimson and silver" (p. 87). A version also appears in *By the Shores of Silver Lake* (p. 67).

18. *Cousin Charley Quiner. . . . and cousin Louisa.* Charley Quiner, the bad boy of Wilder's Wisconsin childhood, would have been about seventeen in 1879; Louisa Quiner would have been twenty. Apparently, Docia and Hiram Forbes had recruited all available family members to work on the railroad, and the cousins' father, Henry Quiner, was also at the camp in 1879, a fact that Wilder included in *By the Shores of Silver Lake* (p. 68). In a letter to Lane, Wilder noted that Ma, who was always calm, was not even "excited at finding Uncle Henry at the R. R. camp. . . . I know we all hated a fuss, as I still do" (LIW to RWL, [1938]). In 1880, the Henry and Pauline ("Polly") Quiner family were living in McLeod County, Minnesota.

19. *the cook shanty and boarded all the men.* The cook shanty and boarding arrangements factored into Charles Ingalls's bookkeeping duties. In June 1879, he recorded one worker's board bill as "$4.80" (LIW to RWL, n.d., [1937 or 1938]).

20. *the new shanty the men had built for us.* "Our shanty was built out at one side of the camp," Wilder told Lane, "away from the boarding shanty and bunk house and the other shanties. We were supposed to keep ourselves a little apart" (LIW to RWL, Jan. 25, 1938, Box 13, file 194, Lane Papers).

21. *The shantys were in a scattered group.* In Bye, the shanties are identified as "the long cook-shanty, the bunkhouse, the stable shanty and the Company store, all built of raw new lumber" (p. 88).

22. *Silver Lake . . . mile each way (160 acres).* Silver Lake, like Lakes Henry and Thompson mentioned later, depends for its water on rain and snowmelt, which can fluctuate wildly. Silver Lake was drained

The sun sank lower and lower until, looking like a ball of pulsing, liquid light it sank gloriously in clouds of crimson and silver. Cold purple shadows rose in the east; crept slowly around the horizon, then gathered above in depth on depth of darkness from which the stars swung low and bright. The winds which all day had blown strongly, dropped low with the sun and went whispering among the tall grasses, where the earth lay breathing softly under the summer night falling softly over the prairie and tucking them gently in.[17]

We drove on and on under the stars and at last saw the twinkling lights of the camp ahead.

When, tired and hungry, we stopped before the largest shanty, Cousin Charley Quiner came out to meet us and lifted us down from the high wagon. Cousin Charley whom we had not seen since we left Wisconsin so long ago! He was a man now and Cousin Louisa[18] was inside dishing us up a hot supper. She kept the cook shanty and boarded all the men[19] who did not have their families with them.

After supper we went to the new shanty the men had built for us,[20] spread the beds on the floor and slept soundly until morning. The camp was awake and stirring early and after the men had gone to their work we went to breakfast at the cook shanty. It had been a pleasant surprise to find Louisa and Charley and we were glad we were to have them in the camp with us.

The shantys were in a scattered group[21] on the north bank of a lake. Silver Lake was only about a half mile each way (160 acres)[22] but the water was clear and cool. It lay in its little basin with a high bank on the south. On the north the bank was low but firm and dry, while at the west end the Big Slough began and extended in a curve southward. At the east end the bank was very low and from it another slough[23] extended east and north.

In these sloughs the thick slough grass grew five and six feet high. The rest of the way around the lake the upland prairie grass grew thickly.

There were no trees. The only tree in sight from all the surrounding country was a giant cottonwood called Lone Tree which could be seen for miles across the prairie.[24] It grew between the twin lakes Henry and Thompson.[25] Lake Henry was the nearest three miles to

in the early 1920s to "turn the wet marsh into hay and pasture land" and to keep nearby roadways "passible" when the lake flooded after heavy rains ("Extensive Ditching," *De Smet News*, Aug. 24, 1923). During the 1930s and into the 1980s, it was unusual for the lakebed to fill with water, but due to higher precipitation in recent years, Silver Lake and its surrounding slough are once again thriving wetlands, although both are considerably smaller than they were when the Ingalls family first arrived. The lake is less than a mile southeast of town and is now classified as a marsh. The rendering of the text in parentheses seemed the best solution to the fact that Wilder added the enclosed words in between the lines above "mile each way." "Silver Lake lives again!" p. 1; U.S. Fish & Wildlife Service, "Special Places to Visit."

23. *slough*. In the northern United States and Canada, "slough" is the term commonly used for a marsh or other reedy, swamp-like area.

24. *a giant cottonwood called Lone Tree . . . miles across the prairie.* On the Great Plains, from Manitoba to Texas, a single, massive plains cottonwood (*Populus deltoides*, subspecies *monilifera*) often towered above the prairie landscape, acting as a landmark for early travelers. For example, the Lone Tree near Egan, South Dakota, planted in 1881, was credited with saving the life of a teacher and her pupils during a blizzard. Cottonwoods are fast growing (two to five feet per year) and relatively short lived. In 2002, the largest cottonwood in South Dakota stood nearly one hundred fifty feet tall and was over twenty-six feet around. Ode, *Dakota Flora*, pp. 26-27; Hunt, *Brevet's South Dakota Historical Markers*, p. 87.

25. *twin lakes Henry and Thompson*. Lakes Henry and Thompson are two naturally formed lakes southeast of De Smet, South Dakota, in the prairie pothole region. Aubrey Sherwood, who grew up in De Smet in the early twentieth century and published the town's newspaper, recalled that Lake Thompson had "vast stretches," confirming Wilder's memory that it was the bigger of the twin lakes. Lake Henry was deeper, providing "sufficient depths in any rains to serve the public well" ("I remember Silver Lake," p. 3). Lake Thompson went dry in the 1930s and again in the late 1970s and early 1980s; today, due to higher precipitation and the draining of surrounding wetlands, it is the state's largest natural body of water. U.S. Fish & Wildlife Service, "Special Places to Visit"; Holden, *Dakota Visions*, p. 63; Johnson, "Decade of Drought," p. 228.

26. *choke cherry trees and wild grape vines.* The choke-cherry (*Prunus virginiana*) tree is actually a shrub, one of the most abundant and tallest on the Northern Great Plains. It was a favorite of the Lakota Indians, who named July the "black cherry moon" for this summer addition to their diet. *Vitis riparia*, the riverbank grape, grows wild along lakes and streams throughout South Dakota. Its dark purple fruit is harvested during August. Ode, *Dakota Flora*, pp. 155–56, 175–77.

27. *Spirit Lake with the old Indian mound on its bank.* Burial mounds occur throughout eastern South Dakota, and most are associated with American Indian cultures that pre-date European contact. The lake may have been named for Spirit Lake, Iowa, or for the spirits of the dead within the mound on its bank. Wilder and her husband revisited the area in 1931, and as they drove toward Spirit Lake, she noted, "Country looks as it used to, but there are houses and barns where the prairie used to sweep unmarked" (*LHT*, p. 311). Rothaus, *Survey of Mortuary Features*, pp. 17, 77; WPA, *South Dakota Place Names*, p. 388.

28. *Wild gray geese; ducks of many kinds . . . queer little water birds.* "Wild gray geese" may be a catch-all term for several species that migrate through eastern South Dakota: the greater white-fronted goose (*Anser albifrons*), snow goose (*Chen caerulescens*), Ross's goose (*Chen rossii*), and Canada goose (*Branta canadensis*). The mallard (*Anas platyrhynchos*), with its glossy green head, remains the area's most common duck, while the blue-winged teal (*Anas discors*) is distinctive for its diminutive size and characteristic wing patch. The "mud hen," or American coot (*Fulica americana*), looks like a duck, but it is more closely related to the sandhill crane (*Grus canadensis*), a long-legged bird with an impressive seven-foot wingspan. The whooping crane (*Grus Americana*), now rare, also migrated through the region. Sometimes confused with the sandhill crane is the great blue heron (*Ardea Herodias*); five other heron species frequent the area, as well. Wilder would have seen the white pelican (*Pelecanus erythrorhynchos*), a buoyant bird with a

the south-east. Lake Thompson was beyond Lake Henry with only a narrow tongue of land between, high enough not to be overflowed but only wide enough for a good road with scattered choke cherry trees and wild grape vines[26] on each side close to the water.

Nine miles north-west from Silver Lake was Spirit Lake with the old Indian mound on its bank.[27] There were quite a good many trees at Spirit Lake but they were not large and the breast of the prairie swelled gradually to a higher level between so they could not be seen from the line of the railroad.

Lake Thompson was the largest of the group. Spirit Lake was next in size; its water was deep and the banks high and rocky except for a slough on one side.

Wild gray geese; ducks of many kinds from the large Mallard and the Teal down to the Mud hens and the little Hell Divers; pelicans, swans, herons, Sand Hill Cranes, gulls and different kinds of queer little water birds[28] stopped at this chain of lakes going south ahead of the winter. The sky was filled with flocks of them, resounding with their cries and any time we could see them rising from or settling down on the lake or on the prairie. They fed in the sloughs during the day but slept on the water through the night.

It was very pleasant when we were comfortably settled in the new shanty, with the great, new country clean and fresh around us. I was so happy to be out in it that I never gave a thought of regret to Walnut Grove, where the settlers, Pa said, were getting too thick. None of us were lonesome or homesick.

Our shanty was just one large room, but Ma got some calico from the company store and we made curtains of it, to shut off each bed by itself in the far end.[29]

Cousin Louisa, with Charley to help her, was busy all day long cooking and serving food to the men. Aunt Docia's shanty was not far from ours and Lena and I were together some. Always we did the milking together night and morning. The cows were on picket ropes at one side of the camp where the grass was good. We always sang as we went and came and while milking. The cows became familiar with "The Wind Blew Across The Wild Moor, Miss McCloud's Reel, the Gipsy's Warning, Buy A Broom, She Was Only A Bird In

Claim shanty, D.T.
*South Dakota State
Historical Society*

long bill and huge throat pouch. The tundra swan (*Cygnus columbianus*) is a large white bird that tends to stay in large flocks. The "hell divers" are grebes, six species of which occur in the area, as do five species of gulls. Wilder's "queer little water birds" are likely any number of plovers, stilts, avocets, and sandpipers—wading and shore birds that live along the edges of lakes and marshes. The birds feed on the rich plant, animal, and insect life of the area. Despite the reduction in habitat that came with agriculture, hundreds of thousands of individual birds migrate through or nest in the region today, giving a hint of the abundance Wilder must have seen in 1879. In *By the Shores of Silver Lake*, Wilder's description of waterfowl on Silver Lake contains fewer species but is more vivid: "Ducks quacked among the thick grasses. . . . Screaming gulls flew over the lake, beating against the dawn wind. . . . geese flew with a beating of strong wings into the glory of the sunrise" (pp. 71–72). For more on the birds, *see* individual species accounts in Tallman et al., *Birds of South Dakota*, and Peterson, *Peterson Field Guide*.

29. *Our shanty was just one large room, . . . in the far end*. Wilder devoted almost two pages to unpacking and decorating the new shanty in *By the Shores of Silver Lake*. The passage includes a reference to Ma's china shepherdess, which apparently was a prized possession that belonged exclusively to the fictional family (pp. 73–74). None of the *Pioneer Girl* manuscripts mentioned it. However, in responding to schoolchildren in 1943, Wilder wrote, "Sister Carrie has the china shepherdess" (LIW to Longfellow School, June 6, 1943, Detroit Public Library).

30. *"The Wind Blew Across The Wild Moor, . . . Where Oh Where Has My Little Dog Gone.* "The Wind Blew across the Wild Moor" is commonly known as "Mary of the Wild Moor" and may date from the eighteenth century. Such modern entertainers as Johnny Cash and Bob Dylan have performed it, and Charles Ingalls apparently thought enough of it to write the lyrics down in a handmade book that Caroline used to record "some of her own poetry" and "some that she liked" (LIW to RWL, Feb. 5, 1937). "Miss [or Mrs.] McLeod's Reel" is a popular fiddle tune, originating in Scotland or Ireland in the late eighteenth century, that goes by many names, including "Hop High Ladies." The lyrics of "The Gipsie's Warning," another nineteenth-century folk song that is still performed today, focus on seduction and a maiden's tragic loss of innocence (it is hard to imagine that Caroline Ingalls approved of the song). The lyrics to "Buy a Broom" date to the 1830s; its tune was published later in Germany. Lena and Laura sing this song while milking the cows in *By the Shores of Silver Lake* (pp. 93–94). "A Bird in a Gilded Cage" is a rare anachronism in *Pioneer Girl*. The song, with words by Arthur J. Lamb and music by Harry Von Tilzer, dates from 1900; it is not mentioned in subsequent versions of *Pioneer Girl*. "Where, Oh Where Has My Little Dog Gone" was originally published in 1864 as "Der Deitcher's Dog," a German-dialect poem that American composer Septimus Winner set to the tune of a German folk song. Cockrell, *Ingalls Wilder Family Songbook*, pp. 356, 360, 388; "Adventurous Story of Poor 'Mary of the Wild Moor'"; "Miss McLeod's Reel"; "Bird in a Gilded Cage"; "Septimus Winner."

31. *Pa's helper, Fred, . . . Ma took him to board.* In a letter to Lane, Wilder identified Fred as "Fred Fields" and noted, "His board money would have paid for our groceries" (LIW to RWL, Aug. 17, 1938, Box 13, file 194, Lane Papers). In *By the Shores of Silver Lake*, Pa does not have an assistant, but a character named Fred is identified as the camp's "foreman" (p. 117). The 1880 census lists a Frederick Fields in Turner County in southern Dakota Territory, working as an "overseer" on a different railroad. He may

a Gilded Cage, Where Oh Where Has My Little Dog Gone["][30] and many others.

Pa's helper, Fred, who slept in the store as watchman, took dinner with Pa one day and then begged so hard to have his meals at our place, instead of at the crowded cook shanty, that Ma took him to board.[31] Fred was Big Jerry's brother-in-law and [Big Jerry] came with Fred to dinner.[32] After that whenever he was in our camp he ate with Pa and Fred. The Co. men when passing through came too and so Ma and I were very busy.

Big Jerry never stayed long in one camp, but at any time might ride up on his white horse, always bareheaded and wearing a flaming red shirt. He would work a few days, long enough to win the men's money gambling at night in the bunk house and then ride away to another camp where he would do the same thing. He was a good worker when he did work and very kind to any one in trouble.

There was a rumor that he was the lookout for a gang of horse thieves operating along the line.[33] One thing was certain no horses were ever stolen where Jerry was in the camp.

It was thought that while he was working he had a chance to see which horses were the best and the place where they stood at night in the in the long shanty-stable, so that it was easier for some one to come in the dark and get a good horse instead of a poor one. Jerry had been seen looking them over as they stood in their stalls and the men had become suspicious of him.

One night a warning came to camp to watch the horses. The men came to the store and bought extra cartridges for their guns and lay around in the dark all night watching the stable, but no one came. They had thought they would catch Big Jerry and swore that some one must have warned him. Next day we learned that two horses had been stolen from the camp west of us.[34]

We were glad nothing had happened to Jerry. We all liked him, he was so quiet and nice around our shanty and so kind hearted.

There was, in camp, a funny, little, old Irishman named Johnny.[35] All his life he had lived and worked in railroad camps, but was now so old that he couldn't work hard any more. He had no money, so Pa made him a water boss and paid him regular wages. He had a

have moved on with Hiram Forbes when Forbes took a contract in that area. Fields, aged twenty-seven, and his wife, Almina, were both from Canada; most of their children were born in Iowa.

32. Squeezed between this sentence and the next, Wilder wrote the word "insert," crossed it out, and then wrote "later." Apparently she planned to insert something at this point but either decided to add it later or realized that it had already been covered later. There is no insertion at any point within this section.

33. *a gang of horse thieves operating along the line*. With close to two hundred teams of horses working on the grade out of Silver Lake camp alone, it and other railroad camps and nearby communities were prime targets for horse thieves. The situation had become so dire by mid-June 1879 that the citizens of Brookings County were calling for creation of "a Horse Thief Protective Association" ("Horse Stolen," *BCP*, June 19, 1879). In Bye, the rustlers drove the stolen horses "into the Bad Lands, where no one cared to go, even if it had not been known that the Bad Lands were headquarters for many gangs of outlaws" (p. 90). The best-known "badlands" of Dakota Territory are located in the southwestern part of present-day South Dakota, more than two hundred miles southwest of the Silver Lake camp. In 1879, however, the thieves were operating much closer to the end of the new railroad line in two areas of wooded ravines and rugged ridges, "that paradise of horse thieves," in what would become Hand County ("Horse Thieves," *Huron Tribune*, July 7, 1881). The Ree Hills, about sixty miles west of Silver Lake, and the closer Wessington Hills were then occupied "by a class of people who did not care to have a record made of their doings" (Peterson, *Historical Atlas of South Dakota*, p. 193). The rough terrain offered hiding places for livestock stolen from "as far south as Nebraska" (Reese, *South Dakota Guide*, pp. 250–51).

34. *they would catch Big Jerry. . . . the camp west of us.* In *By the Shores of Silver Lake*, Wilder devoted an entire chapter (pp. 81–89) to the subject of horse thieves and Big Jerry's possible involvement. Fictional details heightened the tension. For example, the ringleader of the men waiting in ambush for Big Jerry has "already killed one man" and "served a term in State's prison" (p. 85). That night Pa leaves the shanty and later returns with the news that all is well, saying, "The best of it is, Caroline, there'll never be a horse stolen from Silver Lake camp." Big Jerry rides in next day, greets Pa, and the chapter ends with the words, "There never was a horse stolen from Silver Lake camp" (p. 89). The implication is that Big Jerry was in cahoots with the thieves, but because Pa had warned him about the ambush, he had agreed not to rustle horses from Silver Lake. That same implication is not present in *Pioneer Girl*.

35. *little, old Irishman named Johnny*. Johnny apparently left no historical trail except in Wilder's writings. He appears briefly in *By the Shores of Silver Lake* as well (pp. 83–84), where his plight, as here, points up Big Jerry's tenderheartedness. In a letter to Lane, Wilder wrote, "Big Jerry and Little Johnnie and Fred came to our shanty at times. . . . They were absolutely all of the men I knew by sight and name" (LIW to RWL, Jan. 25, 1938, Box 13, file 194, Lane Papers).

wooden yoke that rested on his shoulders and carried a bucket of water with a dipper hanging by a chain from each end. As he walked up and down and around among the men, steadying the buckets with his hands, they helped themselves to a drink whenever they wanted one.

One night Johnny was taken sick and Jerry waited on him most of the night, taking the blankets from his own bunk to put over Johnny [to make him] warmer, for it was cold at night and poor old Johnnie needed more covers. In the morning Jerry came to our shanty and asked for some of Ma's good warm breakfast for Johnny. He took it to Johnny and waited on him while he ate, before he had his own breakfast.

But every man in camp except old Johnnie, Pa and Fred were afraid of Jerry, for he was a terrible fighter with his fists and feet, a dead shot with his gun.

It was because of a fight that Jerry came to our shanty the first time. Looking out of our door toward the cook shanty, where the men had just gone in to dinner, I saw them come piling out so fast they could hardly get through the door. They spread out into a great ring with Jerry and a big Irishman in the center. The two began walking around each other and I said, 'something is wrong down there.'

Pa and Fred were just sitting down to the table, but they came to the door to look. Fred exclaimed, "that dammed fool Jerry will kill him!" And with a flying leap through the door he was running as fast as he could go toward the crowd.

Fred was a small man, almost as small as Old Johnny, and when he broke through the ring of men, jumped between Jerry and the big Irishman and faced Jerry talking fiercely and gesticulating he reminded me of a Bantam rooster. Pa watched and laughed and when Ma looked her astonishment he said "Oh Fred will manage Jerry." And sure enough, in a few minutes Fred came back to his dinner, bringing Jerry, grinning sheepishly, with him and asked Ma to put on another plate.

The next excitement, in camp after watching for the horse thieves, was a prairie fire that came sweeping out of the west after dark and got into the tall grass in the Big Slough. It looked for awhile as though the camp would be burned, but the men were all out with teams plowing furrows to turn the fire and setting back fires whipping them out on the side next camp while they were small and whipping out little fires with grain sacks. They headed it around the camp and it went roaring around on the other side of the lake and away to the east.[36]

Then the men became restless and unruly. Some of them wanted to quit the job and they decided they would not wait for pay day but insisted that Pa pay them at once and up to date.[37] Pay day was the 15th. of each month. On that date they were paid up to the 1st. leaving them always fifteen days behind in their pay and this was their excuse for making trouble, but Pa could not pay them until the money came from Co. headquarters.[38]

He told us at supper that he must stay at the store that night to keep the men from breaking in, and wrecking it. Fred was away for a few days.

Pa went back to the store and, in the darkness, the men began to gather in groups and go toward it until all the 200 men in camp were in a crowd before the door. Then they began to shoot off their guns[39] and call Pa names daring him to come out.

Ma and I were watching through our partly open door and I was shaking, not with fear but with rage. 'Pa's alone,' I said, 'I'm going to help him.' But Ma held me and said to be still! I would only make it worse if I went out there.

Then the store door opend and closed behind Pa and he stood out on the step with his hands in his pockets talking to the men.

Two or three of the men started to talk ugly, but the others were quiet while Pa told them how foolish they were, for he couldn't pay them when the money was not there: that he had always treated them right and would pay them as soon as he could; that if they shot him and wrecked the store, still they wouldn't have their pay, but would be in trouble.

Finally the men began to go away, one at a time then several together until they were all gone, then Pa locked the store door and came home.[40]

36. *it went roaring . . . away to the east.* Wilder did not include this fire in the novel, but the revised description in Bye concluded, "Everything came at us out of the west—storms, blizzards, grasshoppers, burning hot winds, and fire—yet it seemed that we wanted nothing so much as we wanted to keep on going west" (p. 92).

37. *the men became restless. . . . insisted that Pa pay them at once and up to date.* In Brandt Revised, Wilder added, "There was discontent and trouble in all the camps." And indeed there was; this incident may not have been Charles Ingalls's first brush with unruly workers. In mid-June, for example, "the employees on the Chicago & Dakota railway, running west from Tracy, were on strike for their pay." Several hundred gathered at Tracy and "compelled all work to be suspended between that village and Lake Benton. A squad of soldiers were sent there to guard against an outbreak" (news item, *Currie Pioneer,* June 19, 1879). At the camp at Volga, about thirty miles east of Silver Lake, the local sheriff was "busy keeping the pugilistic elements of a gang of railroaders within bounds" through the fall ("Home and Other News," *BCP,* Nov. 27, 1879).

38. *Pa could not pay them until the money came from Co. headquarters.* When Wilder fictionalized this episode in the chapter "Payday" (pp. 109–22), she used all of the material in this railroad section of *Pioneer Girl* to good advantage. She also made some crucial changes—Pa does have the men's pay in "a heavy canvas bag" that he asks Ma to take care of. He also has "the handle of his revolver showing from his hip pocket" (*SL,* pp. 110–11). The men's complaint is about the two-week lag in pay.

39. *they began to shoot off their guns.* No guns are fired in *By the Shores of Silver Lake,* but a crescendo of threatening dialogue increases the sense of menace in the fictional scene: "A growl rumbled from the crowd. The whole mass of men moved in toward Pa as if that growl moved them" (p. 114).

40. *Pa told them how foolish they were. . . . and came home.* In *Pioneer Girl,* Charles Ingalls talked sense to the angry crowd, and the men slowly dispersed. In *By the Shores of Silver Lake,* however, the fic-

Picture copyright 1953 by Garth Williams, copyright © renewed 1981
by Garth Williams. Used by permission of HarperCollins Publishers

tional Pa needs reinforcement, and Big Jerry comes to his rescue
(pp. 115–18) in a scene that takes elements from a later section of
Pioneer Girl. Within the framework of the Little House series, it
is unusual for a character outside the Ingalls family to resolve a
crisis or to function as the hero in a major scene. Giving Big Jerry
a leading role in the "Payday" chapter therefore underscores the
wild unpredictability of the real West. Pa's courage is not enough;
only a mythic figure like Big Jerry can save the family. Laura finds
the untamed West thrilling, despite its inherent dangers. As the
chapter ends, Mary tells Laura that she wants to go back to Plum
Creek, but Laura "did not want ever to go back" (p. 122).

The gun shots, the shouts and loud talking had not been the worst of the affair, but the low, ugly muttering I had heard as a sort of undertone and now that it was over, I sat on the edge of my bed shivering[41] with fright long after I should have been asleep.

The days passed by while the weather grew colder and there was frost in the night.

The railroad grade was nearly finished. The ground had been broken with big plows drawn by great horse teams all the way where the grade stakes were set, then teams, on scrapers, scraped the dirt up into the grade on which ties could be placed and the steel rails laid. Where there was a low place in the ground the grade was raised higher making a fill; where the ground was too high, the roadway was cut through so that the grade was nearly level all the way.[42] All the grading must be finished before winter to be ready for laying the track in the spring, so Pa and Uncle High were hurrying the work along all they could.

But the men were dragging. The weather was unpleasant with a cold wind blowing at times and there was a feeling of coming winter in the air. Added to the discomfort of dust from the grade as the teams and men worked in the dirt it made the men disheartened and rather uncertain in temper.[43]

The Company had put a new man on the work. He was a time keeper over several camps, riding from one to the other down the line one day, then back the next day so that he visited each camp of his string every day, docking the men if they were a few minutes late, spying and prying to be sure that no one got credit for a half day he didn't work.

Naturally the men disliked him and more because he was a town man,[44] very well dressed, wearing always a white shirt and collar and tie.

He made our camp before noon and stopped for dinner at our place, but unpleasantly as though he thought himself above the fare, the place and all the people.

Our men were working on the big fill; scraping the dirt from a nearby high place, loading it on wagons at the dump, hauling it to the fill, unloading and coming back for more.

41. *I sat on the edge of my bed shivering.* This memory of pure fear contrasts sharply with the fictional Laura's response to the payday crisis (*SL*, p. 122).

42. *The ground had been broken with big plows. . . . the grade was nearly level all the way.* In *By the Shores of Silver Lake*, Wilder built one of her most memorable chapters, "The Wonderful Afternoon," around a description of this process (pp. 91–107). Pa takes Laura out to "a little rise" of land (p. 97) to see for herself how the men and their teams use plows and scrapers to make the railroad grade. But as Wilder explained to Lane, the scene is completely fictionalized: "I stretched a point when I had Laura go with Pa to see the work. I never did. He would not have taken me" (LIW to RWL, [late 1937 or early 1938], Box 13, file 193, Lane Papers). Wilder had taken to heart what her daughter had told her about how to

Helen Sewell, 1939

write compelling fiction; she had created this chapter "to have Laura see it first hand and get her reaction" (LIW to RLW, Jan. 25, 1938). Wilder also used the chapter to underscore the differences between Laura and Mary, who cannot see why her sister would "rather watch those rough men working in the dirt than stay here in the nice clean shanty." Laura, on the other hand, "was still seeing the movement of men and horses in such perfect time that she could almost sing the tune to which they moved" (p. 107). The lines illustrate the character's deepening appreciation for the West and the creative spirit it represents.

43. *a feeling of coming winter in the air. . . . the men disheartened and rather uncertain in temper.* Later versions clarified the situation, "Few of the men had money to live on till spring, for Big Jerry and the Company store had got the most of their wages," which made the men "surly" (Bye, p. 93).

44. *Naturally the men disliked him . . . he was a town man.* Subsequent versions identify him as an "eastern man" (Brandt, p. 77; Brandt Revised, p. 60; Bye, p. 94).

The dump was a cut in the high ground just wide enough to drive the teams and wagons through. Planks were laid across leaving a hole in the middle. A team with a scraper full of dirt was driven over the planks while the driver tipped the scraper, spilling the dirt through the hole into the wagon just beneath. When five scraper loads had been emptied the wagon was driven on to the fill making room for the next wagon to be loaded.

The new timekeeper had been making his rounds for some time before Jerry came to camp.[45] Then he rode up on his white horse while the timekeeper was checking the men at the dump.

Jerry sat on his horse and listened for a few minutes then reached and taking the timekeeper's horse by the bridle led him through the dump between the wagons so that he received the scraperful of dirt in place of the wagon it was intended for. At the other side the timekeeper tried to escape, but Jerry wheeled his horse and took him back through just in time for the next scraper. Three times he led him through the dump and three scraperloads of dirt and dust spilled down over the good clothes, the once white shirt and collar, while the men all but Jerry were laughing. Then he let him go.[46] The timekeeper did not stop for dinner and he never came back. We heard later that he rode east to Tracy, took the train and went still farther east, shaking the dust of the west from his shoes — and from all the rest of his clothes.[47]

But the big laugh did the men good. They laughed about it for days and put themselves in a good humor so that the work went merrily on.

Shortly after this there was trouble at a camp far[t]her west[48] where the paymaster had headquarters at the big Company store. The three hundred men in camp did not want to wait until the 15th. for their pay. They thought that five days was long enough for the paymaster to figure their time, so on the 6th, they stopped work and demanded their pay. The paymaster refused to pay until the 15th.

After some drinking and arguing the men decided they would be paid at once and up to date for one month and five days.

The men were quarrelsome and one of the teamsters had some

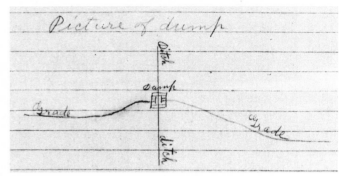

Wilder's diagram of the dump, ca. 1937.
Laura Ingalls Wilder Historic Home and Museum

45. *The dump. . . . The new timekeeper . . . before Jerry came to camp.* Extensive handwritten notes on the Brandt Revised manuscript illustrate how Lane experimented with this scene, adding lines, deleting others (even her own additions), before settling on the Bye version, where the timekeeper arrived just as "the temper of the men was getting dangerous" (p. 94). Big Jerry rode into camp shortly afterwards. From there, Lane included a detailed description of operations at the dump: "The line of wagons moved steadily all the time, each one stopping in the dump just long enough to be loaded, when it moved on and another took its place. It was these wagons that the timekeeper was checking, in an effort to find some way to make the men move the dirt faster" (Bye, p. 94). The level of detail suggests that Lane, who had no firsthand knowledge of railroad construction, worked closely with Wilder to recreate it. Lane's diaries reveal that she and her mother were frequently in each other's company during the summer of 1930. Lane undoubtedly asked her mother to provide specific details, just as she would later ask for specific information in her letters of 1937 and 1938 when Wilder was revising *By the Shores of Silver Lake* and Lane was writing *Free Land*. Ultimately, however, the women probably drew on Almanzo's memories of railroad construction. He had worked as a teamster in a camp west of Silver Lake in 1880. Lane Diary #25, May–Aug. 1930, Lane Papers; LIW to RWL, Feb. 5, 1937, Box 13, file 193, ibid.

46. *taking the timekeeper's horse by the bridle. . . . Then he let him go.* Brandt, Brandt Revised, and Bye added more details to this segment, improving its pacing and broadening its humor. In Bye, Big Jerry took the timekeeper through the dump five times, and "Everyone was happy, except the timekeeper" (Bye, p. 95).

47. At this point in the handwritten manuscript, the number 78 appears at the end of this line near the middle of a page. It is larger and darker than the other text on the page and is probably not in Wilder's hand. It may represent a marker of some kind added during the microfilming or other processing of the manuscript.

48. *there was trouble at a camp far[t]her west.* In *By the Shores of Silver Lake*, this episode is introduced with Pa's announcement, "There's a riot at Stebbins' camp" (p. 117), which was west of Silver Lake in Beadle or Hand County. It was, in fact, the camp in which Almanzo worked. In editing *By the Shores of Silver Lake*, Lane worried that the material was too mature for young readers, but Wilder was adamant. "I don't see how we can spare what you call adult stuff," Wilder wrote, "for that makes the story. It was there and Laura knew and understood it. It was all plain and simple. The riots were just plain rioting. . . . Neither Laura nor the grown ups had any complicated thoughts about any of it." Wilder went on to say, "If grown up readers now see there, the beginings of labor troubles where is the harm. I suppose it was. But what it grew into has no bearing on the story, nor would it prevent a child, then or now, from understanding the simple facts that occured" (LIW to RWL, Jan. 26, [1938], Box 13, file 194, Lane Papers). Lane included a brief synopsis of a similar episode in her novel *Free Land* (pp. 133–34).

difficulty with the man who weighed in the oats he had hauled for the Co. store.

The weigher hit the teamster on the head with one of the heavy weights from the scales. The teamster dropped and the men thought he was killed.

The weigher barely got inside the store ahead of the mob, dodged through the crowd in the store, out the back door and into the tall grass of a big slough that came close to the door. While the friends of the teamster were hunting for him in the crowd a friend of his led two horses into the slough, the weigher mounted and they two followed the slough for some distance before they were seen. Then the mob gave chase but being drunk and so far behind they soon gave it up.

In the store were two clerks and another weigher. The crowd of men went through the store from front door to back, out and in as they pleased. With all their guns and their threats they could not compel the clerks to hand out the goods to them and something kept them from helping themselves. A half drunken, big workman would throw his gun down on a clerk and tell him to hand him some of the goods and the clerk would stand leaning back against the shelf and laugh and talk him into being good natured.

It was a good natured crowd even when ugly so far as the store was concerned, but the paymaster was something else. The paymaster's office was a leanto at the side of the store. He was in there with both doors locked and their pay was in there too.

At last two men climbed on the roof, cut a hole through and dropped a rope down, while others of the crowd were breaking down the door. They intended to put the rope around the paymasters neck and haul him up to hang from the roof while they helped themselves, but when he saw the door splintering he threw open the pay-window and said he would pay, which he did and without being too particular as to a half days time. As they were paid the men went away, men from other camps went home and all was peaceful again. In the morning early our men had followed Big Jerry[49] as he leaped on the white horse and shouted "Come on boys!" They went as fast as they could but no horse up or down the

49. *In the morning early our men had followed Big Jerry.* The edited versions of *Pioneer Girl* put this information in its proper chronological order at the beginning of the neighboring camp episode, where it improves the pacing, clarity, and structure of the entire section. It also helps the reader see how a riot in one camp usually drew men from other camps.

50. *One Irish family. . . . Ma. . . . cured the baby.* Subsequent versions of *Pioneer Girl* do not include this episode, which is one of the few occasions when Caroline Ingalls played a modest but significant role outside of the family.

51. *for their contract on a railroad farther south.* In 1879 and 1880, much railroad construction was taking place in southeastern Dakota Territory. In addition to the Chicago & North Western's Dakota Central Railroad extension, the Chicago, Milwaukee & St. Paul Railroad, known as the Milwaukee Road, was building from the Iowa border through Lincoln and Turner counties to Mitchell. The Chicago, St. Paul, Minneapolis & Omaha, called the Omaha Road, was moving east through Sioux Falls from the Minnesota border. Hiram and Docia Forbes could have contracted with either of these lines, both of which were south and east of Silver Lake. On the 1880 census, the Forbes family was listed in Yankton County, where they may have taken a homestead. Hufstetler and Bedeau, "South Dakota's Railroads," pp. 79, 96.

52. *A contractor did not have capital. . . . over and above expenses.* In subsequent versions of *Pioneer Girl,* Lane struggled to explain compensation arrangements between contractors and the Chicago & North Western Railway in the context of Uncle Hi's situation. In Brandt, she shortened Wilder's original explanation and placed it earlier in the narrative (p. 69), but in Brandt Revised, she returned it to its original place and added background information to create a more sympathetic depiction of railroad contractors: "Whatever supplies the contractor drew were charged against him on the books, together with the money advanced for workmen's wages. At the final settlement, his profit would be whatever might be due him on the contract, after his debt to the Company was paid" (p. 63). In Bye, she concluded with a summary that favored Uncle Hi's position: "Now when the time came to settle up, the contractor found that, on account of the high prices the Company set on its supplies, he not only failed to make anything, but was actually deep in debt to the company. . . .This happened twice to Uncle Hi

line could keep up with Jerry's white pony. Now they came straggling back after night, tired but still hilarious.

Soon afterward the men began to leave our camp for the work was nearly finished and many men were not needed. So singly or in groups, in wagons and on horseback they drove or rode away.

One Irish family, ready to leave, had a sick baby, and could not go. Ma heard of it and went to see if she could help. By great good luck she did know what to do and cured the baby.[50] They wanted to pay her but of course she would take no pay. The morning they left the man came to bid her good by and thank her again. He called on every Saint in the Irish calander to bless her and when he shook hands and hurried away he left a five dollar gold piece in her hand.

Louisa and Charley were gone long since.

Aunt Docia loaded their three big wagons from their shanty and the Co. store and herself driving one, Lena and Gene the other two left for their contract on a railroad farther south.[51]

Uncle High came to board with us until he could make settlement with the R. R. Company. He was in good spirits for on this contract though farther behind than before on the books he had come out ahead.

A contractor did not have capital to finance the building operations, so the R.R. Company paid the men, furnished the goods in the Company store and grain for the teams. Everything used on the job was charged against the contractor. The men paid out of their wages for what they used personally and at the final settlement the contractors profit was what was left over and above expenses.[52]

A contractor did not draw pay for his own teams for on the face of it that would be simply paying himself. But this time Uncle Highs three teams had been put on the work in Pa's name and Uncle High had the pay for them. He had drawn supplies through the Company store and of grain for horse feed as he had the right to do, but he had quietly sent them away by trusted teamsters and sold them keeping the pay.[53] So that, while on the books he was a great deal more than bankrupt, he had made what he had lost, for there was no way the Company could collect what he owed except on another contract and as Uncle High said, there was plenty of work on other railroads.

(p. 96). In a letter to Lane in 1937, Wilder stated this more suc-
cinctly: "All goods for the camp, in the store, feed for the horses
tools etc. were furnished by the R. R. but charged to the contractor. The Co overcharged Uncle Hi on those" (LIW to RWL, Feb. 5,
1937).
53. *three teams had been put on the work in Pa's name. . . . sold them
keeping the pay*. In Bye, "Pa had handed the pay for [the teams']

work to Uncle Hi." At Silver Lake, his second contract, Uncle Hi
had come out ahead by selling supplies from the company store
and "pocketing the money" (Bye, 2d p. 96). "All the contractors
did that way," Wilder later wrote, adding that Old Stebbins, for
whom "Manly was one of the teamsters," had employed "three
teams hauling oats, 100 lbs. to a load, for a month" (LIW to RWL,
Feb. 5, 1937).

54. *This making money by losing it . . . to give him a profit on both contracts.* In Bye, this paragraph began, "The right and wrong of this were too much for me to puzzle out," and the railroad company was not specifically mentioned again, perhaps because the Chicago & North Western was still in business in the 1930s. The morality of this situation became an issue when Wilder was drafting *By the Shores of Silver Lake* and Lane was working on *Free Land*. Wilder wrote Lane: "And here is something, I can't use in a child's story, but you could use it if you have a place for it." She then outlined the same material she had used in *Pioneer Girl* and, as a postscript at the top of the page, scribbled, "You remember the old saying that 'A man who wont steal from the R. R. Co aint honest'" (LIW to RWL, Feb. 5, 1937). When Lane published *Free Land* in 1938, one of the book's characters repeats this very line (p. 108). Although Wilder originally considered this material inappropriate for young readers, Lane encouraged her mother to include it in *By the Shores of Silver Lake*, where a passage justifies Uncle Hi's behavior. Pa tells Ma: "It wasn't stealing. Hi hasn't got away with any more than's due him for his work here and at the camp on the Sioux. The company cheated him there, and he's got even here. That's all there is to it" (p. 131). While editing the novel, Lane had second thoughts about this material, but Wilder was not willing to remove it. "I had not intended to put Aunt Docia's and Uncle Hi's stealing, what was rightfully theirs, into the story but you wrote me that it would be all right for children to read at this time and generation," Wilder reminded Lane. "It was typical. . . . After all even though these books must be made fit for children to read, they must also be true to history and that was the expected, accepted thing. That *was* the way the R. R. was built." Wilder also argued that the stealing was necessary to the structure of the novel; it explained "why Aunt and Uncle went away and left Pa at the camp" (LIW to RWL, Jan. 25, 1938). The next day, still trying to convince Lane, Wilder wrote that she remembered her father saying he wished that Docia and Hi "'would quit railroading and settle down somewhere.' That they never would

This making money by losing it was something new to me, but it was curiously satisfying to know that Uncle High had beaten the Chicago, North-Western R. R. at its own game and made enough to give him a profit on both contracts.[54]

In a few days he made his final settlement and followed Aunt Docia, giving Mary a handful of bills, as she sat in her big rocking chair, when he said good by.[55]

Ma and I had been so hurried with the work, cooking for extra men, as the camp broke up, that we had no time for sewing and alas my dresses wore out until I had no change. Mary had been wearing long dresses and was taller than I, but as she had an extra dress, I put it on. Then I pinned up my hair, because my long braids hanging got in my way and hindered the work. So there I was a young lady with long dresses and hair done up.[56]

I was lonesome after Lena had gone and I didn't feel like singing when I milked. The cow was uneasy and would not stand still and Ma complained about my not getting as much milk as I should. Then having a thought I tried an experiment and learned that when I sang at my milking I got the usualy quantity of milk, but when I did not sing the cow would not give her milk down. (Fifty years ago I learned this and just this winter an Experiment Station discovered with surprise that cows like music and that the flow of milk is increased by playing the radio while milking.)[57]

When the work stopped, Pa was free to hunt as he had been longing to do and as the camp became quieter and the weather colder, sending them south, Silver Lake and the air above it were full of all the migratory birds.[58]

Gulls flew against the wind over the lake in clouds; the big, gray geese honked and swam and flew; ducks were in the water and going and coming in countless numbers. Flocks of beautiful white swans floated on the water; pelicans filled their pouches with little fish and went on their way southward; sand hill cranes lighted on rises of ground where they could watch around them and antelope herds could sometimes be seen feeding on the prairie.

So Pa went to his hunting and we feasted on geese and duck. Ma and I saved all the feathers and that fall we made a large featherbed

have anything until they did for there was 'nothing in this game of trying to out steal a railroad'" (ibid., Jan. 26, [1938]).

55. *giving Mary a handful of bills, . . . when he said good by.* Wilder wrote Lane that the "Silver Lake camp broke up Dec. 1st. Everyone left but us" (LIW to RWL, [1937 or 1938]). In *The Long Winter*, the fictional Mr. Edwards slips Mary a twenty dollar bill as he leaves (pp. 113–14). Perhaps the fictional incident was based on Hiram Forbes's generosity to the real Ingalls family.

56. *So there I was a young lady with long dresses and hair done up.* Wilder's fictional counterpart pins up her hair for the first time when she goes to work making shirts in *Little Town on the Prairie* (p. 38). Later, Laura wears a dress that "came down to the tops of her high-buttoned shoes" (p. 202).

57. *(Fifty years ago . . . while milking.)* This sentence with its reference to an experiment station is similar to other personal observations that Wilder made to Lane. The comment appears in Brandt (p. 80) but not in subsequent versions. Agricultural experiment stations, established at state land-grant colleges and universities after the passage of the Hatch Act in 1887, were intended "to promote scientific investigation and experiment respecting the principles and applications of agricultural science" ("Hatch Act of 1887"). As a columnist for the *Missouri Ruralist* and as a farm wife who valued progressive agricultural practices, Wilder would have been familiar with work published by these stations. While they may not have been the only institution to do so, the University of Wisconsin at Madison experimented with the topic during 1930, when an all-girl band called the Ingenues serenaded the cows in the university dairy barn. "Chart: Wisconsin's ever-more-efficient milk industry."

58. *all the migratory birds.* For a brief description of the various birds, *see* Annotation 28 in this section.

59. *When I was married . . . as soft as the newly bought ones.* In the original manuscript, this sentence is written vertically across the top of the page and set off in a box. Lane incorporated it at this point in the Brandt version but eliminated it in subsequent revisions. These pillows are still in the Wilder home in Mansfield, Missouri.

60. *Pelicans . . . smelled so strong . . . that even the feathers stank.* The pelican uses its expandable throat pouch like a fishnet, scooping up fish and water, which must drain before the bird can swallow the fish. When the bird is not feeding, the pouch is deflated. In *By the Shores of Silver Lake*, Pa brings a pelican to the shanty, opens its bill, and the family watches as dead fish fall out of its mouth (p. 125). "American White Pelican": Peterson, *Peterson Field Guide*, p. 78.

61. *Pa shot one swan. . . . sent it to Uncle Tom . . . for his baby Helen.* Wilder got ahead of herself here. Her mother's brother Tom Quiner married Lillian Graham Hill in December 1879, and their first child, Helen, was born in 1881. Wilder gave the episode a different outcome in her novel, where Ma uses the swan's down to make a collar, hood, and cuffs for Grace's new wool coat (*SL*, p. 177). The swan, however, may have come from an April 1880 hunt, in which "C. P. Ingalls shot a large white swan on Silver Lake. . . . It measured six feet eight inches from tip to tip" (fragment, *Kingsbury County News*, Apr. 1880, in Sherwood, *Beginnings of De Smet*, pp. [4], 38). "Thomas Lewis Quiner."

62. *The R. R. Company had hired Pa to stay through the winter.* Wilder created a fully realized scene to set up this development in *By the Shores of Silver Lake*. Pa announces that the family will have to "go East" for the winter because the shanty is "too thin for zero weather." The family prepares for the move as the "company man" arrives to check Pa's bookkeeping. Then Pa comes "whistling from the store" and asks, "How'd you like to stay here all winter, Caroline . . . in the surveyors' house!" (pp. 132–33).

63. *Mr Boast . . . his wife in Iowa.* Robert A. Boast, born in Canada, was about thirty years old in late

and four large pillows frome the best of the feathers. When I was married Ma gave me two of these pillows and they are good yet, as soft as the newly bought ones.[59] Pelicans we could not use for they smelled so strong of rotten fish in the pouch that even the feathers stank.[60]

Pa shot one swan that measured seven feet from tip to tip of its wings. He skinned it carefully salted the flesh side and sent it to Uncle Tom to have tanned to make a swans down coat for his baby Helen.[61]

There were only a few men lift in camp now and we were feeding them for there was no other place to eat. The R. R. Surveyors were still in the house that had been built for them at the head of the lake, but they were going soon and we were moving in. The R. R. Company had hired Pa to stay through the winter[62] and take care of the house and tools that would be left there until work began again in the spring.

A Mr Boast was eating at our place a few days before leaving to join his wife in Iowa.[63] They had been on the railroad all summer and had taken a homestead two miles east of the camp. When he learned that we were staying he said he would go to Iowa to bring his wife back and they would stay the winter too.

Mr Boast had sold a team to one of the men working on the grade,[64] who promised to pay for them when he drew his pay, now he was leaving without paying.

Mr Boast told Pa about it too late for Pa to take it out of the man's pay, but Mr Boast wanted help to collect it or get the team back so they made a plan.

Dakota was a territory and the counties were not organized.[65] There was no help to be had in that way, but Pa had some of his old Justice blanks and he made out a summons for the man and an attachment for the horses.[66] Then they disguised a friend of Mr Boast's so the man wouldn't know him, gave him an imitation sheriff's star and sent him after the man to bring him and the team back for trial. Mr Boast went along in case the sheriff needed any help.

The man was fooled, not knowing that there were no sheriffs or

Robert A. Boast. *Laura Ingalls Wilder Memorial Society*

1879. In 1870, he and his wife, Ella Rosina Peck, were living in Grundy County, Iowa, almost three hundred miles southeast of De Smet; they had been married in January of that year. The Boasts homesteaded about a mile east of De Smet and lived there until 1898, when they built a house in town. They remained friends of the Ingalls family until their deaths, Ella's in 1918 and

Robert's in 1921. Robert Boast was known for his gardening and landscaping skills and his civic-mindedness; he planted and tended the trees and shrubs in the De Smet park. In *By the Shores of Silver Lake*, Wilder described him as "a big man," with a short, black beard, red cheeks, and black eyes (p. 135). *Ingalls Family of De Smet*, pp. 36–37.

64. *one of the men working on the grade.* Wilder later identified this man as "Sullivan" (LIW to RWL, Jan. 26, [1938]). In *By the Shores of Silver Lake*, she called him Pete (p. 135). In 1880, several Sullivans worked in nearby counties, but there was no Peter or Pete. A young laborer named M. Sullivan worked in Beadle County.

65. *Dakota was a territory and the counties were not organized.* While this may have been Wilder's impression, this statement is not quite accurate. Nearby Brookings County was organized and had a functioning county government in 1879, but Kingsbury County in which Silver Lake was situated did not. The territorial legislature had established the boundaries of Kingsbury County in 1873 but did not finalize them or establish a government until the population was sufficient to request it. With the building of the railroad, the population swelled, and in the fall of 1879, citizens petitioned for a formal organization. In late December 1879, the territorial governor appointed three county commissioners to organize elections and establish a government. "Home and Other News," BCP, Dec. 25, 1879; Peterson, *Historical Atlas*, pp. 198–99.

66. *his old Justice blanks and he made out a summons for the man and . . . for the horses.* When Wilder adapted this experience for *By the Shores of Silver Lake*, Lane worried that it was inappropriate for young readers. Wilder disagreed, saying, "It was just a joke on Sullivan about the sheriff" (LIW to RWL, Jan 26, [1938]). Unlike the real Charles Ingalls, the fictional Pa never served as justice of the peace, and he plays this trick upon Pete using "legal cap," a tablet with large sheets of paper that were "red-lined down the sides" (SL, p. 136). RWL to LIW, Jan. 21, 1938, Box 13, file 194, Lane Papers.

67. *Pa went out to the Land Office and filed on a homestead*. In 1938, Wilder told Lane, "Pa found the homestead when he went to hunt the wolves before Christmas" (LIW to RWL, [1938]). Perhaps when writing *Pioneer Girl* some eight years earlier, this memory had led her to believe that her father had also filed for the homestead in 1879, but Charles Ingalls actually filed on February 19, 1880, with the district court in Brookings rather than at the land office, which was in Sioux Falls at that time. Ingalls himself correctly recorded that he "made a trip to Brookings in February and took a homestead, the N. E. ¼ section 3 town[ship] 110 range 56" ("Settlement of De Smet," p. [4]). As she was revising *By the Shores of Silver Lake*, Wilder found her father's account of settling De Smet, and as a result, her novel presents a more accurate sequence of events. Pa goes hunting and finds the homestead (pp. 172–73) but does not file until the spring land rush begins in late winter. At this point, however, the novel takes an entirely fictional approach to Pa's experience in Brookings when Mr. Edwards appears just in the nick of time to help Pa break through the crowd before a rival can get his homestead ("Pa's Bet," pp. 233–37). When a De Smet newspaperman challenged Wilder about details in the chapter, Wilder replied: "that chapter is fiction. Such things did happen in those days and I placed it there to emphasize the rush for land. You understand how those things are done in writing" (LIW to Sherwood, Nov. 18, 1939). In the novel, Pa pays a homestead filing fee of fourteen dollars for one hundred sixty acres, the standard homestead size (SL, p. 237). Records of the actual transaction, however, reveal that Ingalls paid a filing fee of $13.86 for a homestead of 154.29 acres. Homestead Entry File #2708, pp. 13–14, 16–17; LIW to RWL, [1938].

68. *where the town of De Smet was laid out*. The town of De Smet, Kingsbury County, had been designated and named by October 1879. Its name recognized the contributions of Father Pierre-Jean De Smet, a Jesuit priest born in Belgium who spent almost thirty-five years ministering to American Indians in the Great Plains and Rocky Mountains of the United

Justices within many miles and he was glad to pay for the team and expense of sending after him and be allowed to go on his way.

Mr Boast stayed while Pa went out to the Land Office and filed on a homestead[67] a mile south of where the town of De Smet was laid out,[68] then he went to Iowa for Mrs Boast.

The surveyors went next, the wild birds had gone on south and in place of two hundred men with some women and children and the teams and all the noise and confusion of the camp we were left with only the abandoned shantys and the wind.

We moved at once into the surveyors house and made everything snug for the winter. Pa had laid in a supply of provisions[69] and simple medicines to last the winter and at the last minute a man named Walter Ogden wanted to stay with us. He was taking care of several yoke of oxen for a man whose homestead was several miles to the east[70] and had intended to stay there by himself, but didn't like the loneliness and if Pa would give him permission to keep the oxen in the old company shanty-stable and would board him, he would come and stay with us.

It seemed that it might be wise to have another man around, so Pa told him to come and he moved the cattle and hay to feed them and just got them nicely settled before the first snow.

The surveyors house seemed very large after the railroad shanty. There was one large room, kitchen dining room and living-room in one. From one side of this opened the pantry, a bedroom and the stair door between. On the other side was a large leanto bedroom and storage room. The upstairs was all in one.

It was all very comfortable and homelike, with a good fire in the cookstove which performed the duties also of a heater, Mary in her big rocking chair in the warmest corner and the red and white checked cloth over the drop leafed table that was a kitchen table when bare of cover, a dining table with the leav[e]s up and the tablecloth and dishes on and a center table when the leaves were dropped and the best cloth over it.[71]

An old retired preacher had been alone all summer on his claim two miles north. We thought he had gone out with the other summer people, but in one of his daily walks Pa found him still there.

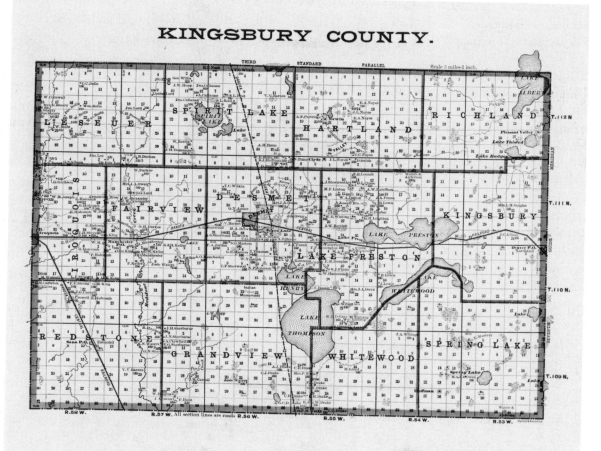

Kingsbury County, 1884.
Andreas' Historical
Atlas of Dakota

States. He wrote extensively of his travels, and his writings are an important historical resource for the period from 1838 to 1873, when he died. The town of De Smet was platted in late March or early April 1880 and organized in 1883. "The Towns," *BCP*, Oct. 8, 1879; WPA, *South Dakota Place Names*, p. 59; Thrapp, *Encyclopedia of Frontier Biography*, 1:396–97.

69. *into the surveyors house. . . . Pa had laid in a supply of provisions.* In *By the Shores of Silver Lake*, Wilder wrote that the surveyors' house "stood on the North shore of the lake not half a mile from the [family's railroad camp] shanty" (p. 141). At some early date, the house was moved from its original location to its current site in De Smet at First and Olivet streets. The Laura Ingalls Wilder Memorial Society restored and maintains the Surveyors' House, which is on the National Register of Historic Places, and it is open to visitors. In *By the Shores of Silver Lake*, Pa says that the surveyors had "laid in coal and provisions" for the winter, includ-

ing "flour and beans and salt meat and potatoes, and even some canned stuff. . . . We can have the whole of it for nothing" (p. 133).

70. *Walter Ogden wanted to stay. . . . He was taking care of . . . oxen for a man . . . to the east.* The fictional Ingalls family lives alone in the surveyors' house, an editorial decision that underscores the family's courage and isolation. Charles Ingalls identified A. W. ("Walter") Ogden as "a young man that was working for Henry Peck . . . taking care of teams that belonged to Peck that were left here for the winter" ("Settlement of De Smet," p. [1]). In 1880, Ogden worked as a laborer and lived in a Beadle County boardinghouse operated by railroad contractor H. J. Stebbins, who is mentioned later in *Pioneer Girl*. Ogden was a twenty-five-year-old bachelor. There were no Henry Pecks in the area in 1880, but also keeping a boarding house in Beadle County was a W. H. Peck. He is listed as William H. Peck in the census for Kingsbury County, where his occupation is given as farmer. The dual listing

suggests that he operated a boarding house for railroad workers in Beadle County and had a homestead in Kingsbury County. Peck was a relative of Ella Peck Boast. Anderson to Koupal, Apr. 24, 2014.

71. *The surveyors house seemed very large. . . . and the best cloth over it.* Wilder's fictional counterpart races ahead of her family to explore the surveyors' house, allowing readers to explore its secrets with Laura. Wilder devoted an entire chapter (pp. 141–49) to the house and to settling in, which she covered here in two paragraphs.

The surveyors' house. *Laura Ingalls Wilder Memorial Society*

He was threatened with consumption and had come out on the prairie to recover if possible leaving his family back east. He was quite feeble and not fit to stay alone and Pa and Ma did not want to be responsible nor have the care of him through the winter. While they were worrying about it not knowing what to do a teamster came driving through, from the Jim river. Pa persuaded him to drive out to Mr Woodworth's in the hope of getting a passanger and for charity's sake. Pa helped Mr Woodworth[72] pack his clothes, dress himself warmly and start on the way home, almost forcing him to go with the very last team going east until spring.

An old batchelor lived alone six miles away at Lake Thompson. We never saw him all winter. Other than that our neighbors were forty miles away to the east and sixty miles to the west.[73]

The cold shut down, the snow fell and blew and drifted into huge drifts though there were no bad blizzards. The lake froze over and was a smooth sheet of ice. At night we heard wolves howl and coyotes slipped around and picked up the crumbs where we shook the tablecloth from the door.[74] We could see them in the moonlight and also the jack-rabbits that drifted like shadows across the snow.[75]

On moonlight nights, Carrie and I would go sliding on the lake. We had no skates nor sled but holding hands we would run as fast as we could, then stop running and slide across the smooth ice. The faster we ran the farther we slid.

Pa had said to not go far away for there were wolves around, he had seen their tracks, but one bright night we were so intent on our play that when we reached the end of a particularly long slide and looked up, we were at the very edge of the shadow cast by the southeast bank and on top of the bank sat a wolf. Our quick slides over were slow to the way we ran and slid back across the lake and just as we reached our home side we heard the wolf howl. As we ran for the house I gave a terrified look over my shoulder and saw the wolf still sitting on the bank, with his nose pointed at the moon. He was a black shadow against the moonlight with the lake, a sheet of silver glistening below him.

Next day, Pa found the wolf den in the bank. He said, by the tracks they were the big buffalo wolves, just a pair. Several times

72. *Mr Woodworth*. In 1880, Horace G. Woodworth was in his early fifties, which would have seemed old to the twelve-year-old Wilder, especially since the man was ill. A decade earlier, Woodworth and his wife, Frances, and their five children had lived in Darlington, Wisconsin, where he worked as a minister. In 1879, the family appeared to be living in Warren, Illinois, while Horace had come west alone for health reasons. He was suffering from tuberculosis, or consumption as it was commonly called because it wasted or consumed the body. In *By the Shores of Silver Lake*, Pa describes Woodworth as nothing but "skin and bones" (p. 151). Tuberculosis, a contagious, life-threatening disease, primarily targets the lungs. The first antibiotics used against *Mycobacterium tuberculosis*, the bacteria that causes most forms of the disease, were not introduced until the 1940s. Before that time, the recommended treatment was a combination of fresh air, a healthy climate, rest, and a proper diet, or as Pa calls it, "the prairie-climate cure" (*SL*, p. 151). Even in the twenty-first century, the disease can be fatal if not treated swiftly and aggressively. "Home and Other News," *BCP*, Jan. 8, 1880; "History of TB"; "Tuberculosis"; Tulloch, "History of the Tuberculosis."

73. *our neighbors were forty miles away to the east and sixty miles to the west*. Charles Ingalls wrote, "We used to keep a lamp burning in the window for fear that some one might try to cross the prairie from the Sioux River to the Jim River" ("Settlement of De Smet," p. [2]). Wilder echoed these lines in *By the Shores of Silver Lake*, "All the way between the Big Sioux and the Jim, there was nobody at all except them" (p. 152). The town of Brookings was near the Big Sioux River, a little less than forty miles east as the crow flies. The James River, familiarly called the Jim, was just over thirty miles west in Beadle County where the town of Huron would soon arise.

74. *coyotes . . . picked up the crumbs where we shook the tablecloth from the door*. Sometimes called the prairie wolf, the coyote (*Canis latrans*) prefers to roam at night in search of prey that can include rabbits, rodents, birds, young deer, and domestic livestock. Similar in size to a medium-sized dog such

as a small German shepherd, a male coyote typically weighs up to thirty-five pounds, about half the size of the gray wolf. Coyotes are less likely to form packs, but they often congregate in family groups and communicate with distinctive, eerie howls. Coyotes have adapted to many environments, including grasslands, woodlands, and urban fringes. Higgins et al., *Wild Mammals of South Dakota*, pp. 164–66.

75. *jack-rabbits that drifted like shadows across the snow.* Unlike the cottontail rabbit, the white-tailed jackrabbit (*Lepus townsendii*) is large, measuring up to twenty-six inches in total length and weighing up to ten pounds, more than twice the cottontail's weight. Keen senses and speed help the white-tailed jackrabbit evade such predators as coyotes, foxes, large raptors, and badgers. It is the only jackrabbit whose gray-brown summer coat turns white in the winter, offering camouflage on a snowy landscape. Higgins et al., *Wild Mammals of South Dakota*, pp. 63–64.

after that we saw or heard them. Once we saw them running across the prairie together and then they disappeared. Pa said the crowds on the railroad had frightened the buffalo herds away. That likely these two wolves had just come by to visit their old den and then followed the herds. Anyway buffalo wolves were never seen there again.[76]

There were lots of the smaller wolves, coyotes and foxes[77] left. Pa set his traps, visiting them every day and soon had a good many skins.

And the fiddle sang again at night.

We had all been so busy and so tired with one thing and another, since our latest coming to Walnut Grove, that Pa had hardly ever played it. Now as we were so nearly by ourselves once more alone in the vast stillness and quiet of the empty prairie, with the cold and whiteness of winter around us, Pa naturally turned again to his music and in the snugness of home with the cold shut out, the fiddle sang all the old tunes and the new ones he had heard even to the railroad ditty about the contractor "Old Stebbins On The North-Western Line," which wasn't music but just a song.[78]

Pa played by ear and a tune once heard he could play and never forgot. He loved to play the hymns we had sung in the little church at Walnut Grove, "Sweet Hour of Prayer, Nearer My God to thee, Let The Lower Lights Be Burning," but of all, "The Sweet By and By"[79] was his favorite. (So much so that it was sung at his funeral)

Pa spent most of his days wandering over the prairie with his gun. Sometimes he would bring home a jack rabbit and always the skins from his traps.

Ma and I cooked and cleaned, washed, ironed and mended. Carrie helped with easy jobs and Mary held Grace on her lap in the warm corner. Pa made a checker board and me and he and Walter Ogden played checkers. I learned to play and at times beat each of them.

We had some books and papers Pa had brought on his last trip out and we read aloud to Mary.

And so with work and play, with music and reading and sleeping

76. *big buffalo wolves. . . . never seen there again.* In the nineteenth-century, explorers, travelers, and settlers reported seeing large wolves that followed the massive herds of American bison and preyed on calves and injured animals. Explorer Stephen H. Long first described the buffalo wolf (*Canis lupus nubilus*) in 1823 near present-day Blair, Nebraska. The buffalo wolf, also known as the Great Plains wolf, is now considered a subspecies of the gray wolf (*Canis lupus*). Gray wolves can weigh anywhere from forty to one hundred seventy-five pounds, but no matter how large, the wolf Wilder encountered would probably not have attacked her. The United States Fish & Wildlife Service reports: "There has never been a verified report of a healthy wild wolf deliberately attacking or seriously injuring a human in North America. Wolves can be very tolerant of human activity if they are not deliberately persecuted" ("Gray Wolf"). While the "crowds on the railroad" did not directly frighten the wolves away, the rapid settlement of the country and the diminishing herds of buffalo and other large animals such as elk caused gray wolves to prey on domestic livestock instead, prompting the institution of federal bounty programs. By the early 1900s, gray wolves had been almost completely eliminated from the lower forty-eight states. In 1978, the animals were listed as an endangered species. Wolf populations have since recovered in several regions of the country, but while individual animals may be present in South Dakota, no wolf packs are known to exist within the state. Laumeyer to Hill, Dec. 28, 2012; U.S. Fish & Wildlife, "Gray Wolf" and "Gray Wolf—Western Great Lakes Region; Hall, *Mammals of North America*, 2:931–32; Chapman and Feldhamer, *Wild Mammals of North America*, p. 460.

77. *foxes.* The red fox (*Vulpes vulpes*) lives on forest edges, in open areas where cover is available, in agricultural areas, and near or in cities. The size of a small dog, the red fox is a stealthy nocturnal hunter. Because of its handsome reddish-yellow coat, it has long been trapped for its fur. More secretive is the common gray fox (*Urocyon cinereoargenteus*),

whose salt-and-pepper fur is also prized by hunters and trappers. Higgins, et al., *Wild Mammals of South Dakota*, pp. 173–78.

78. *"Old Stebbins On The North-Western Line," . . . just a song.* The lyrics to this homegrown tune are apparently lost, but the Bye manuscript included more information: "Stebbins was a contractor, working west of us. A thousand verses were sung about him in all the camps up and down the line. But they were not very proper verses and I never learned any of them" (p. 103). In Brandt Revised, she remembered that each verse ended with "Working for old Stebbins on the Northwest Line" (p. 68). At the time of the 1880 census, both an old and a young Stebbins were working on contracts in Beadle County, due west of Silver Lake. Henry J. Stebbins, forty-nine years old, kept a boarding house and worked as a "R. R. Contractor," while his twenty-eight-year-old son James C. Stebbins, who lived with him, was "one of the grading sub-contractors," who "turned over the first sod west of the Jim" in May 1880; he had fifty teams working directly under him ("Home and Other News," BCP, May 13, 1880). The elder Stebbins also had two more sons working as laborers, and eighteen more men, some with families, boarding with him. Almanzo Wilder and others who worked for Stebbins boarded with William H. Peck or Charles D. Peck, brothers from Iowa, or in other boarding houses in the railroad camp. Clearly, Old Stebbins had figured out the contracting business. He also appeared as a character in Lane's novel *Free Land*, where he was renamed Gebbert: "There were songs about Gebbert. He had been a pioneer, an Indian fighter, a sheriff; he was a square shooter. Gebbert's men bragged about the work they did for him; others said that he was the only honest contractor on the line" (p. 81).

79. *"Sweet Hour of Prayer, . . . "The Sweet By and By."* W. W. Walford wrote the lyrics to "Sweet Hour of Prayer," and William B. Bradbury composed the melody to which his words are still sung today. The lyrics of "Nearer My God to Thee," written by Sarah F. Adam, are usually paired with a melody by Lowell Mason. Philip P. Bliss wrote the words and music of "Let the Lower Lights Be Burning," which was published in 1871. "In the Sweet By and By" dates from 1867, with words by Sanford Fillmore Bennett and music by Joseph Philbrick Webster. The first two lines of this hymn appear in *The Long Winter* (p. 130). "Sweet Hour of Prayer"; Sanderson, *Christian Hymns*, pp. 36, 41, 154; Bliss, *Charm*, hymn no. 14; Cockrell, *Ingalls Wilder Family Songbook*, p. 385

the days and nights passed busily and happily until the night before Christmas.

It was snowing on the already deep drifts. We were sitting around the fire and the lamp on the table reading and talking. Pa had just said "Well! I guess Mrs Boast would'n't come or Boast would have been back before this," when we heard a shout outside.

Pa opened the door while we all crowded around and there were Mr and Mrs Boast[80] on horseback, so chilled they could hardly get off their horses.

The roads had been bad with the snow all the way from the deep snow so that they were many days later than they had planned and at last about six miles back their sled had stuck in a snow drift. Then they had unhitched the team and ridden the horses on.

We helped them in by the fire while Walter put up the horses. While they warmed we fixed them a hot supper then sent them to bed to rest.

The next day Mr Boast and Walter went back after the sled. There was a little, one roomed office building[81] just a few steps from the house and when the sled was brought the things were unloaded into it and Mr and Mrs Boast moved in.

They took their Christmas dinner with us. We had jack rabbit roast, mashed potatoes, beans, warm biscuit and dried apple pie with tea.

We had stealthily made some little gifts for each other. Mary, with Ma's and my help in the hard places, had knit a pair of socks for Pa. Carrie and I had made him and Walter each a tablet of shaving papers from soft; bright colored tissue paper left by the surveyors; we had framed a little picture from a magazine for Ma, with little stars made from writing paper, and a picture book of pictures from papers for Grace.

Ma had a bit of pretty calico from the Co. store and we made Mary a new apron with pockets to hold her ball of yarn which was always rolling from her lap to the floor when she was knitting.

There was some ribbon for Carrie and for me and a bit left to give Mrs Boast and we hastily made a tablet of shaving papers for Mr Boasts [present].

Ella Boast (in chair) with a group of children.
Laura Ingalls Wilder Memorial Society

80. *Mrs Boast.* Ella Peck Boast was twenty-eight when she began keeping house in Kingsbury County, Dakota Territory. She had been born in Illinois, but her family moved to Iowa, where she married Robert Boast in 1870. She developed rheumatism at a relatively young age, was eventually confined to a wheelchair, and died in 1918 at the age of sixty-seven. Although childless, she was well known for her love of children and hosted many parties for those in her De Smet neighborhood. *Ingalls Family of De Smet*, pp. 36–37.

81. *a little, one roomed office building.* In *By the Shores of Silver Lake*, Wilder described the building as "the tiny house nearby that had been the surveyors' office" (p. 199), but Charles Ingalls remembered that it had "been put up . . . by an enterprising land agent" ("Settlement of De Smet," p. [2]). In October 1879, the *Brookings County Press* reported, "C. C. Weilley, of Kampeska, is building a land office at De Smet" ("Home and Other News," Oct. 22, 1879). Land agents were similar to real estate agents; they located land for those who wished to homestead or buy property in a new town. De Smet would be crawling with them in the spring of 1880.

82. *we had to go in the outside door . . . following the scripture that, "The first shall be last and the last first."* In her novel, Wilder described the office as having "no floor" and so tiny "that the double bedstead just fitted across one end." Somehow, the Boasts also squeezed in a stove, two chairs, a table, a trunk, a wall shelf, and a box for dishes. There was just enough room left "for the door to open against the table" (*SL*, pp. 199–200). Wilder's biblical paraphrase is from Matthew 20:16, which in the King James Version reads, "So the last shall be first, and the first last: for many be called, but few chosen."

83. *oysters.* Subsequent versions of *Pioneer Girl* noted that the oysters were "canned" (Bye, p. 105). Fresh or canned, oysters were "something of a mania in America" in the nineteenth century, and "packed in hermetically sealed cans," they "traveled the breadth of the wide trans-Missouri region almost as soon as Americans ventured there" (Hedren, "The West Loved Oysters Too," pp. 4, 6–7). By 1880, the railroad had assured that oysters were "seemingly everywhere" (ibid., p. 14), including isolated De Smet with its population of nine people on New Year's Day. Charles Ingalls's biography referred to the occasion as "the first oyster festival in Kingsbury county" (*Memorial and Biographical Record*, p. 1024).

84. *she exchanged cooking receipts and. . . . loaned us books . . . so Mary could enjoy them too.* While the term is not as common in this context today, a cooking receipt, or a formula of ingredients, is a synonym for recipe. In *By the Shores of Silver Lake*, Mrs. Boast loans Laura an "armful" of *New York Ledgers*, which contain what Ma calls "a continued story." When Mary suggests saving the next installment for the following day to "make the stories last longer," Laura, who "would rather read as fast as she could," keeps her opinion to herself (pp. 207–8). The brief scene quickly reinforces the fictional Laura's and Mary's distinct characters.

85. *Three blind mice.* The music for this well-known nursery rhyme was first printed in 1609. It is one of the best-known rounds and might "be one of the earliest printed secular songs that is still widely per-

The Boasts had brought some candy for us all and we had a jolly Christmas.

After Christmas the weather was much warmer and by New Year's day the snow was nearly gone.

We all had New Year's dinner with the Boasts and it was all the more fun because their one room was so small, that with the table set, we had to go in the outside door and around to our place at the table one by one and leaving the table we must reverse the order and go out the door following the scripture that, "The first shall be last and the last first."[82]

It was so warm we left the door open. The dinner was a treat, there were oysters[83] and honey and sauce [from] home dried fruit the Boasts had brought with them. We told stories and joked and had a happy New Year's day.

We liked the Boasts very much. He was tall and strong, with black hair, the blackest eyes and a laugh that would have made his fortune on the stage. Hearing it, one simply had to laugh too, even though not knowing what the joke was.

She was small and plump and merry with light hair and blue eyes. She slid on the lake with Carrie and me, she exchanged cooking receipts and visited with Ma and Mary. She loaned us books and papers which we always read aloud so Mary could enjoy them too.[84]

All our evenings were spent in our big room, listening to Pa play the violin, telling stories, playing chickers, and always, every evening singing.

Both the Boasts were good singers and his tenor with her alto, joined with Pa's base and my soprano did make music. Hymns from the hymn book, songs from their old singing-school book, rounds— you know where one leads off and when he has reached the end of the first line another starts at the beginning and when the second has reached the end of the first line another starts at the begining until all are signing at a different place in the words and music—

We sang, "Three blind mice, three blind mice
     They all ran after the farmers wife,
     She cut off their tails with the carving knife
     Three blind mice"[85]

until we ended in a roar of laughter. We all laughed because it sounded funny and then the rest of us laughed to hear Mr Boast laugh until we were exhausted.

Mr Boast's favorite song was, "When I was One and Twenty Nell And You were Seventeen." Mrs Boast's name was Ella, he called her Nell and they had been married when he was 21 and she seventeen.[86]

And so the winter was passing quickly and merrily when along in February on another cold, snowy night we heard a shout outside the door and Pa opened the door to let in Rev. Alden, our own Rev. Alden who had started the church in Walnut Grove, whom we had not seen for years, who was still a Home Missionary and had been sent out into the west to plant churches[87] along the line of the new railroad. We were mutually surprised and pleased to meet again.

With him was another missionary,[88] a small, quick, red headed Scotsman, with a slight burr to his tongue. But how he could sing!

They stayed the night, held church services the next day with a congregation of nine counting Grace[89] and went on west. They returned after a week, stayed over night again and went on east, with the promise to return later and organize a church.

Their coming was the begning of the spring rush. Slowly at first one a day then later in crowds they came, wagon loads, hack loads, buggy loads of men stopped on their way to the forts and towns farther west, looking for locations in the new towns laid out on the line of the railroad and for homesteads on the wild lands the railroad was opening for settlement.[90]

We had to take them in and feed them for ours was the only place they could stop in a long days travel in either direction.

It was the end of our jolly evenings and happy days for Ma and I were kipt busy cooking and working for them and the house was always full of strange men.[91]

One day Ma was in bed all day with a sick-headache and I had to manage by myself. I got breakfast and the crowd left. I fed another crowd for dinner and when they began to come in at night, Mrs Boast came over to help me. When supper was over we carried

formed" (Cockrell, *Ingalls Wilder Family Songbook*, p. 398). The song is mentioned in both *By the Shores of Silver Lake* (pp. 212-13) and *These Happy Golden Years* (p. 212).

86. *"When I was One and Twenty Nell. . . . when he was 21 and she seventeen.* "When I Was One-and-Twenty, Nell" was composed by H. R. Palmer and appeared in 1872 in his book *The Song King* (p. 150). The first verse reads: "The hay was newly mown, Nellie,/That year so long ago,/And while the western sky was rich/With sunset's rosy glow,/Then, hand in hand, close linked we passed/The dewy ricks between/And I was one-and-twenty, Nell,/And you were seventeen." Wilder wrote Lane that she did not remember the lyrics because no one else sang it, "and I don't remember that we ever did after that winter in the surveyors house" (LIW to RWL, Aug. 17, 1938). In the *Ingalls Wilder Family Songbook*, on the other hand, Cockrell recorded the song as "The Old Time" (pp. 270, 391), published in three different versions, all with the name Mag or Maggie instead of Nell. In July 1870, the federal census-taker listed Robert and Ella Boast as 22 and 18, respectively, noting their marriage in January 1870, so the story rings true.

87. *Rev. Alden . . . sent out into the west to plant churches.* Wilder told Lane that a lamp burning in their window had led Reverend Alden to the surveyors' house. The Ingalls family began shining the light because the "Boasts told us how they felt when they saw it" on Christmas Eve (LIW to RWL, Feb. 15, 1938, Box 13, file 194, Lane Papers). In November 1876, Edwin H. Alden, the Congregational minister during the Ingallses' first stay in Walnut Grove, had been appointed United States Indian agent at Fort Berthold Indian Agency in northern Dakota. His appointment did not go well. An article in the *New York Times* called him "a pious fraud and a cheat," who had "swindled in a small way." Alden had drawn a fifty-dollar voucher for carpentry work and kept the money (his predecessor had embezzled forty thousand dollars) and had placed his wife in Minnesota on the payroll. The *Times* writer accused Alden of having lied "to the Indians until they came

to regard him as the prince of liars, and threatened to kill him if he did not leave" ("Swindling at the Agencies," Aug. 15, 1878). Alden had resigned his position as agent in February 1878 but continued to serve until April 1879, when his replacement finally arrived. In his official report, Alden referred to "many difficulties and discouragements," but he noted that he "came to this agency with a strong desire to help this people, and their greatest good has been my motive during my stay. When I leave them it will be with the consciousness that though my administration has not been free from mistakes, I have endeavored honestly and faithfully to do my duty" (*Annual Report of the Commissioner of Indian Affairs . . . 1878*, pp. 33–34). Reverend Alden apparently returned to Minnesota in 1879 to work again as a missionary. Wilder devoted an entire chapter ("On the Pilgrim Way") to this surprising reunion in which Reverend Alden also tells the family about a college for the blind in Iowa (pp. 214–23). *Annual Report . . . 1879*, p. 29; "Fort Berthold Indian Agency."

88. *another missionary.* In *By the Shores of Silver Lake*, Wilder called the second missionary "Reverend Stuart" and described him as "not much more than a big boy" (p. 216), but his full name was Rev. Stewart Sheldon, and he was actually in his mid-fifties. Sheldon had moved to Dakota Territory from Lansing, Michigan, in 1869 for his health. He homesteaded near Yankton and served as superintendent of southern Dakota Territory for the American Home Missionary Society from 1874 until 1885. Reverend Alden was thus working for him. "De Smet's Pioneer Church," *De Smet News*, June 8, 1950; Robinson, *History of South Dakota*, 1:571; American Home Missionary Society, *Fifty-seventh Report*, p. 89.

89. *held church services . . . nine counting Grace.* Sources differ about the exact date of this first church service in De Smet, although they agree that it was held in the surveyors' house. An 1898 biographical profile of Charles Ingalls suggests a date of February 2, 1880, but church history places it on Sunday, February 29, 1880, according to notes left by Caroline Ingalls. Wilder's count of the congregation included the Boasts, her family of six, and A. W. Ogden, but twenty-five people actually attended—the spring rush had already begun. *Memorial and Biographical Record*, p. 1024; "De Smet's Pioneer Church."

90. *the spring rush. . . . in crowds they came, . . . for settlement.* In the 1850s, the area between the Big Sioux and Missouri rivers had principally been the home of the Yankton Nakota, or Sioux,

Indians. They had ceded their lands in the Treaty of Washington, D.C., in 1858, but the country had not been accessible to much non-Indian settlement until the railroads began to push into the area in the 1870s. The land rush, known as the Great Dakota Boom, began in 1878 and peaked in 1883–1885, as homesteaders poured into Dakota Territory, lured by the Homestead Act of 1862 and by railroad companies and real-estate interests that promised fertile farm land and ideal conditions. Between 1870 and 1880, the non-Indian population of southeastern Dakota Territory grew from ten thousand to eighty thousand people. By 1885, the number had surged to almost a quarter million. In 1880, Reverend Sheldon told the American Home Missionary Society that hundreds of "new towns are springing up" and the activity "has been without a parallel" (*Fifty-seventh Report*, p. 90). For De Smet, the boom began in the spring of 1879, when the *Brookings County Press* reported, "[F]ifty-one different parties have gone to Kingsbury County during the last two week[s] to start a town. Forty-three more are on the way" ("Home and Other News," May 29, 1879). Most of these people left the area in the autumn of 1879, but they began to return as early as January 1880. "Times are lively here again," Charles Ingalls reported in a February 2 letter to the *Press* (C. [P]. I., "From Kingsbury County," Feb. 12, 1880). The Chicago & North Western Railway had platted towns like De Smet every six to twelve miles along the Dakota Central Division. This interval provided about the "right length of track for a railroad sectional maintenance crew" (Hart and Ziegler, *Landscapes*, p. 193) and about the right distance for most homesteaders to journey to and from town in a day. In the spring of 1880, land agents settled clients on homesteads, while entrepreneurs from Brookings, Volga, and points east visited the new towns, eager to establish businesses to serve the booming population. Hoover and Bruguier, *Yankton Sioux*, pp. 28–31; Schell, *History of South Dakota*, pp. 158–60; "Home and Other News," *BCP*, Sept. 25, Oct. 8, Nov. 13, 1879, Feb. 5, Apr. 1, May 6, June 3, 1880.

91. *the house was always full of strange men.* Wilder later recalled: "Ma charged all those strangers for staying over night and for board, 25¢ a meal 50¢ for a place to sleep over night for travelers. $4.50 a week for board and a place to sleep, not a room, just a bed on the floor" (LIW to RWL, Aug. 17, 1938). Wilder included many of these details in the chapter "Spring Rush" (*SL*, pp. 224–30).

the food and dirty dishes into the pantry and collapsed on the floor. I was so tired I could not eat, but in a few minutes I took Mary up stairs to bed. Carrie went and stayed with her while Mrs Boast and I washed up the dishes. Then she went home and I went upstairs while Pa arrainged eighteen men to sleep for the night in the one bed in the leanto and on the floor of the two rooms using the robes and blankets from their wagons to help out the bedding.

The wild geese began to come back from the South, a sure sign that spring had come. Pa went out one morning hoping to get one and Mary and I disputed about the cooking of it. It should be roasted of course, with dressing, but Mary insisted on sage in the dressing and I didn't like sage. We almost quarreled[92] and were still disagreeing when Pa came back without the goose. As the flocks neared the line of the railroad they had seen the changes made in the landscape beneath them and the movement of men and teams. The wise, old leaders called back to their followers and all the wild geese flew high over Silver Lake[93] and on into the north.

Several men came and started to build on the town site. They became our regular boarders. One young man we liked very much, because he was so quiet and well mannered. He was building a business house but he never told what kind of a business he intended to start.

When his building was finished and his goods came, we learned that the first building on the actual town site of De Smet,[94] was a saloon. The next was a grocery store and the next, to our great relief, a hotel.[95]

Pa bought two corner business lots, diagonally across the street from each other[96] and sent out for lumber to build. All building materials and provisions were hauled in by teams from Brookins.

The business houses were all built one story high with a square, false front a story higher. Pa was building his with the idea of selling.

When the rough sheathing of the building was on the frame and the roof over it, we moved in for the surveyors were back to take over their house and tools.

92. *Mary insisted on sage. . . . We almost quarreled.* In *By the Shores of Silver Lake*, Laura and Mary actually do quarrel (p. 245). Wilder explained the scene to Lane: "I had Laura and Mary quarrel over the stuffing for the goose . . . to show the relaxing from the strain first of loneliness and then the hard work and excitement of so many strangers underfoot. Usually, you know, Laura and Mary disagreed now and then. . . . I thought it very natural that they should snap when at last the letdown came" (LIW to RWL, Feb. 15, 1938). Wilder also shared this quarrel with her *Missouri Ruralist* readers in November 1916. *See Little House Sampler*, p. 30.

93. *As the flocks neared the line. . . . wild geese flew high over Silver Lake.* In *By the Shores of Silver Lake*, this episode occurs after the building boom is underway, and Pa finds, "Not a goose within gunshot. . . . They must have see[n] the new buildings and heard the noise. Looks like hunting's going to be slim around here from now on" (p. 245). One consequence of the settlement that accompanied the Great Dakota Boom was the plowing of the grasslands and the draining of wetlands for crops, which greatly reduced the abundance of wildlife. Even so, the prairie pothole region of northeastern South Dakota remains one of the "duck factories" of North America (Tallman et al., *Birds of South Dakota*, pp. v, vii).

94. *the actual townsite of De Smet.* The railroad surveyor had staked out the lots and blocks of De Smet by March 27, 1880, using the classic T-town formation in which the railroad tracks form the bar of the letter, and main street (Calumet Avenue in De Smet) runs perpendicular and forms the base. The official plat mat is dated April 6, 1880, which is probably when lots officially went up for sale. Miller, "Place and Community," pp. 358–59.

95. *a saloon. . . . a grocery store and . . . a hotel.* Later in *Pioneer Girl*, Wilder identified the saloon owner as Henry Hinze, who appears in the 1880 census as Henry Hinz, a twenty-six-year-old shoemaker. Newspaperman Aubrey Sherwood characterized Hinz's building as "a recreation parlor" and noted that Hinz went on to become "a drayman

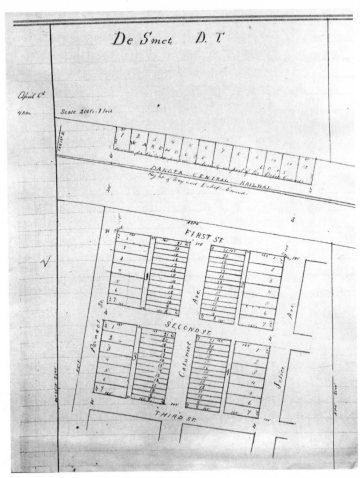

Plat of De Smet. *Kingsbury County Courthouse*

and mail carrier" (*Beginnings of De Smet*, p. 18). Charles Ingalls recalled: "A man by the name of Bierdsly commenced a hotel about [March 1, 1880]. E. M. Harthorn began the erection of a store a few days after. V. V. Barnes came about the 12th of March 1880 with some lumber for a shanty on his claim ½ mile west of De Smet" ("Settlement of De Smet," p. [3]). Jerome C. Beardsley, thirty-nine years old, came to De Smet from New York to start a hotel, and Edelbert M. Harthorn, also thirty-nine, came from Maine to run a grocery store with his son Frank. Visscher V. Barnes, a twenty-nine-year-old lawyer from New York, had settled first in Oakwood, D.T., before moving on to De Smet, where he went "into the land business" ("Home and Other News," BCP, Mar. 11, 1880).

96. *Pa bought two corner business lots, diagonally across the street from each other.* In a letter to Lane, Wilder recalled, "Pa first built on a corner lot facing east with side street on south side. . . . He sold that place at a good profit on the lot because it was the most desirable location in town." She added that he also bought "the lot diagonally across the street, with a west and north frontage." She thought her father had "bought the [first town] lot from the R.R. co. But I don't know how. There was no depot nor R.R. agent there when he built nor, when the first of the other buildings were put up. The town was staked out and I think the first comers simply squatted on the lots they wanted and bought them later. The lots were sold for $50, an inside lot. $75 for a corner lot, and a building worth $250. had to be built on a lot within six months to hold it" (LIW to RWL, Aug. 17, 1938). Wilder's memory was sound. In 1880, a newspaper correspondent gave the same figures, remarking that the $250 building requirement "can be easily done as timber is brought by freight trains direct to the spot" ("New Experiences, BCP, Sept. 30, 1880). When the town of Brookings was platted in October 1879, the newspaper editor had remarked, "In order to get a good location, you have to be on hand" ("Home and Other News," BCP, Oct. 8, 1879). Even before De Smet had been platted, Wilder's father had been on hand and, as a result, got prime lots. He began work on his first building on March 1, 1880. "Settlement of De Smet," p. [3].

We moved on April 3d. a nice, warm day but it turned cold in the night and the wind blew through the cracks between the boards. I felt uncomfortable and waked just enough to know I was cold, so I pulled the covers higher to shelter my head and snuggled closer to Mary and Carrie.

The next I knew, I heard Pa singing,

"Oh I am as happy as a big sun flower
That nods and bends in the breezes
And my heart is as light as the wind that blows
The leaves from off the treeses."[97]

I peeped out. Everything was covered with snow and Pa was standing barefoot in it pulling on his pants. "Lie still all of you," he said, "don't move and mix the snow up! I'll shovel it off in a minute."

And he went on singing about the happy sun flower while he shook the snow off his socks and out of his shoes and put them on. Then he took a large dirt shovel and shoveled the snow off the beds as we lay under the covers, shoveled it off the floor and out doors.

When I saw how deep the snow was over us, I knew why we had all slept so warmly with the snow for an extra cover, but it was'n't warm out in it where Pa was.

He made us all lie still while he made a fire and warmed himself. Then he went out to shovel the snow away from the door while we got up and dressed by the hot stove.

The snow was gone again in a couple of days for it was spring. The prairie was turning a beautiful green and everyone was very busy building a town, while the steel rails came nearer and nearer along the grade from Tracy.

New people were coming all the time putting up little buildings and moving in from their wagons. In one family was a little girl of Carrie's age. She used to come over to play every day and we thought it would be a good way to keep them quiet and out of mischief to have a few lessons each day, but when time for lessons came, Carrie ran and hid and the other girl did not come over any more, so the first school in De Smet closed before it began.

97. *"Oh I am as happy as a big sun flower . . . off the treeses."* This song, "The Big Sunflower," dates from the late 1860s, with words and music by Bobby Newcomb. It was associated with the popular nineteenth-century minstrel Billy Emerson, who also performed "Captain Jinks of the Horse Marines." Pa sings the sunflower song in *By the Shores of Silver Lake* (p. 250) and again in *The Long Winter*, where it is identified as Pa's "trouble song" (p. 37). Cockrell, *Ingalls Wilder Family Songbook*, p. 359; "Captain Jinks."

Depot, De Smet, S.Dak., ca. 1910.
South Dakota State Historical Society

98. *A depot was built. . . . and Mrs Woodworth.*
Horace G. Woodworth, the minister suffering from
consumption in the fall of 1879, returned as station
agent in the spring of 1880. His son, sixteen-year-old
James G. Woodworth, was telegrapher. The family,
who lived upstairs in the two-story depot, also included Horace Woodworth's wife, Frances, and
three more children: thirteen-year-old Benjamin;
ten-year-old Walter; and seven-year-old Richard.
Wilder described the depot in *Little Town on the
Prairie* (pp. 243–51).

99. *De Smet now had a bank, . . . and at last a furniture store.* "During the summer [of 1880]," Charles
Ingalls recalled, "there was 16 buildings put up on
the town cite [*sic*], besides the depot" ("Settlement
of De Smet," p. [4]). These businesses included
Thomas H. Ruth's Kingsbury County Bank; Henry
Hinz's saloon/shoemaker shop; George Wilmarth's
general store; cabinetmaker Charles Tinkham's
furniture store; Charleton S. G. Fuller's hardware
and implement business; Charles L. Dawley's and
Charles E. Ely's lumberyards; the Charles W. Mead
and Jerome C. Beardsley hotels; the Garlands'
boarding house; and Edward McCaskell's black-
smithy. Also started was the *Kingsbury County News*
run by printer Jacob W. Hopp and his associate
G. A. Mathews (only fragments of this early news-

Pa sold the building and lot where we were living to give possession in a week and at once began another building on his other lot.
Before the week was past we were moved into the other unfinished
building.

A depot was built and the agent came, no other then Mr Woodworth, much improved in health. His eldest son Jimmie was to be
telegrapher. There was another son, Ben, and Mrs Woodworth.[98]

The first train came during the latter part of April and then De
Smet was headquarters for the work farther west. Trains brought
the supplies that far and teamsters loaded them on their wagons at
the depot and hauled the[m] the rest of the way.

De Smet now had a bank, a lumber yard, a livery stable, drug
store, drygoods store, another grocery and hotel and at last a furniture store.[99]

Rev. Woodworth held church services at the depot on Sundays,
but not many people attended.

Pa and some other of the first settlers were organizing Kingsbury County,[100] a school district was formed and a school house
was being built.

Then one day a fierce looking old man came and introduced himself to Pa as Rev. Brown, saying that Rev. Alden had sent him to
organize a church.

None of us liked him, he was so rude and rough and unclean.[101]
His hair was white and thick and bushy. His whiskers were thick
and long and he did'n't always spit over them. His fingernails were
dirty and his white shirt and collar soiled and rumpled. He claimed
to be a cousin of John Brown[102] and looked like the picture of him
in the history [book].

We did'n't think Mr Alden could have sent us such a man, but he
had a letter from Mr Alden to Pa, so Pa and Ma helped him get the
people together and a Congregational church and Sunday-school
were organized. The school house was finished and meetings were
held there. Mr Brown was the preacher.

Then one day Rev. Alden came to organize the church as he had
all the time intended to do. He was surprised at what Mr Brown had

paper survive). The editor of the *Brookings County Press* estimated that De Smet was home to two hundred people by the end of July 1880. Wilder provided a vivid picture of the town in *By the Shores of Silver Lake*: "In two weeks, all along Main Street the unpainted new buildings pushed up their thin false fronts, two stories high and square on top. . . . Strangers were already living there; smoke blew gray from the stovepipes, and glass windows glinted in the sunshine" (p. 242). "Home and Other News," *BCP*, Mar. 11, Apr. 15, June 17, Aug. 5, 1880; Sherwood, *Beginnings of De Smet*, pp. 18, 30.

100. *Pa and some other . . . were organizing Kingsbury County.* The governor of Dakota Territory had appointed three commissioners at the end of December 1879 to organize Kingsbury County. The commissioners met for the first time on February 18, 1880, in a claim shanty about six miles east of the De Smet townsite. During their second meeting, which took place in the Ingalls home on March 9, they named De Smet as the county seat and "decided to license saloons at $400. a year" ("County Was Organized," *De Smet News*, June 6, 1930). The county was named for George W. Kingsbury, a newspaper editor and historian, who settled in Yankton, Dakota Territory, in 1862. "Home and Other News," *BCP*, Dec. 25, 1879; *Memorial and Biographical Record*, p. 1024; WPA, *South Dakota Place Names*, pp. 24–25.

101. *Rev. Brown. . . . rude and rough and unclean.* Clergyman Edward Brown and his wife, Laura, and their adopted daughter, Ida B. Wright, came to De Smet from West Salem, Wisconsin. He apparently arrived in May and conducted services to establish and organize the First Congregational Church on June 20, 1880. He was sixty-five years old, had been a schoolteacher and lawyer before joining the ministry, and served congregations in Wisconsin, Minnesota, and Ohio. He retired four years after coming to De Smet and died there in 1895. Wilder's unflattering descriptions of Reverend Brown in *Little Town on the Prairie* echoed the portrait of him in *Pioneer Girl* but added new details. For example, while listening to one of Reverend Brown's sermons, Laura changes "his sentences in her mind, to improve their grammar" (p. 225). "De Smet's Pioneer Church"; Ehrensperger, *History of the United Church of Christ*, p. 115; Miller, *Becoming*, p. 62; *Congregational Year-book, 1896*, p. 20; "A Pastor's Farewell," *De Smet Leader*, Aug. 9, 1884.

102. *John Brown.* John Brown was an abolitionist whose violent stance against slavery along the Kansas and Missouri border gained national attention in the late 1850s. In 1859, he and his followers led a raid on the federal armory at Harpers Ferry, Virginia, hoping to secure arms and liberate slaves. Brown was arrested, convicted of treason, and hanged. His death heightened tensions between anti- and pro-slavery factions and perhaps hastened the coming of the American Civil War. "John Brown [abolitionist]."

103. *one day Rev. Alden came. . . . he would . . . leave Mr Brown in charge.* The southern Dakota superintendent of the American Home Missionary Society had given Rev. Edwin H. Alden a six-month contract to organize the church in De Smet, but finding Brown there, Alden "relinquished" the congregation to him in May 1880 ("De Smet's Pioneer Church"). In 1885, Reverend Alden was living in Spink County, Dakota Territory, about seventy miles northwest of De Smet, where he shared his household with a sixteen-year-old student-boarder. No wife or children were listed within the household. By 1900, Alden had moved back to Vermont, where he worked as a clergyman in Tunbridge and had remarried. Ten years later, he and his second wife, Clara, lived in Chester, Vermont, where he died the following year on May 6, 1911, at the age of seventy-five. Robinson, *History of South Dakota*, 1:571; "Vermont Death Records."

104. *all their worldly good[s], seed grain and provisions for a year in emigrant cars.* The railroad companies offered special shipping rates to those wishing to emigrate to Dakota Territory. For example, in February 1880, the Southern Minnesota Railroad offered "a rate on a car of emigrant movables" between towns in the territory of "only $22.50" ("Home and Other News," *BCP*, Feb. 26, 1880). For less than a carload, the rate was twenty-five cents per one hundred pounds. In April 1880, the editor of the *Press* estimated that since the middle of March "no less than 40 car loads" of "immigrant goods" had rolled into Brookings over the new rails, along with about one hundred twenty head of cattle (ibid., Apr. 8, 1880). In Bye, Wilder added that in De Smet, the immigrants "camped around the town and on the vacant lots" (p. 110).

105. *An old railroader and his wife named Hunt with their son Jack.* While there was a Jonathan Hunt, aged fifty-five, working as a laborer in Beadle County in June 1880, there is no definitive match for the details that follow.

106. *The Hunts had found a claim jumper. . . . he shot Jack. . . . only three years in prison.* In *Territory of Dakota* vs. *George Brady*, the defendant, who shot

said and done. Mr Brown was a retired preacher going west to get a homestead. Mr Alden had given him a letter to Pa out of kindness but he had no authority to organize a church.

They talked it over and Mr. Alden decided to save a scandle in the church, he would let the organization stand and leave Mr Brown in charge.[103]

Settlers for the surrounding country came in on the trains, some as passangers to look the country over, some with all their worldly good[s], seed grain and provisions for a year in emigrant cars.[104]

They were coming too in covered wagons, camping around the town and on vacant lots.

An old railroader and his wife named Hunt with their son Jack,[105] his wife and two babies camped back of our place and we became quite well acquainted. Jack had filed on a homestead several miles south of town, built a claim shanty and broke some ground. Now he was going with his father to work a few weeks on the railroad to get a little more money to use on his farm.

We saw them again the next month as they came back on their way to their homestead and the next day we heard that Jack Hunt had been shot and died while they were bringing him back to town to take him on the train to a doctor.

The Hunts had found a claim jumper in their shanty and he refused to leave. After some words he shot Jack in the stomache.

A crowd of men went out from town to get the claim jumper but he had run away. The sheriff at Brookins caught him. At his trial he pleaded self-defense and was sentenced to only three years in prison.[106]

After Jack was shot, Pa said we must go to our claim to live, for people were getting "too durned thick" and someone might move into our shanty. So we left town and went a mile out onto the sweet prairie.

There was only one room in the claim shanty, but a curtain across the end made a bed room. A bed was spread down at night on the floor of the kitchen-dining-room-sitting-room, By day it was spread on top of the bed in the bed room, covered with a pretty quilt and all was neat and cosy.[107]

and killed homesteader John Hunt, was ultimately found guilty of manslaughter in the first degree and received a sentence of four years in a Detroit prison (the territory had not yet built a penitentiary). The editor of the *Brookings County Press* noted, "It is thought by many that this is a very light sentence" ("Home and Other News," June 23, 1881). In *By the Shores of Silver Lake*, Wilder changed the victim's name to Hunter (p. 257). Lane also drew on the episode for her novel *Free Land*, but in her retelling, the victim's name is Jack Allen, who is shot "before his wife's eyes" (pp. 89–99). One of the witnesses during the trial of George Brady was a Margaret Hunt. "District Court," *BCP*, June 23, 1881, and "County Business," *BCP*, July 14, 1881.

107. *There was only one room. . . . all was neat and cosy.* In *By the Shores of Silver Lake*, Wilder created the chapter "The Shanty on the Claim" (pp. 267–91) to describe the fictional family's first experiences there. At this point in the Brandt Revised manuscript, a curator's note indicates that three pages cannot be found, and the pagination skips from page 74 to 78. However, far more than three pages' worth of material is missing, including the entire section on the hard winter of 1880–1881.

108. *he dreamed the barber was cutting his hair. . . . a tiny blue and white kitten.* Wilder used this episode in *Little Town on the Prairie* ("The Necessary Cat," pp. 19–26), but based on its original placement in *Pioneer Girl*, Lane wondered whether it belonged in *By the Shores of Silver Lake*. Wilder responded that the family did not get the kitten "until the summer after the Hard Winter," implying that the story is out of sequence in *Pioneer Girl*. "We were not civilized enough" earlier, Wilder argued, and the story of the cat would emphasize "the newness and rawness" of life in Dakota Territory "as late as after the Hard Winter." Lane also wanted to bring Black Susan back, but Wilder refused: "That kitten was blue and white and I want it left that way. Leave Susan out" (LIW to RWL, Aug. 17, 1938).

109. *cottonwood trees all the way around.* Today, an old stand of cottonwoods continues to grace the Ingalls homestead site near De Smet.

The first night, as Pa was sleeping, he dreamed the barber was cutting his hair and putting his hand up to his head caught a mouse in his fingers. He threw the poor mouse on the floor so hard he killed it, but in the morning there was a patch of his hair cut close to his scalp where the mouse had been at work.

There was no cat in town and only one in all the country around but she was soon to become a mother. Everyone was speaking for a kitten until there couldn't possibly be kittens enough to go around.

Pa was early on the ground and by the use of persuasion and 25¢ came home one day with a tiny blue and white kitten,[108] with its eyes just opened. She didn't know how to drink and we fed her with a spoon. She couldn't walk well, just crawled around, but we cuddled her and fed her often and soon she was a great pet. She caught her first mouse while still so small that the mouse fought back and kittie would cry when the mouse bit her, but she never let go and finally killed it. Later when grown she could whip any cat or dog in the country in a real fight.

Pa broke a strip of ground around the shanty, leaving a grassy door yard and we planted seeds of cottonwood trees all the way around.[109]

He dug a well down near the edge of the big slough that lay between our place and town. When the well was six feet deep and Pa was in it digging, his feet suddenly sank in quicksand. By leaping and grasping the edge of the hole he clambered out the water following him to within two feet of the top. It was wonderfully good water, cold and sweet and clear.

Pa broke two acres of ground and sowed [them] to turnips for ourselves and the cow and to make a place for the garden next spring after the tough sods had lain and the grass roots rotted all winter.

The prairie sods were so tough that many people used them to build their houses. In breaking the land a furrow was plowed about fourteen inches wide. This turned the sod over in long strips three inches thick, the tough roots of the prairie grass holding them together solid and tight.

To make a sod shanty these strips were cut with an ax into two foot lengths and layed up in the walls one above the other like brick.

Cottonwoods on the Ingalls homestead, 2012. *South Dakota Historical Society Press*

Picture copyright 1953 by Garth Williams, copyright © renewed 1981
by Garth Williams. Used by permission of HarperCollins Publishers

Sod house, Hartford, D.T. *Butterfield & Ralson photograph, South Dakota State Historical Society*

110. *To make a sod shanty. . . . A great many sod houses were built over the prairie.* Wilder's description of the building of a sod shanty indicates how closely she observed what went on around her, and it dovetails with other accounts such as Cass G. Barns's *The Sod House* (pp. 59–60). These dwellings were commonplace on the largely treeless Great Plains. The Bye manuscript added, "everyone in the territory that summer knew and sang the song about them" (p. 113) and included a set of lyrics to "The Little Old Sod Shanty on My Claim." Sung to the melody of William Shakespeare Hays's "The Little Old Log Cabin in the Lane," published in 1871, the sod shanty version probably dated from the early 1880s. The *De Smet Leader* referred to its lyrics on August 15, 1883: "The 'old sod shanty on the claim' is fast disappearing from the gaze, and will soon become a curiosity. The good crops raised on Dakota's soil put the settler in a condition to erect better buildings, and he hastens to do so" (*"Town and Country"*). Wilder did not use the song in her novel, but a chapter title echoes its title: "The Shanty on the Claim" (*SL*, pp. 267–77). Silber and Robinson, *Songs of the Great American West*, pp. 212, 220; Waltz and Engle, *Traditional Ballad Index.*

111. *our house in town.* Both Wilder and her father refer to these buildings on De Smet's main street as houses. *See* Ingalls, "Settlement of De Smet," p. [3]. In a letter to Lane, Wilder explained that this second building, "with a west and north frontage," was "the town house where we lived in Hard Winter and while I taught the Bouchie school" (LIW to RWL, Aug. 17, 1938). The building is also listed as "Residence C. P. Ingalls, Justice Peace" on an 1883 diagram of the business center of De Smet. Miller, "Place and Community," p. 257.

112. *The wild grass, . . . and the blue joint grass.* There are over two hundred species of wild grasses in South Dakota, but one of them, prairie cordgrass (*Spartina pectinata*), is also called sloughgrass. It is one of the tallest wild grasses in the state. Big bluestem (*Andropogon gerardii*), which also goes by the name of bluejoint beardgrass, is considered "the backbone of the tall-grass prairie," and legends sug-

They settled together and made a sol[i]d wall fourteen inches thick. Grass often grew over the outside. A frame work of strips of lumber was put up in the inside and cloth or paper put over it, leaving an air space between it and the wall of sod. Such a house was cool in the summer, warm in the winter and could be perfectly clean. A great many sod houses were built over the prairie.[110]

Pa had been busy all summer finishing our house in town,[111] building the shanty, digging the well, breaking the ground and after the turnip seed was sown he began to make hay. The wild grass, so tall and thick in the sloughs and the blue joint grass[112] on the upland all made good hay. Pa cut and raked the hay. Ma and I helped load it on the wagon and unload and build it into the large stacks[113] to feed our horses and two cows through the winter that was coming. Doing all this work for himself, Pa had not much time to work for pay and besides our living there had been the expense of buying the mowing machine and hay rake.

Nothing was said of money difficulties but I knew our funds must be very low and when I noticed Pa leave the table after eating very little when I knew he must still be hungry, I understood that he was leaving the food for the rest of us.[114] Then my appetite failed me too and I followed his example of eating raw turnips between meals.

When haying was finished Pa worked at carpenter work in town, earning money to last us through the winter.[115]

gest that it once grew so tall that "cattle could vanish from sight into its depths" (Ode, *Dakota Flora*, p. 166). Wilder used the term bluestem grass on the opening page of *The Long Winter* (p. 1). Ode, *Dakota Flora*, pp. 166–71; "Big Bluestem."

113. *Ma and I helped load it on the wagon . . . and build it into the large stacks.* In *The Long Winter*, Laura has to convince Pa that she is strong enough to help him stack hay. Ma agrees reluctantly because she "did not like to see women working in the fields. Only foreigners did that. Ma and her girls were Americans, above doing men's work" (*LW*, p. 4). It is unclear why Wilder made this change in the fictional Caroline Ingalls's attitude. In other books in the series, Ma performs both established homemaking chores and nontraditional ones, as she does here in *Pioneer Girl*. For example, she helps Pa build their cabin in *Little House on the Prairie* (p. 58). The fictional Caroline Ingalls's statement that only foreign women worked in the fields could be Wilder's attempt to depict a social attitude from an earlier frontier period (the idea that Yankee women did not work outside the domestic sphere) as a way to illustrate Laura's blossoming independence from convention. In reality, during the Dakota settlement period, "women of all European and European American cultures took on farm tasks widely considered to be men's work. . . . by need or by choice" (Handy-Marchello, *Women of the Northern Plains*, pp. 57–58). They often "worked outside of their homes in jobs ranging from herding cattle to breaking sod" (Riley, "Farm Women's Roles," p. 92).

114. *Nothing was said of money difficulties . . . he was leaving the food for the rest of us.* In *The Long Winter*, Wilder wrote: "The mowing machine had cost so much that Pa had no money left to pay for help. He could not trade work, because there were only a few homesteaders in this new country and they were busy on their own claims" (p. 4). Wilder was sensitive about how to portray the fictional family's economic struggles. In a letter to Lane about *By the Shores of Silver Lake*, Wilder argued against an opening that focused on a recitation of woes and took offense when Lane characterized the family's situation as "poverty worse than ever" (LIW to RWL, Aug. 17, 1938).

115. At this point in the manuscript, there is a break in the text that coincides with the end of a tablet. Usually, the story continues from tablet to tablet without any pause in the action.

Picture copyright 1953 by Garth Williams, copyright © renewed 1981 by Garth Williams. Used by permission of HarperCollins Publishers

DIAGRAM OF DE SMET

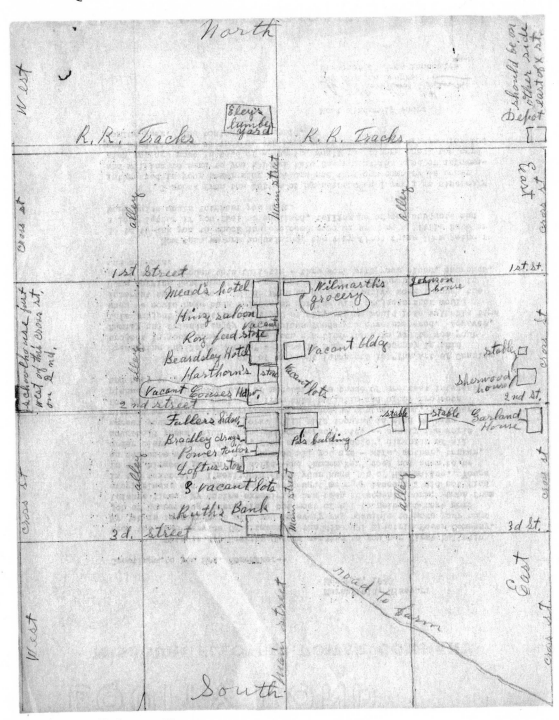

Wilder's diagram of De Smet, ca. 1939.

Herbert Hoover Presidential Library and Museum

Dakota Territory, the Hard Winter of 1880–1881

The 25th. of September the fall rains began.[1] The first of October it cleared for a few days and we were thinking of going back to town for the winter when it began again to rain.

It was dreary and drizzly all day the 8th. and 9th.[2] All work in town was stopped and Pa had been hunting both days, bringing in some ducks but no geese. He said the ducks and geese were not stopping to feed in the sloughs but were flying high and fast going south and he didn't like the looks of the weather.

The dull, gray days were disheartening and I didn't feel like picking and dressing the ducks but did my work as cheerfully as I could not wishing to add to the gloom.

It was raining harder when I went to sleep and there was a drip, drip of rain on the bed-covers over my shoulders where it came through a hole the wind had torn in the tar paper covering the roof.

We never paid any attention to so slight a discomfort and so I slept soundly until some time in the night. I suppose the stopping of the noise of the drip waked me, for I found it was no longer raining and was colder and, snuggling closer under the covers, I slept again.

When next I waked, Pa was building a fire and singing,

"Oh I am as happy as a big sun flower
That nods and bends in the breezes
And my heart is as light as the wind that blows
And comes and goes as it pleases."

I glanced at the window but it seemed to be covered with a whiteness I could not see through.

When the fire was going good Ma got up, but when I started, she told me to lie still. We were all to lie still under the covers for there was no use of our all being cold and there was an awful blizzard outside.[3]

1. *The 25th. of September the fall rains began.* Much of September 1880 appears to have been rainy, affecting the quantity and quality of the harvest across eastern South Dakota. "Fall work of all kinds was three or four weeks behind," the editor of the *Moody County Enterprise* of Flandreau, D.T., explained (news item, Oct. 21, 1880). Some farmers struggled to get crops such as potatoes out of the ground before it froze. Ibid.; "Home and Other News," BCP, Sept. 2, 9, 1880.

2. *It was dreary and drizzly all day the 8th. and 9th.* These dates are just slightly ahead of the actual events.

3. *there was an awful blizzard outside.* Wilder's sequence of events is similar to newspaper reports of this early blizzard. It began raining on Wednesday, October 13, and rain turned to snow on Thursday evening. Friday evening, October 15, the winds picked up, and a full-fledged blizzard raged for at least the next twenty-four hours. In Bye, Wilder explained that during a blizzard "the wind comes from every direction at once. No matter which way you turn, the stinging, blinding snow is driven straight into your face. It is impossible to see an inch, and impossible to get your direction from the wind" (p. 116). When the blizzard ended, drifts lay six to eight feet deep, and the railroad cuts east of Brookings contained ten to twelve feet of snow. The storm covered much of the southeastern quarter of what is now South Dakota and extended into Minnesota and Iowa. "The Blizzard," BCP, Oct. 21, 1880; "The Storm West of Us" and related items, *Moody County Enterprise*, Oct. 21, 1880; Kingsbury, *History of Dakota Territory*, 2:1148–50.

4. *Pa went out. . . . they could not see at all. They were tired out by their struggle with the storm.* In *The Long Winter*, the fictional Laura goes with Pa to check on the motionless cattle, which are not only blinded by their own breath but are smothering in it, with their heads "frozen to the ground" (p. 50). The loss of livestock in the October 1880 blizzard was heavy because the farmers were not prepared for it and had "thousands of head . . . out on the prairies at the time" (Kingsbury, *History of Dakota Territory*, 2:1148). Near Madison, D.T., southeast of De Smet, a herd of one hundred twenty cattle perished as "they seemed to travel with the storm until they came to the railroad grade where the snow had drifted so they could not get farther and all perished near the grade" ("Storm West of Us"). Large numbers of hogs, horses, and oxen also died without sufficient shelter. A similar storm in early October of 2013 killed twenty to thirty thousand cattle in western South Dakota, along with three to five thousand sheep. Most animals died from hypothermia and stress, while some suffocated in deep drifts or drowned when they fell into bodies of water. "Home and Other News," Oct. 21, 1880; "Stress Caused Many Cattle Deaths," *Missoulian*, Nov. 8, 2013; "SD Vet Updates Blizzard Death Totals," *Agweek*, Nov. 11, 2013.

5. *Pa brough[t] in several birds that had fallen exhausted in . . . the stacks of hay.* In *The Long Winter*, Pa rescues just one special bird, which the family identifies as resembling the great auk (pp. 51–52).

Pa bundled up warmly and struggled through the storm to the barn going by the wagon that nearly touched the house and a big hay stack just beyond that nearly touched the barn.

When he came back, Ma gave us some warm breakfast and I insisted on getting up, but Mary, Carrie and Grace stayed in bed all day to keep warm, while Pa, Ma and I hovered over the stove for it was frightfully cold and the wind howled and shrieked, with the sound of nothing else under heaven but a blizzard wind. Trying to look out of the window or door, we could not see an inch into the storm, which lasted all day and night and the next day and into the night. Sometime that night the wind moderated a little and on the morning of the third day we could see a short distance, for while the snow was still blowing, it was rolling along closer to the ground instead of filling all the air. We could see over it.

Just beyond the door yard were some cattle standing motionless with their heads hanging. Poor things, we thought, they are tired out.

Later when they had not moved we wondered why they didn't go to the hay stacks and because they looked strange, standing still so long with their heads hanging, Pa went out to see what was the matter with them. He found that their breath and the snow, blown into their eyelashes and the hair around their eyes, had formed ice over their eyes until they could not see at all. They were tired out by their struggle with the storm,[4] drifting before it for no one knew how many miles. There were twenty five of them and Pa went up to one after another and tore the ice from their eyes. As soon as they could see, they bawled and ran from him a few steps, then stopped and stood still again, they were so tired. He came in and left them standing there looking around at the desolate land with the snow blowing low across it. I suppose they were glad they could see it.

After awhile they drifted down to the shelter of a haystack where they stayed resting and eating until the next morning sometime and then went away when we wern't noticing them.

Pa brough[t] in several birds that had fallen exhausted in the shelter of one of the stacks of hay.[5] Some of them were strange to us, we never saw any like them before nor afterward. We kept them where they would not freeze until they were rested and the storm was entirely over, then turned them loose.

The storm was always called "The October Blizzard." Hundreds of cattle perished in it and some people were frozen to death.[6]

There was a nice spell of weather after it, but an old Indian passing through town warned the people that a terrible winter was coming. He said the seventh winter was always harder than those before; then the winters would be mild again until another seven, which would be harder than the first. Mild winters would follow again until the third seven which would be much worse than either of the others. He said it had always been so; that the winter coming was the third seven and there would be "heap big snow" and the winds would blow and blow.[7]

During the good weather we moved into town for the winter. Pa was one of the county commissioners and also a Justice of the Peace. He had his office in the front room,[8] while we lived in the one room and the leanto room at the back, with the bedrooms upstairs. Everyone staying for the winter was living the same way in small rooms back of their places of business or upstairs over them or in the few shanty houses on the back streets.

George Masters, the eldest son of Uncle Sam Masters of Walnut Grove going through De Smet on his way to work farther west,[9] stopped to see us and begged Ma to let his wife Maggie stay with us to be nearer him.[10] Maggie came the next week, a large, cheerful Scotch girl. We liked her but we did not care for George who was much like his father.

A widow named Garland,[11] with two grown daughters, Florence and Vene[12] and a son about my age named Edward but called Cap,[13] had built a boarding house on the street back of us. Florence was hired to teach the school which began the first of November[14] and Carrie and I started to school again.

There were only fifteen pupils all strangers to each other, but begining to feel acquainted, when one still, sun[n]y day as we were sitting quietly, studying[,] the school house cracked and shook from a blow of the wind that struck the northwest corner like a mighty

6. *"The October Blizzard." Hundreds of cattle perished . . . people were frozen to death.* While people would freeze to death before the winter was over, the loss of human life in the October 1880 blizzard appears to have been minimal, and no deaths were reported in the new towns along the Dakota Central Railroad. The fact that temperatures were mild kept people from freezing, although most were unprepared and ended up burning "bran, corn, hay, and, in fact everything except wood and coal" ("Home and Other News," BCP, Nov. 18, 1880). Huron had three hundred extra laborers in town waiting for the weekend train, and they "came very near being starved out during the storm" and the week-long railroad blockade that followed (ibid., Oct. 21, 1880). Across the region, railroad and telegraph lines took a week to ten days to repair, and snow from this storm remained on the ground until the end of the winter. Kingsbury, *History of Dakota Territory*, 2:1148–49; "Home and Other News," BCP, Oct. 28, 1880.

7. *an old Indian. . . . there would be "heap big snow" and the winds would blow and blow.* In Brandt (p. 94) and Bye (pp. 117–18), this American Indian man came to town specifically to warn people about the coming winter. This occurrence was not without precedent. The *Redwood Gazette* had reported two similar instances in 1878. In January, "Joe Connall, a half breed, who has lived in Minnesota forty eight years," informed a newspaper editor that the month of "December just closed was much the warmest December he had known in the state" (front page item, Jan. 17, 1878). Three months later, the *Gazette* reported: "An old Indian at Traverse de Sioux predicts that there will be a great freshet in June and July, this season; that the Mississippi river would be as high as in 1851 and in 1852; and that the lowlands or flats in the upper Mississippi valley would be terribly inundated" (ibid., Apr. 4, 1878). An early territorial historian also reported that Yankton Indians, "who had been born in this Upper Missouri Valley seventy-five and eighty years prior to" the October 1880 blizzard, "could recall no occurrence of such a wintry visitation during October"

(Kingsbury, *History of Dakota Territory*, 2:1148). Whether their advice and knowledge was solicited or volunteered, American Indian residents of the region shared their long-term awareness of weather patterns with the new settlers, who valued and recorded that knowledge. For her part, Wilder created what may appear to contemporary readers to be a dated and patronizing portrayal of an American Indian man. She recorded his use of a stereotypical phrase—"heap big snow"—to convey his warning. In the novel, she added an improvised sign language, and Wilder's description of his blanket, bare brown arms, and scalp-lock (*LW*, p. 61) seems more consistent with the Osage men she remembered from her childhood than with the Dakota, Lakota, and Nakota men living on reservations in Dakota Territory. Yet, Pa's respect for the "very old Indian" (p. 61) underscores the wisdom and intelligence this man and others offered to white settlers in the region. What strikes readers today as stereotypical may, in fact, be a reflection of Wilder's creative milieu rather than an ethnic slur. As Donna M. Campbell points out, to view Wilder's "vision of other races" as "a monolithic whole is to deny the ways in which [her work] raises questions about racial identity even as it affirms some negative stereotypes" ("'Wild Men' and Dissenting Voices," p. 111).

8. *Pa was one of the county commissioners and also a Justice of the Peace. . . .his office in the front room.* Charles Ingalls's name does not appear on the list of county commissioners and justices of the peace published in a fragmentary issue of the *Kingsbury County News* on February 24, 1881. Instead, he was first appointed as a constable in March 1880 until elections could be held, and then, when one of the town's original justices "moved away in May . . . Mr. Ingalls succeeded him" ("Ingalls Was First Resident De Smet," *De Smet News*, June 6, 1930). His front-room office was known as "the County Office (Ingalls Building)," and it was here that the first school district was organized in July 1880 (Records of Kingsbury County Superintendent of Schools, p. 6). The "Official Directory" of the *De Smet Leader* lists Ingalls as justice from the first issue of January 27, 1883, through March 19, 1884, when he lost the election, but he was re-elected in March 1885. "Justice Ingalls has sustained the dignity of court and the majesty of the law in large chunks of late," the *Leader* editor reported on January 27, 1883. Six court cases recorded in his handwriting from 1883 and 1884 show that he presided over cases ranging from the illegal sale of liquor to assault with intent to kill. In *The Long Winter*, Wilder wrote that Pa had a "boughten desk and boughten chair" (p. 67) in his front room, but the fictional Charles Ingalls,

while civic-minded, was always a farmer and not an elected official. Sherwood, *Beginnings of De Smet*, pp. 39-[40]; "County Was Organized"; "Pa's Century-Old Justice of the Peace work," p. 7; "Election Returns," *DSL*, Mar. 8, 1884, Mar. 7, 1885.

9. *George Masters . . . on his way to work farther west.* In April 1880, George E. Masters was twenty-seven years old and working as a clerk in the railroad's company store in Volga, east of De Smet. He also worked as far west as Blunt during his stint on the railroad. The names of George Masters, his wife, and their infant son appear just below the Ingalls family listing in the census taken in June 1880. Charles P. Ingalls is listed as a forty-four-year-old farmer; forty-year-old Caroline L. is "Keeping House." Both Mary A. (fifteen) and Laura E. (thirteen) are providing "Help in Keeping house." Nine-year-old Caroline C. and three-year-old Grace L. (a mistake; Grace's middle name was Pearl) are also listed as part of the household. "Arthur Masters Born," *De Smet News*, June 6, 1930.

10. *begged Ma to let his wife Maggie stay with us to be nearer him.* Margaret Masters was twenty-two in June 1880, and she, too, was a

Charles P. Ingalls. *South Dakota State Historical Society*

housekeeper, whose parents had been born in Scotland. In a letter to Lane, Wilder explained the family's decision to let the Masters share their home during the winter of 1880–1881:

> When Maggie came, Ma saw she would soon have a baby, much too soon after the time she was married.
>
> Maggie didn't want the baby to be born at her folks' and disgrace them. George's folks were mad because he married her and wouldn't have her there.
>
> Maggie had always been a nice girl and Ma was sorry for her and let her stay, the baby was born before winter came.
>
> Work stopped and George came. We thought they were leaving but George put it off.
>
> Then winter set in and caught them. There was no where else they could stay. Every house was full and Pa couldn't put them out in the street (LIW to RWL, Mar. 7, 1938, Box 13, file 194, Lane Papers).

Wilder's decision not to include George and Maggie Masters in *The Long Winter* was a deliberate one, although Lane initially disagreed with her mother's decision. She urged her to add another set of characters—if not the Masters, then perhaps the Boasts. Wilder objected. "We can't have anyone living with us," she argued. It "would spoil the story." If she substituted the Boasts, Wilder noted, "the point of the situation would be blunted." She added that, given the Boasts' generous characters, they would help haul and twist hay and participate in the household chores. Wilder concluded that the fictional family "must be alone" to heighten the deprivation and emphasize the help they received from the Wilder brothers (ibid.).

11. *A widow named Garland.* Margaret F. Pettit Garland was forty-two in June 1880, when she listed her occupation as "farmer." She had married Walter B. Garland in 1854 in Wisconsin, and they had five children, two of whom died in childhood. After her husband's death, she moved to Dakota Territory in 1879. She opened her boarding house, which was a family affair, on the corner of Second Street and Joliet Avenue in 1880. She had been encouraged to do so "by several of the young bachelors who were dissatisfied with the food at the hotel" (Fugate, "Grandma Garland," p. 90). Sherwood, *Beginnings of De Smet*, p. 30.

12. *two grown daughters, Florence and Vene.* Florence Garland was eighteen in June 1880. Her fictional counterpart in *The Long Winter* is "a smiling young lady, with curled bangs" (p. 81). Florence married Charles Dawley, a lumber dealer, in 1887, and

Florence Garland. *Laura Ingalls Wilder Memorial Society*

they had two sons; Florence died in 1935 and is buried in the De Smet cemetery. Sarah Lovenia ("Vene" or "Venie") Garland was twenty-three in June 1880. She learned millinery and later married Albert Cornwell; they had at least one daughter. By 1910, the Cornwells were living in Watertown, South Dakota, where they provided a home at times for the aging Margaret Garland. Lovenia died in 1942. Fugate, "Grandma Garland," p. 90; "South Dakota Death Index."

13. *a son about my age named Edward but called Cap.* Oscar Edmund ("Cap") Garland was fifteen in 1880. He had been born in Wisconsin in late 1864, making him about two years older than Wilder. In *The Long Winter*, Wilder devoted an entire chapter to his first appearance, "Cap Garland" (pp. 75–95). Throughout the remaining novels in the series, Garland frequently shares the heroic spotlight with Almanzo Wilder. In 1883, Cap Garland

Oscar Edmund ("Cap") Garland. *Laura Ingalls Wilder Memorial Society*

and his sisters took homesteads in Clark County, east of De Smet. Garland never married and died when a threshing machine exploded near Hetland, South Dakota, on November 3, 1891. He was twenty-six. He and his mother are buried at the Collins Cemetery in Willow Lake, South Dakota. Fugate, "Grandma Garland," pp. 90–91; "Terrible Accident," *Lake Preston Times*, Nov. 6, 1891; "Oscar Edmund Eddy Cap Garland"; "Oscar Edmund Garland."

14. *Florence was hired to teach the school which began the first of November.* School began in a building constructed in "the latter part" of 1880 by the citizens of De Smet, who provided both the labor and the materials. Florence Garland "received a salary of $20.00 per month for teaching the dozen pupils" in several grades ("History of the De Smet Schools," *De Smet News*, June 6, 1930). When Wilder and her husband visited Florence in De Smet in 1931, they "talked of the old days of the hard winter when she taught the school before it was closed for lack of fuel and because it was too dangerous to go to the schoolhouse" (LIW, *LHT*, p. 310).

sledge. The sun was blotted out and all we could see from the windows was a white blur for all outside was a whirling chaos of snow.

Miss Garland looked frightened and said we would all go home;[15] for us to put our wraps on quickly and fasten them good; that we must all stay close together and go with her.

Just as we were ready to start a man named Holms came from town[16] to help us get safely through the storm, for the school house was three blocks west of the business street and there were no homes nor anything but bare prairie between.

We started all close together following Mr Holms and Miss Garland, but after a few minutes Cap Garland left the others and went farther to the south. We shouted at him but he disappeared in the storm running. We were blinded by the snow, buffeted by the wind until we could hardly keep our feet and awfully cold. It seemed to me that we had already gone too far and still there was no sign of buildings when suddenly we ran against the back of a building that stood at the very end of the street, the last building in town on the north. We didn't see it until we bumped against it and if we had gone just a few feet farther north we should have missed it and been out on the open prairie lost in the blizzard.[17]

Cap Garland went straight, told the men down town that we had gone wrong and a crowd was just starting after us when we came walking up the street beside the buildings.

For three days, the blizzard raged and no one thought of doing anything but staying safely at home. Then the sun shone on the snow, packed in hard drifts by the wind, the wind was still and people moved about again.

The snow had filled the cuts on the railroad and it was several days before the snow plows and men with shovels could clear the track so trains could run again.

Maggie Masters baby was born[18] in her room upstairs with only Ma and Mrs Garland to help her. There was no doctor to be had. George came back from the west on the first train going east. His job was finished until spring and winter was setting in in earnest.

Storms followed storms so quickly that the railroad track could not be kept open. The Company kept men shoveling snow and snow

15. *Miss Garland looked frightened and said we would all go home.* Wilder added new details in later versions of *Pioneer Girl*, the most interesting of which concerned the fuel supply: "There was enough coal to last for some time, and we could have burned the seats" (Bye, p. 119). In *The Long Winter*, Wilder heightened the drama. "There was only a little fuel at the schoolhouse," she wrote. "The school board was buying coal, but only one load had been delivered. Laura thought they might outlive the storm in the schoolhouse, but they could not do it without burning all the costly patent desks" (p. 85). Rural school teachers often had frightening decisions to make when blizzards struck without warning during the school day. A sudden blizzard in 1888 is remembered as "the children's blizzard" because so many youngsters perished trying to make it home in the storm or survived through the heroism and wise decisions of their teachers. *See* Kingsbury, *History of Dakota Territory*, 2:1512–14; Laskin, *Children's Blizzard*, pp.161–66, 239.

16. *a man named Holms came from town.* A twenty-six-year-old bachelor named Silas Holmes held a homestead in Kingsbury County in 1880. He was in the livery business, which probably meant that he worked in town or had moved to town for the winter. In *The Long Winter*, the man is identified as Mr. Foster (p. 86).

17. *We started all close together. . . . lost in the blizzard.* In the Bye account of this narrow escape, Wilder focused on the need to protect her younger sister Carrie, who is not mentioned in the original. "I kept tight hold of Carrie," she began as they started out and then added later: "I was very anxious about Carrie, feeling responsible for her. After struggling on for some time longer, I was sure we were lost, and I remembered how Nora Robbins had saved the baby" (p. 119), a reference to an incident during the Ingalls family's second stay in Minnesota earlier in *Pioneer Girl*. In *The Long Winter*, Carrie's safety becomes even more central to the story (pp. 86–94).

18. *Maggie Masters baby was born.* According to the 1880 census, George and Maggie's son was born in April 1880, and he is listed as George E., Jr. The

family, however, eventually settled on the name Arthur Kingsbury Masters, and his date of birth is officially recorded as May 23, 1880. He was the first child born in the new town of De Smet. He lived out his life in South Dakota and died in 1963. "Arthur Masters Born"; "South Dakota Births."

Children of George and Maggie Masters, including Arthur K. Masters, standing at right. *Lucille (Masters) Mone Collection*

Snow plow on Chicago & North Western railroad, Minnesota, March, 1881. *Elmer and Tenney photograph, Minnesota Historical Society*

plows working all they could, but the snow plows stuck in the snow and snow blew back faster than the men could shovel it out.[19]

On the 20th. of November a train went up the line and made the trip back. The next train through was a passanger and mail train on January 4th. It went west to Huron but could not get back and stayed there the rest of the winter.[20]

The Suprentendent of the Division was much displeased at the failure of his men to get the trains through and came out to the deep cut west of Tracy to suprentend the work himself.[21]

They were using two snow plows hitched together, but the snow was packed so hard that they could drive them only a few feet when they stuck fast and had to be shoveled out.

The suprentendent ordered them to put three plows on and drive them through. Then the engineer refused to drive the engine in front saying they would all be killed.

The suprentendent replied that he wouldn't ask a man to do anything he wouldent do himself and—with an oath—he'd drive the engine himself. They put the other plow on, backed the train for a mile, then came as fast as they could and struck the snow in the cut with all the power of the engines, their weight and speed. And stopped! The front engine and its plow were completely buried, even the smoke stack covered. By a miricle the enginers were not hurt and crawled and were shoveled out. The impact, the heat and steam from the engine in front melted the snow close around it and it froze again in solid ice. When the men had shoveled the snow away so they could get to it they had to use picks to cut the ice from the wheels and gearing. It took two days, with all the men that could work around them to get the engines loose. By that time another blizzard was raging and the Suprentendent ordered all work on the track stopped[22] with the snow one hundred feet deep on the track at the Tracy cut and Twenty-five feet deep on the track in the cut just west of De Smet.

All the men in De Smet had worked at the shoveling. Most of them were glad of the $2. a day pay, but even those who didn't need the money worked because they wanted the trains to run.[23] The last shoveling they did took three men to get one shovel full of snow to the top

19. *Storms followed storms. . . . snow blew back faster than the men could shovel it out.* Journalist and historian George W. Kingsbury of Yankton observed that these recurrent storms, which stretched over five months, were "of the most damaging and disheartening character." He also noted that trains bound from Minnesota for eastern Dakota Territory remained snowbound on the tracks, buried in drifts, and "human power was inadequate to remove them" (Kingsbury, *History of Dakota Territory*, 2:1149).

20. *It went west . . . and stayed there the rest of the winter.* The editor of the *Kingsbury County News* noted on February 24, 1881, "The leading question is, when shall we have a train from the east?" (Sherwood, *Beginnings of De Smet*, p. [40]). According to the editor of the *Brookings County Press*, the last freight train to reach Brookings from the east arrived on December 24, 1880, and the final passenger train on January 19, 1881. "Home and Other News," May 5, 1881.

21. *The Suprentendent of the Division . . . himself.* The Brandt version added that the superintendent "was an easterner" (p. 97). Both the Brandt and the Bye manuscripts presented the episode in a slightly different sequence, jumping ahead to describe how all the men in De Smet worked at shoveling snow for the railroads, then returning to the action at Tracy. The Bye version, which is particularly well developed, suggested: "Everybody welcomed the superintendent when he came out of his warm offices to take charge of the situation. The foreman on the job was only too willing to turn over the responsibility to him" (p. 121).

22. *ordered all work on the track stopped.* Once he failed to make it through the cut, the superintendent returned "east to his offices, leaving the foreman in charge" (Bye, p. 123). In *The Long Winter*, Pa tells this story in the chapter "The Hard Winter" (pp. 215–22), which appears toward the end of the novel as the fictional family begins to feel hardship more keenly. Pa relates the story to illustrate a point: the superintendent failed because he did not have patience, which the Ingalls family would need to see the hard winter through.

23. *All the men in De Smet. . . . were glad of the $2. a day pay, . . . wanted the trains to run.* On February 24,

1881, the editor of the *Kingsbury County News* reported: "A dollar and a half a day for shoveling snow on the Dakota Central takes most of our business and professional men out. It's more fun to shovel snow than to go without bread or coal." In *The Long Winter*, Pa takes a handcar from De Smet to Volga to help dig out the tracks (pp. 105–15). The next day, a work-train pulls into De Smet, and Pa returns, bringing Mr. Edwards with him. He leaves a twenty dollar bill in Mary's lap before he catches the train west.

24. *It did its best to blot out the town, . . . that it couldn't quite manage.* This line and the three paragraphs that follow hint at creative techniques that Wilder developed later in *The Long Winter*, especially her ability to personify the winter and describe its destructive force tangibly and dramatically. "Sometimes in the night, half-awake and cold, Laura half-dreamed that the roof was scoured thin," Wilder wrote. "Horribly the great blizzard, large as the sky, bent over it and scoured with an enormous invisible cloth, round and round on the paper-thin roof, till a hole wore through and squealing, chuckling, laughing a deep Ha! Ha! the blizzard whirled in" (p. 225).

25. *There were about 100 people in De Smet.* One hundred sixteen names appear on the three pages devoted to De Smet in the 1880 census taken on June 7 and 8.

26. *Two grocery stores.* In *The Long Winter*, Wilder named the proprietors, Mr. Harthorn and Mr. Loftus. Edelbert M. Harthorn and his son Frank operated the Harthorn establishment. Born in Maine, the senior Harthorn was thirty-nine in June 1880; his son, born in Minnesota, was listed as twenty-three, but subsequent census records place his birth in July 1864, making him about fifteen in 1880. He may have fibbed about his age in order to file on a homestead. Twenty-eight-year-old Daniel H. Loftus appeared as a land agent on the 1880 census. He had started a business first in Volga, but he and his partner, Billy Broadbent, set up a general merchandise store in De Smet sometime in 1880. Loftus later bought out his partner and oper-

of the bank. One stood at the bottom and threw it as far as he could; the man above him threw it from his shovel as high as he could. The third man could throw it to the top of the bank. Then in the night more snow fell; the wind blew and in the morning the cut was again full, tight packed with the snow to the top of the snow banks on each side which were as high as the snow fences which were supposed to hold the snow back from the cut. At last the wind could blow the snow, across the tops of the snow fences across the snow on top of the track and away on the other side, in its age old sweep across the prairie, the man made obstacle overcome and hidden.

It did its best to blot out the town, but that it couldn't quite manage.[24] Here in his ages long war with the elements, Man won though it was a hard, long battle. During the night the one street in town might be filled with snow packed so hard teams were driven over it and so high a man sitting on a low sled could look on a level into the second story windows of the hotel and across the roofs of the other buildings. The next night another blizzard would come and the wind striking at a little different [angle] would cut the snow away and sweep the street clean so the length of it would be bare ground in the morning.

We would lie in our beds those nights, listening to the wind howl and shriek while the house rocked with the force of it and snow sifted in around the windows and through the nail holes where nails had been withdrawn for the houses were only shells at best.

Once during the winter our little stable was entirely covered with snow and Pa had to dig a tunnel through it from the back door to the stable door to get in and care for the stock. It had the great advantage of being a shelter for Pa going and coming and he was sorry when one night the wind swept it all away and he had to meet the full force of the storm again.

There were about 100 people in De Smet[25] and town and country were so newly settled that no crops had been raised except a few sod potatoes.

The two grocery stores[26] were small and started with only a little capital. Not having much money to buy with and expecting to be

Men clearing snow, Chicago & North Western railroad, Minnesota, March, 1881.
Elmer and Tenney photograph, Minnesota Historical Society

Daniel H. Loftus. *Laura Ingalls Wilder Memorial Society*

ated the store until his death in 1921. According to his obituary, his store "became widely known for the quality of dress goods on his shelves" ("D. H. Loftus Obituary"), which is consistent with the fictional portrait Wilder created in *The Long Winter*. When Laura and Carrie search for a Christmas present for Pa, they find a pair of "plain, dull gray" suspenders at Harthorn's, but at the Loftus store they find blue suspenders with red, machine-made flowers (p. 178). "Loftus Obituary"; "South Dakota Death Index"; "Home and Other News," *BCP*, Mar. 11, 1880.

27. *both food and fuel were running short.* According to George W. Kingsbury, when the first blizzard struck in October 1880, the railroads "had not yet shipped in the winter's supply of coal or other fuel, so that this essential was one of the earliest 'necessities of life' that was discovered to be lacking" (*History of Dakota Territory*, 2:1149). Supplies did not run short quite that soon on the Dakota Central into De Smet, for the weather improved in November, and the trains ran semi-regularly until mid-December, when, according to the *Brookings County Press*, the "railroad company rushed up five or six car loads of coal and wood this week. Wonder whether this is any indication of another blizzard? P.S.—The blizzard is here" ("Home and Other News," Dec. 16, 1880).

28. *orders came over the telegraph wires to lay off all work.* The *Brookings County Press* indicated that the passenger and mail train came through on January 19. In addition to the order suspending work, the telegraph was probably the source of the story about the superintendent's efforts to open the Tracy cut. During the same time period, the Chicago, Milwaukee & Saint Paul Railroad, south of De Smet, issued a "general order" suspending "the running of all trains west of Mason City, Iowa." Railroad blockades "were so prolonged that in some cases the employees at the stations, having no employment, were temporarily suspended" (Kingsbury, *History of Dakota* Territory, 2:1150).

29. *they hoped we would enjoy the Christmas turkey.* The Bye manuscript added: "But we knew that Christmas barrel was still on the other side of the Tracy cut. We took this as a good joke on us, and long before spring 'our Christmas turkey' had become a by-word in the family that always made us laugh" (p. 123).

30. *the old story of the colored man . . . whar is ye."* The origin of this witticism is not clear, but a version appears in Henry Hupfeld's *Encyclopedia of Wit and Wisdom*, first published in 1877: "Cuffy said he'd rather die in a railroad smash up than a steamboat bust up for this reason: 'If you gits off and smashed up, dar you is; but if you gits blowed up on the boat, whar is you?'" (p. 655).

31. *the terrible cold.* Temperatures had turned cold in

able to replace the stock as it was sold the store keepers had only a small supply on hand when the trains stopped running and it was to[o] late to get more. It was the same with the coal sold at the lumber yard. Now with no way of getting more supplies of both food and fuel were running short.[27]

The storms were so terrible and so frequent that teaming from Brookins could not be done and supplies were short even there for no train could run west of Tracy and the country was all new.

We were wondering how we would get through the winter and were so relieved when on January 4th we heard the train whistle. Everyone ran to the depot but it was only a train carrying passangers and mail. We thought surely there must be another train coming behind with food and fuel but none came and that night there was the worst storm yet; the track was buried again, orders came over the telegraph wires to lay off all work[28] and we knew we could expect no help from outside. We must depend on ourselves.

Anyway we had, from the last train, a letter from friends in Chicago, dated in November, saying they had sent us a Christmas barrel and they hoped we would enjoy the Christmas turkey[29] and the warm clothing it contained.

We knew the old story of the colored man who when asked which he prefered a wreck on land or on the water replied he'd wreck on land, because "in a railroad smash up dar ye is, but in a steamboat bust up whar is ye."[30] And we knew that, in this wreck of the railroad, there we were.

There was no meat to be had, no butter, the potatoes were nearly gone. The only fruit there had been in town was dried fruit and that was long since gone from the stores. We had a little yet and a little bit of sugar.

Coffee was gone and tea. Pa had a little wheat he had bought for seed the next spring and Ma browned that, ground it and made us a hot drink. What with the terrible cold[31] and just dry hay to eat our cows were nearly dry. Pa got about a quart at a milking and the most of that went to Grace and Maggie on account of the baby.

Our sugar was gone and the last sack at the store had sold for 50¢ a pound.

Then the flour was all gone the last sack of that sold for one dollar a pound.[32]

There was no more coal nor kerosene.

For light Ma put a bit of rag around a button, tied the button in with thread and leaving the loose end of the rag standing up about two inches set the button in a saucer of axel grease that Pa had for greasing his wagon. When the end of the rag was lighted the heat of its burning drew the grease into the rag and made a sort of candle that gave a little light after a fashion. There was not much grease and we did not use the light long at night but went to bed early, saving both light and fire.

When the coal was gone we twisted the long, coarse, slough hay into sticks and burned that. It was quite a trick to take a handful of the hay[,] an end in each hand, twist it until it kinked on itself in the middle, then twisting the two sides upon each other until the ends were reached, make a sort of knot and tuck the ends in to hold it tight. If well done it made a hard twist from 18 inches to a foot long about as large around as a stick of split cook wood. We called them sticks of hay and they could be handled like sticks of wood. They made a suprisingly good fuel, a quick, hot fire, but burned so quickly that some one must be twisting hay all the time to keep the fire going.[33]

Pa filled the storm shed over the back door with the loose hay and he and Ma and I took turns twisting it. Carrie was too little and though she wanted to help was not allowed to do much. Mary had never been strong and we would not let her stay out in the cold storm shed.

It is times like this that test people and we were getting to know George and Maggie. We had not asked nor wanted them to stay with us, but they were out of money and had no other place to go, so they just stayed on. George promised to pay his share of the living expenses after work opened up in the spring and I'll say in passing that he paid a scanty part the next fall, though our own milk and potatoes and hay were not counted.

We could not keep the whole house warm, so we shut off the front room and kept the fire going in the kitchen stove, using it both

December, with local newspapers reporting 22, 26, and 34 degrees below zero. "Home and Other News," *BCP*, Dec. 9; local news, *Moody County Enterprise*, Dec. 9, 16, 1880.

32. *the last sack . . . sold for one dollar a pound.* In *The Long Winter*, Pa reports that the last sack of flour sold at this price to "Banker Ruth" (p. 193). The editor of the *Brookings County Press* took note of such price gouging on March 24, 1881. "Owing to the Minnesota snow banks it has for the past twelve weeks been impossible to get any freight west of Sleepy Eye," he wrote. "This fact has of course made it necessary for persons living along the line of road to pay whatever price has been asked for provisions, etc." As a result, "enormous prices have been charged for everything. Fifty cents per gallon for kerosene and six pounds of sugar for one dollar and other things in proportion have been the ruling prices." By comparison, kerosene, for example, had been twenty cents a gallon in January 1880; twelve pounds of dried apples usually cost one dollar; tea ran anywhere from thirty to seventy cents; seed potatoes cost forty cents a bushel in April 1880; hard coal sold for $10 per ton, soft for $7.75; flour ran $3.25 per hundred in July 1880; and coffee could be had at one dollar for four and a half pounds. The cost of sugar varied according to grade, but the best cost one dollar for about nine pounds in 1880. Advertisements, *BCP*, Jan. 8, 29, Feb. 19, Apr. 15, July 1, 1880.

33. *we twisted the long, coarse, slough hay. . . . twisting hay all the time to keep the fire going.* "Hay when well twisted makes a fire much like dry basswood or pine," wrote the editor of the *Brookings County*

Hay twist. *Laura Ingalls Wilder Memorial Society*

Press, "and were it not for the litter, which burning it in a common stove necessitates, it would be fully equal to either of them." The editor, like most territorial journalists, was a Dakota boomer, and he was writing to correct the misconception "in the east" that the burning of hay meant that a person was "in a suffering condi-tion." Many farmers burned it all year long, he claimed, because it cost the farmer nothing but time in putting it up and twisting it ("Home and Other News," May 26, 1881). Wilder, however, did not share the editor's opinion. For both her real and her fictional families, twisting hay was a hardship.

for cooking and warmth. Mary had her rocking chair on one side, close up to the oven door and Maggie with her baby had a rocking chair in the other warm place on the other side of the stove, with the heat from the open oven door on her feet and knees and the baby in her lap.

George would crowd next to Maggie getting part of the warmth from the oven, while the rest of us did the best we could. Grace sat most of the time in Mary's lap while Ma and Carrie and I hovered in front or crowded in at the back to stand between the stove and the wall, always giving Pa room when he came in from the chores, for Pa did all the chores while George sat by the fire.[34]

Pa would get up in the bitter cold and start the fire singing "Oh I am as happy as a big sun flower that nods and bends in the breezes" while George lay snug and warm in bed until breakfast was nearly ready.

George was always first at the table at any meal and though the rest of us ate sparingly and fairly because food was scarce, he would gobble, not denying himself even for Maggie as we did because of her nursing the baby.

As our potatoes became scarce, he would help himself first to them and hurry to eat them so quickly that he always burned himself on them. Then clapping his hand to his mouth he would exclaim "Potatoes do hold the heat!" This happened so often the rest of us made a byword of it.[35]

George was nearly always underfoot in his place at the stove, but Pa was quite a favorite among the other men and used to spend some time where they gathered with the Wilder boys[36] who were batching a little way down the street or at Fuller Bros. hardware store just across the street from us.[37] At those places there were no women or children to be first and they each had an equal chance at the fire. They told stories and sang songs and played games. They didn't eat and drink but at least they were merry for tomorrow they might die in a blizzard.

Henry Hinze and his saloon were still there and his supplies of drink were lasting, the only supplies in town that lasted through the winter.

34. *Pa did all the chores while George sat by the fire.* Many years later, Wilder wrote that George "never went with Pa for a load of hay, he never twisted any. He just sat. He would have done differently or I'd have thrown him out, but Pa wouldn't. Sweet charity!" She also told Lane that she could not include the Masters in *The Long Winter* because "they must be as they were and that would spoil the story. If we make them decent it would spoil the story for we would lose Manly's kindness" (LIW to RWL, Mar. 7, 1938).

35. *This happened so often the rest of us made a byword of it.* The Bye version reads, "He did this so often that 'Potatoes do hold the heat!' later became a family byword for selfishness" (p. 126).

36. *the Wilder boys.* Royal and Almanzo Wilder arrived in Dakota Territory in 1879 and, along with their sister Eliza Jane Wilder, filed adjoining claims on land about a mile north and west of De Smet. Each sibling also acquired a tree claim. They spent the winter of 1879–1880 in Spring Valley, Minnesota, and then returned to Dakota Territory, where they were listed as farmers on the 1880 census. Almanzo, however, was also listed as living in a boarding house kept by a C. D. Peck in Beadle County, where he worked as a teamster at the Stebbins railroad camp. Born in Malone, New York, on February 13, 1857, Almanzo was twenty-three, making him ten years older than Laura Ingalls, the young woman he would marry in 1885. One of six children, Almanzo was a member of the prosperous farming family of James and Angeline Day Wilder, who had moved to southeastern Minnesota in the 1870s. Wilder's second novel, *Farmer Boy,* focused on Almanzo's childhood on the family farm in Malone, New York. Royal G. Wilder, born in 1847, was thirty-three in 1880. He opened a feed store next to Fuller's Hardware, where he and his brother spent the winter of 1880–1881. In 1893, he married Electa Averill Hutchinson, a widow. Census records show that Royal moved back and forth between De Smet and Spring Valley, Minnesota. In 1895, for example, he was a "general merchant" in Spring Valley, living with his wife and their infant daughter, Bernice Angeline, born in 1894.

Almanzo J. Wilder. *Laura Ingalls Wilder Historic Home and Museum*

In 1900, he is listed both in De Smet, where he was a partner in Wilder Brothers, Variety and Notions, a general merchandise concern, and with his family in Minnesota. From 1910 until his death in 1925, he lived in Minnesota. Sherwood, *Beginnings of De Smet*, p. 7; Final Patent #200, #410, #1490, #1505, #2263, #10979, BLM-GLO Records; Anderson, *Laura Ingalls Wilder Country*, p. 66; "Minnesota, Marriages Index"; Wilder Brothers letterhead, Laura Ingalls Wilder Memorial Society.

37. *Fuller Bros. hardware store just across the street from us.* C. S. G. Fuller, whom all the newspapers called "Alphabetical Fuller," established his hardware business with his brother Gerald at the intersection of Calumet Avenue and Second Street in 1880. Although the 1880 census lists the brothers' birthplace as New York, they had actually emigrated from England as children in 1849. Later in

Pioneer Girl, Wilder identified Charleton and Gerald as fraternal twins, and the census taker recorded their ages as thirty in June 1880. Charleton's occupation was listed as "Dealer Hardware," while Gerald's was "Dealer Agr. Imple[ments]." Other records, however, suggest that Charleton, whose full name was Charleton Sumner George Fuller, was the older of the two. The 1900 census recorded his birth in June 1847 and Gerald's in October 1848. The *Brookings County Press* referred to Gerald as "Mr. Fuller, jr., who started for De Smet on [April 13], taking with him a supply of agricultural machinery to fill the wants of that country" ("Home and Other News," Apr. 15, 1880). Gerald's full name was Gerald Cannings Reginald Fuller. Charleton Fuller married Chloe Dow in 1883 (her brother Nate Dow married Grace Ingalls in 1901). Charleton died in 1905 at the age of fifty-seven. Gerald Fuller married his wife, Luella, in 1883 and eventually moved to California. Sherwood, *Beginnings of De Smet*, p. 18: "New York, Passenger and Immigration Lists"; "Fuller's Son Reports," p. 5.

Charleton S. G. Fuller. *Laura Ingalls Wilder Memorial Society*

A man might have taken a drink ocassionally but we never saw or heard of anyone drinking and no one got drunk through all the hardships.

When the thermometer stands at from 25 to 40 below zero and a blizzard wind blows most of the time it takes a good deal of twisted hay to keep an unfinished house warm enough to live in.

Everyone had been burning hay except the banker who would not condescend to such. He had bought lumber at the lumber yard for $28. a thousand feet until he had burned it all. Now he must burn hay too[38] or freeze. And the hay that had been stacked in town had all been burned. Hay must be brought in from the country or everyone would freeze.

A blizzard lasted three days, then there would be a clear, still day, then the next blizzard would strike. There might be a few hours less than three full days storm and again there might be less than a whole clear day. Two days between storms was a remarkable event. It gave the impression of a malignant power of destruction wreaking havoc as long as possible, then pausing for breath to go on with the work.

Or as Pa forcably put it, "The blizzard just let go to spit on its hands." (This is an old woodsman's saying. Do you get it?)[39]

During the storm, people stayed close. On the still day, they hurried here and there to do what must be done before the next storm.

So on these clear days hay must be hauled in but by whom and how.

Some of the men were afraid to go out of town at all.[40] They might be caught in a storm, they came so suddenly sometimes. Some could not stand the cold. Besides it was very difficult to get to the haystacks which were in or beyond the Big Slough.

The snowdrifts on the uplands were hard enough to drive a team over, making only slight marks on the snow with their hoofs, but it was different in the Slough. There, in places, the tall grasses were twisted and lodged by the wind, leaving a cavity underneath. The snow had blown in and over them, forming a crust above, while the warmth from the ground and the shelter of the grass kept the snow soft underneath. A horse was heavy enough to break through the crust into these holes; the sled would be pulled in on top of him and

38. *Everyone had been burning hay except the banker. . . . Now he must burn hay too.* On February 24, 1881, the *Kingsbury County News* noted, "Hay fire is all the rage now in town," which may be the time frame in which the banker acquiesced to the need to burn hay as fuel. In April 1880, lumber had been selling for sixteen to eighteen dollars, so the price had almost doubled. Although two brothers were listed as bankers on the 1880 census of De Smet, Thomas H. Ruth, thirty-two, was the man in charge at the Kingsbury County Bank on the corner of Calumet Avenue and Third Street. He and his wife, Laura or Lora Galbraith, had their own household, while William H. Ruth, twenty-nine, and his sister, Laura or Lora B. Ruth, boarded with the Arthur Sherwood family that summer. The Ruths, who had come from Carmichaels, Pennsylvania, via Iowa, established a bank first in Volga, D.T., before moving permanently to De Smet in June 1880. Thomas Ruth also sold insurance, and in 1889, he became mayor of De Smet. In 1890, he successfully ran for South Dakota commissioner of school and public lands on the Republican ticket. "Home and Other News," BCP, June 17, 1880; Miller, "Place and Community," p. 357; *Memorial and Biographical Record*, pp. 235–36.

39. *"The blizzard just let go to spit on its hands." (This is an old woodsman's saying. Do you get it?).* Not surprisingly, the aside to Lane does not appear in subsequent *Pioneer Girl* manuscripts. The saying itself appears to have been current at the end of the nineteenth century, when it was applied to the gripping of an ax or other tool used by woodsmen or quarrymen. A poem entitled "The Woodsman's Philosophy," published by Madge Morris Wagner in 1917, illustrates the context: "When the handle gets slick and commences to slip/I spit on my hands and take a fresh grip" (*Lure of the Desert Land*, p. 18).

40. *Some of the men were afraid to go out of town at all.* The fact that her father went out to the homestead to supply his family with fuel was an important point for Wilder. She viewed her father's and the Wilders' commitment to hauling and stacking hay as heroic. In 1937, she told Lane: "People became numbed and dumb with the awfulness of those storms and ter-

rible cold. There were only a few who kept normal and very much alive. Pa and the Wilder boys did. They were the only ones [who] would go to haul hay or hunt or anything. The others cowered in the house" (LIW to RWL, [Mar. 20, 1937], Box 13, file 193, Lane Papers). In her novel *Free Land*, Lane also included a similar act of winter heroism. Her main character, David Beaton, loosely based on her father, and Mr. Peters, who resembles Charles Ingalls, agree to haul hay between blizzards for a neighbor, whose claim is "a mile and a quarter east of town." The two make it back to town just before the next blizzard strikes (pp. 158–60).

there was one mess. If a team fell through they were likely to injure each other floundering around, for naturally they were terrified to suddenly fall into a pit and sink into snow above their backs.

Our hay was at the farm and the Big Slough must be crossed to get it.

One of our horses was very wise and gentle with a great confidence in Pa. Him, Pa hitched to the sled alone with the traces made longer so when he fell through the snow crust, the sled would not be pulled in after him. Then with his hay fork and snow shovel on the sled he and Charley, the horse, would go after a load of hay and working together they would bring it safely home.

When Charley broke through the crust into a pit of soft snow he would be quiet while Pa shoveled the snow from in front of him, cut steps in the hard snow bank and, taking him by the bridle, helped him out. The sled meantime at the end of the long traces stood still on the hard bank. When Charley was out, he drew the sled around the hole and they went on until the snow crust broke again and the process was repeated. Arrived at the stack, snow must be shoveled again before the hay could be got at. It took all of the short winter day to make the trip. The hay would last for the stock and the fire through the blizzard that always came at once and on the next still day the trip must be made again in the same way for the blizzard had obliterated all signs and there was no way of knowing where a hole was in the snow until Charley fell through.[41]

The Wilder boys hauled hay in the same way for most of the other people in town. There were no more fires kept than were necessary. School had been closed soon after our experience coming home through the storm. It was not safe to be so far out even when we could get there and the fuel was needed in the homes.

When the last flour in town disappeared[42] in the grand final at one dollar a pound was Ma discouraged? She was not. Pa brought in his seed whea[t] and we ground it in the hand coffee mill. With this whole wheat flour she made mush or biscuits raised with soda and souring made by putting a little of the flour into warm water and setting it under the stove to keep warm and sour. It made a usuable substitute for sour milk.

41. *until Charley fell through*. The Brandt version added, "We always prayed that Pa would return before a blizzard struck" (p. 103), and the Bye concluded, "Our anxiety was great, all the time Pa was gone, until he got safely home again" (p. 129).

42. *When the last flour in town disappeared*. In *The Long Winter*, Pa presents Ma with seed wheat and says, "It's a pity there isn't a grist mill in town." Ma replies that they have their own and reaches for the coffee mill. Wilder then describes the grinding process thoroughly (pp. 193–94). Later in the chapter, Ma serves brown sourdough bread for supper. "It had a fresh, nutty flavor that seemed almost to take the place of butter" (p. 196).

Caroline Quiner Ingalls. *South Dakota State Historical Society*

43. *Wishing to save their seed if possible.* Wilder devoted the chapter "Seed Wheat" (pp. 161–67) in *The Long Winter* to the Wilder boys' hidden supply. The action in that chapter, as well as portions of "Three Days' Blizzard" (pp. 96–104), focuses entirely on Almanzo and Royal. This switch in perspective signals to readers that Almanzo will be a central character in *The Long Winter* and foreshadows his role as leading man in subsequent novels. Even in *Pioneer Girl*, Wilder perhaps unconsciously shifted into Almanzo's point of view, including motivations and thoughts that properly belonged to him rather than herself.

44. *Something more had to be done.* In *The Long Winter*, Wilder switched point of view again for the chapter "Free and Independent" (pp. 255–59) and built a scene between Almanzo and Royal in which the two discuss the town's dwindling supply of wheat and their own responsibility to families who were starving. "Take Ingalls, there's six in his family," Almanzo tells Royal. "You notice his eyes and how thin he was?" (p. 255).

Baking powder was not used then. The best cake makers used soda and cream of tartar in proper combination to raise their cakes. But we were not making cakes that winter.

Everyone was grinding the seed wheat, in town, the same way and using it for bread.

It was slow work grinding enough wheat to make flour to make bread to feed eight people and whoever was not twisting hay for fuel must be grinding wheat for bread. Mary helped with this a good deal for she could sit in her warm place by the fire, hold the mill between her knees and grind.

But George and Maggie took no part in the labor.

As our supply of wheat became low, Pa used to go down to the Wilder boys place and get some of theirs. Wishing to save their seed if possible,[43] they had boarded up their wheat bin, which was in one end of the room in which they lived, so that it looked like the end of the room and no one knew the wheat was there.

They bored a hole through the boards into the wheat which they plugged with a piece of wood. When we had to have more wheat, Pa would pull the plug let the wheat run out into his bucket the[n] put the plug back.

But soon the other supplies of wheat in town were used up and even if the Wilder boys had let their seed be used it would not have been enough. Something more had to be done.[44]

Living twelve miles southeast was a farmer who had raised some wheat the year before and if we were all to live until spring someone must go after it.

A merchant named Loftus said he would furnish the money to buy it and sell it out to the people as they needed it. It was dangerous to go after it and no one wanted to go, but finally the youngest Wilder boy and Cap Garland each with one horse, on a sled used to haul hay from the slough, started.

I think no one really expected them to get back, for twelve miles, a good part of it through sloughs where the horses would break through and have to be dug out, looked almost hopeless of being done in one day and it must be done between storms.

It was a clear, still, cold day and helping the horses through the drifts as Pa did, they made the trip safely, getting back some time after dark.

A blizzard struck again before morning.[45]

The boys had charged nothing for making the trip at the peril of their lives,[46] but had cheerfully gone for the sake of the community. They had paid the farmer $1.50 a bushel for the wheat, which he had not wanted to sell as it was his seed.

Now when Loftus sold it to the people he charged them $2.50 a bushel. He had sold only a little at this price when it became generally known. Then the men in town gathered together and went to Loftus' store in a body. After they had talked to him, he paid back the overcharge to the men who had bought the wheat at $2.50 and he sold the rest of it at $1.50 a bushel.[47]

There was a yoke of cattle in town belonging to a man named French a batchelor[48] who had moved in from his farm for the winter. They were his work team, but he was persuaded to butcher them and sell out the meat, so we had a little beef to go with our whole wheat bread.

There was in town a lawyer named Waters who had expected to go east early in the winter to be married but had got caught by the storms.

Now the wedding day was drawing near and no way to get transportation out. He decided to walk and in the middle of January he started before daylight one morning as the blizzard wind was dying down and the sky cleared.

It was a scant day's calm this time and we were afraid he was caught in the next storm, but he walked the miles to Brookins safely and after resting walked on to Tracy.

The next spring we learned that he arrived safely in time for his wedding, but both feet were so badly frozen that he was unable to walk on that day. However his feet recovered and he came back in the spring, bringing his wife with him.[49]

January went by and February with my 15th. birthday.[50] March was stormy still and we began to wonder if spring would ever come. It seemed as though we had been grinding wheat and twisting hay for years.[51] We were getting shorter tempered. Pa did not sing in the

45. *A blizzard struck again before morning.* In *The Long Winter*, a chapter entitled "Four Days' Blizzard" (pp. 286–94) follows the chapter about Almanzo and Cap's search for the seed wheat (pp. 264–85). According to historian George W. Kingsbury: "One of the most severe of the winter storms came on the 7th of February, 1881, and continued thirty-six hours and in some sections forty-eight hours. It embraced the entire territory" (*History of Dakota Territory*, 2:1150).

46. *The boys . . . making the trip at the peril of their lives.* Wilder wrote Lane, "Manly did go after the wheat to feed the town. . . . He got it before anyone

"He rode down main street on the hay-sled." *Helen Sewell, 1940*

went hungry." She explained what she called "the stoicism of the people" — their acceptance of hardship and their occasional bravery, which defined her view of Almanzo and Cap. "Living with danger day after day people become accustomed to it. They take things as they come without much thought about it and no fuss, in a casual way" (LIW to RWL, Mar. 7, 1938).

47. *Now when Loftus sold it. . . . at $1.50 a bushel.* In *The Long Winter*, Wilder created a pair of memorable scenes, written from Almanzo's point of view, that depict first the men's anger at Loftus and then their confrontation with him. Almanzo suggests that since "Mr. Ingalls" has no wheat left to feed his family that he should be the spokesman for the group. "His face," Wilder wrote, "had shrunken to hollows and jutting cheekbones above his brown beard, and his blue eyes glittered bright" (p. 303), but he accepts the role and persuades Loftus to charge townspeople a fair price (pp. 304–7). Then, weakened by hunger, he accepts Almanzo's help in shouldering his share of the wheat (p. 308). By writing the scene from Almanzo's perspective instead of Laura's, Wilder provided readers with a view of Pa as he appeared to someone outside the immediate Ingalls family.

48. *French a batchelor.* No one named French appears on the 1880 census for Kingsbury County. In *The Long Winter*, Wilder renamed this character Mr. Foster and gave him a recurring role. A Peter J. Foster, forty-five, born in New York, was farming within nine miles of De Smet in 1880. He could have spent the winter in town. A man named Will Foster, from Volga, was also in De Smet in February 1881. Sherwood, *Beginnings of De Smet*, p. [40].

49. *There was in town a lawyer named Waters. . . . bringing his wife with him.* A. N. Waters and his partner, A. A. Anderson, owned a "Law, Loan, and Land" business next to the feed store on Calumet Avenue in De Smet. Both the Brandt and Bye versions contain additional details about the lawyer's story. His fiancée, for example, was waiting for him in Massachusetts (Brandt p. 105). Wilder also recalled that the wife's stay in Dakota Territory was short, "But after two summers in De Smet and two winters spent visiting her sisters in the east, she divorced him because she could not stand the hardships of the west" (Bye, p. 132). Miller, "Place and Community," p. 357.

50. *my 15th. birthday.* Wilder actually turned fourteen on February 7, 1881.

51. *we began to wonder if spring would ever come. . . . twisting hay for years.* The Ingalls family were not the only ones to find the winter interminable. A correspondent from "Town 109–Range 49" reported: "We still live, which we think is saying a good deal. . . . We think we have had a taste of prison life" (BCP, Apr. 7, 1881). Another writer said: "If blizzards were only beautiful streams, dotted with mill sites! With what ecstasy should we see them dammed!" ("Home and Other News," BCP, Jan. 20, 1881).

morning about the happy sunflower and I had even told George if he was not warm enough to suit him he could go twist some hay for I was tired. And in spite of Ma's frown offered to hold the baby while Maggie washed the dishes.

One day a herd of antelope[52] was sighted near town and all the men went hunting.

The antelope were wandering in search of food looking for places where the wind had bared the ground and they could reach the buffalo grass.[53] They were in a little valley like depression in the surrounding prairie and the men went on horseback hoping to surround them.

All the men were on were on horseback. Those without horses had borrowed. It was agreed that each should ride so that they would reach the herd from all sides at about the same time.

French had borrowed a horse from the youngest Wilder boy. It was the fastest horse in town but afraid of the sound of a gun and French had been warned to be sure to hold her fast when he shot off his gun. But when he saw the antelope he was so excited he forgot everything. Without paying any attention to the others he ran his horse closer[;] then, while still out of range, he jumped off let go of the reins and shot.

He didn't hit any antelope, being too far away, but he scared the horse so she rain away and in among them. The antelope bunched close around her and away they all went across the prairie. The other men dared not shoot for fear of hitting the horse so the antelope, all but one, got clear away. Pa shot one[54] and it was divided among the crowd making only a taste apiece. My sympathy had been with the antelope. They had been having a hard winter too and I could have cried when I saw the poor, little, starved one they had brought home although our wheat was getting low again and the beef was only a pleasant memory.

The horse ran with the antelope herd for two hours before she became quiet enough to let the antelope go on without her and her master on her mate to come up and get her.[55]

With the first of April the weather turned warmer and there were

52. *a herd of antelope*. Although the word "antelope" is used throughout the American West, the proper name for this swift and graceful creature is the pronghorn (*Antilocapra americana*), a reference to its distinctive short horns, which extend up and curl back. Reaching speeds of up to sixty miles an hour, pronghorns travel in herds and are the fastest land animals in North America. Shaped like deer, they have distinctive white markings on their faces, necks, stomachs, and rumps. Their fur is usually a warm-reddish brown. In Wilder's day, the animals were common in all areas west of the Mississippi River, and a herd of "over 1,500" was seen grazing near

Pronghorn (antelope). *Chad Coppess photograph, South Dakota Tourism*

Huron in December of 1880 ("Territorial News," *Moody County Enterprise*, Dec. 16, 1880). "Pronghorn"; Higgins, *Wild Mammals*, pp. 237-40.

53. *wandering in search of food . . . buffalo grass.* Buffalograss (*Buchloe dactyloides*), which is prevalent in western South Dakota, is known for its short, curly leaves that resemble the coat of a buffalo. However, across North America, many grasses bear this name because buffalo historically grazed on them. In 1881, the plight of the antelope, which were searching for places to get at the grass under the snow, was shared by range cattle, and in March, one ranch owner near Medicine Creek, about fifteen miles east of Pierre, D.T., estimated that he had lost nearly seven hundred head of cattle due to "actual starvation, the snow being so deep that the grass in the gulches cannot be reached by them" ("Home and Other News," *BCP*, Mar. 31, 1881). Ode, *Dakota Flora*, p. 116.

54. *Pa shot one.* In *The Long Winter*, no one other than Foster gets a shot at the herd, and the hunters return to town empty-handed (p. 204).

55. *The horse ran . . . and her master on her mate to come up and get her.* Again switching point of view, Wilder devoted almost four full pages in the chapter "Antelope!" to Almanzo's perspective in his successful attempt to bring his wayward horse home (*LW*, pp. 205-8). The section further highlighted his heroism. Even Pa would not risk searching for the horse.

no more bad storms. Bare prairie showed in spots and farmers went back to their claim shanties and began their springs work. Men were at work on the railroad too and soon the trains would be running again. But it was the 9th. of May before the first train could get through.[56] We knew it was coming and when it whistled all the men ran to the depot to welcome it. Our mouths watered at thought of good food for we were on short rations of even our wheat bread.

The train came rolling in while everyone cheered and then it was found that it was a whole train of farm machinery, sulkey plows, seeders, harvester, mowing machines, rakes, even a threshing machine that couldn't possibly be used before fall—all the tools necessary to raise us something to eat for next winter. In the meantime———

The mob of men came near wrecking the train and would have done so if they had not found on the very end an emigrant car.

Mr Woodworth broke open the door and divided the food among the people according to the number of persons in the family, for it had come to rationing.

In the car were provisions of all kinds enough to last the emigrants family for some time, besides seed wheat and potatoes.

Everyone went home carrying his share, a little sugar, some flour a bit of salt pork, some dried fruit a little tea.

What rejoicing there was when Pa came. I think none of us had realized the strain we had been under until it broke.

Pa got some sacks and went back for his share of the wheat and potatoes. The train could not go on until the next day for the track through the cut west of town was not clear before then.

A train came the next day but it was a train load of telegraph poles. Unreasonable as it was I think no one who was there at that time could ever feel kindly toward a R.R. Co.[57]

Finally food came in and at last our Christmas barrel, with the turkey still solidly frozen.

The prairie turned a beautiful green and at last the Hard Winter of 1880-81 was over.[58]

56. *With the first of April, the weather turned warmer. . . . the 9th. of May before the first train could get through.* In Bye, Wilder created a greater sense of desperation in the Ingalls household before the first freight train arrived: "On the 8th of May, Ma scraped into the kettle the last grains of ground wheat, and that day there was not enough mush to go around. But we had word that a train was coming, was on the way" (p. 134). The first work train had reached Brookings on May 2, followed by a freight train and then a passenger train, all heading west as soon as the track was clear. Besides snow packed into the cuts, the railroad company had faced multiple obstacles in getting a locomotive that far, including washouts caused by melting snow and desertions of work crews. On May 5, however, the *Brookings County Press* noted that a "large force" was now "working west," and trains would reach the end of the line "in a few days" ("Home and Other News," May 5, 1881). Wilder does not mention the work train in *Pioneer Girl*, although she does in *The Long Winter*, placing it on "the last day of April" (p. 317). "Home and Other News," BCP, Apr. 28, May 5, 1881.

57. *I think no one . . . could ever feel kindly toward a R. R. Co.* In Bye, Wilder added: "When the men tried to buy the telegraph poles for fuel, the only answer they got was that the poles were not for sale. Then they swarmed upon the train, took the poles and carried them away, and sawed and burned them. We all had plenty of wood and stopped twisting hay. The railroad company was never paid a penny for those poles. We felt, as one of the men said, 'The man that wouldn't steal from a railroad company isn't honest'" (p. 135).

58. *The prairie turned a beautiful green and at last the Hard Winter of 1880–81 was over.* Wilder originally intended to use the title "The Hard Winter" for the novel, but her editor at Harper & Brothers objected, fearing it was "too depressing" for young readers ([George Bye] to RWL, ca. June 3, 1940, Brown Papers). Lane responded, "My god, if THE HARD WINTER as a title is too depressing, what is the book?" (RWL to Bye, June 5, 1940, ibid.). Wilder herself confessed, "It has been rather trying, living it all over again as I did in the writing of it and I am glad it is finished" (LIW to Bye, May 7, 1940, ibid.).

BIRD'S-EYE VIEW OF DE SMET

BIRD'S EYE VIEW OF
DE SMET, DAK.
COUNTY SEAT OF KINGSBURY COUNTY
1883.

Published by A. J. Stoner, Madison, Wis.

B School House.
A Church.
C DeSmet Flouring Mill, G. W. Elliott & Co.
D Elevator, L. E. Sasse, Agent.
E R. R. Depot.
F Exchange Hotel, J. E. Smith, Proprietor.
G Empire Lumber Co., Chas. E. Ely, Agent.
H Yeoman Bros. & Hodgins Lumber Co., Chas. L. Dawley, Agent.
J Kingsbury County Bank, T. H. Ruth, Cash'r.
K Bank of DeSmet. Town lots for sale.
U. V. Barnes, Attorney, Calumet Ave.
Thomas, Bros., Real Estate Dealers, Calumet Ave.
G. C. Bradley, Druggist, Calumet Ave.
Waters & Anderson, Attorneys, Calumet Ave.
E. M. Harthorn & Sons, General Merchandise, Calumet Ave.

Loftus & Broadbent, General Merchandise, Calumet Ave.
Geo. Wilmarth & Co., General Merchandise, Calumet Ave.
Peirson & Cooley, Meat Market, Calumet Ave.
E. R. Bennett, Groceries and Provisions, Calumet Ave.
Peter Holburg, Real Estate Dealer, Calumet Ave.
C. H. Tinkham, Furniture, Calumet Ave.
Lyngby Bros., Blacksmiths, Calumet Ave.
Frank H. Schauls, Harness, etc., Calumet Ave.
H. Hinz, Billiard Parlor, Calumet Ave.
C. S. G. Fuller & Sons, Hardware and Farm Machinery, Calumet Ave.
Hopp & McDonald, Editors The News, Calumet Ave.
DeSmet Publishing Co., Publishers The Leader, Calumet Ave.
G. H. Scofield, General Merchandise, Calumet Ave.
J. J. Shockley, Blacksmith, Cor. First St. and Joliet Ave.

Bird's-eye view of De Smet, 1883. *South Dakota State Historical Society*

Dakota Territory, 1880–1885

Seeding was done by those already there as fast as seed could be obtained and emigrants came in every day to settle on the land or start a business in town.[1]

Soon after work started on the railroad west from Huron we heard that there was going to be an Indian outbreak.

Everyone was uneasy[2] for a couple of weeks, then we learned that everything was quiet again.

A doctor, from Chicago, stopping at Old Stebbins railroad camp on Turkey Creek[3] had found the body of an Indian baby, carefully wrapped in soft cloths in a basket, hanging in the top of one of a grove of trees on the bank of the creek. The body was perfect and so beautifully mumfied that he sent it to Chicago, for examination to discover, if possible how it had been done.

Then the family to which the baby had belonged came to the funerial grove, from the reservation, to complete the funeral rites according to their custom[4] and found the body was gone.

The Indian came to the R.R. camp and demanded that the body be returned. Mr Stebbins promised it should be given back and tried to find the man who had taken it, but the Dr. had left hurridly at first sight of the party of Indians and could not be found. So Mr Stebbins did no more about it.

After repeated efforts to recover the body the Indian with his family went back to the reservation. A few days afterward the three hundred men, in the R.R. camp, waked one morning to find six hundred Indians, dressed in nothing but war paint camped near by.

As soon as they saw the men astir, the Indians leaped on their ponies, without saddle or bridle and rode furiously around and around the camp. Each Indian carried a rifle lying across the pony's back in front of him. After circling the camp a few times, they rode through it here and there and as their ponies ran would snatch up their rifles and point them qucckly at a man on one side and then at a man on the other side as if to shoot him.[5] Then they rode back to

1. *Seeding was done . . . and emigrants came in every day . . . in town.* In 1881, wheat was "from three to ten inches" high by the second week in June. The trains were again "loaded with people seeking homes on our beautiful prairies" ("Home and Other News," *BCP*, June 9, 1881), and as many as six hundred people a week visited the new towns on the Dakota Central Railroad (ibid., June 16). The newly released census numbers showed that the population of Dakota Territory had increased by 854 percent since 1870. The Great Dakota Boom was nearing its height. "Dakota Beats Them All," *Huron Tribune*, Aug. 11, 1881.

2. *an Indian outbreak. Everyone was uneasy.* On June 24, 1880, the *Brookings County Press* reported, "A great Indian scare has been pervading the West for a few days. It is reported that 300 Indians have raided the Wessington hills and killed a number of men" ("Home and Other News"). In the summer of 1880, white settlers in Dakota Territory were "uneasy" about American Indian activities because the notorious Battle of the Little Big Horn had taken place only a few years earlier (1876), and Sitting Bull and his people, who had been living in Canada as refuges following the event, were beginning to move south again in scattered bands. "The Indian agent at Poplar river . . . is preparing to be massacred by Sitting Bull's Indians," the editor of the *Fort Pierre Signal* reported in August ("The Indian agent," Aug. 25, 1880). The Brookings editor, however, put little credence in reports of marauding Indians, concluding, "There is little foundation for a scare of this kind" ("Home and Other News," *BCP*, June 24, 1880). And there were no recorded deaths in the story that Wilder related in *Pioneer Girl*. Pope, *Sitting Bull*, pp. 4–5.

3. *Old Stebbins railroad camp on Turkey Creek.* With this episode, Wilder clearly stepped back in time to mid-summer 1880, when Stebbins's railroad camp

Chicago & North Western construction workers in camp. *South Dakota State Historical Society*

would have been located on Turtle (not Turkey) Creek in Hand County, near what would become the town of Saint Lawrence. By the fall of 1880, all grading on the railroad had been concluded, and the track had been laid through to Pierre on the Missouri River. Henry Stebbins and his family had retired from the contracting business, opening a "first-class hotel" with twenty-four sleeping rooms in Pierre in December 1880 (*Pierre Signal*, Dec. 8, 1880). Throughout this section of *Pioneer Girl*, Wilder recounted episodes from 1880 to 1885 without any firm reference to identifiable dates. Wade, "Small-town Survival," pp. 319, 322; *Fort Pierre Signal*, July 28, Aug. 11, Sept. 1, 1880; *Pierre Signal*, Nov. 24, 1880.

4. *carefully wrapped . . . hanging in the top of one of a grove of trees. . . . according to their custom.* Among the Sioux (Dakota, Lakota, Nakota), "burials" typically took place above ground. The deceased person was wrapped in hides or blankets and set atop a scaffold or, as with this baby, within the branches of a tree. The custom may have arisen because of the difficulty of performing in-ground burials in winter or because wild animals dug up shallow graves. Built eight to ten feet above the ground, scaffolds were constructed from four forked branches set into the ground with other branches or boards laid across to create a platform, which could also be built within the branches of a tree. Food and personal possessions were sometimes placed with the body. After a period of time had passed, members of the family or tribe would return to collect the bones for safekeeping or for burial elsewhere. In drier environments, the body would sometimes dehydrate rather than decompose, resulting in the appearance of mummification. Desecration of such burials by curious and insensitive settlers such as the doctor of this story was not uncommon. The *Hand County Press* of Miller, D.T., reported an incident in the Ree Hills on January 18, 1882, in which three white men, "while prospecting for ancient relics," found the body of an Indian man and his bow in a tree and removed it to the newspaper office for the curious to observe. Bushnell, *Burials*, pp. 19–21, 23–25; Sanders, "Trail of the Ancient Sioux," pp. 384–85; "Dakota in the Fifties," p. 144.

5. *dressed in nothing but war paint. . . . as if to shoot him.* In times of war, Sioux warriors acted both to intimidate the enemy and to demonstrate individual bravery. Decorating themselves and their horses with paint, feathers, and other items, galloping through camp with weapons drawn, and holding victory dances were all traditional practices in warfare and raiding. These warriors, who went quietly home to their reservation when they achieved their objective, probably came from the Crow Creek Indian Reservation on the eastern side of the Missouri River or from the Lower Brule Agency, across the river on the Great Sioux Reservation, which then covered most of the western half of what would become the state of South Dakota. Holm, "Warriors and Warfare," pp. 666–68; Hassrick, *Sioux*, pp. 32–33, 80, 82–83; Sturtevant, *Handbook of North American Indians*, 2:781–82, 797.

their camp and their chief came and asked for the chief of the white men. He demanded that Mr Stebbins return the body of the Indian baby and that the man who had taken it be delivered to them. If this was not done, he said, they would massacre everyone in the camp.

Mr Stebbins had a difficult time explaining to him that the man who had stolen the body had run away and could not be found; that the body had been sent a long ways away but would surely be returned if the Indians would only wait until it could be brought back.

But at last the Chief agreed to wait, but the men must stay in camp, excep the one they sent to Huron, the little railroad station forty miles east,[6] to get the body.

Mr Stebbins sent a man out, who learned at the depot to where the mummy had been expressed and telegraphed there for its immediate return, explaining the urgency for haste.

It was ten days before the man came back to camp with the mummy and every night, of that time, the Indians had a war dance at their camp and every day they rode around and through the railroad camp threatening the men with their rfles.

When the mummy was returned to their Chief, they went quietly back to their reservation and work was resumed on the grade as usual.

The youngest Wilder boy and two other boys, Homer and Horace Heath, from near De Smet, were in the railroad camp when all this happened, so later we heard, from them, the story.[7]

George and Maggie went west, the middle of May to a job he had at one of the new towns. We parted frendly enough,[8] but I at least was glad to say good by.

Pa rented the house, for a month to a new comer and we moved home again, for the farm was home to us. Town was just a place to spend the winter.

We had several neighbors now near the farm. Delos Perry owned the farm joining our 160 acres on the south and his father Mr Perry owned the one just south of his. Mr Perry had another son still at home a young man named Ernest.[9]

Southeast of us lived a family named Ross, with a son and daughter, Gaylord and Jenny of about Mary's age. Near them lived Mr Ross'es brother Dave who had married Mr Perry's daughter Fanny.[10]

6. *Huron, the little railroad station forty miles east.* Like De Smet, Huron had been surveyed and platted by the railroad company in the spring of 1880. "In less than twenty minutes twenty-six lots were located by as many parties," the *Brookings County Press* reported, predicting that it was "one of the towns that is going to boom" ("Home and Other News," May 6, 1880). Huron became the county seat of Beadle County and played a prominent role in territorial affairs.

7. *The youngest Wilder boy and . . . Homer and Horace Heath, . . . we heard, from them, the story.* In 1880, Almanzo J. Wilder worked in the Stebbins railroad camp, and so did twenty-four-year-old Horace Heath and nineteen-year-old N. H. Heath. The Heaths, who were also listed in Brookings County, appear to have been making extra money while homesteading, just as Almanzo was. In Bye, Wilder added that the laborers in the railroad camp thought it "best to give the Indians an impression of their calm confidence and fearlessness, so they went on working as usual with their plows and wagons and scrapers, shaping up the railroad grade" (Bye, p. 136). With additional information from her father, Lane expanded the episode in *Free Land* (pp. 109–30), where Stebbins appears as the railroad contractor Gebbert, and the man who leaves the camp to telegraph for help is David Beaton, the main character based on her father.

8. *George and Maggie. . . . We parted frendly enough.* George Masters moved to a railroad camp near Blunt, about one hundred thirty miles west of De Smet, where the "supply store of the Chicago & North-western" was located (local news, *Pierre Signal*, Aug. 25, 1880). He returned to De Smet and became an agent for the Empire Lumber Company before moving to Spencer, South Dakota. George Masters served as one of Charles Ingalls's witnesses when he applied for his homestead patent in 1886; Robert Boast was the other witness. "Town and Country," *DSL*, Mar. 22, 1884; Sherwood, *Beginnings of De Smet*, p. 15; Final Certificate #2708.

9. *Delos Perry. . . . a young man named Ernest.* The Perry family originated in Pennsylvania, and in

1880, they were located in Minnehaha County in southeastern Dakota Territory. The patriarch of the family was Oliver D. Perry. Fifteen-year-old Ernest Perry and thirty-two-year-old Delos (also spelled De Los and Deloss) Perry were his sons. Delos had begun a household of his own. It is not clear when they moved to the De Smet area, but they took homesteads just south of the Ingalls place. Final Patent #2572, #2708, #3834, BLM-GLO Records.

10. *a family named Ross. . . . Fanny.* The Ross family also hailed from Pennsylvania. Russell Ross and his wife, Viola, both in their early forties, had homesteaded in Kingsbury County by 1880. Their oldest children, Jennie Ross (twenty) and Gaylord (eighteen), still lived at home.

All these people passed our place to go to town and as they stopped now and then we soon got acquainted.

Pa was working in town at Carpenter work and hired Ernest Perry to break some ground for him. In that way I got acquainted with him. He was a large, strong boy and walked, with his big feet bare, in the cool, soft, black earth of the furrow behind the plow as his big horses pulled it turning the prairie sod over.

I didn't care much for all these people. I loved the prairie and the wild things that lived on it, much better.

In the early morning[11] I was always on my way to the well, at the edge of the slough, for a bucket of fresh water as the sun rose in a glory of wonderful colors throwing streamers of light around the horizon and up across the sky.

The meadow larks were singing in the dew wet grass[12] and jack rabbits hopped here and there with their bright black eyes watching and long ears twitching nibbling the tender grass that pleased them best for breakfast.

Later in the day, when the sun shone warmly, little reddish brown and black striped gophers[13] would pop out of their holes in the ground and sit straight up on their hind legs with their front paws down close at their sides, so motionless they could hardly be distinguished among the grasses and if seen looking like a stick stuck up in the ground. With their bright eyes they looked, with their sharp ears, they listened for danger. At a sharp sound, a quick motion, or the shadow of a large bird overhead, they slipped back into their holes like a flash, but if all seemed safe to them, they scurried away, through the grass, about their business.

When corn was planted the striped gophers would follow the row, dig down, with their little paws, till they got the kernels and eat them or run off with them to their hole in the ground. They never made the mistake of digging anywhere in the row except where the corn was planted, though how they could tell where the grains were when the ground was all soft plowed was a mystery.

The little garter snakes[14] came out in the warm sunshine too and slithered across the path. They [were] perfectly harmless not poi-

11. *In the early morning.* Wilder used this passage as the basis for an extended description of Laura's experiences in the chapter "Springtime on the Claim" (pp. 3–18) in *Little Town on the Prairie*: "In the dawns when she went to the well at the edge of the slough to fetch the morning pail of fresh water, the sun was rising in a glory of colors" (p. 4).

12. *meadow larks were singing in the dew wet grass.* The western meadowlark (*Sturnella neglecta*) is a common sight, and sound, on the open grasslands and small-grain croplands of the North American plains and prairies. Its melodic song is one of the first

Western meadowlark. *Chad Coppess photograph, South Dakota Tourism*

signs of spring. Meadowlarks nest in grass-lined depressions on the ground and weave together grasses and shrub stems over the nest to create a waterproof canopy. Johnsgard, *Birds of the Great Plains*, pp. 426–27; "Western Meadowlark."

13. *little reddish brown and black striped gophers*. Commonly known as the striped gopher, the thirteen-lined ground squirrel (*Spermophilus tridecemlineatus*) ranges widely across North America, from Canada to Texas and from the Rocky Mountains to Ohio. These rodents burrow in cultivated fields and feast on seeds and green vegetation, making them a perennial enemy of farmers. In some areas, county or other officials offered bounties to help control gopher populations. Higgins, *Wild Mammals*, pp. 78–82, 85–87; West, "Dakota Fairy Tales," pp. 140–41; Rogers, "Almost Scandinavia," pp. 328–29.

14. *The little garter snakes*. Wilder probably observed the common gartersnake (*Thamnophis sirtalis*), which prefers a wet habitat, or the plains gartersnake (*Thamnophis radix*), which lives in drier climates. Fully grown, both species measure sixteen to twenty-six inches long and vary in the color of their stripes. Gartersnakes are not venomous, but they will bite, and they release a pungent musk when alarmed or handled. Wilder included a similar description of gartersnakes in *The Long Winter* (p. 3). Keisow, *Field Guide to Amphibians*, pp. 130–35.

son at all and lived [on] grasshoppers and bugs. I thought they were very pretty and graceful and we never killed them.

It was fun to explore the farm and surprising how much variety and how many things of interest could be found on 160 acres that at a carless glance looked like all the rest of the prairie.

Pa had built an addition to the little slant roofed claim shanty so that the roof had its other half and we had two very small bedrooms. The house was in the N. W. corner of the farm.

The cottonwoods we had planted around it were growing splendidly.

The stable was west of the house, dug into the side of a little rise in the prairie.

The stable was roofed with the long slough hay and banked around with hay in cold weather. The rise of ground behind the barn was a little sand hill where the grass grew sparcely because the soil was so thin. On the northwest corner the grass had not been able to make its way against the strong wind that whittled away at the hill cutting the soil away from the grass roots and shifting the sand.

Just beyond the sand hill was the western line of our farm and the country road to town which was just a wagon track across the prairie.

South of the house, about half way across the farm, was an old buffalo wallow of about two acres.

It was grassed over and early in the spring the whole hollow was covered with beautiful purple violets,[15] so fragrant that one would smell them before reaching the hollow and a saucerful of the blossoms would perfume a room.

The grass grew well in this little natural meadow and when haying time came Pa cut it for hay.

The east side of the farm was just level prairie, but the Big Slough lay all along the north line just beyond the well.

Our road to town led straight north across the Big Slough, but all the sloughs were full of water after the big snows and we had to go first south along our west line then west from our south line and

15. *an old buffalo wallow. . . . was covered with beautiful purple violets.* Buffalo wallows, created when bison rolled in the dust to shed fur and pests, also played a role in prairie ecosystems by distributing seeds that had tangled in the buffalos' coats. The depressions also collected water that allowed plants, such as Wilder's purple violets, to take root. Today, the most common purple violet in eastern South Dakota is the prairie violet (*Viola pedatifida*). The meadow violet (*Viola pratincola*) also blooms in the spring. The fictional Ingalls family first discovers the buffalo wallow at the end of *By the Shores of Silver Lake*, when Grace suddenly goes missing and Laura finds her there among "a lake of violets" (*SL*, pp. 279–81). Lott, *American Bison*, pp. 66–67; Barkley, *Flora of the Great Plains*, pp. 261–62; Larson and Johnson, *Plants of the Black Hills*, pp. 366–67.

16. *the old rule for housework, "Wash on Monday . . . bake on Saturday."* Wilder left out Thursday in this old rule, which may reflect how she first learned it. For example, in 1862, Mary Hooker Cornelius's *The Young Housekeeper's Friend* suggested two variations for managing the household work, the second of which assigned no specific duties on Thursday: "wash on Monday; bake, and do other things necessarily omitted, on Tuesday; iron on Wednesday; Thursday, do no extra work; Friday, sweep and clean; Saturday, bake; distribute clean bed linen, and see that everything is in readiness for the Sabbath" (p. 18). Wilder herself provided another version in *Little House in the Big Woods*: "Wash on Monday, Iron on Tuesday, Mend on Wednesday, Churn on Thursday, Clean on Friday, Bake on Saturday, Rest on Sunday" (p. 29).

17. *breeding place for mosquitoes. . . . screened with mosquito bar.* Mosquito bar was a type of fine netting that served, when stretched on a frame, as wire-mesh screen windows do today. "Mosquitoes are as thick as hair on a dog and as large as small sized rats in these parts," the *Brookings County Press* complained on July 17, 1879. Pa wages war against mosquitoes in *By the Shores of Silver Lake* (pp. 287–88).

18. *In June the wild roses bloomed.* Sweetly fragrant, the prairie rose (*Rosa arkansana*) blooms in May and June. The short shrubby plant has prickly stems and deep-pink, five-petaled flowers. The flower's base, or cup, ripens to a bright orange in the fall. In *Little Town on the Prairie*, Wilder wrote, "The roses scented the wind, and along the road the fresh blossoms, with their new petals and golden centers, looked up like little faces" (p. 47). Larson and Johnson, *Plants of the Black Hills*, p. 544; Johnson and Larson, *Grassland Plants*, p. 262.

19. *(You are their namesake, my dear.)* Personal messages from Wilder to Lane became more frequent in the final two tablets of *Pioneer Girl*. For the most part, they do not appear in the revised manuscripts.

20. *grass flowers, may flowers, . . . and wild sunflowers.* The wildflowers Wilder mentioned here are difficult to identify definitively, in part because common names for these plants have evolved. A Wiscon-

cross the slough much farther from the lake. Later in the summer we would go straight across.

Again I cared for the cows. We kept them on long picket ropes, pulling the picket pins morning and night after milking and driving them in a different place so the cows would have fresh grass each day and night. Their calves were on short picket ropes near by.

Ma and I milked the cows, changed the picket pins, carried the milk to the house and strained and set it in pans in the cellar under the house.

Then while Ma got breakfast, I took the skimmed milk out and fed the calves and changed their picket pins.

After breakfast Pa went to his work and Ma and I and Carrie washed dishes made beds, swept, scrubbed, washed or ironed or baked or churned as the task might be, usually following the old rule for housework, "Wash on Monday, iron on Tuesday, churn on Wednesday, clean on Friday and bake on Saturday,"[16] with mending and sewing and knitting scattered along through the week mixed with the care of the hens and little chickens, working in the garden and feeding the pig. Feeding the pig followed work in the garden no matter how many other meals he had for being kept in a pen, the pig always got all the weeds we pulled or hoed from the garden.

Sometime during the day we led the cows to water at the well.

So much water in the sloughs mad[e] a wonderful breeding place for mosquitoes and at night we had to build a smudge for the cows, a fire that smoked heavily so placed that the smoke would drift over the two cows and their calves. We had doors and windows screened with mosquito bar[17] to keep them out of the house, but any one crossing the slough after sundown would be badly bitten by them.

In June the wild roses bloomed.[18] They were a low-growing bush and, when in bloom, the blossoms made masses of wonderful color, all shades of pink, all over the prairie. And the sweetest roses that ever bloomed.

(You are their namesake, my dear.)[19]

There were grass flowers, may flowers, thimble flowers, wild sweet Williams, squaw pinks, buffalo beans and wild sunflowers,[20] each blooming in its season. There were several different kinds of

sin horticulturist, for example, found "the same common name might be applied to a number of different species. . . .There were pinks without end, bunch pinks, squaw pinks, prairie pinks, Indian pinks" and more (Toole, "Domesticating Our Native Wild Flowers," p. 92). In 1937, as Wilder worked on *By the Shores of Silver Lake*, she was unsure about this subject herself and promised Lane that she would write to her sister Grace about the wildflowers to "refresh óur memories" (LIW to RWL, Feb. 5, 1937, Box 13, file 193, Lane Papers). Still, grass flowers might be blue-eyed grass (*Sisyrinchium montanum* and *Sisyrinchium campestre*), a plant in the iris family that forms tiny grasslike leaves. The meadow anemone (*Anemone canadensis*), which grows in prairie wetlands like the Big Slough, could be Wilder's may flower. The candle anemone (*Anemone cylindrica*) is a likely candidate for Wilder's thimble flower because of its distinctive thimble shape. The buffalo bean (*Astragalus crassicarpus*) has pinkish-purple blossoms and bears edible fruits. Several sunflowers are native to the area, including the common sunflower (*Helianthus annuus*), the Maximilian sunflower (*Helianthus maximiliana*), and the sawtooth sunflower (*Helianthus grosseserratus*). Barkley, *Flora of the Great Plains*, pp. 954–55, 1262–63; Johnson and Larson, *Grassland Plants*, p. 220; Larson and Johnson, *Plants of the Black Hills*, pp. 206, 312–13.

21. *buffalo grass. . . . buffalo feeding on it*. Wilder's observations about the value of buffalograss (*Buchloe dactyloides*) for livestock and wildlife are borne out by science. Today, buffalograss remains among the best forage grasses of the short- and mixed-grass prairies for livestock, big game, waterfowl, and game birds. Fresh or cured, it is a good source of energy and protein. Howard, "Buchloe dactyloides."

22. *Spanish needles. . . . often killing them*. Given the injurious nature of the grass that Wilder described in *Pioneer Girl* and later in *Little Town on the Prairie* (p. 87), it was most likely porcupine grass (*Hesperostipa spartea*) rather than another plant more commonly known as Spanish needles (*Bidens bipinnata* L.), which is not native to the territory. The large flower head of porcupine grass produces a bristle-like plume that coils and uncoils to "drill" the sharp base of the seed into the soil. It will also break off on animals or humans who brush against it and can harm livestock in the ways in which Wilder described. The *De Smet Leader* reported the deadly effects of what it called simply "needle grass" in July 1884, when "2,700 sheep passed through here on their way to the Sisseton Reservation. . . . The needle grass proves too much for about ten head per day" ("From Spirit Lake," July 19, 1884). The grass is most destructive when it matures but can provide good forage at other stages in its development. "Porcupine Grass"; "*Hesperostipa spartea*."

23. *a lawyer named Barnes*. In 1880, Visscher V. Barnes had also become probate judge of Kingsbury County, a position in which he had "proved himself a most determined and indfatigable [*sic*] worker in cases entrusted to his care" ("Town and Country," *DSL*, Mar. 17, 1883). "Home and Other News," *BCP*, Mar. 18, 1880.

24. *one of the drygoods stores the merchant and his wife, with her mother*. In a letter Wilder wrote to Lane in 1937 or 1938, she identified the owner of the dry goods store as Clayson. On the 1880 census, Chaucey or Chauncey L. Clayson was listed as "Dealer [in] Dry goods," living in De Smet with his wife, Ella, and their three-year-old daughter, Nettie. Ella's parents, Horace and Martha White, were also

grass. Slough grass grew in all the low places. On the uplands was blue-joint or blue-slem a tall grass and buffalo grass which never grew tall. It was short and grew thick and curley. Instead of drying up when it ripened and losing its goodness, it cured standing, retaining its food values and made wonderful pasture for stock or wild game through the winter. It got its name from buffalo feeding on it.[21]

There was an ugly grass that ripened in July early in the fall. It was called Spanish needles.

The seeds had a fine, very hard, needle like point an eighth of an inch long. The seed pod itself was one inch long with stiff hairs over it all pointing back from the point [and] at the opposite end from the point was a strong, tough, twisting beard, like a barley beard, about four inches long.

When the seeds were ripe, if anything brushed against the grass, they would brush the beards which would pull the seeds loose. The needle like point would stick in and once started the stiff hairs on the seed would prevent its falling out, while the screw like beard would twist it ever farther in. These needles would work through our clothing like a needle in sewing. If stock got them in their mouths they made painful sores and had to be cut out. If sheep got them in their wool they would work through it into the body and throught the body often killing them.[22]

Farmers killed out the Spanish Needle grass later by burning it over at just the right time.

There was a fourth of July celebration in town with speeches and singing and reading of the Declaration of Independence in the morning and after noon horse and foot races.

Pa and Carrie and I took a picnic dinner in a basket and walked in for the day. Ma stayed with Mary and Grace at home.

It was a tiresome day, I thought. The best part of it was eating our dinner in our empty house and afterward setting off a bunch of firecrackers a lawyer named Barnes[23] had given Pa for us. I didn't like the crowd and would much rather be home where it was quiet.

But it seemed I couldn't stay there. At one of the drygoods stores the merchant and his wife, with her mother,[24] lived in two rooms at the back and the attic.

The mother-in-law made shirts as ordered from goods in the store and she needed help, so I sewed for her for 25¢ a day, slept with her in the attic and ate with them[25] in the kitchen. Mrs Clancy quarreled constantly with her son-in-law,[26] so that at times it was unpleasant.

For some reason, there was a scare about the Catholics getting control of the government and the awful things they would do to protestents. The daughter would wring her hands and pace the floor declaring that the Catholics should never take her Bible away from her.[27] Then a comet appeard in the sky and both women thought it meant the end of the world and were more frightened than ever.[28] But I couldn't see how I could be afraid of both comet and Catholics at the same time so I worried about neither.

The store was across the street from the saloon and as we sat sewing we could look across and up and down the street. I often saw Bill O'Connell go into the saloon and was sorry. His father had brought him west onto a farm[29] hoping to break him from drinking. Bill was very tall, and when he was drunk would walk very straight and dignified stepping as far as he could with his long legs. One day I saw him come out of the saloon, turn, and solemnly and deliberately put his foot through the screen door that had swung shut behind him. Facing out again, he met Tom Power, the tailor. He was a very short little man, but extremely dignified too when drunk as he was now. He and Bill linked arms and walked up and down the sidewalk, Tom trying to keep pace with Bill's long stride and chanting at the top of his voice "My name is T. P. Power and I'm drunk."[30] While Bill wouldn't say his name was Power, he would every time chime in with hiss bass voice, "And I'm drunk," sounding like a bullfrog in a pond. Sorry as I was about Bill I laughed until I cried. I was very glad when I could go home again away from all these people, funny and otherwise.

Pa had planted corn on the land Ernest Perry had broken. It grew surprisingly rank and strong and a vivid green.

When the ears were large enough to roast, great flocks of the most wonderful black birds came and helped themselves.

There were thousands of them, just the common blackbirds and yellow headed blackbirds and red headed blackbirds with a spot of

part of the household. Wilder herself worked for Mrs. White, who "made shirts from the store goods for all the unattached [men] in the country" (LIW to RWL, [1937], Box 13, file 193, Lane Papers).

25. *so I sewed for her for 25¢ a day, slept . . . and ate with them.* Wilder wrote Lane that Mrs. White paid her ".75 cents the first week," adding, "I sewed so well and so fast she wanted me to keep on and as I didn't like to work a whole week and board myself for 75¢ she gave me $1.50 a week" (LIW to RWL, [1937]). In *Little Town on the Prairie*, Laura also makes "a dollar and a half," which she turns over to Ma at the end of every week (p. 48). She does not board with the storekeeper's family, but she stays long enough to make nine dollars (p. 56).

Picture copyright 1953 by Garth Williams, copyright © renewed 1981 by Garth Williams. Used by permission of HarperCollins Publishers

26. *Mrs Clancy quarreled constantly with her son-in-law.* In Bye (p. 141), Wilder continued to refer to the mother-in-law as Mrs. Clancy, but she correctly identified her as Mrs. White in *Little Town on the Prairie* (p. 37). However, Wilder continued to use the name Clancy rather than Clayson for the son-in-law and his family. Wilder wrote Lane that she actu-

ally worked at the Claysons' dry goods store for only three weeks. "I stopped working," Wilder said, because Mrs. White "and her son-in-law quarreled all the time and the daughter sided with her. Sometimes the man got so angry he would strike his wife. Once he dragged her by her long hair from one room to the other." Wilder then added, "Pa said he wouldn't have me working at such a place any longer" (LIW to RWL, [1937]). In the novel, Wilder also depicted the Clancy family as dysfunctional, but when Pa asks Laura how she feels about working for pay, she only says, "Mrs. White spoke well of my buttonholes" (p. 46).

27. *a scare about the Catholics. . . . never take her Bible away from her.* During the nineteenth century as Roman Catholics from many countries migrated to the United States, the majority Protestant population began to fear "that Catholics would attempt to reassert Roman control over the new American republic" (Lauck, "Anti-Catholicism," pp. 8–9). Catholics, on the other hand, feared that the "proselytizing of their children might occur in the Protestant-dominated public schools" and objected to the daily Bible reading and hymn singing that was considered nonsectarian by many school systems and state legislatures, including the Dakota territorial assembly (ibid. pp. 28–29). In 1884, for example, territorial activist Marietta Bones declared it a "GREAT WRONG" that "the most dominant are allowed to steal in upon the rights of others" by forcing their faith to be taught in the public schools (quoted in Koupal, "Marietta Bones," pp. 71–72). The result was a crisis in the relationships between Protestants and Catholics.

28. *a comet appeard . . . were more frightened than ever.* The Great Comet of 1881 (C/1881 K1) was first sighted on May 22 by an amateur astronomer and farmer living near Sydney, Australia. It became visible to observers in the northern hemisphere on June 22, 1881, and "drew immediate attention. . . . The tail continued to grow, and at its best the comet was a truly impressive sight" (Orchiston, "C/1881 K1," p. 36). Its "sudden appearance" over Dakota Territory at the end of the month convinced a Brookings resident that it was "killing off the dogs." The editor agreed, "There is always something terrible following one of these monsters" ("Home and Other News," BCP, June 30, 1881). It remained visible to the naked eye in the evening sky until late August, when the *Press* announced, "Another comet is coming" (ibid., Aug. 18, 1881). Some astronomers considered Comet C/1881 K1 to be "the finest object of the kind since 1861" (Orchiston, "Forgotten 'Great

Comet,'" p. 40), but the one that followed, the Great Comet of 1882 (C/1882 R1), eclipsed it in brilliance and was visible to the naked eye even during the day. In Bye, Wilder added: "I sat sewing and did not say anything. I did not believe what they said about the Catholics or the comet, but it made me feel sick to hear them talk" (p. 141). Orchiston, "C/1881 K1," pp. 33, 41–42.

29. *Bill O'Connell. . . . His father . . . onto a farm.* The younger William O'Connell was twenty-two in 1880 and listed his occupation as "farmer." He had been born in Minnesota. William O'Connell senior was forty-seven and, like his son, was a farmer. He had been born in Canada to Irish parents. In De Smet, the two men boarded with Arthur and Jennie Sherwood. In the novel, the younger man appears as Bill O'Dowd (*LTOP*, p. 55).

30. *Tom Power, the tailor. . . . "My name is T. P. Power and I'm drunk."* Thomas T. Power and his wife, Elizabeth, had both been born in Ireland. They lived for many years in Kasson, Minnesota, before moving to De Smet. In 1880, he was fifty and listed his occupation as "tailor." He and his wife had six children. In the Bye manuscript, Wilder changed the chant to reflect Power's Irish accent, "My name is Tay Pay Power and I'm drunk" (p. 142). In the novel, she also changed his last name to Pryor (*LTOP*, p. 54). In 1883, the editor of the *De Smet Leader* commented about "drunken men reeling and yelling on the streets," concluding, "There is room for some vigorous temperance work in De Smet" ("Town and County," May 5, 1883).

De Smet, 1883. *Laura Ingalls Wilder Memorial Society*

red on each wing.[31] The red headed and yellow headed birds were much larger than the others.

It looked as though they would destroy the whole field. Pa shot them and drove them off, but they only rose, whirled in clouds, then came drifting back and settled down again.

At first Pa shot them and let them lie where they fell. Our kitten, grown up, brought some to her kittens, but they were so full of mice and gophers they couldn't eat the birds.

Then Pa brought several in and asked us to cook them. Said he had never heard of any one eating them but they looked good.

So Ma and I dressed a frying pan full. We split them down the back and fried them whole. They were so fat they fried themselves and were tender and delicious. We understood why four and twenty blackbirds made a dish fit to set before a king.[32]

After that we ate all we could of them every day and by much shooting Pa saved most of his corn.[33]

When haying time came, Pa stopped work in town long enough to put up his hay with Ma's and my help.

All summer we had been talking about sending Mary to the Iowa College for the Blind at Vinton, Iowa,[34] and after haying Ma and I got Mary's clothes ready[35] for she was really going.

Jennie and Gaylord Ross were to stay with Carrie, Grace and me while Ma and Pa went with Mary and got her settled. Gaylord would do the chores and Jennie would look after us all.[36]

Pa and Ma were gone only a week but it seemed an awfully long time. I didn't like either of the Rosses. Gaylord was just unpleasant in a way I couldn't explain, but Jennie was much worse. She told dirty stories that I only half understood, tormented our pet cat and was lazy and quarrelsome besides. She and Gaylord were always quarreling. Carrie and I were very glad when Pa and Ma came walking in from town one night and Jenny and Gaylord went home in the morning.

We were all happy too that Mary was where she would be warm and comfortable, with good food and good company and that she could go on with her studies. She had always loved to study, had been the bright one always while I had been slower and stupid at my

31. *common blackbirds . . . a spot of red on each wing.* Wilder's depiction of common blackbirds corresponds to the behavior of the common grackle (*Quiscalus quiscula*), a noisy, darkly iridescent bird that gathers in large flocks and raids farmers' crops. The yellow-headed blackbird (*Xanthocephalus xanthocephalus*) and the red-winged blackbird (*Agelaius phoeniceus*) prefer wetlands with dense vegetation but, like grackles, often forage in cultivated fields. Tallman et al., *Birds of South Dakota*, pp. 394, 397; "Common Grackle"; "Yellow-headed Blackbird"; "Red-winged Blackbird."

32. *four and twenty blackbirds made a dish fit to set before a king.* Wilder is referring to the nursery rhyme that begins with the line "Sing a song of sixpence." In *Little Town on the Prairie*, Ma bakes a blackbird pie, and the family recites the rest of the first two verses of the rhyme (p.105).

33. *Pa saved most of his corn.* The Bye version changed the outcome, ending the scene with, "But the corn crop was gone" (p. 141). In *Little Town on the Prairie*, Wilder tied the crop loss to paying for Mary's college tuition. Pa plans to sell the heifer instead, telling Mary, "It's time you were going to college. . . . A flock of pesky blackbirds can't stop us" (p. 107).

34. *Iowa College for the Blind at Vinton, Iowa.* In 1853, the Asylum for the Blind opened in Iowa City, but it became the Iowa College for the Blind in 1872, ten years after it moved to Vinton. Because Dakota Territory did not have a similar school for the blind (South Dakota would not build one until 1900), it boarded its visually impaired citizens (only three in 1883) at the Iowa school, "at a merely nominal expense" ("The Blind," DSL, Feb. 17, 1883). On October 3, 1881, the Kingsbury County superintendent of schools certified that Mary Ingalls, sixteen, was blind and "unable to obtain an education in the common schools." She was therefore "entitled to the benefit of the Institution for the Blind of Dakota for the term of five years, she not having passed any time in a like institution" (copy of certification dated Oct. 3, Dakota Territorial Records, roll 74). Territorial governor Nehemiah Ordway approved the certification on October 15, and Mary Ingalls

Mary A. Ingalls in Vinton, Iowa, 1880s.
Laura Ingalls Wilder Memorial Society

entered the Iowa College for the Blind on November 23, 1881. The Ingallses had to find the resources to provide suitable clothing, spending money, and transportation to and from Vinton. Over the next eight years, Mary Ingalls received the equivalent of a junior-college education with additional training in music and industrial skills such as sewing, net tying, and beadwork. "Miss Mary Ingalls, while in the blind asylum, worked a beautiful watch-case of beadwork, as a present to Rev. E. Brown," the *De Smet Leader* reported in 1883 ("Town and Country," July 14, 1883). She graduated in 1889. "Education: Iowa Braille School"; O'Leary and Goddard, *Gleanings from Our Past*, chap. 3; Commissioners'

Record, p. 46; Dakota Territorial Records, roll 74; Mary Ingalls Diploma, Laura Ingalls Wilder Historic Home and Museum.

35. *Ma and I got Mary's clothes ready.* While Wilder did not dwell on Mary's clothing here, she described it at length in *Little Town on the Prairie* (pp. 90–97), where Ma buys much of the material for Mary's best dress, a silk mitt, and velvet hat from the nine dollars that Laura earned making shirts for Mrs. White. In reality, however, Wilder had brought home just $1.19 for her work. In the 1930s, Wilder found the notes she kept at fourteen of her "Account with Mrs. White" and copied them for Lane. The account reveals that Wilder spent $2.56 of her actual $3.75 earnings on four yards of calico, a steel thimble, a pair of cloth shoes, a charm, a plume, and a half yard of silk. It is not clear if any of these materials were for Mary's college wardrobe, but perhaps the silk was for a mitt. Mrs. Clayson charged twenty-five cents to sew "the plume on the hat," which may have been for Mary (LIW to RWL, [1937]).

Picture copyright 1953 by Garth Williams, copyright © renewed 1981 by Garth Williams. Used by permission of HarperCollins Publishers

36. *Jennie and Gaylord Ross. . . . and Jennie would look after us all.* Jennie Ross would have been a responsible twenty-one in 1881. She

books.[37] Now Mary would have a college education and a manual training besides. She would learn music and sewing even cooking and housework. Ma said it was wonderful what they learned to do without seeing.

In hunting for something a few days after Pa and Ma came home, I found where Ma had hidden it a beautiful book of Scotts' Pomes.[38] Because it was hidden, I knew I was not expected to know about it and so said nothing. It was awfully hard to leave it alone but I did. Ma gave it to me for my Christmas present. She had brought it from Vinton, Iowa, for me.

Our school was opened again in the fall and Carrie and I walked in. The teacher was Eliza Wilder a sister of the Wilder boys.[39]

We liked walking to school except that on the way we had to pass several cows and a pure bred Jersey bull[40] belonging to the banker Ruth. They were alowed to run loose and in the morning and at night would be beside our road, just out of town. The bull would lower his head, bellow and paw the dirt at us. His horns looked awfully sharp and I was afraid to pass him, not so much for myself. I had the feeling I could outrun him, but Carrie had never been strong, was very thin and spindly and I was afraid I could not take her with me fast enough.

One night, going home, we saw him beside the road and went far to one side and into the Big Slough on a path we followed until the tall grass was away above our heads so we could not be sure just where we were coming out.

We knew the road we traveled in the spring went through the slough still farther over and if we kept on we must come to it. So we went until we came out of the grass onto a mowed place. There we saw a team hitched to a load of hay. A tall man on the ground was pitching more hay up onto the load. On top of the load a big boy or young man lay on his stomach, kicking up his heels and just as we saw them, the man on the ground pitched a great forkful of hay square on top of the other. We passed by saying good evening while the man on top of the load scrambled out from under the hay and looked at us.

was also a schoolteacher for School District No. 32. In 1883, she married local farmer Walter H. Wheat. Neither the Bye manuscript nor *Little Town on the Prairie* included the Ross siblings' stay with the Ingalls girls. In the novel, Laura is charged with looking out for Carrie and Grace while Ma and Pa take Mary to college (p. 114). Harding, *I Recall Pioneer Days*, p. [8]; "Wedding Bells," *DSL*, May 5, 1883.

37. *She . . . had been the bright one always while I had been slower and stupid at my books.* The Brandt version amended the second half of this line to read, "had been the bright one of the family." The next paragraph added, "And I, who wanted a college education so much myself, was so very happy in thinking that Mary was getting one" (p. 114). The novel says: "Mary had always so loved to study. Now she could revel in studying so much that she had never before had a chance to learn" (p. 121).

38. *book of Scotts' Pomes.* Sir Walter Scott (1771–1832) was a Scottish poet, biographer, and novelist, who is often credited with developing the modern historical novel. Among his works still read today are the Waverly novels, *Ivanhoe* and *Rob Roy*. In *Little Town on the Prairie*, Laura finds a copy of *Tennyson's Poems*, not a collection by Scott (p. 138).

39. *Eliza Wilder a sister of the Wilder boys.* According to the 1880 census, Eliza J. Wilder was a twenty-nine-year-old farmer living in Kingsbury County. Her homestead was adjacent to one held by her brother, thirty-two-year-old Royal, which adjoined one held by another brother, twenty-two-year-old Almanzo. Eliza Jane, also known as E. J., was born in 1850, the third child of James and Angeline Wilder. She grew up on the farm near Malone, New York, attended the Franklin Academy there, and became a teacher at nineteen. After the family moved to Spring Valley, Minnesota, she joined them in the mid-1870s. In an account of her life as a homesteader, Eliza Jane opened the narrative in April 1879, when she taught school in Valley Springs, D.T., about eighty miles southeast of De Smet. Between terms, she filed on "homestead entry N. 20¼, Sec. 28, T. 111, R 56," as well as a timber claim about two miles from her

homestead (quoted in Anderson, *Wilder in the West*, p. 9). She hired Almanzo to build a sod house on her claim, completed her school term, and moved to Kingsbury County in April 1880. She spent the winter of 1880–1881 in Minnesota, then returned to her claim "before the 10th of May, 1881 on the first or second train that entered the Territory" after the Hard Winter (ibid., p. 15). In August, she returned to Minnesota, where she remained until early 1882. She did not, therefore, teach school in De Smet during the fall of 1881, which is when *Pioneer Girl* suggests that she did. Instead, Eliza Jane began teaching the fall term in De Smet in September 1882, "with the understanding that I could continue the year if I wished" (quoted ibid., p. 17). The chronology of events throughout *Pioneer Girl* is sometimes fluid and not necessarily in historical sequence. It is impossible to know whether this chronology resulted from a deliberate creative choice, but throughout the final sections of the memoir, Wilder described events that are factual, although their timing sometimes does not correspond to the historical record. In *Little Town on the Prairie*, Miss Wilder teaches school in the autumn following the long winter. This sequence strengthens the plot and advances the story.

In *Little Town on the Prairie*, Eliza Jane Wilder initially appears as "a very pleasant person. Her dark gray dress was stylishly made, like Mary's best one, tight and straight in the front, with a pleated ruffle just touching the floor, and an overskirt draped and puffed above a little train" (p. 127). Eliza Jane also appears as a "fashionable figure" in Rose Wilder Lane's novel *Free Land*, wearing French calico, "bangs frizzed above her narrow forehead and earrings swinging" (p. 4). Final Patent #1490, #1505, #2263, BLM-GLO Records; Anderson, *Wilder in the West*, pp. 2–4, 8–10, 14–15.

40. *pure bred jersey bull*. With bloodlines that extend back six centuries, Jersey cattle are among the world's oldest dairy breeds, prized for their high production of butterfat-rich milk. This breed originated on the Island of Jersey in the English Channel. The muscular males range in weight from twelve hundred to eighteen hundred pounds. Dairy bulls have a reputation for being dan-

Eliza Jane Wilder. *Laura Ingalls Wilder Historic Home and Museum*

gerous, and Jersey bulls are especially temperamental, as young Thomas Callahan of the De Smet area could attest. In late July 1884, while herding the family's Jersey bull, he was "furiously attacked" and tossed into the air on the bull's horns "about twenty times." The young man's neck and shoulders were "beaten into a black and blue pulp," but he survived ("Town and Country," *DSL*, Aug. 2, 1884). "Cattle: Jersey."

As we went on, I said to Carrie. 'That man on the ground was Wilder. The other must be the youngest Wilder boy.' I had never seen him before.[41]

When we told Pa how Ruth's Jersey bull had pawed and bellowed at us so that we came the long way home, Pa was angry.

I never saw Pa angry but two or three times. When he was, his intensely blue, eyes seemed to flash sparks of fire and his voice always a bass grew deeper. This time he only said, "I'll speak to Ruth.["]

He took us to school the next morning, past the cattle and we never saw the Jersey again.

There were several new girls at school. Mr Brown had brought his wife and adopted daughter Ida[42] out in the spring.

Then there was Mary Power daughter of the tailor Tom Power,[43] and Genieve Masters from Walnut Grove. Uncle Sam Masters[44] had come out with his whole family in the spring and taken a homestead west of town.

There was Minnie Johnson[45] and Laura Remington[46] among the younger girls.

There was quite a large school this time and they were all strangers except some of the smaller children and Genieve.

It was hard for me to meet the strange girls and the strange teacher and Genieve was the last unbearable straw.

She was not changed in disposition since the Walnut Grove days but had grown tall and slim with a beautiful complexion and was always dressed in pretty clothes.

I was still a rolly, polly, half pint of cidar and my clothes were nothing to speak of.[47] There had been no money nor time for my clothes and though they were good enough they were not attractive.

It seemed some mornings as though I simply could not face the crowd on the school grounds and the palms of my hands would grow moist and sticky on my my books.

But there was Carrie no better dressed and no more used to people than I. She must not be made to feel badly, so I stiffened my courage and no one not even Carrie ever knew how I felt.

It was strange considering all this that I should become a leader

41. *I had never seen him before.* Wilder wrote a similar scene in the opening pages of *The Long Winter*, when Laura and Carrie take a shortcut through the Big Slough and encounter the Wilder brothers (p. 23). Laura and the younger Wilder boy have a conversation that foreshadows the important role he will play in her life: "His blue eyes twinkled down at her as if he had known her a long time" (p. 24). Wilder had struggled to find the right way to introduce Almanzo in the series, and this scene is actually Laura's second brush with him. In *By the Shores of Silver Lake*, she catches a glimpse of him driving his horses (p. 262). Wilder's letters and notes to Lane indicate that the pair initially considered other scenarios. Lane, for example, apparently suggested that Laura go with Pa on a hunt that would take them near Almanzo's claim in *By the Shores of Silver Lake*. "I don't know what to say about Laura seeing Almanzo's shanty," Wilder replied, adding, "Seems to me it would be very improbable to have Laura go with Pa on a hunt." Instead, Wilder suggested introducing the name "Almanzo Wilder" on an envelope and let Laura "puzzle over the name herself" (LIW to RWL, [late 1937 or early 1938]). Later, as Wilder was working on *The Long Winter*, she considered having Laura and Almanzo "meet when the blizzard closes the school. You remember when the school wouldn't follow Cap Garland and nearly got lost. I don't know how it will work out, but I'm going to have Laura go with Almanzo to town" (LIW to RWL, Feb. 19, 1938, Box 13, file 194, Lane Papers). Perhaps what guided Wilder toward the right creative decision was a keen awareness of her readers' high expectations. "They all seem," she told Lane, "wildly interested and want to know how, where and when Laura met Almanzo. . . . lots of their letters want me to hurry up and write about it" (LIW to RWL, Jan. 26, [1938]).

42. *adopted daughter Ida.* In Brandt Revised (p. 79) and Bye (p. 143), Wilder described Ida as "a pretty French girl," perhaps because her middle name was Belle. While her photograph suggests that she was indeed pretty, Ida Wright was not French. The 1880 census lists thirteen-year-old Ida B. Wright,

Ida Wright. *Laura Ingalls Wilder Historic Home and Museum*

born in Illinois, as part of the household of Edward Brown and his wife, Laura, in West Salem, Wisconsin. Ida's natural parents were listed as English. Ten years earlier, Ida was listed as a three-year-old, born in Illinois and living in Chicago in a household headed by a twenty-eight-year-old seamstress named Catharine Wright, who had been born in Pennsylvania. Her household also included ten-year-old Henry, who was holding down a job in a store, and seven-year-old Mary, both born in Kansas. The census taker noted that everyone in the Wright household had parents "of foreign birth," but other census records suggest that Ida's parents were both born in Illinois. A different source, based apparently on family records, contends that Ida Belle Wright was born in Chicago in September 1866 as the fourth child of Thomas and Catharine Wright and that only she and her older brother Henry survived the Chicago fire of 1871. The circumstances of the adoption by the Browns are unclear, although the fictional Ida tells Laura, "Mother Brown took me out of a Home" (*LTOP*, p. 133). Cleaveland, "Ida B. Wright," p. 83.

43. *Mary Power daughter of the tailor Tom Power.* Mary Power was born in Tuscara, New York, in 1866 and moved with her family to De Smet from Kasson, Minnesota, probably in 1880, when she was fourteen. She was one of six surviving children of Thomas and Elizabeth Power. Her sister Susie, five years older than Mary, married early De Smet newspaperman Jacob Hopp in 1883. Terranna, "Mary Power," p. 85.

44. *Genieve Masters from Walnut Grove. Uncle Sam Masters.* Genevieve Masters was the youngest daughter of Samuel and Margaret Masters. In *Little Town on the Prairie*, Wilder would cast another old Walnut Grove acquaintance in Genevieve's role. In 1938, Wilder wrote Lane, "I think I will let Nellie Oleson take Jennie Masters' place in Prairie Girl [the original name of the book] and let her be the only girl from Plum Creek. Their characters were alike" (LIW to RWL, Mar. 15, 1938, Box 13, file 194, Lane Papers).

45. *Minnie Johnson.* Minnie Johnson was born about 1869 to Timothy H. and Susan Johnson, who moved from Wisconsin sometime after 1880 to take a homestead claim south of De Smet. In *Little Town on the Prairie*, Wilder ages Minnie Johnson slightly, identifying her as one of the "big girls" at school and Mary Power's seatmate (p. 132). Final Patent #4592, BLM-GLO Records.

46. *Laura Remington.* The 1880 census includes one family named Remington in Kingsbury County: Francis P. Remington and his wife, Ellen. They had one daughter named Grace—not Laura—and she would have been about six years old in the fall of 1881.

47. *dressed in pretty clothes. I was still a rolly, polly, half pint of cidar and my clothes were nothing to speak of.* The subjects of clothes and style played a more central role in *Pioneer Girl* and in Wilder's last two novels as both the real and fictional Laura Ingalls moved into adolescence. In *Little Town on the Prairie*, Miss Wilder and Nellie Oleson bond, in part, over their shared sense of eastern fashion. When Nellie enters the schoolhouse, Laura notices every detail of her costume: "a fawn-colored dress made with a polonaise" and deeply pleated ruffles "around the bottom of the skirt, . . . and falling from the edges of the wide sleeves. At her throat was a full jabot of lace" (p. 129). In contrast, an early photograph of Wilder and her sisters reinforces her statement that her own clothes "were nothing to speak of." Laura and Mary wear matching checked dresses adorned with simple ribbon ties and narrow pieces of lace along the cuffs and at the neckline. Like most adolescent girls, Wilder and her fictional counterpart were insecure about their personal appearance. Wilder called herself "rolly, polly" in *Pioneer Girl* and "round and dumpy as a little French horse" in the

novel (*LHOP*, p. 129). This depiction is endearing, especially to young readers, and as the fictional Laura gains confidence and her financial situation improves, she becomes distinctly more fashionable but never vain and frivolous like Nellie Oleson. When Wilder learned in 1937 that an old schoolmate had praised her appearance, she wrote: "I am so surprised that she said I was good looking. I always thought I was the homeliest girl ever and the only way I could endure myself was because I could outdo the boys at their games, and forget that I wasn't pretty" (LIW to [RWL], on letter from Helen Stratte to LIW, Dec. 17, 1937, Box 13, file 193, Lane Papers). Another contemporary observed: "Laura as a girl could hardly have been called pretty. She was a medium blond, with large blue eyes, but there was such sparkle and aliveness in her expression that she was very attractive" (Harding, *I Recall Pioneer Days*, p. [23]). Neumann, "Ingalls Girls' Dresses," p. 1.

Carrie, Mary, and Laura Ingalls, ca. 1879–1881.
Laura Ingalls Wilder Historic Home and Museum

48. *she had no idea how to govern a school*. In *Little Town on the Prairie*, Miss Wilder says she does not believe in punishment and tells her class that she "meant to rule them by love, not fear." Wilder added, "Even the big girls were embarrassed by her way of talking" (p. 152). Many years later, another early Kingsbury County resident, Alvin H. Greene, stood up for Eliza Jane: "I guess she had trouble with the class . . . but let me tell you. This was the homestead [era] and in the winter those big boys, men really . . . they'd go to school and sit in the back. They weren't mean but restless, not too interested in studying, just keeping things stirred up. Eliza Jane couldn't manage them and they didn't get a teacher that could until they hired Mr. [Owen] and the big guys quit coming" (Cramer, "Alvin Hensdale Greene," p. [2]). Wilder indicated that Eliza Jane's teaching ended before the big boys came to school, but her timing could be off; Eliza Jane herself indicated that she did not leave the area until after Thanksgiving. In any case, Eliza Jane had her supporters. Alvin Greene remembered her "walking across the prairie holding a book out in front of her reading as she went. She was a no-nonsense lady" (ibid., pp. [1–2]). Anderson, *Wilder in the West*, p. 17.

49. *Pa was a school director*. Charles Ingalls had been a member of the original De Smet school board, which was organized in July 1880, when the school district served sixty-three students. Digest of School Records, Laura Ingalls Wilder Memorial Society.

in the school. Ida Brown was my seatmate and both she and Mary Power were my good friends. They both for some strange reason looked to me to decide whatever questions came up. The younger children all liked me and would come running to me to settle their disputes or tell them what to play. There were no big boys in school, they were all working.

Ida, Mary and I did try to be frendly to Genieve but she still thought that being from New York made her far above common peopele, but after some slighting remarks and elevations of the nose we left her alone. Then she became "teachers pet," spending all the playtime with her.

School had not been going on many days until it became plain that though Miss Wilder was well educated she had no idea how to govern a school.[48] She had no sense of fairness and was uncertain as to temper. What she allowed one day she might punish severely the next.

Of course she lost control of the school, the children all became unruley.

I was a little sorry for Miss Wilder and really wanted to study so I tried to be her friend. All my influence was used to help her and a look from me would quiet the children quicker than a word from their teacher. At recess I would persuade them against plots to annoy her. When Ida or Mary or even Genieve would propose something to bother her for fun, I would sa[y] 'Oh! Lets don't['] and we didn't. This was perhaps easier for me to say, because I felt certain Genieve would have gone straight to the teacher with it, to get us into trouble. She did try to get us to say things that she could repeat and was not alway[s] particular to repeat truthfully. We knew this from what we happened to overhear and what Miss Wilder would say to us later.

We moved to town directly after Pa and Ma came back from Iowa so it was easier going to school. The school was rapidly going from bad to worse. Miss Wilder had it firmly fixed in her mind, by Genieve, I thought, that I expect to be favored because Pa was a school director,[49] while Pa was cautioning me all the time to behave myself and I was helping her all I could.

Her ill feeling included Carrie and I began to see that she watched her and at every chance said cutting, insulting things to her.

The seat where Carrie and her seatmate[50] sat had become unfastened from the floor and as they sat studying their lessons, one day, they rocked it gently back and forth. It made a little soft thud, but they were really studying and tipping the seat rather unconciously. Their seat was ahead of mine and I was looking at them when Miss Wilder said "You girls seem to like to rock that seat. You may put away your books and just rock it!"

They put away their books but after a minute the other girl sat over in an empty seat just across the aisle, leaving Carrie to rock the heavy seat alone. Miss Wilder paid no attention to the girl who left although she had been equally at fault with Carrie, but she would not let Carrie slacken the motion in the least.

I knew it was too much for Carrie's strength and that Miss Wilder must know it too for Carrie once in awhile fainted quietly away, so I expected Miss Wilder to stop her any minute.

Then she said to her, "Rock harder Carrie!" and I saw Carrie slowly turning white.

I leaped to my feet and said "Miss Wilder if Carrie isn't rocking that seat hard enough to suit you, let me do it!"

"You may do just that," she said pouncing on me joyfully it being the first chance she had been able to get at me in all the time she had been watching for one.

So I went over to the seat and sat down by Carrie, whispering to her to sit perfectly still and rest.

Then I rocked the seat, no gentle rocking and soft sounds, but thud, thud, back and forth I sent the seat with as much noise as I could manage to make.

There was no studying possible in the room and by all signs it was making teacher's head ache. I kept my eyes steadily fixed on her and rocked. She tried to stare me down, but couldn't face the blaze I knew was in my eyes and looked away.

After about twenty minutes she said we should stop rocking and go home and, with a final thud, we did.

Pa shook his head when I told him about it and said I was to go

50. *her seatmate.* In *Little Town on the Prairie*, Wilder gave Carrie's seatmate a name: Mamie Beardsley (p. 154). In 1880, Jerome C. Beardsley ran a hotel in De Smet, and he and his wife, Martha, had a four-year-old-daughter named Mary. Much of the chapter "Sent Home from School" (*LTOP*, pp. 159–64) focuses on this incident and follows the account in the original draft of *Pioneer Girl* closely.

51. *We went back in the morning . . . behave as they pleased*. The Bye version reads, "Carrie and I went back next morning and to the very letter I behaved myself perfectly, but in spirit I encouraged lawlessness" (p. 145). Much of "The School Board's Visit" (pp. 166–73) in *Little Town on the Prairie* focuses on the students' undisciplined behavior.

52. *her name being Eliza Jane*. The Bye manuscript adds, "She had told us that she never liked the name, which was the reason she didn't use it, and even her brothers called her, 'E.J.'" (p. 146).

back in the morning and "behave myself," but neither he nor Ma said I shouldn't have done as I did.

We went back in the morning and I did behave myself, but I left everyone else to behave as they pleased.[51] And they did!

Boys played leap frog down the aisles during school hours; they threw spit balls and whistled between their teeth.

The girls and boys both drew pictures and wrote messages on their slates and passed them up and down among the seats, while I sat trying to study.

It is hard to describe or to imagine if one has never seen thirty children from seven to sixteen completely out of hand.

During the first of the term, Miss Wilder had been unwise enough to tell us all that when she went to school the other children, to tease her, had called her "lazy, lousey, Liza Jane," her name being Eliza Jane.[52]

One day Ida Brown drew on her slate the picture of a woman, which was anything but pretty and wrote under it, "Who would go to school to Lazy, Lousey Liza Jane.["]

I erased what she had written and wrote in its place.

'Going to school is lots of fun
By laughter we have gained a ton
For we laugh until we have a pain
At lazy, lousey, Liza Jane.'

This was my sole contribution to the general disorder. I have no excuse to make. I should have been whipped. But there you are!

Ida passed the slate around and at recess the doggrel was shouted and sung all over the school yard.

This state of affairs had not come on all at once, but every day, since Carrie and I had rocked the seat, was worse than the one before, until we were surprised one day by the school board, in a body, walking in to look us over.

The teacher told her sad tale and said that I had made her trouble from the start, that everything would have been all right but for me and went into details that were also untrue, though very skillfully twisted from the truth.

I raised my hand, but Pa shook his head at me and put his finger on his lips. I subsided.

The school board one after the other told us we must be good, mind the teacher and study hard.

They told Miss Wilder they would stand by her and see that she was obeyed until the month was finished. At the end of the month a Mr Clewett took the school to finish out the term.[53]

When cold weather began, the big boys came. There were Cap Garland, Ben Woodworth, Frank Harthorn and Arthur Johnson.[54] School became more interesting. Again I played baseball.[55] Ida Brown and Mary Power played with me but Genieve stayed in the house. Afraid of spoiling her complexion, we said.

But she was always on hand when Cap brought candy as he often did, a little paper bag full. She asked for it the first time so he gave it to her, with an apologetic look from his blue eyes, under their white lashes, at Mary and me. Genieve passed it once and gobbled the rest.

After that she would simply take it, pretending she thought it was for her even when he had offered it to Mary, and keeping up a stream of flattering talk. "Cappie was such a dear boy. He was so tall and strong" etc. Cap tried for several days to give the candy to Mary and every time he had to let Genieve have it or be very rude.

One time I said 'Oh Cap! That's nice of you,' and took it fairly out of Genieves fingers. Mary and I and Ida ate it all that time and Cap grinned.

Genieve always made fun of Cap behind his back and going home that night she did so saying among other things, "I like Cap's candy, but Cap! Faugh!["] with a curl to her lip and a sniff.

Then she didn't like the things I told her and we had our only violent quarrel.

Among other things she called attention to my being fat and made fun of my clothes. In return for which I explained to her about the size of her feet, they were very large, and said that at least my clothes were my own and not my aunt's and cousins cast off garments sent to me because I was a poor relation.[56] Mrs Masters and Nannie at Walnut Grove, did send Mrs Sam Masters their old clothes and she

53. *a Mr Clewett took the school to finish out the term.* Frank B. Clewette was in his early twenties when he taught school in De Smet. He grew up in Wisconsin, was educated in the state's "common schools," and appears on the 1880 census as a farm laborer in Middleton, Wisconsin. In 1883, he married Edith Hawes in Willow Lake, Dakota Territory, and the couple eventually moved to Los Angeles, where Frank worked as a salesman, a superintendent in a grain and poultry supply company, and a packer for a furniture company. He died in California in 1928. In *Little Town on the Prairie*, Wilder described the fictional Mr. Clewett as "quiet but firm, a good disciplinarian" (p. 185). The editor of the *De Smet Leader* noted simply, "Mr. Clewitt closed a very successful term of school last week" ("Town and Country," Mar. 31, 1883). For her part, Eliza Jane Wilder did not mention a dismissal from the De Smet school and stated only, "When the term of school ended I was worn out and unfitted for any labor" (quoted in Anderson, *Wilder in the West*, p. 17). She returned to Minnesota for the winter but came back in the spring and continued to work on her homestead and invest in other property. She sold Caroline Ingalls a lot for one hundred dollars on Third Street, where Charles Ingalls built the family's final home in 1887. Eliza Jane left Dakota Territory permanently in the mid-1880s, moved to Washington, D.C., and worked as a secretary for the Department of the Interior until 1892. Returning to Minnesota, she married Thomas Thayer, a widower eighteen years her senior, and moved to his property near Crowley, Louisiana. Their only child, Walcott Wilder Thayer (known as Wilder), was born there in 1894. Thomas Thayer died less than five years later, but Eliza Jane continued to live in Crowley with their son. In 1903, Rose Wilder Lane spent a year with them while finishing high school. "California, Biographical Index"; "California, Death Index"; Anderson, *Wilder in the West*, pp. 17, 24, 26–33; *Ingalls Family of De Smet*, p. 11.

54. *Cap Garland, Ben Woodworth, Frank Harthorn and Arthur Johnson.* The older boys usually worked on family farms until weather put an end to the season's

work. In late 1881 or early 1882, Cap Garland would have been about sixteen; Ben Woodworth about fourteen; Frank Harthorn about sixteen; and Arthur Johnson, the older brother of Minnie Johnson, would also have been about sixteen.

55. *I played baseball.* The familiar story of baseball's origins—that Abner Doubleday invented the game in 1839 in Cooperstown, New York—does not reflect the complexities of the game's early history in the United States. Immigrants introduced a variety of bat-and-ball games in the eighteenth century, most notably the English games of rounders and cricket. Over time, players in different parts of the country developed variations of a game that came to be known as baseball. The New York version—played in the 1840s by the Knickerbocker Base Ball Club—laid the foundation for the game as Americans know it today. By 1883, De Smet had its own "base ball club" ("Town and Country," DSL, May 5, 1883). Brandt Revised (p. 82) and Bye included additional recess activities: "when deep snow came we snowballed each other and rode on handsleds which the boys pulled, for there were no hills to coast on" (Bye, p. 147).

56. *not . . . because I was a poor relation.* In *Little Town on the Prairie*, Laura and Nellie argue more overtly over status. Nellie tells Laura, "I'm glad I don't have to be a teacher. . . . My folks can get along without my having to work." Laura replies, "Of course you needn't, Nellie, but you see, we aren't poor relations being helped out by our folks back East" (p. 186). Wilder used the argument to advance the plot, emphasizing Laura's worry about passing her teacher examination (p. 186).

Schoolyard games, Huron, D.T., 1880s. *W. E. Snell photograph, South Dakota State Historical Society*

made them over, which explained the fine, beautiful materials of Genieve's dresses.

It was then I learned, may years ahead of the scientific discovery, that anger poisoned one, for I went home and to bed sick at my stomache and with a violent headache.

We studied hard with Mr Clewett and played hard too. When the snow came, we snowballed and rode on hand sleds with the boys pulling them, for there was no hill so we couldn't coast.

Once the four big boys coaxed us four girls into a hand cart that was all too small so that we were piled up with feet sticking out at all angles. Then they ran away with us taking us down-town on a run. Only my personal appeal to Cap saved us from being hauled the length of main street in our rediculous positions.

Ben Woodworth had a birthday party. He came with a sleigh, gathered us all up and took us over to the depot wher the Woodworths lived upstairs. It was my first party and I felt very awkward. There were nine of us, our four from school and Jimmie Woodworth. The long dining table was set and ready when we got there. It was beautiful with its silver and china its beautiful linen tablecloth and napkins.

At each place, on a pretty little plate was an orange standing on end with the peel sliced in strips half way down and curled back making the orange look like a golden flower. I thought them the most beautiful thing I had ever seen, even prittier than the birthday cake in the center of the table.

The oranges were a real treat too.[57] We finished peeling them laying the peeling on the plate, then separated the sections, one at time, daintly with our fingers and ate them, putting the seeds on the plate with the peel. (There were plenty of seeds in oranges those days and the membrane between the section was tough so they separated eaisly without spilling a drop of juce.[)]

After we had eaten our orange we were served hot oyster soup and crackers. After that the cake was cut and we were each helped to a generous piece.

When supper was over we went down into the waiting room of the depot and played games. Jimmie arranged us all in a circle holding

57. *The oranges were a real treat too.* Because oranges were a cultivated warm-climate fruit that had to be transported long distances on the railroad, their appearance on the frontier represented a luxury.

58. *Jimmie . . . gave us a shock, . . . from his telegraph instrument.* Woodworth's telegraphic shocks were not reserved for party occasions. "Highly interesting experiments in electro-magnetism are conducted by Prof. James Woodworth at the depot," the *De Smet Leader* reported. "They are most deeply interesting to the experimentee. The look of pained astonishment which he assumes is only equaled by the gentleman who discovers that some guileful plebian in whom he confided has worked on him a twenty-cent piece for a quarter" ("Town and Country," Jan 27, 1883). James G. Woodworth, who was nineteen in 1883, resigned in March of that year to "take a position as private secretary of the general [freight] agent of the Omaha division, whose office is in Minneapolis" (ibid., Mar. 24, 1883).

59. *the aid society gave a social at Mrs Tinkham's . . . over their furniture store.* "The ladies of the benevolent societies of De Smet will hold a sociable, with mush and milk appendage, at the church on Tuesday of next week," the *De Smet Leader* announced on March 3, 1883. Whether or not this sociable was the one that Wilder mentioned is unknown, but it was probably fairly typical of such events. The object was "to procure lamps" for the church, and the editor urged everyone to attend "and be liberal as well as sociable." The newspaper did not mention the location of the social, but both Adeline Tinkham and her husband, Charles H. Tinkham, were active in the community. In 1880, Charles Tinkham, a cabinetmaker from Maine, had walked to De Smet "ahead of his load from Volga to start his furniture store, having but a few chairs to sell in the Hard Winter to come" (Sherwood, *Beginnings of De Smet*, p. 18). His wife joined him later. Tinkham also became the first undertaker in De Smet, retiring in the 1930s. In *Little Town on the Prairie*, an entire chapter is devoted to the event ("The Sociable," pp. 201–9), which, as here, Laura and her friend found disappointing. Later in *Pioneer Girl*, Wilder attended another social, which she also found "stupid." Poppen, *De Smet Yesterday and Today*, p. 309.

60. *organized a literary society. . . . and had debates.* By 1883, the literary society of De Smet was a well-

hands and gave us a shock, that made us tingle, from his telegraph instrument.[58] We went home early well pleased with the evening.

Just after the party, the aid society gave a social at Mrs Tinkham's where she lived over their furniture store.[59] It cost 10¢ to go and each one was served a dish of ice cream, home made of course and frozen with the natural ice of which there was plenty out doors. Mary Power and I went together, but it was a very stupid time and we left early wishing we had saved our 10¢.

The grown people organized a literary society that met at the school house every Friday night.

They spelled down, spoke pieces and had debates.[60]

One night "Mrs Jarleys Wax Works" were shown. They were people we knew, dressed and made up to resemble wax figures, who when described and called upon by "Mrs Jarley" went through stunts with stiff, jerky movements, like wooden men and women.[61]

That same night a vaudavill sketch was given by some men blacked up as negro minstrels,[62] "The Mulligan Guards." They went through a clog dance while they sang.

"Oh Talk about your Mulligan Guards
These darkey's can't be beat
We step in time and cut a shine
Just watch this darky's feet."[63]

Gerrald Fuller was the star performer. Charlton and Gerald Fuller were twin brothers owning one of the hardware stores. Charlton was very tall and thin and dignified a typical Englishman, while Gerald was short and square, not fat, with no dignity whatever[,] a rough, tough, disgrace to his family, but good hearted, generous, kind, a regular clown at times, always a good fellow and liked by everybody, except his twin brother Charlton.

Gerald was a good singer and there were several others. Mrs Bradley, the druggists wife[64] and Mr Trousdale the drayman[65] and Mrs Sassie[66] with Gerald Fuller made a quartett that furnished the music for the meetings of the literary society.

I often saw the Wilder boys and their hired man Oscar Rhuel[67] sitting in a front corner of the room. Oscar Rhuel was a romantic

Charles H. Tinkham in his furniture store, 1920s.
South Dakota State Historical Society

established enterprise. It originally met at the schoolhouse on Friday or Saturday evenings, but switched to the Congregational church when the stove proved faulty. Readings and debates were common, with the topic of February 17, 1883, being, "Resolved, that the expenses of the U. S. Government should be met by direct taxation," followed the next week by "the power of education in this country as opposed to that of wealth." Written essays on such topics as "Woman's Rights," musical arrangements, and the reading of a weekly "paper" were performed to applause, "cheers and hilarity" as the occasion dictated. In March, the literary society "suspended operations" for the season, "and its eloquent ones may bottle up their gas until another winter" ("Town and Country," *DSL*, Jan. 27, Feb. 17, Feb. 24, Mar. 10, 1883). In *Little Town on the Prairie*, Wilder devoted the chapter "Literaries" (pp. 214–20) to the creation of the town's literary society and its first meeting, in which Pa plays a critical role in proposing a loose and democratic structure. In the chapter that follows—"The Whirl of Gaiety"—she described several meetings in detail (pp. 221–39).

61. *"Mrs Jarleys Wax Works."*. . . *like wooden men and women.* In Charles Dickens's novel *The Old Curiosity Shop* (1840), Mrs. Jarley is the proprietor of Jarley's Wax-Work, a traveling exhibit she advertises as "the only stupendous collection of real wax-work in the world" (p. 242). Dickens based Mrs. Jarley's character on Madam Marie Tussaud, who had a traveling wax-works exhibit before opening her famous museum in London in 1835, and a Mrs. Salmon, who owned a similar establishment. During the mid-nineteenth century, several publications gave directions on how to stage a wax-works exhibit or pageant, including George B. Bartlett's *Mrs. Jarley's Far-Famed Collection of Wax-Works* (1873). It offered "full Directions for their Arrangement, Positions, Movements, Costumes, and Properties," as well as a narrative to introduce the various figures (p. 1). Bartlett's cast of characters included Mrs. Jarley, Dickens's Little Nell, a two-headed girl, Blue Beard, a mermaid, Mother Goose, Little Red Riding Hood, and Lord Byron, among others. The members of the Congregational church in De Smet put on "Mrs. Jarley's Wax Figgers" on Thursday evening, March 19, 1885, as a fundraiser. "These life-like representations cannot be fitly described in a few words," the editor of the *De Smet Leader* wrote before the production, "but must be seen to be appreciated. We are desired by the management to say that all those who throughout the entertainment refrain from laughing will be presented the price of admission at its close for their good behavior" ("Town and Country," Mar. 14, 1885). A "large and appreciative audience" attended the spectacle, which brought in about twenty-five dollars for the church (ibid., Mar. 21, 1885). In *Little Town on the Prairie*, Wilder wrote that the faces

of the life-size figures in this production "were white as wax, except for painted-on black eyebrows and red lips. Draped in folds of white cloth, each figure stood as motionless as a graven image." Gerald Fuller played Mrs. Jarley who then introduced George Washington, Daniel Boone, Queen Elizabeth, and Sir Walter Raleigh (pp. 237–38). Bloom, *Waxworks*, pp. 191–92; Barlett, *Mrs. Jarley's Far-Famed Collection*, pp. 1–4; Fisher, "De Smet's Famous Wax Works," pp. 66–67; "Town and Country," *De Smet Leader*, Feb. 28, Mar. 7, 14, 21, 1885.

62. *blacked up as negro minstrels.* Most historians trace the origins of minstrelsy to Thomas Dartmouth Rice, a white performer known as the "Father of Minstrelsy." In 1831, he took to the stage wearing ragged clothes and a burnt-cork black mask and, assuming the character of an old African American man, sang and danced to a song entitled "Jump Jim Crow." His performance launched a unique and, by today's standards, disturbing form of American musical theater that enjoyed sustained popularity into the early twentieth century. In the 1840s, white minstrel troupes toured the United States and Europe giving shows that included music, dance, and comedy served up with irreverence, exaggeration, and racial stereotyping. Yet, before the American Civil War, many abolitionists embraced minstrelsy as a way to reach a broader American audience, and some minstrel troupes performed songs with distinctly abolitionist themes. American lecturers and humorists also developed a kind of blackface writing, built around popular racial stereotypes, and this writing influenced Harriet Beecher Stowe's vision for some of her characters in her abolitionist novel *Uncle Tom's Cabin* (1852). Stephen Foster's popular and often sentimental songs were also written for minstrel shows. After the Civil War, some African American entertainers also began to use the traditional conventions of minstrelsy, including blackface. Their shows promised audiences authenticity and often countered racial stereotypes with messages of political activism. Still, white male entertainers continued to dominate the genre, including Billy Emerson, who popularized Charles Ingalls's trouble song, "The Big Sunflower." Minstrel shows began to wane in popularity during the early twentieth century, but just three years before Wilder wrote *Pioneer Girl*, Al Jolson appeared in blackface in *The Jazz Singer*, the first full-length talking film. Wilder described De Smet's minstrel performers in detail in *Little Town on the Prairie* (pp. 257–60). Reynolds, *Mightier Than the Sword*, pp. 77–86; "History of Minstrelsy"; "Blackface Minstrelsy"; Spitzer, "The Lay of the Last Minstrels," pp. 12–13, 118.

Sheet music for "The Skidmore Guard," 1875. *Library of Congress*

63. *"The Mulligan Guards." . . . Just watch this darky's feet."* The Mulligan Guard, an Irish American militia, appeared in a series of skits, sketches, and plays created by lyricist, actor, and playwright Edward Harrigan with his theater partner, Tony Hart. "The Mulligan Guard" was Harrigan's most popular song from this series and dates to 1878. However, the lines Wilder quoted in *Pioneer Girl* and *Little Town on the Prairie* are adapted from "The Skidmore Guard," also with lyrics by Harrigan, music by William Carter, and musical arrangement by Dave Braham. The African American Skidmore Guard—white actors in blackface—was a rival militia in Harrigan's series. "Harrigan, Edward," p. 447; Cockrell, *Ingalls Wilder Family Songbook*, pp. 154–59, 375.

64. *Mrs Bradley, the druggists wife.* Hattie L. Suffron Bradley was twenty-two in 1880 and married to registered pharmacist George C. Bradley, who was twenty-four. The couple came from

Wisconsin and spent time in Luverne, Minnesota, on their way west. Bradley started the first pharmacy in De Smet. In *Little Town on the Prairie*, Mrs. Bradley sings a beautiful solo at one of the first literaries, and "Laura could hardly bear the sadness" of the song she selected (p. 223). *Memorial and Biographical Record*, pp. 362, 365.

65. *Mr Trousdale the drayman*. The drayman was C. W. ("Charley") Trousdale. In December 1883, he called "for a share of work from those who have draying to do" ("Town and Country," DSL, Dec. 1, 1883) and announced his "New Dray Line" in February 1884 (ibid., Feb. 9, 1884). A drayman was a person who made his living by transporting heavy goods on a two-wheeled cart or wagon called a dray. By 1885, Trousdale also shipped packages "by express or freight" (ibid., Aug. 1, 1885).

66. *Mrs Sassie*. Elizabeth Pearson had married Louis or Lewis E. Sasse of Saint Charles, Minnesota, in 1880. A year later, they moved to De Smet, where he originally bought and shipped grain. He also worked as a building contractor before establishing a drugstore with Dr. E. G. Davies, "putting a fine glass front on the building" in 1884 (Sherwood, *Beginnings of De Smet*, p. 33). Two years later, Sasse bought out his partner and became a registered pharmacist. By the early twentieth century, the business was known as the Sasse Pharmacy. *Memorial and Biographical Record*, pp. 341–42; "De Smet . . . Business Directory."

67. *Oscar Rhuel*. Despite the details Wilder provided about Oscar Rhuel, a search of census records proved unsuccessful, even when using the alternate spelling of Ruhl, which appeared in Brandt Revised (p. 84) and Bye (p. 149).

68. *Alfred Thomas came. . . . to take me.* In 1883, Alfred Thomas was a prominent member of the De Smet community. He worked as a lawyer and land agent, was clerk and board member of the De Smet School Township, and became an elected trustee of the Baptist church in October. The attention he and other single men paid Wilder as a schoolgirl reflected the fact that De Smet was "a bachelor community." Unmarried men were "here in force," the local newspaper editor reported. "They are not here alone for fun, nor their health. . . . They have come to prepare the way for the building up of happy homes when they have brought the wilds under subjection." The editor continued: "Dakota wants more women—young women especially. Send on your girls from the overcrowded East." Not only were there opportunities of all types for these young women, he asserted, but they would also find "an homage unknown where they are less rare" ("A Bachelor Community," *DSL*, June 23, 1883). "Story of the De Smet Schools," *De Smet News*, June 6, 1930; "Personalities," *DSL*, Apr. 14, 1883; "Town and Country," *DSL*, Oct. 6, 27, 1883.

69. *a Women's Christian Temperance Union (W.C.T.U.). . . . Ida Brown had joined.* The Woman's Christian Temperance Union (WCTU) was formed in the mid-1870s as American women took a stand against alcohol and the personal and social problems it created. Initially organized in Ohio, the movement spread across the United States. Among the group's defining principles were the concepts of moderation in all things and a total abstinence from alcohol. The Kingsbury County chapter of the WCTU met quarterly at the Congregational church in De Smet. The March 1883 meeting agenda included papers, essays, addresses, music, and a children's program, along with consideration of this specific question: "Why do we urge that the nature of alcohol and its affects on the human organism be taught in our public schools?" ("Meeting of the W.C.T.U.," *DSL*, Mar. 24, 1883). At this same meeting, "The singing of the children, led by Miss Ida Wright upon the organ, was said to be very fine" (ibid.). *Woman's Christian Temperance Union.*

figure. At his home in Sweden he had fallen in love with and become enga[g]ed to a girl, whose parents objected, Oscar being poor and they rich.

They had taken their daughter to America to keep her away from him and were settled in California as far away as they could get.

Oscar had followed but his money would bring him only so far and he was now working to get money to go on to California, where his girl was waiting for him. Later he did go on and marry her. But at this time we girls felt a great sympathy for him and I thought him quite handsome.

On one of these entertainment nights a young lawyer name Alfred Thomas came in and stayed and kept on staying for no reason that I could see, until I was afraid Pa and I would be late. At last he asked Pa if he were going to the meeting and to my surprise Pa said "No!" Then he asked me if I were going and I thinking if Pa didn't go of course I wouldn't said 'No!' too.

So Mr Thomas went away alone and then Pa laughed at me and said all Thomas had come for was to take me.[68] I had refused my first offer of an escort and I was indignant. If he wanted to take me why couldn't he say "Come go with me!" and not be such a coward. Not that I wanted to go with him, but I hated to miss the fun and now Pa and I couldn't go, but sat home all the evening.

The church and Sunday-school were going along nicely, and Mr Brown dropped in unexpectedly whenever he could to eat with us.

One noon Ma had prepared a kettle of beans with only the small piece of meat necessary to cook with them. As we sat down at the table Mr Brown came. Being company the food was passed to him first. After helping himself to a huge plate of beans, he took the plate of meat, looked at it and around the table, then scooped all the meat onto his own plate saying, "Might as well take it. There ain't much of it anyway." The church women met at Mrs Browns and organized a Women's Christian Temperance Union (W.C.T.U.). Their next meeting was at our house and they insisted I should join. Ida Brown had joined[69] and because of that the[y] urged me harder, but I refused for no very good reason. I just had a distaste for everyone at the meeting except Ma.

Again I worked at my old trade, taking care of a baby at night so its mother could be gone. I often stayed with Mrs Barnes baby[70] so they could go to church in the evening. They were very strict church people. One week Mr Barnes was away and did not get back on Saturday. Sunday morning at Sunday-school, Ma said to Mrs Barnes that perhaps Mr Barnes would come on the morning train. Mrs Barnes was horrified and said "Oh No!" She was sure he would not. He would never do so wicked a thing as to travel on Sunday. And just then Mr Barnes came from the depot off the morning train.

(Later Barnes was attorney for Zion City,[71] near Chicago, and helped organize it.

The new church building was finished[72] and the women gave a New England Supper in it. Two tables were set the length of the room and the food placed on them. A little roast pig with an apple in its mouth was given the place of honor. Roast chicken with dressing[,] cold ham, sausage, baked beans & bread were scattered along the tables. There was cake and pumpkin, mince and dried apple pies and coffee. Everyone sat down at the table and helped themselves. The price was fifty cents.[73]

Ernie Perry came in from the farm one morning and asked me to go, with him, to a party at Ross'es that night. I liked Ernie and was glad to go.

There were sixteen young folks there, all country people. We danced square dances and played games, "Drop The Handkerchief, London Bridge, Miller Boy, Postoffice, Spat them Out, Snap and Catch 'Em" and Forfeits. I didn't like the kissing games[74] and always managed to let the kiss land on my ear.

I could have danced waltzes, polkas or shottishes as Pa had taught me so long ago, but had never learned the square dances, so I went through them awkwardly. But the sleighride home across the moonlit snow was pleasant so I really had a good time.

The next week Ernest came for me again. This time I liked the crowd and the kissing games less than before. I went through the square dances better with Ernest's help but Jennie and Gaylord spoiled them for me by the remarks they made about us.

70. *Mrs Barnes baby*. Mary La Belle Evans married Visscher V. Barnes in 1876, and according to the 1900 census, their daughter, Mary Vere, was born in Dakota Territory in 1879. "Visscher Vere Barnes."

71. *Barnes was attorney for Zion City*. Visscher V. Barnes was living in Lake County, Illinois, in 1900. By 1920, he was in Zion City, Illinois, and died nearby in Waukegan in 1924. "Illinois, Deaths."

72. *The new church building was finished*. The First Congregational Church in De Smet held its first service in its new building on August 30, 1882. "The structure was 28x48, the roof steep and the ceiling vaulted . . . with two small vestry rooms" (Sherwood, *Beginnings of De Smet*, p. 31). In late 1883, a "new church bell was hung in the belfry" (ibid., p. 24). In *Little Town on the Prairie*, Wilder wrote that the new church building "still looked raw" when members gathered for the first services (p. 225).

Original congregational church building in De Smet, ca. 1909.
Laura Ingalls Wilder Memorial Society

73. *a New England Supper. . . . The price was fifty cents*. The New England church supper was, and still is, a reliable fundraiser for which church women donate food and labor. The suppers began after the Revolutionary War when "towns and states gradually abandoned the practice of using levies to pay the local minister." The menu varies from place to place, but bean suppers are popular "everywhere" (Collins, "J. D. Salinger's Last Supper"). In *Little Town on the Prairie*, Ma contributes a "mammoth pumpkin

pie" and a "milkpan full of baked beans" for the supper, which is characterized as a Ladies' Aid event to "help pay for the church." Laura and Ida Wright Brown wash and dry dishes, eat, then wash and dry dishes again (pp. 227–32). The ladies of the De Smet Baptist church hosted just such an event on February 14, 1884. The bill of fare included Boston baked beans, chicken pie, boiled ham, suet corn cake, gingerbread, doughnuts, and pumpkin and mince pies. "New England Supper," *DSL*, Feb. 9, 1884.

74. *We danced square dances and played games, . . . Forfeits. I didn't like the kissing games.* Square dances are partnered dances of two or more couples arranged in a square(s), with the men facing the women. Most of the games Wilder listed involved movement, physical contact, and sometimes kissing. In Miller Boy, for example, boys and girls moved in circles, held hands, and changed partners while singing a song. In some versions, boys grabbed partners and gave them a full circle swing. Lyrics varied, but another De Smet teenager who attended one of these parties recalled this verse: "Happy is the Miller who lives by himself;/While the wheel turns 'round he is gaining on his wealth;/One hand in the hopper, while the other holds the bag:/As the wheel turns 'round, he cries out 'Grab'" (Harding, *I Recall Pioneer Days*, p. [9]). Post Office and Forfeits often involved kissing. In Post Office, girls and boys divided into two groups, one of which went into a separate room—the post office—and when individuals went to collect their "mail," they had to kiss everyone to receive it. Forfeits usually required guests to "forfeit" items—a handkerchief or glove—and to perform a task (kissing, perhaps) to redeem them. Baldwin and Watts, "We've Got a Pig"; Abernethy, *Texas Toys*, p. 209; *Cassell's Household Guide*, pp. 163–64, 202–3.

Going home, Ernest pulled the robes higher around me and forgot to take his arm away. I was too shy and embarrassed to do anything about it but I made up my mind not to go again. Anyway I didn't want to go in that country crowd and it was time to stop. (a snob even then)[75]

When Ernest came again the next week, I told him that I didn't like the games and couldn't dance, so I didn't care to go. I was sorry to hurt his feelings and thanked him for the invitation, smoothing my refusal the best I could. After awhile the crowd surprised me by having a party at our house and that was the end of that. (Ernest Perry went to Oregon with the rest of the Perrys a few years later and stayed a batchelor for the sweet sake of his ideal of me until just a few years ago.)[76]

A revival meeting was started soon afterward and we attended nearly every night. It did not seem, to me, so interesting as those we used to have in Walnut Grove, but I had a brown dress that I liked and a brown velvet turban, with a touch of red, that was very becoming.[77]

I sat demurely with Pa and Ma, well up toward the front, but I did notice the Wilder boys, Oscar Rhuel and Cap Garland always in the same place at the back of the church. To be perfectly truthful I was noticing Cap.

Passing them one night on our way out, I felt a touch on my arm and some one said in my ear, "May I see you home?"

It was the youngest Wilder boy, Liza Janes brother.[78] In sheer astonishment I made no reply, but he took my arm and dropped into step beside me, behind Pa and Ma. Ma looked around, but Pa propelled her gently on and we went out the door and home. I'm sure not a dozen words were said on the way, I was tongue tied wondering why he of all people should pay any attention to me.

Later I learned that Oscar had dared him to ask the girl who walked just behind me and they had made a bet that he would not see her home, but Oscar did not make it plain which girl he meant, so although he knew perfectly well[,] the Wilder boy asked me as he had intended and collected the bet from Oscar, by claiming a

75. *I didn't want to go in that country crowd. . . . (a snob even then).* This insightful personal observation from Wilder to Lane foreshadows Nellie Oleson's prejudice against country parties in *On the Banks of Plum Creek* (p. 171).

76. *(Ernest Perry . . . stayed a batchelor . . . until just a few years ago.)* In 1900, Ernest Perry, still an unmarried farmer, was living in Troy, Idaho, with his father, Oliver, and stepmother, Martha. Ten years later, Ernest and his wife, Mary, several years his junior, were living with his father in Finley, Washington. Although Ernest married later in life, he did not wait as long as Wilder implied in her note to Lane. He died in January 1946. "Washington Deaths."

77. *A revival meeting. . . . I had a brown dress . . . that was very becoming.* Although Wilder described this revival at length in *Little Town on the Prairie* (pp. 276–77), it is clear that the teenage Wilder was primarily interested in her clothes and beaus. From this point forward in *Pioneer Girl*, Wilder's clothes become more sophisticated and fashionable; the transition is more gradual in the novel. While this dress is described as "new" in the revised manuscripts (Brandt, p. 124), in *Little Town on the Prairie*, Laura lets down the hem of her old brown school dress so she can wear it over a fuller set of hoops. The transformation is "clever," but Laura still feels "that all the other girls were better dressed" (p. 271).

78. *It was the youngest Wilder boy, Liza Janes brother.* In *Pioneer Girl*, Wilder waited until much later to introduce Almanzo's first name, a creative strategy that she abandoned in her fiction. In *By the Shores of Silver Lake*, Laura is aware of Almanzo's name almost from the moment when she first sees him (p. 262), and after the revival meeting in *Little Town on the Prairie*, she knows instantly that the person who touched her coat sleeve "was Almanzo Wilder" (p. 279).

79. *Mr Louis Bouchie.* Canadian-born Louis H. Bouchie was in his early twenties when Robert Boast introduced him to the Ingalls family. In 1880, he was living in Grundy County, Iowa, and working as a cattle herder. He filed on various claims in Kingsbury County in 1882, but he and his wife ultimately settled on adjoining claims about six miles (not twelve and a half, which would be a round trip) southwest of De Smet. In *Little Town on the Prairie* and *These Happy Golden Years*, he appears as Lew Brewster. In correspondence with Lane and in her initial outline for "Prairie Girl," which ultimately became the last two novels in the Little House series, Wilder continued to use the surname Bouchie (LIW, "Prairie Girl" outline, Box 16, file 243, Lane Papers; LIW to RWL, Jan. 25, 1938), but the depiction of the Bouchie family is at once so memorable and so disturbing that Wilder must have decided to use a fictional name to protect herself as a novelist and to shield the identities of the people she depicted. Wilder knew when she was taking literary liberties and when she was not. "Unfortunately," Wilder wrote, "we have used real names in these books and must stick closer to facts than otherwise we would need to do" (LIW to RWL, Aug. 17, 1938). Hicks, "Searching for the Brewster School," pp. 71–72; Final Patent #3510, #5537, #9256, BLM-GLO Records.

80. *Two months was all their district could afford.* In 1883, the legislature of Dakota Territory formalized a new set of laws for public schools that dictated that school townships or districts must conduct at least a "four months' school." The four months could be spread over the entire year and were usually broken into two-month terms, depending on the preferences of individual school boards. "The New School Laws," DSL, Mar. 31, 1883; Levisee, *Annotated Revised Codes,* p. 604.

81. *I was not old enough. . . . One must be sixteen and I would not be that old until February.* In 1883, Dakota Territory required that county superintendents "hold public examinations of all persons over the age of eighteen years, offering themselves as candidates as teachers of common [public] schools" (Levisee, *Annotated Revised Codes,* pp. 558–59).

misunderstanding. After that it was the usual thing for him to "see me home."

Before the meetings were ended, Mr Boast came to see us bringing a Mr Bouchie, a friend and distant relative who lived twelve and a half miles south of town. Mr Louis Bouchie[79] was looking for some one to teach the little school in his district and Mr Boast had recomended me. Two months was all their district could afford[80] to have and $20. a month all they could pay.

Pa told them I was not old enough to get a certificate. One must be sixteen and I would not be that old until February.[81] But Mr Boast and Mr Bouchie said they would fix that with the county suprentendent if I would go and I promised to teach the school if I could get a certificate. When I went to the suprentendent I passed the examination and he did not ask my age. So I got my certificate[82] and went out to Bouchie's the first of December[83] to begin the first school in their district.

There were five scholars, Marth and Charles Patterson,[84] and Clarance, Ruby and Tommy Bouchie,[85] brothers and sister of Louis Bouchie, who lived with their parents close by the school house.

The school house was an abondened claim shanty,[86] one thickness of boards with cracks between, through which the snow blew. There were six seats with desks, a huge heating stove, a small blackboard, a little table and a chair for the teacher.

I boarded at Louis Bouchie's, one half mile across the prairie and no road.

Mr Bouchie took me out the day before school was to begin and I was nearly sick, with my dread of being among strangers, when we reached the house.

Mrs Bouchie was quiet and sullen, putting supper on the table and her little boy was crying.[87] Supper was eaten almost in silence and soon after, I went to bed.

My bed was on a sofa so narrow that, even asleep, I kept my mind on not falling off. It was curtained off with calico from the rest of the room where the Bouchies slept. The one other room was kitchen, dining and sitting room.

Mornings, before breakfast, Mr Bouchie would go build a fire in

Clearly, the official age requirement for teachers was eighteen, not sixteen. Prior to 1883, the territory had placed no age restrictions on schoolteachers. Wilder herself turned sixteen in February 1883. These critical historical details contradict Wilder's narratives in *Pioneer Girl* and *Little Town on the Prairie*. Her published work and private correspondence also deliver conflicting answers to the question of how old the real Laura Ingalls was when she received her teaching certificate. In an autobiographical column for the *Missouri Ruralist* in 1924, Wilder wrote that she first taught school when "I was only 16 years old and 12 miles from home during a frontier winter" (*Little House Sampler*, pp. 38–39). This recollection placed the real sixteen-year-old Laura Ingalls at the Bouchie school in 1883–1884—still an underage teacher but a full year older than the Laura of *Pioneer Girl* or the novel. On the other hand, in a letter focusing on the chronology of the novels, Wilder wrote: "I would be 14 the [February of the] Hard Winter and 15 the next winter. That was the winter I began teaching at Bouchies in December two months before I was 16 years old" (LIW to RWL, Aug. 17, 1938). According to this chronology, Wilder would have received her teaching certificate in 1882 at age fifteen. The context of the letter implies that she viewed the Bouchie/Brewster school sequence as historical not fictional: "I think it [Laura's age] is important. It shows how few teachers there were. How glad the people were to find someone to teach their little schools" (ibid.). Wilder continued to argue this case in several letters to Lane during 1938 (LIW to RWL, Jan. 25, 26, Feb. 19, Aug. 17, 1938), and to emphasize it further, she included a specific date in *Little Town on the Prairie*, a detail at odds with the usual timelessness of her fiction. An image of Laura's teaching certificate appears in the novel, dated December 24, 1882, and signed by "Geo. A Williams, Supt. of Schools, Kingsbury county, D.T." (p. 306). This phrasing follows Wilder's actual certificate closely, but one detail is significantly different: the real certificate is signed and dated December 10, 1883, when Wilder was sixteen. For the most part, the historical record contradicts Wilder's chronology. George A. Williams was Kingsbury County superintendent of schools in 1883 and could not have signed a certificate for her in 1882. As a writer of fiction, Wilder could certainly have taken creative license with the timing of historical events, Dakota Territory's official teaching requirements, and even with the fictional Laura's age. However, Wilder's account in *Pioneer Girl* is more difficult to explain because it is nonfiction. Perhaps she was genuinely confused about her actual age and, years later, changed the date on her fictional certificate to conform to her memories. Regardless of Wilder's

exact age when she began teaching, the basic circumstances that she recorded about her first teaching experience were accurate. She was, in fact, an underage teacher for most of her teaching career, and the county superintendent overlooked the territory's stated public education policy when he granted Wilder a teacher's certificate. D.T., *Session Laws*, 1862, 1864, 1879, 1883; Ludeman, "Studies in the History of Public Education," pp. 442–47; Records of Kingsbury County Superintendent of Schools, pp. 1, 114, 147; Teacher's Certificate, Dec. 10, 1883, Laura Ingalls Wilder Historic Home and Museum.

82. *he did not ask my age. So I got my certificate.* In 1938, Wilder told Lane, "the suprentendent of schools forgot to ask me how old I was, because they wanted me to teach that school" (LIW to RWL, Aug. 17, 1938). It was within a county school superintendent's role to adapt the teacher examination process to his personal "knowledge and information of the candidate's . . . knowledge and understanding, together with aptness to teach and govern" (Levisee, *Annotated Revised Codes*, p. 558). In *Little Town on the Prairie*, the superintendent comes to Laura's home to give her an informal test after having seen her perform at a school exhibition (the actual event took place in April 1884). "There's not much need to give you an examination," he says, "I heard you last night. You answered all the questions" (p. 303). Like her fictional counterpart, Wilder received a third-grade certificate, which allowed her to teach for the ensuing twelve months. The teacher's examination covered "orthography [spelling], reading, writing, arithmetic, geography, English language and grammar, and United States history." Holders of third-grade certificates

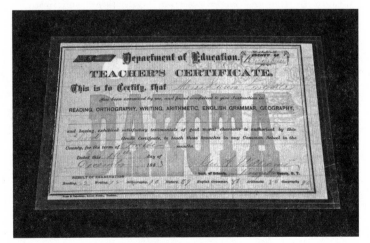

Laura Ingalls's teaching certificate, Dec. 10, 1883.
Laura Ingalls Wilder Historic Home and Museum

like Wilder's were not required to be certified in American history (Levisee, *Annotated Revised Codes*, p. 558). When fictionalizing the teacher's certificate in *Little Town on the Prairie* (p. 306), Wilder dropped the orthography category from her test results (perhaps she thought readers would not understand the term) and improved her history score—from 69 on the original to 98 on the fictional version—as well as her geography score—from 70 to 85. She also added "History" to the list of categories in which she was qualified to teach to emphasize Laura's outstanding performance at the exhibition. "School Exhibition," *DSL*, Mar. 29, 1884, and "Town and Country," *DSL*, Mar. 29, Apr. 12, 1884; Teacher's Certificate, Dec. 10, 1883.

83. *went out to Bouchie's the first of December.* This date is problematical. Wilder received her teaching certificate on December 10, 1883, and would not have been eligible to teach on December 1, which was a Saturday in 1883. Wilder may have started immediately after she received her certificate, Tuesday, December 11, or the following Monday, December 17, both of which are compatible with Wilder's *Missouri Ruralist* column about Almanzo driving her home for Christmas during her first term of school (*Little House Sampler*, p. 38). Wilder's outline for her last novel in the series noted, "Bouchie School to begin Jan. 1st" (LIW, "Prairie Girl" outline), which is consistent with the December 24, 1882, date on her fictional certificate.

84. *Marth and Charles Patterson.* Historical records reveal no school-aged children named Patterson or Harrison (the surname Wilder gives the pair in *These Happy Golden Years* [p. 16]) living in the Bouchie school district during the winter of 1882–1883 or 1883–1884.

85. *Clarence, Ruby and Tommy Bouchie.* These children were probably half-siblings of Louis. Their father, Joseph A. Bouchie, had two families. He married his first wife, Mary Ann Law, in 1858, and Louis was their firstborn, the oldest of six children. She died in 1870, and Joseph married Elizabeth Currier the following year. In 1880, the couple lived in Grundy County, Iowa, with five children of their own and one of his daughters from his previous marriage. By the time Joseph filed on his claim in Dakota Territory in early 1883, he and Elizabeth had two more children. Dakota Territory identified school-aged children as "over seven and under twenty years of age" (Levisee, *Annotated Revised Codes*, p. 574), so several Bouchie children would have been eligible, but only one, Clarence, who was about twelve, had a name that corresponded to Wilder's list. "Gilchrist Camera Family Tree"; "Town and Country," *DSL*, July 19, 1884.

86. *The school house was an abondened claim shanty.* Brandt, Brandt Revised, and Bye added that the schoolhouse was about half a mile away from Louis Bouchie's claim shanty, "with no road leading to it" (Brandt, p. 125). The claim shanty used for the Bouchie school during the winter of 1883–1884 probably belonged to homesteader David Gilbert, who built the structure in September 1883 but was away during most of the winter. Hicks, "Searching for the Brewster School," pp. 73–74.

87. *Mrs Bouchie was quiet and sullen, . . . and her little boy was crying.* Oliv Delilah Isenberger Morrison, who is the model for Mrs. Brewster in *These Happy Golden Years*, moved to Kingsbury County a few months after Louis Bouchie, and the two of them filed on adjoining quarter sections of land on the same day in November 1882 (Louis had earlier filed a preemption claim about three miles northeast of this second one). Like Louis, Oliv (Olive in census records), who had a two-year-old-son, had moved to Dakota Territory from Grundy County, Iowa. It is unclear whether she was widowed or divorced, but in 1880, she was a married woman living with her parents. Homestead records indicate that she paid Louis to build her a claim shanty during the final weeks of 1882 and that they were married on Christmas Day of that year. In March 1883, the Bouchies moved into her improved shanty, which was situated on the property line dividing their adjoining claims, and their first child, Leonard, was born there in October 1883. "My house and my husband's are the same," Oliv explained in 1889, "and is built on both claims and across the line, and my part of the house is on my claim, and his on his claim" (Final Certificate #5537). This arrangement allowed the pair to meet the residency requirements and prove up on both claims simultaneously. It also gave them more room in which to board a teacher, and it fits the description of the Brewster house, which "looked like two claim shanties put together. . . . The partition stood under the peak of the roof, and divided the house into two equal parts" (*HGY*, pp. 4, 6). The fragmentary evidence about the Bouchies' first two years in Dakota Territory offers conflicting insights into the questions surrounding Wilder's real-life experiences. If Wilder taught the Bouchie school when she was fifteen during the winter of 1882–1883, Oliv and Louis would not have been living in the appropriate school district or in this two-part house. On the other hand, in all versions of this story, Wilder described only one young child in the Bouchie household—he is unnamed in *Pioneer Girl*, but Wilder identified him as a toddler named Johnny in the novel (p. 8). In late 1883, when Wilder was sixteen, Johnny Morrison would have been three and his half-brother Leonard Bouchie would have been an infant. It is tempt-

the school-house. After breakfast I walked the half mile through the snow carrying my dinner bucket, and at night walked back again.

Mrs Bouchie was never pleasant, she was always sullen and seldom spoke. Breakfast was a silent meal and I was glad to be gone all day.

At night, before bed time, I had a refuge in my books for I was keeping up with my class, still in school. Sometimes after I went to bed, I could hear Mrs Bouchie raging, seemingly perfectly able to talk.

At school, Martha and Charles were good but stupid. Martha studied, but Charles would sit day-dreaming with his book open before him and his eyes on the pages that I knew he was not seeing. In class he did just well enough to pass. I tried my best to get him interested in his studies, but I couldn't wake him up. They were both taller than I. Martha was fourteen and Charles sixteen years old.

I much prefered Clarence Bouchie who, though a mischievous, trouble making boy, was at least awake and quick. He could learn his lessons well and still have plenty of time to pinch Ruby, stick a pin in Charles and pull Martha's hair and he did them all. My sympathies were strongly with him and the pin.

He would do whatever I asked him but always his manner was a rebelion. It said plainly that he did not have to mind a teacher who was smaller and younger than he. For he was already sixteen and I would not be sixteen for two months yet.

Struggling with these problems at school, going back at night to the Bouchies and the unpleasantness there[,] a week passed.

All day Friday I couldn't keep my thoughts off the next two days, How could I endure Saturday and Sunday all of the two long days with Mrs Bouchie?

I dreaded to dismiss school, but when we were putting on our wraps, there was a jingle of sleigh bells and a prancing team hitched to a cutter (small sleigh)[88] drove up to the door.

Clarence rushed out and then put his head back to shout, "Some one after you teacher!"

To my surprise it was the youngest Wilder boy and when I came

ing to dismiss the absent infant in both *Pioneer Girl* and *These Happy Golden Years* as a simple editorial change, Wilder's decision to streamline her story, but there is no evidence to suggest that Wilder worried about identifying too many characters in her memoir. Final Certificate #5537 and #9256; "Gilchrist Camera Family Tree"; Hicks, "In Search of the Brewster School," pp. 71–73.

88. *a cutter (small sleigh).* In *These Happy Golden Years,* Almanzo tells Laura that he made this cutter himself, and it is "smaller than the boughten ones. It's only five feet long, and twenty-six inches wide at the bottom. Makes it snugger to ride in," he adds, "and lighter for the horses to pull" (p. 32). In a letter to his daughter dating from 1937, Almanzo Wilder included drawings to illustrate the differences between a bobsled and a cutter. Essentially, he said, a cutter is a sled with a buggy body, and a "box cutter . . . is all on a curve both sides. . . . The body curves out side ways as well as front & back." Sometimes, he continued, they did not even weigh a hundred pounds, "so you see a good team can take them over the snow mighty easy" (AJW to RWL, May 12, 1937, Box 13, file 193, Lane Papers).

Almanzo Wilder's drawing of a cutter, 1937.
Herbert Hoover Presidential Library and Museum

89. *home over Sunday and fully intended to stop as soon as my school was out.* Wilder's phrase "home over Sunday," used here for the second time, and the situation she described in *Pioneer Girl* inspired Lane's short story "Home over Saturday." Published in the *Saturday Evening Post* on September 11, 1937, Lane's story fictionalized her mother's experiences with the Bouchies and her father's weekend rescues that brought Wilder home over Saturday. These same elements provide the tension in chapters 2 through 10 (pp. 11–88) of *These Happy Golden Years*, the last novel published in Wilder's lifetime.

90. *['']I am going with you.'. . . "Well!" he answered. "It is . . . anyway."* Wilder gave Laura essentially the same speech in *These Happy Golden Years*, but she deep-

out the door, he asked me if I would like to go home for over Sunday. Would I like to go home!

We drove to Bouchie's where I got the things I wished to take with me and then away over the snowy road with the horses dancing and the sleigh bells ringing. In an hour we were at home to the surprise of the home folks.

As he left me Wilder, as Pa called him, said he would take me back to school Sunday afternoon.

So after Saturday and Sunday were short days and the drive back to Bouchie's was much too short, for every step of the horses took me nearer there.

After that, for two months, "teacher's beau," as Clarance called him never failed to be waiting outside the school house when school closed on Friday night, to take me home, nor to bring me back on Sunday afternoon.

I felt that he was going to a lot of trouble and that the long, cold drives could be no pleasure to him. We were so bundled up to keep warm that talking was not easy. I was no good at talking anyway and with a thick hood over my ears and a thick brown veil over my face I was no beautiful thing to look at.

Much as I wanted to go home, I did not want to be unfair nor deceitful. I was only going with him for the sake of being home over Sunday and fully intended to stop as soon as my school was out.[89]

So one day on the road I took fast hold on my courage and told him so. ['']I am going with you,' I said, 'because I want to get home, but when I am home to stay, I'll not go with you any more. So if you want to stop now and save yourself these long, cold drives, you can.'

"Well!" he answered. "It is quite a while before school will be out anyway."[90]

It was cold, though it was nothing like the Hard Winter, still it was bad enough. The thermometer ranged from twenty to thirty below zero.[91]

On a Thursday morning, Mr Bouchie came running back from building the fire at the school house. He dashed into the house, tore off his boots and began violently rubbing his feet, which had nearly

ened the emotional resonance by adding: "The words sounded horrid to her as she said them. They were abrupt and rude and hateful. At the same time, a dreadful realization swept over her, of what it would mean if Almanzo did not come for her again" (p. 62). Wilder further enhanced the drama by placing the episode just before one of the most disturbing scenes of the series, Mrs. Brewster and the butcher knife. Laura believes she will have to endure the terrors of the Brewster household without a break until the end of the school term. Almanzo's fictional response to Laura's declaration is subtle and leaves Laura convinced that he will no longer drive her home: "After a startled moment, Almanzo said slowly, 'I see.' There was no time to say more" (p. 62).

91. *The thermometer ranged from twenty to thirty below zero.* Various records suggest that the winters of 1882–1883 and 1883–1884 were extremely cold. Weather records from Huron, roughly thirty miles west, indicate that high temperatures did not rise above zero and low temperatures ranged from twenty to thirty below during parts of both winters. Beginning in 1884, the De Smet newspaper kept a monthly tally of weather conditions, possibly to substantiate its prediction that it was going to be a hard winter. "The Indian and old trapper's sign of a winter of deep snow—large muskrat houses—is unusually conspicuous," the editor had reported in October. "They tower up all over the marshes like young haystacks" ("Town and Country," *DSL*, Oct. 20, 1883). Wilder had used this same image in *The Long Winter*, when Laura points out to Pa that he has missed a haycock. "That isn't a haycock, Half-Pint; that's a muskrat house," he says. Pa, a seasoned trapper, recognizes that the thick walls of the muskrat den indicate a hard winter to come (pp. 10–12). The records kept by the *Leader* show that January 1884 was especially harsh, with a six-day cold snap in which temperatures did not rise above zero. Barb Boustead, "These Happy Golden Years, Chapter 8"; "Weather Report," *DSL*, Feb. 2, 1884.

frozen before he could get home. He forbid my going to school at all that day. When I wanted to go for fear the children would come, he said he had made a fire and if they did come, they could get warm, but he didn't think anyone would come on such a day.

The next morning was still frightfully cold but everyone was at school as usual.

All day the snow blew low across the prairie and toward night it grew colder still.

I did not have any hope of going home, the storm was so bad and the cold so intense and I wanted so much to get away for Mrs Bouchie had made up for being a little pleasanter the day before, by being in an awful temper at breakfast time.

With my mind made up to staying, I did not listen for the sleigh bells as I always did when four oclock drew near. I usually heard them while they were still some distance away, but disappointment had so dulled my hearing that I was completely taken by surprise when there was a dashing jingle of bells at the door and as we all looked out of the window, Clarance Bouchie exclaimed aloud, "That Wilder is a bigger fool than I even thought he was!"

It lacked twenty minutes to four but I said, 'Put away your books! School is dismissed.[']

It was too cold for anyone or the horses to stay outside waiting. It was growing colder every minute and the sooner everyone got home, the better.

When we stopped at the house Mr Bouchie tried to dissuade me from going, but Mr Wilder was going back and I would go with him if I froze for it. There was danger at that of the storm thickening and our becoming lost.

I was dressed warmly, high necks and long sleeves in both under-clothes and dress, two warm petticoats woolen stockings, and high shoes. I wore a heavy coat, a thick, wool, knit hood, two thicknesses of woolen veil over my face the ends wrapped and tied around my neck.

There was a heavy blanket under the buffalo robe over our laps and tucked tightly in around us and a lighted lantern underneath among our feet which added a great deal to the warmth.

And so we started into the north facing the wind.

There was no loitering on the way to make the drive last longer. We drove as fast as possible and not hurt the horses but had to be careful of that for they were trotting into the wind.

About every two miles the frost from the horses' breath would become frozen over their nostrils so they could not breathe. Then we would stop and Mr Wilder would climb out into the cold and the snow, cover each nose with his hands an instant and then he could strip the ice of[f], climb back into the cutter and we would go on. At times he would slip one hand beneath the robes, out of the wind into the warmth from the lantern, for a few minutes.

It seemed that the twelve and a half miles would never end that day.

Mr Wilder told me on the way that he had hesitated to go, but that, as his team stood blanketed at a hitching post in town, Cap Garland had passed him, looked at the team and simply saying, "God hates a coward," had passed on. Then he had taken the blankets off the horses and gone.

It was forty-five below zero when he left town. Thermometors were frozen so they wouldn't tell how cold it was soon after he started and it grew colder steadily after that, and the wind blew harder.[92]

I had sensed no feeling of cold for some time before we got home and when Mr Wilder would anxiously enquire if I were cold would answer 'No!'[93] but when I tried to get out of the cutter at [the] door of home, I would have fallen if Ma had not caught me and could not walk into the house without help.

(There used to be an old story of a man who found his sweetheart frozen to death at the end of some such drive)[94]

The next week the county suprentendent visited my school.

He sat by the red hot stove while snow drifted in through the cracks in the wall. He listened to the children recite their lessons. He saw me let one after the other come to the fire, when they would ask, "Please may I come and warm?"

Then as he was about to go, when I asked him if he had anything to say, he said, "Yes!"

92. *It was forty-five below zero. . . . and the wind blew harder.* The Bye manuscript reads, "No one ever knew how cold it was that day. After registering forty two degrees below zero, the mercury in the thermometers shrank into the little bulbs at the bottom and did not register any more. After that it seemed to grow steadily colder, and the wind blew harder" (Bye, p. 157). In *These Happy Golden Years*, Almanzo says, "The mercury was all down in the bulb, below forty, and the wind blowing colder every minute" (p. 77). Mercury freezes or becomes solid at –37.89 Fahrenheit, making it impossible for Almanzo to know exactly how cold it was. Meteorologist Barb Boustead has suggested Friday, January 4, 1884, as a likely date for this fiercely cold ride. The *De Smet Leader* reported that the morning temperature on January 4 had been thirty-nine below zero, and at 3 P.M., it was thirty-four degrees below zero with a strong northwest wind. Other candidates would be Christmas week 1883, when temperatures dipped below minus twenty degrees for a number of days, or early February 1884. Boustead, "These Happy Golden Years, Chapter 8"; "Weather Report"; "Town and Country," Dec. 29, 1883.

93. *I had sensed no feeling of cold . . . would answer 'No!'* In Bye, Wilder added: "It surprised me that I was so comfortable, but this I supposed was because of the heavy buffalo robe, the blanket, the lantern and my many thicknesses of warm woolen clothes. Watching the snow anxiously, I saw it rising higher in the air and knew that we might be lost in the storm if we did not reach town soon. But I had confidence that Mr. Wilder would do all that could be done, and in any case no good would be done by worrying" (p. 157). In the novel, Laura grows used to the cold and begins to fall asleep. Almanzo jolts her awake, and Laura "knew what he meant. If you go to sleep in such cold, you freeze to death" (*HGY*, p. 74).

94. *(There used to be an old story . . . at the end of some such drive).* The revised versions of *Pioneer Girl* referred to a song instead of a story and included its lyrics. The Bye version begins: "We used to sing a ballad about such a drive. It was called Young

Charles and Charlotte, and it must have been written by someone who knew winter weather. It went like this:

"Her bonnet and her cloak were on, she jumped into the sleigh,
And away they rode into the storm and over the desolate way.

There's music in the sound of bells as over the drifts they go,
What a squeaking and screeching the runners make as they cleave the frozen snow.

Such a night as this I never saw, the reins I scarce can hold.
Young Charlotte replied in these few words, I am exceedingly cold.

He cracked his whip, he urged his team much faster than before,
Until five other weary miles in silence they passed o'er.

Says Charles, How fast the snow and ice is gathering on my brow.
Young Charlotte replied in these few words, I am getting warmer now.

And away they rode o'er the frozen drifts through the frozen air of night
Until they reached the village inn, the ballroom was in sight.

He drove to the door, Young Charles jumped out and offered his hand to her,
Why do you sit like a monument that has not power to stir?

He asked her once, he asked her twice, but she never said a word,
He asked her for her hand again, but Young Charlotte never stirred.

He took her lily hand in his, it was cold and hard as stone,
He tore the bonnet from her face and the cold stars on her shone.

Then quickly to the lighted hall her lifeless cor[p]se they bore,
Young Charlotte lying stiff in death will speak to me no more.

He twined his arms around her neck, he kissed her marble brow,
And his thoughts went back to when she said, I am getting warmer now (Bye, p. 158).

Known as "Young Charlotte" or "Fair Charlotte," the song's origins are not entirely clear, but it is likely that Seba Smith's poem from the early 1840s, "A Corpse Going to a Ball," inspired the ballad's lyrics. Maine Folklife Center, "Young Charlotte."

He rose to the full highth of his six feet, while my heart stood still. Had I done anything wrong? (After all I was'n't sixteen yet)

Then with his head almost touching the ceiling he smiled at us all and said, "Whatever you do keep your feet warm!" And with another smile and a handshake he was gone.

The days were so cold that I had the children crowd on the front seats, or stand by the stove to keep warm, moving around as they pleased, just so they were quiet and studied their lessons during school hours.

And now surprisingly Clarance Bouchie began to behave well and even go out of his way to be kind to me, sharpening my pencils and fixing the fire without being asked.

He had been making me trouble from the begining until it seemed as though I must punish him or have the school ruined.

Every week, when I went home, Pa would ask me about him and when I would threaten to punish Clarance in some way, Pa would say I'd better be patient, try not to tell him to do things, unless I felt that he would do as I asked and just manage him. "For," Pa would say, "you can't whip him, he is bigger than you. There is no other way you can punish him for he wouldn't have to take a punishment of any kind. Better just manage!"[95]

So I had done my best and to my surprise had made a friend of him and a sort of partner. For instance at first he often would not study the whole lesson and at recitation time would say "I didn't study that. The lesson was too long," when I knew that it was not.

I learned to assign his lesson and then say, 'or is that too long Clarance? Perhaps it is and better take only to here. I really don't think you could learn so far as I first said.' And he would exclaim, "Oh yes I can teacher." He had now gotten to the point where he would add a little more to my first suggestion and learn it too, to prove that he could. This is just a sample of how I handled him.

Pa would laugh when I told him these things and say "I knew you could manage him if you tried."

If it had only been pleasant at Bouchie's I would not have been so terribly homesick as I was.

At first every night I counted the days of school that had gone by.

95. *Better just manage!"* Wilder used this phrase as the basis for the chapter "Managing" (pp. 53–59) in *These Happy Golden Years*, where Ma, as a former schoolteacher, also provides Laura with advice on how to manage Clarence. "I'd give way to Clarence," Ma says, "and not pay any attention to him. . . . Clarence'll come around" (p. 54). Brandt Revised (pp. 91–92) and Bye (p. 158) do not describe Clarence's academic progress but jump directly to the episode with Mrs. Bouchie and the butcher knife.

Picture copyright 1953 by Garth Williams, copyright © renewed 1981 by Garth Williams. Used by permission of HarperCollins Publishers

96. *waked by Mrs Bouchie screaming in fury. . . . I lay awake the rest of the night.* In leading up to this climactic episode ("A Knife in the Dark," pp. 60–68) in *These Happy Golden Years*, Wilder included more scenes that dramatize the fictional Mrs. Brewster's bitterness and disturbing behavior. Her rants, which usually begin at night, are directed at her husband, but Laura realizes that they are also directed at her, "Mrs. Brewster wanted her to hear. . . . it was a sound that enjoyed hurting people" (p. 22). Neither in the novel nor in *Pioneer Girl* did Wilder attempt to explain the woman's behavior. When Lane adapted the material for her short story "Home over Saturday," however, she did provide an explanation, adapting an incident from later in *Pioneer Girl* that had nothing to do with the Bouchies. Lane's protagonist, Mrs. Hite, is suffering from depression brought on by the loss of two little boys during a tornado. While it is an interesting juxtaposition of Wilder's material, this fictional explanation offers little help in understanding the real Mrs. Bouchie's behavior. Oliv Bouchie's marriage survived until

Then, when half the time had passed, I began counting the other way and every night would say to myself, 'only so many days left.'

There were only eleven more days to go when at night I was waked by Mrs Bouchie screaming in fury. "You kicked me," she screamed, "You kicked me."

"No I didn't," Mr Bouchie answered. "I didn't kick you. I only pushed you off with my foot, but go put up that butcher knife or I will!"

I peeped between the curtains, I was so terrified I must see, and Mr Bouchie lay on his back on the bed, with one foot out from under the covers. He seemed to be lying quietly but I could see that every muscle was tensed.

Mrs Bouchie stood beside the bed with a large butcher knife in her hand. This was the picture for just an instant, then she turned and took the butcher knife to the kitchen, muttering a jumble of words as she went. I lay awake the rest of the night.[96]

And this was one thing I didn't tell when I went home for badly as I hated to go out there again, there was only one more week and I wanted to finish my school.[97]

Things were still very wrong as I saw at once when I went into the house on getting back that last Sunday night. Mrs Bouchie didn't speak to me, the little boy had been crying and Mr Bouchie was out at the barn. He didn't come in until supper was almost ready and when he had his outdoor things off and sat down by the stove, Mrs Bouchie snatched her shawl from the nail where it hung and went out into the cold slamming the door behind her.

The minutes went by and I grew uneasy wondering if she would stay out until she froze or if she had gone at that time of night to some neighbors leaving us alone and if so what, for I knew that would be a dreadful thing.

Mr Bouchie seemed unconcerned, played with the little boy and after some time finished making the supper and put it on the table. I was making myself as small as possible pretending to study my history, but when Mr Bouchie said to come to supper, I sat up at the table. When supper was nearly over Mrs Bouchie came in, hung up her shawl and stood by the stove. She had been gone an hour. I

Louis died in Kingsbury County in 1894. She remarried about three years later and died in 1919, after her fourth marriage. She is buried in De Smet. RWL, "Home over Saturday," pp. 7, 53; Final Certificate #9256.

97. *one more week and I wanted to finish my school.* In *These Happy Golden Years*, Wilder placed the knife episode before the cold ride with Almanzo to heighten the tension and make Laura's decisions more dramatic. Laura has similar feelings about finishing her school, but Wilder added the professional ramifications that she might face: "A teacher could not walk away and leave a term of school unfinished. If she did, she would not deserve another certificate, and no school board would hire her" (p. 82).

98. *Clarance was a fireman in Chicago . . . he died a hero.* This segment about Clarence Bouchie is baffling given what happened to his family in 1884. During that summer, Clarence and his mother, Elizabeth, and his older half-brother Isaac quarreled violently, and "Clarence threw a bone which struck Isaac in the face, producing lockjaw, from which he died" (*Daily Huronite*, Apr. 1, 1887). Three years later, Elizabeth Bouchie and Clarence were convicted of second-degree manslaughter. Wilder almost certainly would have been aware of this case, but she did not mention it in *Pioneer Girl*. Her reference to "the little house behind the church" places the visit from Clarence between August 1892 and July 1894, when Wilder, Almanzo, and Rose were living in De Smet after a brief stay in Florida and before moving to Missouri. It is possible that the real Clarence Bouchie visited De Smet in the early 1890s, but no record places him in Chicago shortly thereafter. He died in 1902, possibly as a result of a hunting accident, and is buried in De Smet. "Town and Country," DSL., July 17, 1884; Bouchie Case Records.

never knew what she was so furious about nor where she spent the hour, but Mr Bouchie appeared to be used to such spells.

I didn't rest well nights that last week, but the children were sorry to see me go when Friday night came and told me so. I enjoyed that ride home more than any before for I was going home to stay, but Mr Wilder was more silent than usual.

(I never heard of any of those school children when the[y] grew up, except Clarance. Many years later, when we were living in the little house behind the church, he came through town on his way home for a visit and Manly saw him. Clarance told Manly that he never appreciated until he was grown, how hard I tried to teach him something that winter, but that he had always been sorry he made it so hard for me. Clarance was a fireman in Chicago and soon after Manly saw him he died a hero,[98] saving people from a burning building)

DIAGRAM OF DE SMET, 1883

Diagram of central De Smet from the *De Smet News*, Sept. 22, 1883. *Redrawn by Steve Mayer. South Dakota Historical Society Press*

Don't forget the Date OF THE
Kingsbury Co. Agricultural Fair
AT DE SMET.
Sept. 26, 27, AND 28, 1883.

EMPIRE Lumber Co. C.E. Ely, Agent.
Office.

Youmans Bros. & Hodains
C. L. Dawley, Agent.
Lumber Yard!
Office.

Weona Mill Co. Warehouse. A. Graham, Agent.

Elevator, C.W. Seefeed. L.E. Sasse, Agent.

G. W. Vonhamm & Co. Flour, Salt and Seed. W. Fonger, Agent.

Dakota Central Railroad.   Water Tank.   Depot, Geo. R. Newman, Agent.

Engine | DeSmet Flour Mill. G.W. Elliott & Co.

Wind Mill.

Res.

FIRST STREET

Thomas Brothers
Real Estate & Loans
Abstracts of Titles.
Insurance in Reliable Companies.

PUBLIC SCHOOL

AVENUE | STREET | AVENUE | AVENUE

Exchange Hotel Stable

Exchange Hotel, Howland & Smith, Props.
Henry Hinz, Billiards.
T.B. Talbot, Shoes.
C.P. Barker, Restaurant.
Feed Store.
Waters & Anderson, Law and Land.
Kingsbury House, J. Sturgeon, Prop.
E.M. Harthorn & Son General Store.

Residence H.P. Hanson.

E. H. Couse, Hardware Co. Treasurer

Geo. Wilmarth & Co. General Store.
"Leader," Brown & Sherwood.
F.X. Schaub, Harness.
Residence Rev. P.L. Hooker.
Pierson & Cooley, Market.
E. R. Bennett, Groceries.
Geo. Morris, Paint.
Thomas Bros., Land.
E. McCray, Barber.
S. J. Johnson, Boots and Shoes.
Bank and P.O., J.H. Carroll, P.M.

F. A. Jordans, Blacksmith.
T.H. Johnson, Wagon Shop.
D. Floyd, Blacksmith.
Residence T.H. Johnson.
Residence A.A. Anderson.
Residence D. Floyd.

COURT HOUSE SQUARE

County Jail.

SECOND STREET

H. MERRILL,
DISTRICT AGENT DAKOTA
FIRE AND MARINE
Insurance Compn'y.

Congregational Church, costing $2,000. Edward Brown, Pastor

Residence E. H. Couse.

E. H. COUSE,
Hardware
AND
Agricul'tl Implem'ts

C.S.G. Fuller & Bro., Hardware.
Geo. C. Bradley, Drugs.
Loftus & Broadbent, General Store.
E.G. Davies, M.D. Office.
Thos. P. Power, Tailor
C.H. Tinkham, Furniture.
G.H. Scofield, Gen'l Store.
D.C. Noyes, General Store.
S.B. Owen & Son, Shoes and Livery.
Residence J.J. Shackley.
Residence Carey Bros.
Kingsbury Co. Bank, Thos. H. Ruth, Cash.

Residence C. P. Ingalls, Justice Peace.
Office Clerk of Courts in Postoffice.
L.E. Fellows, Farm Machinery.
J.B. Hall, Law, Office in News Building
Residence W.E. Whiting.
"News," Hopp & Macdonald, Eds.
Carey Bros., Farm Machinery.
Residence J.E. Howland.
Miss F.E. Bull, Mill'ry
John A. Owen, Law.

Boarding House, Mrs. M.F. Garland.
Residence C.B. Macdonald

Residence I.E. Sasse.

A. N. Waters.   A. A. Anderson.
WATERS & ANDERSON,
Law, Loan
AND LAND.
SPECIAL ATTENTION GIVEN TO DEEDED LANDS. IMPROVED FARMS FOR SALE OR RENT.
8,000 acres of choice farming lands for sale. Lots in DeSmet. Correspondence solicited.

THIRD STREET

C. S. G. Fuller & Brother.
HARDWARE, STOVES
Tinware and Farmers' Implements.
Walter A. Wood's Harvesters and Mowers

C. H. TINKHAM,
UndertakeR
AND DEALER IN FURNITURE, WALL PAPER
Carpets, Trunks, Valises, Etc.

SECOND | POINSET | CALUMET | JOLIET

Office W.E. Whiting, Register of Deeds.
V.V. Barnes, Probate Judge.
Lyngbye & Son, Blacksmith.

Residence A.N. Waters.
Residence O. Fonger.
Residence Fonger Bros.
Fonger Bros., Livery.

Residence A.S. Sherwood.

FONGER BROS.,
Livery, Sale & Feed Stable.
Barn at South End of Town, E.S.
V. V. BARNES,
Attorney AT Law

Dakota Territory, 1881–1888

The next day was bright and beautiful. The weather had moderated until it was only 20 below and there was hardly any wind.

Sleigh bells were ringing and laughing people in sleighs and cutters drove up and down the street while I sat at home looking out of the window. Home was a fine place to be, but I didn't want to stay exactly in the house all the time, not when everyone else was out sleigh riding.

Sunday afternoon was just as beautiful weather and again the bells were ringing and gay laughter floating on the wind.[1] I did want to be out with the others, but I had been away for two months, a long time at sixteen, and they all seemed to have forgotten me.

Mary Power and Cap Garland went by in a cutter built for two. I hadn't seen Cap for a long time. He might have taken me this once, I thought. There were Frank Harthorn and May Bird,[2] Alfred Ely and Laura Remington,[3] Fred Gilbert and Minnie Johnson,[4] Arthur Johnson and Hattie Dorchester.[5] They were all having such a good time while I sat at home and looked on until the afternoon was nearly gone.

It seemed as though I couldn't bear it any longer and when I heard a jingle of bells that stopped at the door I went quickly and opened it.

There stood the team, hitched to the same little cutter, with the same driver that had taken me so many times over the road to Bouchie's.

"Would you like to go sleigh riding?" asked the driver and I went as soon as I could put on my coat and hat, not the hood and veil.

It was only when we were will mixed with the gay crowd that I remembered and when I did, I laughed aloud with pure enjoyment of the joke even though it was on myself.

[']Why did you come for me,' I asked, 'when I told you out at Bouchie's that I wouldn't go with you after school was out?'

Cutter in the good old "sparking" days, Cedar Creek, D.T.
South Dakota State Historical Society

1. *Sleigh bells were ringing. . . . and gay laughter floating on the wind.* Newspapers document the prevalence of this wintertime activity in early De Smet. "The festive sleighbells have jingled numerously since the last snowfall, and have made us sigh for the days when we too were young and frisky," the De Smet editor reported, for example, on February 24, 1883. On January 12, 1884, he noted that the "unexpected good sleighing had brought out the most motley and amusing array of extemporaneous sleds and pungs [boxes on runners] ever seen. A pair of two by sixes, with a dry goods box spiked on top, seems to afford as much fun to the linear mile as the most elegant cutter" ("Town and County," *DSL*). Wilder built an entire chapter (Jingle Bells," pp. 89–94) in *These Happy Golden Years* around sleighing and Laura's delight in it.

2. *Frank Harthorn and May Bird.* By the fall of 1883, grocer Frank Harthorn and a partner were running a store in nearby Lake Preston, where Harthorn probably met Mabel K. Burd. She appears on the 1880 census as the only child of George (a cooper) and Samantha Burd. Mabel was roughly two years

older than Wilder. Frank and May were probably newlyweds during these sleigh rides. They married on October 28, 1883, in Lake Preston, and Frank dissolved his partnership there and moved the merchandise back to De Smet in March 1884. "Town and Country," *DSL*, Nov. 3, 1883, Mar. 15, 1884.

3. *Alfred Ely and Laura Remington*. Alfred Ely was the son of lumberman Charles E. Ely, who with his family came from Winona, Minnesota. The elder Ely worked as an agent for the Empire Lumber Company in De Smet and, in 1884, became a building contractor for area schoolhouses. He was also chairman of the new De Smet Board of Trade. His son Alfred was about five years younger than Wilder. Laura Remington is not easily identified and may also have been significantly younger. "Town and Country," *DSL*, Feb. 9, 23, Mar. 23, Apr. 19, 1884.

4. *Fred Gilbert and Minnie Johnson*. Fred Gilbert was about seventeen years old in the winter of 1884–1885 and part of a large family that had moved to Kingsbury County from Minnesota via Wisconsin. Minnie Johnson was a few years younger than Wilder.

5. *Arthur Johnson and Hattie Dorchester*. Arthur Johnson was Minnie's older brother. Hattie Dorchester was born in Illinois in the early 1860s, and her family had moved to Kingsbury County from Summersett, Iowa. Hattie was between four and five years older than Wilder. Her father, David W. Dorchester, sold horses in partnership with the Ruths. In May 1884, the Catholic church society "prevailed upon Miss Hattie Dorchester" to allow her name to be entered against another young woman in "a contest for a new dress bonnet." Votes cost ten cents apiece, and the proceeds went toward furnishing the new Catholic church ("Town and Country," *DSL*, May 31, 1884).

"I thought you'd have changed your mind and be ready to go by now, after watching the rest of the crowd so long," he answered.

'I fully intended not to go with you any more,' I said. 'I was going to stay home until some one else asked me, but now I'm here, what am I going to call you?[6] I'm tired of saying Mr Wilder and then explaining that I mean the youngest Wilder boy and the crowd will laugh at me if I call you Mr Wilder to them.[']

He told me his folks called him Manzo except his brother Roy who called him Mannie.

'Manzo is ugly', I said. [']I'll call you Manly like Roy does' and when he had told me of my mistake I said I would call him Manly anyway for Mannie was silly.

"And what shall I call you?" Manly asked. "I have a sister Laura[7] and I never did like the name. What is your second name."

So I said the old nursery rhyme, "Elizabeth Elispeth, Betsy and Bess went over the river to seek a birds nest. They found one with three eggs in. They each took one and left two in" and he said he would call me Bessie.[8]

We were going, with the crowd, the length of the street, around the circle on the prairie where the street ended, back down the length of the street around the circle at the other end and repeat, laughing and shouting from one sleigh to another, while sleigh bells rang their merry chimes, sleigh runners squeaked on the cold snow, the wind blew, but not too hard and we were happy and gay for it was only twenty below zero and the sun shone.[9]

On Monday I went back to school and found that I had gone ahead of my class in my studies, but I was glad to go over the lessons again with them. On pleasant Sunday afternoons there was always the sleigh ride, sometimes with Cap and Mary Mary in a two seated sleigh but more often by ourselves in the cutter, which Manly had made himself and that was the nicest one in town. The team he drove was the best too and much the prettiest, tall, slim, brown horses,[10] with slender legs and dainty feet, heads held high and proudly tossing as the sleigh bells sang.

Uncle Tom made us a surprise visit[11] this winter. He was the same dear Uncle Tom that I remembered in Wisconsin, a small, quiet,

6. *what am I going to call you?* Until this point in all versions of *Pioneer Girl*, Wilder referred to Almanzo as the Wilder boy or Mr. Wilder. This conscious creative decision in writing the manuscript gave their eventual exchange of names more dramatic weight, but it also reflected the conventions of the period, when the manner in which a man and woman addressed one another reflected the status of their relationship. For example, Alice Bower, a contemporary of Wilder's who lived in southern Dakota Territory, would not allow her beau to address her by her first name until he had proposed and she had accepted. *See* Nelson, *Sunshine Always*, p. 9. In contrast, the reader of the Little House series knows from the beginning that the younger Wilder boy is Almanzo even though Laura does not use the name. In *These Happy Golden Years*, Laura and Almanzo do not use nicknames for each other, although Nellie Oleson calls him "Mannie" later in the novel (p. 175), implying a deeper relationship than exists. The name "Almanzo" never occurs in the original *Pioneer Girl* manuscript, an oversight corrected in Brandt (p. 133).

7. *"I have a sister Laura.* Laura Ann Wilder was the oldest of James and Angeline Wilder's children. Born in 1844, she was almost thirteen years older than Almanzo. She was the first of her immediate family to move from Malone, New York, to Spring Valley, Minnesota, following an uncle to the area. She married Harrison Howard there in 1874. Laura Ann Wilder does not appear as a character in *Farmer Boy*, Wilder's novel about Almanzo's childhood. Anderson, *Story of the Wilders*, pp. 4–6; Miller, *Becoming*, p. 72.

8. *"Elizabeth Elispeth, Betsy and Bess. . . . he would call me Bessie.* Wilder's middle name was Elizabeth, which had many variations. She quoted the riddle to allow Almanzo to choose his own nickname for her. It is traditionally quoted as: "Elizabeth, Elspeth, Betsy, and Bess,/They all went together to seek a bird's nest./They found a bird's nest with five eggs in,/They all took one, and left four in" (Wheeler, *Mother Goose Melodies*, p. 34). The Bye version does not include this part of the scene, nor Almanzo's de-

Wilder family. Left to right, Royal, Almanzo, James (front), Perley (front), Laura, Angeline (front), Eliza Jane, and Alice (front). *Laura Ingalls Wilder Historic Home and Museum*

cision to call Wilder "Bessie" (p. 160). The name stuck, and Lane, too, often called Wilder "Mama Bess."

9. *sleigh bells rang their merry chimes, . . . for it was only twenty below zero and the sun shone.* In *These Happy Golden Years*, Laura is so happy that she breaks into song, and other voices join her in singing "Jingle Bells" (pp. 92, 94). An item from the *De Smet Leader* on December 29, 1883, echoed her words, "Sleigh-bells fill the wintry air with melody by spells." The editor also noted, "Mercury has occupied the lower story of the thermometer much of the time for a few days past" ("Town and Country," Dec. 29, 1883).

10. *the prettiest, tall, slim, brown horses.* In *These Happy Golden Years*, Wilder identified Almanzo's horses as Prince and Lady (p. 92).

11. *Uncle Tom made us a surprise visit.* "Mr. T. L. Quiner, of Fountain City, Wis., arrived in De Smet this week with a carload of lumber, with which he proposes to build a store," the *De Smet Leader* reported on December 12, 1883 ("Town and Country"). Quiner, who worked for Laird, Norton Lumber Company, stayed for a week and may have visited De Smet to explore the lumber market in the area and engage in some speculative building. By the end of April 1884, his brother-in-law Charles Ingalls was building a house for him on Third Street, which, when completed, "will be occupied by liveryman Pierson" (ibid., May 5, 1884). Wilder wrote more about the visit in Brandt Revised (pp. 94–95) and Bye (pp. 162–63), where Uncle Tom recounts his trip to the Black Hills in western Dakota Territory with the 1874 Gordon party (Appendix C). When Wilder was planning her last novels, Lane worried about introducing a new uncle and asked about substituting Uncle George Ingalls, whose personality had so impressed Laura in *Little House in the Big Woods*. Wilder wrote back, "There are records of that first party of white men in the Black Hills and there was no Ingalls among them. To make it historically correct, it should be Uncle Tom" (RWL to LIW and LIW to RWL, [1938], Box 13, file 194, Lane Papers). Historical accuracy prevailed, and Uncle Tom appears in *These Happy Golden Years* (pp. 105–10).

kind man with a pleasant smile that made me feel at home with him. It didn't seem reasonable that for years his business had been handling log drives and the rough men who made them on the Mississippi river.

But he handled both fearlessly. Once although unable to swim, he had plunged in among the floating logs and by clinging to a log had dragged an injured man out of the water to safety.

He still looked young and Manly[,] stopping for me on Sunday afternoon, seeing him through the door asked feroceously as soon as we were in the sleigh "Who is that young fellow?"

Mary Power and I were delighted and laughed at Manly as we drove away.

This was one of the times we were in the two seated sleigh with Cap and Mary on the front seat.

It was a jolly ride. We teased each other and laughed and joked. Finally Cap began pulling the hairpins out of Mary's hair to her consternation, for Mary had hardly any hair of her own and wore a switch.[12] With too many pins out it would surely drop off. When Mary could not stop him and I saw what was going to happen, I picked up a hard piece of snow, that had landed in the sleigh from the horses flying feet, and threw it past Cap's shoulder hitting one of the horses. Then both Cap's hands were needed on the reins and he had something to think about besides hairpins. (Local color)[13]

When I came back from Bouchie's I had rather hoped to leave Manly and go with Cap, but when one day Cap drove up to the door and asked me to go sleigh riding I discovered that I didn't want to make the change, so I told him I would go if he would take Mary too and he did and that was that.[14] Then Arthur Johnson took me home from church one night when Manly was not there and I found I didn't want to go with him either.

So I kept on going with Manly and people began to take it seriously. Rebecca Newhall[15] told me at school one day that her Mother said I'd "marry Wilder yet, for he meant business. No old batchelor would go with a young girl like that unless he did."

Becky Newhall's father kept the first Leghorn hens[16] I ever saw. They were small and brown, looked like birds and laid very, very

12. *and wore a switch*. A switch is a hairpiece. In *These Happy Golden Years*, Wilder explained, "if Mary lost any more hairpins, her beautiful large knot of hair would come off" (p. 112).

13. *(Local color)*. "Local color" is a literary term that applies to writing that focuses on the unique speech, dress, habits, and mannerisms of a specific geographic region. It is usually linked with the rise of American realism in fiction and dates from the late nineteenth century. One of the most important practitioners in the region was Hamlin Garland, who was also homesteading in Dakota Territory in 1883–1884. In an important essay on the topic, he wrote: "Local color in fiction. . . . is the native element, the differentiating element. It corresponds to the endless and vital charm of individual peculiarity. . . . Literature would die of dry rot if it chronicled the similarities only, or even largely" (*Crumbling Idols*, p. 57). Gish, "Hamlin Garland's Dakota," pp. 198–200.

14. *I would go if he would take Mary too and he did and that was that*. In May 1884, Mary Power was teaching the junior class at "the first regular Catholic Sunday school" ("Town and Country," *DSL*, May 24, 1884). A year later, she took the lead role in the De Smet Dramatic Company's spring play, showing "talent of a superior order" (ibid., Mar. 28, 1885). In *These Happy Golden Years*, Laura learns that Mary Power is "going with a new clerk in Ruth's bank" (p. 183), which may be one reason why Cap Garland at last came knocking on Wilder's door. Mary's real-life clerk was Edwin P. Sanford, who had been born in Prairie City, Illinois, in 1865. In 1884, he took a position as bookkeeper in the Kingsbury County Bank in De Smet and eventually became a stockholder and cashier. The couple did not marry until 1890. They lived across from Charles and Caroline Ingalls until the early 1900s. The Sanfords had no children. In 1907, they moved to Bellingham, Washington, where Mary died in 1929 at the age of sixty-three. *Ingalls Family of De Smet*, p. 40; "Washington, Deaths"; Terranna, "Mary Power," pp. 85–86.

15. *Rebecca Newhall*. A census search for Rebecca Newhall proved unsuccessful, but a farmer named F. W.

Newhall advertised for a farmhand in the *De Smet Leader* in 1883. "Town and Country," Mar. 3, 1883.

16. *Leghorn hens*. In 1925, Lane wrote, "For thirty years my mother has been a servant to hens" (*Little House Sampler*, p. 129). In fact, when Wilder moved to the Missouri Ozarks in 1894, a coop of squawking hens went with her. Wilder launched her professional writing career with a poultry column for the *St. Louis Star Farmer* and, according to a *Missouri Ruralist* profile, was able to get "eggs in the winter when none of her neighbors gets any" (Case, "Let's Visit Mrs. Wilder," in *Little House Sampler*, p. 7). Leghorn chickens originated in Italy and were brought to the United States in the early nineteenth century. They are prized for their egg production. Hens usually weigh between four and five pounds; roosters are slightly heavier. RWL, *LHT*, p. 16; Hill, *Laura Ingalls Wilder*, p. 96; Cheryl Tuttle to Hill, May 13, 2013.

small eggs, so small that the merchants objected to their size in buying them. Mr Newhall answered in his whining voice, "I know they are small but they lay so many of them.["]

The teacher at school was a man named Seeley.[17] He was a very good teacher, but made one feel that he was not quite clean.

It was a habit of his to chew the end of his pointer as he sat listening to recitations. At intervals as he felt the urge, he would run the pointer inside his collar and down, sometimes almost its length to scratch his back, then withdraw it and resume chewing the point.

We girls grew more and more disgusted, until one of us proposed that we doctor the pointer.

So one day we came back early at noon each bringing something unpleasant to the taste. My contribution was cayenne pepper.

We put all these things into the little kettle of water kept on the heating stove, stirred up the fire then held the end of the pointer in the mess and boiled it.

We had it dried off and back in its place, the kettle emptied and refilled with clear water, when Mr Seeley came.

It was not long before he put the end of the pointer in his mouth, rolling it around his mouth and chewing it. He took it out of his mouth quickly, spat on the floor and looked at the point. Then he touched it experimentally with his tongue, looked up quickly at me where I was innocently diagraming a sentence on the blackboard, spat again and laid the pointer down.

Cousin Alice and her husband Arthur Whiting made us a weeks visit. We had not seen Alice since we left the Zumbro river to go to Iowa.

She was much as she used to be[,] like Mary very quiet and sober. Arthur was very pleasant. Alice and Ella had married brothers Arthur and Lie Whiting. They lived near Mitchell,[18] sixty miles south of De Smet.

We were having good reports of Mary. She had been very happy in her college life ever since she had gone there. She could write very well in the usual way and also in Braille, a system of writing,[19] through a slate or frame divided into squares; by making raised dots

17. *The teacher at school was a man named Seeley*. In 1880, Willard Seelye was a twenty-five-year-old married schoolteacher living in Fillmore, Minnesota. Once again, Wilder's chronological reconstruction of events is faulty. Seelye taught school in De Smet during the winter of 1881–1882, preceding Eliza Jane Wilder. He, his wife, and a nineteen-year-old son were still living in De Smet in 1900, but by then Seelye was in the insurance business. During the summer of 1884, he did a "big business" insuring crops against hail ("Town and Country," *DSL*, Aug. 2, 1884). The revised *Pioneer Girl* manuscripts do not contain this episode. Records of the Kingsbury County Superintendent of Schools, p. 55.

18. *Cousin Alice and her husband. . . . Arthur and Lie Whiting. They lived near Mitchell*. Alice Ingalls, Peter's daughter, married Arthur S. Whiting in 1881 in Wabasha, Minnesota, and they had five children. Her sister Ella married Leslie Lee Whiting (Wilder described their visit to De Smet later in *Pioneer Girl*) and had four children. Mitchell, D.T., was on the rival Chicago, Milwaukee & St. Paul Railroad. Both couples eventually moved to southern California. In *These Happy Golden Years*, Laura immediately recognizes Alice, who "was so much like Mary" (p. 141). When she was planning her final novels, Wilder intended to have both cousins "and their husbands come visiting in the last book" (LIW to RWL, Aug. 17, 1938), but she must have changed her mind; only Alice and Arthur visit the fictional family. "Alice Josephine Ingalls."

19. *Braille, a system of writing*. Louis Braille developed the raised-dot, touch reading system for the blind in the early 1820s while he was a student at the National Institute for Blind Youth in Paris. "200 Years."

20. *Mrs McKee, wife of the man who ran the lumber yard.*
James and Martha McKee along with their eight-
year-old daughter, Mary, were living in De Smet by
1880. His occupation was listed as dry-goods dealer.
In *These Happy Golden Years*, Pa describes the
McKees simply as "nice folks" (p. 115). In Bye, this
section opens with the sentence, "In March I had
my second ride on a train" (p. 164).

21. *Manchester.* Manchester, about nine miles west of
De Smet, was established in 1881 as another stop
on the Dakota Central railroad. On August 4, 1883,
the *De Smet Leader* reported, "Manchester village
is humping itself right along these days. It will be
a town in fact as well as name very soon" ("Town
and Country"). Manchester remained a small South
Dakota town until June 24, 2003, when a tornado
destroyed it.

22. *A family must not be away . . . not get their deed
from the government.* In Bye, Wilder added, "As
the settlers in Dakota said, 'Uncle Sam bets us 160
acres against $14.50 that we can't live on the land
five years'" (p. 164). The initial filing fee on a homestead was fourteen dollars, with a residency requirement of six months each year for five years. Wilder
expanded on this idea in *These Happy Golden Years*.
"Whoever makes these laws ought to know that
a man that's got enough money to farm, has got
enough to buy a farm," the fictional Mrs. McKee
complains. "If he hasn't got money, he's got to earn
it, so why do they make a law that he's got to stay on
a claim, when he can't? . . . If women were voting
and making laws, I believe they'd have better sense"
(p. 119). The McKees, however, had actually filed on
a tree claim in April 1883, which James McKee pre-
empted and paid for before the first of November.
On October 27, 1883, the *De Smet Leader* reported:
"J. W. McKee, of Manchester, came to the county
seat on Thursday to 'prove up,' and . . . he expects
soon to remove to Pierre" ("Town and Country").
Wilder could only have stayed with Mrs. McKee on
the claim during the spring/summer of 1883. Cleaveland and Linsenmayer, *Charles Ingalls*, p. 3; Final
Certificate #4956.

in different orders in the squares with a stylus. This writing the blind read with their fingers as they did the raised print of their books.

Ma and I were busy after school and saturdays now making some new clothes to send her and a Mrs McKee, wife of the man who ran the lumber yard,[20] was helping us. Mrs Mc Kee did a great deal of sewing for other people and I often helped her, so that we got to be very good friends.

Mr Mc Kee had taken a homestead near Manchester,[21] the next town west and by spring the family must go live on it or they would lose it. A family must not be away from their homestead for more than six months or they could not get their deed from the government.[22]

Mr Mc Kee would have to stay with his lumber business, but Mrs McKee said, if I would go with her, she and Mary, her ten year old girl, would go and live on the claim.

It was arrainged that we would go early in March. As we got on the train on our way to Manchester, the brakeman who helped us on kept hold of my arm[,] guided me to a seat and sat down beside me saying, "Hullo Laura! How are you?" I looked at him and when he smiled I knew him. He was Will Barnes from Walnut Grove,[23] whom I hadn't seen since we left.

Mrs Mc Kee, Mary and I would have to stay in the hotel at Man-chester until her things could be hauled by team from the depot to the claim. We found we would have to wait all day and the next night before we could get a teamster to take them.

He sat with us at the supper table that night and was so overcome by the presence of two strange women that he could hardly eat.

In his anxiety to show good table manners, he spread a whole large slice of bread with butter, then laid it in his plate, cut it up with his knife and fork and shoveled the pieces into his mouth with the knife. As he worried at it his plate worked nearer and nearer to the edge of the table and while I was torn with a desire to warn him, it over-balanced as, with both elbows up, he cut down on the bread and plate and bread fell into his lap.

To say that his face was crimson doesn't tell it, and knowing

23. *Will Barnes from Walnut Grove*. A census search for a Will Barnes in Redwood County, Minnesota, proved unsuccessful. There was, however, a W. J. Barnes in De Smet from 1883 onward, and in 1884, a Will Barnes erected "a small building south of Ingall's house" for use as a machinery office ("Town and Country," DSL, May 5, 1884). In Bye, Wilder added that she and Will "talked about old friends all the way to Manchester, and none of them were still in Walnut Grove. They were all steadily moving west" (p. 166). In *These Happy Golden Years*, the brakeman is not an acquaintance (p. 116).

24. *an anxious time crossing a large slough. . . . we came safely through*. In Bye, Wilder provided more detail: "Sloughs were treacherous places. Solid to the eye, they were really only thin sod over bottomless mud. It was not safe to let one wheel follow in another's track, for it would cut through and let the wagon down to the axle, at least. When putting up hay in the sloughs, men always drove on a slight circle to prevent the rear wheels from following the front ones exactly, and often kept a wagon moving slightly all the time while they loaded it." This episode ended well, for "the teamster whipped up his horses and swinging across the slough on a run he got us safely to hard ground" (pp. 166–67).

25. *doctorine of foordination*. In Brandt, the spelling is corrected to fore-ordination (p. 136), and Wilder apparently intended to describe what is also known as preordination and predestination, a Calvinistic principle that maintains that God has predetermined all events in human history. Individuals are unable to change the course of fate or even the outcome of their lives, including whether they will find salvation or damnation after death.

just how he felt I suffered with him. But Mrs McKee, Mary, and I laughed about it as long as I stayed with them.

In the morning we were wakened by the hotel-keeper and his wife quarreling, but this time it was the man whose voice I heard.

"I will not get up and build the fire," he said. "Do it yourself! You're just like you dammed old mother, but I'll not wait on you."

We rode out on the load of household goods and had an anxious time crossing a large slough, for the ground, in the sloughs, was still soft from melting snow and the spring rain. But the teamster handled his horses better than he did his knife and fork and we came safely through.[24]

When we came to the house, he set up the stove for us and two bedsteads, one in each room, then drove away and left us at home.

The house had only the two rooms, but was new and tight. There was a small stack of hay at the back for our summer fuel, for we had taught others the trick we learned in the Hard Winter.

Mr Mc Kee came Saturday and stayed until Sunday afternoon, when we all walked the two miles to Manchester with him and he took the train back to his work.

Sunday's were stupid for Mr McKee was a very strict Scotch Presbetrian. Mary and I were not allowed to play, there must be no reading other than the Bible and we must not laugh aloud.

He used to lecture me for the good of my soul, trying to persuade me to join the church and at the same time explaining to me his doctorine of foordination.[25]

My reply, varied a little, always was, if that were true, I was already saved, or not saved, so why bother about it and he would shake his head and say "Oh! My! My! That Laura Ingalls!"

He used often to talk to us about how wicked it was to get angry. When his own temper, which was quick, got the better of him, I would look at him and grin. Then he would swallow his wrath and say a man had a right to his "righteous indignation." But there would be a twinkle in his eye. He was a very human man trying to live at peace with his Scotch conscience and really trying to help us all along the straight and narrow way.

All the week while Mr Mc Kee was away, we played and laughed, ate and slept and worked when and how we pleased.[26]

Mrs Mc Kee often said to me, "You'll marry that Wilder boy yet, because you'll be afraid you'll hurt his feelings if you say no." And when I would reply that he'd likely never give me the chance to say no, she would say, "Oh yes he will! A man of his age[27] doesn't fool around with a girl so long for nothing."

But I thought there was no danger and if it did happen, I would surely say no, for I was still writing to Clarance Huealett, the red headed Irish boy, I had known so long ago in Wisconsin.

The first of June I was home again on the farm and glad to be there, though I had liked the Mc Kee's.

It was good to help with the cows again, to drink all I wanted of fresh, sweet milk and to hunt for eggs where the hens hid their nests around the hay stacks and in the thick grass.

The little kitten we had bought for 25¢ was a grandmother now as well as a mother once again and thought she must hunt for the whole family. She would bring in striped gophers for them until they were stacked in piles.

I had been home only a little while when I began sewing for the milliner and dressmaker in town, Miss Florence Bell.[28]

Every morning I walked to her shop taking my dinner and being there by seven oclock. I sewed all day, with only a few minutes off at noon, until six oclock. Miss Bell paid me fifty cents a day. Of course I got tired and my back sometimes ached but I liked to sew and once on a rush order, I made twenty medium sized button holes, staying, overcasting and working them in thirty minutes and Miss Bell said it was a good job.

I worked for Miss Bell through June, July and August. Manly's other sister Laura worked there too a part of the time and that way I got acquainted with her. She and Eliza lived together on Eliza's homestead[29] north and a little west of town. Manly and Roy each lived on his homestead north of town.

In September Carrie and I began school again, walking in from the farm.

26. *All the week . . . how we pleased.* In Bye, Wilder added: "And in the evenings when the sunset colors were fading and darkness creeping across the prairie, we sat on the doorstep watching the stars brighten and swing low, and we sang to the twilight and the empty land all the songs we knew. One of them was,

Come away, come away, come away I say,
Come away, O come away, come right away,
Come to this country and don't you feel alarm,
For Uncle Sam is rich enough to give us all a
farm" (p. 167).

This song bears a relationship to the chorus of "Uncle Sam's Farm," with words by Jesse Hutchinson, Jr., of the Hutchinson Family Singers. Wilder included a version in *By the Shores of Silver Lake* (p. 62). Cockrell, *Ingalls Wilder Family Songbook*, pp. 170, 172, 377.

27. *A man of his age.* Brandt Revised (p. 96) and Bye included more information about Almanzo's age: "Manly was really nineteen, but in order to file on his homestead the summer before the Hard Winter, when he was seventeen, he had given his age as twenty one. So people thought of him as an old bachelor" (p. 164). Almanzo was actually ten years older than Wilder, and, in fact, had been twenty-one when he filed on his claims in Kingsbury County, although Wilder, who was confused about her own age, could easily have lost track of Almanzo's. Wilder also made the fictional Almanzo younger. In *The Long Winter*, for example, he is "twenty-one . . . or as good as" (pp. 258–59); in fact, the real Almanzo was twenty-four in 1881. Homesteading was open to heads of households or any persons (including single women) who were at least twenty-one years of age. The underage homesteader in Lane's "Home over Saturday" met the requirement by getting married (p. 60).

28. *Miss Florence Bell.* Florence E. Bell, a Pennsylvania native in her mid-thirties, announced in March 1883: "I shall keep constantly on hand the latest in Millinery and Fancy Goods. A complete assortment of

Fichus, Scarfs and Collars, Spanish, French and plain Laces, and embroidery material. Ribbons of all kinds, Plushes, Velvets, and Satins. Ladies' Furnishing Goods, Ladies' and Children's Hoods. Cutting and fitting, dressmaking and family sewing" (ad, *De Smet Leader*, Mar. 24, 1883). She set up shop on Calumet Avenue (main street) across from the Kingsbury County Bank. In *These Happy Golden Years*, Wilder described the shop as a "pleasant, new place, with the pretty hats in two windows, bolts of ribbon in a glass showcase, and silks and velvets on the shelves behind

it" (pp. 130–31). In her early forties, Bell married businessman William H. Ruth.

29. *Manly's other sister Laura. . . . and Eliza lived together on Eliza's homestead*. While Eliza Jane Wilder did not mention her sister's work at Miss Bell's shop, she did record Laura Wilder Howard's assistance in improving her homestead during 1882 and 1883. In the late summer of 1883, however, "sister's little boy was taken ill and required every minute of her time" (quoted in Anderson, *Wilder in the West*, pp. 17–19).

Seeley was teaching again and school went on much the same as ever, except that the big boys of our classes had quit school and were working. Frank Harthorn and May Bird were married[30] and Frank was a full partner in his father's grocery store. Cap Garland was working here and there with his team. Ben Woodworth was working at the depot. Arthur Johnson had gone to the farm with his folks.

Ida Brown and I were still seatmates as were Mary Power and Genieve Masters.

Geneve was not popular any more. It was a common saying that, "her tongue is hung in the middle and runs at both ends"[31] and not much attention was paid to anything she said.

Carrie had been helping with the chores and the housework through the summer. I hadn't been any help even after I came back from Manchester because from seven to six were long hours and when I walked home after six oclock there wasn't much time left for working.

Of course the money I earned had gone into the home fund and now that Carrie and I both were going to school, we helped with the chores and the housework night and morning.

Pa had been working very hard all summer at Carpenter work[32] and on the farm. He and Ma had put up the hay and now he was harvesting his little fields of wheat and of oats with the old hand cradle, because he couldn't afford a harvester and the fields were too small to pay to have one. Pa was very thin and tired from the hard work of harvesting but strong and hard as nails.

I think though that he was not very happy. People had crowded in too thick for him some time before. He wanted to go to Oregon.[33] The man who had left western Minnesota in grasshopper times, because "even a bee couldn't make a living" there had written him to come on out, the country was fine. Although he and Pa had seen each other only the one night we camped on his place on our way to Uncle Peter's the grasshopper plague had been a bond between them and they had written each other once in awhile ever since.

He wanted Pa to come and Pa wanted to go, but Ma said she was tired of wandering around "from pillar to post" and would not go.

30. *Seeley was teaching again. . . . Frank Harthorn and May Bird were married.* Once again, Wilder's chronology is shaky. Seelye taught during the 1881–1882 school year, and Harthorn and Burd were married in October 1883.

31. *"her tongue is hung in the middle and runs at both ends."* This old saying implies that the person is deceitful or false; a modern equivalent might be, "she talks out of both sides of her mouth."

32. *Pa had been working very hard all summer at Carpenter work.* The *De Smet Leader* reported in the fall of 1883: "Carpenters are in such demand in this neighborhood that some people who wish to build at once are unable to do so for want of mechanical help, which is not to be had for love or money. Laborers are extremely scarce, and get their own prices for their work" ("Town and Country," Oct. 6, 1883). Among the projects that Charles Ingalls worked on in the 1880s was the Congregational church building, completed in the summer of 1882. The family attends the first services in the new church in *These Happy Golden Years* (p. 134). Sherwood, *Beginnings of De Smet*, p. 31.

33. *He wanted to go to Oregon.* As in Dakota Territory, the coming of the railroads to the Pacific Northwest in the 1880s accelerated growth in the region. In Bye, Wilder explained her father's desire: "Dakota territory was too settled-up to suit him, and he said the winters were too cold and the summer heat and drought too much for a man to contend with. He wanted to go on, west" (p. 169). In *These Happy Golden Years*, Laura sympathizes with him as his gaze drifts "over the rolling prairie westward from the open door where he stood" (pp. 138–39).

V. S. L. Owen. *Laura Ingalls Wilder Memorial Society*

34. *Mr Ven Owen was finishing out his term*. V. S. L. ("Ven") Owen was hired as principal and teacher of township school No. 2 in De Smet on September 8, 1883. He received forty dollars a month for a six-month school divided into two terms, the first of which started September 24. Owen was ten years older than Wilder, about the same age as Almanzo. College-educated, Owen taught for a number of years in De Smet and then continued his career in Minnesota schools into the twentieth century. He and his wife, Sophia, had six children. He died at the age of ninety-six in 1953. Mr. Owen makes his first appearance in *Little Town on the Prairie*: "He was not very old, but he was serious and industrious and enterprising" (p. 269). Another student remembered him as "a builder of character as well as a teacher" (Harding, *I Recall Pioneer Days*, p. [26]).

We moved back to town when cold weather came so that we could be nearer school and Pa's work.

Mr Seeley had been asked to resign from the school because of conduct unbecoming "a gentleman and a scholar["] and Mr Ven Owen was finishing out his term.[34]

It was a pleasure to study now. Mr Owen was neat rather dapper in fact quick and sharp and all for the business in hand.

One of the smaller boys in school was coming to be thought of as foolish. He had not been at first, but had learned to bring a perfectly blank, witless expression to his face when unable to answer a question in class. Teachers would stare at him aghast and let him go unpunished.

Then he tried it at recess for the amusement of the other boys. He seemed to make his mind a blank at the same time, unhinge it and leave it flapping. At last he was in such a condition that he was actually becoming foolish. He was falling behind in his studies and the other children were begining to call him a fool.

The first time Will Bennet[35] becam a blank before Mr Owen he looked at him curiously and let it pass. The second time it happened, Mr Owen took his flat ruler from his desk, said "Will come with me!" and walked out into the entry, Will following. Then we heard shrieks from the entry and soon they came back. Will sat down in his seat very carefully.

The next day the scene was gone through again, but that was the last time. After that Mr Owen had only to look at Will and the blank look would disappear before it had quite arrived.

Will kept control of his face and his mind recovered almost at the same time. He became an ordinarily bright boy.

Charley Power, Mary's younger brother[36] had to try out the new teacher. Charley was a black-haired, droll, Irish boy who could keep a perfectly straight face while making others rock with mirth.

He bent a pin and put it in his own seat. When school was called, he sat lightly on the pin and lept wildly, clear off the floor with a yelp. His yell and his leap were so comical that the whole school shrieked with laughter.

Mr Owen said quietly, "Come here Charley" and when he came

"Town and Country," *DSL*, Sept. 15, 1883; "Meeting of School Board," *DSL*, Sept. 22, 1883; "Laura's writing teacher," p. 4; "Vidocq S L Owen"; "Washington Death Index."

35. *Will Bennet.* In 1883, the *De Smet Leader* reported that E. R. Bennett, who ran a grocery store in town, was "building a good-sized addition" to use "as a dwelling" ("Town and Country," Oct. 6, 1883), and Will may have been his son. A year later, Bennett had "sold out his grocery stock and gone out of the business" (ibid., Nov. 15, 1884). Brandt and Brandt Revised do not include this episode, but it is reinstated and expanded in Bye (p. 171). In *Little Town on the Prairie*, Will Bennet became Willie Oleson, who begins acting foolish when Eliza Jane Wilder teaches school (pp. 269–70).

36. *Charley Power, Mary's younger brother.* Nine years old in 1880, Charley Power was five years younger than his sister Mary. In her fiction, Wilder put his misadventure with the pin during Miss Wilder's tenure (*LTOP*, pp. 167–68, 180–81).

Silliman and Emma Gilbert family, including Stella, standing, far right. *Laura Ingalls Wilder Memorial Society*

37. *Gilbert. . . . after the hard winter.* In 1880, Silliman and Emma Gilbert had seven children ranging in age from four to twenty-one. Contrary to what Wilder remembered, the family had arrived in Kingsbury County prior to the hard winter. In fact, nineteen-year-old David A. Gilbert, the second son in the family, was the mail carrier who outraces a blizzard and safely delivers the mail from Preston in *The Long Winter* (pp. 157, 168). Stella was about three years older than Wilder; Fred was about Wilder's age. Baby Luella was born about 1881. In *These Happy Golden Years*, Wilder used Stella as a model for the fictional Nellie Oleson. When planning the book, Wilder listed her cast of characters: "Mary Power and Ida Brown, perhaps Stella Gilbert, though I think I'll combine Jennie Masters and Stella in

Charley was laid neatly across Mr Owens knee and the ruler applied where the pin had failed to stick.

That night, Pa said to Charley, "I hear you got a whipping for sitting on a pin."

"Oh no!" said Charley, "I got whipped for getting off it."

After that we could give our full attention to our studies for there were no more disturbances.

Some people named Gilbert lived on a farm north and east of town. There were Pa and Ma Gilbert, Al and Fred and Stella and Leona Gilbert.

They had come early in the spring after the hard winter[37] and by the next winter Ma Gilbert had become bedridden and had not been out of her bed since though she looked well enough, with bright eyes and color in her cheeks.

Stella and her father did the work and cared for Leona who had been born since her mother refused to try to get up.

I got acquainted with Stella at Sunday-school and had been out to the house and seen the rest of the family. Now Fred was going to school and seemed to want to be very attentive to me.

There was a dancing club[38] in town with dances every Friday night and I had been thinking I would like to go, but when Fred told me he had bought a membership and asked me to go with him, I couldn't bear to think of being with Fred so much and refused. He was nice enough for anything I could explain, even to myself, but he was a green country boy and I didn't like his style, nor the Gilbert family.

(Later the Gilberts went to Oregon[39] bought land in just the right place and became millionairs on the rise in value)

Speaking of style—we girls all began to wear hoops that fall. Walking to school in the wind, the wires would creep up and up until they would all be bulging in a circle above our knees, taking our skirts with them. That would never do and we learned to walk a little way, then whirl around and around like a top to let them fall down. So on our way to school we would walk a little way and then twirl, walk and twirl, all the way.

De Smet residents wearing masks, ca. 1880. *Laura Ingalls Wilder Memorial Society*

Nellie Oelson" (LIW to RWL, Aug. 17, 1938). "Gilbert was Mail Boy," p. 20.

38. *a dancing club.* Early De Smet had an active social life. The Cornet Band played frequently and built a dance hall to hold dances, where admission, often including supper, was typically from seventy-five cents to one dollar. Eventually, the band also turned the hall into a roller-skating rink, playing music for skaters and holding "masquerades" at which skaters were required to wear masks. Mrs. Jarley's Wax-works were also shown at the rink. In December 1885, the band announced that it "had arranged for a series of society dances for the winter." Admission would be seventy-five cents at the door or one dollar for season tickets for ten dances ("Town and Country, *DSL*, Dec. 5, 1885). "Town and Country," *DSL*, Aug. 16, 1884, Jan. 10, Mar. 14, 21, 28, June 27, Dec., 5, 1885.

39. *(Later the Gilberts went to Oregon.* In 1900, Silliman and Emma Gilbert, along with their youngest child, Luella, were still living in De Smet, as were David Gilbert and his wife, Sarah Lyngby. By that time, a Christopher L. Gilbert, probably the oldest son in Silliman's family, had moved to the Pacific Northwest, locating first in Portland and later in Zillah, Washington.

40. *hoops, . . . fringe of bangs.* In *These Happy Golden Years*, Wilder described Laura's new hoops in detail: "They were the very latest style in the East. . . . Instead of wires, there were wide tapes across the front, almost to her knees, holding the petticoats so that her dress would lie flat. These tapes held the wire bustle in place at the back, and it was an adjustable bustle. Short lengths of tape were fastened to either end of it; these could be buckled together underneath the bustle, to puff it out, either large or small. Or they could be buckled together in front, drawing the bustle down close in back, so that a dress rounded smoothly over it" (pp. 161–62). In *Little Town on the Prairie*, Laura cuts a fringe of bangs that Ma called a "lunatic fringe" and Laura termed "so stylish" (p. 203). According to the *Wheeling Daily Register* of July 24, 1875, " 'Lunatic Fringe' is the name given to the fashion of cropping the hair and letting the ends hang down over the forehead." Wilton, "Lunatic Fringe."

"Laura curled all the bangs." *Helen Sewell, 1941*

41. *(You may . . . to do so).* Lane chose not to include the story in the edited versions.

We wore full draped skirts over our hoops, tight waists and sleeves and a thick fringe of bangs[40] across our foreheads.

Once out at Gilberts, Fred was bringing Stella and me to town. He helped Stella into the buggy. She sat down and he helped me in and I sat down. Our bulging hoops touched each other and filled the buggy full. Fred looked at them and said helplessly "But where am I going to sit?" We crowded the hoops to the sides until he could sit down between us, but when he did nothing of his feet or legs from the knee down could be seen.

(You may put in here Manly's story of the girl in hoops who jumped from the buggy—if you wish to do so)[41]

The school gave an exebition in the church building the last night before the Christmas holidays.[42]

We all sang "The Star Spangled Banner," while the littlest one waved the flag. There were other songs and dialogus and pieces spoken, but the main feature of the exebition was given by the history class which was Ida Brown and I.

We had just finished the history and two thirds of the book was assigned to me the rest to Ida.

Each of us had written and committed to memory a synopsis of her portion giving dates and names and all important events. With the pointer we indicated the illustrations of our stories in maps and pictures hung on a curtain across the end of the church.

It was a great success. Ida and I covered ourselves with glory and Mr Owen told Pa that I had a wonderful mind and memory and ought to be given every chance for an education.

He knew nothing of the trick I had learned of repeating any lesson to a corner of the bedroom just before I fell asleep and of finding it there by looking at the corner when I waked in the morning.[43] Not knowing this he would never think that as I talked so quietly in the church, I was seeing that corner of my bedroom instead of the faces of the crowd.

For Ven Owen too, our class wrote our first compositions. The subject given the class was "Ambition."

Not having been at school the day before, I did not know what

42. *The school gave an exebition . . . before the Christmas holidays.*
The School Exhibition actually took place on April 4, 1884, at
the Congregational church to close "the most successful term of
school ever taught in De Smet" ("Town and Country," DSL, Apr.
12, 1884). Admission was twenty-five cents for adults, ten cents
for non-schoolchildren, the money to be used to purchase "clocks
and other necessaries for the school, which is sadly in need." The
event, consisting of "readings, recitations, declamations, dia-
logues, personations, songs and choruses, etc.," raised thirty dollars and resulted in circulation of a petition to the school board
to retain the teachers ("School Exhibition," DSL, Mar. 29, 1884).
As Wilder began work on her last books in the late 1930s, she
drew heavily on *Pioneer Girl* but shifted the sequence of events.
As late as 1938, Wilder planned to write just one more book after
The Long Winter, a project she called "Prairie Girl" (LIW to RWL,
Mar. 15, 1938). Her original outline for the project more closely
followed the narrative in her memoir, and the school exhibition
appeared in a section called "Home Again," after Laura's term at
the "Bouchie School" (LIW, "Prairie Girl" outline). As "Prairie
Girl" evolved, Wilder realized that she had enough material for
two books and rearranged several scenes to build satisfying plots
for both. Thus, the fictional school exhibition occurs toward the
end of *Little Town on the Prairie* (pp. 283–97), not in the middle
of *These Happy Golden Years*.

43. *He knew nothing of the trick . . . when I waked in the morning.*
Wilder chose not to reveal this "trick" to readers of *Little Town on
the Prairie*, where Laura gains strength from Pa. In the crowded
church, his face stands out from the rest and their eyes meet. Only
then is she able to launch "upon the great history of America."
As Wilder's symbol of the American West, Pa adds conviction
to Laura's presentation about "freedom and equality in the New
World" (pp. 291–92).

44. *Not having been at school the day before. . . . compo-sition from the dictionary. . . . so well the first time."* In *These Happy Golden Years*, Laura has been away from school for two months, teaching at the Brewster school. The fictional Laura also seeks inspiration from the dictionary and turns in a hastily written draft (p. 97). In reality, however, Wilder rewrote her composition. Her handwritten copy, preserved in Mansfield, includes a scratched-out rough draft on one side of the page and a rewritten text on the other, which reads:

> Ambition is, like other good things[,] a good only when used in moderation. It has worked great good for the world, and great evil also.
>
> [Ale]xander is an example of a man completely carried away by ambition: so much so that when he had conquered the whole world (which one would suppose was enough to satisfy ambition); he wept because there were no more worlds to conquer.
>
> Ambition is a good servant, but a hard master; and if you think it is likely to become your master: I would say to you in the words of the immortal Shakespere: "Cromwell, I charge thee fling away ambition, by that sin fell the angels."

The quotation is from *Henry VIII* (Act III, Scene 2). Wilder rewrote the essay again for *These Happy Golden Years*, where she used almost the same phrasing and dialogue to convey Mr. Owen's reaction (p. 98).

45. *I had not seen Manly all summer.* In fictionalizing this material, Wilder combined this scene with the earlier episode in which Cap Garland asked her to go riding to create Laura's first ride behind the colts (*HGY*, pp. 141–45).

46. *the Perry school in April, May and June.* At its meeting on April 11, 1884, the De Smet Township school board "voted that Miss Laura Ingalls be contracted to teach school No. 3, for the summer term at $25 per month" ("School Board Meeting," *DSL*, Apr. 19, 1884). According to her signed contract, however, she taught school No. 5, and the two-month term began on April 28. School No. 5 was on the Delos

was expected of us until a few minutes before recitation. The others had prepared their papers at home the night before.

I couldn't make a start and in despair went to the dictionary to see what it had to say about ambition, hoping to get an idea.

I wrote my whole composition from the dictionary definition of ambition, closing with the quotation from Shakespear it included, "Cromwell I charge thee fling away ambition. By that sin fell the angels."

Mr Owen looked sharply at me when I had finished reading it and said, "You have written compositions before."

"Oh no Sir!" said I, "This is my first."

"Well you should write more of them," he said. "I wouldn't have believed any one could have done so well the first time."[44]

I had not seen Manly all summer,[45] but since the snow came I had seen him a few times with Cap in the cutter driving the prettiest, wildest pair of brown horses I had ever seen.

And one day after he and Cap had driven all over town he came for me and I went for a sleigh ride.

The horses were so wild that we couldn't talk very well, but he told me that he had been working on his farm all summer. He had no buggy and no driving team but he had broken these colts to be ready to drive on the cutter when snow came.

After this time we went for sleighrides quite often but not long ones and he never came for me until he had driven the colts quite awhile first. They were so high lifed he didn't think it safe but I often wished I might go first instead of waiting while all the boys in town rode with him to take the edge off the team.

As usual we went out to the farm early in the spring and I left school before the term was finished to teach the Perry school in April, May and June.[46]

The Perry schoolhouse was on a corner of Delos Perry's farm, just a little way from our south line.

It was a new little school-house with nice desks and teacher's table and a big Websters unabridged dictionary but there were never more than three scholars and a part of the time only one, little Clyde Perry, seven years old.

I did enjoy those three months. In my walk to school in the morning, I passed close by the little violet-covered meadow, so close that I could smell the perfume from the blossoms.

Then I had most of the long, quiet day for my own studies, with the big dictionary to help me. At recess and noontime I kntted lace and there was plenty of time to watch the cloud shadows chasing each other across the grass outside the windows.

The children were all good and bright too, so that helping them with their lessons was a pleasure. After a long, happy day there was a pleasant walk home at four oclock and for this I was drawing $25. a month.

On saturdays I sometimes walked across the prairie to Mr Brown's. It was a long walk but pleasant and usually Ida and I extended it by going to the highest point of a rise of ground behind their house, from which we could see the Wessington Hills, sixty miles away, looking like a blue cloud on the horizon.

Mrs Brown was literary and wrote for several church papers, neglecting her personal appearance and her house which was always in a dirty disorder.[47]

Ida worked hard and was always cheerful. She couldn't do all the work and keep the house while she walked two miles each way to school every day. I disliked both Mr & Mrs Brown, but I did like Ida, who was no relation to them but had been adopted from a Home.

Mary graduated from college in June[48] and came home. She was much happier than when she went away, with pleasant college memories to dwell upon, able to sew and knit and make beadwork, to read her raised-print books and to play the organ that Pa and I together had bought for her as a surprise when she came home.[49] All my school money went for the organ and Pa made up the rest. We couldn't afford it but we all felt that it was little to do for Mary and we wanted her to be happy at home. Pa had als[o] built another room on the end of the house[50] so we had a sitting room that could be turned into a bedroom at night by opening up the home-made cot.

One Sunday in May a team and buggy came dashing around the corner of the livery barn, in town and out along the road across the

Perry homestead south of the Ingalls claim. In *These Happy Golden Years*, Pa is the contractor for the new school building, and Laura teaches a three-month term (pp. 147, 149). Apparently, Wilder did not consult her contract but relied on her memoir when writing the book. Teacher's Contract, Apr. 22, 1884, Laura Ingalls Wilder Historic Home and Museum; Final Patent #3834.

47. *Mrs Brown was literary . . . dirty disorder.* Mrs. Laura J. Brown was active in church and temperance causes, serving as corresponding secretary of the Kingsbury County Woman's Christian Temperance Union. Neither she nor Reverend Brown are sympathetically portrayed in *Pioneer Girl* or Wilder's novels. At times, they are almost stereotypical. The literary Mrs. Brown, for example, echoes Charles Dickens's Mrs. Jellyby, "sitting in quite a nest of waste paper," who drank coffee all night and talked and wrote about various causes while neglecting her children (*Bleak House*, p. 68). She is also reminiscent of the neglectful modern woman of much anti-suffragist literature. Wilder was far more tolerant of Mrs. Brown when she wrote about her poor housekeeping in a 1917 *Missouri Ruralist* column (reprinted in Hines, *Little House in the Ozarks*, pp. 301–10). "Open Letter," DSL, Apr. 19, 1884.

48. *Mary graduated from college in June.* Mary Ingalls actually graduated from the Iowa College for the

Graduation certificate of Mary Ingalls, 1889.
Laura Ingalls Wilder Historic Home and Museum

Blind in June 1889, after Wilder and Almanzo had been married for almost four years. She attended the school for a total of seven years, missing the 1887–1888 term because of illness. In *These Happy Golden Years*, Mary returns home after her first year of college and then decides to spend the following summer vacation visiting her friend Blanche, much to the family's disappointment. Mary also comes home the summer that Laura and Almanzo wed (pp. 123–38, 179, 246). O'Leary and Goddard, *Gleanings from Our Past*, chap. 3.

49. *She was much happier . . . when she came home.* In *These Happy Golden Years*, Mary returns for her first visit home from college seeming "more sure of herself." She even laughs after sharing a funny story with the family. "Mary had often smiled," Wilder wrote, "but it was a long time since they had heard her laugh out, as she used to when she was a little girl. All that it had cost to send Mary to college was more than repaid by seeing her so gay and confident" (p. 126). The real family's decision to buy Mary an organ was probably directly linked to her academic pursuits. Music was an integral part of the curriculum at the Iowa College for the Blind, which offered classes in "vocal, harmony, piano, pipe organ, violin, guitar, flute, clarinet, and cornet" (O'Leary and Goddard, *Gleanings from Our Past*, chap. 3).

50. *Pa had als[o] built another room on the end of the house.* In the novel, Wilder described this room as being "across the east end of the house, with a door in the north looking toward town" (*HGY*, p. 158). By the time Mary Ingalls graduated from college in 1889, the family was living at 210 West Third Street in a house that Charles Ingalls built in 1887. The house, maintained by the Laura Ingalls Wilder Memorial Society, is on the National Register of Historic Places.

Big Slough. I could see it plainly from the dooryard where I happened to be.

The buggy was new for the sun flashed and sparkled from the wheels and top. The horses were brown and beautiful as they trotted so evenly and swiftly.

I wondered who it could be as I saw the team turn in toward the house. Then I saw it was Manly.

"Would you like to go for a buggy ride?" he asked.

So we tried out the new buggy and the beautiful horses, whose mother was a purebred Morgan and their father a Thoroughbred[51] and who though still nervous and highstrung were gentle and kind.

We drove to Lake Henry, around the lake and home in the moonlight, a drive of forty miles altogether and the horses were still fresh, still needing to be restrained a little.

I had not seen Manly since the sleighing had gone, nearly three months, but he had come as soon as he could buy a buggy.

I hadn't known that I missed him, but it was good to see him again, gave me a homelike feeling.

After all we had been through blizzards, near-murder and danger of death together and those things do create a "tie that binds," more or less. He told me that he had been working hard on his farm all spring, but as soon as he could get the buggy he had come to see if I still liked driving. We decided that we did and after that every Sunday afternoon, his team on the top buggy would come swinging around Pearson's livery barn[52] and with manes and tails flying in the wind come trotting across the Big Slough after me.

Sometimes we drove to Lakes Henry and Thompson again we would go to Spirit Lake and drive along the shore, watching the waves lap against the rocks. In June when the prairie roses bloomed we would stop and gather them filling the buggy with their fragrant blossoms.

Often we went to make the Boasts a call where they lived on their farm. On one such call I spoke of going home, early in the evening, Mr Boast insisted that we stay until the moon came up, thinking to play a joke on us, for he knew the moon didn't rise till morning.[53]

51. *a purebred Morgan . . . a Thoroughbred*. Almanzo Wilder's horses were bred for speed. The Morgan is a light breed originating in Vermont, and the Thoroughbred is an English racing breed. Twelve-year-old Alvin H. Greene, whose family settled about a mile from Wilder's claim in 1884, later recalled Wilder's skill with horses: "About chore time in the morning he'd come flying by here with a wild team of Morgans he was breaking. Their tails would be back and they were running hard. . . . [He was] holding on to the lines, so busy he couldn't wave. . . . there wasn't anything for them to run into, no fences, just wide open prairie. I'd sometimes be outside about twenty minutes later when he'd come by again. . . . Those horses were sweaty and tired and walking. Now he would wave and give me a big grin. Almanzo Wilder was maybe the best horseman I ever knew" (Cramer, "Alvin Hensdale Greene," p. [1]).

52. *swinging around Pearson's livery barn*. An 1883 diagram of De Smet placed "Fonger Bros., Livery, Sale & Feed Stable" on the southeast end of Calumet Avenue (main street) leading out of town toward the Big Slough. Later in the year, White and Pierson, described as "some parties from Nebraska" ("Town and Country," *DSL*, Oct. 20, 1883), took over the establishment. Charles Ingalls did carpentry work on a house for Pierson the following spring. That summer, Pierson gave his livery barn "a coat of red paint, which greatly improves its appearance" and probably increased its visibility from the Ingalls farm (ibid., July 12, 1884). Ibid., May 5, 1884; Miller, *Little Town*, p. 32.

53. *he knew the moon didn't rise till morning*. Morning in this context is the hours just after midnight. The moon's revolution around the earth affects the times of moonrise and moonset, which appear somewhat later each day. Observant people like Mr. Boast might be able to guess the approximate time of a moonrise based on the previous days' times; for the less observant, moonrise times were frequently listed in almanacs.

54. *a sage-green, rough straw, poke bonnet.* Wilder used similar wording to describe this hat in *These Happy Golden Years*, adding: "It completely covered Laura's head and framed her face with its flaring brim. . . . Wide blue ribbons tied under her left ear and held the bonnet securely in place" (p. 163). A poke bonnet featured a fitted crown that perched on the back of the head with space to accommodate the bulky hair styles of the 1880s. Women could "poke" their hair into the back of the crown, giving the bonnet its name. A wide brim protected the wearer's face.

55. *a brown silk, open work, dress a present from the friends in Chicago.* The unknown "friends in Chicago" also sent the Christmas turkey in 1880–1881. In *These Happy Golden Years*, however, this dress was made from ten yards of "beautiful brown poplin" that Miss Bell "ordered from Chicago" and that Laura paid for. Openwork refers to a design that features loops or openings in fabric, lace, or embroidery that add a lattice-like embellishment to a piece of clothing. Poplin is a strong fabric in plain weave with crosswise ribs.

56. *bustles were out. . . . flounce. . . . gored.* A bustle was a padded or structured undergarment designed to enhance the drapery at the back of a woman's skirt below the waistline—or in other words, to make the wearer's backside more shapely. A flounce is a gathered strip of fabric that creates a ruffled edge across a bodice, at the hemline, or in tiers down a skirt. A gored skirt is cut from several triangular pieces and stitched together to form a flattering shape that hugs the waist and hips, then flares into fullness to the hemline.

57. *a polanise.* A polonaise was a close-fitting bodice or cutaway coat, tight at the waist, then flowing over the skirt like a tunic. Polish folk costumes had inspired the design, which enjoyed a revival in the late nineteenth century. Wilder included many period fashion details in her novels, giving her readers a sense of a historical style and culture. This technique continues to be used in contemporary young adult fiction, whether historical or futuristic. Suzanne Collins in *The Hunger Games* (2008), for example,

He did fool us for we had not kept track of the moon, but when we saw we had been fooled we kept on staying waiting for the moon.

Poor Mr Boast went to sleep in his chair and Mrs Boast could hardly keep her eyes open.

We thought the joke was on Mr Boast when the moon came up at two A.M. and we went home. We did drive quickly home and as quietly as possible up to the door. A light was burning in the sitting room. I slipped in quietly and blew it out hoping to get to bed without waking any one, but Ma's voice asked "What time is it Laura?"

"Oh! I didn't look at the clock," I replied. "We stayed too long at Boast's," I added and no more was said.

That spring, I bought, from Miss Bell, a sage-green, rough straw, poke bonnet,[54] lined with shirred silk, blue the color of my eyes.

With the hat, I wore a brown silk, open work, dress a present from the friends in Chicago.[55]

The dress was made with a skirt that fitted smoothly around the top, bustles were out, and was of the lining material only to within a foot of the bottom which reached the ground. The last twelve inches was covered with a flounce of the material. Where it was sewed to the skirt, the seam was covered with a strip of plain brown silk an inch wide and the bottom of the flounce was bound with an inch wide of the same silk. The skirt was gored[56] so the bottom would go over my hoops.

With the skirt was a polanise,[57] fitting tightly at the waist, smoothly over the hips and buttoned all down the front with brown silk buttons. The polanise was bound at the bottom with a band of the plain brown silk and reached to the flounce on the underskirt. The sleeves fitting my arms easily, were smooth and long with a narrow strip of plain brown silk at the wrists. The neck was high with a smooth band of the plain silk around the throat. Over the neck band I wore a blue ribbon, matching the hat trim, about two inches wide pinned together at the throat with Ma's pearl, bar pin. The ends of the ribbon fell to my waist.

Hoops had been improved. There were now tapes across the front almost to the knees, letting the dress lie close in front. There was a wire bustle attached at the back and a tape fastened to it by one end at each side. If a bustle was wanted these tapes were buck-led together at the back underneath the bustle, the size of the bustle being regulated by how tightly the tapes were drawn. If no bustle was wanted the tapes were buckled together tightly in front, hold-ing the wires of the bustle tight and smooth against the back. The hoops were a great nuisance, though Ma said they were not nearly so large as the ones she used to wear.

I had begun wearing corsets the first spring we were in De Smet, but I refused to wear them at any time except when I was dressed up and never would wear them as tight as the other girls did or as Ma thought I ought to, if I were to have a pretty waist.

Pa could span her waist with his hands when they were married, she said and when I said I did not want any ones hands around my waist she shook her head at the girls of to day,[58] but let me do as I pleased.

Of course I wore my brown silk dress, hoops, corsets sage-green bonnet and all on Sunday afternoons, but I always tied the bustle down tight and smooth. My stockings were white cotton open-work and my shoes were black and high and buttoned.

Our usual Sunday afternoon drive was around forty miles. We had the top of the buggy up to shade us from the sun, or shelter us from the rain if a shower should come up, and when it rained we buttoned on the side curtains, fastened the rubber laprobe to the dashboard, drew it over our laps, buttoned it to the ends of the seat and rode all snug and dry.

When the sun set, we put the top down so that the beautiful moon-drenched or star-spangled sky was directly over our heads.

The sunsets were gorgeous, flaming spectacles; the night winds were soft and sweet; little animals scurried across the road ahead of us; now and then a night bird called and once two little black and white spotted skunks played along beside the buggy as we drove slowly.

Sometimes we drove over to Gilbert's and took Stella with us. Manly said the poor girl worked so hard it would be nice to give her a good time.

I didn't object to her going with us but I did think of how she lay

Polonaise coats, 1879. Godey's Lady's Book and Magazine

gives readers vivid descriptions of costumes for her main characters.

58. *shook her head at the girls of to day.* In *Little Town on the Prairie*, Laura tells Carrie, "I think it was silly, the way they dressed when Ma was a girl," although from the context it is clear that Wilder is actually making a subtle comment on the almost universal disregard young people have for the conventions of their parents' generation. Laura is, after all, wear-ing a hoop skirt and corsets as her mother did, and

Laura's lunatic fringe is no less silly than Caroline Quiner's youthful decision to comb her hair off her ears (pp. 271–73). Wilder noted, too, that Laura's "corsets were a sad affliction to her" (p. 93). These close-fitting, boned support undergarments extended from above or beneath the bust to below the hips and were hooked or laced to form an artificially narrow waist. Corsets continued to plague Wilder even into her seventies. In 1939, she wrote Lane, "Do you wear corsets yet? If not how can you wear a dress? I think I'll be eccentric and wear smocks, making them myself so they will be loose" (LIW to RWL, Apr. 10, [1939], Box 13, file 195, Lane Papers).

in bed in the morning and let her father get the breakfast, of how she was often too sick to work and lay in bed all day, but would get up at night and go to a dance. But I said nothing about all this. If she had worked on his sympathy, what did I care.

One Sunday we were coming home rather late on a road that led by our house first, so naturally I got out and Manly took Stella on home by herself. The next Sunday, he picked Stella up first as his farm was much nearer Gilbert's than ours. We went on South from our place to Lake Henry and again came back so that I stopped first.

The next Sunday again Stella came with Manly after me. I went pleasantly enough, but Stell's smugness gave her scheme away to me. She was trying her best to edge me out of the drives. It was even more plain when she made plans for the next Sunday's drive and kindly (?) included me in them.

Never, thought I, did I try to hold any one that wanted to go and I'll not enter into any competition for Manly.[59] But I wanted a clean break and to do it myself not just hang on until sometime they neglected to come by for me.

I manuevered that drive. Let's go this road I would say, indicating one that would swing us toward Gilbert's. Stella could have no reason to object. "Let's go by Boasts now we are so near," I said. That brought us across the railroad track and north of my home. I suggested one more turn and then we were nearer Gilbert's than my home so we went that way and left Stella.

The ride from there home was quiet. Manly got out of the buggy and helped me down. As we stood there, Manly said, "Well, I suppose we'll all go next Sunday?"

"No!" I answered "We'll not all go. If you want Stella, take her. You need not think you have to come by for me. Good night!" and I went in and shut the door.

I had cause for speculation as to the outcome[60] when next Sunday afternoon came, but promptly at 2 oclock the brown horses came dashing around the corner by the livery barn, with Manly alone in the buggy and we did not go by for Stella nor was she mentioned on that afternoon. Neither was she included any more in our

59. *I'll not enter into any competition for Manly.* In *These Happy Golden Years*, Laura's decision to continue driving with Nellie and Almanzo hinges more on displeasing Nellie than winning Almanzo's affections. "If she refused to go, Nellie would be pleased," Wilder wrote, "that was what Nellie wanted. . . . Laura made up her mind to go with them" (p. 174).

60. *I had cause for speculation as to the outcome.* In the novel, Laura decides, "If he didn't [come for her], he didn't; that was all," and she goes about her business (p. 178). Yet, by Saturday night, Laura is convinced that Almanzo will choose Nellie (p. 180). The emotional differences between Wilder's depiction of her own rivalry with Stella Gilbert and the fictional one between Laura and Nellie Oleson are significant. In *Pioneer Girl*, Wilder's younger self exerts more control over the resolution of the developing rivalry; she is a shrewd, nearly adult woman, full of pride and self-confidence. In the novel, Laura is more tentative, unsure that she wants to admit even to herself that she is interested in Almanzo. Like so many young adult heroines, she is reluctant to embrace the roles and responsibilities of adulthood. She also seems less confident of her feminine charms. These qualities make Laura a more sympathetic and endearing heroine for young readers. When Almanzo arrives the following Sunday, Laura asks without guile, "Wouldn't Nellie go?" On that ride, however, something shifts between Laura and Almanzo, and they reach an unspoken understanding that signals a more permanent relationship (*HGY*, pp. 180–84).

61. *a whole circus in himself, Manly named him Barnum*. Phineas T. Barnum (1810–1891) was an American showman and promoter who entered the circus business in 1870. His name became synonymous with the circus, although it was only one of Barnum's many entertainment ventures. In *These Happy Golden Years*, Almanzo tells Laura, "I wasn't sure how you'd like this circus I'm driving" (p. 189). Maher, "P. T. Barnum."

drives. Well anyway it was much more comfortable on hot summer days with only two in the seat.

We took Mary for a short drive once in a while but she did not care to go far.

Manly sold his beautiful gentle team in July and bought another. One of the team was a large, rangy brown horse with white spots on his sides and one on his neck, which in connection, with a waving white streak in his mane to form the tail, resembled a rooster, with the use of only a little imagination. This horse had never been known to walk a step, though he had been around town for a year. He would trot or run or leap around, or stand up on his hind legs and, with his front feet pawing the [air], hop like a kangaroo, but walk he would not.

Because of his actions and his spots, because he was a whole circus in himself, Manly named him Barnum.[61]

Barnum's mate, Skip, was a bay, a little smaller not quite so raging, but a good second to anything Barnum might do and determined to run away.

Manly was staying in town now boarding at Garland's and Cap always helped him hitch up the team and held them by the head until Manly got in the buggy and sat down, being very careful not to move the top which was always down.

When Cap let go of them the horses would leap and go on the run, running all the way to our house. When I saw them coming, I would put on my hat and be out the door when he drove up.

He never stopped the horses, for then would have been a circus indeed. It really was not safe so soon after starting. He didn't stop them, but as he passed the door he would turn the buggy to make a greater space between the wheels and check the horses just a little. Just the little check and Barnum would rear up and, reaching as high as he could with his front feet, paw the air. Skip would plunge and rear, while I made a leap for the buggy.

If I calculated the time exactly right and were quick enough, I would touch the step with one foot as I jumped and land in the buggy.

If I failed, Manly would drive around the house and I would try again. Once he drove around three times before I succeeded, but practice made perfect and I soon got so that I would leap in easily and away we would go as fast as the horses could run for several miles. Then they would settle down to a fast trot.

Whenever we came to a bit of water in the road, a little creek, or a narrow wash, they jumped it taking the buggy with them clear over it.

We extended our drives going fifty and even sixty miles. The buggy top was left down until about half the way was passed, then we would, both together, raise the top and quickly so that Manly could get both hands back on the reins, for when the top came up both horses were frantic and would try their best to run away. There wasn't a man in town would ride behind the team. Ma said Manly was trying to kill me,[62] but it was the greatest fun I'd ever had.

Fourth of July came with a grand celebration in De Smet.[63] I had made a new dress for the occasion. It was of lawn,[64] a very pale tint of pink, with a little spray of blue and rose flowers scattered over it.

The waist was tight, buttoned down the front with small pearl buttons. On each side [of] the closing and on each side down the back were two tucks a half inch wide. The neck was high with a band, the sleeves were long and close fitting.

The skirt was made of straight breadths, very full, so full that the gathers had to be crowded and packed into the waist band. There were half inch tucks runing around the skirt about three inches apart, the full length of the skirt and a three inch hem at the bottom. It just touched the ground and the hoops held it out beautifully.

I had a new hat to go with this dress. It was of cream colored straw, with a ribbon a little darker in shade around the crown and three ostrich tips, shading from the light cream of the straw to a little darker than the ribbon, standing upright at one side. The hat sat on top of my head and had a narrow brim with a little roll to it.

My hair was worn, these days, combed smoothly back and braid[ed] in a thick braid that was wound around and around at the back of my head covering the whole back and pinned snugly in place.

My bangs had grown out.

62. *Ma said Manly was trying to kill me.* The revised versions of *Pioneer Girl* credited Pa with this line, but Wilder returned to the original in the novel, where Ma tells Laura: "I do believe he wants to break your neck! And I hope he breaks his own, first." Pa replies, "Wilder will manage the horses, Caroline. . . . If ever I saw a born horseman, he's one" (pp. 186–87).

63. *Fourth of July . . . grand celebration in De Smet.* Elaborate Fourth of July celebrations were a hallmark of small-town America and had become almost standardized by the time the De Smet community held them in the 1880s. The program usually included "a parade, a speech, . . . lunch, a baseball game or games, street sports, fireworks, and a dance" (Miller, "Fourth of July," p. 121). De Smet's Independence Day committees met a month or more in advance to coordinate all these elements. "The Glorious Fourth," DSL, June 30, 1883; "Town and Country," DSL, June 7, July 6, 1884, June 6, 1885; "Program," DSL, July 4, 1885.

64. *It was of lawn.* Lawn is a sheer, lightweight fabric of linen or cotton. In *These Happy Golden Years* (pp. 243-44), this dress is the first that Ma makes on her new sewing machine.

65. *to see the races*. All kinds of races, from foot races to sack races to wheelbarrow races, were part of such festivities. Horse races, however, were a special feature of the 1883 and 1884 Fourth of July celebrations. In June 1884, the De Smet Trotting Association began construction of a half-mile racetrack "on Fred Dow's tree claim, about one half mile east of the village" ("Town and Country," DSL, June 7, 1884). On the Fourth, a large crowd gathered "to witness the contests," for which "a purse of about five dollars" had been raised, but the newness of the track kept the horses from making "good time" (ibid., July 6, 1884). In *These Happy Golden Years*, the Fourth of July celebration is held the summer before Laura and Almanzo's wedding and does not include races (pp. 247–49). "Glorious Fourth," DSL, June 30, 1883.

66. *Cousin Ella and her husband Lee Whiting*. Grace Ingalls recorded a later visit from this pair in her schoolgirl diary: "Cousins Lee and Ella came to day with their baby Earl, they came with a covered wagon and a stove" (quoted in Anderson, *Little House Reader*, p. 24). The couple may have been en route to California, where they ultimately settled.

Manly and I did not go to hear the speeches but in the afternoon we drove in to see the races.[65] I wore my new outfit but alas no one got to see it but Manly. Barnum and Skip were so wild that we dared not drive them into the crowd. We had to keep them moving and so we drove them around and around the crowd, out on the prairie and back, with their manes and tails flying in the wind, their feet beating a tatoo on the hard ground or their front feet flailing the air as they danced on their hind ones, when the crowd cheered.

A particularly violent jump of the horses combined with the wind that blew strongly, tore the bunch of ostrich tips from my hat and I just barely caught them as they were sailing away.

"Put them in my pocket!" Manly said between his teeth, as he struggled with the plunging team and I tucked them into the coat pocket nearest me.

When we went home, he left me at the door with the understanding that we would go to the fireworks in the evening.

I was angry as I showed my damaged hat to Ma. [']If you want anything done,' I said 'do it yourself. I never sewed a feather on, for Miss Bell, that would come loose.'

We saw the fireworks from the buggy well on the outside of the crowd, with plenty of room around us.

When a rocket went up, the horses would leap and as Manly turned them to circle away from the crowd ahead, we would see it burst, which made the horses wild. Manly would swing them in a wide circle and bring them facing the fireworks in time to see the next rocket go up. Then we would swing on another circle.

But we saw them all and then drove home in the starlight, with the horses seeming almost to fly, so swiftly and so smoothly they trotted.

Cousin Ella and her husband Lee Whiting[66] drove up one Saturday and stayed three days.

Sunday afternoon when Manly drove up the horses were worse than usual and Ma didn't want me to go. But Lee told her I was safe enough. "That fellow knows how to handel horses," he said.

But that night he said to me, "Don't trust the driver too far, Laura, It isn't always safe."

I laughed and answered, 'If the driver fails me, I can do the driving myself.'

Soon after this Manly sold Skip and the buggy and drove Barnum single on a new buggy.

We did not make such long drives with one horse and we had driven all the roads so many times that we were a little tired of them, so we were glad when a singing school was started. It was held in the church every Friday night.[67]

We drove Barnum. I sat in the buggy and held the reins while Manly tied him tightly to a strong hitching post. Then we went inside and sang the scales and the rounds and "We're All Here, Don't Leave The Farm Boys, The Sleighing Glee, Dearest May, Don't Go Out Tonight My Darling, Blame Yourself If You're Sold, We All Have A Very Bad Cold[,] Wine I[s] A Mocker," and others.[68]

(If you want the spirit of these times, you should read over these old songs.)[69]

We always had to leave at recess, for we must get Barnum away without a crowd around. We would slip quietly out, and I would get into the buggy, while Manly stood at Barnum's head. I would unwind the lines from around the whip, without letting Barnum feel my touch on the reins, for as soon as he felt that he would jump.

Then while I sat with the reins loose but tightly in my hands, tensed and ready, Manly would untie Barnum and with the tie strap in his hand, wait while I turned Barnum on his Jump, so the buggy would not strike the post, and make a flying leap for it as it went by. Sometimes he missed and when I brought Barnum around to pass him again, would make another try. Usually it took several times trying before he could get in the buggy and once Singing school was over and the people coming out of the church before we got away.[70]

One Sunday afternoon, Manly came for me to go driving, with Barnum single on a new buggy. I took the reins to drive before we got to town, for Barnum and I had become used to each other and a certain sympathy passed between us over the lines.

He had been acting in his usual manner, but I had driven him only a little way, when, of himself, he dropped into a walk.

I hardly dared breathe and I kept trying to feel quiet and cool so

67. *a singing school. . . . every Friday night.* Singing schools became popular in the nineteenth century as a way to improve singing in churches and to provide wholesome entertainment. They were often held in churches and organized by a self-appointed singing master, who worked from manuals that included basic music principles as well as secular and sacred songs. In De Smet, singing schools appear to have been a wintertime activity. Two schools were held in 1884–1885. One began in February 1884, and the other started in December and ran into 1885. The Brandt Revised and Bye manuscripts included a detailed description of the singing school (*see* Appendix D). "Singing Schools"; "Town and Country," DSL, Feb. 16, Dec. 6, 1884.

68. *"We're All Here, . . . and others.* These songs appear in Charles E. Leslie and Ransom H. Randall's *The Conqueror*, a songbook published in 1880. The book may have been the one used in the singing school, and Wilder and Lane certainly consulted it when drafting *Pioneer Girl* and, later, *These Happy Golden Years.* Charles Edward Pollock wrote the lyrics and music for "Don't Leave the Farm, Boys." Wilder mentioned it as one of "the old singing-school songs" in *The First Four Years* (p. 22), and its lyrics supplied the book's closing words (p. 134). "Sleighing Glee" uses words by Lizzie Newbury and music by E. C. Newbury. For the remaining songs, *see* Appendix D. Cockrell, *Ingalls Wilder Family Songbook*, pp. xlii–xliii; Leslie and Randall, *The Conqueror*, pp. 24–25, 33.

69. *(If you want . . . you should read over these old songs.)* This aside to Lane may have prompted inclusion of the extended section on songs and the singing school in Brandt Revised (pp. 109–15) and Bye (Appendix D).

70. *before we got away.* In Bye, Wilder commented wryly, "On account of Barnum, going to Singing School was, for Manly and me, mostly leaving" (p. 188), but even so, "Barnum was fun" (p. 189). Wilder crafted an entire chapter on the topic in *These Happy Golden Years* (pp. 201–8).

"Barnum arched his neck and walked proudly on."
Helen Sewell, 1943

71. *And that way, I drove him.* This moment is so important within the context of *These Happy Golden Years* that Wilder devoted an entire chapter to it ("Barnum Walks," pp. 209–16).

72. *ice cream social at the church.* The "ladies of the M. E. church" gave an "ice cream festival" on Thursday night, September 4, 1884. The *De Smet Leader* pronounced it "a complete success," at which "the cream and cake were excellent, and a very social time was had" ("Town and Country," Sept. 6, 1884).

73. *in the starlight.* "In the Starlight" features music by Stephen Glover and lyrics by Joseph E. Carpenter. Wilder quoted from the song's second verse. Almanzo requests and Laura sings the same song in *These Happy Golden Years* (pp. 213–14). Garson, *Laura Ingalls Wilder Songbook*, p. 100; Cockrell, *Ingalls Wilder Family Songbook*, pp. 250–53, 389.

it would get to him over the lines. He was nervous and I felt his impulse now and then to jump and make a dash, but still he walked with no pulling on the reins, only a firm hold.

And that way, I drove him[71] the whole length of main street, while everyone in sight stopped and stared at Barnum and me. Manly had started to exclaim at the first but stopped and sat without saying a word, while I talked quietly about how Barnum and how nice it was to have him walking.

Going home in the twilight Barnum walked for Manly and he had time to ask me how I liked the new buggy.

I said I liked it but the back of the seat was not quite so high as in the old buggy. Then he laid his arm along the top of the back of the seat behind my shoulders and asked if that were better.

I shrugged my shoulders and said I didn't think it was any improvment 'and you'd better,' said I 'tend to your driving,' for Barnum jumped. So he took his arm away suddenly.

Shortly after that Manly sold Barnum and got a quiet team that he could hitch and stay to supper and for the evening at times. And when we went anywhere we could stay until other people left if we wanted to.

We went one night, to an Aid society, ice cream social at the church,[72] but it was stupid and we left early going the long way, around the Big Slough, home.

There was wind enough so the misquotoes didn't bother and we drove quietly along under the stars. Manly was very quiet, the horses feet beat rythmacly on the hard prairie road while I sang softly.

"In the starlight, in the starlight,[73]
At the daylight's dewy close,
When the nightengale is singing
His last love song to the rose.
In the calm, clear night of summer,
When the breezes gently play,
In the starlight, in the starlight
Let us softly steal away.
Where the silver waters murmur,

By the margin of the sea,
In the starlight, in the starlight
Let us wander gay and free.
In The starlight, in the starlight,
We will wander, we will wander.
In the starlight, in the starlight,
We will wander gay and free.["]

When I stopped signing, the horses were stepping slow and softly and there was silence under the starlight.

Manly was so still I wondered if he had dropped asleep.

'A penny for your thoughts,' said I.

"I was wondering if you wanted an engagement ring," he answered.

I gave a startled gasp. 'That would depend,' I said, [']on who offered it to me?[']

"Would you take it from me?" he asked and I said 'Yes!'[74]

Then we drove on in some more silence until I got down at the door.

I started to go in, then stopped and asked, 'Arn't you going to kiss me good night.'

"I was afraid you wouldn't like it," he said.

Then he kissed me good night and I went in the house, not quite sure if I were engaged to Manly or to the starlight and the prairie.

But I was sure, when Manly brought me a beautiful pearl and garnet engagement ring, the next time he came.[75]

When I showed it to Ma she said "Pa and I havent been blind. We've been expecting it" and she kissed me. Pa said nothing when he saw the ring, he just smiled at me.

The bad storms seemed to have changed their time of coming from winter to summer this year. Early in the spring as Pa was walking across the prairie, he saw what looked like a ball of fire, as large as a wagon wheel, inside a cloud whirling along the ground behind him. As he watched it swung to one side and moved off out of sight across the bare prairie. Pa said it was electricity. All summer there had been terrible storms of thunder and lightening. We often saw

74. *and I said 'Yes!'* In *These Happy Golden Years*, Laura says, "Then it would depend on the ring" (p. 214). The difference is subtle but significant. Wilder's fictional counterpart is more poised, less surprised. When Wilder originally outlined the material, she blocked it this way: "Staying at Boasts until moon comes up. Starlight instead. Ride home in the starlight. 'Do you want an engagement ring?' 'That would depend on who gave it to me.' 'If I should give it to you?' 'Then it would depend on the ring.'" Wilder then added a note to Lane: "Fact! This was Manly's proposal and my answer. It was what you might call laconic and illustrates once more the something about us at that time and place I have tried to express" (LIW, "Prairie Girl" outline). Yet, in all versions of *Pioneer Girl*, Wilder gave Almanzo an affirmative answer right away.

75. *the next time he came.* Wilder initially planned for the novel to end here—with Almanzo's proposal and the ring. The final chapter in her initial "Prairie Girl" outline, titled "One Sunday Night," contained: "A long drive. Barnum walks through town for the first time with me Laura driving. Home in the starlight. Manly has the ring." From there, Wilder wrote what she believed would be the last scene in the series:

The horses stand quietly, beside the claim shanty, within the hollow square of young cottonwoods. There is no light in the windows but the music of Pa's fiddle floats softly out. Laura's voice joins it singing just above her breath—"In the starlight, in the starlight we will wander gay and free, for there's nothing in the daylight half so dear to you and me"—

"And while we wait,["] Manly whispered, "I will build us a little house on the tree claim where the trees will shelter it as they grow."

The End
(Or words to this effect)

Tornado, thirty miles south of De Smet, D.T., August 1884.
South Dakota State Historical Society

76. *There were terrible wind storms . . . down in the cellar.* Today, wildly rotating funnel clouds are called
tornadoes (not cyclones) when they touch down
and begin to move destructively across the land. The
De Smet vicinity appears to have been especially
troubled with such storms during the summers of
1884 and 1885. On August 18, 1884, "three great
water-spouts were seen west of De Smet during the
rain." These clouds were from "ten to fifteen miles
distant." On the same day, a tornado—"a cyclone of
the funnel shaped variety"—demolished buildings
and injured people near Huron ("Town and Country," DSL, Aug. 20, 1884). In July 1885, the *Leader*
editor remarked: "Storms are becoming most un-
pleasingly frequent. If they come up much oftener
people will need to live in their cellars altogether
to be safe. Thus far our citizens have been more
scared than hurt, but there is no telling when it will
change" (ibid., July 4, 1885). In *These Happy Golden
Years*, Wilder described two different summer
storms that happened roughly a year apart (pp. 195-
97, 251-58).

77. *the Catholic church. . . . were twisted around.* On
July 25, 1884, a storm struck De Smet directly, causing "considerable damage." The "unfinished Catholic church was blown down. Loss $800. Insured for
$500. The band hall was moved about six feet and
badly racked. W. S. Lawman's residence was moved

funnel shaped clouds, dip toward the ground and rise, dip and rise
as the body of the cloud rolled by.

There were terrible wind storms and often Pa would wake us in
the night and send us down in the cellar,[76] while he prowled around
outside, watching the clouds, ready to drop down into the cellar
himself, if the cyclone really came.

One Sunday afternoon there was such a bad storm that Manly
did not drive out, but sat with Cap Garland in their room upstairs
and watched the Catholic church lifted from its foundations and set
down at one side with a smash, while several dwelling houses were
twisted around.[77]

We were all watching the storm when Pa shouted to run down
cellar. We thought all De Smet was blowing away and we ran, but
the bad part of the storm did not hit our place, though the cottonwood trees that had grown tall and beautiful around the house were
blown nearly flat to the ground.

One night after an unusually hot day[78] a storm was coming
up and we did not go to bed when bedtime came, but watched
the storm to see if it was going to be a cyclone.

The black clouds rolled and tumbled showing plainly as the
lightening played over and through them, while the thunder
pealed and crashed.

The cloud seemed coming directly over us and the wind blew
harder and harder while the cottonwood trees around the house
thrashed wildly, bending almost to the ground.

Pa said to go to the cellar and they all went but me. I didn't
like to go sit in the cellar and I wanted to see the storm, too. I
thought I could get down as quick as Pa could. And I proved it!

When a dull roaring filled all the air, I dashed for the cellar
and Pa was just behind me.

And in the cellar we all cowered on the floor in a corner,
while we heard that awful roaring pass over our heads and on.

In a few minutes the rain fell in torrents and Pa went up
stairs saying the danger was over when the rain came. In a few
minutes we all followed him and went to bed.

from its foundation" ("Last Night's Storm," DSL, July 26, 1884).
Eliza Jane Wilder also recorded details: "One day I was caught in
a storm about ¾ of a mile from home. The wind blew so hard as
to crush the Catholic Church and several buildings were moved
from their foundations. The town hall among the rest. Hail and
rain came in torrents and with such force that my arms were black

and blue after. Gardens were destroyed, wheat and other grains
seriously injured" (quoted in Anderson, *Wilder in the West*, p. 20).

78. *One night after an unusually hot day.* Wilder added the description of this storm on the back of a page without directions as to
where it should go. All subsequent versions of *Pioneer Girl* place
it here.

79. *One boy and both mules were killed.* Lane used a variation of this outcome (both boys were killed) in her short story "Home over Saturday" to explain the depression of their mother, who was based on Mrs. Bouchie (p. 53). Wilder also used the story in *These Happy Golden Years* (pp. 255-57).

The cyclone struck to the east of us we learned later, but did not do much damage and no one was hurt.

One afternoon we saw a bad storm rising in the northwest. It came up for awhile, then turned and swung around passing to the west of us going south. The large bank of clouds was first black, then turned a queer greenish, purple color and from it a funnel shaped cloud dropped down until its point touched the ground. With its point on the ground and the large end of the funnel in the cloud above it began whirling and traveled southward with the purple green cloud above it.

Then a second funnel point dropped, touched the ground and followed the first, then another and there were three under the cloud and traveling swiftly with it.

The wind was almost still where we were and we stood in the dooryard and watched the cloud and its funnels pass on the west of us.

This storm did a great deal of damage and killed some people. Two boys were caught as they were riding a span of mules home, from where they had just finished stacking the grain on their farm.

One boy and both mules were killed[79] with every bone in their bodies broken, the clothes stripped off the boy and the harness of[f] the mules, no sign of clothes or harness was ever found.

The boy who came through alive and unhurt, said they started home with the mules hitched together, he riding one mule, his brother the other. When the storm struck, the wind lifted them and carried them around in a large circle and up higher and higher, with straw blowing thickly all around them.

They went around so swiftly that he grew dizzy. He called to his brother to hang [on] to the mule and just then, they were snatched apart and he was plucked off his mule.

He didn't see his brother or the mules again and after awhile he felt that he was floating down around a circle instead of rising. As he went around close to the ground he tried to spring up and then struck the ground running ran a few steps and fell.

After a few minutes he got up unhurt, but with no shred of clothing on him, not even his shoes. The great stacks of wheat, the whole years crop had disappeared.

A door, belonging to a house that had been destroyed at one oclock floated down into the street of a nearby town at 4 oclock[80] and never told where it had been for three hours.

School began in September, but it was moved into the new, large schoolhouse and changed into a high school.[81]

Ven Owen was still teacher, only now he was the principal and Gussie Masters, Genieve's older, oh much older sister, taught the downstairs room of little children.[82]

Ida Brown and I were still seatmates and she had an engagement ring too. She was going to marry a Mr McConnel[83] who had worked all summer for Mr Brown, but who had a homestead of his own several miles away.

Carrie and I walked in to school through September and October.

The first of November, Manly and his brother Roy started south with a covered hack and a stock of notions to sell on the road. They expected to travel through Nebraska into and through Iowa and come to Spring Valley where their father lived to spend the winter.[84]

It was lonesome after Manly left. There were no more drives nor evenings out somewhere, but I was studying hard at school hoping to graduate from high school in the spring.

A roller skating rink[85] had been opened in town and one afternoon I went to try the skates, instead of staying at school.

As luck would have it a great many others in school did the same that same afternoon, so the next morning all who had been absent were asked to stand and tell where and why.

It became funny as one after the other said, "At the rink, to skate," and Mr Owen's remarks were not pleasant. I was last being on the back seat and when I said 'At the rink,' a wave of amusement went over the school, but I could see that Mr Owen was surprised, but he only said "You usually set a good example Laura."

I was distressed, for I was the best scholar in school and had taught the downstairs room for two days when Gussie Masters

80. *A door, . . . at 4 oclock*. In Brandt, this incident took place in a town east of De Smet before the storm passed into western Minnesota. The town name was left blank, as if Lane intended to consult with her mother before finalizing the typewritten text (p. 152 [2d]). Brandt Revised and Bye omitted any town reference but provided more detail:

> In this same storm another strange thing happened. At about one o'clock in the afternoon another farmer's house was destroyed. None of this family was hurt, as they were all in the cyclone cellar, but like many families that year, they lost everything they owned. Only some scattered and broken lumber was left of their house.
>
> That afternoon about sunset, the storm having been out of sight for some hours and the sky clear, this family and some neighbors were sadly looking at the scattered wreckage, when they noticed a small dark object overhead, which appeared to be growing larger. It did not look like a bird, and they all watched it. For some time it fell slowly toward them, and they saw it was a door. It came gently down before them, and proved to be the door of the vanished house.
>
> This door was in good condition, not injured at all, nor even scratched. It was a wonder where it had been all those hours, and how it could have fallen from a clear sky directly over the place where the house had been.
>
> Manly and many others went to see the door, and found the farmer quite cheerful, saying that anyway he had saved more from the storm than he had thought at first, and he used this old door in the new shanty he put up (Bye, p. 194).

It could be that Wilder and Lane consulted Almanzo for details about this incident because in *These Happy Golden Years*, his fictional counterpart and Pa witness the door floating back to earth (p. 258).

81. *the new, large schoolhouse and . . . a high school*. The process of building this larger school began in the fall of 1883, when the school board voted to hire a primary teacher "as soon as necessary, and a room

De Smet school, built 1884. *South Dakota State Historical Society*

can be procured" ("Town and Country," *DSL*, Sept. 15, 1883). The board hired Miriam M. ("Minnie") Barrows to teach the primary grades and, after the successful school exhibition in April 1884, promoted her to assistant principal. Voters also agreed to issue bonds for a suitable building, and in July 1884, the "contract for building the new $5,000 graded school building was let to L. E. Sasse" (ibid., July 12, 1884). By mid-August, the building was enclosed, the roof was being laid, and it began to "look imposing" (ibid., Aug. 23, 1884). The community dedicated the building January 1, 1885. It contained four classrooms, "two in each story, each 29 feet square" ("The Schoolhouse Dedicated," ibid., Jan. 3, 1885). Wilder described "the new brick schoolhouse on Third Street" in *These Happy Golden Years* (p. 201). "School Board Meeting," *DSL*, Aug. 18, 1883, Apr. 19, 1884; "Town and Country," *DSL*, Jan. 12, 1884.

82. *Gussie Masters, . . . taught the downstairs room of little children.* The eldest daughter of Samuel and Margaret Masters, "Miss Gussie Masters," arrived in De Smet in April 1883 with the intent to stay ("Personalities," *DSL*, Apr. 14, 1883). About eight years older than Wilder, she began teaching in New York at the age of fifteen, then taught schools in Currie, Minnesota (near Walnut Grove), and Esmond, Dakota Territory. In August 1884, she attended the monthly teacher's institute in De Smet under the name "G. Elgetha Masters," and in January 1885, when the new schoolhouse opened with over eighty pupils, "Miss G. E. Masters" was engaged to take the intermediate grades ("Town and Country," *DSL*, Aug. 2, 1884, Jan. 10, 1885). In 1888, she married Carter P. Sherwood who had become publisher of the *De Smet Leader* in February 1885. After their marriage, Grace Ingalls observed, "Miss Masters is a great deal taller than he so they must

look funny together" (quoted in Anderson, *Little House Reader*, p. 26). Others remembered her for her "gentle, gracious personality" (Harding, *I Recall Pioneer Days*, p. [26]). The couple had three children, including Aubrey Sherwood, who published the *De Smet News* for fifty-seven years. Sherwood, *Beginnings of De Smet*, p. 15; "Town and Country," *DSL*, Feb. 21, 1885; "De Smet publisher retires," *Watertown Public Opinion*, Mar. 25, 1977.

83. *Ida Brown. . . . was going to marry a Mr McConnel.* In *These Happy Golden Years*, "Ida's left hand was resting on the desk where Laura would be sure to see the broad circlet of gold shining on the first finger" (p. 217). Elmer E. McConnell worked the farm for the elderly Reverend Brown during the summers and taught a term of school near his hometown of Nevada, Ohio, in the winter. Ida Wright, who also taught a term of school near Manchester, D.T., in the spring of 1885, married Elmer McConnell on Decem-

G. Elgetha Masters. *Aubrey Sherwood Collection*

Elmer E. McConnell. *Laura Ingalls Wilder Historic Home and Museum*

ber 3, 1885. The couple had three children before moving to Wisconsin, where they had two more. In 1920, the McConnells and two of their children lived in Sacramento County, California, where Ida died in 1926. "Town and Country," *DSL*, Apr. 4, May 16, 1885; Cleaveland, "Ida B. Wright," pp. 83–84.

84. *The first of November. . . . to Spring Valley . . . to spend the winter.* The *De Smet Leader*, however, suggested a different itinerary for Manly and Royal. "The Wilder brothers are supposed to be progressing toward New Orleans on the hurricane deck of a peddler's wagon," the editor reported on November 22, 1884, "expecting to spend the winter on the road and return here in time to put in next year's crop" ("Town and Country"). The 1884 World's Fair, also known as the World's Industrial and Cotton Centennial Exposition, would open in mid-December 1884 in New Orleans, and a number of De Smet residents planned to go. On December 6, the editor wrote, "We hear from the Wilder brothers that they

are progressing well on their way to the Exposition, and enjoying the trip immensely." Whether or not the Wilder brothers ever intended to go so far south is unknown. In the novel, they leave to spend the winter in Minnesota in Royal's "peddler's cart" (*HGY*, p. 220). Eliza Jane Wilder routinely spent winters with her family in Spring Valley.

85. *A roller skating rink.* De Smet's concert band built the town's skating rink in 1884. It had a hardwood floor and "four Electric Sun lamps" that produced "a light equal to twenty common lamps" ("Town and Country," *DSL*, Oct. 11, 1884). The rink was open for skating afternoons and evenings on Wednesday, Friday, and Saturday. Dances and skating events were also held there regularly, including a Christmas Eve ball with an oyster supper at the Exchange Hotel afterward. Ibid., Nov. 20, Dec. 27, 1884; Miller, *Laura Ingalls Wilder's Little Town*, p. 139.

Perley, Royal, and Almanzo Wilder, ca. 1890.
Laura Ingalls Wilder Historic Home and Museum

86. *Pa rented the house in town*. Charles Ingalls actually rented it to George C. Westervelt, who "will devote his time to teaching music this winter" ("Town and Country," DSL, Nov. 20, 1884). *See* Appendix D. The fictional Ingalls family decides to spend its first winter on the claim because "the little house was really a house, no longer a claim shanty" (HGY, p. 222).

87. *Roy had left his pet horse, Lady*. In the novel, Lady and Prince are Almanzo's horses. Almanzo tells Laura that one of his neighbors is keeping Prince (p. 220). This episode, written on the back side of the tablet page, does not appear in subsequent versions of *Pioneer Girl*.

88. *"I couldn't stay away all winter."* The Wilder brothers arrived back in De Smet during Christmas week, "having given up their New Orleans trip after going to southwestern Nebraska" ("Town and Country," DSL, Dec. 27, 1884).

could not be there, but certainly I had not set a good example that time.

Pa rented the house in town[86] and we stayed on the farm that winter. When it grew cold and the snow came Pa took us to school and came after us at night with the horses and sleigh. Sometimes it was bitterly cold and Pa froze the tip of his nose or his ears. He made a joke of it saying that every time they froze they grew larger.

I took one drive for pleasure but failed to find it.

Roy had left his pet horse, Lady,[87] for Pa to take care of while he was gone and told me I might drive her whenever I wanted to.

One day I started for Boast's, when I was a little over half way there, Lady went lame[,] so lame that I hated to drive her. It was nearer Boasts than home and I went on hoping Mr Boast could find the trouble.

He could find nothing wrong and when after a couple of hours I started home Lady went perfectly. There was no sign of lameness whatever all the way hom[e] and she wanted to go much faster than I did.

Manly told me afterward that it was a trick of hers to pretend she was lame when she didn't want to go.

Sunday night before Christmas was cold and stormy and I was feeling blue, because I had just had a letter from Manly reproaching me for not writing. I had written but the letter had not reached him.

We were sitting around the lamp reading when someone rapped at the door. I went and opened it and there stood Manly, huge in his big overcoat covered with snow, for it was storming. "I couldn't stay away all winter,"[88] he said and kissed me before all the folks.

He had no bells on his horses and had driven up and hitched them in the shelter of the stable, without our hearing him.

He had brought me a very pretty gold bar-pin for Christmas.

The rest of the winter went swiftly. We had a few sleigh rides, over to see Stella sometimes and down to Boasts, but Sunday evenings we spent by the fire in the sitting room.

The folks left us alone about nine oclock, but we knew that Manly was expected to leave when the clock struck eleven. He always did except one stormy night when he stopped the clock just before it struck and started it again when his watch said twelve, so that it struck eleven just as he left. I hastily pushed the hands ahead to nearly twelve blew out the lamp and went to bed in the dark.

Manly and Roy were batching together in the harness room of their new barn, near the schoolhouse and after Pa left Carrie and me at school he would drive his horses into the shed there, blanket them and go in and warm himself and sometimes eat buckwheat cakes with Manly and Roy at their breakfast. He did not freeze himself any more because he got thoroughly warm before he drove home.

We only had a few bad storms during the winter and when a blizzard was blowing in the morning we stayed at home.

One blizzard came just before time for school to close,[89] but Pa and the horses together followed the road and we got home safely.

At a country school eight miles north of De Smet, the teacher brought his children to school in a sleigh, stayed all day and drove home at night.[90] The other children lived very near the schoolhouse. In this storm the nearby children got safely home, but the teacher, with his load, was lost on the prairie.

When he knew that he couldn't find his way, he unhitched, unharnessed the horses and turned them loose. Then he spread part of the robes on the ground had the children sit on them, wrapped the rest of the robes around them and turned the sleigh bottom up over them. Then he crawled underneath the sleigh himself and there they huddled together while the snow blew and drifted over the sled keeping out the wind. Their bodies warmed the air in their little cave and they all survived the storm. No one was frozen except the teacher whose hands and feet were frozen, but not badly.[91]

The horses found shelter beside a haystack several miles away and came through safely too.

("No Sir! The storms are not what they used to be! Now in the Hard Winter" —)[92]

As spring drew near I talked to Mr Owen about graduating. He said he would have no graduation exercises that spring. The class

89. *One blizzard came just before time for school to close*. This blizzard likely took place in 1888 and is often called the "children's blizzard," which struck swiftly across the Great Plains on January 12, 1888. The storm "came up while the rural schoolhouses were filled with pupils, many of tender years, and a mile or two, possibly more from home, and raged with such strength and fury that neither strong men or animals could make their way against it" (Kingsbury, *History of Dakota Territory*, 2:1512). In Dakota Territory alone, 148 to 171 people, many of them children, froze to death or died of complications later. "As a rule teachers had been warned against such a danger, and lost no time in dismissing school. Others delayed, expecting the storm would subside and when they ventured forth they were soon bewildered, lost, and fell easy victims to the relentless fury of the maelstrom" (ibid., p. 1514). In 1888, Wilder and her family still lived in Kingsbury County, and Charles and Caroline Ingalls had moved into their new house in De Smet less than a month before the blizzard struck.

90. *the teacher brought his children to school in a sleigh. . . . at night*. The story that follows matches that of Orion E. Stearns, who homesteaded in Spirit Lake Township, about seven miles northeast of De Smet in 1885. He came from Trempealeau, Wisconsin, and at the time of the children's blizzard, he and his wife, Gertrude, had three school-aged children, Guy, fifteen; Nellie, about eleven; and Bessie, about eight. In January 1888, Stearns was teaching school one or two miles northwest of his claim, about seven miles from De Smet. Guy, Nellie, and Bessie Stearns were among his pupils. When the family started for home during the blizzard on January 12 and got lost, Stearns and his son turned the conveyance over to protect the two younger children and shoveled snow throughout the night to keep an airway open. The next day, Guy Stearns, whose feet were badly frozen, crawled away for help, while the telegraph wires reported the family missing. "The Grim Tally," *Wessington Springs True Dakotan*, Jan. 12, 1988; Final Patent #3749, BLM-GLO Records; *Erwin*, p. 52; Laskin, *Children's Blizzard*, p. 218.

91. *No one was frozen . . . but not badly.* The two girls survived the ordeal unharmed, and Orion Stearns, who suffered frozen fingers and toes, was crippled thereafter. Guy Stearns lost both legs and died on February 28, 1888, a circumstance common in the aftermath of this killer storm. Wilder apparently did not know about his death. *Erwin*, p. 52.

92. *("No Sir! . . . in the Hard Winter"—).* Subsequent manuscripts incorporate this aside. The Bye version reads:

"No siree!" the early settlers said. "Storms aren't what they used to be. Now in the Hard Winter—"

We remembered what the old Indian had said, and thought that these were the moderate winters he had said would follow the hard one (p. 197).

was not ready as I was the only one who could pass the examinations.

I was very much disappointed but didn't fuss. Instead I took [the] teachers examination and having secured my second grade certificate, with honorable mention, I applied for the Wilkins' school north west of school and being elected signed the contract to teach a three months school begining the first of April, for thirty dollars a month.[93] This made it necessary that I leave school before the term was finished.

On my last day of school, on my way out carrying my books, I stopped to say good by to Ven Owen. He wished me good luck with my school and then I told him this was good by to him as a teacher for I would be married in the fall and was not coming back to school any more.

When he understood, the tears came in his eyes and he begged me to give up teaching that spring and finish the term. He said he had not been fair to me to hold me back for the rest of the class as he had done all winter and if I would stay he would graduate me from high school by myself, that we still had time and I could do it.

I told him it was too late[94] that there was not time for the Wilkins' school to find another teacher, I had signed the contract and school began next Monday.

Florence Wilkins was one of my classmates. She had hoped to teach the school herself but failed to get a certificate.

She lived with her father, mother, little sister, married brother and his wife and baby[95] within a few rods of the school house where I was to teach. I liked Florence very well but had never seen any of her people and I did dread to go to live again in a houseful of strangers. It seemed as though I just could not.

But Sunday afternoon, Manly came and took me over to Mr Wilkins' and I opened school bright and early on Monday morning.

For scholars there were Jimmie and Mamie and Danny Glover, Irish children as full of mischief as they could hold but bright and quick. There were Mary and Charley and Tommy Webb good and bright enough, but slow minded. Then there was Georgie Dwight,[96] who was the littlest, with his brand new primer.

93. *I applied for the Wilkins' school . . . thirty dollars a month*. The Wilkin school stood about three miles northwest of De Smet on the homestead claim of Thomas C. Wilkin. In 1880, Wilkin lived in Middleville, Michigan, with his wife Mary, a twenty-two-year-old son, Willis, a twelve-year-old daughter, Florence, and an infant daughter, Ethel. He was listed as "Architect & Builder" by trade and, in July 1884, was hired to "be superintending architect to draw plans and specifications in detail for, and to oversee the construction of," De Smet's new graded school building ("School Board Meeting" *DSL*, July 12, 1884). Wilder signed a contract to teach Common School No. 6 for three months starting on April 20, 1885, for twenty-five dollars a month. Final Patent #3328, BLM-GLO Records; Teacher's Contract, Apr. 14, 1885, Laura Ingalls Wilder Historic Home and Museum.

94. *I told him it was too late*. The Brandt Revised (p. 123) and Bye manuscripts added: "This was a very great unhappiness to me. I had always so longed for an education, and had hoped at least to graduate from High School" (Bye, p. 197).

95. *Florence Wilkins. . . . lived with . . . baby*. Florence Wilkin was just a year younger than Wilder, and her family had grown since the 1880 census. Presumably, her brother Willis had married in the interim.

96. *Jimmie and Mamie and Danny Glover. . . . Mary and Charley and Tommy Webb. . . . Georgie Dwight*. Tracing these children and their families through census records under these names was unsuccessful. However, Wilder's memory improved when she was writing *These Happy Golden Years*, and in the draft of that book housed in the Detroit Public Library, she listed "Fanny and Delbert Webb" (p. 256) among Laura's students. They were the children of Rueben Webb, who came from Wisconsin and homesteaded near the Wilkin school district. In 1885, Fanny Webb would have been about fourteen; Adelbert was eleven; and they had an eight-year-old sister named Edith. In the draft of the novel, Wilder also mentioned "little Clarance" as the youngest pupil, and a Clarence Dwight is traceable through census records as one of the four school-aged chil-

dren of Dan and Frances A. Dwight, who came from Fillmore County, Minnesota, and homesteaded in the same general vicinity. In the published novel, Wilder did not name the students, and she skimmed over experiences at the school because Laura "felt herself a capable teacher now, and she dealt so well with every little difficulty that none ever lasted until the next day" (*HGY*, p. 239). Final Patent #1239 and #4265, BLM-GLO Records.

97. *the boy*. The boy was Will Bennet or Bennett.

At first Georgie did not seem to be any obstacle to the success of the school. I started hopefully to teach him his letters and found that he could not learn them. He seemed to try, but from his first lesson in the morning to the next before noon he couldn't remember and tell A. from B.

I tried with all patience. Whenever the other children were not reciting I would have him come to me and I did everything I knew to fix in his mind the first few letters of the alphabet. He wrote them on his slate; He made them on the blackboard with a beautiful long piece of chalk, he read them to me over and over, but he did not learn one of them so he knew it the next time he saw it. This went on for two weeks.

Then I remembered Ven Owen and the boy[97] everyone called a fool and I brought a switch to school one morning.

When he came to me to struggle with the alphabet again, I said, meanwhile toying with the switch in my hand, 'Now Georgie, we will try again the first four letters. If you don't learn them so you can tell them to me the next time, I will whip you.'

Just after recess, I called him up again. There was a sinking feeling in the pit of my stomach. I didn't want to whip the poor little rat.

But Glory Be! He knew them! He could write them as I asked, frontwards, backwards or mixed. He could find them anywhere in his primmer. I praised him and told him he might go out doors and play in the shade until noon.

In the afternoon we went over them again and in the morning he remembered them and we learned four more.

Carefully reviewing so not to lose any of them and always with the switch in sight, we learned the alphabet. It took the term of three months for him to learn the alphabet and begin the words, but the thing of greatest value that he learned was to begin to use his mind.

The children all walked together about a quarter of a mile on their way home before they separated. At first all was pleasant and they had merry times coming and going. Then they divided along family lines and began to quarrel and fight. It was the Irish against the Dutch and it kept growing worse. Each side came to me with complaints of the other.

Then as I dismissed school at night I went with them to the door. 'You must not walk together any more['] I said. [']You Jimmie and Mamie don't go in a straight line, but start from here directly toward your house. Mary and Charley and Tommy, you start directly toward your house from the doorstep.' As the Glovers lived to the southeast and the Webbs to the northeast, every step they took separated them farther and by the time they were beyond my control they were too far apart to fight. They became so eager to be together when it was forbidden, that they were good friends at the schoolhouse where before they had often quarreled. The going home rule lasted the rest of the term.

One night a prairie fire came through where the grass had not been burned the fall before and Florence and I got up and helped fight it away from the buildings and the school house.

I was sick and delerious[98] so that Mr Wilkins went down and dismissed the school.

Manly took me home every Friday night and brought me back Sunday night, quite like old times only now it was the beautiful spring time with no cold wind blowing and I had no intention of quitting him when school was out.

I was soon home again with $60.[99] that after all had been easily earned. The other $30. could not be paid me until some time in the fall.

(This was the $30. that bought the colt, that was sold to buy the sheep that with their increase were sold for the money that bought Rocky Ridge)[100]

One Sunday morning Pa took Mary and me to church. I wore my tucked lawn dress. It was a warm day and the church door stood open.

As the preacher was earnestly preaching a stray kitten came walking up the aisle and stood arching its back and rubbing its side against a corner of the pulpit. Just then a stray dog came in the door

98. *I was sick and delerious.* The Brandt version explained, "The fire nearly got beyond our control and I worked so hard fighting it that next morning I was sick and delirious" (p. 157).

99. *I was soon home again with $60.* In *These Happy Golden Years,* Laura gives part of her salary to Pa, who says, "It will help me out of a pinch. . . . But this is the last one. . . . The town is growing so fast that I am going to have plenty of carpenter work. . . . and next year I win my bet with Uncle Sam and this homestead will be ours. So you need never worry about helping any more, Half-Pint." This passage near the end of the novel signals that the Ingalls family will enjoy good fortune at last. It is Wilder's way of providing a realistic but happy ending for her fictional family (p. 245).

100. *(This was the $30. . . . Rocky Ridge).* In *The First Four Years,* an autobiographical novel that Wilder did not seek to publish in her lifetime, she wrote that after her marriage, "the directors of the school were able to pay Laura the salary for the last month she had taught. . . . Manly told her if she bought a colt with it she could double the money" (p. 30). Later, Laura's cousin Peter Ingalls proposes that Laura and Manly join him in buying one hundred head of sheep. Laura and Manly sell the colt for one hundred dollars, which pays for fifty sheep (pp. 93–95). Ultimately, they sold the sheep for five hundred dollars. Lane later recalled, "My mother had saved one hundred dollars to take to The Land of the Big Red Apple [Missouri]" (RWL, *LHT,* p. 13). That hundred dollar bill was temporarily lost, but when found, it "bought the farm" that the Wilders would live on for the rest of their lives (ibid., p. 94). Miller, *Becoming,* p. 85.

101. *a tree claim.* As required by Congress in 1878, homesteaders taking out a tree claim agreed to plant ten acres of trees on a quarter section of land (one hundred sixty acres). In Bye, Wilder added: "These trees almost always died, as no amount of care would make them survive the dry, hot summers with their scorching winds. But planting and careful cultivation, whether the trees lived or not, would give a man title to the land" (p. 200). Manly's tree claim was in the southeast quarter of Section 9, Township 111, roughly a mile north of his homestead and two miles north of De Smet. In *The First Four Years,* Wilder identified the trees that sat "in a beautiful grove" beside the road as cottonwoods, elms, and maples (p. 15). Miller, *Becoming,* p. 73; Final Patent #10979.

102. *and this Sunday . . . planning a big wedding.* Wilder's two fictional accounts of this episode unfold differently. In *These Happy Golden Years,* Almanzo reveals his family's plans for a big wedding to Laura on Tuesday. His unannounced appearance on a weekday worries Laura. Wearing a "calico work dress," she grabs a sunbonnet and gets into the buggy, where Almanzo asks, "Do you want a big wedding?" (p. 268). The scene conveys a sense of urgency. In *The First Four Years,* Manly drives out to deliver the news on a Monday afternoon, and Laura almost appears to be expecting him. Wearing a good dress "of pink lawn with its small springs of blue flowers," she has "time to put on her hat and pick up her gloves" (pp. 1–2). The details make the episode seem less spontaneous.

103. *I agreed . . . and be married.* In *These Happy Golden Years,* Laura does not agree quite so quickly, telling Almanzo that she had hoped to have "a little longer to get my things made" (p. 269). But in *The First Four Years,* while Laura again worries over her trousseau, she also raises a significant objection: "I don't want to marry a farmer. . . . I do wish you would do something else" (pp. 3–4). Manly persuades her to give him three years to make it as a farmer, and, with a year of grace, that agreement provides the structure for the novel.

and walked up the aisle toward pulpit and kitten. The kittens tail grew large, the hair on its back stood up and spitting it disappeared, while the little dog went hunting it.

While the dog was still hunting, I felt a gentle swaying of my hoop skirt and looking down saw the tip of the kittens tail disappearing under the hem of my dress. It had taken refuge under my skirts and was climbing up my hoops on the inside, like a monkey on the bars of his cage. I had a sudden vision of the dog discovering the kitten and what the consequences might be so that I shook with silent laughter.

Mary, who had missed it all, punched me with her elbow and whispered savagely, "Behave yourself!" which didn't help me any.

When it was time to go, the kitten had disappeared once more and outside I found Manly waiting to drive me home to dinner.

He had been very busy all summer putting in his crops and building a house on the tree claim. He had already proved up on his homestead so we did not have to live there and he thought it would be a pleasant place to live among the trees of the ten acres he had planted and must cultivate to get title to the 160 acres he had filed on as a tree claim.[101] The two claims made him 320 acres of land.

The house was nearly done and this Sunday he told me that his sister Eliza and his mother were planning a big wedding[102] for us in the church. That he had not been able to persuade them out of the idea and unless we were married before fall, they would be out and surely have their way.

Manly didn't want that kind of a wedding. He said he could not afford what it would cost him.

I knew Pa couldn't afford to give me that kind of a wedding either, so I agreed that as soon as the house could be finished, we would drive quietly to Mr Brown's and be married.[103]

Ma and I made my wedding dress of black cashmere,[104] a tight fitting basque, pointed at the bottom front and back, lined and boned with a high collar and plain sleeves rather full at the top, also lined. There was a shirring around the front of each armhole making a fullness over the breast that was taken up by the darts below and

Laura and Almanzo Wilder, ca. 1885.
Laura Ingalls Wilder Historic Home and Museum

104. *my wedding dress of black cashmere.* In 1885, white had not yet become the standard color for a wedding gown in the United States, nor was the dress to be worn just once. By 1943, however, when *These Happy Golden Years* first appeared, white had become traditional, and Wilder used the hasty wedding scenario to explain the black dress to her readers (pp. 267–71). Wilder also described it in detail (pp. 272–73), employing vocabulary and phrasing almost identical to that in *Pioneer Girl*. Cashmere is a soft, supple wool produced from the shearing of Kashmir goats. It has long been considered a luxurious yet durable material. In *These Happy Golden Years*, Ma tells Laura, "Cashmere wears well, and it is always dressy for all but the very hottest days of summer" (p. 266). Later, she also worries over the old saying, "Married in black, you'll wish yourself back" (p. 217).

105. *(You know the dress. It was still my best . . . Missouri)*. Lane did know this dress, which she called her mother's "black cloth wedding dress." She remembered Wilder wearing it in 1894, nine years after the wedding. "She put on the skirt and smoothed the placket," Lane wrote in 1962. "I was sorry that the skirt hid her new shoes. She coaxed her arms into the basque's tight sleeves and carefully buttoned all the glittery jet buttons up its front to her chin. . . . She looked lovely; she was beautiful. You could see my father think so, when she came out and he looked at her" (RWL, *LHT*, pp. 89–90).

106. *On the morning of August 25th. 1885.* The announcement in the *De Smet Leader* on August 29, 1885, noted that Almanzo J. Wilder and Miss Laura Ingalls had been married "at the residence of the officiating clergyman, Rev. E. Brown, August 25, 1885." It was a Tuesday; the fictional wedding takes place on a Thursday (*HGY*, p. 276; *FFY*, p. 9). Reverend Brown, now seventy-one years old, had retired a year earlier, but he was still active in the community. Wilder wrote in *The First Four Years* that he lived on a homestead two miles away, and "it seemed to Laura the longest drive she had ever taken" (p. 10). The newspaper wished the couple well: "Thus two more of our respected young people have united in the journey of life. May their voyage be pleasant[,] their joys be many and their sorrows few" ("Married," *DSL*, Aug. 29, 1889).

107. *Mr Brown had promised me not to use the word "obey". . . he kept his word.* Wilder offered an explanation for this promise in *These Happy Golden Years*. When Laura asks Almanzo, "Do you want me to promise to obey you?," he answers, "Of course not," but then asks if she believes in women's rights. Laura replies that she does not want the right to vote but that she "can not make a promise that I will not keep." Almanzo reveals that Reverend Brown is opposed to using the word "obey" in wedding ceremonies. "You know he is a cousin of John Brown of Kansas," Almanzo points out, "and a good deal like him" (pp. 269–70). In reality, both Reverend Brown and his wife were heavily involved in the Woman's

it was buttoned straight down the front with imitation jet buttons. The skirt was long just escaping the floor as I stood straight. It was plain at the top, but gored so it was full at the bottom. It was lined throught with cambric dress lining and interlined with crinolin from the bottom to as high as my knees.

(You know the dress. It was still my best dress when we came to Missouri)[105]

I had besides a black and fawn color striped silk dress a present from the Chicago friends. It was made very plainly, with a gored skirt and polanaise without any trimming whatever. My brown open work silk dress and my tucked lawn were still good.

On the morning of August 25th. 1885[106] at half past ten oclock, Manly drove up to the house and drove away with me in the buggy, for the last time in the old way.

We were at Mr Brown's at eleven and were married at once with Ida Brown and Elmer McConnell as witnesses.

Mr Brown had promised me not to use the word "obey" in the ceremony and he kept his word.[107]

At half past eleven we left Mr Brown's and drove home to dinner, which Ma had ready and waiting for us.

Then with good wishes from the folks and a few tears we drove over the road we had traveled so many times, across the Big Slough, around the corner by Pearson's livery barn, through De Smet and then out two miles north to the new house on the tree claim, where Manly had taken my trunk the day before.

There were three rooms in the house and a leanto over the back door.

The front door opened into the main room, which was dining and sitting room. At the right hand, as one went in the front door, was the door into the bedroom and a little farther along the door into a most wonderfully shelved pantry, with many drawers of many sizes and a broad shelf across the far end under the window.

Manly's batchelor, kitchen stove was in the leanto over the back door, which was opposite the front door. The dishes Manly had used in his housekeeping were on the pantry shelves, his table in

Christian Temperance Union, the most active organizational supporter of woman suffrage in Dakota Territory, and 1885 was an interesting year for the cause. During February, the territorial legislature was "wrestling with this problem of woman suffrage," the editor of the *De Smet Leader* noted, asking, "Why should any woman who pays taxes for school and for city, county or State government be denied the right of representation?" ("Woman's Suffrage," Feb. 14, 1885). The Kingsbury County representatives helped to pass a pro-suffrage measure through both houses in March. "If Gov. Pierce does not veto it," the editor wrote, "we shall see what the ladies will do with the ballot" ("Town and Country," Mar. 14, 1885). Governor Gilbert Pierce, however, did veto it, citing the possibility that it would delay statehood, and the legislature was unable to override his veto. The women of South Dakota did not get the vote until 1918, two years before ratification of the Nineteenth Amendment to the United States Constitution granted women nationwide the right to vote. Reed, *Woman Suffrage Movement*, pp. 12–13.

108. *Later I was to learn that we owed $500. . . . But that . . . is another story anyway.* This passage, written on the back of a page, does not appear in subsequent versions of *Pioneer Girl*, but Wilder did eventually write the story she alluded to here in her adult novel *The First Four Years* (p. 57). For more about that book and Wilder's early married life, *see* Hill, *Laura Ingalls Wilder*, pp. 66–80, and Miller, *Becoming*, pp. 71–90.

109. *"The moon is at its full. . . . asleep to-night."* Wilder excerpted and slightly misquoted these lines from "The Tides" by American poet William Cullen Bryant:

> The moon is at her full, and, riding high,
> Floods the calm fields with light.
> The airs that hover in the summer sky
> Are all asleep to-night (*Thirty Poems*, p. 78).

110. *I had a house and a home of my own.* Perhaps Wilder chose to end her autobiography on this note of promise because the next few years would prove so difficult for the young couple, including the death of their infant son and a debilitating illness for Almanzo. *These Happy Golden Years* also ends with a deceptively simple scene. Laura and Almanzo sit on the front doorstep of their house, and in her memory, Laura hears "the voice of Pa's fiddle and the echo of a song" (p. 289). This evocative ending leaves readers with the haunting memory of Laura's childhood and a glimpse into the promising fictional future that she and Almanzo will share.

the dining room, and his bed in the bedroom. A neighbour woman had been in and put all in order.

There were provisions of all kinds in the pantry with bread a pie and a cake that Manly had bought from the neighbor.

When the new home had been looked over and admired inside and out, I got supper and washed up the dishes.

Later I was to learn that we owed $500. on the house, which we were never able to pay until we sold the farm.

But that was nobodys fault and is another story anyway.[108]

Afterward we sat on the doorstep in the moonlight and looked out across the prairie.

"The moon is at its full and riding high
floods the calm fields with light.
The winds that hover in the summer sky
are all asleep to-night."[109]

The horses were comfortably resting in their stalls in the stable back of the house. We could hear them move now and again.

The cow Pa had given me was lying in the barn-yard chewing her cud and Old Shep, Manly's dog lay at our feet.

I was a little awed by my new estate, but I felt very much at home and very happy and among the other causes for happiness was the thought that I would not again have to go and live with strangers in their houses. I had a house and a home of my own.[110]

Conclusion
"I Don't Suppose Any One Will Take the Trouble"

PAMELA SMITH HILL

In an exchange with her mother during the writing of *By the Shores of Silver Lake* in 1938, Lane asked, "Would it be possible to substitute Uncle George for Uncle Tom?" She liked the way Uncle George Ingalls had been presented in *Little House in the Big Woods* as "the boy who ran away to the war to be a drummer boy when he was very young." Because Uncle Tom Quiner had not yet appeared in the series, Lane urged Wilder to let the fictional Uncle George live the real Uncle Tom's life in the remaining novels. The substitution would provide more continuity, not to mention dramatic appeal. After all, Uncle Tom had been the real adventurer in the family—a "riverjack" on the Mississippi, an Indian fighter, and a member of the Gordon party that entered the Black Hills illegally in 1874 searching for gold. "I hardly know what to think about this," Wilder replied. "There are records of that first party of white men in the Black Hills and there was no Ingalls among them. To make it historically correct, it should be Uncle Tom." Then she added, "But I don't suppose any one will take the trouble to look it up."[1]

Yet, even before her lifetime ended, readers, scholars, and critics were doing just that—taking the trouble to look up one detail after another about Wilder's life. How would she react to all this scrutiny today—to people not only checking the facts about Uncle Tom, who kept his own life in the Little House series, but about the people, places, and ideas that influenced her? What would Wilder make of all the details presented here in the context of *Pioneer Girl*?

These questions are impossible to answer, of course. But in that note to Lane, it is clear that Wilder considered historical context to be critical. "If you think best, knowing the circumstances, you may make the change from Uncle Tom to Uncle George," she told her daughter, but added, "Remember the date and don't have the first white men in the Black Hills to[o] late. That would be a bad mistake."[2] Historical accuracy

---

1. RWL to LIW and LIW to RWL, n.d. [1938], Box 13, file 194, Rose Wilder Lane Papers, Herbert Hoover Presidential Library, West Branch, Iowa. Wilder's reply is handwritten in response to a typewritten question from Lane.
   2. Ibid.

sometimes had to take precedence over literary license. As she wrote Lane, "Unfortunately we have used real names in these books and must stick closer to facts than otherwise we would need to do."[3]

For Wilder, however, historical context went beyond names and dates. The real challenge, which she viewed almost as an obligation to her readers, was to recreate a three-dimensional world for her characters that depicted the physical, emotional, and cultural forces that had shaped her childhood. She wanted her books to reflect accurately the historical spirit of her time. She argued passionately with Lane over this concept during the writing of *By the Shores of Silver Lake*. In Wilder's view, her daughter did not fully grasp the literary significance of historical and cultural context in the ongoing series and had made editorial suggestions that were "all wrong. . . . Remember this was a little more than 60 years ago," Wilder admonished Lane. "Take your stand there. What girls would do now has no bearing whatever. This is a true story and supposed to show a different (almost) civilization."[4]

For Wilder, the "truth" in *By the Shores of Silver Lake* and, indeed, the entire series centered on her vision of *historical* truth. Although she wrote fiction and sometimes "stretched a point" to tell a better story, she instinctively knew that what set the Little House series apart from other children's books published during the 1930s and early 1940s was its ambitious attempt to portray the American pioneer experience of the late nineteenth century with depth and authenticity. "After all," she wrote Lane, "even though these books must be made fit for children to read, they must also be true to history. . . . I have given you a true picture of the times and the place and the people. Please don't blur it."[5]

Pioneer Girl served as the historical foundation for Wilder's fictional world. Out of the period, places, and people in that manuscript sprang the characters and settings for the novels. Given Wilder's dedication to authenticity, it is hard to imagine that she would disapprove of the historical, geographical, and cultural studies her work has since inspired. Although Wilder once wrote her literary agent George Bye that she believed "one must have a first hand knowledge of their subject"[6] to write compelling fiction, she engaged in research herself, going beyond the pages of *Pioneer Girl* when she recognized that her fiction demanded a clearer or more solid historical founda-

3. LIW to RWL, Aug. 17, 1938, ibid.

4. LIW to RWL, Jan. 25, 1938, ibid.

5. Ibid.

6. LIW to Bye, May 10, 1943, James Oliver Brown Papers, Rare Book and Manuscript Library, Columbia University, New York, N.Y.

tion. When, for example, Wilder could not quite remember where her family had lived in Indian Territory, she and Lane traveled to eastern Kansas and Oklahoma, seeking the precise location of her former home. They did not find it, and Wilder chose to rely on memory rather than historical documentation when she placed the fictional family deep in Indian Territory, forty miles from Independence, Kansas. Wilder also sought historical context for Soldat du Chêne, the Osage chief she remembered from her life on the Osage Diminished Indian Reserve. She requested information about him from the Kansas State Historical Society, but her contact was unable to provide anything useful.[7] Again, once Wilder had exhausted the historical resources available to her at the time, she decided to recreate Soldat du Chêne from her own memories.

During her lifetime, Wilder did not have the wealth of resources and technologies that contemporary readers and researchers now rely upon. For example, the 1870 United States Census, which clearly places the Ingalls family in Montgomery County, Kansas, about thirteen miles from Independence, had apparently not yet been released to the public when Wilder wrote *Little House on the Prairie* in 1934.[8] Moreover, Wilder could not have accessed the information with the ease that researchers do today. In another example, while writing *By the Shores of Silver Lake*, Wilder struggled to track down the lyrics to a song she had mentioned in *Pioneer Girl*. "I do not remember any more of 'When I was One and Twenty Nell and You were Seventeen.' . . . Carrie may have it or remember the song," Wilder wrote Lane. "I will write to her and Grace and try to find it. That would be the only chance."[9] Wilder's search for these lyrics proved futile; she used only the song's title in the novel. Seventy-five years later, an online search traced the song to H. R. Palmer's *The Song King: Collection of New and Original Music for Singing Classes, Day Schools, Conventions. &c.*, published in 1872. The book itself has been digitized and is part of an online collection, a concept Wilder could not have envisioned in 1938. In fact, several of the songs and books mentioned in *Pioneer Girl* or the Little House series are now digitized and available, including Pa's big green book, *The Polar and Tropical Worlds*, and even *The Floweret*, a book of poems that Wilder received when she was five years old.

7. [Kirke Mechem] to LIW, Jan. 10, 1934, Folder 14, Microfilm ed., Laura Ingalls Wilder Papers, Laura Ingalls Wilder Historic Home and Museum, Mansfield, Mo.

8. The United States Census Bureau waits seventy-two years before releasing census information from a particular year to the general public. In 2012, for example, the 1940 census was made public for the first time. What has become known as the Seventy-Two-Year Rule dates from the early 1950s, but official Census Bureau correspondence suggests that this restriction was in place long before it was formalized. *See* Roy V. Peel to Wayne C. Grover, Aug. 26, 1952, and Robert G. Dixon, Jr., to William G. Casselman II, June 14, 1978, census.gov/history.

9. LIW to RWL, Aug. 17, 1938.

Wilder perhaps would have appreciated the inherent contradiction most scholars and historians now embrace—that of using contemporary technologies to gain almost instantaneous access to the past. Wilder once wrote to her friend Aubrey Sherwood, editor of the *De Smet News*, that her novel *By the Shores of Silver Lake* "is not a history but a true story founded on historical fact."[10] In the same letter, she explained how and why she fictionalized a critical scene in the novel. Given her willingness to reveal these distinctions between fact and fiction to Sherwood, she may well have approved of recent efforts to illuminate the historical, social, and cultural influences that have made her work so enduring. The publication of *Pioneer Girl: The Annotated Autobiography* is yet another step in that ongoing process.

In 1943, shortly after the appearance of *These Happy Golden Years*, literary agent George Bye wrote Wilder: "I have been very remiss in not telling you what a beautiful volume I think Harper's produced with your last story. I say 'last' with great reluctance. I hope there will be more—and I predict that this series will become an American fixture, something like Little Women and Little Men."[11] The Little House series certainly has become part of the classic American canon of children's literature. It ranks alongside the works of Louisa May Alcott, Mark Twain, L. Frank Baum, and E. B. White. In 1954, the Children's Library division of the American Library Association established the Laura Ingalls Wilder Award to honor Wilder and future writers and illustrators for "distinguished, creative, sustained contribution[s] to children's books."[12] Yet, Wilder's reputation as an innovative and inspired artist still suffers from the perception that she simply wrote the facts of her life as she remembered them and that the Little House books lack the imaginative depth of great fiction because they are really nonfiction.

The publication of *Pioneer Girl: The Annotated Autobiography* presents new insights into Wilder's past, but it also helps to document her growth as an important American artist who grew from farm journalist to novelist to literary legend. And precisely because the original draft of *Pioneer Girl* lacks the depth, drama, and detail of Wilder's novels, it illustrates how quickly she moved beyond nonfiction and how capably and imaginatively she embraced the unique challenges of writing fiction.

Wilder did not give up on nonfiction entirely, however. Even after the publication of *Little House in the Big Woods*, she continued to hope *Pioneer Girl* would find a larger

---

10. LIW to Sherwood, Nov. 18, 1939, Archives, Laura Ingalls Wilder Memorial Society, De Smet, S.Dak.

11. Bye to LIW, May 5, 1943, Brown Papers.

12. Ursula Nordstrom to Garth Williams, Feb. 11, 1954, in *Dear Genius: The Letters of Ursula Nordstrom*, ed. Leonard S. Marcus (New York: HarperCollins, 1998), pp. 74–75.

audience. "My mother wants to enter PIONEER GIRL in the Atlantic, Little-Brown prize contest for non-fiction work," Lane wrote George Bye in 1933.[13] It has taken more than eighty years, but *Pioneer Girl* is finally finding an audience, although that audience is now far larger than Wilder could have envisioned when she created an improvised writing den at the Rock House, opened that first Fifty Fifty tablet, and began writing the story only she could tell.

13. RWL to Bye, Feb. 15 1933, Brown Papers.

Facsimile of "Juvenile Pioneer Girl"[1]

When Grandma was a little girl she lived in a little gray house made of logs. The house was in the Big Woods, in ~~Michigan.~~ *Wisconsin.* ~~The~~ The great dark trees of the Big Woods stood all around the house, and beyond them were other trees, and beyond them more trees. ~~As far as a man~~ *to the north,* ~~houses~~ As far as a man could go/in a day, or a week, or a month, there was nothing but trees, ~~and then~~ There were no other houses. There were no roads. There were only trees, and the wild animals that lived in the Big Woods.

Wolves lived in the Big Woods, and ~~bears~~ bears, and wild cats. muskrats and mink and otter lived by the streams, and foxes had dens in the hills. ~~~~ But there were no other people. There was only the one little gray house made of logs, where Grandma lived with her father and her mother, her sister Mary and baby Carrie.

~~~~

At night, when Grandma lay in her trundle bed, she could not hear anything at all but the ~~many~~ sound of all the trees whispering together. Sometimes, far away in the night, a wolf howled.

~~~~

It was a scare-y sound. Grandma knew that wolves ate little girls. But Grandma was safe inside the log walls. Her father's rifle hung on the wall, ~~~~ and Jack, the brindle bull-dog, lay by the door. Grandma's father would say, "Go ~~back~~ to sleep, Laura. Jack won't let the wolves get in." *So Grandma cuddled under the covers of the trundle bed and went to sleep again.*

Grandma's name was Laura. She called her father, Pa, and her mother, Ma. When Grandma was a little girl, children did not ~~~~ say, Father and Mother, or Papa and Mama. They said, Pa and Ma.

One night Pa picked her up out of bed and carried her to ~~her~~ *the* window so that she could see the wolves. There were so many of them, all sitting in a ring around the house with their noses pointed up at the big, bright moon. They were all howling. Jack

2

paced up and down before the door and growled. The wolves could not get in.

In front of the little log house were two beautiful large oak trees. Every morning as soon as Laura awoke she ran to look out of the window, and one morning she saw a dead deer hanging from a branch in each oak tree.

Pa had shot the two deer the day before and had hung them in the trees so that the wolves could not get the meat in the night.

That day Pa and Ma and Laura and Mary had fresh venison for dinner. But most of the meat was packed away in salt, to be eaten in the winter. For winter was coming. The days were shorter and frost crawled up the window panes at night.

Soon the snow would come. Then the log house would be almost buried in snow drifts. The lakes and the streams would freeze. In the bitter cold weather Pa could not be sure of finding any wild animal to shoot for meat. The bears would be asleep in their dens. The squirrels would be curled in their nests in hollow trees, with their furry tails wrapped snugly around their noses. The deer and the rabbits would be shy and swift. Pa might hunt all day in the bitter cold, in the Big Woods covered with snow, and come home at night with nothing for Ma and Laura and Mary to eat. All the food for winter must be stored away in the little log house before the winter came.

One morning Pa went away with the horses and wagon and that night he came home with the wagon full of fish. Some of the fish were as big as Laura. Pa had been to Lake Pepin, far away in the Big Woods, and had caught the fish with a net.

Ma cut large slices of juicy fish, without one bone, for Laura and Mary. They all feasted on the good, fresh fish. All that they did not eat that day was salted down in barrels for the winter.

Pa owned a pig. It ran wild in the woods, living on acorns and roots. Now he caught it, and put it in a pen to fatten. He would butcher it as soon as the nights were cold enough to keep the pork frozen.

One night Laura woke up. ~~suddenly~~ She heard the pig squealing terribly, and she saw Pa snatch his gun from the wall and run outdoors. Then she heard the gun go off, once, twice.

3

When Pa got to the pigpen, he saw a big, black bear standing beside it. The bear reached into the pen to grab the pig. Pa saw this in the starlight, and he fired so quickly that he missed the bear. The bear ran away in the woods.

Laura was sorry that Pa did not kill the bear. She liked bear meat very much. But at least, Pa had saved the pig.

The garden behind the little house had been growing all summer. Now the potatoes and carrots, the beets and turnips and cabbage, were gathered and stored in the cellar, for freezing nights had come. Onions were made into long ropes, braided together by their tops, and these were hung in the attic. Pumpkins and squash were piled in great gold and yellow piles in the attic's corners. The attic was a lovely place to play, and many Laura and Mary played there with the large, round, colored pumpkins and squash. They must play in the house now for it was cold outdoors and the brown leaves were all falling from the trees.

Then the first snow came, and the bitter cold.

Pa took his gun and traps and was gone all day, setting the traps for muskrats and mink along the creeks, and for wolves and foxes in the woods. He set out big bear traps, hoping to get a fat bear before they all went into their dens for the winter.

One morning he came back, took the horses and sled and hurried away again. He had shot a bear. Laura and Mary jumped up and down and clapped their hands, they were so glad. Mary shouted, "I want the drum-stick! I want the drum-stick!"

Mary was so little that she did not know how big a bear's drumstick is.

When Pa came back he had both a bear and a pig in the wagon. He had come upon the bear in the Big Woods, just as the bear killed the pig and began to eat it. Pa said the bear was standing up on its hind legs, holding the pig in his paws just as though they were hands.

Pa shot the bear, and as he did not know where the pig could have come from, nor whose pig it could be, he had both bear and pig. There was plenty of fresh meat now, to last a long time. The days and the nights were so cold that the bear-meat and the pork froze and stayed frozen, hanging in the little shed against the back door. When Ma wanted meat for dinner, Pa would take an ax and cut a piece of bear-meat or pork.

4

The snow kept coming until it was drifted and banked against the house. In the morning the window panes were covered with frost. Laura and Mary were allowed to take Ma's thimble, and make pretty patterns in the frost with it. When they put their mouths close to the pane and blew, the white frost melted and ran in drops of water down the glass. Then they could see the drifts of white snow outdoors and the great trees standing bare and black, ~~showernitm~~ making thin blue shadows on the snow.

When the work was done, Ma would cut out paper-dolls for Laura and Mary, and let them cook on the big cookstove for their play-house dinners. And at night Pa came home.

He would come in from his tramping through the woods with iciclyes on the ends of his whiskers. He would hang his gun on the wall by the door, throw off his fur cap and coat and mittens, and call, "Where's my little half pint of sweet cider half drank up?"

That was Laura, because she was so small. Laura and Mary would run to climb on
                                                                              fireplace.
his knees, and sit there while he warmed himself by the ~~stoven~~ Then he would put on his cap and coat and mittens again, and go out to do the chores and to bring in plenty of wood to keep a good fire.

Pa and Ma and Laura and Mary and little baby Carrie were warm and snug and happy in their little log house in the Big Woods, especially at night. Then the fire ~~sh~~ was shining on the hearth, the dark and the snow and the wild beasts were shut out, Jack the brindle bulldog and Black Susan, the cat, sat blinking at the flames in the fireplace. And Pa told stories.

~~Hhm~~ When Laura and Mary begged him for a story, he would take them on his knees, and tickle their faces with his long whiskers until they laughed aloud. His eyes were very blue and merry. "What story shall I tell you tonight?" he would ask, and sometimes they said, "Tell us about Grandpa and the panther."

* * *

The Story of Grandmas Grandpa & the Panther

Grandpa was Pa's father. He

~~Grandpa~~ lived far away in the Big Woods, in a log house just like this one. He went
as he rode his horse through
to town one day and was late starting home. It was dark/~~in~~ the Big Woods, so dark that

he could hardly see the road, and when he heard a panther scream he was frightened, for he

had no gun.

"How does a panther scream?" Laura asked.

"Like a woman," said Pa. "Just like this." Then he screamed so that Laura and Mary

shivered.

The horse, with Grandpa on him, ran fast, for it was scared, too. But the panther

followed through the dark woods, screaming. It was a hungry panther, and it came as fast

as the horse could run. It screamed now on this side of the road, then on the other side,

and it was always close behind.

Grandpa leaned forward in the saddle, and urged the horse to run faster. The horse

was running now just as fast as it could possibly run, and still the panther screamed

close behind.

At last Grandpa had a glimpse of it, as it leaped from tree-top to tree-top, almost

overhead.
~~upon him.~~ It was a huge, black panther, leaping through the air just like Black Susan

after a mouse. But it was many, many times larger than Black Susan. It was so large

that it could ~~catch Grandpa in just a~~ leap on Grandpa and ~~slash him and~~ kill him with

its great, slashing claws.

The panther did not scream any more. Grandpa did not see it any more. But he knew

that it was coming, in the dark woods behind him, leaping after him like a great, black

cat. ~~many instant the~~ The horse ran with ~~him~~ all its might, doing its best to jump

farther and faster than the panther.

The horse ran up to Grandpa's log house. Grandpa jumped off, against the door. He

burst through the door into the house, and slammed the door behind him. When Grandpa
was jumping, too, and the panther
jumped off the horse, the panther ~~jumped, and~~ landed on the horse's back.

The horse screamed horribly, and started to run away into the Big Woods, with the

panther's claws ripping deep into his back. But Grandpa grabbed his rifle and got to the

window just in time to shoot the panther dead.

Grandpa said he would never again go into the Big Woods without his gun.

6

When Pa told this story, Laurs and Mary shivered and cuddled closer against him. They
                                                                    They liked to
were happy, snug and safe on his knees, with his strong arms around them. ~~it was comfort to~~
            before the warm fire,   with
be there ~~in the warm of the light of the fire upon~~ Black Susan purring
~~sleeping~~ on the hearth and good dog Jack stretched out beside her. When they heard a wolf
howl, ~~and no may~~ Jack's head lifted and the hairs rose stiff along his back, but Laura and
Mary listened to that lonely sound in the dark and the cold of the Big Woods and they were
glad. They felt so cosy and comfortable in their little house made of logs, with the snow
                          ~~some higher~~ and the wind crying because it could not get in by
drifted around it and ~~the wind crying~~
the fire.

* * *

~~Sometim~~

Every evening, before he began to tell stories ot to play the fiddle, Pa made the
bullets for his next day's hunting.

Laurs and Mary helped him. They brought the big, ~~spoon~~ long-handled spoon, and the
box full of bits of lead, and the bullet-mold. Then while he squatted on the hearth and
made the bullets, they sat one on each side of him, and watched.

First he melted the bits of lead in the big spoon held in the coals. When the lead
was melted, he would pour it carefully from the spoon into the little hole in the bullet-
mold, and after a moment he would open the mold and out would drop a bright new bullet
onto the hearth. The bullet was too hot to touch, but it ~~was so shining~~ shone so temptingly
that sometimes Laura or Mary could not help touching it. Then they burned their fingers.

But they did not say anything, because Pa had told them never to touch a new bullet.
If they burned their fingers, it was their own fault. So they put their fingers in their
mouths to cool them, and watched Pa make more bullets.

There would be a shining pile of them on the hearth before Pa stopped. He let them
cool, and then with his jack-knife he trimmed off the little lumps made by the hole in
the mold. He gathered up even the tiniest shaving of lead and saved it carefully, and the
finished bullets he put into the bullet-pouch. The bullet-pouch was a little bag
beautifully made of buck-skin, from a buck that Pa had shot.

7

Then it was fun to watch Pa load his gun. He took the gun between his knees, while Laura and Mary stood on either side of him. "You watch me, now," Pa said, " and tell me if I make a mistake." So they watched very carefully, but he never made a mistake.

Laura handed him the smooth, polished buffalo horn full of powder, and he poured a little powder down the barrel of the gun. Then he took the ramrod from its place beside the barrel, and pounded the powder down firmly. When it was hard ~~enoughtight~~ enough, he asked, "Where's my patch-box?" and Mary gave him the little tin box full of bits of greased cloth. Pa laid one of these pieces of greased cloth over the muzzle of the gun, pushed it down the barrel with the ramrod, and pounded it tightly against the powder.

Now that was finished. He would not put the bullet in, until he was ready to shoot.

Next he put the ramrod back in its place against the gun barrel. Then taking a box of caps from his pocket, he raised the hammer of the gun and slipped one little bright cap over the pin that was under the hammer. He always let the hammer down very slowly and carefully. If it came down quick--snap! like that--the gun would go off.

Now the gun was loaded, and Pa would hang it on the wall by the door.

When he went out into the Big Woods next morning, to hunt and to look at his traps, he ~~made sure that he had the powder-horn full of powder and the bullet pouch~~ made sure that the bullet pouch full of bullets, the tin patch-box, and the box of caps were in his pockets. The powder-horn and a small hatchet hung at his belt, and he carried the gun ready loaded on his shoulder.

                         shot

~~Whenever he~~ Whenever he ~~fired the gun~~ shot at a wild animal, he had to ~~immediately~~ stop and
the gun--
load ~~it~~--put in the powder and pound it down, put in a patch and pound it down, put in
                                                            When
a bullet, and then put a cap under the hammer--before he could shoot again. ~~If~~ he shot at a bear or a panther, he must kill it with the first shot. A wounded bear or panther would kill a man ~~quick enough~~ before he had time to load the gun and shoot again.

But Laura and Mary were never afraid in the mornings when Pa kissed them and went
          into   could
off alone/~~in~~ the Big Woods. They knew he ~~would~~ always kill~~ed~~ bears and panthers with the first shot.

                              * * *

After the bullets were made and the gun was loaded, came story-telling time. ~~Mamma~~

8   *The Story of Grandma's Father and the Voice in the Woods—*

"Tell us about the time you went after the cows," Mary would ask. And ~~finn~~ Pa would tell

                he was a naughty little boy.

the story about the time/~~when he was an eight little boy and his father sent him after the cows~~

The Story of Grandma's Father was a Naughty Little Boy

           ***

         eight years old--   afternoon

When I was a little boy,--Pa said--I ~~used to when I was~~ had to go every ~~night~~ to find the

cows in the woods and drive them home. My father told me never to play by the way, but

to hurry and get the cows home before dark, because there were bears and wolves and

panthers in the woods.

    One evening I started ~~an~~ earlier than usual, so I thought I did not need to hurry.

There were so many things to look at and to play with in the woods that I forgot that

dark was coming. There were red squirrels in the trees, chipmunks scurrying through the

leaves, and rabbits playing games together in the open places before they went to bed.

                 from one thing to another,

I went this way and that, ~~looking at them~~ until I came to a creek, and there I went

wading and watched the little fish.

   Then

  ~~At last~~ I began to play that I was a mighty hunter, stalking the game and being

stalked by Indians. I played that I was fighting the Indians, until the woods seemed

full of the wild red men, and then all at once I heard the birds twittering good night. It

was dusky in the path, and quite dark in the woods.

      ~~I had come a much farther from home than I had ever been~~

    I saw that I must get the cows home quickly, or it would be black night before I

had them safe~~ly~~ in the barn. And I didn't even know where the cows were!

    I listened, and I could not hear the bells. I called, ~~and~~ but the cows didn't come.

I was afraid of the dark and the Indians and the wild beasts, but I dared not go home

without the cows. So I ran through the woods, calling and hunting. All the time the

shadows were getting thicker and darker, ~~until~~ and the woods seemed larger, and the trees

and the bushes ~~as they around me~~ looked strange to me. I could not find the cows anywhere.

I climbed up hillsides, looking for them and calling, and I went down into dark ravines,

calling and looking. I stopped and listened for the ~~bell~~ cowbells, and there was not a

                              me   heard

sound except the rustling of leaves in the dark, ~~and other sounds of my own moving things~~

~~scared me about me and me~~ Then I heard loud breathing, ~~which~~ and thought a panther was

there, breathing in the dark beside me. But it was only the sound of my own breathing.

9

My bare legs were scratched by the briars, and when I ran through the bushes their branches struck my cheeks. But I kept on, looking everywhere, and calling.

"Sukey! Sukey!" I shouted with all my might. "Here, Sukey! Sukey!"

Right over my head something answered, "Who?"

My hair stood straight on end. "Who-oo?" the voice said again. And then I did run!

That thing in the dark came after me and called again, "Who-oo?" I ran the faster. I ran until I couldn't breathe, and still I kept on running. ~~When~~ Something grabbed my foot, and down I went. Up I jumped, and then I <u>ran</u>. Not even a wolf could have caught me.

At last I came out of the dark woods by the barn. There stood all the cows, waiting to be let through the bars. I let them in, and then sneaked to the house.

My father looked up and said, "Young man, what makes you so late? Been playing by the way?" But I was so glad to be safe in the house that I ~~couldn't think of anything else.~~ couldn't answer him. I looked down at my feet and saw that one big toe-nail had been torn clean off. I had been so scared that I had not felt it hurt until that minute.

~~"~~ ~~..~~

~~..~~

~~..~~

~~....................~~

Pa always stopped telling the story here, and waited until Laura said, "Yes, Pa, go on! Please go on!"

"Well," Pa said, "Then your Grandpa went into the yard and cut a switch. And he came back and gave me a good ~~thrashing~~, because I hadn't minded him and got home safe before dark. 'If you'll do as you're told,' said he, 'No harm will come to you.'

"Yes, yes, Pa!" Mary would say, bouncing up and down on his knee. 'And then what did he say?"

"He said, 'If you'd ~~mama~~ obeyed me, as you should, you wouldn't have been out in the Big Woods after dark, and you wouldn't have been scared by a screech-owl."

* * *

10

When Christmas time came, the little log house was almost buried in snow. There were
great drifts against the walls, and in the mornings when Pa opened the door

When Christmas time came, the little log house was almost buried in snow. Great drifts
were banked against the walls and windows, and in the mornings when Pa opened the door,
there was a wall of snow, as high as Laura's head. Pa took the shovel and shoveled it
away, and then he shoveled a path to the barn, where the horses and the cow were warm
and snug in their stalls.

The days were bright and clear. Laura and Mary stood on chairs by the window and looked
out across the glittering snow at the glittering trees. Snow was piled in little ridges
all along their bare, black branches, and it sparkled in the sunshine. Icicles hung from
the eaves of the house to the snow snow-banks, great icicles as large at the top as
                                                    They
Laura's arm, and they were many of them were like glass and full of sharp lights.

Pa's breath hung in the air like smoke, when he came along the path from the barn.
He breathed it out in clouds, as though there were a fire inside him, and it froze in
white frost on his mustaches and beard. When he came in, tramping the snow from his boots,
and caught Laura up in a big bear-hug against his cold, big coat, his mustache was beaded
with little drops of melting frost.

Ma was very busy, cooking good things for Christmas. She baked brown bread and white
bread and salt-rising bread. She baked vinegar pies and dried-apple pies, and cakes.
One morning she boiled molasses and sugar and vinegar together until they made a thick syrup
and Pa brought in two pans of clean, white snow from outdoors. Laura and Mary each had a
pan, and they poured the dark syrup in little streams onto the snow. They made circles,
and curleycues and squiggledy squiddledy things, and they hardened at once and were candy.

All this was done because Aunt Eliza and Uncle Peter and the cousins, Peter and
Alice and Ella, were coming to spend Christmas.

The day before Christmas they came. The big bob-sled drove up to the door, with
a loud ringing of sleigh bells. Aunt Eliza and Uncle Peter and the cousins were in it,
all covered up with buffalo robes made of buffalo skins. Even Ella, the littlest cousin,
was wrapped in so many coats and blankets and mufflers and veils that she was like a big,

10

When Christmas time came, the little log houas was almost buried in snow. Snow was
piled in little ridges all along the bare, black branches of the trees

11

shapeless bundle.

When they all came in, the log house was full and running over. Black Susan ran
out through the open door and hid in the barn, and Jack leaped in circles through the
snow, barking, as though he would never stop. Now there were cousins to play with! As
soon as Aunt Eliza had unwrapped them, Peter and Alice and Ella and Laura and Mary
began to run and shout. They ~~played~~ made so much racket, Aunt Eliza said, that she
couldn't think, and Carrie woke up and began to cry.

"I'll tell you what let's do," Alice said. "Let's make pictures." They had to go
outdoors to do it, and Ma thought it was too cold for Laura to play outdoors. But when
she saw how disappointed Laura was, she said she might go, after all, for a little while.
She ~~xxxxxxxxxx~~ put on Laura's coat and mittens and wrapped a muffler around her neck, and
let her go.

All morning Alice and Ella and Laura and Mary played outdoors in the snow, making
pictures. The way they did it was this: Each one climbed up on a stump, and then,
holding her arms out wide, fell off the stump into the soft, deep snow. They tried to
get up without spoiling the marks they made when they fell. If they did it well, there
in the snow was a hole, shaped almost exactly like a little girl--arms and legs, and all.
They played it was the picture of a little girl,
They played so hard all day that when night came they were almost too much excited
to sleep. But they had to sleep, or Santa Claus would not come. So they hung their
stockings by the fireplace, and said their prayers, and were put to bed--Alice and Ella
and Laura and Mary all in one big bed, made on the floor.

Pa and Ma and Uncle Peter and Aunt Eliza sat by the fire, talking, till at last
Ma said she vowed she didn't believe those young ones ever <u>were</u> going to sleep. Then
Pa took down his fiddle. He played Old Zip Coon and Money Musk, the Irish Washerwoman,
and the Red Heifer, and the Arkansas Traveler. And at last Laura went to sleep, while
Pa and the fiddle were both softly singing, My Darling Nelly Gray.

> My darling Nelly Gray, they have taken her away,
> And I'll never see my darling any more---

In the morning, they all woke up almost at the same moment. Alice and Ella and
Laura and Mary in their ~~nightgownxxxxxxxxxxxxxxxxxxxxxx~~ red flannel nightgowns, and Peter
in his red flannel night shirt, all ran shouting to see what was in their stockings.

12

Every stocking had in it a pair of red mittens, and a long, flat stick of striped peppermint candy, all beautifully notched along each side! Alice and Peter and Ella and Laura and Mary were so happy ~~nowhavananchmbeamhfimmpmanmm~~ that they could hardly speak for a few minutes. Then they all looked at each other's mittens, and tried on their own, and Peter bit a large piece out of his stick of candy, but Alice and Ella and Laura and Mary licked theirs, to make it last longer.

"Well, well!" Uncle Peter said. "Not even one stocking with nothing but a switch in it? My, my, so you've all been good children, have you?"

Peter looked guilty. But Laura couldn't believe that Santa Claus ~~mmmm~~ would really have given Peter nothing but a switch, even if he had been naughty. It was so hard to be good, for a whole year.

~~ritmwasmsuchmambeautifulmChristmas~~

For breakfast there were pancakes and molasses, and Ma made a pancake man for each one of the children. It was so cold that they could not play outdoors today, but they sat together on the floor and looked at the pictures in the ~~mmg~~ Bible, and in Pa's big green book, full of animals and birds.

Then there was the Christmas dinner, all the good things they could eat, ~~and~~ ~~mmma~~ Alice and Peter and Ella and Laura and Mary did not say anything at the table, because they knew that children should be seen **and** not heard. But they did not need to ask for second helpings. Ma and Aunt Eliza kept their plates full, and let them eat all the cake and pie they ~~wanteam~~ could hold.

"Christmas comes but once a year," Aunt Eliza said.

Dinner was early, because Uncle Peter, Aunt Eliza and the cousins had such a long way to go. "Best we can do, Uncle Peter said, we'll hardly make it home before dark." They had twenty miles to go.

So as soon as they had eaten dinner, Uncle Peter and Pa went out to put the horses to the sleigh, while Ma and Aunt Eliza wrapped up the cousins. They ~~put~~ pulled heavy woolen stockings ~~mmm~~ over the woolen stockings and the shoes they were already wearing, they put on ~~mmatammdmahawma~~ mittens and coats and shawls, and warm hoods, and wrapped mufflers around their necks and thick woolen veils over their faces. Ma ~~had~~ slipped hot baked potatoes ~~to put in~~ into their

14

pockets to keep their fingers warm, and Aunt Eliza's flatirons were hot on the stove,

ready to put at their feet in the ~~which~~ sleigh. The blankets and quilts and the buffalo

robes, ~~were warm, by the open oven door.~~ had been warming by the fireplace.

So they all got into the big bob-sled, snug and warm, and Pa tucked the last buffalo-

robe around them, and off they went, the horses trotting gaily and the ~~bells~~ sleigh bells

jingling.

In just a little while the merry sound of the ~~sleigh~~ bells was gone, and Christmas

was over. But what a beautiful Christmas it had been!

* * *

Now the winter was long. Laura and Mary began to be tired of staying in the house.

Especially on Sundays, the time went so very slowly. Ø Every Sunday Laura and Mary were

dressed in their clean, best clothes, with fresh ribbons in their hair, and they were

not allowed to ~~run or shout or~~ cook or sew doll clothes or be noisy in their play.

They must sit quietly, while Ma read ~~them~~ Bible stories to them, or stories about

lions and tigers and white bears from Pa's big green book.

Sunday was such a tiresome day. One Sunday Laura could not bear it any longer.

She began to play with Jack, and in a few minutes she was running and laughing. Pa told

her to sit in her chair and be quiet, but when Laura sat down she began to cry and

kick the chair. "I hate Sunday!" she ~~said~~ screamed.

Pa put down his book. "Laura," he said, "Come here."

She went ~~very~~ slowly, for she knew ~~how~~ (naughty, ~~she had been, and~~ she had been) she knew she

deserved ~~the~~ a spanking. But when she reached Pa, he ~~only~~ looked at her sorrowfully

for a moment, and then took her on his knee. ~~When he came home, when he had put his arm around Mary~~

~~he had put his arm around Mary~~ He held out his other arm to Mary, ~~and when he had them~~

~~snug~~ and said, "I'm going to tell you a story about one Sunday when Grandpa was a boy."

The Story of Grandma's Grandpa and the Pig.

When Grandpa was a boy, Sunday ~~was a very much and a very much began~~ did not begin on

Sunday morning. It began at sundown on Saturday night; then everyone stopped work and

play. Supper was solemn. After supper, Grandpa's father read aloud a chapter of the

Bible, while everyone sat very straight and still, then they all knelt down by their

15

chairs and their father said a long prayer. When he said, "Amen," everyone got up
from his knees, took a candle, and went to bed. They must go straight to bed, with no
playing, laughing, or even talking.

Sunday morning they ate a cold breakfast, because no one cooked on Sunday. Then
they all dressed in their best clothes and walked to church. They walked, because
the horses were never hitched up on Sunday.

In the church, Grandpa and his brothers must sit perfectly still for two long hours
and listen to the sermon. They dared not swing their feet, but must sit perfectly motionless.
They dared not turn their heads to look at the windows or the walls of the ceiling
of the church, but must never for a moment take their eyes from the preacher.

When church was over, they walked ~~sedately home~~ slowly home. They might talk on
the way, but they must not talk loudly, or laugh, or play. At home they ate a cold
dinner which had been cooked the day before. Then all the long afternoon the boys must
sit still and study their catechism, until at last the sun went down and Sunday was
over.

Now Grandpa's house was about half way down the side of a steep hill. The road
went from the top of the hill to the bottom, right past the front door. It was the best
place you can imagine for sliding down hill in winter.

One week Grandpa and his two brothers, James and George, were making a sled. They
worked ~~hard~~ at it every moment of their play-time. It was the best sled they had ever
made, because it was so long that all three of them could sit on it, one behind the
other, and slide downhill together. They planned to have it finished so that they could
play with it on Saturday. But that week their father was cutting down trees in the Big
Woods, and he kept them working with him so long every day that they ~~didn't finished~~ ,
couldn't get the sled finished until just as the sun went down, Saturday night.

They could not slide down hill, not even once, after the sun went down. That would
be breaking the Sabbath. So they put the sled in the shed behind the house, to wait
until Sunday was over.

All the two long hours in church next day, while they kept their feet still and

16

their eyes fixed on the preacher, they were thinking about the new sled. At home while they ate dinner they couldn't think of anything else. After dinner their father sat and read the Bible, and Grandpa and James and George sat as still as mice on their bench with their catechism, but they were thinking about the sled.

The sun shone brightly and the snow was smooth and glistening on the road; they could see it through the window. They looked at their catechism and they thought of their new sled, and it seemed that sundown would never come.

After awhile they heard a snore, and looking at their father they saw that his head had fallen against the back of his chair and he was fast asleep.

Then James looked at George, and ~~George looked at Grandpa~~ James got up from the bench and tip-toed out of the room through the back door. George looked at Grandpa, and George tiptoed after James. And Grandpa looked fearfully at their father, but on tiptoe followed George and left their father snoring.

They got their new sled and went quietly up to the top of the hill. They meant to slide down, just once. Then they would put the sled away, and slip back to the bench and their cateshism before their father woke up.

James sat in front on the sled, then George, and then Grandpa, because he was the littlest. The sled started slowly, then it went faster, and faster. It was running beautifully down the long, steep hill, but the boys dared not shout. They were still as mice, to slip by the house without waking their father. There was no sound except the little whirr of runners on the snow, and the wind rushing past.

But just as the sled ~~was sliding~~ was sliding ~~faster~~ so fast that the three boys could hardly see anything, a great black hog [pig] walked out of the woods in front of them. The hog [pig] stood still in their way. They couldn't stop the sled, there wasn't time to turn it. The sled went right under the big hog [pig] and picked him up. He sat down on James with a frightful squeal, and kept on squealing, "Squee-ee-ee-ee! Squee-ee-ee-ee!"

They flashed past their house, the hog [pig] sitting in front, then James, then George, then Grandpa, and they saw their father standing in the doorway, looking at them. They couldn't stop, they couldn't hide, there was no time to say anything. Down the hill they

17

went, the ~~hog~~ *big* sitting on James and shrieking all the way.

At the bottom of the hill the sled stopped. Then the ~~hog~~ *big* jumped off James and ran into the woods, ~~squealing all the way.~~ *still squealing with all his might.*

The boys walked slowly up the hill. They put the sled away. They sneaked into the back door and slipped quietly to their places on the bench. Their father was reading his Bible. He looked up at them without saying a word. Then he went on reading and they studied their catechism.

But when the sun set and the Sabbath day was over, their father took them out to the woodshed and tanned their jackets; first James, then George, then Grandpa.

"So you see, Laura and Mary," Pa said, "You may find it hard to be good, but you should be glad it isn't as hard to be good now as it was when Grandpa was a boy."

"Did little girls have to be as good as that?" Laura asked, and Ma said, "It was harder, *for little girls—* Because they had to behave like little ladies all the time, every day, not only on Sunday. *They could never slide down hill at all.* They had to sit *in the house all the time, and stitch on samplers.*"

* * *

Then one day Pa said spring was coming. In the Big Woods the snow had begun to thaw. It dropped from the branches of the trees and made little holes in the softening snow banks beneath them. At noon all the big icycles along the eaves of the little log house quivered ans sparkled in the sunshine, and drops of water ran down them and hung trembling at their tips.

Pa said that he must go to town to sell the furs of the wild animals he had been trapping all winter. So ~~early one morning~~ *one evening* he made a big bundle of them. There were so many furs that when he had packed them tightly and tied them together they made a package almost as big as he was. *Very early next morning Pa* ~~He~~ strapped it on his shoulders, and started to walk to town. There were so many furs to carry that he did not take his gun.

Laura and Mary had never seen a town. The nearest town was so many miles away that Pa must start before the sun rose, and/walk/~~all day~~ *very fast, all day,* to get back before dark. Laura and Mary were too little to go so far. ~~But they knew that~~ They had never seen a store, nor a sidewalk; ~~nor any~~ they had never ~~even~~ seen even two houses standing close

18

together. But they knew that in a town there were many houses--seven, ten, nineteen houses--
and that there was a store full of candy and calico and other wonderful things. They knew
that Pa would trade his furs ~~in the store~~ to the storekeeper for beautiful things from town.

All day they thought of ~~the wonderful~~ the presents that Pa would bring them. When the
sun sank low in the west, and no more drops fell from the tips of the icycles, they began
to watch eagerly for Pa. But the sun sank out of sight, the woods grew dark, and still he
did not come.

~~That evening Ma took the milk pail and went to milk the cow~~

When he had not come at milking time, Ma took the milk pail and went to milk the cow.
She said that Laura might come with her, and hold the lantern. So Laura put on her coat
and Ma buttoned it up. And Laura put her hands into her red mittens that hung by a red
yarn string around her neck, while Ma lighted the candle in the lantern. Laura was proud to
be helping Ma, and she carried the lantern very carefully. It was a ~~large~~ large lantern for a
little girl to carry. Its sides were of tin, with places cut in them for the candle-light to
shine through.

When Laura walked behind Ma on the path to the barn, the little bits of candlelight
from the lantern leaped all around her on the snow. The night was not yet quite dark, There
was a thick gray light in the Big Woods, and in the sky there were a few faint stars. The
stars did not look as warm and bright as the little lights that came from the lantern.

Laura was surprised to see Sukey, the brown cow, standing at the barn-yard gate. Ma
was surprised, too. It was too early in the spring for Sukey to be let out in the Big Woods
to eat grass. She lived in the barn. But now Ma and Laura saw her ~~in the shadows~~ beyond
the bars, in the dark shadow of the barn.

Ma went up to the gate, and pushed against it to open it. It did not open very far,
because Sukey was standing there. Ma ~~reached across the gate and~~ said, "Sukey, get over!"
She reached across the gate and ~~gave~~ slapped Sukey's shoulder. Just at that moment, one of
the dancing little bits of light from the lantern jumped between the bars and stayed on
Sukey's side, and Laura saw long, shaggy black fur.

Ma said,"Laura, walk back to the house."

Laura turned and began to walk toward the house. Ma came behind her. When they had gone

19

part way, Ma snatched her up, lantern and all, and ran. Ma ran with her into the house,

and slammed the door.

Then Laura said, "Ma, was it a bear?"

"Yes, Laura," Ma said. "It was a bear."

Laura began to cry. ~~Mhinmapnwithhhenaatnfinkappfin~~ She hung on to Ma and sobbed, "Oh

Ma, will he eat Sukey?"

"No," Ma said, hugging Laura tight. "No, Sukey is safe in the barn. Think, Laura--
                    And the door is heavy and solid, made to keep bears out.
all those big, heavy logs in the barn walls./No, the bear can not get in and hurt Sukey."

Laura felt better then. "But he could have eaten us, couldn't he, Ma?" she said.

"He didn't eat us," Ma said. "You were a good little girl, Laura, to do exactly

what I told you, and to do it quickly, without asking why."

Ma was trembling all over, and she began to laugh a little, in a queer way. "To

think," she said, "I've slapped a bear!" But she stopped right away, and wiped her eyes,

and got supper for Laura and Mary.

Pa had not come yet. He did not come. Laura and Mary were undressed and put to bed

in their trundle bed. They said their prayers, and at last they went to sleep.

In the morning Pa was there. He had brought candy for Laura and Mary, and two

pieces of pretty calico to make them each a dress. Ma had calico for a dress, too. And

they were all happy because Pa had got such good prices for his furs that he had been

able to ~~hmy~~ get such beautiful presents.

~~ThenbreamtmackenwameraihhmamnundnthenbacnnpnbntnSnkaymandnthenhormaemwama~~

The bear tracks were all around the barn, but Sukey and the horses were safe inside.

All that day the sun shone, the snow melted, and ~~thermometbes~~ little streams of water ran

from the icicles, which all the time grew thinner. Some of the icicles fell from the

eaves with soft smashing and crackling sounds in the snow. Before the sun set that night,

the bear tracks were only shapeless marks in the soft, wet snow.

After supper Pa took Laura and Mary on his knees, and said he had a new story to

tell them.

The story of ~~Pa~~ Grandma's Father and the Bear in the Big Woods.

20

When I went to town yesterday with the furs--Pa said--I found it hard walking in the soft snow. It took me a long time to get to town, and there I found a great many men with furs coming in to do their trading. The storekeeper was busy, and I had to wait before he could look at my furs. Then we had to bargain about the price of each one, and then I had to pick out the things I wanted in trade. So it was sundown before I started home.

I tried to hurry, but the walking was hard and I was tired, so I had not gone far when night came. And I was alone in the Big Woods without my gun.

The night got darker and darker. I wished for my gun, for I knew that some of the bears had come out of their ~~winter~~ dens. I had seen their tracks when I went to town in the morning. Bears are hungry and cross at this time of year; you know they have been sleeping in their dens all winter long with nothing to eat, and that makes them thin and angry when they wake up. I did not want to meet one.

~~It was a black as pitch when there in the woods were a thick and by and by the stars have was~~ ~~much~~ I hurried along as fast as I could, through the dark. By and by the stars gave a little light. It was still black as pitch where the woods were thick, but in the open places I could see a little, dimly. I could see the road ahead a little way, and I could see the dark woods standing up ~~tall~~ all around me. I was glad when I came into an open place where the stars gave me this faint light.

Then I came into such an open place, and there, right in the middle of my road, I saw a big black bear.

He was standing up on his hind legs, looking at me. I could even see his eyes shine. I could see one of his claws, in the starlight.

My scalp prickled, and my hair stood straight up. I stopped in my tracks, and stood still. The bear did not move. There he stood, looking at me.

I knew it would do no good to try to go around him. ~~If I should go around him~~ ~~and he not seen and in the bear much him~~ He would follow me into the dark woods, where I could not see and he could. I did not want to meet a hungry bear, in the dark,

But I had to pass that bear, to get home. O, how I wished for my gun!

21

I thought that if I could scare him, he might get out of the road and let me by. So I took a deep breath, and suddenly I shouted as loud as I could and ran at him, waving my arms. He never moved. I did not run very far toward him, I tell you! I stopped and looked at him, and he kept on looking at me. Then I shouted again, with all my might. There he stood. I kept on shouting and waving my arms, but he did not budge.

There we were, the bear and I, in the ~~middle~~ Big Woods, in the middle of the night. It would do no good to run away. There were other bears in the woods. I might meet one any time. I might as well deal with this one as with another. Besides, I was going home. I would never get home, if I ran away from everything in the woods that scared me.

So at last I looked around, and I got a good big club, a solid, heavy branch that had been broken from some tree by the weight of snow in the winter. I lifted it up in my hands, and I ran straight at that bear. Yelling and swinging my club as hard as I could, I brought it down, Bang! on his head.

And there he still stood, but he was only a big black burned stump!

I had passed that stump a dozen times. I had passed it on my way to town that morning. It wasn't a bear at all. I only thought it was a bear, because I had been thinking all the time about bears and being afraid I would meet one.

            * * *

"It wasn't a bear at all?" Mary ~~mamma~~ said.

"No, Mary, ~~mamma~~, it wasn't a bear at all."

Laura said, "Ours was really a bear. But we were not scared at first, because we thought he was Sukey."

"Yes, yours was a bear," Pa answered. ~~that just shows that~~ "That just shows what mistakes we all make because we think things aren't what they really are."

"They're too little to understand that, Charles," Ma said.

"Oo-oo! That bear might have eaten Ma and me all up!" Laura exclaimed, and she shivered and snuggled closer against Pa. "Just think, Ma went right up to him and slapped him! He didn't do anything at all, Pa. Why didn't he do anything at all?"

"I guess he was taken by surprise, Laura," Pa answered. ~~mm~~ "I guess he was afraid.

22

When Ma walked right up to him and slapped him, he knew she was not afraid of him."

"Well, I think you were brave, too, Pa," Laura said. "Even if it was only a stump, you thought it was a bear. You'd have hit him on the head with a club, ~~mmmm~~ if he had been a bear, wouldn't you, Pa?"

"Yes," Pa said. "I would. You see, I had to."

Then Ma ~~mama~~ said it was bedtime. She took Mary and undressed her and put her in her red flannel nightgown. Then she undressed Laura and put her in her red flannel nightgown. They both crawled into their trundle bed, and said their prayers.

> Now I lay me down to sleep,
> I pray the Lord my soul to keep.
> If I should die before I wake,
> I pray the Lord my soul to take.

Ma kissed them both, and tucked the covers in around them. They lay there awhile, looking at Ma's smooth, parted hair and at her hands busy with sewing in the lamplight. ~~Theymlookednatmumayanhommmm~~ Her thimble made little clicking sounds against her needle, and then the long thread went softly swish! through the pretty calico that Pa had traded his furs for. They looked at Pa, who was greasing his boots. His mustaches and his long brown beard looked silky in the lamplight, and the colors of his plaid jacket were pretty. He whistled softly between his teeth,

> My darling Nelly Gray, they have taken her away,
> And I'll never see my darling any more---

It was a warm night. The fire had gone to coals on the hearth, and Pa did not build it up. All around ~~nhemhommmm~~ the little log house, in the Big Woods, there were little sounds of falling lumps of snow, and from the eaves there was the drip, drip of the melting icicyles. In just a little while the trees would be putting out their baby leaves, all rosy and yellow and pale green, and there would be wild flowers and birds in the Big Woods. Then there would be no more stories by the fire at night, but all day long Laura and Mary would run and play among the trees, for it would be spring.

* * *

The Benders of Kansas[1]

In the spring when the creek had gone down, Pa went to Independence again. He took the horses and wagon and was gone, it seemed, a long time. At last, in the night, he came driving up to the house, and when Ma lighted the lamp Mary and I woke up and got out of bed in our nightgowns. We had been eagerly watching for Pa and wondering what he would bring us from town. He had brought some candy for Mary and me, and for Ma a jar of sour pickles. They were so good.

We had never been up so late before. Pa held us on his knees and tickled our faces with his whiskers to make us laugh. He said he was glad he had come home. He told Ma that he had had some thoughts of stopping at Benders' for the night. It was pretty late when he got that far, he said, and while he was getting a drink at the well in the yard, and watering the horses, Kate Bender came out and asked him to have supper there and put up for the night. He had a pretty heavy load on the wagon, and the horses were tired, but he had thought best to hurry on.

Mary and I had those names in our minds, Independence Kansas, and Benders.

One night just about sundown a strange man came riding his horse up to the door on a run. Pa hurried out and they talked a few minutes. Then the man went away as fast as he had come, and Pa came into the house in a hurry. He would not wait for supper, but asked Ma to give him a bite to eat right away, saying he must go. Something horrible had happened at Benders.

Ma put bread, meat, and some of those good pickles on the table, and Pa talked while he ate. Mary and I hung at the table's edge, looking at the pickles. I heard Pa say "dead," and thought somebody at Benders was dead. Pa said, "Already twenty or more, in the cellar." He said, "Benders—where I stopped for a drink. She asked me to come in."

Ma said, "Oh Charles, thank God!"

1. The account of the Benders first appeared in the Brandt Revised version of *Pioneer Girl*. This text comes from Bye, pp. 7–10. Selected details in this narrative about the Benders ring true. They did run an inn and grocery store near the Osage Diminished Indian Reserve and frequently served customers from Independence, Kansas. The younger Kate Bender (the older Bender woman used the same name and may have been her mother) reputedly enticed male travelers. Many accounts of their one-room inn or tavern describe it as being "curtained across to make two rooms," and victims were often said to be attacked from behind that curtain. According to the Kansas State Historical Society, "Settlers were easy prey for robbers, and it was not uncommon for people to go missing" ("Cool Things—Bender Knife"), an observation that again corresponds to the Bye description that the country was lonesome, "beyond the reach of postal service." Perhaps most chilling: one of the victims was indeed a little girl, the eight-year-old daughter of George Loncher. Her body was found with her father's on the Benders' property, and many accounts claim that she was buried alive. Between eight and eleven bodies were recovered from the orchard behind the Benders' cabin; some newspaper accounts of the period placed the number of victims even higher.

But in the context of autobiography, the Brandt Revised and Bye narratives are fictional. Charles Ingalls was unlikely to have stopped at the Benders' inn on his way to and from Independence. It was too far out of his way. The Benders' place was across the Montgomery County line in Labette County, seventeen miles northeast of Independence, and about thirty miles northeast of the Ingalls cabin. Furthermore, the murders themselves gained public attention long after Wilder and her family had moved back to Wisconsin. Although the Benders opened their inn for business in the winter of 1870–1871, and the Ingalls family left Kansas later that spring, the first murder charges date from 1873. Vigilante groups tried to track down the Benders when they disappeared from Kansas that year, and one group even claimed that they threw the Benders' dismembered bodies into the Verdigris River. By then, however, Charles Ingalls and his family were living in Pepin County, Wisconsin.

So how did the Benders' story end up in later versions of *Pioneer Girl*? Given Lane's proclivity to mix fact with fiction, it is reasonable to assume that the idea originated with her. Furthermore, the writing style in the Bender episode more closely corresponds to Lane's published work than Wilder's *Missouri Ruralist* columns or her original draft of *Pioneer Girl*. Perhaps the most personal line in the narrative, the one that concludes the section, originally appeared in Brandt Revised in Lane's handwriting: "I have often thought of that wagon with the Benders in it, driving fast across the empty prairie, overtaken at last and stopped by those men on horseback" (p. 6b). The Brandt manuscript had not sold; Lane may have reasoned that attaching a wholesome family's brush with a notorious one would tease out a sale. In Brandt Revised, the sequence appears as a tentative insert, covering pages 6, 6a, and 6b. The page numbers 6a and 6b are handwritten scribbles over sequential typewritten page numbers. It could be that Lane wanted her mother's approval of the sequence before it was incorporated into the final draft.

Yet, it is possible that the Ingalls family skirted the Benders' property when they left Kansas in 1871. In fact, several of the Benders' victims had been traveling either to or from Independence when they stopped at the tavern, which was near the Osage Mission on the road to Fort Scott. The Ingallses certainly headed northeast and could have taken a route that would have led them past the Benders' inn. In a speech delivered at the Detroit Book Fair in 1937, Wilder included this personal memory of the Bender place: "We stopped there, on our way in to the Little house, while Pa watered the horses and brought us all a drink from the well near the door of

I did not understand and felt confused. Mary kept asking Ma why she thanked God, and Ma did not answer. She poured some coffee for Pa and Pa blew on it to cool it, while I watched him and kept hoping he would give me a piece of pickle. Then Pa said, "They found a little girl, no bigger than Laura. They'd thrown her in on top of her father and mother and tramped the ground down on them, while the little girl was still alive."

I screamed, and Ma told Pa he should have known better.

Pa took his gun, jumped on Patty and rode away, while Ma tried to quiet me. She said it didn't mean anything, that no one would hurt a little girl like me, that I was mistaken and mustn't think of it any more. She gave me mush and syrup and told me to eat my supper.

I was afraid, even when Ma pulled our trundle bed from under the big bed and put Mary and me in our nightgowns. We said, "Now I lay me down to sleep, I pray the Lord my soul to keep, if I should die before I wake, I pray the Lord my soul to take." I could say it all, by following just a little behind Mary. But I was still afraid, and Pa was gone, and Ma did not seem the same as usual.

Pa wasn't there when we woke in the morning, and Ma did not tell us where he had gone. All day he didn't come, and Ma kept looking across the prairie. Mary and I looked, too.

That night, or perhaps the next night, at sundown Pa came riding home on Patty, all tired out. Mary and I hung onto him, as soon as he got to the ground. He said to Ma something like, "Yes, Caroline. Kate Bender with the rest. She deserved it just as much as they did."

Somehow Mary and I were both frightened when we heard that word, "Bender."

For a long time, even for years, after that, I dreamed sometimes about a little girl thrown on top of her father and mother and buried alive. Sometimes I was the little girl.

I was a woman grown before I ever spoke to Pa about the Benders. He used to listen when other men told about the roadhouse Kate Bender kept between Independence Kansas and Indian territory, and the travelers who were murdered there. The roadhouse was curtained across to make two rooms, and when a man sat eat-

THE BENDERS OF KANSAS {355

ing, on a bench against the curtain, one of the Benders would come stealthily behind the curtain and kill him by a blow on the head with the blunt end of an ax. All that country was so far beyond the reach of postal service that no one was troubled when no word came back from men who went into it.

When at last the eastern relatives of a man who had disappeared began to make careful inquiries, and aroused some suspicion of the Benders, more than forty bodies of men, women and children were dug up in the cellar and around the house.

Just before the alarm was raised, the Bender family got away across the prairie, and though the Vigilantes followed them, it was never known what had become of them. From time to time we would hear a rumor that Kate Bender had been found living somewhere. Pa would listen, and never say a word.

One day when we were alone I asked him if he had not stopped once to water his horse at the Benders, but had refused to stay all night when Kate Bender asked him. Wasn't he one of the Vigilantes who went after the Benders, and didn't they catch them?

He only said, "We thought you were too little to understand." As for what became of the Benders, he would not answer. He said, "Don't worry. They'll never find Kate Bender anywhere."

I have often thought of that wagon with the Benders in it, driven fast across the empty prairie, overtaken at last and stopped by those men on horseback.

the house. I saw Kate Bender standing in the doorway" (p. [9], Box 13, file 197, Lane Papers). But this memory is itself flawed. The Benders were not in Kansas in 1869, when Wilder and her family were on their way into Indian Territory; yet, the Benders were certainly there when the Ingallses were on their way out. Wilder was two years old when she moved to Kansas, four years old when she left. She could have easily confused the circumstances that created the memory.

In any case, Wilder elaborated on her memory in the book fair speech. She talked about Pa's involvement with the vigilantes and even included details about how victims were discovered at the Bender place. Given the fact that both Wilder and Lane were confused throughout *Pioneer Girl* about the chronology of Wilder's life, they may not have been aware that the vigilante activity actually took place after the Ingallses had left Kansas. Perhaps Wilder grew up on those stories. Charles Ingalls may have inserted himself into the Benders' saga years later, when dates and places had become distant and hazy. Or perhaps the story of the Loncher girl's murder had attached itself, in Wilder's memory, to Ingalls family lore surrounding that stop at the Benders' place for a drink of water. What harm could there be, Wilder and Lane may have concluded, in embellishing this connection? Lane herself fictionalized the Benders' story in her novel *Free Land* (New York: Longmans, Green & Co., 1938), where the Benders became the Bordens, perhaps as a deliberate echo of yet another sensational American murder case—the Lizzie Borden axe murders of 1892.

The issue of fictionalizing what is presented as autobiography or memoir continues to be controversial. Recent bestsellers from James Frey's *A Million Little Pieces* (2003) to Margaret Selzer's *Love and Consequences* (2008) generated controversy when their authors revealed that they had fictionalized details, episodes, and characterizations in these autobiographical works. Their publishers came under fire as well. How could they not know what was real and what was not? *Pioneer Girl*, of course, was not published in Wilder's or Lane's lifetime,

The Bender Ranch, 1872.
*G. R. Gamble Photograph,
Kansas State Historical
Society*

and the Little House books were published as fiction. Yet Wilder
and Lane promoted the novels as being absolutely true. Perhaps
they instinctively recognized that what is billed as a "true" story
often seems to resonate more deeply with readers than a fictional
one. "Every story in this novel [*On the Banks of Plum Creek*],"
Wilder pledged at the Detroit Book Fair, "all the circumstances,
each incident are true. All I have told is true but it is not the whole
truth" (p. [8]).

APPENDIX C. The Gordon Party[1]

This was not his first trip into Dakota territory. Uncle Tom had been in the party of twenty one men and one woman with her husband, who had been the first white people in the Black Hills. This had been in 1874.

Uncle Tom told us all about it in his mild, gentle way, but he was really very bitter. He told how the party in covered wagons and on horseback traveled across the plains from Sioux City to the Black Hills, how they went on into the hills, stopping at last and building a stockade to protect them against the Indians. He told how they prospected, how they found gold and staked out their claims, how well they liked the country and how hopeful they were, how they settled in for the winter and were beseiged by the Indians.

The weather was bitter cold, their provisions ran low and they could not hunt because of the Indians. But they hung on, rationing their food, tightening their belts and keeping watch day and night. They knew if they could manage to survive the winter and hang on till spring, they would be all right.

They had come into the Black Hills while the land was still Indian territory, but before spring the government would take possession of the land and throw it open to settlement, and the rush of settlers would start. Uncle Tom and the men with him were first on the ground, their claims already staked and gold found, and this thought fortified them to bear their sufferings through the winter.

They did hold out till spring, and what was their joy one day to see white men coming—soldiers! Soldiers in the Black Hills meant nothing more to fear, for the soldiers were coming to drive out the Indians. The American flag was on the stockade, they had kept it flying there all winter. The men were so thin their clothing hung on them like coats on scarecrows, but they threw open the stockade gate and went out to meet the soldiers, cheering.

The soldiers put them under arrest, hauled down the flag and set fire to the stockade, burning everything they owned in the world.

1. This text from the Bye version of *Pioneer Girl* (pp. 162–63) describes Uncle Tom's experiences as a member of the historical Gordon party, a group of twenty-eight led by John Gordon who made their way into the Black Hills in 1874. The group included a woman and a child, the family of one of the prospectors. The episode also occurs in the Brandt Revised version (pp. 94–95) and *These Happy Golden Years* (pp. 105–10), where Uncle Tom appears less bitter and more resigned. Ma is shocked by the outcome of the story, but he frankly replies, "It was Indian country. . . . Strictly speaking, we had no right there" (p. 109). Neither Fred Grant nor the eventual opening of the Black Hills is mentioned. The difference in tone between the narrative in Bye and the one published in *These Happy Golden Years* could be a reflection of their distinct target audiences—adults versus young readers. It could also reflect ideological differences between Wilder and Lane, who was more outspoken in her criticism of federal power. As her mother's editor and with an eye toward making the Bye manuscript more marketable, Lane may have reasoned that politicizing the details of Tom Quiner's experiences would appeal to more prestigious national magazines and make an essentially historical story more relevant.

Tom Quiner was a member of the Gordon party, but he and his comrades were not the first European Americans to enter the Black Hills. In fact, the military expedition accompanied by Second Lieutenant Frederick D. Grant, the son of President Ulysses S. Grant, and led by Lieutenant Colonel George Armstrong Custer left the Black Hills two months before the Gordon party even started from Sioux City, Iowa, in October 1874; newspapermen attached to the Custer expedition publicized the discovery of gold, providing the final incentive for men like Tom Quiner to seek their fortunes in territory forbidden by the Fort Laramie Treaty of 1868. The group

Members of the Gordon party, 1875, with Tomas L. Quiner, standing, far left. *Laura Ingalls Wilder Memorial Society*

evaded capture by military units set on alert to enforce the treaty and reached the Black Hills in December 1874.

Neither of the participants who later recorded the adventure mentioned any conflict with Indians at the stockade, although they expected the Lakotas to challenge their intrusion. In the end, it was a cavalry company under Captain John Mix that found the party in April 1875 and forced their removal. The soldiers did not burn the stockade and even waited a few days for the prospectors to gather possessions and livestock before bad weather threatened their return journey. To make better time, the party had to abandon its wagons and heavy equipment. Mix assured them that their mining claims would be respected when the land was declared legally open, but contrary to this account in Bye, the Black Hills were not officially opened for nearly two years, although military

efforts to enforce the Fort Laramie Treaty ceased in November 1875. Apparently, Tom Quiner did not return to take possession of his claim.

In *These Happy Golden Years*, Wilder contrasted Uncle Tom with Pa, who paces across the room and bristles, "I'll be durned if I could have taken it!" Ma adds, "To this day I think of the house we had to leave in Indian Territory" (p. 109). But instead of drawing direct conclusions, Wilder lets Laura, and by extension her young readers, absorb the complexity of the two sets of experiences. Aken, *Pioneers of the Black Hills*, pp. 111–45; Schell, *History of South Dakota*, pp. 129, 139; Hedren, *Ho! For the Black Hills*, pp. 6–8, 12–14; Parker, "Report," pp. 385–96; Power, "Distance Lends Enchantment," p. 47; Tallent, *Black Hills*, pp. 66–86.

Then the soldiers took them out of the hills and turned them loose on the plains, stripped of everything but the clothes they wore and their rifles.

A little later Fred Grant, the President's son, led a party of white men into the Black Hills and was acclaimed as the first white man who had ever gone into that wild country.

Uncle Tom was bitter about this, because he said that while his party had [g]one into the hills before they had a legal right to, the land had been taken over by the government while they were there, and was government land legally open to settlement by white men at the time the soldiers came in, burned everything they owned, and drove them out. He said it was done because Fred Grant wanted the credit of being the first white man to penetrate into the Black Hills.

The Singing School[1]

Mr. Clewett, our old schoolteacher, started it. Terms were $2. a pupil for the six week's school to be held from half past seven to ten o'clock every Tuesday and Friday night in the church building in town.[2] Knowing it would cost so much, I hardly expected to be able to go. But when Manly asked me to go with him, I answered by singing a bit that we had sung with the Boasts that winter in the surveyor's house on Silver Lake.

Oh, childhood's joys are very great,[3]
A-swinging on your mother's gate,
A-eating candy till your mouth
Is all stuck up from north to south,
But though I have to mind the rule,
I'd rather go to Singing School.

So Manly paid for two pupils and bought a singing book,[4] and every Tuesday and Friday night we went, driving Barnum single.

Mr. Clewett taught us the names and values of the notes and accents, the base, tenor and treble clefs, the holds and the slurs and the rests. Then he practiced us on scales and exercises, Three Blind Mice[5] and The Bramble Bush[6] — rounds I had sung with the Boasts.

At the last meeting of the second week he prepared to start us on the first easy song in the book. He seated the base singers in a group by themselves, the tenors in another group, sopranos and altos the same, saying we could sing better that way. Of course we could have, but it spoiled the fun of going to Singing School to be separated from one's beau all evening, so this way of sitting lasted only one meeting. At the next, bases, sopranos, altos and tenors were inextricably mixed again, and with a smile Mr. Clewett left us so.[7]

I wore my tucked lawn dress and the hat with the ostrich tips on these evenings, and Manly and I sat side by side, though not very close because of my hoops, and sang from the same book.

The evening always began with our singing the scales to lim-

1. The following description of the singing school appears on pp. 181–88 of the Bye version of *Pioneer Girl*.

2. *Mr. Clewett . . . in town.* The *De Smet Leader* does not mention a singing school conducted by Mr. Clewette, but it does mention two others. On February 16, 1884, E. A. Forbush began a singing school on Monday and Saturday evenings at the Congregational church; in March, it expanded to three times a week but cut back in April to accommodate the season's farm work. On December 6, 1884, the *Leader* announced that G. C. Westervelt would begin a singing school, which it later described as "an advanced class in choral singing" ("Town and Country," Dec. 27, 1884). Also organized at the Congregational church, this class moved to Westervelt's home and met twice a week on Mondays and Saturdays. The singing school seems to have been a winter-only phenomenon. "Town and Country," *De Smet Leader*, Feb. 9, 16, 23, Mar. 1, 8, 22, 29, Dec. 6, 27, 1884, Jan. 10, 1885.

3. *joys are very great.* These lyrics come from "The Singin Skewl," an 1869 song by P. Benson, a pseudonym for Charles Miller. The lyrics occur again in *These Happy Golden Years* (p. 212). Cockrell, *Ingalls Wilder Family Songbook*, pp. 280–83, 392–93.

4. *bought a singing book.* The Laura Ingalls Wilder Historic Home and Museum in Mansfield, Missouri, holds a copy of a singing-school book called *Thompson's Class and Concert*, compiled and published by Will L. Thompson in East Liverpool, Ohio, in 1880. This book could be the one that Almanzo Wilder bought for the singing school, but musicologist Dale Cockrell has demonstrated that a different book was consulted for *Pioneer Girl*. The songs mentioned or quoted in the various versions do not appear in *Thompson's Class and Concert*. With one exception, however, they can be found in *The Conqueror*, compiled by Charles E. Leslie and Ransom H. Randall

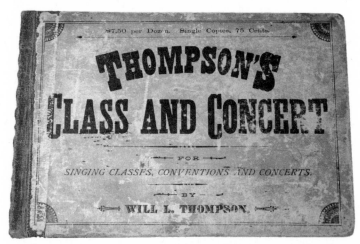

Thompson's Class and Concert. Laura Ingalls Wilder Historic Home and Museum

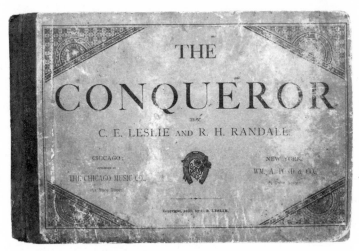

The Conqueror. South Dakota Historical Society Press

and published in 1880 by the Chicago Music Company. In *These Happy Golden Years*, Wilder also referred to the song "The Heavens Declare the Glory" and gave its correct page number in *The Conqueror*, "page one hundred forty-four" (*HGY*, p. 213). The only song mentioned that does not appear in *The Conqueror* is "The Singin Skewl." No existing copy of *The Conqueror* has been connected to Wilder or Lane. Cockrell, *Ingalls Wilder Family Songbook*, pp. xlii–xliii.

5. *Three Blind Mice*. This round, discussed earlier, appears in Leslie and Randall, *The Conqueror*, p. 8.

6. *The Bramble Bush*. This song also appears on page 8 of *The Conqueror*; the round in three parts is based on a children's rhyme of unknown origin. A variant text, using "quickset hedge" rather than bramble bush, can be found in Wheeler, *Mother Goose's Melody*, p. 121.

7. *with a smile Mr. Clewett left us so*. Even the wholesome singing school was once regarded as a corruptive influence. The *De Smet Leader* ran the following item on April 25, 1885: "The Rev. Henry Ward Beecher said, in response to one of his cranky people, who is opposed to roller skating: These places are said to be immoral, are they? Well, the same was said of our old New England singing schools, which also brought our young people together. However, I think too highly of our American young men and girls to believe that they would misbehave themselves in being brought into contact."

ber up our voices. Mr. Clewett gave us the pitch with his tuning fork and kept us trying until we got it. Once started we usually did very well, leaping vocally from crag to crag or sliding gracefully up and down the scales. When the voice of some unfortunate leaped too high or fell down past rescue, we all smiled, and Mr. Clewett had us go back and begin again, giving him another chance. Some learned easily and were soon singing with the best, while those who couldn't sing and couldn't learn, having neither voice nor ear, enjoyed themselves well trying.

After the scales, the evening's real pleasure began. The first song we learned was The Song of the Freedmen, "We're All Here."[8] We let ourselves go on this and sang with a will:

> When Paul and Silas were bound in jail,
> Do thy-seffa no harm,
> One did sing and the other did pray,
> Do thy-seffa no harm!
> If religion was a thing that money could buy,
> Do thy-seffa no harm,
> The rich would live and the poor would die,
> Do thy-seffa no harm!
>
> As I go down the steeps of time,
> Do thy-seffa no harm,
> I leave this sinful world behind,
> Do thy-seffa no harm!
> If you get there before I do,
> Do thy-seffa no harm,
> Tell them I am a-coming too,
> Do thy-seffa no harm!

With the rousing chorus:

> We're all here, we're all here,
> Do thy-seffa no harm,
> We're all here, we're all here,
> Do thy-seffa no harm!

8. *"We Are All Here."* Written by Louis Murray Browne in 1880, this song appears on p. 22 of *The Conqueror* in an arrangement by Randall. Cockrell, *Ingalls Wilder Family Songbook*, pp. 323–24, 399.

9. *"Who Was It?"* Leslie arranged this song using an anonymous text. Leslie and Randall, *The Conqueror*, p. 23.

10. *"Don't Go Out To-night, My Darling."* This song featured both words and music by Leslie. Ibid., pp. 88–89.

Another song we all enjoyed, though it was more difficult, was "Who Was It?"[9]

Who was it picked up all my chips,
And strewed the floor with strings and whips,
And in the washtub sailed his ships?
My brother, Oh my brother.
Who was it taught me how to skate,
And set me on the ice to wait,
While he went home with Cousin Kate?
My brother, Oh my brother.

Who was it when he older grew
To tops and marbles bid adieu
And tried but could not learn to chew?
My brother, Oh my brother.
Who does a tiny mustache wear,
And oils and curls it up with care,
And in the middle parts his hair?
My brother, Oh my brother.

Who talks to me about his clothes,
And all my little secrets knows,
And teases me about my beaux?
My brother, Oh my brother.
Who is it that I love the best
Of all the boys in east or west,
Although he is a perfect pest?
My brother, Oh my brother.

This was a very happy six weeks for all of us. Mr. Clewett had eighteen pupils, at two dollars each, so the Singing School was a success and he had a good profit from it. As for us, we looked forward eagerly to every Tuesday and Friday night, and enjoyed to the full every moment of those evenings.

Not all the songs were gay; some were deeply religious in feeling, some pathetic. We sang with emotion The Faithful Wife's Pleading to Her Drunken Husband, "Don't Go Out Tonight, My Darling."[10]

Don't go out tonight, my darling,
Do not leave me here alone,
Stay at home with me, my darling,
I am lonely when you're gone.
Though the wine-cup may be tempting,
And your friends are full of glee,
I will do my best to cheer you,
Darling, won't you stay with me?

In the chorus the quartet was very affecting.

Don't go out tonight, my darling,
     (My darling, do not go,)
Do not leave me here alone,
     (All alone)
Stay at home tonight, my darling,
     (My darling, stay at home)
I am lonely when you're gone.
     (When you're gone.)

Oh my darling do not leave me
For my heart is filled with fear,
Stay at home tonight, my darling,
Let me feel your presence near.
Oh my God, he's gone and left me,
With a curse upon his lips,
Who can tell how much I suffer,
From the accursed cup he drinks?

Hear the tread of heavy footsteps,
Hear that rap upon the door,
They have brought me home my husband,
There he lays upon the floor.
No caress of mine can wake him,
All he craves is rum, more rum,
And the fondest hopes I cherished,
All have faded, one by one.

11. *"Blame Yourself If You're Sold."* Randall wrote the words and music of this selection using the slang of the time. Ibid., pp. 96–97.

After such a sad and harrowing song, the recess was a relief. We always had a fifteen minute recess, during which we ate candy and talked gaily, moving about from group to group or sitting shyly in our places, according to our dispositions.

I was one of the shy ones, for it was always hard for me to mingle with people, but Manly always stayed by me, and as he had usually brought a paper sack of candy the others clustered around us more or less.

There were many gayer songs, and funny ones, though we did not really enjoy them more than the pathetic ones, only in a different way. We were much amused when we sang, "Blame Yourself If You're Sold."[11]

Oh, this world of ours is a very queer place
And the people all find it so,
For you never can tell what a day may bring forth,
And the future no man can know,
And the many mistakes of a comical king,
Committed by young and old,
Is the fault of him who gets in the scrap,
So blame yourself if you're sold.

So blame yourself, so blame yourself,
            (So blame yourself)
So blame yourself, so blame yourself,
            (So blame yourself)
So blame yourself if you're sold.

I remember well of a very nice girl,
And the fellow she met one day,
For he fell in love at the very first glance,
And wanted to marry straight way.
But the sorrow and grief that he suffered that day,
Can never, no never be told,
She was married, she said, to a better looking man,
So you see, my friends, he was sold.

Oh the ways by which we are many times sold,
Are so comical, strange and queer,
As to make us a mark for the lovers of fun,
And we have a just cause to fear.
But if ever you get into any such scrape,
By being too timid or bold,
Recollect, my friend, whose fault it is,
And blame yourself if you're sold.

Another song, which left us all quite exhausted with laughing, was "We All Have a Very Bad Cold."[12] The verses of this, very short, called on each group for their best efforts.

The tenor now your Sol Fa Mi with vigor you must sing,
Let every note be loud and clear, this room with music ring.

The alto next their Mi Re Do will sound so sweet and low,
And mind I do not hear you say you can not sing today.

Now Madam, you can surely sing, your voice has had a rest,
I love to hear your upper notes, I'm sure they'll bear the test.

But the fun was in the chorus, with we sang lustily as well as we could for laughing, after each verse.

Tenor: Excuse me, sir, I cannot sing,
          I ab so very hoarse, (sneeze)
          Ad every tone I try to sig,
          Is very rough and coarse. (cough)

Alto: O dear, O dear, I fear you'll scold,
          I too have got a cold (ply handkerchief vigorously)
          I cough and sneeze with perfect ease (cough, sneeze)
          But cad nod sig to please.

Soprano: O please sir, now my part excuse, (sneeze)
          My cold is very bad, (cough)
          Ad father says I must not sing—

12. *"We All Have a Very Bad Cold."* Charles E. Leslie wrote the music for this "comic quartet," with words by Allie B. Leslie (ibid., pp. 106–7).

13. *Temperance Anthem*. Wilder referred to this song in the original *Pioneer Girl* as "Wine I[s] a Mocker." Leslie again set lyrics of unknown origin to music, although the opening verse comes from Proverbs 20:1. Ibid., pp. 117–19.

Base, indignantly:
> Who cares about your dad?

All together:
> We all have a very bad cold,
>> (bad cold)
>
> That's a story that's often been told,
>> (been told)
>
> But with us you'll agree,
> For you surely can see (everyone cough, sneeze,
>> blow noses)
>
> That we all have a very bad cold.

A serious song which was a great favorite with all of us was the Temperance Anthem.[13] It was beautiful when we had learned to sing it properly.

Base solo: Wine is a mocker and strong drink is raging,
And whosoever is deceived thereby is not wise.

Full chorus: Wine is a mocker and strong drink is raging,
Wine is a mocker and strong drink is raging,
And whosoever is deceived thereby is not wise.

Duet, sopranos and altos:
> Touch not the wine, the beautiful wine,
> Shun its temptations bright though they shine,
> Thousands today are fast in its snare,
> Shun its temptations, of it beware.

Quartet:

> Dare not to trust yourself in its snare,
> Goodness and mercy dwellest not there,
> Misery and woe the wine cup will bring,
> Ever it biteth and endless its sting.

Solo obligato:

> Wine is a mocker and strong drink is raging,
> Wine is a mocker and strong drink is raging,
> And whosoever is deceived thereby is—not—wise.

Prayer, in solemn chant:

> O God, be merciful to those who are weak,
> And crave strong drink.
> Be unto them a strong tower against a monster
> That would swallow them up.

We did so well with this that Mr. Clewett became ambitious to teach us a song called, "O Hail Us, Ye Free,"[14] which our book said was an "Accompaniment In 'Opera Chorus Book'." Mr. Clewett told us that the man who had written this song, Verdi, was an Italian. But whether because it was difficult, or whether because we did not find it very interesting, we never did learn to sing it and Mr. Clewett soon gave up trying to teach it to us.

While the words of this song did not make very good sense, I liked some of them, with their music:

> The lightnings lit our path with wild and lurid flame,
> The thunders spoke in wrath and storm clouds darkly came,
> Where fearful breakers flashed as o'er the waves we dashed,
> We rushed to land in tempests, we bowed to proud old forests,
> Then crushed the monarch oak. Thus on and on we flew,
> Till all the wide world knew ['Twas] Freedom's voice that
>   spoke.

We did learn, and love, "Dearest May."[15] The pages of our books on which this song appeared were well worn before the end of Singing School.

> Now darkie[s] listen to me, a story I'll relate,
> It happened in the valley in the old Car'lina state,
> 'Way down in the meadows where I used to mow the hay,
> I always worked the harder when I thought of lovely May.

> Oh May, dearest May, you're lovely as the day,
> Your eyes so bright, they shine at night,
> When the moon am gone away.

> Old Massa gave me holiday, I wish he'd give me more,
> I thanked him very kindly as I shoved my boat from shore,

14. *"Oh Hail Us, Ye Free."* This selection uses music from the opening chorus *"Evviva! Beviamo!"* of Giuseppe Verdi's opera *Ernani*. The lyrics are a remarkably high-toned, Romantic adaptation of what is, in the Italian libretto, a bandits' drinking song. Ibid., pp. 70–74; Verdi, *Ernani* libretto.

15. *"Dearest May."* With lyrics by Francis Lynch and music by James Powers, this song was described as "an old and favorite Negro Melody," that would "be well received in the concert room" (Leslie and Randall, *The Conqueror*, pp. 78–79).

Then gently down the river, with a heart so light and free,
To the cottage of my dearest May I long so much to see.

Oh May, dearest May, you're lovely as the day,
Your eyes so bright, they shine at night,
When the moon am gone away.

On the banks of the river where the trees they hang so low,
The coon among the branches play while the mink remain
  below,
Oh there is the spot and May she looks so neat,
Her eyes they sparkle like the stars, her lips are red and sweet.

Oh May, dearest May, you're lovely as the day,
Your eyes so bright, they shine at night,
When the moon am gone away.

BIBLIOGRAPHY

MANUSCRIPTS AND
MANUSCRIPT COLLECTIONS

Bouchie Case Records, 1884–1887. *Dakota Territory* v. *Clarence and Elizabeth Bouchie.* Clerk of Courts Office. Kingsbury County Courthouse. De Smet, S.Dak.

Brown, James Oliver. Papers. Rare Book and Manuscript Library. Columbia University. New York, N.Y.

Commissioners' Record, 1880–1901. Auditor's Office. Kingsbury County Courthouse, De Smet, S.Dak.

Congregational Conference of Minnesota. Papers. BA3.1/C749c. Minnesota Historical Society. St. Paul, Minn.

Dakota Territorial Records. Microfilm ed. University of North Dakota. Grand Forks, N.Dak.

Ingalls, Charles P. "The Settlement of De Smet." N.d. Laura Ingalls Wilder Memorial Society Archives. De Smet, S.Dak.

Lane, Rose Wilder. Papers. Herbert Hoover Presidential Library. West Branch, Iowa.

Laura Ingalls Wilder Historic Home and Museum. Archival and Artifact Collections. Mansfield, Mo.

Laura Ingalls Wilder Memorial Society. Archives. De Smet, S.Dak.

Laura Ingalls Wilder Museum. Research Files. Walnut Grove, Minn.

London, Jack. Papers, 1866–1877. Huntington Library. San Moreno, Calif.

London, Jack and Charmian. Correspondence and Papers. Utah State University Special Collections and Archives. Logan, Utah.

Minnesota. State Census. 1875–1885.

Records of Kingsbury County Superintendent of Schools, 1880–1889. Auditor's Office. Kingsbury County Courthouse, De Smet.

Redwood County Courthouse. Deed Record Book, no. 5. Redwood Falls, Minn.

South Dakota. State Census. 1885–1905.

South Dakota Historic Preservation Office. National Register Files. Pierre, S.Dak.

Town Lot Record Book, no. 1, 1879–1887. Register of Deeds Office. Kingsbury County Courthouse. De Smet, S.Dak.

U.S. Department of the Interior. Bureau of Land Management. General Land Office Records. Springfield, Va. glorecords.blm.gov.

U.S. Department of the Interior. General Land Office. Land Entry Files. Records of the General Land Office. Record Group 49. National Archives and Records Administration. Washington, D.C.

———. Cash Entry File for Final Certificate #7410, issued to Charles P. Ingalls.

———. Homestead Entry File. Final Certificate #1490, issued to Almanzo J. Wilder. Also available at "Today's Document from the National Archives." archives .gov.

———. Final Certificate #2708, issued to Charles P. Ingalls. Also available at "Land Records: Ingalls Homestead File." archives.gov.

———. Final Certificate #4956, issued to James McKee.

———. Final Certificate # 5537, issued to Oliv D. Bouchie, formerly Oliv D. Morrison.

———. Final Certificate #9256, issued to Delilah Tibbs, formerly Delilah Bouchie.

Wilder, Laura Ingalls. Letters, Manuscripts, and Clippings. Laura Ingalls Wilder Historic Home and Museum, Mansfield, Mo.

———. Manuscript draft of *These Happy Golden Years.* Detroit Public Library. Detroit, Mich.

———. Papers. Laura Ingalls Wilder Home Association. Mansfield, Mo. Microfilm ed. LIW Papers, 1894–1943. Western Historical Manuscript Collection. Ellis Library. University of Missouri. Columbia.

Wisconsin. Census Records. 1905.

BOOKS, ARTICLES, AND WEBSITES

Abernethy, Francis Edward, ed. *Texas Toys and Games.* Publications of the Texas Folklore Society 48. Dallas, Tex.: Southern Methodist University Press, 1989.

"Adaliza A. Symms." Iowa Gravestone Photo Project. iowagravestones.org.

"The Adventurous Story of Poor 'Mary of the Wild Moor.'" justanothertune.com.

Aesopica: Aesop's Fables in English, Latin & Greek. Mythfolklore.net.

Aken, David. *Pioneers of the Black Hills; or, Gordon's Stockade Part of 1874.* [Milwaukee, Wis.]: By the Author, [1920].

Alcott, Louisa May. *Little Women.* New York: Scholastic, 1995.

Alexander, W. E. *History of Winneshiek and Allamakee Counties, Iowa.* Sioux City, Iowa: Western Publishing Co., 1882.

"Alice Josephine Ingalls." "Courtney/Newman Tree." trees.ancestry.com.

Allexan, Sarah S., Carrie L. Byington, Jerome I. Finkelstein, and Beth A. Tarini. "Blindness in Walnut Grove: How Did Mary Ingalls Lose Her Sight?" *Pediatrics* 131 (Mar. 2013): 1–3.

"American Badger — *Taxidea taxus.*" *Badger Info.* badger.org.

American Home Missionary Society. *The Fifty-seventh Report of the American Home Missionary Society.* New York, 1883.

"American White Pelican." *All about Birds.* Cornell Lab of Ornithology. allaboutbirds.org.

Anderson, William T. *Laura Ingalls Wilder Country*. New York: Harper Perennial, 1990.

———. *Laura Ingalls Wilder's Walnut Grove*. Walnut Grove, Minn.: Laura Ingalls Wilder Museum, 2013.

———. "The Literary Apprenticeship of Laura Ingalls Wilder." *South Dakota History* 13 (Winter 1983): 285–331.

———, comp. *Laura's Album: A Remembrance Scrapbook of Laura Ingalls Wilder*. New York: HarperCollins, 1998.

———, ed. *A Little House Reader: A Collection of Writings by Laura Ingalls Wilder*. New York: HarperCollins, 1998.

———, ed. *A Little House Sampler*. By Laura Ingalls Wilder and Rose Wilder Lane. Lincoln: University of Nebraska Press, 1988.

———. *The Story of the Wilders*. N.p.: By the Author, 1983.

———, ed. *A Wilder in the West: The Story of Eliza Jane Wilder*. De Smet, S.Dak.: Laura Ingalls Wilder Memorial Society, 1985.

Andreas' Historical Atlas of Dakota. Chicago: A. T. Andreas, 1884.

August Schell Brewing Company. schellsbrewery .com.

"Badger." *Columbia Encyclopedia*. 6th ed. 2013. encyclopedia.com.

Baldwin, Rebecca, and Patsy Watts. "We've Got a Pig in the Parlor: A Collection of Ozark Play Party Games." *Bittersweet* 6 (Fall 1978). thelibrary.org.

Baldwin, Sara Mullin, and Robert Morton Baldwin, eds. *Nebraskana: Biographical Sketches of Men and Women of Achievement Who Have Been Awarded Lifetime Membership in the Nebraskana Society*. Hebron, Nebr.: Baldwin Co., 1932.

Barkley, T. M., ed. *Flora of the Great Plains*. Lawrence: University Press of Kansas, 1986.

Barns, Cass G. *The Sod House*. Lincoln: Bison Books, University of Nebraska Press, 1970.

Barrington, Judith. *Writing the Memoir: From Truth to Art*. Portland, Ore.: Eighth Mountain Press, 1997.

Bartlett, G[eorge] B. *Mrs. Jarley's Far-Famed Collection of Waxworks, Part I*. London: Samuel French, 1873.

Bergen, Fanny D., ed. *Animal and Plant Lore Collected from the Oral Tradition of English Speaking Folk*. Boston: Houghton, Mifflin & Co., American Folk-Lore Society, 1899.

"Big Bluestem." *Plant Guide*. United States Department of Agriculture. Natural Resources Conservation Service. plants.usda.gov.

"A Bird in a Gilded Cage." New York Public Library Digital Gallery. digitalgallery.nypl.org.

"Blackface Minstrelsy." *American Experience*. pbs.org.

Bliss, P[hilip] P. *The Charm: A Collection of Sunday School Music*. Chicago: Root & Cady, 1871.

Bloom, Michelle E. *Waxworks: A Cultural Obsession*. Minneapolis: University of Minnesota Press, 2003.

Blum, Stella, ed. *Victorian Fashions and Costumes from Harper's Bazar, 1867–1898*. New York: Dover Publications, 1974.

Bollet, Alfred Jay. *Civil War Medicine: Challenges and Triumphs*. Tucson, Ariz.: Galen Press, 2002.

Boustead, Barb. "These Happy Golden Years, Chapter 8: A Cold Ride." *Beyond Little House*. beyondlittlehouse.com.

Brandt, Terry. "Children's Games." *Bittersweet* 1 (Fall 1973). Springfield-Greene County Library District. thelibrary.org.

Bryant, William Cullen. *Thirty Poems*. New York: D. Appleton & Co., 1871.

Burns, Louis F. *A History of the Osage People*. Tuscaloosa: University of Alabama Press, 2004.

"Burr Oak Township." *IAGenWeb*. iagenweb.org.

Bushnell, David I., Jr. *Burials of the Algonquian, Siouan and Caddoan Tribes West of the Mississippi*. Smithsonian Institution, Bureau of American Ethnology, Bulletin no. 83. Washington, D.C.: Government Printing Office, 1927.

"California, Biographical Index Cards." ancestrylibrary.com.

"California, Death Index, 1905–1939." ancestrylibrary.com.

Calloway, Colin G. *The Indian History of an American Institution: Native Americans and Dartmouth*. Hanover, N.H.: Dartmouth College Press, 2010.

———. *One Vast Winter Count: The Native American West before Lewis and Clark*. History of the American West Series. Lincoln: University of Nebraska Press, 2003.

Campbell, Donna M. "'Wild Men' and Dissenting Voices: Narrative Disruption in *Little House on the Prairie*." *Great Plains Quarterly* 20 (Spring 2000): 111–22.

"Captain Jinks, [of the Horse Marines]." Washington State University Libraries Digital Collections. kaga.wsulibs.wsu.edu.

Carson, Gerald. "T. R. and the 'Nature Fakers.'" *American Heritage* 22 (Feb. 1971). americanheritage.com.

Cart, Michael. *From Romance to Realism: 50 Years of Growth and Change in Young Adult Literature*. New York: Harper Collins, 1996.

Cassell's Household Guide: Being a Complete Encyclopædia of Domestic and Social Economy, and Forming a Guide to Every Department of Practical Life. Vol. 1. London: Cassell, Petter, and Galpin, 1869.

"Cattle: Jersey." *Breeds of Livestock*. Oklahoma State University, Department of Animal Science. ansi.okstate.edu.

Chapman, Berlin B. "Removal of the Osages from Kansas." *Kansas Historical Quarterly* 7 (Aug. 1938): 287–305.

Chapman, Joseph A., and George A. Feldhamer, eds. *Wild Mammals of North America: Biology, Management, and Economics*. Baltimore: Johns Hopkins University Press, 1982.

"Chart: Wisconsin's ever-more-efficient milk industry." Wisconsinwatch.org.

Chase, Carole F., comp. *Madeline L'Engle Herself: Reflections on a Writing Life*. Colorado Springs, Colo.: Shaw Books, 2001.

"Civil War: 25th Infantry." *Dictionary of Wisconsin History*. Wisconsin Historical Society. wisconsinhistory.org.

"The Civil War and Medicine." *Scientific American*, 14 July 2011. scientificamerican .com.

Clark, Edward B. "Roosevelt on the Nature Fakirs." *Everybody's Magazine* 16 (June 1907): 770–74.

Cleaveland, Nancy. "Ida B. Wright, Laura's Friend." In *The Best of the* Lore, pp. 83–84. De Smet, S.Dak.: Laura Ingalls Wilder Memorial Society, 2007.

———, and Penny Linsenmayer. *Charles Ingalls and the U.S. Public Land Laws*. N.p.: By the Authors, 2001.

Cockrell, Dale, ed. *The Ingalls Wilder Family Songbook*. Music of the United States of America, vol. 22. Middleton, Wis.: A-R Editions, Inc., for American Musicological Society, 2011.

"Colby Family & Others." Freepages.genealogy .rootsweb.ancestry.com.

Collins, Jim. "J. D. Salinger's Last Supper." *Yankee* (Jan. 2011). yankeemagazine.com.

"Common Grackle." *All about Birds*. Cornell Lab of Ornithology. allaboutbirds.org.

The Congregational Year-book, 1896. Boston: Congregational Sunday School & Publishing Society, 1896.

"Cool Things — Bender Knife." kshs.org.

Cooper, George. "Frogs at School." *The Nursery: A Monthly Magazine for Youngest Readers* 16 (1874): 101.

Curtiss-Wedge, Franklyn, comp. *The History of Redwood County, Minnesota*. Vol. 1. Chicago: H. C. Cooper, Jr. & Co., 1916.

———, comp. *The History of Wabasha County, Minnesota*. Winona, Minn.: H. C. Cooper, Jr. & Co., 1920.

Cutler, William G. "Montgomery County." In *A History of the State of Kansas* (1883), pt. 1. kancoll.org.

"D. H. Loftus Obituary." *Laura Ingalls Wilder Lore* 17 [Spring–Summer 1991]: 3.

"Dakota in the Fifties." *South Dakota Historical Collections* 10 (1920): 130–94.

Dakota Territory. *Session Laws*. 1862. 1864. 1879. 1881. 1883.

Danz, Harold P. *Cougar!* Athens, Ohio: Swallow Press, Ohio University Press, 1999.

Dary, David A. *The Buffalo Book: The Full Saga of the American Animal*. Rev. ed. [Athens]: Swallow Press/Ohio University Press, 1989.

"De Smet, Kingsbury Co., SD — 1909 Business Directory." *USGenWeb Archives*. files.usgwarchives.net.

"Despite scientific skepticism, black panther sightings reported in St. Tammany." *New Orleans Times-Picayune*, 30 Nov. 2011. nola.com.

Dickens, Charles. *Barnaby Rudge; a Tale of the Riots of 'Eighty*. London: Chapman and Hall, 1841.

———. *Bleak House*. Vol. 1. New York: Hurd and Houghton, 1870.

———. *The Old Curiosity Shop: A Tale*. Illus. George Cattermole and Hablot K. Browne. London: Chapman and Hall, 1841.

"Docia Waldvogel Forbes." liwfrontiergirl.com.

"Dr. George Tann." liwfrontiergirl.com.

"Dugout." *Encyclopedia of Oklahoma History and Culture*. Oklahoma Historical Society. digital.library.okstate.edu.

"Education: Iowa Braille School — Vinton." *History of Blindness in Iowa*. iowablindhistory .org.

Ehrensperger, Edward C., ed. *History of the United Church of Christ in South Dakota, 1869–1976*. N.p.: United Church of Christ in South Dakota, 1977.

"Emeline Hurley." "Masters Family Tree." trees.ancestry.com.

Encyclopedia of Chicago. encyclopedia.chicago history.org.

Erwin: The First 100 Years. [Erwin, S.Dak.]: n.p., [1987].

Ferguson, Natalie. "A Brief History of the Dolly Varden Dress Craze." *A Frolic through Time*. Zipzipink.blogspot.com.

Find a Grave. findagrave.com.

1st Minnesota Regiment, Minnesota Heavy Artillery. en.wikipedia.org.

Fisher, Richard A. "De Smet's Famous Wax Works." In *The Best of the* Lore, pp. 66–68. De Smet, S.Dak: Laura Ingalls Wilder Memorial Society, 2007.

Fite, Gilbert C., ed. "Some Farmers' Accounts of Hardship on the Frontier," *Minnesota History* 37 (Mar. 1961): 204–11.

Flandrau, Charles E. *The History of Minnesota and Tales of the Frontier*. St. Paul, Minn.: E. W. Porter, 1900.

Folwell, William W. *A History of Minnesota*. Vol. 3. St. Paul: Minnesota Historical Society, 1926.

"Fort Berthold Indian Agency [North Dakota]." familysearch.org.

"Frequently Asked Questions." Laura Ingalls Wilder Memorial Society. discoverlaura.org.

Fridley, Russell W. "Charles E. Flandrau, Attorney at War." *Minnesota History* 38 (Sept. 1962): 116–25.

Fugate, Mary. "Grandma Garland." In *The Best of the* Lore, pp. 88–91. De Smet, S.Dak.: Laura Ingalls Wilder Memorial Society, 2007.

Fuller, Jake. "Polka." centralhome.com.

"Fuller's Son Reports on the Early Days of De Smet," *Laura Ingalls Wilder Lore* 6 (Spring–Summer 1980): 5.

Garland, Hamlin. *Crumbling Idols: Twelve Essays on Art Dealing Chiefly with Literature, Painting and the Drama*. Chicago: Stone and Kimball, 1894.

Garson, Eugenia, comp. and ed. *The Laura Ingalls Wilder Songbook: Favorite Songs from the "Little House" Books*. Arr. Herbert Haufrecht. New York: HarperCollins, 1968.

"The Genealogy of Almanzo and Laura Ingalls Wilder." pennyn.tripod.com.

"General Map of Redwood County, Minnesota." Library of Congress. loc.gov.

"Genevieve Masters Renwick." "Sherwood Family Tree." trees.ancestry.com.

"Genevieve M. Renwick." "Cook County, Illinois, Deaths Index, 1878–1922." ancestrylibrary .com.

"George Cooper." *Hymnary.org*. hymnary.org.

Gibbs, Laura. *Aesop's Fables: A New Translation*. Oxford: Oxford University Press, 2002.

Giezentanner, Veda. "In Dugouts and Sod Houses." *Chronicles of Oklahoma* 39 (Summer 1961): 140–49.

"Gilbert was Mail Boy through *The Hard Winter*." In *The Best of the* Lore. De Smet, S.Dak.: Laura Ingalls Wilder Memorial Society, 2007. P. 20.

"Gilchrist Camera Family Tree." trees.ancestry .com.

Gish, Robert F. "Hamlin Garland's Dakota: History and Story." *South Dakota History* 9 (Summer 1979): 193–209.

Godey's Lady's Book and Magazine 99 (July 1879): plates.

"Gopher Removal." *Minnesota Nuisance Wildlife Control*. mn-wildlifecontrol.com.

"Graphical Climatology of Minneapolis-St. Paul Area Temperatures, Precipitation, and Snowfall (1820–Present)." climatestations .com.

"Gray's Atlas New Railroad Map of Minnesota and Iowa 1873." geographicus.com.

Greene, Alvin Hensdale (Allie). Interview by Marian Cramer. Transcript [1970].

Greiner, Alyson L. "Dugout." *Encyclopedia of Oklahoma History and Culture*. digital.library .okstate.edu.

Gries, John Paul. *Roadside Geology of South Dakota*. Missoula, Mont.: Mountain Press Publishing, 1996.

Griswold, Hattie T. "Under the Daisies." *Magazine of Poetry* 3 (Oct. 1891): 425–26.

Hale, Edward E. *Sunday-School Stories on the*

Golden Texts of the International Lessons of 1889. Boston: Roberts Brothers, 1880.

Hall, E. Raymond. *The Mammals of North America*. 2 vols. New York: John Wiley & Sons, 1981.

Hallowell, Wayne. "Bloody Bender Family, 1871–1873: Keepers of the Devil's Inn." leatherockhotel.com.

Handwerk, Brian. "Ball Lightning: A Shocking Scientific Mystery. *National Geographic* (May 31, 2006): news.nationalgeographic.com.

Handy-Marchello, Barbara. *Women of the Northern Plains: Gender and Settlement on the Homestead Frontier, 1870–1930*. St. Paul: Minnesota Historical Society Press, 2005.

Harding, Neva. *I Recall Pioneer Days in South Dakota*. Brookings, S.Dak.: By the Author, 1961.

"Harrigan, Edward." In *McGraw Hill Encyclopedia of World Drama*. Vol. 2. 2d ed. New York: McGraw Hill, 1984.

Hart, John Fraser, and Susy Svatek. *Landscapes of Minnesota: A Geography*. St. Paul: Minnesota Historical Society Press, 2008.

Hassrick, Royal B. *The Sioux: Life and Customs of a Warrior Society*. Norman: University of Oklahoma Press, [1964].

"Hatch Act of 1887." Mississippi Agricultural and Forestry Experiment Station and Mississippi State University Extension Service. msucares .com.

"The Heart and Home of Rose Wilder Lane." *Kansas City Star*. Reprint, *Springfield* (Mo.) *Leader*, July 5, 1925.

Hedren, Paul L. *Ho! For the Black Hills: Captain Jack Crawford Reports the Black Hills Gold Rush and Great Sioux War*. Pierre: South Dakota State Historical Society Press, 2012.

———. "The West Loved Oysters Too!" *Montana, the Magazine of Western History* 61 (Winter 2011): 3–15.

"*Hesperostipa spartea* (Trin.) Barkworth, porcupinegrass." Plants Database. United States Department of Agriculture. plants.usda.

Hicks, Jim. "Searching for Brewster School." In *The Best of the Lore*, pp. 70–74. De Smet, S.Dak.: Laura Ingalls Wilder Memorial Society, 2007.

Higgins, Kenneth F., et al. *Wild Mammals of South Dakota*. Pierre: South Dakota Department of Game, Fish and Parks, 2000.

Hill, Pamela Smith. *Laura Ingalls Wilder: A Writer's Life*. South Dakota Biography Series, no. 1. Pierre: South Dakota State Historical Society Press, 2007.

Hines, Stephen W., ed. *Little House in the Ozarks: The Rediscovered Writings*. Nashville: Thomas Nelson, 1991.

"Historical Note." American Missionary Association. Amistad Research Center. amistadresearchcenter.org.

"Historical Value of U.S. Dollar (Estimated)." mykindred.com.

"History of Brookings." Brookings Area Chamber of Commerce and Convention Bureau. brookingschamber.org.

"History of Maiden Rock." maidenrock.org.

"History of Minstrelsy." University of South Florida Libraries Special & Digital Collections. exhibits.lib.usf.edu.

"History of Pepin County" co.pepin.wi.us.

History of Southeastern Dakota. Sioux City, Iowa: Western Publishing Co., 1881.

"History of TB." New Jersey Medical School Global Tuberculosis Institute. globaltb.njms .rutgers.edu.

Holden, David J. *Dakota Visions: A County Approach*. Sioux Falls, S.Dak.: Center for Western Studies, Augustana College, 1982.

Holm, Tom. "Warriors and Warfare." In *Encyclopedia of North American Indians*, edited by Frederick E. Hoxie, pp. 666–68. Boston: Houghton Mifflin, 1996.

Holtz, William. *The Ghost in the Little House: A Life of Rose Wilder Lane*. Columbia: University of Missouri Press, 1993.

Hoover, Herbert T., and Leonard R. Bruguier. *The Yankton Sioux*. Indians of North America

Series. New York: Chelsea House Publishers, 1988.

Howard, Janet L. "Buchloe dactyloides." In U.S., Department of Agriculture, Forest Service, Rocky Mountain Research Station, Fire Sciences Laboratory, *Fire Effects Information System*, 1995. fs.fed.us.

Howe, Charles W., comp. and ed. *A Half Century of Progress: Walnut Grove, Minn. and Vicinity—1866 to 1916*. Walnut Grove, Minn.: *Walnut Grove Tribune*, 1916.

Hufstetler, Mark, and Michael Bedeau. "South Dakota's Railroads: An Historic Context." Rev. 2007. South Dakota Historic Preservation Office, Pierre, S.Dak.

Hunt, N. Jane, ed. *Brevet's South Dakota Historical Markers*. Sioux Falls, S.Dak.: Brevet Press, 1974.

Hupfeld, Henry. *Encyclopedia of Wit and Wisdom: A Collection of Over Nine Thousand Anecdotes, . . . Pathos* (Philadelphia: David McKay, 1897.

Hymnsite.com.

"Illinois, Deaths and Stillbirths Index, 1916–1947." ancestrylibrary.com.

The Ingalls Family of De Smet. De Smet, S.Dak.: Laura Ingalls Wilder Memorial Society, Inc., 2001.

"Introduction." *19th Century Baseball*. 19cbaseball.com.

Jameson, Elizabeth. "In Search of the Great Ma." *Journal of the West* 37 (Apr. 1998): 42–52.

"John Brown [abolitionist]." en.wikipedia.org.

"John Brown's Body." en.wikipedia.org.

Johnsgard, Paul A. *Birds of the Great Plains: Breeding Species and Their Distribution*. Lincoln: University of Nebraska Press, 1979.

———. *Wings over the Great Plains: Bird Migrations in the Central Flyway*. Zea E-Books, 2012. digitalcommons.unl.edu.

Johnson, A. J. *Johnson's Kansas and Nebraska*. 1870. alabamamaps.ua.edu.

Johnson, James R., and Gary E. Larson. *Grassland Plants of South Dakota and the Northern Great Plains*. South Dakota Agricultural Experiment Station, Bulletin 566 (rev.). Brookings: South Dakota State University, 1999.

Johnson, Lyle R. "Decade of Drought: A Year-by-Year Account of Weather-related Changes in 1930s Kingsbury County." *South Dakota History* 43 (Fall 2013): 218–44.

"The Kansas Murders: A Terrible Tale of Crime." *Jackson Sentinel* (Maquoketa, Iowa), 22 May 1873. newspaperarchive.com.

Karolevitz, Robert F. *Challenge: The South Dakota Story*. Sioux Falls, S.Dak.: Brevet Press, 1975.

Kaye, Frances W. "Little Squatter on the Osage Diminished Reserve: Reading Laura Ingalls Wilder's Kansas Indians." *Great Plains Quarterly* 20 (Spring 2000): 123–40.

Keisow, Alyssa M. *Field Guide to Amphibians and Reptiles of South Dakota*. Pierre: South Dakota Department of Game, Fish and Parks, 2006.

Kingsbury, George W. *History of Dakota Territory*. George Martin Smith. *South Dakota: Its History and Its People*. 5 vols. Chicago: S. J. Clarke Publishing Co., 1915.

Koupal, Nancy Tystad. "Marietta Bones: Personality and Politics in the South Dakota Suffrage Movement." In *Feminist Frontiers: Women Who Shaped the Midwest*, edited by Yvonne J. Johnson, pp. 69–82. Kirksville, Mo.: Truman State University Press, 2010.

Lane, Rose Wilder. *Free Land*. New York: Longmans, Green and Co., 1938.

———. "Home over Saturday." *The Saturday Evening Post* 210 (Sept. 11, 1937): 5–7, 53–54, 57–58, 60.

———. *Let the Hurricane Roar*. New York: Longmans, Green and Co., 1933.

———. "Long Skirts." *Ladies Home Journal* (Apr. 1933): 11, 83–84, 86, 88–89.

———. "Object, Matrimony." *The Saturday Evening Post* 207 (Sept. 1, 1934): 5–7, 57–58.

"Lansford Whiting Ingalls." geni.com.

Larson, Gary E., and James R. Johnson. *Plants of the Black Hills and Bear Lodge Mountains*.

South Dakota Agricultural Experiment Station, Bulletin 732. Brookings: South Dakota State University, 1999.

Laskin, David. *The Children's Blizzard*. New York: HarperCollins, 2004.

Lauck, Jon. " 'You can't mix wheat and potatoes in the same bin' ": Anti-Catholicism in Early Dakota." *South Dakota History* 38 (Spring 2008):1–46.

Laura Ingalls Wilder, Frontier Girl. liwfrontiergirl.com.

Laura's Prairie House. laurasprairiehouse.com.

"Laura's writing teacher, V.S.L. Owen." *Laura Ingalls Wilder Lore* 23 (Spring-Summer 1997): 4.

Lauters, Amy Mattson, ed. *The Rediscovered Writings of Rose Wilder Lane, Literary Journalist*. Columbia: University of Missouri Press, 2007.

"Legends of Kansas: The Bloody Benders of Labette County." legendsofamerica.com.

"Leonard Hathaway Rev. Moses." "Family Roots, Stews, Chowder and Gumbo lines." trees.ancestry.com.

Lerone, Bennett, Jr. "What's in a Name? Negro vs. Afro-American vs. Black." *Ebony* 23 (Nov. 1967): 46–54.

Leslie, Charles E., and Ransom H. Randall. *The Conqueror*. Chicago: Chicago Music Co., 1880.

"Le Soldat Du Chene, Osage Chief." accessgenealogy.com.

Levisee, A. B., and L. Levisee, eds. *The Annotated Revised Codes of the Territory of Dakota, 1883*. Vol. 2. St. Paul, Minn.: West Publishing Co., 1884.

Linsenmayer, Penny T. "Kansas Settlers on the Osage Diminished Reserve: A Study of Laura Ingalls Wilder's *Little House on the Prairie*." *Kansas History* 24 (Autumn 2001): 169–85.

"List of real-life individuals from Little House on the Prairie." en.wikipedia.org.

"Local History Items." *Minnesota History* 16 (1935): 257.

Lockwood, Jeffrey A. *Locust: The Devastating Rise and Mysterious Disappearance of the Insect That Shaped the American Frontier.* New York: Basic Books, 2004.

Lott, Dale F. *American Bison: A Natural History.* Berkeley: University of California Press, 2002.

Love, William DeLoss. *Wisconsin in the War of the Rebellion.* Vol. 1. Chicago: Church & Goodman, 1866. At "20th Wisconsin." Second Wisconsin Volunteer Infantry. secondwi.com.

Ludeman, Walter W. "Studies in the History of Public Education in South Dakota." *South Dakota Historical Collections* 12 (1924): 375–502.

Lurie, Alison. *Boys and Girls Forever: Children's Classics from Cinderella to Harry Potter.* New York: Penguin Books, 2003.

"Lyrical Legacy." Library of Congress. loc.gov.

McHugh, Tom. *The Time of the Buffalo.* Lincoln: University of Nebraska Press, 1972.

McKenney, Thomas L., and James Hall. *History of the Indian Tribes of North America.* Vol. 2. Philadelphia: J. T. Bowen, 1849.

McKnight, William J. *A Pioneer Outline History of Northwestern Pennsylvania.* Philadelphia: J. B. Lippincott Co., 1905.

Maher, Kathleen. "P. T. Barnum (1810–1891)—The Man, the Myth, the Legend." The Barnum Museum. barnum-museum.org.

Maine Folklife Center. "Young Charlotte (or Fair Charlotte)." *Maine Song and Story Sampler.* digitalcommons.library.umaine.edu.

Marcus, Leonard S., ed. *Dear Genius: The Letters of Ursula Nordstrom.* New York: HarperCollins, 1998.

"Mary Jane Holmes." Project MUSE-Legacy. muse.jhu.edu.

Mathews, John J. *The Osages: Children of the Middle Waters.* Norman: University of Oklahoma Press, 1961.

"Measles." historyofvaccines.org.

Meier, Peg, comp. *Bring Warm Clothes: Letters and Photos from Minnesota's Past.*

Minneapolis, Minn.: Minneapolis Star & Tribune Co., 1981.

Memorial and Biographical Record: An Illustrated Compendium of Biography, Containing a Compendium of Local Biography, . . . of Prominent Old Settlers and Representative Citizens of South Dakota . . . etc. Chicago: Geo. A. Ogle & Co., 1898.

Miller, Brenda, and Suzanne Paola. *Tell It Slant: Creating, Refining and Publishing Creative Nonfiction.* 2d ed. New York: McGraw Hill, 2012.

Miller, John E. *Becoming Laura Ingalls Wilder: The Woman behind the Legend.* Columbia: University of Columbia Press, 1998.

———. *Laura Ingalls Wilder and Rose Wilder Lane: Authorship, Place, Time, and Culture.* Columbia: University of Missouri Press, 2008.

———. *Laura Ingalls Wilder's Little Town: Where History and Literature Meet.* Lawrence: University Press of Kansas, 1994.

———. "The Old-fashioned Fourth of July: A Photographic Essay on Small-town Celebrations prior to 1930." *South Dakota History* 17 (Summer 1987): 118–39.

———. "Place and Community in 'The Little Town on the Prairie': De Smet in 1883. *South Dakota History* (Winter 1986): 351–72.

Minnesota. *General Laws of Minnesota for 1875.* St. Paul, 1875.

"Minnesota, Death Index, 1908–2002." ancestrylibrary.com.

"Minnesota, Marriages Index, 1849–1950." ancestrylibrary.com.

Minnesota Historical Society. *Minnesota Place Names.* mnplaces.mnhs.org.

———. *The U.S.–Dakota War of 1862.* usdakotawar.org.

"Miss McLeod's Reel." desertdulcimers.com.

"Miss McLeod's Reel—from Scotland to Appalachia." fiddlingdemystified.com.

Mott, Frank Luther. *A History of American*

Magazines, 1850–1865. Cambridge, Mass.: Harvard University Press, 1938.

"Mpls.-St.Paul Area Annual Mean Temperatures, by Year, 1820–2012." climatestations.com.

Murphy, Sandra. "Irish Folk Remedies." *eHow.* ehow.com.

Nachtrieb, Henry F., Ernest E. Hemingway, and J. Percy Moore. *The Leeches of Minnesota.* Geological and Natural History Survey of Minnesota. Zoological Series, no. 5. Minneapolis, 1912.

Neill, Edward D. *History of the Minnesota Valley, Including the Explorers and Pioneers of Minnesota.* Minneapolis, Minn.: North Star Publishing Co., 1882.

Nelson, Paula M., ed., and Maxwell Van Nuys, comp. *Sunshine Always: The Courtship Letters of Alice Bower & Joseph Gossage of Dakota Territory.* Pierre: South Dakota State Historical Society Press, 2006.

Nettleman, Mary D. "Scarlet Fever." *Medicine Net.* onhealth.com.

Neumann, Connie Ryle. "The Ingalls Girls' Dresses: A Study in Textiles." *Laura Ingalls Wilder Lore* 39 (Fall/Winter, 2013): 1, 3.

"New York, Passenger and Immigration Lists, 1820–1850." ancestrylibrary.com.

"The *New York Ledger*: History and Context." *Fanny Fern in* The New York Ledger. spacely.unl.edu.

"Northern Pocket Gopher." *Species Profile: Minnesota Department of Natural Resources.* dnr.state.mn.us.

"Notes on Classification of Materials and Excavation, and Contractor's Responsibility in Railway Grading." *Engineering-Contracting* 27 (Jan.-June 1907): 157–60.

"Obit of Mrs. Charles (Martha Jane Quiner) Carpenter, Wabasha Co., MN," *USGenWebArchives.* usgwarchives.net.

Ode, David J. *Dakota Flora: A Seasonal Sampler.* Pierre: South Dakota State Historical Society Press, 2006.

O'Leary, Dorothy Petrucci, and Catherine G. Goddard. "Chapter 3: Mary Ingalls Era, 1877–1889." In *Gleanings from Our Past: A History of the Iowa Braille and Sight Saving School, Vinton, Iowa*. Vinton: Iowa Braille and Sight Saving School, [1984]. ibsssalumni.org.

Orchiston, Wayne. "C/1881 K1: A Forgotten 'Great Comet' of the Nineteenth Century." *Irish Astronomical Journal* 26 (1999): 33–44.

"Osage Indian Tribe History," accessgenealogy.com.

"Oscar Edmund Eddy Cap Garland." Baroudi, Cooper, Cowles, Fish, Mead Family Tree." ancestry.com.

"Oscar Edmund Garland." findagrave.com.

"Overview of Measles Disease." Centers for Disease Control and Prevention. cdc.gov.

Palmer, H. R. *The Song King: Collection of New and Original Music for Singing Classes, Day Schools, Conventions. &c.* Cincinnati, Ohio: John Church & Co., 1872.

"Parasites—Scabies." Center for Disease Control and Prevention. cdc.gov.

"Pa's Century-Old Justice of the Peace work comes to light." *Laura Ingalls Wilder Lore* 8 (Fall-Winter 1982–83): 7.

"Pertussis, Whooping cough." ncbi.nlm.nih.gov.

Peterson, E. Frank, comp. *Historical Atlas of South Dakota*. Vermillion, S.Dak.: By the Compiler, 1904.

Peterson, Roger Tory. *Peterson Field Guide to Birds of Eastern and Central North America*. 6th ed. Boston: Houghton Mifflin Harcourt, 2010.

"Physiological Responses to Anger." *Family Works*. University of Illinois Extension. urbanext.illinois.edu

"Plant guide: Wild Plum, *Prunus americana* Marsh." United States Department of Agriculture. Natural Resource Conservation Service Plants Database. plants.usda.gov.

"Pleasant Prairie Cemetery." rootsweb.ancestry.com.

"Pocket Gophers." University of California Agriculture & Natural Resources Statewide Integrated Pest Management Program. ipm.ucdavis.edu.

"Pom-pom-pullaway." *Dictionary of American Regional English*. dare.wisc.edu.

Pope, Denis C. *Sitting Bull, Prisoner of War*. Pierre: South Dakota State Historical Society Press, 2010.

"Pop Goes the Weasel." *Nursery Rhymes Lyrics and Origins*. rhymes.org.uk.

Poppen, Caryl Lynn Meyer, comp. and ed. *De Smet Yesterday and Today*. De Smet, S.Dak.: De Smet Bicentennial Committee, 1976.

"Porcupine Grass." Grasses of the Eloise Butler Wildflower Garden. friendsofeloisebutler.org.

Power, Fred W. "'Distance Lends Enchantment to the View': A Diary of the 1874 Black Hills Expedition," edited by Thomas R. Buecker. In *Beyond Mount Rushmore: Other Black Hills Faces*, edited by Mary Kopco. Pierre: South Dakota State Historical Society Press, 2010.

"Pronghorn." National Wildlife Federation. nwf.org.

"Red-winged Blackbird." *All about Birds*. Cornell Lab of Ornithology. allaboutbirds.org.

Reed, Dorinda Riessen. *The Woman Suffrage Movement in South Dakota*. 2d ed. Pierre: South Dakota Commission on the Status of Women, [1975].

Reed, Ethel Irene, and William ("Bruce") Willford. "Genealogy and History of William Herbert Reed and Emma Lucetta Webster." silasknight.com.

[Reese, M. Lisle, ed.] *A South Dakota Guide*. Comp. Federal Writers Project. Pierre: South Dakota State Historical Society Press, 2005.

"Research: Watermelons and human health." June 25, 2005. Agricultural Research Service. ars.usda.gov.

"Rev. Leonard H. Moses." justme-ingrid.blogspot.com.

Reynolds, David S. *Mightier Than the Sword:*

Uncle Tom's Cabin and the Battle for America. New York: W. W. Norton & Co., 2011.

Rice, Irvin. "Traditional Games." Missouri Folklore Society. missourifolkloresociety.truman.edu.

Riley, Glenda. "Farm Women's Roles in the Agricultural Development of South Dakota." *South Dakota History* 13 (Spring/Summer 1983): 83–121.

Robinson, Doane. *History of South Dakota*. 2 vols. [Logansport, Ind.]: B. F. Bowen & Co., 1904.

Rogers, Elwin E. "Almost Scandinavia: Scandinavian Immigrant Experience in Grant County, 1877–1920." *South Dakota Historical Collections* 41 (1982): 273–452.

Roosevelt, Theodore. "Nature Fakers." *Everybody's Magazine* 17 (Sept. 1907): 427–30.

Rose, Arthur P. *An Illustrated History of Lyon County, Minnesota*. Marshall, Minn.: Northern History Publishing Co., 1912.

Rothaus, Richard. *Survey of Mortuary Features in Brookings, Deuel, Kingsbury, Lake and Moody Counties, South Dakota*. Sauk Rapids, Minn.: Trefoil, 2011.

Rule, Deb Houdek. "Ingalls-Wilder Family Genealogy." dahoudek.com.

"Saint Paul Daily Maximum/Minimum Temperatures for 1875." climatestations.com.

Sanders, W. E. "Trail of the Ancient Sioux: An Introduction to Their Ethnic History." *South Dakota Historical Collections* 26 (1952): 278–433.

Sanderson, L. O., ed. *Christian Hymns: Number Two*. Nashville: Gospel Advocate Co., 1948.

Schell, Herbert S. *History of South Dakota*. 4th ed., rev. John E. Miller. Pierre: South Dakota State Historical Society Press, 2004.

"Selected U.S. Federal Census Non-Population Schedules, 1850–1880." ancestrylibrary.com.

"Septimus Winner." en.wikipedia.org.

"Shawnee Trail." Oklahoma Historical Society. digital.library.okstate.edu.

"Shawnee Trail." RedRiverHistorian.com.

"Shawnee Trail." Texas State Historical Association. tshaonline.org.

"The Shawnee Trail." theshawneetrail.com.

Sherwood, Aubrey. *Beginnings of De Smet*. De Smet, S.Dak: By the Author, 1979.

———. "I remember Silver Lake." *Laura Ingalls Wilder Lore* 10 (Spring-Summer 1984): 1, 3.

———, ed. *Heritages of De Smet, South Dakota* [De Smet, S.Dak.]: By the Editor, 1981.

———. Interview by Marian Cramer. Transcript [1969–1970].

Shutter, Marion D. *History of Minneapolis: Gateway to the Northwest*. Vol. 2. Chicago: S. J. Clarke, 1932.

Silber, Irwin, and Earl Robinson. *Songs of the Great American West*. New York: Macmillan Co., 1967.

"Silver Lake lives again!" *Laura Ingalls Wilder Lore* 10 (Fall-Winter 1984-85): 1.

"Singing Schools." *Library of Congress Performing Arts Encyclopedia*. lcweb2.loc.gov.

Smith, Tara C. "Aetiology: Scarlet fever—past and present." *ScienceBlogs*. scienceblogs.com.

"South Dakota Births, 1856-1903." ancestrylibrary.com.

"South Dakota Death Index, 1905-1955." ancestrylibrary.com.

Spaeth, Janet. *Laura Ingalls Wilder*. Twayne's United States Authors Series. Boston: Twayne Publishers, 1987.

Spitzer, Marian. "The Lay of the Last Minstrels." *The Saturday Evening Post* 197 (Mar. 7, 1925): 12-13, 117-18, 123.

"State of Minnesota-Crayfish Species Checklist." iz.carnegiemnh.org.

Stradley, Linda. "Ice Cream—History, Legends, & Myths of Ices and Ice Cream." whatscookingamerica.net.

Sturtevant, William C., gen. ed. *Handbook of the North American Indians*. Vol. 2, pt. 2: *Plains*, edited by Raymond J. DeMallie. Washington, D.C.: Smithsonian Institution, 2001.

"Sweet Hour of Prayer." cyberhymnal.org.

"Take a Tour." Laura Ingalls Wilder Park and Museum." lauraingallswilder.us.

Tallent, Annie D. *The Black Hills; or, The Last Hunting Ground of the Dakotahs*. St. Louis: Nixon-Jones Printing Co., 1899.

Tallman, Dan A., David L. Swanson, and Jeffrey S. Palmer, *Birds of South Dakota*. [Aberdeen, S.Dak.]: South Dakota Ornithologists' Union, 2002.

Terranna, Gina. "Mary Power, From the Prairie to the Pacific Coast." In *The Best of the* Lore, pp. 85-86. De Smet, S.Dak.: Laura Ingalls Wilder Memorial Society, 2007.

"Texas Road." Oklahoma Historical Society. digitial.library.okstate.edu.

"Thomas Lewis Quiner." pioneergirl.com.

Thrapp, Dan L. *Encyclopedia of Frontier Biography*. 3 vols. Lincoln: Bison Books, University of Nebraska Press, 1991.

Thurman, Evelyn. *The Ingalls-Wilder Homesites: A Diary of Visits, 1872–81*. Bowling Green, Ky.: By the Author, 1982.

Toole, William. "Domesticating Our Native Wild Flowers." *Forty-ninth Annual Report of the Wisconsin Horticultural Society* 49 (1919): 89-94.

Townsend, George F., trans. *Aesop's Fables*. 1867. mythfolklore.net.

"Township and railroad map of Minnesota published for the Legislative Manual, 1874." Library of Congress. loc.gov.

"Tuberculosis." medical-dictionary.thefree dictionary.com.

Tulloch, Margaret. "The History of the Tuberculosis." Ed. Richard Sucre. Blue Ridge Tuberculosis Sanatorium. faculty.virginia.edu.

Turnbull, William W. *The Good Templars: A History of the Rise and Progress of the Independent Order of Good Templars*. N.p.: B. F. Parker, 1901.

Turrell, Orlando B. "The Early Settlement and History of Redwood County." *Collections of the Minnesota Historical Society* 9 (1901): 279-90.

"200 Years: The Life and Legacy of Louis Braille." American Foundation for the Blind. afb.org.

"Under the Daisies!" (lyrics sheet). University Library Libraries. library.duke.edu.

"Union Drums." *The Price of Freedom: Americans at War*. National Museum of American History. amhistory.si.edu.

U.S. Bureau of the Census. *Seventh Census of the United States*. 1850.

———. *Eighth Census of the United States*. 1860.

———. *Ninth Census of the United States*. 1870.

———. *Tenth Census of the United States*. 1880.

———. *Twelfth Census of the United States*. 1900.

———. *Thirteenth Census of the United States*. 1910.

———. *Fourteenth Census of the United States*. 1920.

"U.S. City Directories, 1821–1989 [Beta]." ancestrylibrary.com.

"U.S. Civil War Soldiers, 1861–1865." ancestrylibrary.com.

U.S. Congress. House. *The War of the Rebellion: A Compilation of the Official Records of the Union and Confederate Armies*. Series 1, vol. 8. Misc. Doc., no. 27. Washington, D.C.: Government Printing Office, 1883.

U.S. Department of the Interior. Office of Indian Affairs. *Annual Report of the Commissioner of Indian Affairs to the Secretary of the Interior for the Year 1878*. Washington, D.C.: Government Printing Office, 1878.

———. *Annual Report of the Commissioner of Indian Affairs to the Secretary of the Interior for the Year 1879*. Washington, D.C.: Government Printing Office, 1879.

U.S. Fish & Wildlife Service. "Gray Wolf—Western Great Lakes Region: Status under the Endangered Species Act." fws.gov.

———. Mountain-Prairie Region. Madison Wetlands Management District. "Special Places to Visit within the Madison Wetlands Management District." fws.gov.

———. South Dakota Field Office. "Gray Wolf." fws.gov.

"U.S. Federal Census Morality Schedules Index, 1850–1880." ancestrylibrary.com.

U.S. Forest Service. *Celebrating Wildflowers*. fs.fed.us.

Verdi, Giuseppe. *Ernani*. Libretto by Francesco Maria Piave. *Verdi 200*. giuseppeverdi.it.

"Vermont Death Records, 1909–2008." ancestrylibrary.com.

"Victorian Combs and Hair Accessories, 1870–80." *ebay*. ebay.com.

"Vidocq S L Owen." "Leslie Family Tree." trees.ancestry.com.

"Violin Makers of the Amati Family." *Encyclopedia Smithsonian*. si.edu.

"Visscher Vere Barnes." "Gysegem/McKeldin." trees.ancestry.com.

Wade, Louise Carroll. "Small-town Survival on the Great Plains: Miller, Dakota Territory, in the 1880s." *South Dakota History* 16 (Winter 1986): 317–50.

Waltz, Robert, and David G. Engle, eds. *The Traditional Ballad Index: An Annotated Bibliography of the Folk Songs of the English-Speaking World*. fresnostate.edu.

"Washington Death Index, 1940–1996." ancestrylibrary.com.

"Washington, Deaths, 1883–1960." ancestrylibrary.com.

Waskin, Laura. "Nellie Oleson: Lost and Found." *Laura Ingalls Wilder Lore* 23 (Fall–Winter 1997–1998): 1, 3–6.

———. "The Nellie Olson Story Continues." *Laura Ingalls Wilder Lore* 24 (Spring-Summer 1998): 1, 4–5.

Watson, J. Madison. *Independent Fifth Reader: Containing a Simple, Practical, and Complete Treatise on Elocution, . . . and a Complete Supplementary Index*. New York: A. S. Barnes & Co, 1876.

West, Mark I. "The Dakota Fairy Tales of L. Frank Baum." *South Dakota History* 30 (Spring 2000): 134–54.

"Western Meadowlark." *All about Birds*. Cornell Lab of Ornithology. allaboutbirds.org.

"What is Homeopathy." National Center for Homeopathy. nationalcenterforhomeopathy .org.

Wheeler, William A., ed. *Mother Goose's Melodies; or, Songs for the Nursery*. Boston: Houghton Mifflin Co., 1878.

"Whooping cough." mayoclinic.com.

Wilder, Laura Ingalls. *A Little House Traveler: Writings from Laura Ingalls Wilder's Journeys across America*. New York: HarperCollins, 2006.

———, and Rose Wilder Lane. *A Little House Sampler*, edited by William T. Anderson. Lincoln: University of Nebraska Press, 1988.

Wilton, David. "Lunatic Fringe." Wordorigins .org.

Wisconsin. Adjutant General's Office. *Roster of Wisconsin Volunteers, War of the Rebellion, 1861–1865*. 2 vols. 1886.

Woman's Christian Temperance Union. wctu.org.

Works Projects' Administration (WPA). *South Dakota Place Names*. Enl. & rev. ed. Vermillion: University of South Dakota, 1941.

"Yankee Doodle." In "Lyrical Legacy," Library of Congress. loc.gov.

"Yellow-headed Blackbird." *All about Birds*. Cornell Lab of Ornithology. allaboutbirds.org.

Yoon, Carol Kaesuk. "Looking Back at the Days of the Locust." *New York Times*, Apr. 23, 2002. nytimes.com.

Zochert, Donald. *Laura: The Life of Laura Ingalls Wilder*. Chicago: Contemporary Books, 1976.

NEWSPAPERS

Brookings County Press, 1879–1881.

Currie (Minn.) *Pioneer*, 1878–1879.

Dakota Pantagraph, 1879.

Decorah Iowa Republican, 1876–1877.

De Smet Leader, 1883–1885.

Hand County Press, 1882.

Huron Tribune, 1881.

Moody County Enterprise, 1880–1881.

Pierre Signal (originally *Fort Pierre Signal*), 1880.

Redwood Gazette, 1874–1880.

Wessington Springs True Dakotan, Jan. 12, 1988, Special Edition.

CORRESPONDENCE

Anderson, William T., Wilder biographer, to Nancy Tystad Koupal, Mar. 3, 2013, Feb. [14], Apr. 24, 2014.

Laumeyer, Phil, U.S. Fish and Wildlife biologist, to Pamela Smith Hill. May 10, 2010, Oct. 8, Dec. 28, 2012.

Palmlund, Cheryl, Director, Laura Ingalls Wilder Memorial Society, Inc., De Smet, S.Dak., to Pamela Smith Hill, Feb. 23, 2012.

Sheets, Arian, curator of National Music Museum, Vermillion, S.Dak., to Pamela Smith Hill, Feb. 21, 2010.

Tuttle, Cheryl, poultry farmer, to Pamela Smith Hill, May 13, 2013.

INDEX

Page numbers in italics refer to illustrations and captions; n refers to the number of the marginal annotation.